Real Estate Investment and Finance

Real Estate Investment and Finance

Sherman J. Maisel, Ph.D.

Stephen E. Roulac, J.D., Ph.D.
Schools of Business Administration
University of California, Berkeley

McGraw-Hill Book Company

New York St. Louis San Francisco Auckland Düsseldorf Johannesburg
Kuala Lumpur London Mexico Montreal New Delhi Panama
Paris São Paulo Singapore Sydney Tokyo Toronto

Real Estate Investment and Finance

1 2 3 4 5 6 7 8 9 0 K P K P 7 8 3 2 1 0 9 8 7 6

This book was set in Times Roman by Creative Book Services, subsidiary of McGregor & Werner, Inc. The editor was James J. Walsh; the cover was designed by Rafael Hernandez; the production supervisor was Judi Allen. The drawings were done by Fine Line Illustrations, Inc.
Kingsport Press, Inc., was printer and binder.

Library of Congress Cataloging in Publication Data

Maisel, Sherman J
    Real estate investment and finance.

      1.   Real estate investment.   2.   Real estate investment
—Finance.   I.   Roulac, Stephen E., joint author.
II.   Title.
HD1375.M276   332.6'324   75-35950
ISBN 0-07-039730-9

Contents

Preface

The mid-1970s have been critical years for the fields of real estate investment and finance. A virtual explosion of activity was followed by a drastic recession, failures, foreclosures, and then gradual recovery. Lenders and investors found that they could not depend solely on inflation and the relationship between growing population and limited land to ensure the success of their investments or the security of their loans. Even those who had been skeptics began to recognize the value of understanding the factors which cause some loans and investments to be successful while others fail. Those who had been convinced that good decisions require good analysis were reinforced in their beliefs.

Real Estate Investment and Finance is designed for classroom use in introductory courses in real estate finance or investment. It is also intended for use by individuals who—as potential investors, lenders, salespeople, or professional participants in activities related to real estate—want to understand the fundamentals of this field. Our principal goal has been to show how financing, the tax system, and supply and demand interact to create values. At the same time, we explain the institutional background of real estate finance and the techniques necessary to judge values, and we introduce some of the concepts required for making investment decisions and choosing an investment strategy.

We decided to include both financing and investment in a single book because of our own general experience and that of others in the field. The traditional division between a debt position and an equity position has become blurred in recent years. Many of the basic concepts in one sphere interact so closely with those in the other that their joint exposition greatly increases understanding.

The general field of finance has made rapid advances in recent years. Those wanting to teach in real estate have been unhappy to find that many works contain few if any concepts based on the new knowledge in the general field. While keeping our exposition at an introductory level, we have made progress toward filling this gap by combining both finance and investment.

Depending upon the length of a particular course, its emphasis, and the background of the students, instructors may want to assign some of the chapters as supplementary, rather than required, reading. The Instructor's Manual available from the publisher illustrates various possible combinations of chapters related to specific objectives.

The field of real estate is one in which both men and women have been active and successful. Although masculine pronouns have occasionally been used in the text for convenience and succinctness, we fully recognize that concepts under discussion apply equally to women and men.

We are indebted to a large number of people for assistance in preparing this book. Lawrence D. Jones, Maury Seldin, Stephen D. Messner, James A. Graaskamp, Dennis J. McKenzie, Ronald F. Poe, and John McGuire all read parts or all of the manuscript and made valuable suggestions, many of which we gladly accepted. Research aid was furnished by Michael J. Hanrahan and Jacqueline Bernier. The manuscript was ably typed by Claire Gilchrist, Cheryl E. Dale, and Susan E. Ward. The staff and library facilities of the Center for Real Estate and Urban Economics at the University of California, Berkeley, were exceedingly helpful. Our debt to Lucy C. Maisel for editorial work and other major assistance is substantial. For those errors of fact and analysis which still remain despite the best efforts of others, we accept full responsibility.

Sherman J. Maisel
Stephen E. Roulac

Real Estate Investment and Finance

Chapter 1

Introduction: Decisions to Invest, Borrow, and Lend

The earth is composed of real estate which is continuously being bought, sold, cultivated, developed, and redeveloped. The field of real estate investment and finance is consequently one of the largest and most active in our economy. In a simple form, it touches everyone who uses space—whether by renting or buying living space or engaging in commerce or industry. Many real property deals, however, are extremely complex. Every transaction is unique, and many involve a number of unusual features. In addition to the profit-making opportunities which lure investors into real estate, the field offers fascinating intellectual challenges that attract many people. Typically, detailed analysis of large transactions will reveal an intricate interweaving of numerous complex elements. The success and profitability of a real estate operation depend on the proper analysis of many different factors, the effective use of a number of specialized financial and legal institutions, and a critical sense of timing. Intuition and good luck must be reinforced by sound knowledge.

The high profit potential inherent in many real estate activities gives them a broad appeal. Most people would like to make a million dollars. Many people *have* made a million dollars or more in real estate, and this fact has been widely publicized. That is one reason why so many study real estate investment and finance. Unfortunately, however, while the profit potential is high, it is frequently necessary to take great risks in order to reap extremely large gains with limited capital. This means that most people want all the knowledge they can get before investing, lending, or embarking on a career in one of the fields related to real property. They hesitate to invest their savings or their future without a more detailed understanding of where they might be going.

Real estate values have increased at a rapid, although not steady, rate. While estimates are rough, the value of real estate in the United States was $65 billion in 1900, $295 billion in 1929, $235 billion in 1933, $880 billion in 1955, and $2,650 billion in 1973. In past decades, many of the great American fortunes were created through real estate investments. It is believed that in the postwar period, more millionaires made their money in land development, building, and real estate than in any other industry.

The industries concerned with real estate investment and finance form one of the largest sources of jobs in our economy. Millions of people are employed in the occupations surrounding real property. While many perform their work without knowing what the industry is all about, added knowledge can enhance both job performance and understanding of what is happening and why. For many, such information is not merely useful or entertaining; it is vital to their day-to-day success.

The purpose of this book is to make clear both the profit-making possibilities and the other challenges of real estate. It points out the basic, underlying factors which create real estate values and make successful investing and lending possible. It contains information on the significant institutions which play a crucial role in the field. The book also explains how those who invest in, or work with, real estate can be phenomenal successes or nearly as great failures. It details the specific information and analytic models used by both successful investors and successful lenders.

A few people intuitively make sound decisions that pay off time after time, whether they are acting as investors or lenders or are offering specialized services. Most, however, do much better when they understand the basic forces at work shaping values and when they recognize the constraints and opportunities they face. With knowledge and practice, people can estimate both profit potentials and the risks involved. They can increase their income without risking a complete debacle.

Real Estate Know-How

Unfortunately, despite the major role of real estate investment and financing in our economy, the information and techniques needed to analyze them have not kept pace with the expansion of the field. Although over 3.9 million pieces of property are bought and sold every year and although the number of real estate loans made is even larger, there is a great dearth of information about what actually goes on in the real estate market.

Libraries abound with data on stocks and bonds. The literature on how to value and invest in these securities is huge. This is decidedly not the case for real estate. Knowledge of why property values grow and change is the foundation of both successful investment and successful financing. Yet one of the most common complaints of those interested in real estate concerns the lack of material to assist them.

This book is almost unique in presenting a practical, integrated view. It explains the forces causing real estate values to wax and wane, and it shows how these values can be analyzed and predicted. It makes clear the necessarily close interrelationships between investor, promoter or broker, developer, lender, borrower, and government.

The book is planned for both the investor and the lender. In addition, it contains the type of information and analysis required by all those in the real estate and construction industries who prepare the land and buildings and who handle on a continuing basis real estate brokerage and lending transactions. Emphasis throughout is on the creation of values through the constant interaction of financing and investing. Why the two cannot be separated becomes clear. The development proceeds from the knowledge required for lending and borrowing to that needed for buying and selling.

Those who are interested primarily in finding out what is required for successful investing may, after concluding this chapter, wish to read Part Seven first and then return to the earlier parts for more specific answers to the questions that will arise as they move to implement their investment strategies.

Part One introduces the field of real estate financing. It explains why people borrow and lend, and it presents the basic concepts which underlie this activity.

Part Two describes the ways in which property is owned, as well as the significant modern developments in this sphere. In many cases, recent changes cause the traditional roles of owning and lending to overlap and to be far less clear-cut than in the past.

Part Three explains the institutional structure of real estate finance. It shows how and why, as a result of its unique institutions, this market is subject to tremendous fluctuations, buffeting, and major changes in values when the vital flow of money periodically drops to low levels.

Part Four describes the critical functions of the federal and state governments in real estate. Most real estate transactions are heavily influenced by governmental actions. Understanding what governments do and why has been the basis of the vast majority of real estate fortunes made in the past 40 years.

Part Five presents the analysis necessary for both lenders and investors to control their risks. A key factor in real estate is that high profits are paid for taking risks. To realize actual profits over and above payments for risk, those in the market must understand, calculate, and properly control these risks.

Part Six explores the knowledge and techniques required for successful investing. The number of factors impinging upon each real estate venture makes it vital that decisions to invest or not, as well as decisions concerning how much to invest, be made in an organized, logical manner.

Part Seven may well be the proper starting point for many readers. It explains how to develop a successful investment strategy. It makes clear the critical factors one needs to look at in investing in real estate. While it draws on the language and analysis of the previous parts, many readers will find that even without reading the preceding material carefully, they will find answers to many of the questions they face when trying to decide whether to invest in real estate.

REAL ESTATE IN OUR ECONOMY

Real estate constitutes the largest share of American wealth. Over 43 million families own homes. For most families, their real estate far exceeds all their other assets in value. In addition, millions own other real estate, either directly or through partnerships, syndicates, investment trusts, and corporations. Because real property is everywhere and because it is possible to make a great deal of money by buying and selling it, real estate investment has become increasingly popular.

Except for governments and retail trade, more people are employed in the various sectors of real property development, management, and sales than anywhere else. The market for mortgage lending is the largest and most widespread of any credit market.

Some idea of the vast scope of the real property market and related activity can be gained from Table 1-1. The value of real property in the United States is roughly estimated at close to $3 trillion. This is between 60 and 70 percent of our total national wealth. Housing makes up the largest share—about one-third—of this wealth. The total value of dwellings, both single-family and apartment or multifamily units, is close to one-half of the value of all real property. Land and buildings owned by governments are the second largest component of real property. Next come lots, raw acreage, and land. Even though commercial and industrial users pay the most for their land and many individual properties tend to be large, these categories are lowest in total value.

The annual amount spent on the construction of buildings is close to $100 billion. Not included in Table 1-1 is over $30 billion spent on other types of construction, such as highways, sewers, and public utilities.

Table 1-1   A Broad Estimate of Real Estate Investment Activity in the United States in the Early 1970s

Category	Value of real property (in billions of dollars)	Annual construction (in billions of dollars)	Number of sales	
			In millions of units	In billions of dollars
Structures:				
One-family dwellings	1,000	30	2.40	60.0
Multifamily dwellings	200	20	.20	4.0
Commercial	90	15	.45	3.0
Industrial and others	30	15	.15	1.0
Land:				
Farms	180		.25	4.0
Other	500		.50	5.0
Governmental	650	15		
Total	2,650	95	3.95	77.0

Firms involved in real property activities	
Contract construction	900,000
Real estate brokerage and management	850,000
Real estate finance	50,000
Total	1,800,000

Source: Based on data in Census Bureau and Internal Revenue Service reports of governments, construction, and establishments.

Sales of real property include new and used houses, vacant lots, and acreage, as well as some new industrial units, apartment houses, and commercial buildings. The estimate indicates that over 3.9 million individual sales of property take place each year. Their annual value totals over $75 billion. The importance of income-producing properties in the industry is greater than their sales indicate because most are sold only after a period spent under their initial owner and user.

Over 1.8 million firms are engaged in the planning, design, development, construction, maintenance, management, financing, and sale of real property. In addition, large numbers of lawyers, accountants, and other consultants spend a good deal of their time on real estate problems. We have no estimate of the number of individuals who own and invest in property except for the more than 43 million people who own various types of housing.

Most firms concerned with real property are extremely small. While in the financial sphere, giants such as the Bank of America and Prudential Insurance play significant roles, the single construction tradesman, the one- or two-person real estate office, and the apartment owner-manager are far more typical. The average size of firms in the real estate business is among the smallest of any industry, although the trend is toward an increasing influence of larger firms. Turnover is heavy. There are few barriers to entry. Almost anybody can strike out alone and take a chance at entrepreneurship. Lack of knowledge and other handicaps cause far more to fail than to achieve success, but the opportunities exist.

THE KNOWLEDGE REQUIRED FOR SUCCESSFUL REAL ESTATE INVESTMENT AND LENDING

Just as the nature of real estate endows it with vast profit potentials, it also makes individual investments hard to analyze and to complete successfully. Risks are great:

1 Each piece of property is fixed in location. Its future income will be tied to the economic health of the surrounding neighborhood and community.

2 The sums required for the purchase or development of a piece of property are large. Money must be borrowed. The terms of financial agreements can be crucial.

3 The agreements between promoters, lenders, and owners are complex. They can make or break a transaction.

4 Tax rules are intricate. In recent years tax considerations have dominated real estate investments.

5 The information essential to wise decisions is imprecise, hard to find, and likely to be inaccurate.

A successful loan or investment in real property requires a proper forecast of the profit and loss potential in each individual case. This means that successful investors must be able to recognize the possible alternatives for a piece of property. They must be able to choose the best of these alternatives and negotiate the necessary deal. Obviously, all predictions of the future are fraught with danger. Therefore, success also depends on recognizing potential risks and on adopting plans which can minimize the consequences of wrong judgments. No one will always be right, but on average, winners make more good forecasts than losers do. Furthermore, they make necessary contingency plans to control the bad effects of errors.

What are the primary factors which must be examined to make good forecasts and proper decisions? They are the forces which cause property values, returns, and risks to shift. They must be properly estimated and analyzed if an investment or loan is to work out. They can be discussed under five headings:

1   Projections of income
2   Projections of costs
3   Management
4   Financial arrangements
5   Governmental influences

Income

The income from a property depends partly upon events in the general economy and partly upon factors specific to the property itself. Real estate values are affected by changes in (1) population, (2) location, (3) incomes, and (4) prices (inflation). Each of these forces must be examined as part of any real estate transaction.

Population will continue to expand, but at a slower rate than in the past. While the rate of growth helps us determine total demand, more crucial to our understanding of real estate markets is the actual composition of the population. For example, during the past two decades, an explosion of apartment building occurred. This trend was predicted by those aware of our changing age distribution. In contrast, a shortage of schools and problems of financing them dominated much of suburban growth. Now schools built only 15 years ago are standing empty. Even with the population explosion, many areas were stable or declining even as others were expanding sharply. This trend toward differentiated growth may well accelerate. Some believe that our whole transportation technology is shifting. This, too, will cause population to move and property values to shift. Yesterday's "hot market" may today have a larger population of vacancy signs than of people.

Location is the key factor in projecting the effect of local influences on a property's future income. The nature of the geographic location will vary with transportation, neighborhood conditions, competition, city services and taxes, and a host of other local factors. Each of these influences the desirability or value of a specific location. For the most part, real estate investments are permanently tied to their sites. Investments are typically large, and income is generated over long periods.

It is the uniqueness of each property that creates both opportunities and difficulties for the real estate investor. We can buy a million dollars' worth of a common stock in a 30-second phone conversation. We know what we will be getting. On the other hand, because each property is unique, even small transactions require a good deal of detailed investigation, complicated negotiations, and specialized legal knowledge.

Gross National Product   In addition to demand arising from population growth and locational factors, rents for a property depend on the amount of money people have to spend, or on the gross national product (GNP)—the total spending of the nation. When business is booming, rents and property values rise. In major depressions, it is difficult even to give property away.

Dollar income has the greatest effect on rents. People earning more can afford higher rents. Some rents are tied to their tenants' dollar sales. As prices rise, owners of real estate can expect to increase their rent income. That is why real estate is generally a good hedge against inflation.

Costs

Income is only one side of the picture. Outgoes and costs are the other. Cash flow or profits are the difference. While costs tend not to fluctuate as much as income, their variations often spell the difference between success and failure.

In estimating costs, one must understand various definitions. There are cash costs, accounting costs, costs for tax purposes, development costs, operating costs, and others. While in many endeavors the variety of costs is significant, rarely is it as critical as in real estate transactions. Much of the success of a particular investment may depend on the proper structuring for loans and taxes of the costs. On the other hand, all too often investors spend so much time on financial juggling that they sadly underestimate the real costs of development or operations. The result is that any advantages the careful structuring might have produced are nullified. It is hard for investors to come out whole when the fundamentals go awry.

Management

We use the term "management" in a broad sense to include both the furnishing of information to lenders and investors and the planning, development, and ongoing operational responsibilities of a property. Because the real property market is so large—although fragmented and diverse—literally hundreds of thousands of firms are involved in the industry. While their skills are often crucial in determining whether an investment succeeds or fails, the expertise and ability of these firms vary greatly. The maxim "Investigate first, then invest" holds only too true in the real estate field. Important in the process of investigation is an assessment of the management and personnel of the firm with which one is dealing. Its ability to provide good management for both development and operations will determine the bottom line. Too many bad deals have made true an old saying: "Developers start with knowledge, and investors with money. After a time, the investors have the knowledge, and the developers have the money." Clearly, investors must beware.

Financial Arrangements

The years 1966, 1970, and 1974–1975 mark difficult periods for all real estate lenders, builders, and promoters. These have also been years of sharp fluctuations in the short-term money markets. The two sets of facts are interrelated. Over the past decade, shifts in financial markets have been among the most crucial factors influencing real estate. Widespread misunderstanding of the relationship between financial markets and successful investment has caused many in the industry to commit major errors. As we shall see, such ignorance is not necessary. Although complicated, how the money markets work and how they affect real estate are not really mysterious or unfathomable subjects.

Financing is critical in most real estate transactions because it determines the amount of equity required for a purchase. The relationship of the amount borrowed to that invested by the owner—or the leverage—is a major determinant of both risk and potential profits.

Intermediation Because most real estate investments are large and complex, lending normally takes place through financial intermediaries. The money flows to real estate markets are dominated by the shifting relationships between the institutions in the field and by the reaction of these institutions to what is happening in other markets for credit. This means that the whole concept of intermediation must be understood. Specialized lenders gather the funds of individual savers as deposits and lend them out in larger and riskier situations than the individuals themselves could handle. The efficiencies of size and the general principles of the sharing of risks and the law of large numbers make such loans possible. Costs and efficiency, however, also depend on the proper planning, lending skills, and portfolio policies of the financial institutions.

Interest Rates Frequently, there is a lack of understanding of interest and of what happens when rates change. Because borrowed money often provides 75 percent or more of the total financing, interest is a major cost. Furthermore, in investment analysis, the role that interest plays in determining the present value of a future income stream is as significant as its cost. What a property sells for now, what it will sell for in the future, and what will be its total yield or profitability depend on movements in the level of interest rates.

Governments

The real estate market is closely entwined with all levels of government. How governments affect individual deals is also a major factor in investment analysis. In recent years, the federal income tax has probably been the largest single factor influencing real estate transactions. Carefully and properly structured tax effects have been the big thrust both in creating a market for sales and in making profits. Understanding the concepts of depreciation, "soft dollars," and capital gains has been vital to a good working knowledge of the field.

The federal government's involvement goes far beyond income taxes, however. It is the single largest factor in financial markets and in the operations of financial institutions. Most large institutions are chartered, regulated, or insured by the government. Every week the government borrows and repays billions of dollars. A speech by the Secretary of the Treasury or the Chairman of the Federal Reserve Board can cause interest rates and lending to react sharply.

The federal government has hundreds of special programs for housing and for other types of real estate. It spends large sums for urban renewal, highways, and transportation systems. It subsidizes housing, sewers, water supplies, and schools, in addition to being the largest owner of land and purchaser of construction.

States and localities are engaged in many of the same activities as the federal government. Frequently they act as the local agents for the administration of federal programs. They also have key functions in planning, zoning, and environmental protection. The actions required of developers by localities and the energy such actions entail can be as time-consuming as all the other parts of the process of development. Politics and real estate investment and development are not strangers. To understand the market for real estate investment and lending, we need a basic grounding in what governments do and in why and how they do it.

PARTICIPANTS IN REAL ESTATE INVESTMENT AND FINANCING

The hope of substantial gain, protection against inflation, an opportunity to help build a better urban environment, the attraction of dealing with many people, and the chance to lead a varied and active life—these are some of the factors that have drawn hundreds of thousands of individuals into the industries concerned with real property. The actual number active in buying, selling, advising, developing, constructing, and lending on real property runs into the millions. It is a livelihood for many, a hobby for others, and a source of income and capital gains or losses for still another group.

The market is occupied by so many specialties that even a mere listing would be overly long. One rather simple grouping classifies participants as investors, developer-builders, broker-promoters, advisers, financiers, and the government. These classifications often overlap. Many developers, builders, brokers, and promoters are also investors. Developers may also do their own brokerage and promoting. Many advisers—such as lawyers, appraisers, and consultants—are active participants in some transactions and counselors in others. Financial institutions such as insurance companies are rapidly increasing both their loans and their equity investments. Governments own a great deal of property.

Differences in roles are important, however, because each looks at a real estate parcel and the transactions surrounding it from a unique point of view. In the sense that they all want as much of the profits as they can get, they are competitive. But the fact that their approach to profits and to risks may be very different enables them to cooperate. Some may be interested in immediate values, and some in long-run ones. Some may want to minimize risks; others may be willing risk takers.

An increase in the value of a property will be welcomed by all, since the larger the pie, the easier it will be to get agreement on how to divide it. The developer, the investor, and the financier all want a successful project; so does the government, although it may measure success in somewhat different terms.

While relationships tend to be cooperative, a constant tension prevails. All participants want to further the project but also to protect their own interests. The problem of an analyst is to understand what each needs and wants. If the tensions and their causes can be recognized, they may often be resolved with mutual benefits. The better all participants understand both the totality of the real estate investment and financing picture and its component parts, the better their chances of achieving their own goals.

The following sketches illustrate the great variety of people and firms active in the real estate field. They serve also to introduce some of the specialized language and some of the problems which will be explained and analyzed later in this book.

Investors

Small Owners   Larry and Sally Roberts are both 31. Larry is a buyer for a large department-store chain. They own their own home—or, more precisely, have a 14 percent equity in it. (That is, they have invested $4,200 of their own money, while a savings and loan institution has lent them $25,800 on a mortgage.) They also own a resort condominium. They bought their home 3 years ago, when their second child was born. Even though Larry knows he is almost certain to be moved, he decided to buy a house, primarily because he could not find a suitable one to rent. He also figured that because of the tax break given owners, and provided he was not moved for 3 years, owning would be a little cheaper than renting. Furthermore, he would gain stability. His monthly payments would be more or less fixed, and he could not be forced to move by a landlord.

Larry and Sally bought the condominium as a speculation with some hope of income and capital gains. When Sally's father died, he left her $50,000 in stocks and bonds. She and her husband were impressed by the rapidly expanding leisure market and disappointed by their lack of success in the stock market. The real estate firm that sold them their house was developing a condominium of attached units bordering a golf course on a mountain lake 200 miles away. Because the firm handled the renting of the units for a fee, the investment was considered a security with a prospectus similar to that for common stocks. Larry and Sally could buy one for a $20,000 downpayment. The promoter projected that the rental income would cover their mortgage payments, and they could spend their own vacations in the unit. If good recreational property rose in price as rapidly as they expected, they would end up better off than if they had continued to hold their stocks.

High-Income Investor   Dr. Harold Goldsmith, a successful radiologist, is 45. He owns his own home, a quarter of the 20-unit office building which contains his office, 10 percent of each of three apartment buildings, $50,000 in shares of a $3 million vineyard, and 5 percent (about $35,000) of a mobile-home park. Dr. Goldsmith was first introduced to real estate investing by a lawyer friend. It seemed to the doctor that high taxes were a recurring topic in most conversations with his colleagues. The tax collector was getting a large share of the substantial fees they were earning. Taxes averaged 55 percent on the top $30,000 of Harold's income each year. The lawyer friend suggested that instead of going to the government, the top $15,000 or $20,000 of Harold's taxes could be used to buy real estate. This lawyer had put together partnerships of doctors for the medical office building and three separate apartment buildings. Dr. Goldsmith bought shares in syndicates for the vineyard and the mobile-home park himself.

Small Apartment Developer   Edward Frank is 66. He owns seven 16-unit apartment houses, three stores on Main Street, and a warehouse. Up until 10 years ago,

Ed owned a hardware store. Several of his best customers were small contractors. In 1957, one of them ran into financial difficulties and offered to sell Ed a small 3-year-old apartment building at a good price. Ed has found the building very profitable. He has used his experience to develop an additional building about every 2 years. By the time Ed was 56, running the hardware store was requiring a great deal of effort, and he was making very little money from it, even as he was making excellent profits from his apartments. He sold his store and became a full-time owner-manager of real estate investments. In addition to managing his own buildings, he bought and sold about one property every year.

Investors Using Real Estate as a Hedge The Hansa Land Company is the holding concern for a European industrial family—one of the wealthiest in the world. Hansa owns farms in California and Arizona, a shopping center in Florida, and a major office building in New York. The properties are owned free and clear, with no debt outstanding. The owners do not think of Hansa primarily as a source of income, but rather as a method of diversifying their capital and ensuring future income for themselves. As is true of many European families, they are all too aware of what happened to the wealth of some of their friends as a result of the German inflation, the gradual erosion in value of the French franc, and the takeovers in Poland, East Germany, and Hungary. They do not want to be down to their last million if they can help it. They can afford to sacrifice income (although they try not to) in order to make sure that no matter what happens in their home country, they will be able to get along somewhere in the world.

Large Investors Zenith Fund is part of one of the largest insurance companies in the country. This company manages and invests the assets of a large number of pension funds, which are not subject to income tax. The insurance company set up a real estate fund (which now has $250 million in assets) to invest for the pension funds in real estate. Such investments take advantage of the pension funds' tax-free status and their much longer time horizon compared with that of most other investors. The pension funds can get higher yields than in other investments, share in income of a property when it exceeds certain levels, and hold residual rights that may augment their income by a good deal more than currently estimated.

Developer-Builders

Large Builders A to Z Homes is a division of a large conglomerate. It is currently building homes in the suburbs of seven cities. One of its subsidiaries builds apartment houses, usually in the same areas in which the firm is selling single-family homes. The apartment houses are sold to syndicates, for which A to Z acts as the general partner. Sales and underwriting of the syndicate shares have been handled through stockbrokers and investment advisory firms.

The syndicates pay A to Z a 7 percent construction fee, a profit on the land, and a mortgage brokerage fee. In addition, A to Z gets a 5 percent annual management fee. It shares in all current income which surpasses the first 10 percent average return to the investors and in any capital gains.

Individual Developer   Peter Bonelli is an independent developer. Over the past 20 years he has put together seven apartment complexes and three shopping centers. He still owns a share in, and his firm manages, four of the apartments. On the last three projects Pete worked entirely with a large insurance company, and he is doing so on two more now in progress. He is responsible for obtaining the land, securing the design, getting necessary approvals, contracting, and supervising the construction. He has a small personal staff to assist him, but he depends primarily on outside consultants. Each project requires an initial investment of about $100,000 of his cash, which he recoups as the project develops. The insurance company puts up all other money. As the project is constructed, Bonelli earns a 5 percent fee for his efforts. On top of this, his management firm will be paid 5 percent annually of rents. He and the insurance company will split all profits: one-third to Bonelli and two-thirds to the insurance company.

Broker-Promoters

The F&M Corporation has been in the real estate business for 50 years. It has 10 offices and 190 employees scattered over a major metropolitan region. While most of its business is brokering of existing houses, it also sells all other types of property. It has built several subdivisions, 5 shopping centers, and 15 apartment houses. It has a property management subsidiary which rents these and other properties. The firm is also the general partner of an $8 million real estate fund. It underwrote the fund, selling shares through its own sales force and some stockbrokerage firms. The fund owns a shopping center, several apartments, and a small industrial park. F&M receives brokerage commissions for buying and selling the fund's properties. It is also paid 6 percent a year for its property management functions. It receives 5 percent of all capital gains calculated after the return of capital and a 9 percent per annum yield to the investors.

SUMMARY

The markets for real estate are among the largest in the United States. More people actively participate in buying, selling, lending, or borrowing on real property than in all but one or two other fields of endeavor. The real estate markets include a tremendous variety of individuals and firms, ranging from part-time individuals to some of the country's wealthiest families and largest corporations.

Successful real estate investing and lending require an understanding of the profit and loss possibilities attached to each property or real estate security. These, in turn, depend on future income and costs, management, financing, and governmental influences. Profits result from an ability to put all these factors together.

The real estate field has something to offer almost everyone. How well one fares depends upon knowledge, analysis, and hard work—as well as luck.

QUESTIONS AND PROBLEMS

1   The majority of the wealth of the United States consists of real estate. Why would you expect this to be so?
2   What factors increase the level of knowledge and skills required for real estate transactions?
3   Explain why population, location, an area's real income, and the level of prices should each be expected to influence the price of a property.
4   What are some of the reasons for investing in real estate?
5   Given the information in Table 1-1, what parts of the real estate lending and selling markets would you expect to be most active?
6   What factors separate successful investors from less successful ones?
7   Who are the participants in the real estate business? What roles do they play?
8   Do all investors in real estate have similar objectives? Why?

SELECTED REFERENCES FOR CHAPTER 1

Casey, William J.: *Real Estate Desk Book*, 4th ed. (New York: Institute for Business Planning, 1971).

Cooper, James R., and Karl L. Guntermann: *Real Estate and Urban Land Analysis* (Lexington, Mass.: Lexington Books, 1974).

Hoagland, Henry E., and Leo D. Stone: *Real Estate Finance*, 5th ed. (Homewood, Ill.: Irwin, 1973).

Pease, Robert H., and Louis O. Kerwood (eds.): *Mortgage Banking*, 2d ed. (New York: McGraw-Hill, 1965).

Ring, Alfred A.: *Real Estate Principles and Practices*, 7th ed. (Englewood Cliffs, N.J.: Prentice-Hall, 1972).

Smith, Halbert C., Carl J. Tschappat, and Ronald L. Racster: *Real Estate and Urban Development* (Homewood, Ill.: Irwin, 1973).

Smith, Wallace F.: *Housing: The Social and Economic Elements* (Berkeley: University of California Press, 1971).

Weimer, Arthur M., Homer Hoyt, and George F. Bloom: *Real Estate*, 6th ed. (New York: Ronald, 1972).

Part One

FINANCING
REAL ESTATE

These chapters introduce the fundamentals of real estate finance, painting the background against which the remainder of the book unfolds. They provide information needed to understand what real estate financing is all about: Why do people borrow? Why do they try to borrow so much? What are the advantages and disadvantages of reducing monthly and annual payments of principal to a minimum? Before a property can be built, there must be a financial plan. The plan indicates where the money will come from as development proceeds.

Chapter 2 presents an overall view of who lends and on what types of properties and mortgages. In Chapter 3, some of the unusual features of the mortgage and the legal restrictions surrounding it are considered. Chapter 4 covers the economics of large mortgages and lengthy periods for repayment. In Chapter 5, the role of financial planning in real estate is introduced, particularly in the process of development and construction. Chapter 6 emphasizes the time value of money and some of the mathematics encountered in interest rates and borrowing.

Real Estate Lending

The financing of real estate is one of the most fascinating sectors of the United States economy. More money is borrowed each year on mortgages than in any other way. That real estate financing is a major American business is obvious from the number of borrowers and the amounts involved. In 1973, more than $170 billion, representing more than 3.5 million loans, was borrowed on mortgages, and the net increase in mortgage debt was over $70 billion. The largest share of the financing of most transactions was made available by borrowing. In 1975, more than 25 million American firms and families owed over $700 billion on debts secured by mortgages.

To supply this vast demand for credit, over 22,000 institutions—including savings and loan institutions (S&Ls); commercial banks (CBs), savings banks (MSBs), and mortgage banks; life insurance companies (LICs); pension funds; and real estate investment trusts (REITs)—actively engage in mortgage lending. Since many of these institutions have numerous branches, real estate loans can be obtained at over 45,000 lending offices.

For most financial institutions, mortgages rank among the most important sources for investments and income. In recent years, about a third of the net flow of funds from financial institutions to the capital markets has taken the form of mortgages. Their net mortgage investment recently has been more than three times their new investment in corporations through bonds and stock combined. It far exceeded lenders' portfolio additions of all types of government obligations.

The profitability and safety of the more than 22,000 mortgage lenders are directly related to their proficiency in this kind of lending. As their managers and employees gain a better understanding of the possibilities and problems associated with the mortgage market, our entire financial structure and our economy become more efficient.

THE MARKET FOR REAL ESTATE LOANS

Most construction, selling, and ownership of real property is financed by mortgage loans. Although we speak of the "market" for real estate mortgages, it is far different from most markets usually studied, as well as more complex. Only in recent years has there been any significant progress toward making it possible to buy and sell mortgages in an organized, national market. While major mortgage brokers and dealers are now beginning to interact by phone, wire, and computer, the mortgage market remains primarily local and dependent on personal contacts. A notable exception has been the introduction of organized trading in Government National Mortgage Association (GNMA) mortgage interest rate contracts on the Chicago Board of Trade. This trading is in contracts for future delivery similar to trading in commodities. It came about after a number of dealers and brokers began to make markets in these certificates.

For actual mortgages, however, no single organized market for funds or price quotations exists. Not only is there no large exchange (as for listed stocks), but there are few dealers or over-the-counter brokers. Instead, there are thousands of submarkets in cities and towns throughout the country, each trading in a variety of mortgages, bonds, and notes covering all types of loans on real property. Mortgages are originated in amounts which, while they can range from a few dollars to millions, are usually small. Most borrowers are unsophisticated. The terms and interest rate of each loan vary both with prevailing capital-market conditions and with the specific factors affecting each loan, such as the credit-worthiness of the borrower; the location, type, age, and quality of the security offered; and the time covered, which may itself vary from 1 day to 50 years.

Still, despite these substantial contrasts with an organized market, it is possible to speak of a mortgage market and to analyze what goes on within it. By a "mortgage market" or "loan market," we mean the interrelated points where requests to borrow are negotiated, interest rates and fees are determined, transactions occur, and money is borrowed and lent. The significant fact is that even though such loans are widely disparate, each one has some influence on the overall mortgage market. Price movements in the many parts tend to be related.

Funds flow from one location to another. Borrowers and lenders are willing to substitute investments in one place for those available elsewhere. When a corporation in Boston expands and requires a loan, one of the consequences may be that it becomes harder to buy a house in Dallas. The Boston corporation may seek funds from an insurance company or a local or New York bank. The bank, in turn, must decide whether to make the loan and, if it does, what other potential customers not to accept. Each lender or borrower makes adjustments as a result of experiencing a slightly altered situation with respect to supply or demand. It is the existence of these interrelationships that enables us to analyze the mortgage market in overall terms, while recognizing that the form and magnitude of impact at each separate lending point will vary.

A VIEW OF THE MORTGAGE MARKET

Even though the number of lenders is vast, there may be periods when many potential borrowers are handicapped in obtaining funds because the structure of the mortgage market is so complex that lenders do not compete vigorously. Lenders are not evenly distributed geographically. All must meet specific legal requirements. Their skills and knowledge vary widely.

These geographic, legal, and institutional differences fragment the market into pieces like those of a jigsaw puzzle. A unified view is possible only after a careful piecing together of the parts and a recognition of their interdependence. Only through an overview of the completed picture can we examine the total United States mortgage market. Only by understanding the uniqueness of each part can the borrower and lender avail themselves of the full opportunities within the market.

The Market's Unifying and Divisive Forces

The market is held together by the fact that all lenders make some funds available as long-term credits on real estate. Diversity arises from their methods of operation, their reasons for making mortgage loans, and their legal and informal organizational structures. What are some of the major factors differentiating their market performance?

Lending institutions vary in their primary reasons for existence; each group was organized to meet a separate credit or saving need. As a result, they have highly distinct policies as to the position of mortgage credit in their operations and as to whether they feel a continuing responsibility to particular classes of potential borrowers.

Another contrast is evident in the source and stability of their funds. Since mortgages are relatively frozen assets, lenders must relate their holdings to their possible cash requirements. Some lenders consider a large share of their deposits to be temporary or subject to rapid withdrawal. Others expect that funds will remain with the institution over long periods.

Firms have many different approaches to lending. Some specialize in mortgages made only in their immediate vicinity; others operate over the entire nation. Some make and service their own loans; others purchase almost all mortgages through intermediaries. Some can handle small, individual properties; others find it easier to place their money in larger sums through tracts or expensive buildings.

Significant variety exists in the types of property upon which loans will be made, the terms or conditions of typical mortgages, and the prevailing interest rates charged.

Lending institutions range from banks and savings associations so small that they may make only one loan a week to mammoth financial institutions—institutions so large, whether banks, savings and loans, or insurance companies, that they process hundreds of loans weekly.

The Diversity of Mortgages

A mortgage is a personal and highly differentiated claim. Differences between mortgages are caused by variations in the laws of each state, in the practices of each lender, in the types and needs of borrowers, and in the property used as collateral.

Borrowers are highly diverse. They include individual consumers, investors and corporations desiring funds primarily for use outside the real estate field, and investors and corporations needing money for their real estate transactions. Loans may be required for the development or construction of new property, for the purchase of existing buildings, or perhaps to remove equity accumulated in real estate in order to use elsewhere.

Mortgages may be classified according to location, borrowers, and type and use of the property. Thus mortgages are said to be on (1) one- to four-family residential structures; (2) other multifamily dwellings; (3) commercial properties, including stores and office buildings; (4) hotels and motels; (5) industrial plants; (6) farms; (7) special-purpose buildings (churches, theaters, service stations, bowling alleys, etc.); and (8) unimproved land.

There may also be differentiation between government-insured or government-guaranteed and conventional types of mortgages.

Legal Factors

Each state or supervisory authority establishes complex legal requirements specifying what the lenders under its supervision may hold in their mortgage portfolios. Frequently particular terms are set forth with respect to minimum equities or downpayments (for example, loans may not be more than 90 percent of value), the maximum period of amortization and its form (say, 25 years of level payments), and the amount of interest that can be charged. In recent years, some states have seen mortgage lending grind to a halt because usury laws set maximum interest rates below the cost of money to potential lenders.

In addition, the area within which many institutions can lend is limited. Much savings and loan lending must be transacted within the home state. Almost all institutions must meet special requirements as to the percentage of assets that can be invested in particular kinds of loans.

Legal influences are felt still more strongly through the differences in the real property laws of the 50 states. Foreclosure procedures, for example, vary dramatically. The period required for foreclosure may run from under a month to over 2 years. Costs incurred range from small sums to over $1,000. Clearly, all these legal factors cause every mortgage to differ from every other.

In new development projects, other difficulties arise because of the need for construction supervision. Since the structure forms a major share of the security, the manner of construction and how plans are followed influence the worth of the final loan. A need for interim financing also exists. As in most industries, builders require loans for working capital. Much of this capital is furnished through construction loans, funds advanced as building is accomplished and paid off either when the structure is completed and sold or when a final loan is granted. The fact that the amount lent is tied to construction progress means that lenders must walk a fine line, desiring to furnish sufficient capital but not wanting to pay out more than the builder has invested in the partially completed unit. Only astute judgment and continuous loan supervision during construction can assure lenders that they actually receive the security upon which they thought they lent their money.

Loans or Commitments

The analysis of the data in the mortgage market is complicated further by the fact that there may be a wide difference between conditions when the loan was agreed to and those prevailing when it was actually made. The data available on flow of funds and on rates of interest and other terms usually apply to the time that the money was paid out. There is frequently a long lag between the time of commitment and the actual loan. Buildings usually cannot be started without a guarantee that a loan will be made upon completion. A lender makes a commitment to lend money when and if the unit is finished and the potential borrower wants to take up the commitment. Such an arrangement ties up future funds. In cases of large structures, tracts, or shopping centers, the money will not be paid out for 1 to 3 or 4 years, during which time money markets may shift drastically. In addition, because so many propositions fall through before completion, the lender can never be certain that the money will actually be used. While lenders are striving to ensure that loans will be made by increasing commitment fees and other devices, many borrowers continue to find more favorable terms in the interim and fail to exercise the option implicit in an advance commitment.

THE LENDERS ON MORTGAGES

Over 22,000 major financial institutions make mortgage loans. Tables 2-1 and 2-2 present a bird's-eye view of the institutional mortgage lending market. Because the 1974 data give a somewhat distorted picture, since lending was off by $23 billion from 1973, in this chapter we frequently show the 1973 data in parentheses following the 1974 data. Thus total loans acquired by institutions in 1974 amounted to $152 (175) billion, or down from $175 billion in 1973. From Table 2-2, their total outstanding loans were $672 (616) at the end of 1974. In addition, the table notes that there are probably at least 15,000 institutions which are eligible to make mortgage loans but made none. These firms tend to be the smaller ones in their respective spheres.

These data do not cover all mortgage lenders. There are thousands of credit unions, fire and casualty insurance companies, real estate corporations, welfare funds, and individuals who also occasionally lend on mortgages. With these other minor lenders included, outstanding mortgage loans exceeded $730 billion in 1975.

The importance of mortgage financing to any particular institution depends upon that institution's position in the saving and lending markets as well as upon its own individual portfolio policy, which in turn is determined by law, by traditions, and by its management. However, the share of the total assets each group holds in mortgages does serve as an indicator both of the importance of mortgages to that particular industry and of the probability that any given firm within it will be active in the mortgage field. Thus lending on real property will be the core of the operations of almost any S&L, MSB, or mortgage bank. On the other hand, while mortgage lending is important to insurance companies, CBs, and pension funds, there are firms in all these industries which direct minimal or no resources to opportunities in the mortgage field.

Table 2-1   An Overview of the Mortgage Market, 1974
(In Billions of Dollars)*

Type of lender	Construction loans				Long-term mortgages				Total
	One- to four- family	Multi- family	Other	Sub- total	One- to four- family	Multi- family	Other	Sub- total	
Originations of mortgage loans									
S&Ls	6.5	1.1	1.4	9.0	30.9	3.3	3.6	37.8	46.8
CBs	6.5	3.4	9.7	19.6	15.8	.7	10.8	27.2	46.8
LICs	†	.1	.3	.3	.4	2.0	7.4	9.8	10.1
MSBs	.5	.4	.3	1.1	3.9	1.4	1.7	7.0	8.1
State agencies and pension funds	†	.7	†	.8	.7	.6	.5	1.8	2.6
REITs	.8	2.6	2.3	5.7	†	.3	.8	1.1	6.8
Mortgage companies	2.0	1.9	1.4	5.3	12.3	.6	.8	13.8	9.1
Federal agencies	†	†	†	†	2.5	2.9	4.9	10.2	10.2
Total	16.3	10.2	15.3	41.8	66.5	11.7	30.5	108.7	150.5
Net acquisition of mortgage loans									
S&Ls	6.5	1.1	1.4	9.0	32.7	3.5	4.0	40.2	49.2
CBs	6.5	3.4	9.7	19.6	14.5	.6	10.7	25.8	45.4
LICs	†	.1	.3	.3	.5	2.2	7.7	10.4	10.7
MSBs	.5	.4	.3	1.1	4.7	1.6	1.8	8.1	9.2
State agencies and pension funds	†	.7	†	.8	1.1	.7	.7	2.4	3.2
REITs	.8	2.6	2.3	5.7	†	.3	.8	1.1	6.8
Mortgage companies	2.0	1.9	1.4	5.3	−1.2	†	.1	−1.1	4.2
Federal agencies	†	†	†	†	14.3	3.5	5.0	22.8	22.8
Total	16.3	10.2	15.3	41.8	66.5	12.3	31.0	109.8	151.6
Net increase in outstanding mortgage loans									
S&Ls	−.3	−1.3	−.1	−1.7	14.8	2.2	2.3	19.3	17.5
CBs	−.5	.3	3.5	3.2	7.0	.3	3.1	10.4	13.6
LICs	†	†	†	†	−1.4	1.1	5.1	4.9	4.9
MSBs	−.1	−.3	†	−.4	.5	.7	1.0	2.1	1.7
State agencies and pension funds	.1	.7	−.1	.7	.8	.7	.7	2.1	2.8
REITs	−.1	.1	−.1	−.1	†	†	.3	.3	.2
Mortgage companies	−.1	−1.7	.5	−1.3	−1.0	†	.5	.5	−1.8
Federal agencies	†	†	†	†	11.1	3.0	2.9	17.1	17.1
Total	−1.0	−2.2	3.7	.5	31.6	8.2	15.9	55.7	56.1

*Figures will not add to totals because of rounding.
†Less than $50 million.
Source: U.S. Department of Housing and Urban Development, *Survey of Mortgage Lending Activity*, March 1975.

TYPES OF LOANS

The tables, plus other supplemental data, give a perspective as to who lends and on what. Table 2-1 shows that in 1974, major institutional lenders acquired $110 (126) billion of long-term mortgage loans. In addition, they acquired about $42 (49) billion of construction loans, making a grand total of about $152 (175) billion. Total repayments were about $54 (65) billion on long-term loans and $41 (39) billion on construction loans, to give a net increase in outstanding loans of over $56 (71) billion.

Since some firms originate loans and then sell them to others in the secondary market, net acquisitions do not present a complete picture. The three sets of figures in Table 2-1 make this clear. The first section shows the mortgage loans made (originated) by each type of lender. The second section shows net acquisitions by lending groups. The differences between these sections are sales and purchases of loans to other groups. Net acquisitions also record the gross mortgage funds made available by the lending groups in 1974. The third section—net increase in outstanding mortgage loans—shows the amounts lent on mortgages after account is taken of repayments against all outstanding loans; that is, the change in net loans measures the increase or decrease in a group's mortgage loan assets. Outstanding loans shown in Table 2-2, for example, are equal to the outstandings at the end of 1973 plus the net increase in 1974.

The principal difference in amounts of originations and acquisitions is found among mortgage companies, the government agencies, S&Ls, and MSBs. Mortgage companies sell loans to these other institutions in the secondary market.

Table 2-2   Total Mortgage Loans Outstanding, 1974
(In Billions of Dollars)

	No. of insti-tutions	Construction loans				Long-term mortgages				Total	Assets
		One-to four-family	Multi-family	Other	Sub-total	One-to four-family	Multi-family	Other	Sub-total		
S&Ls	5,400	5.2	1.9	1.9	9.0	197.2	21.7	21.5	240.5	249.4	296
CBs	14,200	5.8	4.1	10.4	20.3	66.1	3.0	42.4	111.5	131.8	840
LICs	1,800*	†	.1	.3	.4	18.4	18.9	46.2	83.5	83.9	256
MSBs	480	.2	.4	.3	.9	48.7	12.2	12.8	73.7	74.7	110
State agencies and pension funds	17,000*	.1	2.0	.1	2.1	7.7	6.8	4.9	19.3	21.4	222
REITs	200	1.1	4.3	3.4	8.8	.2	.9	5.9	7.0	15.8	17
Mortgage companies	1,500*	1.6	1.7	1.4	4.6	3.3	.1	2.1	5.6	10.2	11
Federal agencies	10	†	†	†	†	52.1	12.2	20.5	84.8	84.8	103
Total	40,590	14.0	14.5	17.7	46.2	393.7	75.9	156.4	625.9	672.0	1,855

*In these groups only 10–60 percent of firms may actually hold mortgages. Some banks will also not hold mortgages
†Less than $50 million.
Source: U.S. Department of Housing and Urban Development, *Survey of Mortgage Lending Activity*, March 1975.

TYPES OF LENDERS

S&Ls are the largest lenders on mortgages. They acquired $40 (50) billion, or 36 (40) percent, of new long-term loans in 1974. They also lend by far the largest share of their total assets on real estate.

CBs are the largest construction lenders and the second largest long-term lenders. They did about a quarter of the long-term lending in 1974 and nearly half of construction volume. They hold the largest share of financial assets, but their mortgage share is less. Traditionally, in response to the ebb and flow of demand for commercial loans, banks have varied their mortgage lending more than others, but this has been less true recently.

In 1974, the 10 federal agencies were the third largest long-term lending group. Their totals somewhat overstated the funds they furnish, however. They include $21 billion of mortgages, against which bonds and notes have been issued to other lenders. Inclusion of these bonds and notes in the lending figures for other intermediaries would considerably expand their totals.

LICs rank fourth in total mortgage loans outstanding, and MSBs fifth. MSBs hold a far greater share of their assets in mortgages than insurance companies do. As the competition from corporate bonds for lenders' money has increased, both types of institutions have placed a somewhat lower percentage of their lending into mortgages. LICs as a group have been letting their one- to four-family-home mortgages run off by only partially replacing them.

As a group, all other institutional lenders showed only a small increase in 1974 in their outstanding long-term mortgage loans. They made a substantial number of loans, but they sold many and received sizable repayments against their existing portfolios. As a result of past volume, the other institutions together hold about 7 percent of outstanding mortgages.

TYPES OF MORTGAGES

Construction Loans

Tables 2-1 and 2-2 present an overall view of where one might expect to obtain loans for particular types of transactions. Examine the four columns headed ''Construction loans.'' The share of outstanding construction mortgages appears relatively unimportant—less than 7 percent of total mortgage loans. On the other hand, they usually average about a third of the total originations. There is a good reason for this difference. Because construction loans turn over at such a rapid rate, a table showing outstanding loans underestimates their share of total activity. On the average, construction money is outstanding for roughly 1 year, while other types of loans last an average of 8 to 10 years. Furthermore, the availability of construction money determines whether construction and development can take place. For this reason and because of their importance in mortgage lending activity, construction loans are far more significant than they appear to be when one looks simply at the total amount of money outstanding on mortgages.

CBs are the most important construction lenders, accounting for over 47 (40) percent of the total volume of such loans. They lend on all types of properties. The next most important construction lenders are the S&Ls, but a higher percentage of their loans is concentrated in the one- to four-family-home category. Many of these construction loans are preliminary to a final long-term mortgage made by the same association.

REITs, also called *mortgage investment trusts* (MITs), and mortgage companies rank next as construction lenders. Their construction activity is far more significant than their role in the long-term market. Mortgage investment trusts originated comparatively few long-term loans. In the construction market, they rocketed to prominence in 1973 and 1974 and then dropped drastically, making few new commitments in 1975. In 1974 they were the second largest construction lenders on apartment houses and nonresidential structures. The volume for mortgage companies dropped sharply, but not quite as much. They ranked just behind mortgage investment trusts in income property lending in 1974.

MSBs lend on all types of construction, but their totals are relatively low because they exist in only a limited number of localities. Construction lending takes place primarily in areas where an institution has an office and thus is familiar with local laws and customs and where it is close enough to inspect the work as it progresses. For this same reason, the remaining institutional lenders make few, if any, construction loans. Because construction loan operations differ so greatly from those of regular long-term lending and because risks have been high, borrowing in this sphere has been particularly difficult and expensive.

Long-Term Loans

Examining the origination of long-term mortgages, we see striking differences depending on the type of property. For the one- to four-family home, S&Ls are by far the largest lenders. They account for nearly half of both originations and outstanding mortgages. In 1974, their net lending in this market reached almost 50 (66) percent of the total funds advanced by all institutional lenders.

Mortgage companies are the third (second) largest originators in the one- to four-family-home area. They differ considerably from other types of lenders because of their continued high concentration on government-insured or government-guaranteed mortgages (FHA-VA). A family borrowing on such a mortgage is most likely to obtain its funds from a mortgage company. In this category, they originated considerably more than half the loans, but then sold them either to government agencies or to other lenders through the instrument of mortgage-backed bonds guaranteed by the government.

In contrast to the single-family market, no lender dominates the market for apartments or for nonresidential borrowing. However, in particular markets, such as farms, raw land, or commercial property, shares are more concentrated than in mortgage markets as a whole. Thus banks and the federal credit agencies are the largest lenders on farms. Similarly, MITs and mortgage companies are far more important in the market for loans to develop property or to warehouse land for future development, than in mortgage lending as a whole.

Table 2-2 does not break down loans between those on new buildings and those to finance or refinance the ownership of existing property. About 60–65 percent of mortgage loans are made on existing properties, but again with major differences by type of property and type of lender. Insurance companies, for example, lend primarily on new properties.

Local Markets

Table 2-2 shows national data. When we examine the local mortgage picture, we find it still more complex. We see a market divided among a variety of institutions and individuals. Many of the institutions which are significant at the national level may not be active in a particular locality. The number of institutions in any local market depends upon the area's size. Local markets tend to be competitive. In all but the smallest of them, there is usually some competition from each of the main financial intermediaries plus mortgage companies and REITs in the case of income property. Rarely will there be a single firm that dominates the entire market. The number of active participants is more likely to range between 5 and 100. Even the 10 largest firms will not account, as a rule, for more than half of the total loans made in any local market.

However, when different types of structures and particular terms desired in loans are taken into account, this degree of competition may not exist. Because there is a more limited interest in specific types of loans and since the number of potential lenders for any individual property may drop drastically if money is tight, borrowers looking for terms they can meet on a given structure may find only a single lender, or perhaps none at all. Still, because the diversity is so great and because lenders may be actively seeking loans at a time when others are out of the market, it is worthwhile for individual borrowers to shop the mortgage market.

LENDERS

We may get a better feeling for what occurs in the mortgage market by examining the following sketches of a few typical lenders.

Small Lenders

Joe Johnson is manager, savings officer, and chief loan officer of the Home Mutual Savings and Loan Association, a firm with assets of $20 million. Although being manager and savings officer takes up most of his time, the firm's income and safety depend primarily on his skills as a mortgage officer. Home Mutual is close to the middle range of S&Ls. Joe has a staff of 10 people and an operating budget in the vicinity of $300,000. On the average, three or four customers come in every day to talk seriously about the possibility of a loan. In the course of the interview, Joe must learn enough about the property, the amount of money needed, and the customer's income and asset situation to decide whether Home Mutual is interested in the particular case.

If there is a mutual interest and an informal agreement, a loan application will be filled out. It lists the proposed amount of the mortgage and its terms, the property description, and the customer's personal credit information. Joe then has to get a credit check and see that the property is appraised, either by himself with part of his management committee or by an independent appraiser. Finally, on the basis of his report, recommendation, and discussion, the loan or management committee may approve the loan.

The money will be paid out only after numerous forms, documents, and ledgers have been prepared and after a formal closing procedure has taken place to ensure that all legal and administrative requirements are met. Then the loan is added to the 1,000 to 1,200 already existing loans which Home Mutual is servicing. Johnson, with the aid of his clerk, has to check carefully the papers and the entire procedure. As each loan is completed, he hopes that it will fall into the routine category which requires only his minimal attention. Unfortunately, though, this is frequently not the case. Payments slow up, and the account becomes delinquent. Now extra time and special efforts are required. Mail communications, interviews, working out of new payment agreements, or a decision to ask for transfer of title or start of foreclosure may be necessary. Johnson may even have to manage the rental and eventual sale of the foreclosed property.

If Joe worked for the considerably larger commercial bank across the street, he would probably be a loan officer. He might find himself spending about the same or not quite as much time handling mortgage problems, but the rest of his work would be concerned with other types of lending. Many customers who approached him for money for their businesses would end up with their loans secured by a mortgage.

If the business were not an S&L but the Johnson Mortgage Company, the size of operation would be about the same. Instead of spending time in attracting savers, Joe would have to spend an equivalent amount of time in finding and negotiating correspondent and lending agreements with out-of-town lenders. Travel to the main insurance capitals would be necessary to line up commitments to purchase the mortgages his firm would originate. He would need to negotiate a line of credit with his local bank. Very frequent contacts would be required as he borrowed on his loans in progress (warehousing). He would also be far more active in calling on builders and real estate brokers so that they would come to him when their clients needed money to finance purchases.

Middle-sized Lenders

In its 80 years of existence, the Provident Mutual Savings Bank has accumulated about $100 million in assets. It is one of the smaller mutual banks, with an operating budget of around $1.5 million. Like most of these institutions, it is in a Northeastern state. Its mortgage department makes between 800 and 1,000 new loans a year and services over 6,000. There are 12 people in the mortgage loan department.

Jack Roberts might hold any of four or five different jobs in this unit. If he were head, he might carry the title of vice president and have a carpet on his floor. In general charge of all mortgage activity, he would spend less time with borrowers for individual homes but more time on specialized loans, such as store or apartment loans. Recently, Provident Mutual has experienced some abrupt shifts in its inflow of savings and overall demand for funds. It has bought and sold mortgages in the secondary market and has varied considerably its ratio of bond investments to other assets. All these activities require greater skill, a constant reexamination and determination of policy, and negotiations with other lenders, borrowers, and officers. Roberts is so occupied by these negotiations, committees, and overall supervision that in the normal course of events he handles only individual loans that are problems or exceptional for some other reason.

If Jack had not reached the top of the mortgage department, he might spend most of his time making appraisals, or he might be in charge of loan servicing and particularly of attempting to clear up delinquencies. Provident has an active construction loan program. One person spends almost full time on builders' sales and contacts. Another loan officer does most of the interviewing and qualifying of customers coming in for individual loans. Still another officer specializes in government-underwritten loans and in negotiations with the FHA or the VA.

The mortgage unit of Provident could be transplanted in size and general functions to a large CB or a slightly smaller S&L. In the S&L field, units of this size or larger account for more than half the lending.

Some, but not many, functions would differ if this were a unit in one of the other institutions. Depending on what type of lender the unit serviced, more or less time might have to be spent on problems of the general money market, the demand for loans, and competitive terms and interest rates. Actually, functions would probably vary more with the geographic area and size of city that the mortgage unit was in than they would vary by type of lender.

Large Lenders

In 1948, Paul Mosher founded Urban Mortgage Company, and it has grown steadily ever since. Urban now has 10 offices and 400 employees, places over $300 million in loans annually, and services over $1 billion in outstanding mortgages.

As president of Urban, Mosher spends almost all his time and effort concentrating on overall problems of policy and management and in meetings with lenders, large-scale builders, and industry and community groups. He attributes his company's success and rapid growth to its willingness and ability to follow the market carefully and to some of its successful innovations that have helped to shape the patterns of the mortgage industry. Servicing contracts, prices, commitments, and interim financing—all have changed constantly. Mosher has had to improvise and find new lenders as major sources of funds have dropped out of the market. Shifting interest rates have given him sizable profits and losses on his inventory of loans.

Urban has built up a fairly large management staff. Most now specialize in very specific tasks even though, as a rule, they have had experience in many of the other functions performed by the firm. One group of officers is charged with producing the customers for loans by working with builders, large-sized real estate firms, and land developers. At the other end, several executives handle relationships with final lenders, traveling to their home offices, placing mortgages, obtaining commitments, and smoothing out servicing problems.

In between are the numerous officers who handle individual loans. These include appraisers, loan processors, and those who interview loan applicants. A firm of this size requires accountants, treasurers, and computer specialists. There is a section for loan closings and a legal division. Another unit handles construction supervision and lending and the obtaining of interim financing. The actual servicing of the loans, for routine and for delinquent cases, requires both large clerical staffs and skilled management.

While some of these functions of a large-scale mortgage company are unique, similar-sized staffs, having many of the same skills and performing related duties, are found in large CBs and MSBs, in the largest S&Ls, and, with somewhat curtailed size and duties, in large LICs.

THE MORTGAGE MARKET IN RELATION TO CREDIT MARKETS

In addition to knowing the size of the mortgage market and its main participants, it is useful to relate mortgage lending to the other credit markets. Table 2-3 provides a general perspective of all lending during the years 1964–1974 by type of lender and type of loan.

Several factors stand out from the table. In the 10 years ending in 1974, the amount of funds borrowed or lent in the credit markets of the United States nearly tripled. Some growth was due to inflation, but far more reflects a greater dependence of our economic system on debt. Among institutions, the CBs experienced a tremendous rate of growth, as did finance companies and REITs. Government-sponsored agencies showed an even larger percentage rate of increase. Thrift institutions—the S&Ls and MSBs—did well for most of the period, but their lending fell off drastically in 1973–1974. Lenders dependent on other than deposit funds during these years had a below-average growth rate.

The table reflects the much more aggressive attitude of the deposit institutions, particularly CBs, to risk taking, lending, and growth. During this period, banks rapidly raised the rates they paid to depositors and other suppliers of funds. They aggressively sought money to lend. They succeeded both in creating new sources of funds and in attracting large amounts into their institutions. They then lent these greatly enlarged flows at profitable rates.

We shall constantly return to another important fact demonstrated in the table. The flow of funds through the deposit institutions and credit markets fluctuates violently. In 1966, 1969, and 1973–1974 the funds advanced by deposit institutions all dropped sharply. In each of these years, the government and individuals increased their lending. These shifts of funds to and from deposit institutions have crucial impacts on real estate lending. They show up even more clearly in quarterly data such as those displayed in Table 10-4. Chapter 10 discusses in detail the reasons for these movements and their effects.

Uses of Funds

Mortgage borrowers take the largest slice of the total credit pie. On the average, about 30 percent of funds lent flow through the mortgage market, while the share of long-term borrowing held by mortgages is well over 50 percent. To obtain this money, mortgage borrowers compete in terms of yield, risk, and profitability with all other potential users of funds. The interactions between these forces determine the actual flows of funds.

Table 2-3   Total Funds Advanced and Raised in Credit Markets, 1964–1974
(In Billions of Dollars)*

	1964	1965	1966	1967	1968	1969	1970	1971	1972	1973	1974
Advanced by:											
S&Ls	11.0	9.6	4.2	9.2	10.2	9.9	11.6	29.2	36.4	27.1	21.0
CBS	23.0	28.4	17.0	35.3	38.2	12.7	33.2	50.3	68.8	80.9	58.1
LICs	7.4	8.2	8.0	8.4	9.0	8.4	9.0	11.8	13.8	15.6	16.0
MSBs	4.4	3.9	2.7	5.2	4.3	3.2	4.1	10.0	10.4	5.4	3.9
State agencies and pension funds	7.3	8.5	10.5	9.3	10.5	11.6	13.1	13.5	14.3	16.5	20.4
Other financial institutions	7.3	10.0	8.5	4.5	13.0	15.3	13.1	12.5	20.9	22.3	18.2
Government	6.9	8.8	13.5	9.3	11.9	16.0	17.8	15.3	9.9	32.5	37.8
REITs	0	0	0	0	.2	.9	2.1	2.5	4.9	4.5	0.7
Other	7.8	5.7	15.3	3.2	16.8	47.5	6.7	18.7	19.0	34.6	41.7
Total	75.2	83.2	79.6	84.4	114.3	125.5	110.8	163.9	198.3	239.4	217.8
Raised by:											
Mortgages, residential	20.0	18.9	13.8	16.0	18.6	20.4	19.2	36.8	51.2	50.3	39.4
Mortgages, other	5.9	6.6	7.5	7.0	8.8	7.4	7.2	12.1	17.7	21.6	15.0
U.S. government	6.3	1.8	3.6	13.0	13.4	-3.6	12.8	25.5	17.3	9.7	12.0
Sponsored credit agencies	.7	2.1	4.8	-.6	3.5	8.8	8.2	3.8	6.2	19.6	22.1
State and local	5.7	7.3	5.6	7.8	9.5	9.9	11.2	17.6	14.4	13.7	17.4
Corporate and foreign bonds	7.1	8.6	11.8	17.2	15.0	14.5	23.8	24.8	20.2	12.5	23.3
Corporate equities	3.5	3.5	4.8	5.5	6.4	10.0	10.3	14.8	12.9	8.0	5.4
Consumer credit	8.5	9.6	6.4	4.5	10.0	10.4	6.0	11.2	19.2	23.0	9.6
Bank loans and open market paper	12.0	18.3	14.1	11.5	20.9	31.6	4.6	13.3	31.9	63.8	52.7
Miscellaneous loans	5.8	6.5	6.9	2.5	8.3	15.8	7.2	3.9	7.4	17.2	21.1
Total	75.2	83.2	79.6	84.4	114.3	125.5	110.8	163.9	198.3	239.4	217.8

*Figures may not total because of rounding.
Source: Board of Governors of the Federal Reserve System, *Flow of Funds Accounts* (Washington).

Figure 2-1 provides a clear picture of the relative importance of mortgage lending for each type of institution. In 1974 the thrift institutions—S&Ls and MSBs—lent about 80 percent of their new money on mortgages. LICs lent slightly less than a third of their new money, while CBs lent less than 20 percent of their new funds in 1974 to real property owners. The ratio for the other types of lenders, except for REITs, tended to be much lower.

The rate of mortgage lending has been unstable. While on an annual basis the total flow of funds to mortgages does not seem too erratic, annual data can hide some very drastic movements from quarter peaks to quarter troughs. Corporations make sharp shifts in investment funds borrowed, especially from the short-term credit markets. These actions seem to cause opposite movements in other flows.

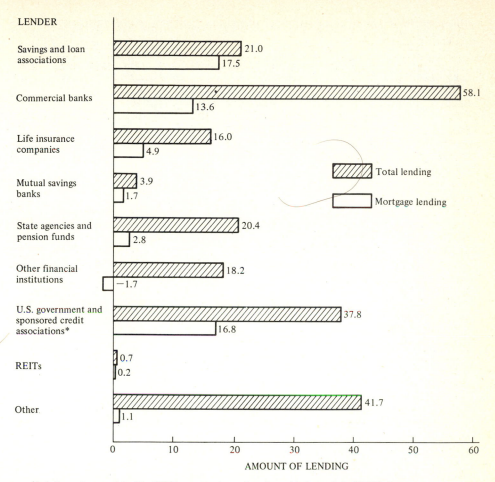

*Includes mortgage pools backing GNMA–guaranteed pass–through securities but excludes FHLBB advances.

Figure 2-1   Financial institutions: total and mortgage lending, funds advanced, 1974 (in billions of dollars). [*Source: Board of Governors of The Federal Reserve System, Flow of Funds Accounts (Washington).*]

This erratic movement of mortgage lending, as well as its rapid growth, appears even more clearly when we examine Figure 2-2. Figure 2-2*b* depicts movements in net mortgage lending since 1946. Lending in 1946 was $6 billion, a very large increase over the war and prewar periods. By 1973 the level had reached over $70 billion. Again, however, the expansion has been far from smooth. Important dips in mortgage activity occurred in 1949, 1951, 1956, 1960, 1966, 1970, and 1974.

The movement of interest rates on mortgages shown in Figure 2-2*a* reveals somewhat similar fluctuations. The level of rates doubled from under 4.5 percent to over 10 percent. There have also been significant short-period variations. While mortgage interest rates and yields move more sluggishly than other rates, substantial changes do take place. When movements in interest rates are translated into quoted prices or the

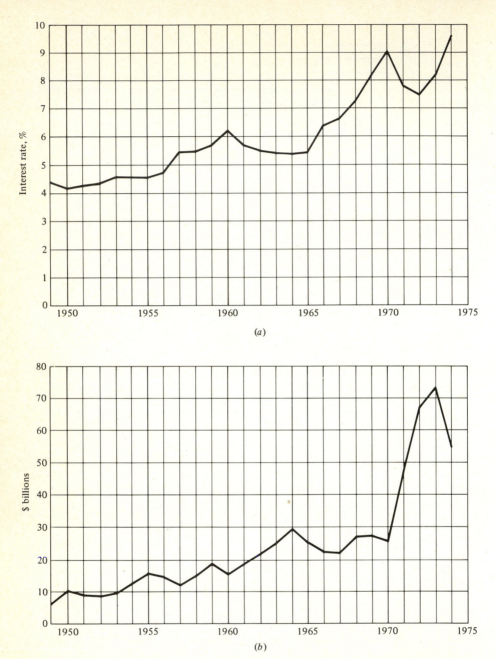

Figure 2-2 Mortgage interest rates and mortgage lending. (*a*) Annual yields on FHA mortgages; (*b*) net mortgage lending in year. (*Source: Federal Reserve Bulletin*.)

values of existing mortgage loans, the price of existing mortgages can fluctuate fairly rapidly and by 20 percent or more, as shown in Figure 19-1.

These fluctuations in net lending, in current yields, and in the value of existing loans are of great importance to those engaged in real estate finance. Rarely will any part of the market escape untouched when such movements in funds occur. Shifts in the demand for, and supply of, mortgages cause rapid changes in the bargaining positions of borrowers and lenders and in the terms they agree upon.

SUMMARY

The market for real estate lending is intimately related to the existence and the growth of financial intermediation through our financial institutions. This relationship is particularly close for those which gather funds from the public through deposits.

As we shall see in greater detail, how and where one can borrow for a specific type of property is related closely to particular institutions and their regulation.

Even a cursory examination of the flow of mortgages through the market over time immediately calls attention to the instability of such lending. Understanding how and why such shifts occur is essential for anyone involved with real estate investment and finance.

QUESTIONS AND PROBLEMS

1 How does the mortgage market compare and contrast with other markets?
2 From Table 2-1 it can be seen that mortgage companies in 1974 originated $19 billion in mortgages; sold $15 billion, to have net acquisitions of $4 billion; and yet ended the year with less money loaned on mortgages than at the start. Explain how this happened. Trace changes for other major lenders.
3 Most comments on mortgage availability are concerned with long-term loans, and yet nearly 30 percent of loans are for construction. Which do you think would be more important for those concerned with real property?
4 Contrast activity changes in the credit and mortgage markets between 1972 and 1974.
5 The importance of different types of mortgage lenders varies greatly among states. How would lending in your state compare with the national picture?
6 LICs as a group, which were once one of the largest lenders on single-family homes, are now one of the smallest. Why do you think this change occurred?
7 How can mortgages be classified?
8 Contrast the objectives of lenders concentrating on construction loans with those of lenders emphasizing long-term loans.

Chapter 3

The Mechanics
of Mortgages

The development of real estate lending has been fostered by the unique legal features of mortgages. These complex legal relationships allow more money to be lent, for longer periods, and at lower risks than is possible with other lending. The basic factor that differentiates the borrowing of money on real estate from other loans is the concept of a secured debt. When lending with unsecured loans, a lender receives a promise to pay. If the borrower fails to pay the debt, the creditor must go to court to obtain a judgment against the borrower. The lender's ability to collect depends upon receiving a judgment which makes certain assets or part of the income of the debtor available to him. Whether he can collect anything will depend on the debtor's income and net worth. In many cases he gets nothing. The decision to lend on an unsecured basis requires a complete analysis of the borrower's current and future income and wealth.

In contrast, in a secured loan, a lien or encumbrance is recorded against a specific property. Upon proper legal action, the lender can force the sale of the property in order to make money available to pay the debt. In the great majority of cases, because of the existence of the secured loan for real property, the success of the loan depends on the future selling price or income-producing capability of the individual property. Only occasionally are other assets of the owner available to pay off loans. Other assets are significant primarily because borrowers may use income from other sources for temporary periods to avoid defaulting on a loan.

USES OF MORTGAGES IN LENDING

Most important for analyzing real estate lending are:

> **1** The terms of the debt contract, most often contained in a promissory note
> **2** The pledge of the security through a mortgage or trust deed
> **3** The procedures whereby the lender can obtain possession of the pledged

security in case of default

Problems arise from attempts to be equitable to both creditors and debtors, while keeping costs low enough so that the price of borrowing is not inordinately increased. Legal costs for initiation of loans, transfers, and foreclosures can become very high. Relative risks can be shifted from the borrower to the lender, or vice versa. Finding sound and desirable compromises in these decisions is most difficult.

The Major Instruments

The three most common methods of obtaining real estate financing over and above an individual's equity are the mortgage, the deed of trust, and the contract of sale, or land contract. While each serves the same basic purpose, there are significant differences in the legal concepts of these three instruments and also in the rights which the borrower and the lender have under each type of loan. The types are listed and discussed in descending order of rights of the borrower, who is also called the "debtor," "mortgagor," "trustor," or "vendee," depending on the instrument. In contrast, moving from the land contract through the mortgage, the lender, also called the "creditor," "mortgagee," "beneficiary," or "vendor," has a more difficult time and meets with greater formalities and costs in obtaining possession of the property which has been used as security for the loan.

Throughout this volume, the term "mortgage" describes the various methods by which money is lent on real property. Included are all the various types of written contract which pledge real estate as a security for repayment of debts. The debts may be long- or short-term. They may arise from real estate transactions or may reflect other purposes:

> **1** A mortgage is a contract which pledges a specific property as security for the repayment of a debt. Both a contract to repay a debt and a pledge of security must exist for a mortgage to exist. The two parts may, however, be in separate documents. The majority of states operate under the so-called lien theory. In these states, the underlying property is merely hypothecated, or pledged. A lien is created against the property in favor of the mortgagee. If the borrower (mortgagor) fails to pay, the lender can go to court to enforce the lien. In a minority of states, the mortgage is considered an instrument which conveys the title of the property to the lender in order to secure the debt. The transfer of title is defeated, or becomes void, when the debt is repaid. Such actual transfers of title by a defeasible deed go back to the common-law theory of mortgages.
>
> **2** The trust deed conveys the title to the property to a third party (trustee). The trustee has a power of sale which he or she is to exercise if the trustor (debtor) fails to meet the conditions of the loan which the trust deed secures. The trustee applies the

proceeds of the sale to pay the obligation held by the beneficiary (creditor). The trustee takes only such title as is necessary. When no default is in existence, the trustee's title lies dormant. Subject to the encumbrance of the debt and trust deed, the trustor has all the normal rights of ownership.

In some states mortgages may carry a power of sale. The effect of such powers is to enable lenders to have the property sold without a judicial procedure. The results are much like the results when there is a trust deed, but no third-party trustee exists.

3   The long-term, or installment, land contract differs considerably from the mortgage, even though it serves the same general purpose. In a land contract, the selling owner, or vendor, agrees to convey title to the purchaser, or vendee, at some future time when the contractual payments have been met. The contract gives the purchaser equitable ownership. Normally this includes the right to use the property while continuing payments. Vendees may sell or borrow on their interest in a property. They can compel that they be granted full title when they have met their side of the bargain, with only such encumbrances as are spelled out in the initial contract. Vendors also may sell or borrow on their interest in a property subject to the terms of the land contract.

Recording of Mortgages

Any interest in land can be borrowed against and pledged under a mortgage. In addition to the usual borrowing against ownership of land and buildings, a common example is borrowing against a long-term lease. The mortgage must be in writing. While not essential everywhere, most mortgages are recorded. This means that the laws regulating recordings must be followed. The mortgages must contain the necessary legal descriptions and acknowledgments required by law. Recording is a filing of the mortgage and related documents with the proper public official so that they may be copied into the public records and made readily available for public inspection. In most states, records are maintained by county recorders, and mortgages must be filed with the recorder in the county or counties where the property is located.

Recording is necessary so that we can tell by looking at the record for a piece of property who owns it or has claims against it. Recording gives a constructive notice— one available to all who search the public records—of the existing interests in the property. Lenders must give such notice in order to protect the priority of their lien or claim. In most cases, the priority of a lien depends on the specific time and order of acceptance by the public official for recording. A first mortgage is first because it is recorded first; others recorded later are junior mortgages. While priority is usually granted in order of recording, certain other liens may be given preference. This is usually true of tax liens or assessments. Depending on the particular state and circumstances, mechanics' liens (arising from work done on a property) also gain priority. The mortgage itself or later subordination agreements may spell out a change in the order of preference from the simple order of recording. Such arrangements are especially important in land development agreements.

Because the order of recording is so important, in many states the process of closing the loan and examining the record to make certain of the order of priority remains an extremely important ritual. In many other states the process of escrow is used, whereby a neutral party is given both the mortgage and the funds to be loaned. Escrow agents are instructed to pay the money to the borrowers only after they have assured themselves that the mortgage has been recorded with the proper priority.

The Promissory Note

The obligation secured by a mortgage is usually evidenced by a promissory note or notes (bond). These notes may be negotiable instruments in and of themselves. Their owner has the right to sue to collect on them in the normal manner. The mortgage lien is simply an additional form of security. The critical factor is the debt. The mortgage has no standing without the note. The mortgage may contain a description of the obligation, or, more commonly, the note may simply be referred to in sufficient detail to put other parties on notice of its existence.

The obligation may refer to money previously lent, to future advances (as in construction lending), or to optional future advances (open-end mortgage). The priorities and rights of other parties may differ depending on the type of advance. Commonly, purchase-money mortgages, which are extensions of credits as part of a purchase, are treated specially. They are given extra priorities, but in many states they cannot claim deficiency judgments.

Mortgages frequently spell out certain duties and rights. Acceleration clauses are common. These specify that upon default of certain conditions, such as failure to meet amortization payments or failure to insure or to pay taxes, the entire debt becomes due and payable. Action may be taken to collect the whole sum rather than merely those parts otherwise due. Under assignment-of-rents clauses the lender can step in and collect rents to apply to the debt. This stops the borrower from collecting moneys and putting them to other uses. Similarly, borrowers are required to maintain properties and to avoid waste or injury to property.

In the usual case, owners can sell properties which are mortgaged, while lenders can sell the mortgages to others. The sale or assignment of the debt to a third party can be recorded, which puts all on notice as to the new creditor. Borrowers can sell their property subject to the mortgage debt.

In some cases, however, a form of the acceleration clause states that the total debt is due in case of a sale. Such clauses may be costly. In periods of rising interest rates or when money is hard to get, the right of the new owner to continue the debt (assume the loan) at its existing terms may mean that the property will sell more easily and for a considerably higher price than if a new mortgage must be obtained. Because the "due-on-sale" clause is a complex technical subject, careful legal planning in drafting documents is of particular importance.

In contrast, loans may also contain clauses restricting the right of the borrower to pay off the loan more rapidly than established in the original agreement. These clauses may specify particular prepayment penalties—sometimes as high as a year's interest—or they may "lock in" the borrower by forbidding repayment during a certain number of years. Clearly, such clauses can be expensive to the borrower if interest rates drop. They must be carefully negotiated to maintain a proper equity between the rights of the borrower and lender.

The Land Contract

The land contract, or contract of sale, is another way for the seller to extend credit and yet attempt to avoid some of the difficulties and costs of foreclosure. Such contracts are particularly common where the buyer puts up only a small equity. They are used because the seller can regain the property in a much simpler manner. As a corollary, they mean that the buyer has fewer rights.

The contract is made between the vendor (seller) and vendee (buyer). It usually provides that the vendor will pass the legal title when the agreed-upon price has been met through installments, which may be accompanied by a fixed lump-sum payment. The seller retains title and can sell his or her rights, including those for future payments, to a third party. In other cases, sellers may simply assign their rights to the payments. They can mortgage whatever interests they have under the contract. Judgments can be entered as liens against their interests. The contract continues even if the vendor dies.

The purchaser, or vendee, receives equitable ownership and many rights pertaining to it. Purchasers can sell or borrow against their interests. While not necessary, many contracts give them the right of possession. Their interests can be made subject to a judgment lien, and their rights, like those of vendors, are not terminated by death.

In many areas, sellers are unwilling to record the contract, since they would then be forced to clear the title if the sale did not go through. In some cases, however, recording is necessary, and the vendee frequently desires it for added protection. This is typically true when vendees are not in possession, since it is the act of possession that gives them much protection. When purchasers meet their obligations, they are entitled to a title free of any circumstances except those they have agreed to in the contract.

If buyers fail to meet payments, vendors can, in most states, take various actions. They can evict a vendee, or they can sue for specific performance, foreclose, sue for damages, and declare a forfeiture of previous payments under the contract. Normally the cost and expense of gaining possession are less than under a mortgage or deed of trust.

Buyers normally use contracts of sale because they have no choice. They lack sufficient funds to obtain ownership with a mortgage. Their interest is harder to transfer and borrow against. Claims against the vendor may cause difficulties in obtaining a clear title. The final title may turn out to be defective or at least will require expensive court action. If the buyer defaults, the losses of prior payments may be considerably greater than under a mortgage.

Just as with the mortgage, the rights of the contracting parties under land contracts have been subject to continual revision, primarily by legal interpretations and occasionally by statute. As a result, in some states there is very little difference in fact between the rights obtained and retained through a contract of sale transaction and those of a normal sale with a loan secured by a mortgage or deed of trust.

Bonds and Debentures

Real estate bonds have a long and undistinguished record. They came into prominence as part of the speculative boom of the 1920s but almost disappeared under a wave of defaults during the 1930s. Originally, bonds were used to attract additional mortgage money to the real estate market. The bonds looked like those issued by industrial or utility companies. They were backed by a mortgage on individual properties.

Most bonds were backed by first mortgages, but second- and third-mortgage bonds also existed. The concept was similar to that of mortgage borrowing. The property owner promised to meet the bond payments. If the payments were not met, the trustee for the bondholder foreclosed and became the owner of the property. Problems arose both because of the great deflation in real estate values and because many firms underwriting and issuing bonds used unduly optimistic appraisals of current and future values. Their profits arose from developing properties and selling the bonds. While successfully tapping a new source of financing, they were not sufficiently careful in evaluating the real worth of their properties. The value of the building used for security fell far below the amounts paid by most subscribers. The problems of operating buildings by bondholders' committees were great. The investments were not liquid. To raise cash, many buildings had to be sold at well below their real value.

The reappearance of real estate bonds in the postwar period has been on a somewhat different basis. Many have been issued by capital-short but promising industrial or merchandising corporations. They have been able to increase the amount of money they could borrow on a property above that possible on a mortgage. Small chain stores, drugstores, and discount houses have difficulty raising capital to purchase properties. By issuing debentures backed by both their general credit and a mortgage, they can borrow more than they could through a mortgage alone. In many cases debentures have made 100 percent loans possible.

In some cases convertible debentures have been used. In others, the bonds have had stock warrants attached. Some lenders believe that since they put up a large share of the capital, they should have an opportunity to share in any potential growth. Such arrangements have been particularly common for new shopping centers when the major leases are not from well-known national firms with excellent credit ratings.

In other cases debentures have been used in syndicate operations either as a form of tax saving or to differentiate risk. Where the syndicate is a corporation, interest on bonds is an expense, not a profit. The limits to which bonds instead of stock can be used in financing depend on complex tax rulings. Ratios of stocks to bonds have to be carefully planned. They differ for each situation. Some cases of this type are discussed in Chapter 21.

A very important new form of bond and debenture is the mortgage-backed security. These are bonds usually issued against portfolios of mortgages held by a trustee. The payment of interest and principal is often guaranteed by the issuer. This concept is explained in the discussion of government agencies, for that is where most of these bonds originate. It is probable, however, that variations of this concept by private organizations will become more and more common.

DEFAULTS AND REMEDIES OF LENDERS

Many observers are surprised when they learn that in recent years, foreclosures or sales under deeds of trust have averaged well over 130,000 per year. Moreover, this is only the tip of the iceberg, since many deficiencies and defaults under loan contracts are corrected without the necessity of going through a formal foreclosure procedure, as a result of forbearance on the part of lenders, or by means of transfers of properties to lenders under deeds. The number of loans in which deficiencies—often minor—arise may be as high as 2 million per year.

A default on a loan is a failure to meet the terms of an agreement. Examples of defaults would include failing to make agreed payments under the note, pay taxes, or maintain necessary insurance, and allowing waste to occur.

Foreclosure

When debtors fail to make payments or default on their agreements in other ways, lenders have the right to attempt to satisfy their claim against a property. We use the term "foreclosure" loosely to apply to this procedure even though several alternative techniques may be involved.

Foreclosure is the sale of whatever right, title, and interest in the property the mortgagor had when the mortgage was executed. The mortgagee goes to court to claim his or her rights. Parties whose claims are superior to those of the mortgagee are not affected. The court determines the amount due. It orders a public foreclosure sale. This usually requires that cash bids be made except for mortgagees, who may bid the unpaid balance due to them. The sums received by the court are used to pay off the unsatisfied liens according to their priority, with any balance (which rarely occurs) going to the original mortgagor or borrower.

In most states mortgagors have a right called the *equity of redemption*. This allows them to pay the debt plus certain penalties up to the time of the foreclosure sale even though the mortgage is in default. In some states an additional statutory redemption period runs following the foreclosure sale for up to a year or more. As a rule, mortgagors cannot waive their rights to redeem. In many states the mortgagor may remain in possession after the foreclosure until the period for redemption has ended.

The cost of judicial procedure is likely to be high. The problems of gaining possession and of potential losses during the redemption period are great. These are among the reasons for the use of the trust deed or mortgage with a power of sale. Under this procedure, the trustee or mortgagee records a notice of default. From the time of the notice, a fixed reinstatement period usually exists. An announcement of a public sale is published. The sale then takes place with public bidding. The trustee or the mortgagee with power of sale passes title. In most cases the deed carries the right of possession. The effect of both the judicial process and the trustee sale is normally to eliminate most junior liens but not federal tax liens.

To save the expense and costs of foreclosure or the public sale, the lender will sometimes seek to obtain a deed in lieu of foreclosure. Since this deed is valuable to the lender to save expenses, courts may scrutinize the transaction with considerable care to be certain that a bona fide sale took place. They want to avoid situations where lenders, because of their superior knowledge and financial strength, could take advantage of the debtor.

Example of Foreclosure or Sale   To understand how these provisions work in a specific state, we can examine the procedures in California, the most populous state and the one with the greatest amount of real estate activity. This will also enable us to contrast procedures under a power of sale in a trust deed and foreclosure in a court of equity. In California, the trust deed is normally used, but the right to foreclose does exist. One or the other of these procedures is typical of most other states:

1   The initial step which a creditor—beneficiary or lender under a trust deed—must take is to give official notice of the existence of a default to either (*a*) the trustee who has the right of sale or (*b*) a court of equity by taking legal action against the debtor to foreclose the property and obtain a deficiency judgment.

2   The trustee will record the default in the recorder's office. The debtor (trustor) will be notified as well as all those who have requested notification. These would include all junior lienholders.

3   During the 90 days following the recording of the default, the debtor or others such as lienholders can clear the default by taking the necessary action to make delayed payments, pay taxes, or correct whatever caused the default.

4   After this 90-day period, the trustee or court-appointed commissioner will hold a public sale. It must be preceded by 20 days of public notice consisting of notices posted on the property and at the point of sale, and published once a week in a newspaper of general circulation. The sale is by public bid. Any sum realized greater than the debt of the holder of the trust deed goes first to other lienholders and then to the owner-borrower. Usually, however, the lender is the highest bidder. The lender makes sure of obtaining possession by bidding, if necessary, the amount loaned, unless the sum bid by others is more than the lender expects to get through taking possession and eventually selling the property.

5   In the case of sale by trustees, they give a deed to the property covering whatever rights the owner had. In addition, the property is cleared of all junior liens.

6   When foreclosures occur through a court of equity, debtors have 12 months to redeem their property by paying their debts. The court transfers a foreclosure title to the purchaser only at the end of this year.

The delays caused by the redemption period, the higher costs, and the difficulty of obtaining a deficiency judgment explain why foreclosure through the courts is rarely used in California. In other states, the procedures followed depend on what remedies are available to the lender. The sale by a trustee can be thought of as the extreme most favoring the lender, with foreclosure through a court the opposite. Each state may differ between these poles. Each will also have different periods of redemption and rights of possession.

Deficiency Judgments

We note that in some cases, no one in a foreclosure sale bids a sum sufficient to cover the outstanding debt, unpaid interest, and the costs of foreclosure. In a judicial procedure, the court may award the lender a judgment against the borrower covering the deficiency between this total amount owed and the amount received by the lender from the public auction.

The problems of these so-called deficiency judgments vary greatly from state to state. In theory, such a judgment can be extremely serious, since it makes the income and the other assets of the borrower available, in addition to the mortgaged property, to meet the debt and any deficiency. As a result, the risk of borrowing is greatly increased. In practice, in many states such judgments have become more and more difficult to obtain. In some states they have been abolished completely, particularly for owner-occupiers. In others a judgment must be based on fair market value rather than merely the amount bid in the sale.

There are numerous ways of reducing the risk of deficiency judgments. One method is through the use of corporations and limited partnerships. Another is by taking title to a property "subject to an existing mortgage." While the property remains as security of the mortgage, the new owner does not assume the liability for the debt. It remains as a liability of the seller. In contrast, if the new owner assumes the mortgage, he or she becomes the principal debtor. The seller, or original mortgagor, however, remains liable for any deficiency, as does the new buyer unless there is a specific agreement by the lender to substitute the new owner in place of the original borrower.

In some cases, a corporation may be used to hold property temporarily, assume the liability on the note, and then transfer the property to an individual. In other cases, the lender may agree that the property shall be the "sole security" for the debt, thus relieving the buyer of personal responsibility. In all these cases, of course, what can be and is done depends both on state law and on the relative bargaining power of the borrower and lender and buyer and seller at the time the sale and loan are made.

TRUTH-IN-LENDING

Real estate lending plays such a vital part not only in American family life but also in the whole national economy that in recent years governments have devoted a steadily increasing amount of attention to regulating the industry. A number of laws have been aimed at protecting and informing consumers. An important milestone was the "truth-in-lending law," enacted in 1969, together with regulation Z, issued by the Federal Reserve Board to implement the law.

Among the provisions of the law is the requirement that all nonbusiness borrowers on real estate be fully informed as to various characteristics of the credit arrangements into which they are entering. In addition, if the loan establishes a lien against the principal residence a borrower already owns, the borrower has the right to cancel or rescind the contract within 3 business days.

Disclosure

For all nonbusiness real estate loans, prospective borrowers must be given a written statement of the finance charges and the annual percentage rate of interest they have agreed to pay. The list of finance charges must be complete and include such items as points or discounts, inspection fees, required credit insurance, and loan fees. Other charges which are often part of a sale but not part of the cost of financing, such as title insurance, surveys, appraisal or inspection fees, and legal charges, are also included, but not as part of the statement of finance charges.

The key concept of truth-in-lending is to make clear to the borrowers the actual annual percentage rate of interest they are paying, that is, the proportion that all charges for finance, including interest, are of the amount borrowed. Usually the rate turns out to be higher than the quoted interest rate on a loan because payments include all costs imposed by the lender for making the loan and because loans are frequently quoted on a discount or other basis which is well below the true annual rate.

Further, the disclosure statement given to the borrower must show when charges start, when payments are due, delinquency charges, prepayment penalties, the total sums to be paid for financing over the life of the loan—except for first mortgages on a house purchase—security retained, ánd similar features. It is assumed that if consumers know all the facts, they will be better able to make logical choices and to shop around for lenders with the lowest rates.

The Right of Rescission

One concern of the lawmakers was that people have too often been talked into junior mortgages without recognizing that they could lose their homes if they failed to meet the required payments. So-called suede-shoe operators, home improvement and book salesmen, and others often pressure unsophisticated buyers into such loans. The law therefore specifies that if the lender acquires a lien on a home as a result of a credit transaction, the borrower must be given the right to cancel or rescind the arrangement.

Borrowers must be made aware of their rights by creditors, who must give them two copies of a formal notice. This notice informs borrowers of the danger of foreclosure of their homes if they fail to pay, tells them that they can call off the deal, and includes a rescission form, the address to which it should be sent, and a deadline. During the rescission period, except for agreed-upon emergencies, no work can be performed. Upon rescission, any deposits must be returned in full. The would-be borrower cannot be charged for expenses.

REAL ESTATE SETTLEMENTS

The concept of disclosure behind truth-in-lending was moved one step further by the Real Estate Settlement Procedures Act of 1974. This act resulted from various controversial issues surrounding real estate settlements and mortgage closings. The act applies to all federally assisted mortgages. Since all mortgages made by federally aided lending institutions are included, coverage is extensive. Because problems have arisen in the functioning of the act, the specific requirements are likely to be altered.

The Settlement Statement Under the act, every lender, whether an individual or an institution, must disclose information on mortgage settlement costs. The lender must supply the prospective borrower with a copy of the uniform settlement and truth-in-lending statement containing an itemized list of such costs as appraisal fees, lawyers' fees, fees for title searches and title insurance premiums, taxes, and other charges. The estimated charges must either be precise or be based on a "good-faith estimate." Failure to meet the requirements of the act can lead to a penalty payment to the borrower as well as a liability in future court action.

The lender must also furnish the borrower with an HUD-prepared booklet explaining the reason behind various settlement and closing costs.

Other Features The settlement act also prescribes certain other relationships between borrowers and lenders for covered loans. The borrower cannot be required to deposit into an escrow account more than a pro rata share of property taxes or insurance. The buyer must be informed of the previous purchase price of a house bought within the past 2 years and not used as a residence by the seller. This provision is aimed at curbing speculation in properties.

A provision forbids requiring title insurance from a specific company as a condition of sale. Tie-in sales are usually illegal, but they have been hard to prove. In addition, people desirous of getting a loan usually have not wanted to make waves; they would rather have their money than a lawsuit. The settlement act established penalties for title companies or lawyers giving kickbacks to those who steer business to them.

Consumer groups have pushed for mandatory ceilings on closing costs. HUD was granted such authority in 1970 but did not use it. The concept of ceilings on charges is extremely controversial. If too low, they can make lending on real estate unprofitable and cause mortgage funds to dry up.

ADDITIONAL FINANCING

Most of this book is concerned with the traditional first mortgage or deed of trust, which remains the basic means of borrowing on real property. However, other devices are important, some of which have a long history of use. Employment of additional financing devices tends to rise and fall as money becomes harder or easier to obtain. In recent years, some of these devices have been featured in new and more complex real estate transactions. They appear as part of what are often called ''creative financing techniques.''

Three techniques aimed at increasing the sums that can be borrowed without disturbing prior lending arrangements are (1) the open-end mortgage, (2) the junior mortgage, and (3) the wraparound mortgage.

Open-End Mortgages

Over the years, the open-end mortgage has been touted as a potential solution to the problem of borrowing additional funds without incurring heavy expenses. Most states have passed laws making such mortgages legal. They have been authorized by Congress and included in the government mortgage programs. Their actual use, however, remains infrequent.

Open-end mortgages provide that existing borrowers can borrow specified additional funds without the necessity of executing a new mortgage by increasing the outstanding principal on their existing loan. The form of the instrument and what advances may be covered vary with the state. Usually advances must cover repairs or improvements on the house. In some states the additional advances must be specified and required in the initial mortgage. In others they may be optional.

The theory is that the improvements or repairs will increase the value of the underlying security by more than the amount advanced. With an open-end mortgage, an owner needing more money can avoid the expense of a new title search, recording expenses, and other fees which make it very expensive to borrow by taking out a new mortgage, particularly if it increases the loan by only a limited amount.

The open-end mortgage gives the new advances the same priority as the initial sum advanced. The idea is to enable owners to use their property as security for added funds. Since property is much better security than most assets available to the average family, borrowing on an open-end mortgage can be done at far less interest than borrowing on a personal or installment loan. Difficulties arise, however, because with rising interest rates lenders have not been willing to advance additional funds at below current market rates. In fact, lenders often use the desire of a family for more money as an opportunity to renegotiate the existing interest rate as well as other terms.

Junior Mortgages

Junior mortgages or liens (those subordinate or with lesser rights than the first mortgage or deed of trust) play a significant part in making many transactions possible. Many of these mortgages originate as part of the transactions in the sale of an existing house, income properties, and land. In many of these cases, the mortgages are retained as part of the deal by the seller. However, junior mortgages are also vital in raising money for the development of many projects and income properties.

Junior mortgages are found in other markets as well. A major one is the market for home improvement loans. People who want to add a new room, put on a new roof, or buy a new furnace frequently find that while they cannot use their existing mortgage, they can get the needed money at a better rate by borrowing through a junior mortgage than by taking out a personal installment loan. Lenders in such cases are more secure because they have a lien against the property. These home improvement loans may also be insured through the FHA, in which case no mortgages are needed.

Consumer Credit   Another group of junior mortgages arises specifically from the consumer or installment loan market. In most large cities, there are companies that specialize in making larger-than-normal consumer loans by using as security the equity a family may have built up in its house. For example, if a family bought a house for $20,000 and paid off $3,000 on its first mortgage and if, in addition, inflation caused the value of the property to go up to $23,000, then the family would find that, including the small downpayment it might have made initially, it would have a $6,000 or $7,000 equity. In such cases, a second-mortgage company might be willing to loan $3,000 or $4,000. This would be more than would be available on a personal loan. In addition, repayments would be spread over a longer period than would normally be available from other types of finance companies. Families in financial trouble frequently use such mortgage loans to consolidate their debts. While these second mortgages are a type of consumer financing, their rates may or may not be competitive with those of other loan agencies. Frequently the yield or interest rate to the lender is higher.

Purchase-Money Mortgages   Risks in the junior-mortgage market are great. Discounts exist, and interest rates are high. Why, then, do people participate in this market? Frequently, this lending takes place either because prospective purchasers do not have adequate funds for the required downpayment or because in buying income property, they want to use increased leverage to raise the amount of property they can control with a small amount of equity.

In a typical sale of a single-family house, the owner might find that a prospective buyer lacks $3,000 of the required downpayment. The seller may find herself with the choice of accepting a $3,000 second mortgage as part of the downpayment, even though she knows she may lose $1,000 on the mortgage, or of waiting for a future purchaser to show up with the necessary cash. The seller might then decide that it is worth $1,000 to sell immediately instead of waiting.

Typically, terms on such a loan might call for 10 percent interest. The principal would be payable at the rate of 1 percent per month for 5 years. The remaining 40 percent of principal would then become due and payable. This is called a *balloon payment*. The mortgage would also contain an acceleration clause carrying the proviso that it would become due immediately if the house were resold.

The seller may decide to hold the second mortgage for a time, or she can ask her broker to attempt to sell the loan. Most localities have individuals or firms that specialize in such mortgages. Or real estate brokers, as part of their business of selling homes, may develop lists of people who will occasionally purchase junior mortgages. Such loans are often sold at 20, 30, or even 40 percent discounts.

Going back to our seller who accepted a $3,000 second mortgage as part of her downpayment, assume the loan is sold for $2,000. By accepting and then selling the second mortgage, the seller in effect has cut her cash price by the $1,000 she felt was necessary. The new owner has been able to buy a house before accumulating sufficient capital. He pays $1,000 more for the house than he would have had to pay if he had had the required downpayment. His monthly payments for the first 5 years are as much as $50 more than on the first mortgage alone. Consequently, the risks to himself, the first-mortgage lender, and the second-mortgage lender are higher. This risk is also increased by the fact that he is expected to pay the balloon of $1,200 at the end of 5 years (60 months).

The new second-mortgage owner has a high prospective yield. By the procedure shown in Chapter 6, her annual yield, if all payments are met on time, can be calculated as over 20 percent. This, however, will be a gross and not a net yield. Since the monthly payments are small, she will incur considerable administrative costs and effort. In addition, her risk will be relatively great, at least during the early years of the loan. On the other hand, she will have her cash back near the beginning of the fifth year. The high theoretical returns attract investors to this market. Firms exist to handle buying and selling of these loans, and even collections.

Reinstatement   The high risk on junior liens arises from the fact that they are subordinate to the first mortgage in all respects. If the first mortgage is foreclosed and the property is sold, the junior lien will be wiped out unless the amount of the sale is sufficient to pay off both mortgages. To avoid being wiped out, the holder of the second loan has the right of reinstatement. This means that if borrowers default on their payments on the first mortgage or deed of trust, holders of second mortgages may take over the payments (reinstate the first loan) and at the same time may foreclose or sell the property themselves.

This can be illustrated by the previous case. Assume the seller had asked a price of $25,000. This was covered by a mortgage from the bank of $20,000, $2,000 in cash, and the second mortgage of $3,000. The first $20,000 would be secured by a note and deed of trust which the buyer would give to the bank, while the second loan for $3,000 would be secured by a note and junior deed of trust. If the buyer then defaults on his payments to the bank, the bank would record a notice of default and order the property sold under the deed of trust. At this point the original seller, who holds the second deed of trust, could reinstate by meeting the payments due to the bank. If she fails to do so, the trustee will sell the property, and the original seller's junior security would probably be wiped out. The sale by the trustee under the terms of the first deed of trust wipes out all rights of the junior lien unless an outside buyer appears at the sale and bids a sufficient sum to cover both liens—an unlikely occurrence.

If the holder of the second deed of trust reinstates the first loan, she must continue to meet its payments. At the same time, by ordering the property sold under her lien, she can reobtain possession of the house she had sold. The procedures will be the same as if the property had been sold under the first lien; but when she reestablishes her title, the mortgage to the bank will still be outstanding because she received the money from the mortgage when she sold the house.

Because the complications are great, and legal costs not inconsequential, in many cases holders of second mortgages will not go through the process of foreclosing unless they feel the value of the property has gone up. It is this danger that they either will be wiped out or will have to go through the cost of foreclosure that raises the risks on second mortgages and makes their interest rates high.

Wraparound Mortgages

The wraparound mortgage, also known as the *all-inclusive deed of trust* and the *overlying (or overriding) note and deed of trust*, is another device using a mortgage which is subordinate or junior to a permanent (usually preexisting) mortgage. It is more common on large-income properties. It is frequently used when a mortgage exists with a lower interest rate than currently available but with a low outstanding principal. Sellers or lenders on wraparound mortgages retain responsibility for payments on the permanent mortgage. They advance only funds equal in amount to the difference between the face amount of the wraparound mortgage and the existing outstanding mortgage balance. They receive payments on the new, enlarged sum and continue to make the payments on the existing original loan. The wraparound mortgage lowers the required downpayment, but at a high cost in interest.

Example   Consider a wraparound mortgage granted for $1,000,000 at 10 percent interest, based on a property with an $800,000 permanent mortgage at 8 percent. In this case, the wraparound lender is advancing $200,000. He receives 10 percent interest on the entire $1,000,000 and pays 8 percent interest on the $800,000 permanent loan. In the simplest case, he is receiving a return of 18 percent on his $200,000 investment.

This is calculated by examining the wraparound lender's receipts and payments. The composition of the $100,000 in interest paid by the borrower for the first year can be broken down as follows:

8% paid on the $800,000 permanent mortgage	$ 64,000
10% paid on the $200,000 additional financing	20,000
2% (10% − 8%) received by the wraparound lender on $800,000	16,000
	$100,000

The wraparound lender's initial return on his $200,000 is $36,000, or 18 percent, calculated either

```
Receipt of 10% on $1,000,000          $100,000
Less payment of 8% on $800,000          64,000
    Return on $200,000                 $ 36,000
```

or

```
2% (10% − 8%) on $800,000      $16,000
Plus 10% on $200,000            20,000
    Return on $200,000         $36,000
```

Earnings over the life of the mortgage will differ depending on the amortization agreements discussed in later chapters. Depending on the repayment terms, the wraparound lender's share of the outstanding debt will vary. From the example, it is clear that if his percentage of the total amount still lent rises, his rate of return will fall. If a point were reached where the original loan was paid off but he was still owed money on his loan, his yield would fall to 10 percent.

Clearly, 18 percent is a high return. The actual 10 percent rate paid by the borrower may, however, be less than he would have to pay for a new $1,000,000 loan, or there may be other sound business reasons for using this specialized financing device. The wraparound is often used by a developer who wants to reduce the amount of downpayment required from the buyer. Sometimes the seller can get better financing terms than the buyer can, and the wraparound can facilitate the transfer to the buyer. It provides the seller more protection than a second mortgage since the seller receives the total payment and then forwards the amount due on the first mortgage. Thus the seller can exert direct control over the payments on the permanent debt.

Extended Terms   The wraparound mortgage generally allows much greater flexibility of debt-service payments. The term is usually longer than available with traditional secondary financing. In fact, it is not unusual for the term of the wraparound to be longer than that for the underlying permanent financing. Often the wraparound will have an extended term with a balloon payment due when the permanent loan is paid off. With more flexibility as to payment terms, the debt-service payments can better match the cash-flow pattern of the property. Also, because of the larger face amount of the wraparound, more interest can be prepaid.

Because the wraparound mortgage generally has a higher interest rate and longer term than the underlying permanent loan, there will be differences in the annual interest deductions and principal payments. More of the debt service in the early years of the mortgage is interest. Thus when the property is sold or refinanced, a larger relative amount of the wraparound, more interest can be prepaid.

The effective rate of interest on the additional funds will be significantly higher than the rate on a regular first mortgage and may well exceed that legally allowed under the usury laws. Consequently, use of the wraparound may be a means of avoiding usury problems, although again legal interpretations are uncertain and varied.

SUMMARY

The distinguishing factor of real estate lending is the secured loan. The mortgage or lien makes it possible to raise money to pay a debt through forced sale of a property. However, this is a drastic remedy protected by numerous laws and legal complications. The expense of foreclosure may greatly lower the value of a security. The amount of risk accounts for part of the interest paid on borrowings. It may be high, particularly in the case of secondary or junior mortgages.

In recent years, borrowers have received more favorable treatment than in the past. This is especially true with respect to deficiency judgments in many states. Changes have also caused more attention to be paid to methods of adjusting debts in order to avoid the cost of foreclosure. As we shall see in the next chapters, security has also been increased by the introduction of many forms of mixed methods of raising funds.

QUESTIONS AND PROBLEMS

1 Explain the principal differences between a mortgage, a deed of trust, and a land contract (contract of sale).
2 What is the main feature of a secured loan?
3 What danger would you run if you failed to record a mortgage?
4 List the steps which take place when a lender forecloses against a property.
5 Explain the critical features of the Real Estate Settlement Procedures Act.
6 If you hold a specific lien against a property, must you look solely to the property to satisfy your claim?
7 Why might it be advantageous to both buyer and seller to use a land contract?
8 What is a junior mortgage?
9 Describe the process and importance of reinstatement.
10 Does the mortgagor require the approval of the mortgagee to sell a property?
11 What is a wraparound mortgage? Why would it be used?
12 What public policy questions are raised by the issue of deficiency judgments?
13 What is the rationale of usury laws?

Chapter 4

Leverage and the Thrust to Borrow

Buildings and pieces of real property are large and expensive. Only rarely do people possess enough cash or available funds to finance a major investment by themselves. Even if they could, in most cases they would not, since they would be unwilling to risk so much capital in a single investment. Consequently, outside financing is utilized for most real estate purchases.

The way in which the relationship between the owner and the lender is structured is very significant for both. How money is provided for a real estate venture, whether in the form of equity or debt, determines its risks and profitability. Usually, people who purchase a property pay part of the price with their own resources and the rest with borrowed money.

Much of the analysis of this book deals with determining when it is worthwhile to borrow or lend and where funds are available. A loan increases borrowers' ability to purchase property. With a loan, borrowers may achieve either the right to occupy a property or the right to profit from its operations and future sale. In turn, they agree to make certain payments, and they take the risk that they may lose their own capital. Sound investing and successful lending depend upon making good decisions as to when and how much to borrow.

BORROWING MONEY ON REAL ESTATE

When negotiations take place between lenders and borrowers, they usually revolve around three prime questions: (1) How much of the value of the property shall the lender or lenders furnish in the form of the debt in comparison with the amount to be put up by the owner as equity? (2) What amount of money will the owner have to pay to the lender each month, quarter, or year? (3) How much of the payment will be considered interest to pay for the loan of the money, and how much will be credited as a repayment of the initial debt?

Equity

The difference between the value of the property and the sum of all debts is called the *owner's equity*. Owners of equity assume major obligations. They must pay certain sums and meet other conditions of the debt agreement. If they fail to do so, they will be in default and may lose their property through foreclosure. However, if they meet their debt and other obligations, they have the right to all the residual returns from the property. These may include periodic cash payments, substantial tax benefits, and an increase in the value of their equity. Their profits or yield will depend upon the relationship of these returns to their investment.

The Amount of Debt and Equity

The relationship between the debt and equity of a property is spoken of in several ways. One is the *loan-to-value ratio*, or the percentage of the cost of a property covered by loans. Thus if a house is purchased for $50,000 and the mortgage is $40,000, the loan-to-value ratio is 80 percent. We can also say that the downpayment is $10,000, or 20 percent, or that the owner has a 20 percent equity in the house. If he got a good buy and the house shortly becomes worth $60,000, we would say that his equity is now $20,000, or 33 percent.

The loan-to-value ratio in many cases determines whether a purchase can be made, the risks involved, and the potential profit or losses. Much of the growth of homeownership in this country has been made possible because loan-to-value ratios have increased and downpayments have decreased as a percentage of cost. These changes have allowed families with lower incomes to buy homes and have also increased the price and size of houses a family can buy.

The higher-percentage loans also increase the risk of foreclosure and the potential loss to the lender. With smaller downpayments, a small drop in value can wipe out the owner's equity. The debt will be greater than the value of the house. The chances that lenders will have to foreclose and that they will lose on the foreclosure both rise.

Downpayments

Homeownership in the United States has expanded rapidly in the past 25 years as changes in mortgage terms have brought about lower downpayments and longer periods over which to retire debts. Two factors limit the ability of a family to buy and the amount it can pay for a house: (1) It must have enough savings to make the required downpayment, and (2) the monthly payments for mortgage interest and amortization must not exceed a certain percentage of its income.

While the need to accumulate savings for a large downpayment has kept many families from buying homes in the past, this is far less true today. The government, through the programs of the FHA and the VA, showed that low-downpayment mortgages could be sound. Today private mortgage lenders and mortgage insurers require downpayments only 15 to 20 percent as large as those demanded 30 years ago.

If no downpayment is required, a family needs no accumulated savings, no matter what the value of the house. If a 100 percent downpayment were required, there would be very few families with sufficient savings to own their own homes. In 1975, under the FHA program, a family could get an insured loan for 97 percent of the value of a $25,000 house. This meant they would have to accumulate or raise only $750 for their downpayment.

While savings rates vary greatly among families and by income, an average family making $10,000 a year could be expected to save the amount necessary for such a downpayment in a year or so. Even families with considerably lower incomes could be expected to accumulate the necessary downpayment in not too long a period. Consequently, under the FHA program, the downpayment has become a rather negligible hurdle for a $25,000 house. Even for a $45,000 house, the required downpayment would be only $3,750, or less than 9 percent.

These sums contrast strikingly with the amounts of downpayment required before the FHA and even during its early days. In 1934 under the initial FHA programs, a family would have had to pay $9,000 down on a $25,000 house. Of course, at that time such a house price was typical of a comparatively wealthy family. Without FHA, a family probably would have had to pay more than $10,000 down on a $25,000 house and between $15,000 and $20,000 on a $45,000 house. Accumulating savings of such magnitudes was a real hurdle which the average family could not surmount.

Downpayments on Income Property

Just as it does for the potential borrower, a reduction in the percentage downpayment on income properties increases an investor's ability to buy a property or to buy more properties with a given amount of capital. This added ability to buy is called *leverage*, which can be defined in two ways. With reference to the funds needed for a purchase, leverage is the relationship between the owner's equity and the total value of a property. Consider the example of Table 4-1. The table shows a property which sells for $1,000,000 and which has a cash flow of 12 percent of its value, or $120,000 per year. Loans are available to the investor at 9 percent interest, with the debt to be repaid in monthly payments over 25 years. Under these terms Table 4-2 shows that the borrower must pay $8.40 per month for each $1,000 borrowed, or $10,080 per year for each $100,000 borrowed.

A comparison of the property value in column 1 and the investor's equity in column 2 gives us a measure of leverage. Examine the two cases in the first and last rows of Table 4-1. In row 1 the investor would put up $500,000 to purchase a $1,000,000 property. His leverage is 2 to 1. In the last row, he would put up $100,000 for the same property, and so his leverage would be 10 to 1. The larger mortgage increases his leverage fivefold. If the investor had $500,000 and a number of similar properties offered to him, in the first case he could control $1,000,000 in property, as compared with $5,000,000 in the second case.

Table 4-1 Leverage Resulting from Increases in the Ratio of Mortgage Debt to Cost

Ratio of mortgage debt to total cost	Total cost (1)	Equity investment (2)	Cash flow before debt service (3)	Debt service (4)	Net cash flow after debt service (5)	Percent cash flow of equity investment (6)
.50	$1,000,000	$500,000	$120,000	$50,400	$69,600	13.92
.60	1,000,000	400,000	120.000	60,480	59,520	14.88
.70	1,000,000	300,000	120,000	70,560	49,440	16.48
.80	1,000,000	200,000	120,000	80,640	39,360	19.68
.90	1,000,000	100,000	120,000	90,720	29,280	29.28

Financial Leverage

A second way of measuring leverage is based upon the difference between required loan payments and the overall rate of return on a property. Most frequently, leverage refers to this second concept. Leverage is the relative spread per dollar of equity between a project's cash flow (or net operating income) and the required payments on the debt. Investors receive not only the return on their own invested funds but also the spread between what the property earns and the cost of the borrowed funds.

Again consider Table 4-1, particularly columns 5 and 6. With a $500,000 equity and a $500,000 mortgage (row 1), net cash flow after debt service is $69,600. This sum divided by the equity gives a cash-flow percentage of 13.92 percent. For the last row, the cash flow after debt service is $29,280, which, divided by the $100,000 in equity, gives a flow of 29.28 percent. Since the ratio of equity and debt change over time, it is important to recognize that initial rates of return or rates of gain on initial equity differ from actual yields or rates of return. The more precise methods of calculating actual returns are explained in later chapters.

Leverage exists because the 12 percent net operating income exceeds the 10.08 percent which must be paid on each dollar borrowed. One way of thinking about this is to divide the cash flow on the property into the portion paid for by the owner's equity and that paid for by the loan. The owner receives any return on the part he paid for with his own funds plus any spread on the part paid for by the loan. For example, in the first case the owner receives a 12 percent cash flow on his $500,000 equity, but he also receives the difference between 10.08 percent and 12.00 percent on each dollar of the loan. His equity and the loan are both $500,000, and so he earns 12 percent on his half plus 1.92 percent on the second half, or 13.92 percent on his equity. In the second case, he earns 12 percent on his $100,000 equity, but he also receives the 1.92 percent spread on each of the $900,000 borrowed. This is equal to $17,280, which, added to the $12,000 gross flow on his $100,000, gives a total return of 29.28 percent [12% + (1.92% × 9)].

Operating Leverage Because leverage is a dynamic force, its importance for real estate financing far exceeds these initial examples. For most properties the spread will not remain fixed. In many situations, the cash flow before debt service can increase while the debt service remains constant (see Table 4-5). This means a greater spread per dollar of debt, with the return to the equity being multiplied still more. Such potential movements are called *operating leverage*.

Leverage at Sale   A third type of leverage arises when the property changes in value over time. All the change in value accrues to the equity holder. For example, suppose the property in Table 4-1 is sold for $100,000 above the purchase price after subtracting all costs of sale, taxes, etc. The person who put up $500,000 in equity will realize a 20 percent gain. On the other hand, the purchaser who invested only $100,000 and borrowed $900,000 will have made a 100 percent gain on the investment.

Tax Leverage   Income tax benefits in the form of tax shelters, shifting of the time at which taxes must be paid, and the ability to pay lower rates are an extremely important part of the total benefits an investor receives from ownership of properties. These benefits are explained in detail in Chapter 21. At this point, we merely note that most tax benefits are based on the total value of the property; yet they accrue entirely to the owner of the equity. As a result, owners' tax benefits will increase with their leverage. In many cases, tax leverage has been the most significant of all.

All these types of leverage work in the same way as in the example of Table 4-1, and their effects can be generalized. The smaller the downpayment over which the total property returns—whether from operations, appreciation in value, or tax benefits—are spread, the greater the percentage return on the equity. In addition, the greater the positive spread between the average earnings and the debt service, the more leverage will work in favor of the owner. However, spreads are not always positive. In a loss situation, leverage works in reverse (tax leverage is an exception). The greater the negative spread between earnings and debt service, the more leverage will work against the owner.

DEBT-SERVICE PAYMENTS

The fact that downpayments may not be a major hindrance for many potential homeowners does not mean that everyone can easily buy the type of house he or she wants. Having jumped one hurdle, families encounter a second—their ability to make the necessary monthly or annual debt-service payments on the house they desire. The amount they are able to pay is determined by their expected income. The amount they must pay depends on (1) the price of the house or the amount they borrow and (2) the debt contract, which establishes the amount of money to be paid on the loan each year. Thus how much a family can spend on a house is a function of the relationship between its monthly or annual income and the required monthly or annual payment per dollar of loan.

In the same way, the degree of leverage that can be handled in an income investment also depends on the expected cash flow and tax benefits related to the amount of money which must be paid annually for each dollar borrowed. The amount which must be paid each year per $100 of the initial amount borrowed is called the *annual constant*. Much analysis of income properties is concerned with the size of this constant.

The desire to keep leverage high leads to a need to keep the constant low and within the earnings potential of a property. The desire for higher loans with lower annual payments is so great that investors are willing to make considerable sacrifices to achieve this goal. They may agree to pay higher interest rates, to pay much more cash at a future date, or to share profits with the lender. They do this (although they try to avoid giving up income) because they hope to gain from the leverage, because they may have an extremely high time value for money, because the payments as structured give them higher tax benefits (see Chapter 21), or simply because if they have to try to meet higher current payments, it becomes impossible to borrow and buy.

The most common type of payment plan, particularly on home mortgages, is to agree that payments will be equal in each period. However, on income properties many other methods of payments exist. In many cases owners want to maximize the cash flow they obtain from a property. This means they want the constant to be as small as possible, particularly in the early years of an investment, so that they can recover the money they put up as rapidly as possible. As a result, more and more contracts contain a variety of conditions for the loan payments. For example, some might provide for no repayment of the principal for 3 to 5 years while a property is building up its flow of income. Others might move from very low repayments of principal to very high ones after a period in order to force a refinancing of the loan.

The Annual Constant

To understand what possibilities exist in structuring or restructuring the debt service of a property, one must recognize the basic factors which enter into these decisions:

1 The amount of money owed as debt is called the *principal*. Lenders may furnish cash, or the debt may represent payment for other rights. Not infrequently the principal includes added sums or fees above the funds advanced.

2 The amount charged for the use of money is called *interest*. Interest is usually expressed as a percentage, or a given percent per year of the principal. Thus a charge of $10 (the interest) for 1 year on a loan of $100 (the principal) gives an *interest rate* of 10 percent per year.

3 It is agreed that the loan will extend for a certain period. This is called the *term* of the loan—say, 10, 20, or 30 years. The date at which the final payment is due is the maturity date for the loan. Agreements also specify how often payments will be made during the life of the loan. Payments are usually made on a monthly, quarterly, or annual basis, but split agreements which specify no payments or odd payments for some periods are becoming more common.

4 The amount of the principal repaid in any period is called an *amortization* payment. If upon maturity the principal has not been completely amortized, or paid off, a *lump-sum* payment is required. If the unpaid balance is considerably larger than the typical previous amortization payment, the lump sum is called a *balloon payment*.

Decisions taken as to each of these four factors determine the size, the number, and the costs of each periodic payment—that is, of the monthly or annual constant. While the amount for each payment is usually found by looking in a mortgage table, the impact of the size of the constant on all lending and investing decisions is so important that we must understand just what is happening when these decisions are made. We must look within the mortgage table.

Fixed-Term and Level Payments

The typical home mortgage is based on an agreement that payments will be equal in each period. Bargaining usually takes place primarily with respect to the length of time over which the loan is to be repaid, that is, over what time period the principal is to be amortized, or reduced to zero. Agreements commonly specify periods of anywhere from 15 to 40 years in length.

These mortgage payments have the effect of paying the interest or cost incurred during that month and simultaneously reducing some of the outstanding principal amount of the debt. The size of a monthly payment and how much of a payment goes toward interest and how much toward repaying the principal depend upon the term or number of monthly payments to be made and the interest rate charged on the loan. Looking down any column in Table 4-2, it is clear that the greater the number of payments, the smaller each payment must be. On the other hand, the decrease in the size of payment is not proportional to the increase in number of payments. Thus looking at the 5 percent column, we see that to extend the term of a loan from 5 to 20 years enables us to cut the monthly payment by over 60 percent. However, if the term of the loan is extended another 15 years to 35, the cut in monthly payments is less than 25 percent.

We also note that as we move across the table, considering loans at each interest rate, the amount of the monthly payment rises. The effect of an interest rate increase, however, is much larger at longer maturities than it is at the shorter ones. Thus if a mortgage is to be paid off in 5 years, increasing the interest rate from 5 to 11 percent increases the monthly payment by about 15 percent. On the other hand, at 40 years the same increase in interest rates means that the monthly payment must be more than 90 percent higher.

Interest and Principal

These differences arise because when a loan is amortized with level payments, the size of the starting payment must be greater than the interest charge. Some of each payment goes to cover the interest, and some goes for repayment, or amortization, of the

Table 4-2   Monthly Payments to Amortize a $1,000 Loan in a Given Period*

Term in years	Monthly payments	Interest rates						
		5%	6%	7%	8%	9%	10%	11%
5	60	$18.88	$19.34	$19.81	$20.28	$20.76	$21.25	$21.75
10	120	10.61	11.11	11.62	12.14	12.67	13.22	13.78
15	180	7.91	8.44	8.99	9.56	10.15	10.75	11.37
20	240	6.60	7.17	7.76	8.37	9.00	9.65	10.33
25	300	5.85	6.45	7.07	7.72	8.40	9.09	9.81
30	360	5.37	6.00	6.66	7.34	8.05	8.78	9.53
35	420	5.05	5.71	6.39	7.11	7.84	8.60	9.37
40	480	4.83	5.51	6.22	6.96	7.72	8.49	9.29

*For example, to amortize a $1,000 loan in 10 years at 8 percent interest, the borrower must pay $12.14 per month for each of 120 months.

Source: Derived from P. Wendt and A. R. Cerf, *Tables for Investment Analysis* (Berkeley: University of California, Center for Real Estate and Urban Economics, 1970).

principal. Since each payment reduces the amount owed, the interest payable next time is based on a smaller outstanding balance and therefore is lower. It follows that in each succeeding period, the amount of the constant payment credited to principal is greater, and the amount for interest is less.

Table 4-3 shows how this works. This table shows the amount paid annually on a $10,000 loan at 9 percent, to be paid off in 20 years through 240 equal monthly payments. The $1,097.67 paid in each year is (except for rounding errors) obtained from the $9 per month per $1,000 of loan found in Table 4-2 at the intersection of the 20-year row and the 9 percent column.

We see in the table that in the first year, most of the payments—$892.40, to be exact—goes to cover the interest charged by the lender. This charge is identical to the interest the lender would receive if he or she had deposited the $10,000 in a savings account paying 9 percent interest.

We also note, however, that some of each monthly payment has gone to pay off part of the loan. In fact, at the end of the year, $187.27 has been paid off. The outstanding balance is $9,812.73. At the end of each month and year, the amount of the outstanding principal on which interest must be paid decreases. As a result, the amount in each successive monthly payment going toward interest is reduced, and the amount going to repay principal rises.

This is clear from the table also. In each year, the amount shown as interest paid falls. Thus in year 1 almost 90 percent, or $892.40, goes to interest, while in the last (or twentieth) year the interest part is $50.84, or under 5 percent of that year's payments. In the first year, interest is being paid on the average outstanding balance, which is $10,000 at the start and $9,812.73 at the end of the year. In the twentieth year the balance is $1,028.83 at the start and zero at the end.

MONTHLY PAYMENTS AND HOMEOWNERSHIP

Table 4-2 enables one to say more about the relationship of housing purchases and monthly payments. The relationships between income and mortgage payments deter-

Table 4-3   Annual Summary of Monthly Amortization

Year	Annual debt service	Interest	Principal	Cumulative principal payments	End-of-year principal balance
1	$1,079.67	$892.40	$ 187.27	$ 187.27	$9,812.73
2	1,079.67	874.83	204.84	392.11	9,607.89
3	1,079.67	855.62	224.05	616.16	9,383.84
4	1,079.67	834.60	247.07	861.23	9,138.77
...	...	...	...	...	...
17	1,079.67	293.49	786.18	7,170.65	2,829.35
18	1,079.67	219.74	859.93	8,030.58	1,969.42
19	1,079.67	139.08	940.59	8,971.17	1,028.83
20	1,079.67	50.84	1,028.53	10,000.00	0.00

Source: Derived from P. Wendt and A. R. Cerf, *Tables for Investment Analysis* (Berkeley: University of California, Center for Real Estate and Urban Economics, 1970).

mine the amount which can be spent for a house as well as the risk of default. How a payment is divided between interest and amortization affects the risk as well as the real cost to the owner.

Ability to Buy

From the data in Table 4-2 we can see the joint effect of higher interest rates and shorter amortization periods on the amount of income a family needs to purchase a particular house. We see that required monthly payments rise with interest rates and fall with the length of the amortization period. Obviously, they also rise with the price of the house or the amount of the loan. The table shows payments per each $1,000 of a loan. We must multiply each figure in the table by the number of thousands of dollars borrowed. To illustrate, a loan of $25,000 at 9 percent amortized over 25 years would require payments of $210 a month (25 × 8.40). On the other hand, the same house purchased with a similar $25,000 loan with 5 percent interest payable over 35 years would require monthly payments of only $126.25 (25 × 5.05). If we now assume that a family can pay 20 percent of its income for its mortgage, then the family would have to earn over $1,000 per month to live in the $25,000 house with the higher interest rate and shorter amortization period (5 × 210 = 1,050). But with the lower interest rate and longer loan, the family's income would have to be only about 60 percent as much. Because other expenses of owning a house are considerable—taxes, maintenance, and so forth—many families would find it difficult to pay 20 percent of their income for the mortgage payment alone. As a rule of thumb, they might pay 25 percent of their income for all housing expenses.

As costs of housing have risen and interest rates have gone up, the ability of the average family to buy a new house has fallen drastically. Immediately after World War II, almost any family making more than the minimum wage could afford to buy a typical house being produced by large builders almost everywhere in the United States. At present, in most parts of the country a family probably has to earn three times the minimum wage to be able to afford even the lowest-cost new house meeting FHA standards.

Risks and Costs

The larger the outstanding balance compared with a property's value, the larger the risks are likely to be. If a borrower defaults, the probability is greater that the loan balance will exceed the house's value. The larger the share of interest in a payment, the greater the outstanding balance will be at any time. Furthermore, the larger the share of interest in the payment, the greater the real cost to the owner is likely to be. At any time, the principal outstanding will be larger, and this will require higher interest payments over a longer period.

Note that while the payments fall as the amortization period lengthens, the higher the interest rate, the less effective longer amortization is in reducing payments. As a corollary, when amortization periods are long, a relatively small amount of a loan is repaid in the early years. In the case of a loan at 9.0 percent interest, how much would be repaid in the first 5 years with differing amortization periods? The answer is that with a 15-year loan 20 percent will be repaid in the first 5 years. Repayment is 6.7 percent on a 25-year loan, 2.5 percent on one of 35 years, and less than 2 percent on a

40-year loan. The fact that so little has been repaid on the longer loans at the end of 5 years means that the amount required for interest payments remains high, since the amount of principal outstanding on the loan is only slightly reduced.

The amount of interest in each contract and payment varies also: (1) If we pay off a $1,000 loan charged at 5 percent·yearly in 60 quarterly payments over 5 years, we will pay $1,132.80 in total, or $132.80 in interest. (2) For a similar $1,000 loan paid off in 480 payments over 40 years, we will pay $2,318.40, or $1,318.40 in interest. We are borrowing the money for a longer period and therefore pay more. (3) If the loan carries an interest rate of 10 percent (that is, if its time value is doubled), then to pay it off in 60 monthly payments over 5 years will require payments totaling $1,305.00 or $305 in interest. We will have more than doubled the amount paid in interest. However, since each payment includes a payment on both interest and principal, our actual monthly payments will not rise by anywhere near the over 100 percent increase in interest payments.

We should, however, differentiate carefully between more interest paid because we borrow for a longer period and more interest paid because the rate goes up. Thus although the 40-year loan at 5 percent requires interest payments nearly 10 times as great as those required by the same loan for 5 years, its economic cost to a house buyer may be far less than that of the shorter loan. The real cost depends upon the value of money to individuals and on their own discount rate (see Chapters 6 and 25).

INVESTING AND THE ANNUAL CONSTANT

The larger the loan and the smaller the equity on a property, the greater are the effects of leverage. Investors recognize that, just as with home mortgages, each reduction in the annual constant increases the maximum loan a given operating income can support.

Some properties are bought by conservative investors who are concerned with underlying values rather than with leverage. They fear the dangers of default and foreclosures which come with borrowed money. They look upon high interest rates as expenses that far outrun the real value of money.

In recent years, however, many more properties have been sold to investors convinced that leverage is the secret to amassing a fortune. Many investors were sure that the greater the leverage on a property, the more likely it was to be worth buying. They have been willing to increase their leverage. They have accepted added costs in order to reduce the equity required for a purchase.

There are several ways of increasing leverage: (1) The period over which a loan is amortized can be extended. This reduces the annual constant so that a given cash flow can pay for a larger loan. (2) Annual amortization payments and even interest payments can be delayed. This is accomplished through agreeing to make after a few years—say, 5—a single large or balloon payment that includes all amounts owed. Such agreements are particularly common on purchases of land which lacks a current income. (3) The size of the debt can be increased, and equity reduced, by borrowing through additional loans. The use of second or third mortgages may lead to very large current payments, or some of the payments may be delayed by promising much larger ones in the near future.

To obtain such agreements from lenders often means paying higher interest rates, offering a share of the profits, and reducing the usual buildup of equity which results from repayments of principal. Such agreements may also increase the risks of a complete loss (1) by removing any cushions for possible falls in income, (2) by forcing the refinancing of a loan at a time when borrowing terms may be extremely unfavorable, (3) by selecting an index such as the bank prime lending rates to determine future interest payments (the movements of interest rates so determined may be completely unrelated to a property's income), or (4) by reducing the cushion an equity gives if a sale must take place in a depressed market.

Changes in Required Payments

Table 4-4 exemplifies the leverage effects of altering the required annual debt-service payments. The property is the same as in Table 4-1. Four investment possibilities are illustrated:

   1   In row 1, the property is bought without a loan. The cost and the equity are both $1 million.
   2   In row 2, the investor finds that it is possible to arrange a first mortgage of $800,000 with a 9 percent annual constant payment. The interest is 8 percent, and so the mortgage will be paid off in approximately 30 years.
   3   Row 3 illustrates what happens when there is an existing $700,000 mortgage with an 8 percent constant payment (7 percent interest) and the seller agrees to accept a $200,000 second mortgage with a 15 percent constant (12 percent interest). The total annual debt payments on the two mortgages are $86,000.
   4   In row 4, the required equity is only $40,000, but the annual constant is 12.5 percent (all interest, no amortization), and the borrower must agree to pay off the mortgage at the end of 5 years. The annual payment required during this period is $120,000.

   Columns 3 and 4 show the initial expectation of return under the assumption that the cash flow of $120,000 continues. In case 1, no debt, the property returns 12 percent. (The relationship between a percentage return on equity and profits or yield is explained in Part Six.) In case 2, with a $200,000 equity, the return is 24 percent. The equity earns 12 percent directly plus its right to the spread of 3 percent between the earnings rate and required debt payment. Since there is $4 of mortgage for each $1 of equity, this adds (4 × 3 = 12) 12 percent, to give a total return of 24 percent for the equity. In the third row, the spread is less than 2.5 percent, but $9 is borrowed for each dollar of equity. As a result, the leverage from the spread adds 24 percent, to give a total return of 34 percent. In the final case, there is no spread, and so no current return is expected on the small equity.

   Operating Leverage   The final four columns show what happens when the cash flow alters while the debt service remains constant. In columns 5 and 6, the cash flow increases by 25 percent to $150,000. The return on a property purchased without leverage rises by the same amount. In each of the other cases, the rate of return rises far more rapidly, depending on the amount of leverage. As an example, in line 3, in addition to the basic 15 percent return, the spread on each dollar borrowed more than doubles to over 5.5 percent and the total return on equity rises to 64 percent. It is now five times

Table 4-4   The Effect of the Annual Constant and Operating Leverage on the Ratio of Cash Flow to Equity

| | | | Cash flow of: | | | | | |
| | | | $120,000 | | $150,000 | | $90,000 | |
Equity	Mortgage debt (1)	Annual debt service (2)	Net cash flow after debt service (3)	Percent cash flow of equity (4)	Net cash flow after debt service (5)	Percent cash flow of equity (6)	Net cash flow after debt service (7)	Percent cash flow of equity (8)
$1,000,000	0	0	$120,000	12	$150,000	15	$ 90,000	9
200,000	$800,000	$ 72,000	48,000	24	78,000	39	18,000	9
100,000	900,000	86,000	34,000	34	64,000	64	4,000	4
40,000	960,000	120,000	0	0	30,000	75	−30,000	−75

as great as on the property without a loan. Each added dollar of income will cause the differences in rates of return to widen still more.

Negative Operating Leverage   Usually discussions of leverage tend to emphasize only the positive. Indeed, the historical experience of increasing prices and inflation pressures has caused many in the real estate business to approach projects optimistically. Unfortunately, however, leverage is a two-edged sword, as is demonstrated in columns 7 and 8 of Table 4-4. This shows what happens when the actual cash flow from a venture fails to meet projections. In such a situation, the greater the leverage, the greater the probability of default on the mortgage.

In the third example, the cash flow falls 25 percent below the initial projection. In case 1—the all-cash purchase—the rate of return goes down by that amount. In the second case, the return on the $200,000 downpayment falls by 62.5 percent to 9 percent. In the third case, the drop is by 88 percent to a 4 percent yield. But complete disaster strikes the most highly leveraged purchase. In the final case, the return on each dollar of the debt falls below the amount required for its service. In fact, with $960,000 of debt, a net cash-flow deficit of $30,000 occurs.

Leverage is working in reverse. The earnings on the nominal downpayment are not enough to meet the cash deficit on the mortgage. The low downpayment and higher constant on the mortgage, even without amortization, increases risks and the required interest rate. As creative financing lowers the owner's share of the total financing package, it raises the chances of a complete failure.

Fixing the Annual Constant

Because leverage increases the potential risk to the lender without large potential gains, it becomes the focus of much of the bargaining between lender and borrower and buyer and seller (since the latter may initially lend some of the money). Inherent in the bargaining is the fact that the lower the required payment per dollar of loan (the annual constant), the more dollars of borrowing can be carried by any cash flow. Bargaining occurs with respect to the amount that can be borrowed, the interest rate charged, and the annual constant which must be paid. The relationship between these factors will determine how much principal is paid off and how much is outstanding at any time. In many cases when the borrower and the lender fix the size of the loan, the interest rate, and the constant, the number of payments agreed to will not run for a long-enough period to pay off the loan. A large sum, or a balloon, remains which must be paid as the final payment.

Table 4-5 shows the type of information necessary for such agreements. It indicates how long it takes to repay a loan with a given annual constant in relation to a particular interest rate. It also shows how much of the loan will be repaid at the end of any period. Thus if we look at a 9 percent annual constant, we find that with a 7 percent interest rate it will take over 20 years to repay the loan. At the end of 10 years, less than 30 percent of the initial principal will have been paid off. Over 70 percent will still be outstanding. In contrast, with a 12 percent constant, the loan at 7 percent interest will be repaid in slightly over 12 years. Of course, at a 9 percent constant loans with interest

Table 4-5   Annual Constants

Annual constant	Interest rate (percent)	Percent paid off in:				Full term	
		5 years	10 years	15 years	20 years	Years	Months
8	5	17.0	38.8	66.8		19	8
	6	11.6	27.3	48.5	77.0	23	2
	7	6.0	14.4	26.4	43.4	29	10
	7.5	3.0	7.4	13.8	23.1	37	1
9	5	22.7	51.8	89.1		16	4
	6	17.4	41.0	72.7		18	5
	7	11.9	28.8	52.8	86.8	21	7
	8	6.1	15.2	28.8	49.1	27	7
10	5	28.3	64.7			13	11
	6	23.3	54.6	96.9		15	4
	7	17.9	43.3	79.2		17	3
	8	12.2	30.5	57.7	98.2	20	3
	9	6.3	16.1	31.5	55.7	25	9
11	5	34.0	77.6			12	2
	6	29.1	68.3			13	3
	7	23.9	57.7			14	6
	8	18.4	45.7	86.5		16	4
	9	12.6	32.3	63.1		19	1
	10	6.5	17.1	34.5	63.3	24	1
12	6	34.9	81.9			11	7
	7	29.8	72.1			12	7
	8	24.5	61.0			13	10
	9	18.9	48.4	94.6		15	6
	10	12.9	34.1	69.1		18	
	11	6.6	18.1	37.9	72.1	22	9

rates above 9 percent would never be paid off. Unpaid interest would cause the amount of the outstanding loan to grow steadily.

Constant Payments on Principal

The previous examples covered constant payments in each period. It is not uncommon, however, to find agreements that specify a constant level of payment on principal, rather than in total. Interest is paid only on the remaining, or unamortized, principal.

Since the remaining principal is less each period, both interest charges and the level of total payments for interest and principal decrease each period. For example, assume again that $100,000 is borrowed at 9 percent interest but that the borrower agrees to pay the prior year's interest and 5 percent of the principal each year. The borrower's payments would be $14,000 the first year ($5,000 amortization and $9,000 interest), $9,500 the eleventh year ($5,000 amortization and $4,500 interest on the remaining principal of $50,000), and $5,500 the last year ($5,000 amortization and $500 interest).

SUMMARY

What are some of the significant conclusions that can be drawn from this discussion of periodic payments with respect to what happens when bargaining occurs over the form and number of payments?

1 We note that as the amortization period lengthens, the amount of the loan which can be paid for by a given amount increases, but not by as much as the payment. Thus from Table 4-2 we see that a person with the ability to pay $100 monthly can, with a 9 percent loan, borrow $7,893 on a 10-year loan and meet the payments. (When we divide the $100 payment by the required monthly payment of $12.67 per $1,000, we get $7,893.) On the other hand, the $100 payment, still at 9 percent interest, will enable the person to borrow $12,422 if the term of the loan is 30 years. Moreover, we see that even though the length of the loan has tripled, the actual amount that can be borrowed is increased by less than 60 percent. On a longer loan, much more interest must be paid.

2 The division of a given payment between interest and principal varies greatly. From Table 4-3 and its discussion, we see that the share of interest in a constant payment is much higher near the start of the loan.

3 As a corollary, the percentage of principal repaid in each period rises and at an accelerating pace. Thus for the 20-year loan in Table 4-3, less than 4 percent is paid off in the first 2 years, while nearly 20 percent is paid off in the last 2.

4 Again it is clear that the longer the amortization period, the larger the total interest paid on a loan of a given size. With longer amortization periods, more is borrowed on average. The extra time for which the principal is available must be paid for.

5 Similarly, as interest rates increase, a given amount pays off a loan more slowly. Thus from Table 4-5, if a borrower pays 10 percent of a loan annually, the loan will be repaid in approximately 15 years at 6 percent interest, compared with over 25 years if it is a 9 percent loan.

6 At high interest rates the amount of a loan repaid in the early years is well below that of a similar loan with lower interest rates. Table 4-3 shows that it will take a payment of approximately $1,080 a year to amortize a $10,000 9 percent loan in 20 years. Someone taking out a similar-sized loan at 5 percent for the same period need pay only three-quarters as much in monthly payments. Even so, at the end of 5 years the amount of principal paid off on the 5 percent loan will be over 17 percent, compared with an 11 percent repayment for the 9 percent loan. Longer terms and higher interest rates entail greater risks. Either factor causes the amount of principal repaid in earlier periods to be less. If property values fall, there is less equity to protect the lender.

7 Higher interest rates always cause problems for borrowers. Their costs rise.

Unless they trade the higher rates for a longer amortization period or a balloon, their monthly payments will rise also. Moreover, the higher the interest, the less the effect of spreading payments over longer terms. Owners can borrow more if they spread their payments over a longer period, or reduce the amortization part of each payment. However, their costs of money will be higher. The increase in the cash from a property must grow rapidly, or owners are not likely to gain.

Leverage is a very powerful tool. It increases the amount of property which can be controlled. If operations increase income, yields may rise rapidly. If property values appreciate, the return to those who share in the equity will go up even more. In either case, tax considerations which apply to the entire property will be concentrated in the hands of the equity owners. Of course, if a project is less successful than projected, leverage works in reverse.

Much analysis of real estate investment deals with the fundamental relationships between income and debt. One of the critical skills for both borrowers and lenders is making a proper evaluation of the likelihood that debt-service payments will be met and what costs will arise if they are not.

QUESTIONS AND PROBLEMS

1 What causes the amount and percentage of an owner's equity, or the loan-to-value ratio, to change over time?
2 Under what circumstances would you recommend that a prospective homeowner pay a larger downpayment than required?
3 Describe important types of leverage.
4 In what ways can the annual constant or monthly payment be reduced?
5 Explain why doubling the term of a loan does not cut monthly payments in half.
6 What are the critical factors which determine whether a family can afford a specific home? How can the ability to buy be increased?
7 In Table 4-3, add a line to show what the result would be if the mortgage loan was $500,000 with a 9 percent annual constant.
8 Calculate the approximate annual payments on a $1-million mortgage at 9 percent interest with the mortgage to be amortized between 25 and 26 years. About how much would still be owed at the end of 10 years of payments?
9 Would it ever make sense to get a loan that cost more than the free and clear yield of a property?
10 What is negative leverage?
11 What impact do prospects for inflation have on borrowers? On lenders?

Financial Planning

At the heart of the real estate process is the financial plan required to develop, construct, or buy and to own or sell a piece of property. A couple buying their first house, a family building their dream house, a firm buying a warehouse, or a developer starting out to build an entire community—all need a financial program to pinpoint when they will need money and where they will get it. The program should include the funds required both for the construction or purchase of the property and for the income and outlays necessary for continued ownership.

Plans range from the simple statement of a family's available savings and future income, needed to buy a house in a development, to complex masses of documents and projections required for borrowing hundreds of millions of dollars. Looking at a simplified financial plan is a useful introduction to some of the basic concepts of the financing process.

DEVELOPMENT AND CONSTRUCTION

Chapters 1 and 2 show that roughly half of all real estate lending is generated in the initial development, construction, and sale of a property, while half originates from resales or refinancing. The percentage of resales is much higher for single-family houses than for most other types of property.

The share of glamour and rewards reaped by successful developers is far higher than their share of the total business. The development and construction processes are where values are created. The developer starts with a piece of land, plans a project, packages it into a real estate venture, and finally nurses it through the construction phase.

Origination is the most critical phase of each investment since it is here that the basic decisions are made. Throughout the development process the risks and potential rewards are great. The successful developer achieves a higher ratio of reward to risk than others through careful planning and analysis and through individual knowledge and skills.

The Developer

Chapter 1 showed the wide variety of firms which perform the development function. Some may be individual developers and promoters; others may be large firms specializing in this work. Builders and real estate companies also are active in the development process.

Developers find land. They then determine both the concept of land use and the type of building, as well as the way in which the venture will be put together. They carry the project through the planning process and frequently the construction process. Developers may sell the completed property, own and manage it, or participate in the ownership.

The tasks of developers are complex and frequently frustrating. They must combine and hold together the land, the architect, and the general design of the development; see that market analysis is adequate; obtain government approval; obtain financing; and supervise construction and the actual marketing of the project.

None of these steps is simple. Few will occur smoothly. There is a constant need for rushing and then waiting—expediting and then trying to relax, as one stage is held up by others who can be motivated and hurried only with difficulty.

Risk-Reward Relationships

The risks to all those who invest money early in a project are high. With many things under way, the odds increase that something may go wrong. The general applicability of Murphy's law—"If anything can possibly go wrong, it will"—to land development and construction must be emphasized. The process is so complex, the variables so numerous, and the relationships so delicate that some unforseen problem is almost certain to arise.

The approval process for a real estate project has become much more complicated. A great deal of specific information is required by prospective lenders, investors, and the public agencies, each of whom can halt the project. The cost of planning for all these contingencies has shot up. The approval process takes longer and costs more. The number of decision points that the developer must pass to get a project off the ground has increased. The possibility of being turned down somewhere along the way is much higher. These changes in the financing, promoting, and land-use approval process have been superimposed on traditionally high developmental risks.

The long lead time of the development process represents a basic danger. The decision maker must commit major resources today on the basis of projections of future costs and market acceptability. Increasingly, developers find that by the time they are ready to contract for work, costs have shifted dramatically, and some materials or labor may be in short supply. Prices are up, and the potential delays are greater. A market that is strong when a job is planned may soften significantly because other projects, though begun after the proposal reached the negotiation stage, actually finish earlier.

THE FINANCIAL BUDGET

Preparing a financial plan or budget for a real estate project is analogous to preparing a financial budget for a company. The budgeting process involves planning future expenditures and scheduling the funds likely to be available for them. The emphasis is on identifying the sources and uses of funds. Cash-flow analysis is indispensable in planning future dollar needs and in evaluating the basic feasibility of the project.

The development process starts with various possible uses for the land. The initial concept must be worked up from a sketch into the design stage. With a rough idea of the project an economic analysis can also be made. The project formulation includes the type of improvements to be put on the land, the size and scope of the proposed building, projected price or rent levels, and costs of construction. Timing questions are of critical concern, particularly as to when units will be sold or space rented. Assumptions as to market absorption rates have a major impact in determining whether the project is feasible. Slight timing variations can completely cancel a project's appeal.

The basic economic analysis begins with a definition of a project and an estimate of probable revenues and costs. It ends with a final determination that the project is worth pursuing because it will be profitable.

Tables 5-1 and 5-2 are extremely simplified budgets. They illustrate the type of financial planning engaged in by a developer. He is offered a tract of land which he believes can best be used for constructing 400 single-family homes to be sold for $40,000 each, plus an apartment house with 200 units to rent on average at $350 per month each.

At this initial stage, the developer constructs a budget from simple unit costs based upon information from properties completed in the recent past. Before time and money are spent on the proposal, it must seem to make sense.

A For-Sale Project Table 5-1 presents an estimate of the time and money it will take to build and sell the 400 houses. The eight expenditure categories of land, construction, site development, marketing, administration, real estate taxes, interest, and contingencies will be broken down at a later date into many subcomponents. At the point of more specific planning the estimates of costs will become more exact, as will those of the specific times at which funds will be required. The more precise the timing, the more useful and reliable is the resulting budget. For parts of the budget, quarterly time periods may be sufficient; in the actual period of construction the funding may well be shown on a monthly basis. Longer intervals can prove to be very long, particularly if all the costs must be incurred at the start of the period, while the anticipated revenues do not occur until the end.

Another division of costs might be into "hard" and "soft," the former being for

Table 5-1   Financial Budget: Single-Family Units

(In Thousands of Dollars)

	Year					
	1	2	3	4	5	6
Single-family operations:						
Units constructed	60	140	175	25		
Units sold	25	125	150	100		
Gross cash outlays for:						
Land purchase	225	530	665	95		
Construction	1,260	2,940	3,675	525		
Site development	280	660	825	115		
Marketing	180	420	525	75		
Administration	60	120	140	55		
Real estate taxes	20	50	60	10		
Interest	150	350	440	60		
Contingency	75	175	220	30		
Total	2,250	5,245	6,550	965		
Income from sales	1,000	5,000	6,000	4,000		
Net outlays	−1,250	−245	−550	3,035		
Financing:						
Construction borrowing	1,920	4,480	5,600	800		
Construction loan						
repayments	−800	−4,000	−4,800	−3,200		
Net cash from loans	1,120	480	800	−2,400		
Cash flow from net outlays						
and net loans	−130	235	250	635		
Cumulative net cash flow	−130	105	355	990		

physical items such as land and construction, and the latter for financing and services. The term "soft" refers to the fact that these costs are not for physical expenses and also that they may be more subject to developer decisions as to amount. In addition, some of them may be obtained on longer credit or as investment contributions from those supplying the services. Among the soft costs are professional fees for architectural and engineering work, legal services, and economic-feasibility analysis, as well as the costs of required permits, marketing costs for advertising and promotion, and administrative and overhead costs.

The budget shows an estimate of when income will be received from sales. The sales money flows in only after the units have been completed, whereas the builder requires funds for the development and construction process. He plans to cover these needs through construction loans against the houses as they progress. At a maximum, in the middle of the third year, the developer hopes to have about $2,500,000 in loans covering his site development and the construction costs of the individual homes.

The Apartment Development   Table 5-2 lays out a similarly simplified financial plan covering the first 6 years of the apartment development. The land must be

Table 5-2   Financial Budget: Apartments and Joint
(In Thousands of Dollars)

	Year					
	1	2	3	4	5	6
Apartment operation:						
units available for rent	0	25	175			
Gross cash outlays for:						
Land purchase	135	540				
Construction	1,825	2,500				
Operations and maintenance	15	45	168	176	185	194
General and administration	50	55	38	40	42	44
Real estate taxes	15	20	122	128	135	141
Interest	110	370	388	386	383	379
Repayment of mortgage principal	—	—	30	32	35	39
Total	2,150	3,520	746	762	780	797
Income from rentals	—	45	760	800	840	880
Net cash receipts	−2,150	−3,475	14	38	60	83
Financing:						
Construction loan	1,825	2,500				
Construction loan repayment			4,325			
Permanent mortgage			4,325			
Net cash from loans	1,825	2,500	0			
Cash flow from net receipts and net loans	−325	−1,085	14	38	60	83
Cumulative net cash flow	−325	−1,410	−1,396	−1,358	−1,290	−1,207
Joint cumulative net cash flow from both operations	−555	−1,290	−1,041	−468	−300	−217

purchased, and the units built. There are costs for operation and maintenance, administration, and taxes. Money must be borrowed on an interim basis to cover construction, and then on a permanent or long-term basis for the continuing investment in the building.

After construction, the building is rented out. Expenses rise. Mortgage payments must be met. The plan shows large initial expenses partially covered by a construction loan and then by a permanent mortgage. In the third year, according to the budget, the property will start returning a cash flow to the owners.

Financing the Project   The bottom lines from each section show the total financing needs. Adding the two together, it appears that in the first year, expected outlays will total $3,400,000. The developer hopes he can finance $2,945,000 of this through construction loans. He needs $555,000 of funds from other sources. At the end of the second year, the outstanding construction loans would be $4,100,000, and he would need $1,290,000 of other money. In the third year, part of the construction funds would be repaid from the permanent apartment mortgage. Sales income would be rising. The outstanding construction loans and the need for other money would be starting to decline.

Although analysis of profitability would be a major part of a real financial plan, this specimen budget says nothing about the possible profitability of the venture. It does not even show expected profits from the sale of the individual homes, although they are an important source of potential funds. The reason for excluding profit calculations from this schedule is that they are complex. They are explained in detail in Part Six. At this stage, they would merely confuse the exposition of the financing process.

The financial budget contains three different types of funds: (1) There are final, or permanent, loans. A major one will be for the apartment building. But in addition, the developer will have to arrange permanent mortgages for each buyer of the single-family houses. Without them, sales would be minimal. (2) If permanent mortgages have been assured, funds can be borrowed for the development and construction process. These are interim (in contrast to permanent) loans to be repaid from the proceeds of the permanent mortgage. (3) However, lenders will not furnish all the necessary funds. The final line in the plan shows a maximum cash need of at least $1,290,000 and probably at least $1,500,000 over and above available mortgages. This gap between expenditures and income from loans and sales measures the need for "front money" and equity. The builder must have these additional funds available before he can start to build.

FRONT MONEY

The riskiest period in any project is that during which the proposals are completely fluid. Anyone putting up money during this period expects a high reward because of the risks. The term "front money" is used to describe the money that developers or promoters must put up prior to the time that they can draw on financing through mortgage debt. Developers need money for their preliminary plans, to make the necessary studies for their presentation, and to control the land which they will develop. These expenditures must be made before they can arrange the debt financing. As the number of approvals to be obtained and requirements to be met have proliferated, the amount of front money developers need has grown rapidly.

The concept of front money also applies to the money needed during the actual process of land development and construction. Even though some loans are available from financial institutions during this period, developers must find enough money to bridge the gaps between the phases or times at which the financing becomes available.

Developers look to several sources for their front money. One, of course, is their own capital, which provides the maximum discretion and fewest restrictions. But few developers enjoy the luxury of having substantial financing of their own.

Other Credit

A second possible source for developers' front money is their regular credit lines. Frequently, however, these too are inadequate, and so they obtain the necessary credit from their suppliers or consultants. Thus it is common to find that the lawyer, the architect, and even the market analyst delay their billing in return for a share of the potential profits.

Again, during the construction phase suppliers frequently act in the role of lenders. Even though they may not be compensated for it, they find that their bills are simply paid late. This whole problem of loans during the construction process is one of the factors raising the cost of construction. Suppliers who find themselves continually with debts owed to them reflect this in their prices. Suppliers who must anticipate waiting to be paid for their work will very likely tend to overcharge. They add an extra increment both for the time they must wait and, more importantly, for the uncertainty associated with collecting the account at all.

Of greater concern, needs for credit may well be reflected in the quality of goods or services provided. If payment is not immediately forthcoming, suppliers may be motivated to provide less than top-quality materials. In the case of consultants providing professional services, objectivity may be noticeably influenced by what form the payments take. Clearly, consultants whose payments depend on the successful availability of financing will be highly motivated to make certain that such funds become available. Consequently, the objectivity of their advice may be impaired.

Joint Ventures

Because of the enormous difficulties of coming up with the needed front money, developers often turn to the joint venture (see Chapter 9) in order to have financial partners who can assume a major burden for these expenditures. This is obviously one reason why some of the largest developers have gone into partnerships with insurance companies or pension funds.

If the venture is to be a form of syndication, a considerable amount of information is required before other parties can be admitted. A good deal of the planning must have taken place. The dimensions of the project must be defined, possible economic benefits must be identified, and a projected set of financial statements must be in existence. Without considerable detailed information of this type, joint-venture partners cannot know whether they ought to become involved.

This means again that substantial resources are required even before a developer is in a position to admit financial partners. Even if the developer seeks to minimize front-money requirements through preselling the project before it becomes necessary to incur capital expenditures, a fair amount of up-front work must have been done, and payments made, to get the venture to the point where it can be considered by a potential purchaser.

Land Development and Subdividing

Probably the prime source of front money is through a favorable deal with landowners. Essentially, developers seek to have landowners allow them to defer the time when the money must be put up for the land. At the same time, they will attempt to obtain the flexibility they need to borrow during the construction phase.

One frequent method of ensuring the availability of the land during the planning period is through a series of options. These might include a lease of the land with an option to buy at some later time. The lease payments could start at a very nominal amount, or the payments might be deferred until the property is completed and income is being produced. In other cases, developers may purchase the land on an extended purchase contract with only small early payments required. Developers usually insist that there be no recourse if they fail to meet the remainder of the contract. The entire security will be the land itself.

In another procedure, the owner retains title while the land is being developed and may even furnish part of the capital for improvements. As individual lots are sold, the owner transfers title to the purchaser. Part of the income from the sale is paid to the owner for his or her land and risk, while part goes as a return to the developer.

In still another method, the builder buys the land, but the original owner retains a large purchase-money mortgage against the property. The lien is usually a blanket mortgage covering all the land. When an individual lot is sold, the mortgage holder receives payment for the amount of land involved. To this is added an additional sum so that the mortgage becomes an ever smaller percentage of the value of the still unsold land. Upon receipt of payment, the mortgage holder releases his or her claim, and the purchaser gets a clear title.

As an example, assume that you purchase 25 acres of land for $12,000 an acre, paying 10 percent down. The total land is worth $300,000, and you put up $30,000, with the remainder financed by a blanket mortgage of $270,000. The land is divided into 100 lots. Each time a lot is sold, you pay $3,150 to the mortgage holder, who releases the lot to the new owner. The amount owed on the mortgage becomes a decreasing percentage of the value of the unsold land. The $270,000 mortgage will have been completely paid off when 86 lots have been sold, and so the developer retains all sums after that point.

If the land is to be built upon or improved before sale, the firm making a construction loan usually requires a subordination agreement. Under such an agreement, the holder of the blanket mortgage agrees to allow his or her claim to be junior, or second, to the construction loan even though it was recorded first in time. The conditions of such subordination clauses and the release clause which specifies the conditions for transferring titles on individual lots are an important part of the bargaining in land sales. Such conditions, as well as the use of options and developing on others' land, are usually paid for through the fact that the price of the land becomes higher than it would be in a cash sale. For example, in the case of land purchased for $300,000 including a subordinated mortgage, the cash price might be only $225,000.

Credit for construction of land improvements is expensive but not quite as hard to obtain as credit for purchasing raw land. Developers who have used their own capital to buy the land or who have received financing through the owner or other land investor are frequently able to borrow the money needed for streets, lights, and other improvements from a combination of financial institutions, material suppliers, and subcontractors, in a system similar to that used for the construction of the house. In fact, in much tract development the construction of the house and land improvements proceed and are financed together.

The problem of front money remains critical. It greatly limits the number of potential developers. It leads to a high reward-to-risk payment for those who actually succeed in successfully putting together a project.

PERMANENT FINANCING

In the mortgage market, a major difference exists between long-term (or permanent) loans and those granted to finance the project (interim loans) before the permanent loan is received. Differences arise because most lending institutions specialize. The permanent lenders—LICs, pension funds, thrift institutions, the government, and some banks—often cannot or will not handle interim financing. Such loans are more important to CBs, mortgage companies, and REITs.

Permanent and interim loans differ in their character, their maturity, and the know-how required to make them successful. Most long-term loans have a maturity of 25 to 30 years. Interim loans include construction and development loans, which average less than 1 year and seldom go over 3—unless they get in trouble—as well as standby and gap financing, discussed later in this chapter.

Most projects cannot proceed without a lender's firm commitment to make a long-term loan when the building is completed and sold. With such a commitment the developer has far less trouble obtaining both construction loans and front money. The planning stage of a project aims at developing a project which will gain the necessary loan commitment.

In Tables 5-1 and 5-2 a key assumption is the availability of permanent loans both for the apartment and for the buyers of the sale housing. The examination of a typical mortgage loan submission package can give a feel for the key factors in the planning process. Table 5-3 outlines a submission package for an income property. It lacks a great deal of the background data which would be required from the developer before a lender would agree to give a commitment for permanent mortgages in the project.

The Submission Package

The submission package includes the loan application and its supporting documentation. Essentially it is intended to include all the information needed by lenders to decide whether to commit their funds to a project. Consequently, it is a partial listing of the factors that developers must take into account in their own planning. Since the sums involved are large, a commitment to provide funds for an interim or a permanent mortgage is a major one. The economic factors and risks that will influence its success must be carefully evaluated. For both interim and permanent loans, lenders want to be as certain as possible of the ability of applicants to pay off the loan, either from proceeds generated by the property or from other sources of financing.

While lenders want all the information they need to make an informed decision, too often they are disappointed. The data are inadequate and undocumented and lack third-party objectivity. Developers and borrowers frequently fail to get the consideration they believe they deserve because their submission packages are deficient or fail to present all the information in an organized manner. When lenders must undertake a great deal of extra work to put a deal together, they are likely to put it aside in favor of one that requires less effort on their part.

At the outset, the submission package must carefully describe what the venture is all about and who is involved. Key questions lenders want answered are: (1) Will the market accept the project? (2) Are the cost projections reasonable? (3) Can the developer perform? The planning process must develop the economic rationale, including

Table 5-3 Mortgage Loan Package: Breakdown of Outline

Mortgage loan proposal: Applicant   Term
Loan amount   Constant
Rate

Security
Indicate project type, number of units, size—shopping center, industrial buildings, etc. Include amenities, parking facilities, design features, rent range—initial description of property securing loan.

Location
1 Give exact location.
2 Describe location in relation to downtown—central business district.
3 Describe streets—two- or four-lane and access to major thoroughfares.

City Data
1 Give information and general data on city, including population (city and metropolitan) for past years (for example, 1950, 1960, 1970).
2 List major employers and current employment—give figures and unemployment rate.
3 Indicate the economic base—what makes the city tick.
4 Give any additional information describing city and its future growth.
5 For a shopping center, include figures on retail sales—use same years as for population and per capita income.

Neighborhood
1 Describe immediate surroundings—residential values, apartment rent ranges, etc.
2 Describe location and access to major work centers—office parks, industrial parks, downtown business district, etc.—and give brief description of facilities.
3 Indicate location of, and access to, educational facilities, churches, hospitals, etc.
4 Describe trend of growth of the area.
5 Give any additional information which would affect subject's location for better or worse.
6 For a shopping center, indicate population of trade area for a 1- to 3-mile radius.

Site data
1 Give size and shape of lot with dimensions. Always indicate frontage size.
2 Briefly describe the land—flat, rolling, wooded, etc.
3 Indicate any easements located on the site.
4 Note any unusual site or soil conditions.
5 List available utilities to site (if industrial, is rail available?).
6 Describe current or anticipated zoning—does project conform to zoning?

Applicant
1 Give information on the borrower and/or tenants; include real estate experience, number and type of projects developed, etc. Give background on principal developer and all applicants.
2 Indicate who will handle management.
3 Comment on financial status. Give a complete analysis in the case of a credit loan.
4 Include photos of subject in the case of an existing project.

Recommendation of broker or lender's local office: include operations and future plans

Loan application: Insert signed application.

Mortgage loan analysis
Data on this sheet cover loan per square foot, room, etc., as well as break-even point, debt coverage, etc.—use forms presently in existence.

Financial information
1 Include signed financial reports on individuals, also income and expense statements and balance sheet on companies and corporations.
2 Include credit reports on individuals and Dun and Bradstreet reports on companies.
3 Include any résumé or background data on individuals or company.
4 For a credit-type loan (for example, an industrial plan), include past 5 years, operating statements.

74

Market

1 Indicate the demand for apartments, office space, shopping centers, etc., for the city or metropolitan area if available, but be sure to have information for general and immediate area of subject. Discuss factors affecting each project used as comparables as well as demand to locate in subject's area; indicate subject's comparison to comparables.
2 Include rent comparable sheets to include all information on each comparable including occupancy, rents, and unit or building size and types, as well as comments on good and bad points.
3 Include photos, usually two pictures of each comparable.
4 The purpose of this section is to indicate the existing and anticipated demand for the type of real estate involved in loan submission. Market analysis should be in detail.

Appraisal

1 Fill out in complete detail to include:
   a Complete building description and materials to be used in construction.
   b Breakdown of units with totals—number of rooms, baths, size, etc.
   c Cost estimate—breakdown between direct and indirect costs. If available, use actual costs on similar properties.
   d Land valuation—include actual land sales of comparable properties. Show sales price per unit, square foot, acre, etc.
   e Income and expense breakdown. Show breakdown on expenses in as detailed a form as possible; for example, for office buildings, show each item per square foot.
2 Use a residual technique on economic valuation approach.
3 Indicate actual market sales of projects, listing price per square foot, unit, etc., as well as net return, equity return, etc.
4 Use general-remarks section to summarize reasons for arriving at final value.

Neighborhood map and photo

1 Map should be in detail showing all development within a radius of about 1 mile. This item is very helpful to a reviewer if the map is in full detail. Show subject boundary lines in *red* on map.
2 Photos should include numerous pictures of subject site and street scenes. Show surrounding property and pictures of neighborhood shopping centers, schools, homes, work center, etc. This section of the submission should make the reviewer as knowledgeable of the area as the appraiser is. Write a brief description beside each photo.

City map

Indicate location of subject, central business district comparables, shopping centers, major work centers, and other items of importance which were included in the city- and neighborhood-data sections. This map is a key in comparing location of subject with that of comparables.

Aerial photo

Show subject and the major projects—apartments, shopping centers, offices, hospitals, etc.—in the general area of subject. Indicate major thoroughfares. Outline subject site in *red*.

Note: The city and neighborhood maps and all photos should enable the reviewer to reach the same decision as the appraiser in regard to a good location for subject.

Plot plan, layouts, and elevations

If a complete set of plans and specs is not submitted with loan package, then these items should be included (original sheets cut down to half size). Outline subject site in *red*, and indicate total livable area, number of rooms, etc., on each apartment unit or total building area for industrial plant. Use elevation sheet or architectural renderings of subject if available. For office buildings, use the typical floor layout. Plot plan should include all buildings, driveways, and parking areas along with clubhouse, pools, tennis courts, and other features of the project.

Summary

Other items which are vital to the success of a real estate project should be included in the mortgage loan package. The purpose of the package is to provide a lender with the complete facts and details about the proposed or existing development. A complete and detailed package enables the appraiser to know every detail of the project and area and indicates to the lender that a thorough analysis has been made, and much time spent in preparing to submit the loan to the lender.

specific information on the market for the project. Lenders are interested in the projected revenues, a breakdown of anticipated costs detailed by source with supporting verification, and the resulting pro forma cash flow. Examining Table 5-3, we find that it includes six basic types of information: (1) location, (2) property and design, (3) the market, (4) financial information, (5) the applicant, and (6) the final overall appraisal:

1 Information on location moves from the general to the specific. Thus it includes information on the economic viability of the city, more detailed information on the neighborhood, and finally very specific information on the site, including its soil conditions, utilities, and zoning. The economic and statistical information is supplemented by maps and photos of the neighborhood and the city.

2 A second set of topics is concerned with the property itself. These include a detailed description of the project, its design, its costs, and its potential or expected revenues. The information includes a general description, as well as very specific plans and specifications. Information concerning such factors as number of rooms, number of apartments, space, amenities, parking, and rent range is needed for the final decision making. The information must be complete enough to show the lender that the cost estimates are accurate and that the building can generate the specific revenue required.

3 The location and property lead into a very specific projection of the market for the project. It is not sufficient simply to know what the potential rent schedule will be. The lender wants an indication of what actual revenues will be. Thus the package includes a good deal of information on comparable and competitive projects as well as an economic-feasibility study indicating that there will be a market for the project when it is completed. This part of the study is often performed by an independent consultant in an attempt to convince the lender that it is based on factual information with disciplined analysis founded on reasonable assumptions taken from an actual field investigation.

4 Financial information will include the actual mortgage being requested and the debt-service provisions, complete with the interest rate and payments on the principal. Equally vital, it will also include the projected financial statements for the life of the project so that the lender can be assured that the terms of the mortgage will be met. Included will be factors such as the amount of the mortgage per square foot and other similar overall items such as the debt coverage, the break-even point, reserves, and other items bearing on the risk of the lender.

5 Of special importance is information on the applicant and the other principals involved in the venture, including the contractors and professionals providing supporting services. The lender wants to see a history of the jobs they have been involved in. He or she is concerned with both their personal and their corporate financial condition. Information on the principals involved must disclose all financial guarantees and contingent obligations. Any past problems should be revealed since they will surface during the credit check. Increasingly, lenders are insisting on seeing verification that basic legal conditions and requirements are being adhered to. The lender will also want relevant title insurance documents, guarantees, bonds or letters of credit, and other documents supporting the venture to be submitted.

6 Finally, the submission package comes down to the bottom line. It requires an analysis which shows that the cash flow of the project should be sufficient to meet the requirements of the debt service. If things go wrong and debt payments are not met, then the lender wants to be as sure as possible that the value of the mortgage security is great enough so that upon foreclosure or sale, the lender will be protected against most dangers of loss. The bottom-line projection is based on both a traditional mortgage appraisal and an analysis of the pro forma financial statements indicating the future revenues and costs.

Clearly, the information required for the mortgage submission is of the identical type which developers require for their own decision making. While for their own purposes they will make modified assumptions as to certain costs, revenues, and profitability, and while they will be far more concerned about their personal tax conditions and ultimate risk and profitability, the planning which they perform will follow that required by lenders. They will not be able to proceed until they have a commitment from both the final and interim lenders.

LOANS FOR DEVELOPMENT AND CONSTRUCTION

In the financial plan, the third type of financing is that required for the development and construction process. The amount needed for land development may be the largest and most difficult to obtain. This is one reason why the owners of the land frequently are not paid substantial sums prior to the actual development process.

Construction loans cover the funds required for materials and labor during the building process. While construction loans are usually distinct from final lending, some lenders do participate in both parts of the market. The financing of development and construction is a specialized part of mortgage lending. It has been among the most lucrative and at the same time the riskiest of the lending markets. Depending on the local legal situation and habits prevailing in particular regions, different types of lenders dominate the construction market.

The single-family construction loan market, as we saw in Table 2-1, is concentrated primarily between CBs and S&Ls. Usually S&Ls lend for construction purposes when they are committed to the final loan. In the case of the CBs, a much larger percentage specialize in construction lending alone.

For residential income properties, the construction loan market is fairly evenly divided among CBs, mortgage companies, REITs, and S&Ls. Again in this case, the deposit institutions are likely also to be final lenders, while the other two are primarily construction lenders.

In nonresidential properties, the market is dominated by banks, with REITs serving as the other major source.

To obtain the interim loan for development and construction, the developer usually has to submit a loan application separate from that for the permanent loan and containing a different type of data. Lenders want to be certain that (1) there is sufficient front money to enable the project to be completed even if things go badly, (2) the developer and his or her team have the skills needed to keep out of trouble and to bring the project in within its budget, and (3) there is a commitment for a permanent loan so that cash will be available to pay off the interim loan when the project is finished.

Additional Risks Lenders must examine construction loan proposals with the knowledge that such lending is the riskiest kind in the real estate market. The builder may not bring the building or tract to completion. Cost overruns may occur. Unforseen events such as strikes, bad weather, and deaths may halt production. Losses on other properties or ventures may cause the builder to default. Any of these eventualities will leave lenders with an unfinished project which will have to be completed if they are to get their money out. In some cases performance bonds are used to ensure against losses arising from noncompletion. In most cases and especially in housebuilding, however, lenders depend on their credit analysis and assume the added risks of noncompletion.

If the building is finished, other risks may still develop. In many states, mechanic's liens may be a problem. Those who work on the building and furnish materials to it may have the right to be paid from the proceeds of its sale prior to any rights of the mortgage holder. If the builder finishes the building but bills remain outstanding, they may have to be paid by the lender. Despite the careful safeguards contained in lending procedures which attempt to protect against this eventuality, it continues to crop up not infrequently.

Finally, it may be difficult to sell the completed house. The construction loan typically continues until the unit is sold. If delays are long, the builder will have difficulty meeting taxes and interest payments. Some buildings may be marketed at prices below the amounts advanced on the construction loan. If the builder's equity has been wiped out, the lender may lose.

Terms and Rates   Construction loans tend to have terms of 6, 9, and 12 months, with the greatest number in the lowest category. In many cases, of course, the loan will be extended. The short term increases lenders' control, since they can take action to avoid prolonged failure to sell.

Because of their risks and considerable administrative requirements, the rates charged on construction loans tend to be high, and heavy charges are imposed in required fees or discounts. The rate of return to the lender depends on the speed of turnover of the loan. For example, consider a loan on a house in which the period from the initial recording of the construction mortgage to sale is 6 months. If the money is advanced evenly over the entire period, the average amount of funds outstanding for the whole period is only half the face value of the loan. A $30,000 construction loan advanced evenly in $5,000 increments over 6 months would have an average outstanding loan balance of only $15,000.

Under typical terms, borrowers might be charged 9 percent interest on the outstanding balance, but they would be required to pay loan fees of from 3 to 5 points, that is, from $30 to $50 per $1,000 loan. On a $30,000 loan advanced over 6 months, the average outstanding money of $15,000 for 6 months is equivalent to $7,500 loaned for a year. If 4 points were charged, the fee would be $1,200. This by itself would be equal to 16 percent simple interest. Added to the 9 percent actual interest charge, it amounts to a gross interest charge of 25 percent on an annual basis.

Of course a good portion of this return may be required to cover the added risk and supervision. On the other hand, fees or discounts may run considerably higher in some parts of the country and in certain periods. The fee schedules on construction loans tend to be volatile, rising and falling as money eases and tightens. These shifting costs and the availability of construction credit appear to be very important in causing the rate of building starts to fluctuate.

On income properties the charges frequently have been 3–5 percent above the prime lending rate of banks. Similar types of fee schedules are added to these loans, and so again the actual simple interest rates run much higher.

Disbursement of Funds

Construction lending is characterized by unique timing, risk, and control problems. Most simply, since the construction process occurs over a span of time, borrowers are interested in keeping their invested equity to a minimum. In order to do so, they would have to be reimbursed for each payment as they make it.

On the other hand, lenders are concerned that they advance funds to borrowers only to the extent that these are reflected in an increasing value for the building. Since the security for the construction loan is the value of the project, completed or in process, lenders want to be certain that this value exists. They want to be sure that if they have to take over the project and complete construction, they will be able to do so within the budget implied by the remaining undisbursed balance of the loan.

The natural diversity of interests between the builder and the lender can create considerable tension and maneuvering for position. Indeed, successful building and successful portfolio management for construction loans both hinge on how the parties cope with and resolve these questions.

The usual procedure for paying out construction loans is through a system of progress payments made at certain stages of the building process. These systems of advances—or *draws*, as they are commonly called—have the purpose of making capital available to builders to replenish most of the amount they have had to pay from their own capital or borrow from suppliers to bring the building to a certain stage of completion. Lenders attempt to ensure that the amount of the loan is less at all times than the amount of value included in the property which serves to secure the advances.

The construction mortgage is recorded prior to the start of building. The note specifies the manner in which advances will be made. Many possible payment methods and rates of advance exist. In contracts to build houses for individuals, it is common to require a deposit of sufficient funds by the owners to cover the difference between the contract and the loan. The lender or his agent then reimburses the builder for receipted bills as they are presented. In other cases, the owner may certify the bills, which are then paid directly by the lender.

Far more common, and particularly applicable to operative (speculative) building, are agreements by the lender to furnish funds when certain amounts of work have been completed or certain stages of construction have been reached. In the most flexible system, but one commonly used only on large construction projects, the lender advances each month a percentage of the total work cost which he and the builder agree went into the structure during the previous period. More usual, particularly for housebuilding, is an agreement to pay a certain percentage of the loan at particular stages of construction.

Schedules for disbursements are negotiated between the builder and lender. Many different forms of agreement are employed, calling for anywhere from three to fifteen payments as the work progresses. A typical agreement based on five advances calls for the bank to pay the builder 20 percent of the contract price at each of five stages of construction: (1) at completion of foundation and rough flooring, (2) at completion of roofing, (3) at completion of plastering, (4) at completion and acceptance of job, and (5) after the end of the mechanic's lien period.

Under such systems, the builder usually calls the lender to report that a particular stage has been reached. The lender then sends an inspector to the site to see that the work has been accomplished and to check both its quantity and quality. The lender ascertains that the plans are being followed and sometimes asks to see receipted bills for the materials included in the work. The degree of care used in checking depends on the builder's credit standing, on the lien laws, and on the general health of the construction market.

Timing
In theory, under this five-stage system, builders may be required to invest personal capital in the project up to 20 percent of the value of the building. When their investment approaches that amount, they reach the next stage and should be able to draw against the mortgage. Their work in progress should be limited to five times their working capital; otherwise there will be periods when they cannot meet their bills because their investments in work in progress exceed their available capital. They may be solvent but illiquid. Builders should, of course, have some additional, but not necessarily liquid, capital to pay for unpredictable setbacks which could cause losses on the property.

The available amount of working capital, however, often falls short. As noted previously, builders are the beneficiaries of an average of 2 or 3 weeks' credit from their workers, trade contractors, and material dealers. At any stage there is likely to be considerable completed work for which they get an advance from lenders but for which they have not paid their suppliers. While this enables builders to double the work they can undertake with a given amount of capital, it is one of the factors which make construction lending so risky.

These complex relationships mean that it is not only the builder and the lender who are concerned with the progress payments. All parties to the venture are interested in minimizing their risk and financial exposure. Consequently, the various contracting parties—the general contractor who manages the entire job, the subcontractors, material supply houses, and individual construction workers—all endeavor to avoid having any other party "get ahead of them."

Lenders attempt to avoid disbursing funds in excess of the value of work done to date by holding back an amount—say, 5–10 percent of the total project—in order to protect their position against future liens that might be filed against the job. The amount of holdback is frequently a matter of bitter debate.

With developers trying to minimize their cash involvement while lenders try to keep their advances below the value of work done, a delicate timing balance obviously prevails. Given the importance of maintaining precise timing as regards the loan, disbursements, and work completed, accounting systems and control measures are very important. The nature of the construction industry, however, is such that record-keeping capabilities and the number of good accounting systems are limited. The amount of paperwork involved is tremendous, with the builder having the responsibility for dealing with all types of schedules, bills, books, and inspections. The plans, specifications, contracts, agreements, and related documents for a job fill many file cabinets. The general contractor works through numerous subcontractors and may have a dozen or more for each job, with several bids received for each subcontract awarded. The problem of merely keeping track of all the paper, let alone that of attempting to set up effective systems for control, is monumental.

Because the problems are so difficult and control is so hard to establish, and also because many contractors start as skilled workers and have limited capital, the building industry has one of the highest bankruptcy rates of all industries in the United States. This puts even more pressure on the lender to ensure that the moneys disbursed on the construction loan are, in fact, spent on the job for which they are paid.

Schemes are constantly being advanced to try to solve the industry's many difficulties. Thus far, however, none have been successful. The best method of keeping solvent is to make certain that the initial budgets are proper and adequate and that the actual progress of a job is checked carefully as disbursements are made.

STANDBY, OR GAP, FINANCING

For a number of reasons, developers may not want or be able to negotiate a permanent or final loan at the time they want to arrange interim financing. As a result, so-called standby, or gap, financing has grown up to handle such situations. Standby financing is money available to carry a property after it has been completed but before a permanent loan is obtained.

1 On many income properties, the permanent mortgage terms depend on the leases in existence when the loan is made. This is particularly true of office buildings and shopping centers. Builders may hope to get both a better mortgage and higher rents by a delay in leasing. They may think that the market for space is tightening, or that a major tenant is holding out in hopes that they will be forced to give good terms to get a decent mortgage. On the other hand, potential tenants may simply be unwilling to sign up until the builder is further along. In all such cases, if builders can delay the need to obtain the final mortgage, they may be able to improve its conditions.

2 In other cases, builders may feel that they will pay less by waiting. Interest rates may turn down. Money may become easier.

3 Finally, terms may be much better if builders are able to show actual operating results instead of only projections. They may therefore want to wait to negotiate the permanent loan until some results are in. This is particularly true when the builder plans to share part of the venture with the lender.

There are several possible solutions to the lack of a takeout commitment:

1 In some cases, construction lenders may be willing to go ahead without a takeout. They will increase their fee to cover added risks.

2 In other cases, developers might obtain a standby commitment. This is a guarantee by a financial institution that it will provide a permanent loan if called upon to do so. A fee of several points is charged for the commitment. A special feature of the standby is that no one—not the interim lender, the developer, or the standby lender— expects the commitment to be used. The terms of the permanent loan to be granted under such commitments are much poorer, and the interest rates higher, than on a conventional loan. They are made sufficiently burdensome so that the builder will accept them only as a last resort. Neither interim nor standby lenders want to keep their money tied up in the project. They expect the builder to negotiate a better permanent loan elsewhere.

    3 In cases where the size of the mortgage constant that can be met depends upon successful leasing—as in apartments and office buildings—the takeout commitment may be a gap loan of a split-level or floor-ceiling type. Lenders agree to make a loan—say, for 60 percent of the value when the building is completed. Furthermore, they agree to increase the loan to 80 percent of value when effective rents reach a certain amount—say, 85 percent of an agreed-upon schedule.

    In such cases, interim lenders know they have a floor or minimum amount that they will receive when the building is completed. The difference between this floor and the ultimate permanent loan may be covered by a commitment to finance the gap between the two amounts. For a fee, either the construction or another lender will give such a commitment. They agree to lend on a second mortgage—at second-mortgage rates—the difference between the floor and ceiling, with the mortgage to be paid off if and when the permanent lender increases his or her loan to the ceiling.

SUMMARY

The core of planning for development and construction is the financial plan. The plan starts as an extremely rough budget which becomes more and more refined as the starting date for construction approaches. The plan shows how much money will be needed for the entire project and where the money will be raised.

    Developers can borrow money on both interim and permanent loans. To obtain an agreement to lend money for the development and construction process, they must prove to the lender that they have sufficient funds to meet costs not covered by the construction loan and that they have a commitment for funds to pay off the construction loan when the building is completed.

    Builders plan to use their own money, that of their partners, and some from suppliers—particularly of the land—to meet costs engendered before the construction loans are available and to cover the ''holdback'' or fact that lenders insist that developers have an investment in the project over and above the loan.

    Construction, or interim, loans are risky and expensive. The lender may have to take over a partially completed project because the developer runs out of money or goes bankrupt. Lenders who must foreclose are almost certain to lose on the venture. Lenders attempt to protect themselves by always lending less money than has actually gone into a project and by insisting that developers have sufficient funds at the start to pay for unexpected cost increases. Even so, in periods such as 1974–1975 many large development and construction lenders saw half or more of their loans go bad.

    Permanent or final or takeout lenders do not need to worry about the construction process. They agree to lend when the building is completed. They want to be sure that the building or family can generate sufficient income to meet scheduled payments for the 20 to 30 years in the future that the loan will last. They require a detailed submission of plans with projected costs and income. They then appraise these plans with a view to ascertaining that there will always be a sufficient flow of income to pay off the loan.

QUESTIONS AND PROBLEMS

1 Why in development lending is so much emphasis put on cash flow rather than on profitability?

2 What is the difference between a permanent and an interim loan?

3 What is front money?

4 Mr. Smith buys acreage containing 200 lots from Mrs. Brown for $300,000 with a downpayment of $40,000 and a blanket mortgage of $260,000. Mrs. Brown agrees to release each lot upon a payment of $4,000. After how many sales would the mortgage be paid off?

5 What protection does a permanent loan commitment give an interim lender? What risks must the lender still bear?

6 Explain how carefully policed progress payments reduce the lender's risks.

7 Why would a builder want a standby commitment?

8 Discuss the conflict between the developer and the lender over the timing of construction loan draws.

9 What factors cause projects to be delayed?

10 What steps can be taken to minimize losses during the construction period?

The Mathematics
of Real Estate Investment
and Finance

In almost every real estate situation someone has to decide what the property or loan will cost over time and whether the investment or loan will be profitable. Calculating yields on real estate equities and figuring the costs of borrowing are closely connected problems. Each requires the accurate estimation of what expected income streams are worth today. In other words, the current value of cash expected to be received in the future must be estimated.

The calculation of current values is complicated because money received today can be invested. Investments or loans made today can earn interest. Because the money received next year will fail to earn interest during this coming year, dollars to be received next year are not worth as much as dollars available now. Because money can earn interest, we say that it has a *time value*. The value to us of a dollar will depend upon when (the time) we receive it. The fact of interest complicates all estimates of future costs and income.

The topic of the mathematics of finance considers both how much invested money earns and what it costs to use or borrow money. People with funds to invest have numerous opportunities. They are eagerly sought after. Each proposal or offer competes with all others. In choosing, investors must satisfy themselves that, all things such as risk considered, the property they pick will earn as much as, or more than, an alternative property could.

In most cases, the actual calculation of how much a property will yield or what payments will be required is made by looking up the required information in a set of interest or mortgage tables, by using a computer, or by applying simplified shortcut techniques. However, every real estate investor or lender must recognize the critical importance of interest rates and must understand the concepts underlying the tables or formulas. The time value of money plays an important role in decisions. A shift of 1 or 2 percent in market interest rates can move a potential investment over the line between sound and unsound.

In this chapter, we use simplified examples to show how the interest factor works. In each case, we then illustrate the underlying mathematics at work. The sections with the mathematical derivations are in indented type. This will enable the reader to recognize sections which will require more careful reading and analysis. Those who are not concerned with the more detailed logic can obtain an understanding of what is involved from the nonindented sections alone.

Time Value   That the value of money differs depending upon the time at which it is received is not a new idea. Many people delay paying for something as long as they can. At the same time, they would like to be paid for their services as soon as possible. This practice of attempting to accelerate one's receipts and defer one's payments is a familiar budgeting technique.

The differing value of money, depending on time, can be illustrated by examining three alternative investments identical in every way except for the time at which their earnings are received. Each investment costs $10 to buy. Each returns the original $10 investment at the end of 10 years. Each pays $10 during its life in "dividends," "interest," or "profits." However:

1   The first pays $10 in dividends at the end of the tenth year.
2   The second pays $10 in dividends at the rate of $1 per year.
3   The third pays $10 in dividends at the end of the first year.

Which is the best investment?

The return on each is $10 over the 10 years, or an average return of $1 a year. One dollar a year on the initial investment of $10 equals 10 percent. However, it does not take any sophisticated mathematics to see that because the investor receives his return at an earlier time, the third investment is preferable. In this third case the investor gets his dividend at the end of the first year. This means that if, for example, he were to place the $10 dividend in a savings account, it would earn additional interest or dividends for each of the last 9 years. This opportunity is completely missing in the first case, where the dividend is paid at the end, and it is greatly diminished in the second case, where the amount that can be reinvested is equal to $1 per year.

This example illustrates a basic maxim of investing: The sooner one gets receipts, the better; the longer one can defer a payment, the better. This principle is straightforward, and if it is understood, it is relatively easy to understand the main features of investment mathematics.

COMPOUND VALUE

Let us start our consideration of the mathematics of real estate finance by considering the mechanics of a savings account. We are all familiar with the idea that if a sum of money can be invested so as to yield a return, it will grow to a larger sum in the future. If a person places $100 in a savings account that pays 5 percent interest compounded annually, how much will she have at the end of 3 years? We can see from Table 6-1 that at the end of 3 years, she will have $115.76.

The table shows that at the end of the first year, the savings balance is $105—the initial $100 plus the first year's $5 in interest. At the end of the second year the balance is $110.25—the initial $100 plus the first year's $5 in interest plus the second year's $5.25 interest on the $105 balance at the end of the first year. Similarly, the third-year interest is based on the $110.25 held at the beginning of the third year.

While the amount that will accrue over time as a result of compound interest can be calculated by hand, an easier and much more common approach is to refer to a compound interest table, as shown in Table 6-2. As can be seen, the longer the time period and the higher the rate, the greater the amount earned. Looking at the 5 percent value, we see that the factors at the end of periods 1, 2, and 3, if multiplied by 100, give the values shown in Table 6-1, with the exception of an error attributable to rounding.

While for most purposes it is sufficient to know that compound interest tables exist and how to use them, some people will find it useful to see how the table is derived. Let us define the following terms:

P_0 = principal or beginning amount at time 0
i = interest rate or yield for one interest-earning period
n = number of interest-earning periods
P_n = principal value at end of n periods

If a person has $1 today and the bank will pay her 5 percent interest, then at the end of the year she will have $1.05, or the principal at time 0 plus the interest earned. This is

$$P_1 = P_0(1 + i)$$

In the second year, she will be lending the bank $1.05 and will again be receiving 5 percent interest. She will get $1.05 \times 1.05 = 1.1025$, or

$$P_2 = P_1(1 + i) = P_0(1 + i)(1 + i) = P_0(1 + i)^2$$

Table 6-1

	Year 1	Year 2	Year 3
Beginning amount (P_0)	$100.00	$105.00	$110.25
Interest calculation $(1 + i)$	× 1.05	× 1.05	× 1.05
	5.00	5.25	5.51
	100.00	105.00	110.25
Ending amount (P_n)	$105.00	$110.25	$115.76

Table 6-2 Future Value of $1 at Annual Compound Interest $(1 + i)^n$

Year	5.00%	6.00%	7.00%	8.00%	9.00%	10.00%
1	1.050000	1.060000	1.070000	1.080000	1.090000	1.100000
2	1.102500	1.123600	1.144900	1.166400	1.188100	1.210000
3	1.157625	1.191016	1.225043	1.259712	1.295029	1.331000
4	1.215506	1.262477	1.310796	1.360489	1.411582	1.464100
5	1.276282	1.338226	1.402552	1.469328	1.538624	1.610510
6	1.340096	1.418519	1.500730	1.586874	1.677100	1.771561
7	1.407100	1.503630	1.605781	1.713824	1.828039	1.948717
8	1.477455	1.593848	1.718186	1.850930	1.992563	2.143589
9	1.551328	1.689479	1.838459	1.999005	2.171893	2.357948
10	1.628895	1.790848	1.967151	2.158925	2.367364	2.593742
11	1.710339	1.898299	2.104852	2.331639	2.580426	2.853117
12	1.795856	2.012196	2.252192	2.518170	2.812665	3.138428
13	1.885649	2.132928	2.409845	2.719624	3.065805	3.452271
14	1.979932	2.260904	2.578534	2.937194	3.341727	3.797498
15	2.078928	2.396558	2.759032	3.172169	3.642482	4.177248
16	2.182875	2.540352	2.952164	3.425943	3.970306	4.594973
17	2.292018	2.692773	3.158815	3.700018	4.327633	5.054470
18	2.406619	2.854339	3.379932	3.996019	4.717120	5.559917
19	2.526950	3.025600	3.616528	4.315701	5.141661	6.115909
20	2.653298	3.207135	3.869684	4.660957	5.604411	6.727500
21	2.785963	3.399564	4.140562	5.033834	6.108808	7.400250
22	2.925261	3.603537	4.430402	5.436540	6.658600	8.140275
23	3.071524	3.819750	4.740530	5.871464	7.257874	8.954302
24	3.225100	4.048935	5.072367	6.341181	7.911083	9.849733
25	3.386355	4.291871	5.427433	6.848475	8.623081	10.834706
26	3.555673	4.549383	5.807353	7.396353	9.399158	11.918177
27	3.733456	4.822346	6.213868	7.988061	10.245082	13.109994
28	3.920129	5.111687	6.648838	8.627106	11.167140	14.420994
29	4.116136	5.418388	7.114257	9.317275	12.172182	15.863093
30	4.321942	5.743491	7.612255	10.062657	13.267678	17.449402
31	4.538039	6.088101	8.145113	10.867669	14.461770	19.194342
32	4.764941	6.453387	8.715271	11.737083	15.763329	21.113777
33	5.003189	6.840590	9.325340	12.676050	17.182028	23.225154
34	5.253348	7.251025	9.978114	13.690134	18.728411	25.547670
35	5.516015	7.686087	10.676581	14.785344	20.413968	28.102437
36	5.791816	8.147252	11.423942	15.968172	22.251225	30.912681
37	6.081407	8.636087	12.223618	17.245626	24.253835	34.003949
38	6.385477	9.154252	13.079271	18.625276	26.436680	37.404343
39	6.704751	9.703507	13.994820	20.115298	28.815982	41.144778
40	7.039989	10.285718	14.974458	21.724521	31.409420	45.259256

Source: P. Wendt and A. R. Cerf, *Tables for Investment Analysis* (Berkeley: University of California, Center for Real Estate and Urban Economics, 1970).

Similarly, at the end of 3 years, she will have $1.05 \times 1.05 \times 1.05 = 1.1576$, or

$$P_3 = P_2(1 + i) = P_0(1 + i)^3$$

In general, we can apply the familiar compound interest formula, which says that the compound amount P_n at the end of any year n is found as

$$P_n = P_0(1 + i)^n$$

If an investor has \$1 in a savings account at 5 percent payable in 3 years, she will have

$$\$115.76 = \$100(1 + .05)^3$$

The values of $(1 + i)^n$, called the *compound interest factor*, are readily available in tables. They can be found in column 1 of Table 6-3, which is an example of such a table. All that is necessary, then, is to multiply the interest factor found for the proper n, or number of years, in the table times the beginning amount to know what the final amount will be.

PRESENT VALUE AND THE YIELD ON INVESTMENTS

This concept of time value plays a significant part when we examine the investment process. The determination of whether an investment is worthwhile most frequently is concerned with attempting to place a current value on a future cash flow. In making this calculation, we must take into account the fact that the money to be received from the investment will come in the future and is not available to be used for other purposes today.

Present Value

Because money now in hand can earn interest, we will not pay as much for \$1 to be received next year as for \$1 today. Thus if we were offered \$1 next year and we knew we could invest our current \$1 at 10 percent interest, we would pay only \$.909 today for next year's promised payment. Similarly, for \$1 payable in 2 years, we would pay only \$.826, and for \$1 payable in 10 years we would pay only \$.386.

How are these sums calculated? The value today of a future payment can be found by seeing how much money would have to be invested today at a specific compound interest rate for today's investment to grow to the future payment in the given number of years. We call the amount which would have to be invested or paid today the *present value* of the future payment. More formally, present value is the current value of a promise to pay at some future time discounted by a given interest rate.

Again, we can easily find such estimates from tables which show discount factors to be applied against future receipts. Table 6-4 is such a table. It shows the present value of a dollar to be received at various future dates, discounted at different interest rates. It, too, is based on the concept of the time value of money.

Table 6-3   Annual Compound Interest Tables; Effective Rate 9.00 Percent

Year	IF_c Amount of $1 at compound interest (1)	IF_s Accumulation of $1 per period (2)	$1/IF_s$ Sinking-fund factor (3)	IF_p Present-value reversion of $1 (4)	IF_a Present value of an annuity of $1 per period (5)	$1/IF_a$ Installment to amortize $1 (6)
1	1.090000	1.000000	1.000000	.917431	.917431	1.090000
2	1.188100	2.090000	.478469	.841680	1.759111	.568469
3	1.295029	3.278100	.305055	.772183	2.531295	.395055
4	1.411582	4.573129	.218669	.708425	3.239720	.308669
5	1.538624	5.984711	.167092	.649931	3.889651	.257092
6	1.677100	7.523335	.132920	.596267	4.485919	.222920
7	1.828039	9.200435	.108691	.547034	5.032953	.198691
8	1.992563	11.028474	.090674	.501866	5.534819	.180674
9	2.171893	13.021036	.076799	.460428	5.995247	.166799
10	2.367364	15.192930	.065820	.422411	6.417658	.155820
11	2.580426	17.560293	.056947	.387533	6.805191	.146947
12	2.812665	20.140720	.049651	.355535	7.160725	.139651
13	3.065805	22.953385	.043567	.326179	7.486904	.133567
14	3.341727	26.019189	.038433	.299246	7.786150	.128433
15	3.642482	29.360916	.034059	.274538	8.060688	.124059
16	3.970306	33.003399	.030300	.251870	8.312558	.120300
17	4.327633	36.973705	.027046	.231073	8.543631	.117046
18	4.717120	41.301338	.024212	.211994	8.755625	.114212
19	5.141661	46.018458	.021730	.194490	8.950115	.111730
20	5.604411	51.160120	.019546	.178431	9.128546	.109546
21	6.108808	56.764530	.017617	.163698	9.292244	.107617
22	6.658600	62.873338	.015905	.150182	9.442425	.105905
23	7.257874	69.531939	.014382	.137781	9.580207	.104382
24	7.911083	76.789813	.013023	.126405	9.706612	.103023
25	8.623081	84.700896	.011806	.115968	9.822580	.101806
26	9.399158	93.323977	.010715	.106393	9.928972	.100715
27	10.245082	102.723135	.009735	.097608	10.026580	.099735
28	11.167140	112.968217	.008852	.089548	10.116128	.098852
29	12.172182	124.135356	.008056	.082155	10.198283	.098056
30	13.267678	136.307539	.007336	.075371	10.273654	.097336
31	14.461770	149.575217	.006686	.069148	10.342802	.096686
32	15.763329	164.036987	.006096	.063438	10.406240	.096096
33	17.182028	179.800315	.005562	.058200	10.464441	.095562
34	18.728411	196.982344	.005077	.053395	10.517835	.095077
35	20.413968	215.710755	.004636	.048986	10.566821	.094636
36	22.251225	236.124723	.004235	.044941	10.611763	.094235
37	24.253835	258.375948	.003870	.041231	10.652993	.093870
38	26.436680	282.629783	.003538	.037826	10.690820	.093538
39	28.815982	309.066463	.003236	.034703	10.725523	.093236
40	31.409420	337.882445	.002960	.031838	10.757360	.092960

Source: P. Wendt and A. R. Cerf, *Tables for Investment Analysis* (Berkeley: University of California, Center for Real Estate and Urban Economics, 1970).

We recognize that the greater the time interval between now and when a dollar will be received, the less the future payment will be worth. Similarly, the greater is the value of time—in other words, the higher the rate of compound interest which can be earned, the less will a dollar to be received in the future be worth today.

Thus from Table 6-4 we see that a dollar to be received in 1 year, if time is valued at 5 percent, is worth $.952 today. On the other hand, a dollar to be received in 30 years, if time is valued at 20 percent, is worth less than 1 cent ($.004, to be exact) today. Table 6-4 shows the relationship between present value, the amount of compound interest to be earned in a period, and the period at the end of which the payment is to be received.

Table 6-5 shows, in the same manner as Table 6-1, the underlying factors at work in these relationships. Thus Table 6-5 shows that if we had $751 to be invested today at 10 percent interest, it would earn $75 in the first year, or its value at the end of that year would be $826. Similarly, that $826 invested in year 2 would earn $83, and so we would have $909 to be invested in year 3. The $91 interest earned in that year would leave us with the $1,000 to be received at the end of year 3. Or, since $751 invested today at 10 percent compound interest would grow to $1,000 at the end of 3 years, the present value of $1,000 to be received 3 years from now is $751 when the interest rate or discount factor is 10 percent.

Again, for those interested in the derivation of this table, we know that finding the present value (or *discounting*) is simply the reverse of compounding. Thus we can transcribe our previous relationships. We find

$$P_n = P_0(1 + i)^n$$

$$P_0 = \frac{P_n}{(1 + i)^n}$$

The discount factor, therefore, is simply $1/(1 + i)^n$. It can be found either in special discount tables such as Table 6-4, or in more general interest tables

Table 6-4   Discount Factors for Present Value of $1 to Be Received at Various Future Dates and Discounted at Various Interest Rates

End of year	Interest rate				
	5%	9%	10%	15%	20%
1	.952	.917	.909	.870	.833
2	.907	.842	.826	.756	.694
3	.864	.772	.751	.658	.579
4	.823	.708	.683	.572	.482
5	.784	.650	.621	.497	.402
10	.614	.422	.386	.247	.162
15	.481	.275	.239	.123	.065
20	.377	.178	.149	.061	.026
30	.231	.075	.057	.015	.004

Table 6-5

	Year 1	Year 2	Year 3
Present value (P_0)	$751	$826	$909
Interest rate (i)	× .10	× .10	× .10
Interest earned	75	83	91
Principal + interest (P_n)(1 + i)	$826	$909	$1,000

such as Table 6-3 under titles like "the present value or worth of 1" or "the present value of the reversion of 1."

Because discounting is so important in real estate transactions, it is worth seeing how rapidly the present value of future income falls, particularly if interest rates are high. Thus we should examine carefully Table 6-4. Look, for example, at the 10-year row. We see that at 5 percent interest rates, a dollar which we expect to receive 10 years from now is worth $.61. On the other hand, at 20 percent interest rates, such a dollar is worth only $.16. Similarly, as we go out in time, future dollars become worth only a small amount. We saw already that this was true for the 30-year dollar at 20 percent, but even at 5 percent, a dollar to be received in 30 years is worth less than a quarter today.

The Present Value of a Stream of Receipts Most real estate investment and financing problems are concerned not with a single sum to be received in the future but with a series of cash payments and receipts, each taking place at a different time. For this reason, we must be concerned with arriving at the present value of a future cash flow or stream of receipts. Such a calculation is shown in Table 6-6.

A potential buyer is offered a piece of income property. Its net cash flow will be $1,000 at the end of year 1, $4,000 at the end of year 2, $4,000 at the end of year 3, and $4,000 at the end of year 4. In addition, at the end of year 4 the building can be sold for $35,000, and so the buyer will receive $39,000 at that time. In other words, as we see from the table, over the next 4 years a cash flow of $48,000 is promised.

We know that because of the time value of money, no one would be willing to pay $48,000 today for this stream of receipts. The question is: How much might one be willing to pay? One possible way of finding the answer is to cal-

Table 6-6   Discounting to Find Present Value

Year	Cash flow	Discount factor*	Present value
1	$ 1,000	.917	$ 917
2	4,000	.842	3,368
3	4,000	.772	3,088
4	39,000	.708	27,612
Total	$48,000		$34,985

*9 percent interest rate.

culate the present value of the expected stream. First an interest rate or discount factor must be picked. Assume it is 9 percent. Then examine table 6-6. We see that the $1,000 received at the end of year 1 must be discounted, according to Tables 6-3 and 6-4, at a discount factor of .917. This means that its present value is approximately $917. Similarly, the $4,000 to be received at the end of year 2 has a discount factor of .842, or a present value of $3,368.

From the total in the present-value column, we see that the cash flow of $48,000 over the next 4 years has a present value of slightly under $35,000. If an investor is satisfied with a 9 percent rate of return and the cash-flow projection is believed, this would be an attractive opportunity if the building could be bought for under $34,985.

The Present Value of an Annuity   Because many real estate problems deal with uneven flows such as in Table 6-6, before the advent of the computer such problems were difficult to solve. As a result, they were frequently simplified by assuming a stream of receipts in which many years were assumed to have the same cash flow. With such simplification, tables such as Table 6-3 can be used to calculate the present values.

What if we were promised the right to receive $1 each year for the next 10 years? How much would that promise be worth? Such a promise is called an *annuity*, which is defined as a series of payments for a specified number of years. Let us assume again that we could earn 9 percent compounded annually through investing in an equally risky venture. Under present value, we saw that the present value of the first year's payment is $.917, that of the second year's payment is $.842, and that of the tenth year's payment is $.422. We can find the present value of all these payments by adding together the worth of what we will receive in year 1, plus year 2, plus year 3, etc., up to and including year 10.

Again we can find the answer to such problems by using Table 6-3. Let us define A_n as the present value of an annuity which runs for n years. Let us define R as the periodic receipt. Then we have seen that the present value of a receipt at the end of year 1 is $R[1/(1 + i)]$, the second year's receipt is worth $R[1/(1 + i)]^2$, and so on. The value of the annuity is the sum of the value of these receipts, or

$$A_n = R\left(\frac{1}{1 + i}\right) + R\left(\frac{1}{1 + i}\right)^2 + \cdots + R\left(\frac{1}{1 + i}\right)^n$$

$$= R\left[\frac{1}{1 + i} + \frac{1}{(1 + i)^2} + \cdots + \frac{1}{(1 + i)^n}\right]$$

$$= R(IF_a)$$

where *IF* is the abbreviation for an interest factor.

In this case, we find the interest factor in column 5 of Table 6-3 under the heading of "Present value of an annuity of $1 per period," or for a 10-year $1,000 annuity at 9 percent (that is, a payment of $1,000 each year for 10 years), we find that the IF_a is 6.4176 and that the present value of the annuity is

$$A_n = R(IF_a)$$
$$\$6,417.60 = \$(1,000)(6.4176)$$

YIELDS, OR INTERNAL RATES OF RETURN

The calculation of the present value of a future cash flow is basic to most real estate investment decisions. Several different methods are in use for making the necessary estimates.

In comparing properties offered us for investments, we usually want to compare the *yields*, or rate of return on either the total property or the equity, that we can expect from each offer. Frequently, we are given a development cost, or a selling price for a property, an expected stream of income, and a final value or sales price, also called a *reversion*, at the end of a given period. From these data we want to calculate the yield. The problem is slightly different from that of Table 6-6 because we have positive cash flows consisting of expected income and the sales price of the property as well as negative cash flows, the costs of acquiring or disposing of the investment, and possible operating losses.

To find the yield, the owner must forecast all future revenues and expenses up to the time he plans either to sell the property or to transfer it to another use. He must also forecast the selling price or the value of the property at the end of this income stream. The problem is to find a given rate which, when used to discount the future income stream and the final worth or reversion, will make their sum exactly equal to today's cost or investment. We define this rate as the *internal rate of return*, or that interest rate at which the present value of all future positive inflows is equal to the present value of all negative outflows.

Internal Rate of Return

Finding an interest rate which will bring to zero the present value of all future flows turns out to be a cumbersome problem because we are valuing both positive and negative flows at many future points in time. To do it accurately, one must have a computer or else solve it through a process of trial and error.

An example of the trial-and-error method of selecting an interest rate and then calculating the present value of all flows is shown in Table 6-7. In that table we see that there are positive inflows of cash in years 1, 2, 3, and 4. On the other hand, there are negative flows, or outpayments, at the start of the period and in year 5.

The problem is to pick a likely rate and then discount the various flows back to see whether they equal zero, the definition of an internal rate of return. To start the table, we have selected an 18 percent internal rate of return. It is similar to the previous example, but we note here that the first outpayment has a discount factor of 1, since it is made at the start of the period in dollars of present value.

We see from the table that after we have calculated the present values at 18

Table 6-7 Illustrative Calculation of Internal Rate of Return

Period	Amount	Discount factor	Present value
		18% internal rate of return	
0	(1,300)	1.000	(1,300)
1	100	.847	85
2	400	.718	287
3	900	.609	548
4	1200	.516	619
5	(500)	.437	·(219)
			20
		19% internal rate of return	
0	(1,300)	1.000	(1,300)
1	100	.840	84
2	400	.706	282
3	900	.593	534
4	1200	.499	599
5	(500)	.419	(210)
			(11)

percent, we end up with a positive value of 20. This indicates that we are not discounting at a sufficiently high rate. Therefore, we try 19 percent in the second part of the table. Here we find that the sum of the present values of the flows is -11. This rate, then, is somewhat too high, or, in fact, the actual internal rate of return is somewhere between 18 and 19 percent.

For many purposes, such an estimate as between 18 and 19 percent ought to be sufficient because to carry out the calculation of the rate of return with extreme precision to several decimal places indicates a greater belief in the validity of the underlying data than probably exists. However, it is useful to see how the actual rate could be approximated. The absolute difference between the present values at 18 and 19 percent interest rates is 31. Then the internal rate of return is equal to 18 percent plus 20/31 (.65) or to 19 percent minus 11/31 (.35). Consequently, the internal rate of return for the illustration is approximately 18.65 percent, derived by subtracting .35 from 19 percent or by adding .65 to 18 percent.

Use of the Computer Because the calculation of the internal rate of return is a cumbersome process and because multiple calculations are required, it can be quite time-consuming, particularly if one wishes to test a variety of different assumptions as to cash flow or the amount that should be offered for the investment. As a result, readily available computer packages have been prepared which can be used for this purpose.

Specific expected cash flows are read into the computer. It almost immediately furnishes the desired internal rate of return. It also, of course, can as easily recalculate the internal rate of return based upon alternative assumptions.

Other Estimates of Yields Because the problems of calculating internal rates of return are difficult and because computers are not always available, investors often use a shortcut to figure the yield. They make several simplifying assumptions such as (1) that the income stream is regular and will not vary over time, (2) that the stream will continue forever—in which case no problems of a lump-sum payment or a reversion upon sale exist—or (3) that the income stream will continue for a given number of years and that the property will be worthless at the end of that time. Again, no problem of a reversion will arise.

Under the first type of calculation, a net income (free and clear income) is estimated before depreciation, financing charges, and income taxes. In this case a net yield can be found directly from the capitalization formula for a perpetual annuity:

$$y = \frac{R}{I}$$

where y = annual yield
R = annual net income
I = total investment, developed cost, or cost to purchase
Thus a property which costs $800,000 and has $86,000 annual income is said to yield 10.75 percent:

$$y = \frac{86,000}{800,000} = 10.75 \text{ percent}$$

In many cases owners wish to calculate the yield on their equity rather than on the total investment. Then R' will be net income after financing charges, while I' will be the equity rather than total investment.

The problem which arises in these cases is that the income is assumed to remain constant forever. The owner must decide how likely this assumption is and must determine whther the yield is high enough to cover the risks that this assumption is incorrect. To be conservative, therefore, some owners take the opposite point of view and assume that the stream of income will disappear completely at the end of a fixed period. The owner may assume that income will continue at the present rate for 25 years and then drop to zero.

It turns out that the yield under this assumption is approximately 9.7 percent. It appears that to assume that no income or reversion will be available at the end of 25 years cuts the estimated yield from 10.75 percent to 9.7 percent, or by about 10 percent. [We find the 9.7 percent from a table such as Table 6-3 using the formula $I = R(IF_a)$.] One method appears overly conservative, and the other not conservative enough. On the other hand, many believe that such estimates are based on such broad assumptions that no greater accuracy ought to be implied and therefore little is lost by using the simplifying assumptions.

The Mathematics of Yields

Again if we do not want to use the shortcut formulas or do not have a computer available, we can calculate internal rates of return or yields from interest tables such as Table 6-3. We use the concepts and interest factors already described in the discussion of the present value of a reversion and of an annuity.

Let us call the amount of investment today I_0, the present value of the expected stream of receipts A_n and of the reversion P_0. The problem, as we have just seen, is to find that interest rate i (also called the *yield* or *y*) which will cause the present value of the expected cash flow to exactly equal the amount of investment, or

$$I_0 = A_n + P_0$$

where P_n^e is the projected reversion and A_n and P_0 are the discounted present values of the expected stream of income and the reversion, respectively. Since

$$A_n = R\left(\frac{1}{1+i}\right) + R\left(\frac{1}{1+i}\right)^2 + \cdots + R\left(\frac{1}{1+i}\right)^n = R(IF_a)$$

and

$$P_0 = P_n^e\left(\frac{1}{1+i}\right)^n = P_n^e (IF_p)$$

$$I_0 = R(IF_a) + P_n^e (IF_p)$$

We have estimates of I_0, R, and P_n^e, but we have to find a particular yield or interest rate so that the two interest factors will be equal and will bring about the necessary equality. The problem is complicated because no table carries the combined yield rate. Instead, we must estimate the expected yield, use it on a trial basis to get the present value of the reversion, subtract this from the investment, and then use the rate on the income stream to see how far its discounted value differs from the remaining investment.

This is the identical problem we solved in Table 6-7 for a complex situation with uneven flows of income. If the expected cash flow is even, we can use the present values found in an annuity table; otherwise we must discount each flow separately.

Let us use as an example a building with a 15-year lease. Let us assume that an investor is offered a store for $188,664 which has a net-net lease of $20,000 per year and an estimated sales price at the end of the lease of $100,000. The investor would like to know the yield on the building. We now know the present value I_0, but we must solve for the yield (*y*), or the rate of return which will exactly cause the discounted value of the future cash flows to equal the present selling price. In other words, we must find the level of interest which will solve the equation

$$\$188,664 = \$20,000(IF_a) + \$100,000(IF_p)$$

where the period of discounting is 15 years.

We must seek these factors by trial and error, but by a lucky hunch we pick 9 percent and find that with this yield, IF_a is 8.0607 and IF_p is .2745, and so the equation can be solved:

$$188,664 = (20,000)(8.0607) + (100,000)(.2745)$$

Income Capitalization

An understanding of the process of calculating the yield on an investment is also basic to an understanding of the income capitalization process, one of the three basic appraisal methods used to determine a property's fair market value. This appraisal method is generally considered to be the most relevant for income properties.

Capitalization in appraising is the determination of the present value of the property from an analysis of its future income stream. The critical factors in such an analysis are the projection of the cash flow (that is, the amount of income to be received in each future period) and the decision as to the proper rate at which this income should be discounted in order to estimate the present value. The discount, or interest rate, used is called the *capitalization rate*.

If we could assume that a property would continue to yield its income at a constant rate forever, the appraisal problem would be fairly easy. We would use the same basic formula just discussed for estimating a property's yield. However, we would put into the formula the estimated cash flow and the discount or capitalization rate. Thus:

$$\text{Present value of property} = \frac{\text{net annual income}}{\text{capitalization rate}}$$

As an example, if a piece of land was expected to have a $100,000 net income forever, "in perpetuity," and our discount and capitalization rate was 10 percent, then the land's current value would be $1 million, or

$$\$1,000,000 = \frac{\$100,000}{.10}$$

A problem arises, however, because we do not expect most properties to maintain their income flows forever. Buildings must be thought of as gradually losing their ability to earn income. They are a wasting investment. As a result, part of the original investment must be recaptured from annual income each year. There are a number of ways to take account of this wasting of the investment.

Frequently a building will have a known income for a number of years. In addition, an estimate can be made for the value of the building (also called its *reversion*) at the end of the period. In the identical manner outlined in Table 6-6 we can use the derived capitalization rate to find the discount factors and calculate the present value of the property. For example, assume a store has a net-net lease which promises $20,000 in rent per year for the next 15 years; in addition, assume that we estimate that the store will sell for $100,000 at the end of the lease. We believe that for the risks involved, a 9 percent capitalization rate is proper.

We can calculate that the value of the store is approximately $188,000. The $300,000 in rents to be received at a rate of $20,000 a year for 15 years has a present value of $161,214, while the $100,000 income to be received at the end of the fifteenth year on the reversion or sale of the property has a present value of about $27,450.

This problem is identical to the one just solved for calculating the yield or internal rate of return for this same building. Instead of knowing the present value of the building (its cost of investment I_0), we are asked to solve for the value—

call it V_0. Instead of having to solve for the interest rate i, we are told the capitalization or discount rate is 9 percent. In other words, instead of

$$I_0 = R(IF_a) + P_n{}^e(IF_p)$$

where $i = y$, we have

$$V_0 = R(IF_a) + P_n{}^e(IF_p)$$

where i = capitalization rate. Or, since we have \$20,000 as the annual return for each of 15 years, \$100,000 as the reversion at that time, and 9 percent as the capitalization rate, the required equation is

$$V_0 = 20,000(IF_a) + 100,000(IF_p)$$

Looking up the present value of an annuity for 15 years discounted at 9 percent interest, we find that IF_a is 8.0607. Under the present value of 1 at the end of 15 years, also discounted at 9 percent, we find IF_p to be .2745. The value is therefore

$$V_0 = (20,000)(8.0607) + (100,000)(.2745) = 188,664$$

Recapture Estimates

This problem of allowing for the recapture of any anticipated loss in value over time can also be handled by incorporating a special added factor in the estimated capitalization rate. Under these techniques the rate will consist of two parts: one based on the desired yield or rate of return and the other reflecting the expected change in the property's value. The two are added together. If property values are expected to decline, the compound capitalization rate is higher. Since the capitalized value is found by dividing this rate into projected income, the present value for the property is lower than if only the desired yield were used. This is as it should be, on the assumption that the property income and value will decline with time.

For example, a building has a return of \$86,000 a year, and the desired rate of return is 8 percent. Then the simple capitalized value of the building is

$$\frac{\$86,000}{.08} = \$1,075,000$$

However, we believe that we should add 2.75 percent to the capitalization rate to allow for the recapture of the loss in value. The capitalized value of the building falls from \$1,075,000 to \$800,000 since

$$\frac{\$86,000}{.08 + .0275} = \frac{\$86,000}{.1075} = \$800,000$$

Sometimes the two parts of the capitalization rate are spoken of as performing separate functions: (1) The normal discount rate provides for the required yield or "return *on* the investment," and (2) the second part provides for the fall in value expected from the wastage or the "return *of* the investment."

There are two ways of thinking about the recapture rate and how it should be calculated. We can assume that the extra sum required from income each period either (1) serves to reduce the amount of investment in the property or (2) is put aside and held in a theoretical pool. The value of this pool at the end of the period should be sufficient so that the investor will have a sum equal to the original investment when the sum in the pool is added to the value remaining in the building.

The three most common methods of adding a recapture factor are the straight-line method, the Inwood level annuity, and the Hoskold safe-rate method.

The Straight-Line Method   The straight-line method is calculated by dividing the anticipated percentage loss in value by the appropriate time period. Thus if a property were assumed to have a 40-year useful life and no value at the end of the period, the capitalization rate would include for recapture purposes an extra 2.5 percent (100 ÷ 40 = 2.5). If the desired return on the investment were 7 percent, the two added together would give an overall capitalization rate of 9.5 percent.

In calculating the effect of the recaptured sums, the straight-line method gives no consideration to the time value of money. If the owner reinvested the 2.5 percent of the value recaptured each year, unless the interest rate were zero, at the end of the 40 years her investment would be considerably above the amount with which she started. Looking at it the other way, we would find that if the 2.5 percent extra return were considered as subtracting from the investment in the building, the actual yield on the remaining investment would grow steadily. For example, at the end of 20 years half the investment has been recaptured; yet the straight-line method calculates the average return for the period as if the value of the investment were the same as at the start.

The Inwood Level Annuity   The Inwood level annuity method of adjusting for recapture, on the other hand, can be thought of as making one of the following assumptions: (1) The amount recaptured from income each year is used to reduce the value of the investment, and therefore the desired yield is figured on the remaining nonrecaptured investment. This is the same assumption which underlies the constant mortgage debt service and the calculation of the internal rate of return. (2) Another way of expressing this is to assume that the amount recaptured each year is set aside and reinvested at a yield equal to the capitalization rate. Through compounding, the annual amounts set aside grow sufficiently so that at the end of the period, they and the sums earned exactly equal the estimated loss in value, or the amount needed to be recaptured.

The addition of the recapture factor reduces a property's capitalized value. The reduction is greatest for the straight-line method because, since it neglects the possible compound earnings, the recapture factor and the capitalization rate which includes it must be large. On the other hand, because it assumes that the amount recaptured can be reinvested at the high capitalization rate, the Inwood method requires a smaller factor in the capitalization rate and gives a larger current value.

The Hoskold Safe-Rate Method   In between these two is the Hoskold safe-rate method. It does not neglect the possible compound earnings on the recaptured amounts. Instead, it assumes that the amounts set aside annually from income to fund the anticipated loss in value are invested at a safe rate, perhaps 3 or 4 percent. Because this rate is lower than the rate under the Inwood method, the amount for recapture entered in the compound capitalization rate under the Hoskold approach will be greater, and the indicated property value less.

Actual versus Agreed-upon Interest Rates

Mortgages sell in competition with other types of loans, notes, and bonds. As we have seen, market interest varies greatly over time. No one who can buy a new $1,000 mortgage yielding 9 percent interest will buy an older one which yields only 6 percent for the same $1,000. Instead, the seller will have to cut the price so that the yield on the old mortgage will equal that on new ones. The difference between the face value or outstanding principal and the market price is called a *discount* or *premium*. If a mortgage has a contract rate of 6 percent interest and the market goes to 9 percent, the drop in price, or the discount, would be large.

In the mortgage market, such discounts or premiums are frequently called *points*. In lending, each percent of discount or premium of the principal is a point. Let us consider a $1,000 30-year mortgage with an agreed-upon interest rate of 9 percent. If interest rates rise, the seller might discount the mortgage by 3 percent, or pay 3 points. The new buyer would pay only $970 for a mortgage which requires the borrower to pay back $1,000 at 9 percent over 30 years. This contract, as we saw in Table 4-2, would call for 360 monthly payments of $8.05 each. The new buyer is interested in calculating his real yield. He will find that his yield depends upon whether the mortgage is outstanding for the full time or, as often happens, is refinanced or paid off in a lump sum at an earlier date.

Because such transactions are so common, convenient tables have been printed showing actual estimated yields for mortgages with particular terms sold at specific discounts or premiums and with separate assumptions as to when they will be paid off. Sections of such tables are shown in Table 6-8. Looking at this table, we see immediately that a 9 percent mortgage with 30 years to maturity bought at a price of 97 has an annual yield of 9.44 percent if this mortgage is paid off at the end of 12 years, an assumption frequently used in the market. The table shows yield calculations for mortgages bought at either discounts or premiums.

The idea behind the changing yields should be clear. The interest collected is figured on $1,000. The actual amount lent was only $970. This means a somewhat higher real interest rate. In addition, though, the actual amount repaid on principal is also more than was lent. This $30 difference is an added interest payment which goes to increase the yield by still more. The yield on the loan repaid at an earlier date is still higher because this $30 is averaged over a shorter period. More of it is added to the return in each period, since it is all repaid in a shorter time.

Table 6-8   Repayment Mortgage Values*
9.00% Monthly Payment Mortgage

	25-year mortgage prepaid in:								30-year mortgage prepaid in:						
Yield	6 years	8 years	10 years	12 years	14 years	16 years	18 years	Yield	6 years	8 years	10 years	12 years	14 years	16 years	18 years
3.50	128.64	136.36	143.20	149.19	154.34	158.66	162.15	3.50	129.06	137.12	144.42	150.99	156.85	162.01	166.50
3.75	127.14	134.38	140.77	146.33	151.09	155.06	158.25	3.75	127.54	135.10	141.91	148.01	153.43	158.18	162.28
4.00	125.66	132.44	138.39	143.54	147.93	151.58	154.49	4.00	126.04	133.11	139.46	145.11	150.10	154.46	158.21
4.25	124.21	130.53	136.06	140.82	144.86	148.19	150.84	4.25	124.56	131.16	137.06	142.28	146.87	150.86	154.27
4.50	122.77	128.66	133.77	138.17	141.87	144.91	147.32	4.50	123.10	129.25	134.71	139.52	143.73	147.37	150.47
4.75	121.35	126.82	131.54	135.58	138.96	141.73	143.91	4.75	121.66	127.37	132.41	136.83	140.68	143.99	146.80
5.00	119.95	125.01	129.36	133.05	136.14	138.65	140.61	5.00	120.24	125.52	130.16	134.21	137.72	140.72	143.25
5.25	118.58	123.23	127.22	130.59	133.39	135.66	137.42	5.25	118.84	123.70	127.96	131.65	134.84	137.55	139.82
5.50	117.21	121.48	125.12	128.18	130.71	132.75	134.33	5.50	117.46	21.92	125.80	129.16	132.03	134.47	136.51
5.75	115.87	119.77	123.07	125.84	128.11	129.94	131.34	5.75	116.10	120.17	123.69	126.73	129.31	131.49	133.30
6.00	114.55	118.08	121.07	123.55	125.58	127.20	128.45	6.00	114.76	118.45	121.63	124.35	126.66	128.60	130.20
6.10	114.02	117.42	120.27	122.65	124.59	126.13	127.32	6.10	114.22	117.77	120.82	123.42	125.62	127.47	128.99
6.20	113.50	116.76	119.49	121.76	123.61	125.08	126.20	6.20	113.70	117.09	120.01	122.50	124.60	126.35	127.80
6.30	112.98	116.10	118.71	120.88	122.64	124.03	125.10	6.30	113.17	116.42	119.21	121.58	123.58	125.25	126.62
6.40	112.47	115.45	117.94	120.00	121.67	123.00	124.01	6.40	112.65	115.76	118.42	120.68	122.58	124.16	125.46
6.50	111.96	114.80	117.18	119.14	120.72	121.98	122.93	6.50	112.13	115.10	117.63	119.78	121.58	123.08	124.31
6.60	111.45	114.16	116.42	118.28	119.78	120.97	121.87	6.60	111.61	114.44	116.85	118.89	120.60	122.02	123.18
6.70	110.94	113.52	115.67	117.43	118.85	119.97	120.82	6.70	111.09	113.79	116.08	118.01	119.63	120.97	122.06
6.80	110.43	112.88	114.92	116.59	117.93	118.99	119.79	6.80	110.58	113.14	115.31	117.14	118.67	119.93	120.96
6.90	109.93	112.25	114.18	115.76	117.02	118.02	118.76	6.90	110.07	112.50	114.55	116.28	117.72	118.91	119.87
7.00	109.43	111.63	113.45	114.93	116.12	117.05	117.75	7.00	109.57	111.86	113.80	115.43	116.78	117.89	118.79
7.10	108.94	111.01	112.72	114.12	115.23	116.10	116.76	7.10	109.06	111.23	113.05	114.58	115.85	116.89	117.71
7.20	108.44	110.39	112.00	113.31	114.35	115.16	115.77	7.20	108.56	110.60	112.31	113.74	114.93	115.90	116.69
7.30	107.95	109.78	111.28	112.51	113.48	114.24	114.80	7.30	108.06	109.97	111.58	112.92	114.02	114.93	115.66
7.40	107.46	109.17	110.58	111.71	112.62	113.32	113.84	7.40	107.57	109.35	110.85	112.10	113.12	113.96	114.64
7.50	106.98	108.57	109.87	110.93	111.76	112.41	112.90	7.50	107.08	108.74	110.13	111.28	112.23	113.01	113.63
7.60	106.49	107.97	109.18	110.15	110.92	111.52	111.96	7.60	106.59	108.13	109.41	110.48	111.36	112.07	112.64
7.70	106.01	107.37	108.48	109.38	110.08	110.63	111.03	7.70	106.10	107.52	108.70	109.68	110.49	111.14	111.66
7.80	105.54	106.78	107.80	108.61	109.26	109.75	110.12	7.80	105.61	106.92	108.00	108.89	109.63	110.22	110.69
7.90	105.06	106.20	107.12	107.86	108.44	108.89	109.22	7.90	105.13	106.32	107.30	108.11	108.77	109.31	109.74
8.00	104.59	105.61	106.44	107.11	107.63	108.03	108.33	8.00	104.65	105.72	106.61	107.34	107.93	108.41	108.79
8.10	104.12	105.03	105.78	106.37	106.83	107.19	107.45	8.10	104.18	105.13	105.92	106.57	107.10	107.52	107.86
8.20	103.65	104.46	105.11	105.63	106.04	106.35	106.58	8.20	103.70	104.55	105.24	105.81	106.28	106.65	106.94
8.30	103.19	103.89	104.45	104.90	105.26	105.53	105.72	8.30	103.23	103.96	104.57	105.06	105.46	105.78	106.04
8.40	102.72	103.32	103.80	104.18	104.48	104.71	104.87	8.40	102.76	103.39	103.90	104.32	104.66	104.93	105.14
8.50	102.26	102.76	103.16	103.47	103.72	103.90	104.04	8.50	102.29	102.81	103.23	103.58	103.86	104.08	104.26
8.60	101.81	102.20	102.51	102.76	102.96	103.10	103.21	8.60	101.83	102.24	102.58	102.85	103.07	103.25	103.38
8.70	101.35	101.64	101.88	102.06	102.21	102.31	102.39	8.70	101.37	101.67	101.92	102.13	102.29	102.42	102.52
8.80	100.90	101.09	101.25	101.37	101.46	101.53	101.59	8.80	100.91	101.11	101.28	101.41	101.52	101.60	101.67
8.90	100.45	100.54	100.62	100.68	100.73	100.76	100.79	8.90	100.45	100.55	100.64	100.70	100.76	100.80	100.83
9.00	100.00	100.00	100.00	100.00	100.00	100.00	100.00	9.00	100.00	100.00	100.00	100.00	100.00	100.00	100.00
9.10	99.55	99.46	99.38	99.33	99.28	99.25	99.22	9.10	99.55	99.45	99.37	99.30	99.25	99.21	99.18
9.20	99.11	98.92	98.77	98.66	98.57	98.50	98.45	9.20	99.10	98.90	98.74	98.62	98.51	98.43	98.37
9.30	98.67	98.39	98.17	98.00	97.86	97.76	97.69	9.30	98.65	98.36	98.12	97.93	97.78	97.66	97.57
9.40	98.23	97.86	97.57	97.34	97.17	97.03	96.94	9.40	98.21	97.82	97.51	97.26	97.06	96.90	96.78
9.50	97.80	97.34	96.97	96.69	96.47	96.31	96.20	9.50	97.77	97.29	96.90	96.59	96.34	96.15	96.00
9.60	97.36	96.81	96.38	96.05	95.79	95.60	95.47	9.60	97.33	96.75	96.29	95.93	95.64	95.41	95.23
9.70	96.93	96.30	95.80	95.41	95.12	94.90	94.74	9.70	96.89	96.23	95.69	95.27	94.93	94.67	94.47
9.80	96.50	95.78	95.22	94.78	94.45	94.20	94.03	9.80	96.46	95.70	95.10	94.62	94.24	93.95	93.72
9.90	96.08	95.27	94.64	94.15	93.78	93.51	93.32	9.90	96.02	95.18	94.51	93.97	93.56	93.23	92.98
10.00	95.65	94.76	94.07	93.53	93.13	92.83	92.62	10.00	95.60	94.66	93.92	93.34	92.88	92.52	92.25
10.25	94.60	93.51	92.66	92.01	91.52	91.16	90.91	10.25	94.53	93.39	92.48	91.77	91.21	90.78	90.46
10.50	93.57	92.28	91.28	90.52	89.95	89.54	89.24	10.50	93.48	92.13	91.07	90.24	89.59	89.09	88.72
10.75	92.55	91.06	89.93	89.06	88.42	87.96	87.63	10.75	92.45	90.90	89.69	88.74	88.01	87.45	87.03
11.00	91.54	89.87	88.60	87.64	86.93	86.42	86.06	11.00	91.42	89.69	88.33	87.28	86.47	85.86	85.40
12.00	87.64	85.31	83.56	82.27	81.33	80.67	80.22	12.00	87.47	85.04	83.18	81.77	80.70	79.91	79.32
13.00	83.94	81.04	78.91	77.37	76.27	75.51	75.00	13.00	83.73	80.70	78.43	76.74	75.49	74.58	73.92
14.00	80.43	77.05	74.62	72.89	71.68	70.86	70.32	14.00	80.18	76.65	74.05	72.16	70.79	69.80	69.11
15.00	77.11	73.32	70.65	68.79	67.51	66.66	66.11	15.00	76.82	72.86	70.01	67.97	66.52	65.51	64.80
16.00	73.95	69.83	66.98	65.03	63.72	62.86	62.32	16.00	73.63	69.32	66.28	64.14	62.66	61.63	60.94
17.00	70.96	66.57	63.58	61.58	60.27	59.42	58.90	17.00	70.60	66.01	62.83	60.64	59.14	58.13	57.46
18.00	68.13	63.51	60.43	58.42	57.11	56.29	55.79	18.00	67.73	62.91	59.64	57.42	55.94	54.96	54.33
19.00	65.43	60.64	57.52	55.50	54.23	53.44	52.97	19.00	65.01	60.01	56.68	54.47	53.03	52.09	51.49
20.00	62.88	57.96	54.81	52.82	51.58	50.84	50.40	20.00	62.43	57.30	53.94	51.76	50.36	49.47	48.91
21.00	60.45	55.44	52.29	50.34	49.16	48.46	48.05	21.00	59.98	54.75	51.40	49.26	47.92	47.08	46.56

*This table shows the price to be paid for a mortgage to return a yield on the investment if the mortgage is prepaid in full prior to maturity. For example, a portfolio of 9 percent 30-year mortgages is offered at a yield of 5.00 percent, assuming prepayment in 12 years. The price is $134.21.

Source: D. Thorndike (ed.), The Thorndike Encyclopedia of Banking and Financial Tables, 1973. Permission to reprint is granted by Warren, Gorham & Lamont, 210 South Street, Boston, Mass., and David Thorndike. All rights reserved.

Discounts on a Mortgage

The same information and formulas already developed can help us to understand the problem of discounting or premiums.

We saw that Table 6-8 enabled us to find immediately the yield on a mortgage bought at a discount, whether paid off at maturity or in advance. What is the logic behind these tables? What the buyer has done is to pay $970 for an annuity which promises to pay $8.05 for the next 30 years. We know that the present value of such a contract discounted at 9 percent is $1,000. Clearly, the contract in this case must be discounted at a higher rate to give the lower present value. We must solve the equation

$$IF_a = \frac{\text{principal}}{\text{monthly payment}} = \frac{970}{8.05} = 120.4969$$

Looking in a set of compound interest tables (but using the table based on monthly rather than annual payments, as in Table 6-3), we find that for 360 months the present value of an annuity of $1 per period is 124.2819 with discounting at 9.00 percent and that it is 118.9267 at 9.50 percent. The 120.50 falls between, and so interpolation is necessary to get the approximate yield (call it X).

We must solve as follows:

Yield	Present-value factor
9.00	124.2819
X	120.4969
9.50	118.9267

$$X = 9.00 + .50\left(\frac{124.2819 - 120.4969}{124.2819 - 118.9267}\right) = 9.353$$

Thus the 3-point discount raises the actual yield by about .353 of a percent.

What happens when the loan is paid off at the end of 12 years? The same general type of calculation takes place, but it is more complex. The problem is to find the interest rate which will equate $970 to 144 monthly payments of $8.05 plus a lump-sum payment of $860, which is the amount which will remain unpaid at that time on the original loan of $1,000. In other words, there is some interest rate or yield (actually the 9.44 percent shown in Table 6-8) which will discount back the monthly-payment series and the final reversion to give a present value of $970, the amount which the new buyer pays for the loan.

There is no simple formula to solve this latter problem analytically. It can be done either by a trial-and-error method or by a computer program. It is complex, like the internal rate of return, because we must find equal yields to discount both the monthly payments and the final reversion. Since the data we get in our normal tables do not enable us to do this, we must look directly into a table such as Table 6-8 that has been properly calculated or use a trial-and-error method.

SUMMARY

Money has a time value. If we have money today, we can invest it and receive interest on it. As a result, most real estate investment and finance problems require either calculating the present value of future income or estimating the interest rate which will cause the present value of all future expenditures and cash flows to be equal. This interest rate is the internal rate of return.

Most such problems can be solved through the use of existing printed tables or through computer programs. When we examine separate types of problems, we find them closely related. They differ primarily with respect to the specific information we are given and that for which we must solve. If the flows are even and continue forever, the use of the mathematical formulas is relatively straightforward. When the flows differ among years, some of the problems become rather complex.

QUESTIONS AND PROBLEMS

1 From the tables in this chapter, find approximately how long it would take a sum to double at compound interest of 8, 15, and 20 percent.
2 If the interest rate is 9 percent, would you prefer to have $1,000 today or an equally risk-free promise of $3,000 in 10 years? Why?
3 What amount would you pay today for a mortgage that consisted of a single payment of $30,000 at the end of 20 years if you wanted to earn 9 percent compound interest?
4 You are offered a mortgage with annual payments of $1,000 for each of the next 20 years, at which time it will be paid off. If you want to earn 9 percent interest, how much will you pay for such a mortgage?
5 What is the value of a stream of income of $50,000 a year capitalized at 20 percent?
6 Discuss the concept of recapture in calculating the value of a building.
7 If you agreed to pay 5 points to borrow $50,000 on a mortgage, how much funds would the lender actually give you?
8 What amount would you pay for a $100,000 9 percent 30-year mortgage if market interest rates fell to 8 percent and you believed the mortgage would be prepaid at the end of 10 years?
9 Is the Inwood or the Hoskold method of providing a recapture factor for a capitalization rate similar to the basic assumption underlying the internal rate of return? Explain.
10 Can a person who discounts the future at a high rate pay more or less for a specific investment opportunity than a person with a low discount rate?
11 Does the use of a recapture factor increase or decrease a property's capitalized value?

SELECTED REFERENCES FOR PART ONE

Adler, B., and C. J. Greene: *Profits in Real Estate: A Reader* (New York: World Publishing, 1971).

Axelrod, A., C. J. Berger, and Q. Johnstone: *Land Transfer and Finance: Cases and Materials* (Boston: Little, Brown, 1971).

Bierman, H., and S. Smidt: *The Capital Budgeting Decision*, 4th ed. (New York: Macmillan, 1975).

Board of Governors of the Federal Reserve System: *Flow of Funds Accounts* (Washington: quarterly and annually).

Bockl, G.: *How to Use Leverage to Make Money in Local Real Estate* (Englewood Cliffs, N.J.: Prentice-Hall, 1965).

Bryant, W. R.: *Mortgage Lending: Fundamentals and Practices*, 2d ed. (New York: McGraw-Hill, 1962).

Goleman, H. (ed.): *Financing Real Estate Development* (Washington: American Institute of Architects, 1974).

Griffin, C. W.: *Development Building: The Team Approach* (Washington: American Institute of Architects, 1972).

Haley, C. W. and L. D. Schall: *Theory of Financial Decisions* (New York: McGraw-Hill, 1973).

Kratovil, R.: *Real Estate Law*, 6th ed. (Englewood Cliffs, N.J.: Prentice-Hall, 1974).

Maisel, S. J.: *Housebuilding in Transition* (Berkeley: University of California Press, 1953).

Pugh, J. W., and W. H. Hippaka: *California Real Estate Finance*, 2d ed. (Englewood Cliffs, N.J.: Prentice-Hall, 1973).

Robinson, R. I., and D. Wrightsman: *Financial Markets: The Accumulation and Allocation of Wealth* (New York: McGraw-Hill, 1974).

Roulac, S. E.: *Real Estate Syndication Digest: Principles and Applications* (San Francisco: Real Estate Syndication Digest, 1972).

Schulkin, P.: *Commercial Bank Construction Lending* (Boston: Federal Reserve Bank of Boston, 1970).

Seldin, M., and R. H. Swesnik: *Real Estate Investment Strategy* (New York: Wiley-Interscience, 1970).

Silber, W. L.: *Portfolio Behavior of Financial Institutions* (New York: Holt, 1970).

Thorndike, D. (ed.): *The Thorndike Encyclopedia of Banking and Financial Tables* (Boston: Warren, Gorham & Lamont, 1973).

U.S. Commission on Financial Structure and Regulation: *Report* (1971).

U.S. Department of Housing and Urban Development: *Loan Transaction Activity* (monthly and annually).

Van Horne, J. C.: *Financial Management and Policy*, 3d ed. (Englewood Cliffs, N.J.: Prentice-Hall, 1974).

Wendt, P. F., and A. R. Cerf: *Tables for Investment Analysis* (Berkeley: University of California, Center for Real Estate and Urban Economics, 1970).

Part Two

Evolving Forms
of Ownership
and Investment

This part examines the forms of real estate ownership, including both traditional and newer techniques. Possible relationships between sellers, buyers, lenders, and investors have multiplied. The differences between an investor and a lender have become far less clear-cut than they were in the past. Why have some types of ownership become so much more prominent? What is gained and what is lost in the new relationships?

Chapter 7 introduces methods of owning property. It examines in greater detail limited partnerships, cooperatives and condominiums, and real estate investment trusts. In Chapter 8 we discuss the growth of real estate securities and syndication, using two famous cases as examples. The chapter also points out areas of potential conflict. Securities based on real estate are examined in Chapter 9. Ownership and sales are increasingly involved with securities regulatory agencies. The chapter concludes with a discussion of other mixed forms of ownership and leasing.

Chapter 7

The Ownership
of Property

When we discuss owning a property, we sometimes joke about the fact that our ownership is mainly nominal because the mortgage covers most of the price and takes most of the income. On the whole, however, only rarely do we pay much attention to the forms and attributes of different ways of owning properties.

This situation changes drastically when one becomes a real estate investor or wants to borrow or lend money on property. How a property is owned can have a significant impact on profits, taxes, and risks. Furthermore, purchasing property can be extremely complicated. Not only are the choices numerous and intricate, but they also depend on real property law, which is complex. The law of property has developed over centuries. Its intricacies have multiplied as the law has changed in an effort to encompass the needs of the newly dynamic field of real estate investment. In modern practice the variations and different forms of legal claims have become paramount. A vast difference exists between the complexities surrounding the purchase and sale of interests in developments and income properties and the negotiations concerned with single-family homes; however, even the latter are in the process of rapid change.

Our discussion of these factors intentionally avoids legal niceties. Instead, we treat fundamental principles as well as the investing and financing logic involved. Few critical decisions in real estate can be made without competent legal advice. On the other hand, the investor and financier need to be aware of the possibilities opened up by new techniques of ownership and financing. They must have a working knowledge of the specialized language involved and the rationale behind each instrument.

METHODS OF OWNING PROPERTIES

The methods by which property can be purchased and owned include individual ownership (sole proprietorship), joint tenancy, tenancy in common, corporation, general partnership, limited partnership, condominiums and cooperatives, and REITs. The legal form elected makes a great deal of difference, particularly for income property, with respect to the owner's liabilities. In deciding how to hold properties, the following characteristics are especially significant:

1 *Taxation status.* Is the entity eligible for single taxation, with the income tax results of the business "flowing through" directly to the investors, or is there double taxation, with taxes being paid twice—both by the entity and by the individual investors?

2 *Investor's liability.* What is the amount of the investor's risk? Is it limited to the amount of the investment, or can the investor be liable for losses and claims in excess of his or her investment?

3 *Management.* What restrictions are there on how management decisions are made? Can all investors participate? Can the decision making be centralized?

4 *Transferability of interests.* Can investors freely trade their interests, or are there restrictions on transferability?

5 *Allowed activities.* Are there limitations on the types of activities in which the entity can engage?

Attempts to merge various of these advantages and disadvantages have led to the establishment of many mixed forms of ownership. Practice in this sphere is changing rapidly. New forms and their desirability shift with tax laws and rulings. Table 7-1 is a summary of major characteristics of various types of ownership.

Individual Ownership, Joint Tenancy, and Tenancy in Common

The simplest and most common way of holding property is through individual ownership. For tax purposes, individual owners report the profits or losses from the property as part of their income. Owners are, however, liable without limit for any debts contracted by them as a result of their property ownership. They are liable for personal injury or similar claims of persons damaged through the property. Furthermore, the property will be subject to liens for any of their other debts.

Joint tenancies and tenancies in common are similar to individual ownership but relate to two or more persons. They differ primarily with respect to the share of ownership and the rights of survivorship. In a joint tenancy, the ownership interests are equal, and the survivor owns the property. In a tenancy in common, there may be unequal shares, and the deceased's interest becomes part of his or her estate. Taxes and liability basically follow the rules of individual ownership. Difficulty with tenancies in common arises when there is disagreement as to management or sale. The owners must agree to all the terms and conditions before a sale is possible.

Table 7-1   Characteristics of Ownership Forms

	Taxation status	Investor liability	Management	Transferability	Restrictions on allowed activities
Individual	Single	Unlimited	Personal	Unlimited	No
Tenancy in common	Single	Unlimited	Flexible (usually sign management contract)	Modified	No
Corporation	Double*	Limited	No restrictions	Unlimited	No
REIT	Modified single (tax losses can not exceed cash distributions)	Limited (with some special exceptions)	Trustees	Unlimited	Yes
General partnerships	Single	Unlimited	All partners (often sign management contract)	Varies	No
Limited partnerships	Single	Limited	General partner(s) only	Varies	No
Condominiums and cooperatives	Combine characteristics of individual ownership, tenancy in common, and corporations, depending on articles of incorporation, leases, and bylaws				

*Subchapter S has single-taxation status but usually is inappropriate because of limitations on number of shareholders and nature of real estate activities.

Corporations

When a business grows to any size, the corporation becomes the most widely used ownership form. This applies in real estate as in other fields. Corporations are creatures of the state and must be chartered by it. What a corporation can or cannot do is limited by its charter. Many states have special rules and taxes applying to real estate corporations.

The disadvantages of corporations are found primarily in the sphere of taxation and record keeping. The corporation pays the state special fees for its charter. Extra legal advice and expenses are also involved. Certain taxes must be paid simply to continue in existence whether the firm is profitable or not. The records of major actions requiring approval by directors must be kept in a specified form. Taxes must be paid to transfer stock. A still more important influence on decisions is the corporate profit tax. All these taxes can be very burdensome. Finally, losses or depreciation allowances accruing to the corporation in the course of its business cannot be passed on to the owners.

The considerable advantages of the corporation frequently outweigh the drawbacks. The corporation is a legal entity distinct from its stockholders and management. It holds property in its own name. While the corporation can sue and be sued, the liability of shareholders is limited in that they can lose no more than their investment in the corporation. If the property goes bad or an unexpected accident and damages occur, stockholders will lose only their investment.

In certain situations, some of the tax disadvantages of the corporation may be minimized. As a result of heavy depreciation charges, a corporation may show a loss or break-even situation in its profit account even though, at the same time, it may have a large cash flow. This cash may be distributed to owners as a repayment of capital. In such cases the repayment or cash receipt by the stockholder is not subject to taxes. It merely reduces an owner's investment in the corporation. In this manner, some of the more important advantages of real estate investment may be available, together with other advantages of the corporate form of ownership.

Partnerships and Joint Ventures

Partnerships are the usual form of holding property among several individuals if there is a wish to remain unincorporated. Partnerships have been a traditional form of ownership in real estate. In recent years the role of partnerships has become far more important. To gather large sums of investment capital, partnerships with thousands of individual partners have been formed. This development has caused basic changes in the entire field of real estate investing and lending.

Both in traditional partnerships and in the new ones, problems arise in the sphere of liability. Where a general partnership exists, each partner can normally bind the group. In addition, each is usually liable individually for the entire debt and personal liabilities created by the property owned by the partnership. The advantage in holding property in a partnership is that the partnership pays no income tax in and of itself. It files its own return, but pays no taxes. Instead, all the partners pick up their share of the total return and include it on their own reports.

In a limited partnership, the control and liability of certain of the partners are curtailed. The partnership is divided into general and limited partners. The general partners are subject to the usual rules of liability and have a voice in management and control. The limited partners may have no voice in management. Their liability is generally limited to their initial capital contribution. The partnership need not dissolve because of the death of a limited partner, whereas it is terminated by the death of a general partner.

A joint venture is a partnership formed for a single purpose. It is most common in real estate and construction, where the purpose is usually the purchase, development, or ownership of a single property. The joint venture is frequently a limited partnership and gives management and control to one individual or a few individuals.

Cooperatives and Condominiums

One of the fastest-growing forms of ownership in the 1970s has been that of cooperative corporations and condominiums, institutions which combine forms of individual ownership of units with group ownership and management of common property. Their more detailed workings are described later in this chapter. They have been a "hot" marketing device because they solve some basic problems, even as they create others. Cooperatives were popular in the 1920s also, but they had a disastrous experience at that time. The history of condominiums goes back to early biblical times. Although they have been among the most common forms of ownership in many European countries and South America, they were late gaining a foothold in the United States. They got an early and rather slow start in Hawaii in the 1940s. Recently, however, their growth has accelerated rapidly.

The impetus for cooperatives and condominiums has come from many sources. After the war they were pushed as part of the FHA program by advocates interested primarily in cheaper housing. Their next big expansion came when developers discovered that because of their tax advantages, they provided a method of reopening the market for luxury apartments. They have also been promoted in recent years by owners who wanted to sell existing apartment buildings either because rent control prevented them from renting profitably or because they had used up most of their tax depreciation allowances. Such investors found they could sell units to individual owners more advantageously than they could sell the whole building to another investor.

Other boosts have come from higher land costs, from people tired of maintaining their own lawns and gardens, and from the boom in retirement and resort homes. In such cases, units may be one-family houses, townhouses (or attached houses), garden apartments, or highrises. The cooperative or condominium association furnishes outside maintenance, lawn and garden care, and recreational facilities, such as swimming pools and tennis courts. In addition, for second homes, managers are provided to rent the units to others. Thus the condominium can serve as a form of investment or, at least, as a method of writing off for tax purposes part of the expenses of a second home.

The concept of cooperatives and condominiums has also spread to professional offices, warehouses, and, more recently, shopping centers. In all these cases occupants want to own rather than lease. By getting together, individuals can own a share of a building that would require too great an investment for any single occupant.

Real Estate Investment Trusts

Another form of response to the changing relations in property ownership and lending has been the REIT. Prior to 1960 only a small number of REITs existed. In 1960 the tax laws were changed to allow REITs meeting certain criteria to be treated as conduits (nontaxable) with respect to income distributed to the trust's beneficiaries. For a period, trusts still grew slowly, but after 1968 they expanded rapidly as the country's largest banks, mortgage lenders, real estate firms, builders, insurance firms, and others sponsored them. By 1974 the total assets of REITs were over $20 billion.

REITs had a rather easy time selling themselves to the public because they followed the familiar pattern of the regulated investment company or "closed-end mutual fund." The REIT has (1) trustees, (2) shareholders or beneficiaries, and (3) investment advisers and consultants or managers. Trustees include some members of management and some outsiders (but frequently with related interests). They are paid for their actual time spent on the business of the trust. The investment advisers are usually a separate firm who receive payments based on the assets in the trust (for example, .8 percent per year of average assets in the year) and who do most of the work and management. However, in some cases the trust may do a good deal of the investing and management itself.

Typically, the sponsors (banks such as Bank of America or Chase Manhattan Bank, insurance companies such as Equitable or State Mutual Life, or mortgage bankers such as Sutro, or Colwell, or Lomas & Nettleton) or an advisory firm files a declaration of trust. They then sell shares to the public through a public underwriting. Some trusts are listed and their shares traded actively on the New York and American Stock Exchanges, while others are traded over the counter. The price of the shares fluctuates from day to day depending on the trust's earnings and market conditions. If the firm meets certain criteria, the income paid to the shareholders or beneficiaries will not be taxed to the trust. These stipulations are similar to those of mutual funds, but they require that at least 75 percent or more of the trust income be derived from real estate (including mortgages, rents, and capital gains).

There are three principal types of REITs which differ as to the type of assets in which they invest: (1) equity trusts, which hold primarily ownership of income properties; (2) holders of permanent (long-term) mortgages; and (3) trusts specializing in construction and development lending, which buy land, make construction and development mortgages, make interim (short-term) mortgages up to 5 years, and also purchase land and leasebacks. In fact, although a particular trust may hold assets predominantly in one or another category, many trusts are a combination of the three types. REITs which hold primarily mortgages are sometimes given the alternative title "mortgage investment trusts."

FACTORS INFLUENCING CHOICES

Table 7-1 summarizes some of the key characteristics of the various ownership forms. The most significant differences appear with respect to liability, taxes, and management.

The Use of Limited Partnerships

While houses and small properties are usually owned individually or by general partnerships, cooperatives, or condominiums, the ownership of large income properties is more and more being concentrated into corporations, limited partnerships, and trusts.

Corporations have the fundamental advantage of limiting liability. In addition, they facilitate centralized control and the transfer of fractional or complete interests. Not only can shares be transferred with ease, but also ownership can be split into innumerable parts. For persons in high-income brackets, the rate of corporate tax may be lower than their personal income tax. On the other hand, corporations have to pay an income tax themselves. As their income is paid out, it becomes subject to tax again. Furthermore, corporations may have trouble passing to the owner losses to be used to offset income from other sources, thereby reducing tax obligations.

The fact that owners pay twice on income distributions from corporations has earned them the title "double-taxation entities." As a result, there has been a push toward other forms. Individual ownership could be used, but because many individuals prefer to join with others in owning property, this is not a preferred form. Among other possibilities, some have chosen the real estate trust, which is a "single-taxation entity." However, because current losses of a REIT are not available as tax losses to the owners and since this is a major advantage of real estate ownership, still other methods have been developed.

To avoid the problems of double taxation and the liabilities of other forms, the preferred form of ownership in recent years has usually been the limited partnership. It is a single-taxation entity which also provides for the flow-through from the partnership's business to individuals of losses which can offset income from other sources (see Chapter 21). Substantial noncash deductions from depreciation can give a real estate limited partnership a negative taxable income in its early years of operation. These losses are used by the partners to shelter income from other sources from taxes. In addition, this form of partnership can limit the liability of most partners and can flexibly structure its ownership and management.

Qualification as a Partnership

Because of some abuses of the limited partnership, the Internal Revenue Service (IRS) has become concerned that associations which in reality are not limited partnerships have been claiming the tax advantages established for other purposes. Consequently, the IRS examines with great care claims of groups holding real estate that they constitute limited partnerships.

An entity can qualify as a partnership for tax purposes if it *avoids* a "preponderance of corporate characteristics." These characteristics include:

1 Having associates
2 Being formed to carry on a business for profit
3 Centralization of management
4 Continuity of life
5 Limited liability
6 Free transferability

If a partnership has a preponderance of these characteristics, it will be termed an *association* and subject to double taxation. Since both partnerships and corporations share the first two characteristics, avoiding a preponderance of corporate characteristics generally means having no more than two of the last four.

Many limited partnerships, particularly large publicly registered programs, have centralization of management and therefore possess the third corporate feature. However, some limited partnerships are organized so as to avoid this characteristic.

The fourth characteristic, continuity of life, may ordinarily be avoided by providing for termination of the partnership on the death or incapacity of the general partner. However, recent interpretations by the IRS have held that many partnership agreements do have continuity of life because the term of the partnership can be extended by a vote of the limited partners and thus no effective limitation exists on the life of the partnership.

The fifth characteristic of limited liability is often avoided when the general partner is exposed to unlimited liability even though the limited partners do, in fact, have limited liability. Because of the general partner's exposure, the entity as a whole is considered to have unlimited liability. This theory depends on the general partner's possessing sufficient assets. If this person is a mere ''dummy'' or a corporate shell with no assets, no effective exposure to the risk of loss exists. In such circumstances, the IRS will deny that the corporate characteristic of limited liability has, in fact, been avoided.

Assuming that both continuity of life and limited liability have been avoided, the partnership could elect to provide for free transferability of interests, thus failing to differentiate the sixth characteristic from a corporation. To provide additional safety, however, many attorneys prefer to restrict the transferability of interests in order to maintain a differentiation from a corporation and to ensure that the partnership is not treated as an association and taxed as such.

THE ADVANTAGES OF COOPERATIVES AND CONDOMINIUMS

Because cooperatives and condominiums have become such an important ownership technique, an understanding of their strengths and weaknesses can be helpful in evaluating individual situations.

Builders and promoters sell cooperatives or condominiums by stressing those factors which have led to the increased demand for them:

1   There is a large tax saving compared with renting. The cooperative qualifies for a tax saving as if it were an individually owned home. In contrast, rental payments on one's residence in most cases offer no tax benefits.

2   Since the owner holds the equity, an inflationary hedge exists.

3   Costs of management and operation are less than for investor-owned apartments. Individual owners handle their own internal maintenance and take an interest in preserving the total property.

4   A purchaser can live in an apartment house rather than a single-family unit and yet enjoy all the status and attributes of homeownership.

5   Owners who prefer single-family units need not be concerned with maintaining lawns and gardens, since these are handled cooperatively.

6   Recreational facilities go far beyond what might be possible on an individual basis and are also owned cooperatively.

7   Finally, a centralized management is possible for maintenance and rental of second homes.

The Form of Ownership

Cooperative groups can own property through a corporation, a trust, or a tenancy in common, or as a condominium. The similarities and differences among these methods are important. Since trusts and tenancies in common are infrequently used, however, we shall not discuss them separately. They follow the same general concepts as the other cooperatives. We shall, however, describe, compare, and contrast the cooperative corporation and the condominium.

Typically, cooperatives and condominiums have been promoted by builders, developers, or owners of an existing structure. The promoter enters into an agreement to sell the structure to a newly formed cooperative corporation, which he or she organizes, or to individuals and a condominium association. In this sale process, five types of documents are essential: (1) the agreement for construction or for sale of the structure as condominiums or to the cooperative corporation, (2) the articles of incorporation and the corporation's stock shares, (3) the proprietary leases from the corporation to the owner-tenants, (4) the cooperative's and condominium's bylaws, and (5) the mortgage or deed of trust.

It is vital for the buyer of a cooperative or condominium to check carefully the sales agreement and any management contract. Buyers have been surprised to find that in come cases the promoter retains ownership of the parking, shopping, and recreational facilities. After they start making payments on their home or apartment, the new owners are stunned when they are billed for services they assumed were included in their agreed-upon payments.

In other cases, they may find that a type of "sweetheart" agreement has been made with the promoter's management or ownership company. A long-term contract gives the promoter's firm the right to manage the property at what may be excessive rates for the service rendered. Other contracts have specified that the properties retained by the promoter need not pay their fair share of common costs.

Another not uncommon experience has been the discovery that the seller greatly underestimated taxes and operating and maintenance costs. The problems experienced by unwary purchasers have led to legislation and increased regulation.

Cooperative Corporations

The cooperative corporation exists to own and to manage the building and to lease apartments to its shareholders. The latter may be either owner-occupiers or investors who sublease to others. The corporate charter, the leases, and the bylaws specify the rights and duties of the individual shareholder-tenants and of the corporation. Financing over and above the equity is obtained by the corporation through a single mortgage or deed of trust on the entire property.

In cooperative corporations, owners buy shares of stock. The number of shares required to lease a particular apartment varies with its size, location, and initial price. But owning stock does not automatically give the right to occupy a unit; stockholders must, in addition, receive a proprietary lease covering their specific apartment.

The cooperative corporation is responsible for the operation, maintenance, and financing of the entire structure, but usually not for maintenance within individual apartments. The corporation is managed by a board of directors elected by the shareholders, each of whom usually has a single vote. The owners as a group, or through the directors, determine the budget, the level of maintenance, and the level of services; hire the manager or management firm; and make similar decisions.

Owners must pay their pro rata share of all the corporation's expenses including taxes, mortgage payments, operating and maintenance expenses, heat, security, janitorial services, insurance, and others. Each owner's share of these joint costs depends on the ratio of his or her shares to the total. Thus if there are 200 shares in the corporation, an owner with 6 shares will be liable for 3 percent of all expenses. As a rule, the stock shares and the leases of owners are pledged to ensure their payments. If they fail to pay, the corporation can depose them, sell their shares, and re-lease their apartments to others in order to cover the delinquency.

In most circumstances, the cooperative corporation has no income tax liability, and in addition owners are able to claim on their own income tax returns their share of those expenses which are normal deductions from income, just as if they had paid them directly on their own individually owned homes. Thus they will benefit from the income tax deductions allowed for property taxes and interest payments.

The bylaws of the corporation, as well as the shares and leases, may limit the owner's use and disposal of a unit. They may forbid signs, occupancy by more than a limited number, excess noise, and similar nuisances. Furthermore, they may limit the owner's right of subletting and of sale or disposal. Frequently, the board of directors must approve a new proposed buyer or tenant before the sale of stock or issuance of a new proprietary lease is authorized. The point of such limitation is to maintain a group of owners who are financially sound and congenial and who take an interest in the cooperative corporation. The extent to which cooperatives can be arbitrary and opinions as to what constitutes a valid reason for granting or failing to grant such approvals have been subject to considerable change as both laws and their interpretation have altered.

Financing Difficulties   Two major disadvantages of cooperative corporations should be stressed. Operating costs and mortgage payments are shared mutually. If some owners cannot meet their payments and so default on their shares, the burden carried by the remaining owners will go up. They may attempt to lease the units on which defaults have occurred as ordinary rental units, but the rent received may be too small to cover all costs. In such a case, the remaining owners' costs rise. The higher each remaining owner's share becomes because of others' defaults, the more probable are additional defaults. The point may be reached where all the remaining owners will be forced to default on the mortgage. That was the typical experience of the 1930s.

Perhaps more important is the difficulty of financing resales in such a cooperative. The existing mortgage covers the entire property. If a mortgage has been in existence for some time, it is likely to have been paid down through amortization. It is hoped that, through appreciation, the value of the shareholders' property rights will have increased as well. This leaves a large potential gap between the value and selling price of the unit and its share of the existing mortgage. The new owner must be able to arrange a loan or have the necessary capital to cover this gap. Many new owners have trouble doing so. They cannot pledge the building as security; they can pledge only their stock and their proprietary lease. A lender's rights will be subordinate to the corporation's claims for funds due for taxes, maintenance, and operating expenses and to the holder of the mortgage granted by the corporation on the entire building. As a result, the markets for these special loans are not as highly organized as those for standard mortgages. A purchaser on a resale in a cooperative is likely to need a larger downpayment and will pay higher interest rates. This limits the resale market. To sell at the full value of their property, owners may have to finance a major share of the total selling price themselves.

Condominiums

Primarily because of the financing problems of cooperative corporations, condominiums have increased in popularity as a means of cooperative ownership. In a condominium, one owns an undivided interest in common property such as land, elevators, halls, swimming pools, and furnaces, while at the same time holding a separate interest in a particular space such as an apartment, office, or store. In a condominium, the specific units which individuals own are taxed separately, and they can be financed with normal mortgages. Lenders' problems are only slightly complicated by the fact that their rights are subordinate to assessments to pay common expenses and by the right of the condominium association to have some say on new tenants or owners. As a result, mortgages on resales tend to be nearly as good as those on sales of existing single-family homes.

The condominium is established by a declaration or master deed which must be filed with the county recorder. This document describes the total property, the common property, and each separately owned unit. It establishes the owners' association and allocates votes within it, as well as determining how the common expenses shall be shared. A unit owner's pro rata share of the common expenses depends upon location, initial price, etc., as in the cooperative corporation. The master deed will also provide for bylaws and methods of amending them. The declaration and bylaws protect the common property and ensure that the funds required for its operation and maintenance become a lien against an individual unit if a member fails to pay his or her share of the common costs.

In actual operation, there seems to be very little difference between condominiums and cooperative corporations. The description of how the cooperative corporation operates will fit a condominium association quite well. Rights and restrictions for property use seem similar. However, some people feel that there are fewer restrictions on individual rights for use and resale in the condominium. Some see this possible difference as an advantage, while others, stressing the closeness of apartment life, view it as a drawback since they feel restrictions are necessary.

The main differences between the two become evident at the time of resale and in the financial arrangements already emphasized. It should be noted that in both cases where new associations are being formed and sold, security laws and regulations may apply. Shares in cooperative corporations sell in the same way as other stock shares. This means that compared with the typical costs of a regular real estate transaction which must be undertaken when a unit in a condominium is sold, transfer costs for the unit in the cooperative corporation are minimal. The records and expenses of the corporation must be examined, but that is simpler than obtaining a clear title for a separately owned unit.

On the other hand, the condominium has the obvious advantage of being taxed and financed as a separate unit. Individual mortgages may be obtained from any type of lender. Their amount will vary with the value of the unit at the time a loan is made. Refinancing is simpler and cheaper. Owners are liable primarily for their own mortgages and taxes. The chances are far less that an owner will have to pay much higher expenses because of the failure of others to pay their share.

THE PROS AND CONS OF REITs

The appeal of REITs lies in the claim that they can make available to small investors the advantages of real estate investment (otherwise difficult for a person with limited capital to obtain), together with expert management. Moreover, in particular cases the speculative appeal of REIT shares has been enhanced by leveraging and by compounding the high risks of real estate and mortgage investment. Thus those interested in "taking a flyer" in hopes of high returns could find a vehicle with extremely high risks tailored to their own speculative instincts. As with mutual funds, a system was established that has made it worthwhile for advisers, underwriters, and security salesmen actively to promote sales of shares to investors.

As we note throughout this book, while investment in real estate can be extremely profitable, there are great problems inherent in the analysis of individual properties, and the risks of error are large. Clearly, small investors in real estate can benefit if they can hire expert management through a REIT to meet some of these dangers. This is particularly true since diversification among numerous properties tends to reduce certain of the risks which accompany single investments. The problem investors face is how to make sure they are not paying more for these services than the services are worth. They also need to evaluate how much of any current return through a REIT is merely payment for the extra risks assumed. In 1974 and 1975 a sizable number of bankruptcies, many failures to pay any dividends, and a tremendous fall in stock prices reflected the large and unsuccessful risks which many REITs took. The result was a severe black eye for the industry, affecting even those trusts which had tried to maintain conservative portfolios.

Mortgage Investment Trusts

Those REITs which have concentrated their emphasis on the ownership position are called *equity trusts*. Other REITs, concerned principally with mortgage investments, are often labeled *mortgage investment trusts* (MITs). Some MITs are primarily investors in permanent mortgages, while others emphasize construction or development loans or the providing of secondary financing. They start from the fact that mortgages usually yield more than other debt instruments. Furthermore, in periods of tight money or by assuming greater risks, the trust lenders may obtain a contingent return ("kicker") or share of the potential increased revenues or capital gains from the property on which a loan is made. Thus they can promise some hope of enhanced returns in the future and some inflationary hedge.

Yields on short-term construction and development loans have been even higher than those on long-term mortgages. This area has lacked available institutional funds. Risks are high. Required management skills are great. MITs sought to fill this void. Again, some hoped to exceed even the normally high yields earned by this type of lending through kickers.

They turned to two other well-known investment techniques to increase both their risks and their potential yields. Many utilized leverage to a high degree. Some attempted to play the term structure (see pages 325 to 326) by borrowing short and lending long. For example, a not untypical REIT balance sheet included—in addition to the beneficiaries' shares—stock warrants, convertible debentures, subordinated debentures, mortgages, bank and Eurodollar floating rate loans, and commercial paper. This type of REIT pays a different rate of interest on each of these kinds of borrowings, related primarily to the differing risks. The shareholder of the trust owns the equity and bears all the residual risks. To the degree that the loans made by the trust to others paid it a higher yield than the trust paid on its own debt and no losses occurred, its return for the shareholders was enhanced. Both the use of leverage and successful gambles on the yield curve can raise profits. However, when rates on borrowings shifted adversely, when builders experienced cost overruns and failed to complete projects, payments were halted on a large number of projects and foreclosures became common. Many REITs could not meet their commitments to their banks. They had to negotiate new agreements which, in many cases, made the banks the senior partners with prior rights to future earnings.

The problem for investors in REITs is to make certain that they purchase shares which meet their own particular needs. Some trusts are as conservatively managed as the proverbial trust for widows and orphans. Others are at the opposite extreme. Investors are always urged to investigate before investing. Because the differences between REITs are so vast, this advice is especially pertinent for investors in all kinds of REITs, whether of the equity, MIT, or mixed type, Information on the trusts, their philosophies, their balance sheets, and their records to date can be found in business libraries and brokerage houses. There are also special books, compendiums, and services specializing in information on REITs. A problem in analysis does arise, of course, because of the relatively short record for many of the trusts.

SUMMARY

Ways of purchasing real estate have been changing. Individual ownership of a single building has become less common. The tax laws, financing needs, and convenience have led to more complex real estate entities.

The traditional forms of ownership—individual, joint tenancy, and tenancy in common—limit the type and size of investment open to the average person. Cooperatives and condominiums make possible ownership of portions of larger projects. At the same time they increase the factors that must be considered in a purchase. The initial promotion agreements as well as the soundness of the overall project may exert an overriding effect on the value of the individual's own unit.

Recently, one of the more popular ownership forms has been the limited partnership. It allows tax flow-throughs while also centralizing management and limiting liability. Real estate investment funds have also achieved a rapid acceptance. They do not allow flow-through of tax losses, but income passed through is taxed only once. REITs have often gained fame and notoriety—as well as poor records—when they have used financial manipulations rather than depending on their underlying advantages as a useful method of investing in real estate.

QUESTIONS AND PROBLEMS

1 What factors should influence the decision as to the legal form in which to hold property?
2 Describe individual ownership—the most common form—with respect to its main features.
3 What is the difference between a general and a limited partnership? What are the main features that have made limited partnerships so popular? When would a limited partnership be elected over a general partnership?
4 What characteristics distinguish the corporate form from the partnership form?
5 Describe the problems of making certain that a limited partnership avoids a "preponderance of corporate characteristics" and thus is not taxed as an association.
6 What are the essential documents to examine in purchasing a cooperative or a condominium?
7 Discuss the key differences between a cooperative and a condominium. As a lender, would you prefer to lend on the purchase of an apartment in a cooperative or a condominium? Why?
8 What caused the greatly increased interest in condominiums and cooperatives?
9 Describe the differences in the three types of REITs.
10 What are the advantages and disadvantages of purchasing shares in a REIT?

Chapter 8

Broadening the Scope
of Ownership

Traditionally owners have purchased property for their own investment or use. To accomplish the purchase, they might borrow money from a lender. An agreement as to amortization and interest on the loan balanced their needs. If unexpected events caused payments to be delayed, the property served as security to pay off the loan.

In recent years, both owning and financing have become far more complex. The growth in size of individual ventures has led to a need for money from more investors. More people have become interested in real estate for a variety of reasons: because they could afford to speculate, for tax benefits, or as a hoped-for hedge against inflation. Creative developers found that by slicing the rights to property into different and at times complex shapes and forms, they could raise the total value of the property. They have been able to give each potential owner a unique set of property rights covering differing degrees of risk, tax benefits, and profit potential. Developers and promoters attract investments from thousands of individuals, most of whom never see the property or properties in which they are investing. Frequently the investment is in securities based on property rather than in real property itself, with the result that investors may be unclear as to exactly what they own. In fact, it may be hard to say in certain situations whether the investment is primarily a method of financing or of ownership.

The complex splitting of property rights and ownership also raises problems for lenders. Whereas the owner as well as the property used to stand behind the debt, lenders now must depend on the property alone. They are further concerned because existing values of mortgages have changed drastically as interest rates have jumped and as the value of the dollar has fallen. Lenders try to protect themselves against these added risks by developing new types of loans, by participations, by variable payments, and by actual ownership of some parts of the property.

As more parties have become involved in a mixed relationship of owning and lending, new and specialized financing arrangements have developed to serve the particular needs of each of the various parties to a deal. These techniques reflect different characteristics in terms of:

1   The form of the return
2   The timing of the return
3   The risk, as to both current income and future value
4   The priority of claim on income
5   The obligations to perform on guarantees

When properly used, these specialized mixed buying and financing techniques create real value by achieving a better allocation of the various benefits and characteristics of the investment among the interested parties. At the same time, they greatly complicate analysis. The process of splitting rights has made some risks far greater than was formerly true in real estate investment and finance. To assure their returns, more investors are dependent on the skill of developers and managers who are not personally known to them. The property no longer bulks as the primary factor giving them security.

Too little emphasized in most offers to sell or borrow is the fact that every venture must possess a basic economic integrity if it is to succeed. ''Creative financing'' does not make a bad deal good, although many plans imply that it can. The ultimate values depend on the sound underlying economics of a venture, its skillful development, and a proper relationship between the amount a party invests in the venture and the bundle of claims and rights he or she receives. Real estate analysis now must look beyond a concern with the basic legal rights of owners and borrowers to a consideration of the fairness and effects of the new relationships. In a well-planned package all may gain, but in too many deals some get the cream, while others end up with the dregs.

Using two well-known case examples, this chapter illustrates some of the reasons behind the complex methods of modern financing.

ZECKENDORF'S HAWAIIAN TECHNIQUE

It is a truism that the money market consists of many different markets. Sellers of money in each market are looking for somewhat different characteristics and priorities. Therefore, money furnished for different types of security demands different interest rates. Each type will be eligible for varying amounts of lending. Splintering a single business into components and selling each one separately results in a higher total market value than the entire business is worth as an entity. Packagers are, in effect, being rewarded by the market for their packaging efforts, even though the inherent economic value of the enterprise is unchanged.

The concept of issuing a variety of equity and debt instruments—such as common stock, preferred stock, bonds, and convertible bonds—when applied to real estate can offer spectacular returns.

The types of factors leading to new relationships between promoters, investors, and lenders are well demonstrated by an early and highly publicized case. The concept of complex subdividing of rights was made famous by William Zeckendorf, one of the more flamboyant real estate speculators, whose rise to a multimillionaire and subsequent fall as his firm went through bankruptcy were widely followed as a result of a barrage of publicity. Zeckendorf called the process of splitting rights his "Hawaiian technique" because the idea came to him suddenly while he was surf-fishing in Hawaii. To illustrate how to use the Hawaiian technique, Zeckendorf described in his autobiography the dramatic increase in returns due to his creative packaging of a building at One Park Avenue in New York. In the early 1950s, the property at One Park Avenue had a $1-million cash flow. Capitalizing this income at 10 percent, the price would have been $10 million. Zeckendorf was able to increase its value to over $15 million in the following manner:

1 The building with its $1 million in income was leased for $750,000 on an outer or operating lease to a tenant who would manage the building, solicit tenants, and collect rents. This tenant had the most risky investment, since the $250,000 spread between the building's current cash flow and the $750,000 rent he had to pay on his lease would vary with the actual revenues and expenses. Still, at that time such returns were valued at 7 percent, to give this lease a value of roughly $3,600,000.

2 The building was sold to a purchaser who received an inner, or "sandwich," claim. He would be paid the $750,000 by the tenant or operator of the building and would pay $250,000 in ground rent. The building owner, in turn, used $350,000 of his $500,000 spread between his ground rent and rent receipts to make mortgage payments. For this $350,000 payment, he was able to borrow $4 million by agreeing to make constant payments of 8.5 percent a year on the first mortgage, of which 6.5 percent was interest. He was willing to pay $2,500,000 for the $150,000 annual income he had left from his $750,000 income after making his mortgage and ground rent payments.

3 At the opposite extreme from the outer lease, the ground was sold. The owner of the ground was promised $250,000 a year in rent from the owner of the building. Since the ground rent must be paid before any other expenses, it is the safest income of the property and at that time could be sold for $5 million at an average capitalization rate of 5 percent. The land purchaser had to put up $2 million in cash, for which he received $130,000 annually, or a 6.5 percent return. He borrowed the remaining $3 million on a land mortgage paying $120,000 a year, or 4 percent. This low cost was due to the fact that this income was protected by being the highest claim against the entire land and building.

Reviewing the results of the Hawaiian technique, the original $10 million property and $1 million in income had been splintered into the parts listed in Table 8-1. Thus, although the underlying operating economic value of the building was unchanged, imaginative packaging had increased the market value of the property by 50 percent. Zeckendorf noted that the owner of the inner lease was like a preferred stockholder,

Table 8-1   Value of Property Components

	Value	Receipts
Mortgage on land	$3,000,000	$120,000
Sale of land	2,000,000	130,000
Mortgage on inner lease	4,000,000	350,000
Sale of inner lease	2,500,000	150,000
Sale of operating lease	3,600,000	250,000
Total	$15,100,000	$1,000,000

since he had a relatively secure return and enjoyed depreciation benefits as well. The holder of the operating lease was in a position not unlike that of a common stockholder, since he was exposed to risk and could benefit from upgrading the income. An increase of 10 percent in the rentals would improve his income by 40 percent, from $250,000 to $350,000.

STRUCTURING THE RENTS AND RETURNS

The above is actually a simplified version of what can be done with the principles embodied in the Hawaiian technique. This creative approach takes advantage of the fact that various suppliers of money have different objectives, needs, risk preferences, and tax positions. An approach that structures an investment to the particular needs of investors generates greater values than one that lumps all investors into one group. Many additional possibilities for such structuring exist beyond those outlined in con-nection with the One Park Avenue building. Among them are:

1   A second mortgage on the land and/or the inner lease.
2   A lease on the land.
3   Sale of the depreciation now taken by the owner of the inner lease.
4   A sublease of the inner lease.
5   A sublease of the operating lease.
6   A dormant second mortgage on the land and/or the inner lease in which there would be no payment until the first mortgage was paid off. This would appeal to someone who wanted a secure income to start at some future time.
7   Sale of the rights to the maintenance contract or parking concession.
8   Arranging for the broker to defer his commission.
9   In the case of a new building in process of being completed, having the contractor and subcontractor defer their fees in the form of a third mortgage.
10   Sale of the right to name the building. Some public relations experts have assigned a several-million-dollar advertising value to having a company's name on a prominent building.
11   Sale of the lease on a specific space for a long term, payable at present time.
12   A variety of subleases and subsubleases, hedged against various possibilities.

As techniques like these have spread, so has the need for greater understanding of what is involved in current real estate transactions.

REAL ESTATE SYNDICATES

The growth of a broader interest in real estate, the development of limited partnerships, the possibility of high gains through leverage, and the sales of tax benefits have all led to rapid expansion in the field of real estate syndication. The field has undergone, and probably will continue to undergo, major ups and downs because the values offered have often depended too heavily on everything's going exactly right for the project. When the economy has weakened or ventures have drifted too far from economic reality, many syndicates have experienced plummeting values.

A syndicate is usually a group of investors gathered together to invest in one or more properties. They may own through a partnership, corporation, or trust. Frequently, joint ventures have been set up in which a promoter contributes entrepreneurial activities and management expertise, while passive investors put up the money. In many cases, the joint venture has one or a few general partners and many limited ones. Real estate ownership, through this normally burdensome form, is possible on the assumption that management problems are small, income distribution simple, and liability coverable by insurance.

Many people think of real estate syndication as analogous to fractionalizing the ownership of real estate into individual shares, just as common stock represents a fractionalized ownership of the company. The investors contribute money without management responsibilities and with limited liability, while the sponsor or promoter assumes the responsibilities of management.

The major problem in real estate development has been finding equity capital. A logical solution was to interest several people—friends, clients, or acquaintances—in the joint purchase of a property. The investment economics could be explained to a few key people, who often would then bring in additional money from friends and relatives. This type of partnership has existed throughout the real estate industry. It is only in the past 20 years, however, that the concept has gone far beyond this simple relationship.

The Empire State Building

A good example of the development of modern syndication, and one that will give some understanding of how this technique works, is the case of the Empire State Building, which has become a real estate financing landmark as well as a physical one. The building was completed in 1931 with a $25-million equity investment plus a $27-million first mortgage to cover its $52-million cost. Occupying the 91,000-square-foot Fifth Avenue blockfront from 33rd to 34th Streets in midtown New York City, it rises 102 stories above the street, has two stories below grade, and at 1,250 feet in height was for many years the tallest building in the world. There is a 22-story television tower on top of the building. The total net rentable area is approximately 1,753,000 square feet.

In 1951 a syndicate purchased the property for $50 million plus $1.5 million for legal and related expenses. Harry Crown, a prominent Chicago business executive who initially owned 24 percent of this syndicate, acquired full ownership by 1954.

A new syndicate was set up in 1961 by Lawrence A. Wien and Harry B. Helmsley, two extremely successful real estate practitioners. They formed the Empire State Building Associates and, through an offering registered with the Securities and Exchange

Commission, raised $26 million through the sale of 2,600 units priced at $10,000 each. In a complex arrangement, various rights were split among several parties.

The Empire State Building Associates venture is significant for several reasons. First, the Empire State Building was the world's tallest and best-known building. Second, the dollar volume of participations offered was substantial. Third, the syndication is in the form of a general partnership, whereas the majority of syndications are organized as limited partnerships. Fourth, the syndication utilizes a combination of a master lease and a sublease. Investors in the syndicate receive a relatively low-risk preferential return but have the opportunity for additional cash distributions. The agreement provides an opportunity for attractive additional profits to the promoters, providing that at the same time they increase the return to the investors.

The Arrangements among the Promoters, Investors, and Lenders The Empire State Building Associates, the syndicate, was formed to purchase the master lease of both the Empire State Building and the land thereunder. With renewal privileges, the lease runs for approximately 114 years, to January 5, 2076. In addition to the syndicate, there were at least five other major parties to the agreement: (1) Lawrence A. Wien, Henry W. Klein, and Peter L. Malkin, of the law firm of Wien, Lane & Klein, who served in various capacities as promoters, syndicators, general partners, lawyers, and partners in a sublease; (2) Harry B. Helmsley, of the real estate firm of Helmsley-Spear, Inc., who acted as promoter, syndicator, real estate broker, building manager, rental agent, and partner in the sublease; (3) Prudential Insurance Company, which owned the building and the land separately; (4) the mortgage lender on the master lease; and (5) the sublessee, or actual operator of the building, which was the Empire State Building Company, a joint venture composed of Lawrence Wien (25 percent interest), Harry B. Helmsley (25 percent interest), Martin Weiner Realty Corporation (12.5 percent interest), and Cargo Dispatch, Inc. (37.5 percent interest), a wholly owned subsidiary of D. K. Ludwig's American-Hawaiian Steamship Company.

The Syndicate The Empire State Building Associates was formed as a general partnership consisting of Wien, Klein, and Malkin, as individual general partners. These three entered into a participation agreement with the other investors, each of whom contributed a minimum of $10,000. Under these agreements, each of the three partners acted as an ''agent'' for the participants in his one-third partnership. Each participant shared proportionately in all profits, losses, or liabilities to persons outside the venture.

The Master Lease This was a net lease to the Empire State Building Associates (the syndicate). This master lease was purchased on December 27, 1961, for a contract price of $65 million plus $3 million for various fees and expenses. The money was raised as follows: $26 million from the sale of participations in the Associates, sale of the building for $29 million to Prudential Insurance Company (which had acquired the land for $17 million in 1951), and a mortgage of $13 million.

The Associates agreed to pay Prudential under the master lease an annual rent of $3,220,000 for an initial term of 30 years and 9 days. There were four renewal options of 21 years each, with a rent of $1,840,000 a year for the first renewal and $1,610,000 for each subsequent term. Prudential, the master lessor, agreed to look solely to the partnership property for collection of any judgment which it might recover against the Associates. This agreement, in effect, eliminated any personal liability of the participants for lease obligations. Prudential also agreed to advance certain additional funds for modernization for a promise of increased rents.

The Associates, as the lessee, was obligated to pay real estate taxes and all other operating and maintenance expenses, to make all necessary repairs, to maintain insurance coverage, and to rebuild or replace the building in the event of fire or other casualty. However, these conditions were all effectively assumed by the sublessee.

The Sublease The sublease from the Empire State Building Associates to the Empire State Building Company was for the same period as the master lease, less 1 day. The Building Company assumed all the tax, operating, insurance, and other obligations of the Associates under the master lease and leasehold mortgage.

The basic annual rent under the sublease was set so as to make possible an annual payment of $900 per $10,000 participation, plus the amounts required to enable the Associates to meet all mortgage requirements, to pay the rent under the master lease, and to defray all administrative costs. The initial minimum payment from the sublessee to the Associates was $6,765,000. Furthermore, one-half of any funds made available upon renewal from reductions in the lease payments to Prudential was to go to the Associates.

Under the sublease, the Empire State Building Company retained the first $1 million of net operating profit. Any net profits in excess of $1 million were to be split evenly with the Associates. Of the Associates' share, 94 percent went to the participants, and 6 percent to the law firm of Wien, Lane & Klein. In effect, the participants were to be paid $900 per share and then to split 47 percent of all net operating profits above the first million.

Promoters' Arrangements The Empire State Building Associates, when formed, paid out $3,000,000 in initial expenses. This covered $1,100,000 to Wien, Lane & Klein, as promoters, for legal expenses and promotional activity; a $500,000 real estate brokerage commission to Helmsley-Spear, Inc.; $100,000 in estimated expenses of the offering; and the balance for all the many costs related to the real estate transfer and closing.

The agreement specified that, in addition, the law firm of Wien, Lane & Klein was to receive $100,000 a year for supervising the Associates' partnership agreement, making distributions to the participants, preparing and filing tax returns and other reports, and acting as general counsel. They were to receive $90,000 a year from the sublessee for similar services, plus 3 percent of all net operating profits over a million dollars.

Helmsley-Spear, Inc., after its initial brokerage fee, received $90,000 a year from the sublessee for building management services plus leasing commissions based on the recommended rates of the Real Estate Board of New York, Inc.

Participants' Income The estimated income and expenses for the first year of ownership, based on a leasehold investment of $39 million, with participations of $26 million and mortgage of $13 million, are shown in Table 8-2. The total cash available for distribution is $2,340,000.

Table 8-2   Estimated First-Year Income Statement

Rent income		$6,765,000
Expenses:		
Master lease	$3,220,000	
Interest on mortgage	837,113	
Supervisory fees	100,000	
Total expenses		4,157,113
Net income before writeoff of leasehold		$2,607,887
Leasehold, writeoff over 30 years, 3⅓% of $39,000,000		1,300,000
Net income		$1,307,887
Estimated cash available for distribution:		
Net income before leasehold writeoff		$2,607,887
Less annual amortization of mortgage		267,887
Cash available for distribution		$2,340,000

This is $900 per $10,000 participation. During 1962, the first calendar year of ownership, $397 of this would represent a return of invested capital and would not be subject to tax as ordinary income. An investor in the 50 percent tax bracket would report $503 as taxable income and would be able to retain $649 after taxes, or approximately 6.5 percent on the $10,000 investment. In the second through the fifth years, the amount of the distribution constituting reportable income would range from $510 to $534, and by 1991 the full amount of all distributions would be reportable as income.

In addition to the initial agreed-upon payment of $900, in 1965 the participants began to receive overage payments as their share in the net operating profits. These payments have increased steadily, as shown in Table 8-3.

Compensation   This deal was structured in an attempt to give congruency to the goals of the promoters and investors in order to avoid some of the problems of conflicts of interest and compensation that plague many syndicates. The promoters were given a substantial incentive to perform. Specifically, they were awarded $280,000 a year for services, plus the first $1 million in operating profits, plus 53 percent of all additional profits. Although high, these are not extraordinary payments by current standards. The indicated total cost of $3 million for the offering is a front load of 11.5 percent of the $26 million raised. This, too, is far lower than many recent offerings, although it should be noted that the size of the venture permitted economies of scale and consequently a reduced front-end load.

Further History

The Empire State Building was part of a burst of syndication activity which occurred in the mid-1950s and early 1960s. Problems developed, however, because properties were sold whose underlying economic value was inadequate to support the prices asked. As a result, the business of syndication went into a decline. In 1968 the Housing and Urban Development Act provided a new impetus. It authorized the formation of the National Housing Corporation, which in turn sponsored the National Housing Partnership. This $50-million syndication limited investors to prominent organizations such as business corporations, labor unions, and financial institutions. The National Housing Partnership

Table 8-3 Payments to Participants in Associates

Year	Overage payment	Total distribution	Payment as percent of $10,000 investment
1962	$ —	$ 900	9.0
1963	—	900	9.0
1964	—	900	9.0
1965	49	949	9.5
1966	166	1,066	10.7
1967	212	1,112	11.1
1968	255	1,155	11.6
1969	305	1,205	12.1
1970	419	1,319	13.2
1971	538	1,438	14.4
1972	490	1,390	13.9
1973	532	1,432	14.3
1974	532	1,432	14.3

attracted a great deal of attention and provided a stimulus to others to organize smaller housing syndicates, which also invested in FHA housing programs.

Additionally, the Tax Reform Act of 1969 restricted certain available tax advantages in so-called tax-shelter investments, but left real estate investment relatively better off than other business sectors. This tax change focused a great deal of investor interest on real estate investments. Inflation and the continuing economic expansion of the country placed substantially more individuals at income levels where taxes were a major concern. These forces fueled the investor demand for real estate securities. More and more, higher-income individuals became concerned with sheltering their incomes from tax liability.

Another major factor behind expansion of real estate syndication was the emergence of publicly held development companies which furnished the supply of properties necessary for syndication to occur. Traditionally, real estate developers have been relatively small, family-held organizations concerned primarily with building for their own account. They held properties for an extended period of time, with the result that the number of properties available for ownership by wider groups was limited. The new publicly held developers, however, had a very different orientation. Because of their obligation to report financial results on a regular basis, they needed to be able to show sales and profits. But this is possible only if a property has been sold in a real transaction. Consequently, whereas most developments had hitherto not been available for sale, now the opposite was the case. Developers needed buyers for their new properties. Syndication provided a natural sales outlet for them.

Volume of Syndication

Indicative of the expansion of real estate offerings are the data in Table 8-4, representing filings with the National Association of Securities Dealers.

After the dramatic jump in volume from 1970 to 1972, the decline in 1973 was

Table 8-4   Volume of Offerings of Syndicates and REITs

Year	Real estate syndication	REIT
1970	$ 256,000,000	Not available
1971	524,000,000	$2,540,000,000
1972	1,911,000,000	1,417,000,000
1973	849,000,000	1,320,000,000
1974	521,458,000	123,000,000

attributable to adverse publicity surrounding real estate syndication offerings. Some of the publicity resulted from the slowdown in sales and profits due to a temporary excess of supply of space relative to demand. The bad publicity discouraged investors and created difficulties for a number of recent syndications. Of even more concern, however, was an aggressive attack by the IRS, which sought to restrict severely many of the basic tax-saving characteristics of syndication that had made the business so attractive in the first place. Poor operating results in 1974 and 1975 led to a still more drastic curtailment in syndicate offerings and an almost total collapse of the market for REITs.

The table shows only public offerings registered with a securities regulatory agency, as opposed to private offerings, whose sponsors claim they are exempt from registration. Some commentators maintain that the volume of private offerings exceeds that of the public ones shown in the table by a ratio of 10 to 1.

The Mechanics of Syndication

The Empire State Building Associates provides a good example of the mechanics of syndication. Typically, the idea of the syndicate originates with a promoter who has an idea for a new development or sees an existing property which he feels is a good buy. He puts together a proposal which requires more capital than he has available. He must then decide what his relationship should be to the ultimate syndicate. In many cases promoters have thought of the syndicate primarily as a way of selling property. For a new development, the syndicate makes construction possible and ensures the promoters a profit.

Chapter 26 discusses in depth the problems of syndicates and how they should be analyzed before a security is purchased. As explained there, syndicates have many advantages. They are usually single-tax entities, they offer the unsophisticated investor expertise and independent judgment, there are significant economies of scale, and they lower risks through diversification.

The key factors in analyzing a syndicate are to determine what type of joint venture is involved; what actual values are contained in the price, income, tax shelter, and financing; the record of the sponsor; and the specific legal terms of the partnership agreement.

The Syndicates and Wall Street   In the last few years, Wall Street's stockbrokerage firms have become increasingly important in marketing real estate securities. Some Wall Street firms assumed the sponsor role, promoting and organizing their own deals.

The majority, however, chose to limit their involvement to marketing real estate syndicates organized by others. For such efforts, the firms have been paid underwriting commissions ranging from 7 to 10 percent of the investor's initial contribution. This level of compensation corresponds roughly to that received by selling load mutual fund shares.

In the past, some of the brokerage firms have been relatively nondiscriminating as to which real estate syndicate interest they offered. However, there has been a greater emphasis on "investment consumerism" recently, as well as an insistence by securities regulators that the financial community assume greater responsibility for the products it offers. The concept of "due diligence," which means essentially that an underwriter is obligated to do what a "prudent person" would do in managing his or her own money, suggests that the brokers may have to become more careful in selecting the real estate syndicate offerings with which they associate. Such a development would make it more difficult for marginal operators. It would allow the investor to commit funds to real estate syndicates with greater confidence.

Although faced with a number of problems, real estate syndicates have expanded in response to basic, fundamental economic forces. The sponsor of the syndicate makes available to average investors a package of skills and expertise that they could not acquire on their own. Substantial economies and more efficient purchases can be realized by aggregating the funds of many small individuals.

However, too many sponsors have failed to meet the fiduciary responsibility they have had as managers of real estate securities programs. In such cases disputes have often led to litigation. A problem for legitimate firms in the real estate securities industry is to differentiate themselves from certain unethical marginal operators, who, unfortunately, have been highly visible and in some cases highly successful in attracting investor funds. The new types of syndicates can prosper only if they provide a product that investors can participate in with confidence, recognizing that they are going to receive a fair return for their money in light of the risks they undertake. When these risks are large, investors should expect a large return. With minimum risks, they should expect returns similar to those from other types of investments.

SUMMARY

Syndicates have proliferated in response to developers' needs for more financing and investors' desires to invest in real estate. The mechanics by which shares in a single property or a group of properties can be sold to thousands of investors have been developed with a minimum of difficulty.

The problem of how an investor, at a distance or through written reports, can evaluate the true worth of a property has remained most troublesome. Some problems have arisen because profits have accrued to developers and promoters as a result of the investment—as opposed to the operation or management—process. Individuals and firms have been willing to take their profits and run. But other problems are more deep-rooted. Real estate investments are risky and hard to evaluate. Even major financial institutions have made damaging errors by failing to take into account some of the unique features of real property.

QUESTIONS AND PROBLEMS

1 How can merely structuring the ownership rights in a property and not altering its income or costs create real values for the owners?

2 It is possible to buy an inner, or sandwich, claim. What is meant by this term? What rights and duties does the holder of such a claim have?

3 In the One Park Avenue case, there are two mortgages; yet neither is a junior mortgage. Each is the first lien against a piece of property. What rights did each creditor lend against?

4 What is a syndicate?

5 In the Empire State Building case, what is the difference in terms of rights and duties between the Empire State Building Associates and the Empire State Building Company?

6 In the Empire State Building case, what is the basic source of the overage payments to the participants in the syndicate?

7 Suppose you were asked to lend money on a secured note to the Empire State Building Company. According to the text, what rights would be available to secure your loan?

8 What factors have made syndicates popular?

9 How are syndicates and REITs similar? Different?

10 Why has the Empire State Building Associates deal succeeded when others have failed?

11 Discuss an application of goal congruency in real estate investing.

Chapter 9

Other Investment Relationships

As types of real estate investment have proliferated, significant shifts have occurred in the relationships among promoters, investors, and lenders. In many cases, determining exactly what role an individual plays is difficult. Is he or she a promoter, a borrower, a lender, or a purchaser? Each new proposal and procedure must be analyzed individually to get a clear picture of how it works and to understand its promises and dangers.

In addition to making relationships less clear-cut, the growth in syndicates and similar offerings has also meant an increased involvement of real estate transactions with the sphere of securities and security law. Knowledgeable real estate professionals have to keep abreast of how developments in securities regulations influence real estate. Changes in the regulatory environment have brought about major alterations in the way investments are managed and sold. In this chapter, we shall first consider some of the questions which arise in the field of securities.

The second half of the chapter analyzes some of the newer developments in owning and financing which alter traditional relationships by allowing the contract payments to vary from those found in the usual mortgage loan. The four types considered are:

1 Contingent payments, in which the amount to be paid depends upon future events

2 One-hundred percent financing based upon sale-and-leasebacks

   3   Options and irregular mortgage payments aimed at giving greater flexibility and accounting advantages to the buyer

   4   Lender participations, also known as "equity kickers," in which the lender receives some of the revenue or profits from the operations of the income property.

REAL ESTATE AS A SECURITY

The development of new forms of investment and financing of real estate has moved many real estate transactions into the sphere of "securities" offerings. Traditionally, real estate was concerned with tangible, real property, while securities involved contract claims such as stocks, bonds, or stock equities. In recent years, this differentiation has been disappearing.

Definition of a Security

What constitutes a security depends upon the federal Securities Act of 1933 and similar state laws. A fundamental concept is that of an "investment contract." When an investment is sold on the basis of a continuing management involvement by either the sponsor or a third party and when investors purchase the property for a return rather than solely for their own personal use, the central attributes of an investment contract are present. The landmark legal case defining the parameters of an investment contract is *Securities and Exchange Commission v. W. J. Howey Company*, 328 U.S. 293 (1946), which considered the offering of a citrus-grove development, coupled with a contract for cultivating, marketing, and distributing the proceeds to the investor. Here, the court stated:

> The transactions in this case clearly involve investment contracts as so defined. The respondent companies are offering something more than fee simple interests in land, something different from a farm or orchard coupled with management services. They are offering an opportunity to contribute money and to share in the profits of a large citrus fruit enterprise managed and partly owned by respondents. They are offering this opportunity to persons who reside in distant localities and who lack the equipment and experience requisite to the cultivation, harvesting and marketing of the citrus products. Such persons have no desire to occupy the land or to develop it themselves; they are attracted solely by the prospects of a return on their investment. Indeed, individual development of the plots of land that are offered and sold would seldom be economically feasible due to their small size. Such tracts gain utility as citrus groves only when cultivated and developed as component parts of a larger area. A common enterprise managed by respondents or third parties with adequate personnel and equipment is therefore essential if the investors are to achieve their paramount aim of a return on their investments. Their respective shares in this enterprise are evidenced by land sales contracts and warranty deeds, which serve as a convenient method of determining the investors' allocated shares of the profits. The resulting transfer of rights in land is purely incidental.
>
>   Thus, all the elements of a profit-seeking business venture are present here. The investors provide the capital and share in the earnings and profits; the promoters manage, control and operate the enterprise. It follows that the arrangements whereby the investors' interests are made manifest involve investment contracts, regardless of the legal terminology in which such contracts are clothed.

To illustrate how widely this concept applies, the Securities and Exchange Commission (SEC) has held that resort condominiums are securities if owners buy them as second homes but the management agrees to rent the units out to others on a regular basis. While in most states a primary residence is not considered a security, in some it may be. Furthermore, the trend is in that direction. The federal Interstate Land Sales Full Disclosure Act of 1968 and similar state subdivision acts, for example, parallel the SEC act in requiring full disclosure of land sales, even for individual use.

Administration

Over 100 government agencies have jurisdiction over real estate securities offerings. At the federal level, they include the SEC, the Department of Housing and Urban Development (HUD), the Federal Reserve Board (over margin requirements), the IRS (with tax rulings), and the quasigovernmental, self-regulatory National Association of Security Dealers (NASD). In each state there is a securities commissioner and a real estate commissioner with some power.

At the federal level, the primary concern is with the full disclosure of material facts for publicly offered securities in order to prevent fraud, misrepresentation, and deceit. Issuers of securities must file registration statements and a prospectus containing significant financial information about the issuer and the offering. The SEC has no authority to control the nature or quality of an offering and does not pass upon its merits. Permitting a registration statement to become effective does not constitute approval or imply that the SEC believes it is a good deal.

While the enabling legislation limits the role of the SEC to that of requiring full disclosure, how it goes about this task can have a major impact on an offering. In practice the SEC often appears to go beyond merely requiring disclosure to requiring some degree of evaluation. This is even more true at the state levels. Many states, in addition to full disclosure, insist on a substantive evaluation as to whether the proposed securities are "fair, just, and equitable." Such requirements are spreading. While states may refuse registration for securities not meeting this standard, the fact that an issue is authorized obviously does not include judgment as to whether money will be lost or gained through the investment.

The overlapping and dual jurisdictions of the federal government and the states frequently lead to conflicts and expense on the part of those desiring to issue securities. The problem is compounded by a third form of regulation. In recent years, members of the NASD have sold the vast majority of real estate securities. The NASD requires that if any NASD members participate in selling a security, no nonmembers may. When an NASD member is to participate, the offering must be reviewed by the NASD, with a separate set of securities regulations in addition to those of the SEC and the various states. The NASD administers a "fair-practice" standard. Most simply, an NASD member violates the fair-practice rule by participating in an offering which, considering all relevant factors including compensation, is unfair and/or unreasonable.

Registration Responsibilities and Available Exemptions

Unless sponsors can qualify for one of the available exemptions, they have the responsibility for registering their offerings with the SEC. For offerings involving $500,000 or less of investor contributions, regulation A allows a "short form" or simplified registration with a regional office of the SEC. For other offerings, at least several months' time and legal fees approaching or exceeding $50,000 are inescapable for registration of a real estate securities program. If a full SEC registration is undertaken, the offering must also be registered in each state in which it will be sold. As a result, most sponsors will seek an exemption. While a variety of specialized exemptions are available, for real estate offerings the intrastate and the private placement exemptions are the most common.

The *intrastate exemption* applies where the sponsor, investors, all officers, and the business of the offering are all contained within the boundaries of a single state. To qualify, the offering must comply with the letter and not merely the spirit of this provision. The specific guidelines as to what is and what is not an intrastate offering are covered in Rule 147, a release by the SEC that interprets and clarifies the basic legislation.

The *private-placement exemption* applies when a transaction is not a "public offering." To qualify, an offering must meet various criteria, such as that there be no more than 35 investors (but some states specify as few as 10). Also significant are the relationships between those involved and their level of sophistication, the manner of the offering, and the size and nature of the investment.

Even if exempt, a private placement must provide an investor with the same information that would be provided in the case of a public offering. While some legal fees, costs, and delays may be avoided, the risks and disclosure standards may be higher. Furthermore, a single offering cannot be considered in isolation. The private-placement exemption may not apply if a pattern of offerings exists.

Disclosure Guidelines

The disclosure standards in real estate offerings have become stricter and more numerous. They are specified in Guide 60, prepared by the SEC staff. Various state commissioners have also developed guidelines for the regulation of real estate securities. The guidelines emphasize more detailed, more specific, and better-organized disclosure. The idea is that what is disclosed is to be "understandable" as well as "full." The new rules reflect a trend toward investor orientation rather than a mere satisfaction of legal requirements. Since exemption from registration does not relieve one of the responsibility to disclose all material facts, these same concepts apply to private placements. Indeed, the disclosure obligation in private-placement offerings is at least as great as, if not greater than, that for public registrations.

Some or all of the following ideas have been adopted as part of the disclosure requirements in various states; they attempt to ensure that the disclosure gives a picture of the underlying economic reality:

1 Information on earnings projections of the project
2 Past track record of the sponsor
3 The requirement that compensation and fees be shown in a comprehensive form and the possibility of limiting their total
4 A discussion of possible risks to the investment
5 Information and specifics on any partnership agreements

6 A detailed discussion of tax considerations

7 Information on the proposed investments, if specified, or on investment policy if the properties are yet to be acquired

The inclusion of detailed projections of probable performance has been controversial. Many have opposed this idea, but the trend is toward inclusion. Others have argued that the investor should have all available information and a standard against which the sponsor's performance can be measured. Information on the sponsor's past results may also be helpful in analysis.

Other requirements preclude the sponsor from self-dealing, from taking insurance commissions, and from providing services at above-competitive rates. In some cases, the qualifications of investors in terms of wealth and income as well as minimum size of investments may also be specified.

Enforcement and Investor Remedies

The fact that a number of real estate securities programs have not achieved performance equal to their expectations and have encountered difficulties has been of increasing concern. The following are among the reasons why real estate programs have had problems: payment of an exorbitant purchase price for a property, excessive and unfavorable leverage, gimmicked tax structuring that achieves no economic benefit, poor property management, poor property selection, changes in economic conditions, and excessive compensation to promoters and their affiliates. Generally, the problems are attributable either to faulty analysis or to a violation of the sponsor's fiduciary responsibility to serve his or her investors' interests.

On occasion the sponsor's misdeeds amount to a violation of the securities regulations. When this occurs, the securities regulators can implement an enforcement action. Among the misdeeds by sponsors that have triggered enforcement actions have been comingling of funds, converting moneys to personal use, failure to keep adequate records, issuance of misleading and erroneous reports, failure to pay debt service on the properties, arranging financing with hidden fees and compensation in favor of the promoter, taking undisclosed fees and markups, using misleading appraisals, preparing unrealistic and erroneous projections, misrepresenting the true conditions of the property, and various deceptive marketing practices including sponsors' representing themselves as "financial advisers" when, in fact, all their "clients" are investment packages they themselves have put together.

Noncompliance with regulatory requirements can result in severe criminal, civil, and administrative actions. In addition, if sponsors violate the securities laws by failing adequately to disclose material information or by acting in a manner that violates their obligation to serve as fiduciaries for their investors, the investors may demand rescission. If the courts find that a sponsor is obligated to make rescission to his or her investors, the investors will receive return of their initial investment plus an appropriate rate of interest. Recently several class-action suits have been filed by investors seeking to achieve rescission as well as damages if the court thinks appropriate. It is clear that there is an increasing trend toward litigation on the part of dissident investors in real estate programs where performance has not matched the promoter's promise.

Due Diligence

The concept of due diligence is receiving increasing attention from securities regulators and professionals in real estate securities matters. Most simply, due diligence refers to the obligation that the underwriter (the party selling the securities) has to make reasonable efforts to investigate the economic disclosure in the registration statement. Reasonableness is determined by the standard of what a "prudent man" would do in the management of his or her own property. Clearly, the due-diligence obligation imposes a very real responsibility on the underwriter, and it is likely that in the future, greater care will be exercised in determining what offerings should be sold to the public. To the extent that the industry responsibility embraces the due-diligence concept, many of the problems that have plagued it to date may be greatly minimized in the future.

CONTINGENT PAYMENTS

In addition to the complexities of securities, types of debts and sales are also becoming harder to analyze. In an increasing number of cases, the relationships between sellers, buyers, and lenders are complicated by agreements as to who will be responsible for future payments and under what conditions payments will have to be made.

For example, in some cases buyers make only nominal downpayments. The seller furnishes or arranges for the bulk of the money needed. If there is no future claim against the borrower, a question may be raised as to whether the transaction is really a sale or merely an option, with the buyer being able, at his discretion, to get out of any obligations. (How such agreements should be valued has caused problems for REITs, syndicates, and firms engaged in development and land sales.) At the opposite extreme, buyers (traditional lenders) may make 100 percent financing available, but only because they have agreements from a seller who retains responsibility to make specified payments if they become necessary. Among various significant contractual agreements we find:

1 Sellers or borrowers who agree to furnish funds from other sources to ensure that loan payments can be met if occupancy or rents fall below projected levels for periods up to 2 or 3 years

2 Sellers who agree that payment of the final portion of the total consideration will be delayed until a designated level of occupancy or receipts is reached

3 Sellers who sign leases which are sufficient to guarantee all debt payments

4 Lenders who agree to give up any claims to payments beyond those which can be raised by sale of the property securing the loan

5 Buyers and lenders who agree to split future profits with the sellers

In both the Zeckendorf and the Empire State Building cases, we noted examples of such agreements. As real estate investors and lenders have recognized the wide possibilities of these arrangements, their use has skyrocketed.

SALE-AND-LEASEBACKS

"Sale-and-leaseback" is a term used to refer to the purchase of a property and the simultaneous leasing of it back to the seller or another party at a previously agreed-upon rent. Many different arrangements exist. We discuss four: (1) The credit-sale-leaseback, where the security is really the signature of a major corporation on a lease. Interest rates and other considerations are close to those found in the market for corporate debt. (2) Leases on income properties, such as in the Empire State Building case. (3) Land purchase-leasebacks aimed primarily at questions of tax shelters and leverage. (4) Sale-condobacks, where the seller of land obtains ownership of a condominium in a larger development.

Credit-Sale-Leasebacks   The most common situation is one in which a large firm sells off store buildings, warehouses, or other property either when newly built or after a considerable period of occupancy. The firm simultaneously enters into net-net (the renter agrees to pay all expenses including property taxes) leases that run for long periods—20 to 30 years or more with a series of options to renew at lower rates. There may be any of a variety of advantages to the leasing firm in these situations:

1   The user of the property can get 100 percent financing. In contrast, if the firm owns a building, it usually can borrow only two-thirds of the value of a property and must furnish equity for the remainder.

2   By using a specific asset (real estate) that is a good security, the company can frequently improve its balance sheet and its accounting financial structure.

The balance sheet improves for two reasons. If the property has been heavily depreciated, its sale will yield a capital gain. The amount of gain less its tax becomes an addition to the firm's capital. Second, the lease appears only indirectly as a liability. It will normally be reported as a footnote to the balance sheet. In contrast, a mortgage is a normal debt. The mortgage's existence affects the firm's debt ratio and can cause restrictions in a firm's lending agreements to take effect.

Furthermore, if a new building is owned, deductions for interest and depreciation may exceed the lease payments. In such situations, the leaseback makes it possible to report higher accounting earnings.

3   The company gets out of the real estate business. Some firms consider this a big advantage; they assume that they can earn more profits in their own line of endeavor. Others take the opposite point of view. Real estate is profitable. They are users of real estate. They may set up a subsidiary to handle their own needs and also to rent or develop properties for others.

4   There may be major tax advantages. The tax benefits arise from the differential tax rates which apply to normal corporations, to high-bracket individual taxpayers, and to tax-exempt colleges or foundations and insurance companies. While the latter have varying rates of taxation, these are almost always well below the amounts paid by a typical successful corporation. Tax benefits depend on the amount of authorized depreciation. This will be low when the proportion of land to structure is high. Sale-leasebacks are more common on central-city properties where such land ratios apply. They are also used when the selling company has a low tax base because of rapid depreciation or a long history of ownership of the building.

Although original owners or sellers in such cases are able to take only a small depreciation deduction against taxes, they can deduct the whole rent payment on the lease for tax purposes. The new owners are not concerned with the depreciation rate because they typically pay little or no income taxes anyway. As noted above, this difference may boost net income after taxes to the original seller by a large amount. An added advantage is that any subsequent improvements may be depreciated over the life of the lease rather than over the improvements' normal life.

In other cases, what may be sold is primarily the right to depreciation when the original owner has already used all that he or she can. As in one of the original Empire State Building sales, the land may be sold to an owner who cannot use the tax benefits of depreciation. Then the building is sold to a high-bracket individual who wants the tax benefits. Depending on bargaining power, the tax benefits are split: part to the lender in higher interest, part to the corporation in lower occupancy costs, and part to the owner in a higher after-tax return.

Lenders also see advantages in the sale-leaseback market. Their return is usually somewhat higher than that on a regular mortgage, with about equivalent risks. Residual values may accrue to the lender after the lease is up. Because they discount at lower rates, the present value of such residuals tends to be higher for lenders than for borrowers. Many lenders who are not equipped to handle small mortgages welcome the large size and comparative investment ease of these sale-leaseback packages.

Terms for sale-leasebacks depend upon the type of properties and the seller's credit rating. Leases of major firms, such as Woolworth or Sears Roebuck, are judged on the company's credit standing. Charges are based upon the amount they would have to pay in the bond market plus a sum to amortize some or all of the loan plus a small premium. Typical payments run from 1 to 3 percent above the bond rate.

Income-Sale-Leasebacks   In contrast to situations where the credit of the renter is of primary interest and leases tend to cover the entire life of the building, some sale-leasebacks cover income properties where the risks to the lender are much higher. Leases may run for only 5 or 10 years. They may cover specialized property, such as a bowling alley or a motel rented by a firm with little or no capital, when the rate may be extremely high. The lender (owner and lessor) increases his or her risk because the percentage of value covered is higher. The lender must be compensated for this added danger.

Land Purchase-Leasebacks   While some land purchase-leasebacks have been used to give a lender greater security, more recently they have been used to add leverage. REITs, in particular, have bought land for or from real estate developers and leased it back to them on long-term leases. This enables developers to reduce their cash investment and removes a segment on which they derive no depreciation.

The leases are often subordinated to a first mortgage, enabling the developer to get maximum leverage. In return, the REITs have frequently obtained rights to participate in the development's rents or profits paid, in addition to an agreed-upon minimum rent to the trust for the lease of the land.

Sale-Condobacks   More unusual are sale-condobacks. Essentially, sale-condoback transactions evolve from agreements by owners to sell their property on the condition that part of the same property will be deeded back to them in condominium form. As the name suggests, these arrangements include transfer of two ownership rights, as opposed to one in the more traditional sale-leaseback.

The form is most common in business condominiums. As is true of residence condominiums, these have arisen to enable firms to enjoy the benefits and risks of ownership in cases where the total space is beyond their needs. Without a condominium form, businesses needing only part of a development either had to be tenants or had to go into the business of renting the extra space to others. As with other condominiums, a business which owns can get better space, can use it more flexibly, may obtain better financing than a developer, and may profit if the real estate appreciates.

These sale-condoback transactions often arise when a company occupies a parcel that is being assembled into a major development. By selling, the company allows the developer to proceed. Simultaneously, the developer deeds back a portion of the space in the to-be-developed project. The original owner may realize a substantial financial gain, while retaining the right to own at its original location.

VARYING AMORTIZATION PAYMENTS AND OPTIONS

Many developers face a constant cash-flow problem. They may be land-poor or have large equities in successful units, but lack the cash necessary to meet traditional mortgage terms. Their problems are particularly acute when interest rates are high. It takes time to "rent up" a new building. In some cases, the development may be somewhat ahead of the market. Its success will depend on future construction in its vicinity, or income may be projected on the basis of recent rates of inflation. In many cases, heavy initial start-up costs for promotion, advertising, and special tenant improvements must be paid from the reduced flows. In these and similar cases, the cash-flow problems may be handled by agreements which allow the payments in a period to vary from the basic or long-run requirements.

Varying Constants   Whereas conventional mortgage terms require constant payments to interest and principal which will pay off (amortize) the entire debt in a fixed period, in recent years many loans have had their payment schedules tailored to the developer's individual needs. Both the amortization schedule and the date of final payment have become more flexible.

In some cases, loans will require only interest payments in the early years and then move to a normal schedule of principal payments when a full cash flow is expected. In others, some of the interest due will be added to the principal for a few years. In still others, the required payments will vary with the actual cash flow. These flexible payments need not change the actual amounts due, although, as we shall note shortly, in some cases lenders will vary their charges in order to increase their participation in the earnings of the property.

Balloon Payments   Another variation involves a schedule of amortization payments extending beyond the term, or due date, of the mortgage. We noted that such payments are frequent in junior mortgages, but they also have become more common in loans on income properties. When the term of the mortgage is reached, the unpaid balance (balloon payment) is all due and payable. The borrower must anticipate covering the amount of the "balloon" from his or her own funds or from a new loan.

When amortization periods run 25 years and the due date is 20 years, such amounts need not be onerous. But recently a number of mortgages have been written with relatively early due dates, with the balloon payment due at the end of anywhere from 5 to 12 years. In such cases, at the time the note is due the amount of principal payments will have been relatively small. The sizable remaining debt can represent an almost impossible burden to the borrower.

Some lenders such as insurance companies or savings banks are not concerned that the balloon may not be paid off. They expect to renew the loan, but they want the early due date so that they can adjust the interest rate upward if rates have risen (a common form of variable rate mortgage) or so that they can insist on a new management or reforms if upon examination they are dissatisfied with the way the property has been managed in the initial period.

On the other hand, when REITs or developers who are not basic sources of funds have made the loans, they may have proceeded on the assumption that the borrower would actually be able to raise the money to meet the balloon payments. If they themselves are squeezed for cash, they may foreclose in the hope that upon resale, the new buyer can raise enough money to pay them off.

In many cases, when buyers obtain properties with very little cash and with minimum amortization payments and when they give no recourse to other assets, the debt-service payments can be considered a series of "optionlike" payments. If the property does not achieve a certain value by the time the balloon payment becomes due, the erstwhile buyer will merely walk away (make no effort to pay) from the deal. In many actions of this type, the seller and the buyer are more concerned with trying to take advantage of lapses in accounting regulations than with the reality of the situation. They enter into the arrangements in order to improve their current earnings statements or tax situations even at the expense of a high risk of future losses.

Options   In other cases, real options may be granted by the developer to the lender at a price that will guarantee the developer a considerable profit. Frequently as part of the option, the developer is given a long-term operating lease to come into effect when and if the option is used. As part of the package, the developer receives a sufficient sum through the loan to guarantee him a good initial profit—he has "cashed out" on the project.

What are the results of such an arrangement?

1   The developer has a guaranteed profit.

2   He operates the development as owner. (*a*) If he is successful, he keeps the current income above the expenses and debt payment. He eventually sells to the lender at the still greater profit provided by the option terms. He then still has an additional opportunity to profit through his operating lease. (*b*) If he is not successful, the lender can take over the property for the amount owed on the debt; however, the developer already has received an initial profit.

3   The lender also sees two possibilities: (*a*) He has made a loan with some, but not much, added risk. If the project does not work out, he will have to take it over in an attempt to hold down his loss. (*b*) If the project is a success, by making an additional payment he can purchase the equity. He gains some of the benefits which his loan has made possible.

LENDER PARTICIPATION

In the option example, the developer gave up part of his potential profits to the lender, but he did so in order to assure himself of the loan which would make the project possible. As real estate agreements have become more complex, tremendous profit opportunities have accrued to developers when all went well. This has been especially true since in many cases their leverage is enormous—in fact, often "infinite." Lenders on real estate, aware that they make these profits possible, began to be dissatisfied because they were not sharing in the gains even though they often bore much of the risk if a project failed. They have also worried increasingly about maintaining competitive yields with other types of financial institutions and about preserving the actual value or real purchasing power of the funds they advance.

Traditionally, developers pursued the entrepreneurial task of creating physical space, while the financial institutions supplied most of the needed funds at fixed interest rates considerably below the return of the total project. Frequently, the aggressive developer could "mortgage out," that is, borrow 100 percent of the necessary funds and thus have no cash investment in the project, while retaining 100 percent equity ownership. When projects could not support 100 percent debt financing, developers either invested their own money or took in silent partners who provided these funds. Leverage made such development activity quite attractive in spite of the risks.

While the development process was dependent on the availability of mortgage debt, as long as the developers could show that they were creating a building whose value based on projected revenues exceeded its costs, lending money for such a venture did not seem imprudent. But the continuing surge of inflation has had a marked impact on this traditional lender-developer relationship. Now financial institutions have become less willing to commit huge sums over time without an inflation hedge. They have demanded equity participation or concessions as conditions for granting mortgages. Consequently, loans are made with various forms of lender participation. Most simply, the lender obtains some aspect of the ownership rights that have traditionally been reserved to the equity position.

Equity Kickers

Popularly known as "equity kickers," lender participations may take a variety of forms. In addition to the option situation just described, we find (1) direct sharing in total revenues collected or in cash flow after payment of operating expenses and debt service; (2) participation in revenues or operating income after a certain threshold level has been achieved; (3) an escalating participation in revenues or rental income over time; (4) "free equity," a form under which the lender conditions the granting of the loan on the developer's assigning to the lender a certain percentage ownership of the project; and (5) various joint-venture arrangements such as (a) full partnership based on the lender's money and the developer's skills or (b) others under which the lender may insist on the opportunity to acquire the land and lease it back to the developer, to provide construction financing at terms especially favorable to the lender, or to acquire an ownership position in the property on favorable terms.

Borrowers are motivated to agree to lender-participation arrangements because these arrangements can enable them to obtain more dollars than they might otherwise.

In some circumstances, they can secure debt financing only by agreeing to such terms. But often, lender-participation deals involve lower constant rates and better overall financing terms. Further, when lenders insist on participating in certain property rights usually reserved for the equity position, they often have a much more flexible attitude toward elections the developer wants to make for tax purposes.

Where lender participation essentially involves additional interest, developers can often enhance their tax position and thereby their overall return by means of such arrangements. A lender insisting on participating in the equity position may ease the burden on the developer by extending the amortization term, thereby lowering the overall constant rate. Yet the overall annual cost of debt service may not be significantly changed. While this saving in the reduction of the constant rate is more than offset by the added equity payments to the lender, more of the payment is interest, as opposed to principal, and is thus tax-deductible. However, this extra increment of tax shelter which reduces current costs is gained at the expense of equity buildup. Consequently, at the time of sale or refinancing, developers will find that they have less equity in the project than they would otherwise have.

Generally, developers prefer a formula whereby the lender participates in a percent of gross or net above a certain level. Under that kind of arrangement, the added burden is felt only after the property reaches a successful operating level. In some lender-participation agreements, developers have claimed that they could not anticipate any cash flow until the project had been operating for at least 5 years.

Joint Ventures

Frequently in recent years, rather than acting as passive lenders, insurance companies and similar investors have been willing to put up all the money for a development except for minor amounts of initial or front money and any sums needed to pay for cost overruns. They have preferred to acknowledge from the start that they were part of a risky joint venture. They have sought to ensure themselves of developers' best efforts by agreeing that developers share fully in all profits and by making them responsible for all cost overruns.

In such a case, an insurance company might be approached by a developer with plans for a new apartment complex. The company would agree that this person act as developer, perhaps as general contractor, and as manager and leasing agent of the completed building. It would agree to pay all costs up to a specified limit. In order to protect its funds, it would have an agent on the ground during development and construction to evaluate and to take action if the project was falling behind the budget and financial plan.

Under a typical agreement, the company might buy the land and lease it to the development, put up equity in the form of participating preferred stock, and take a mortgage or agree that the joint venture would seek the best available financing terms. The rent on the land, the mortgage payments, taxes, and operating and all other expenses would be paid before the net cash flow was calculated. This cash flow would then be divided equally between the developer and the insurance company, with, however, the insurance company receiving an accumulating return on its equity before the developer receives any payments.

Example How such an agreement might work is shown in the following illustration. The apartment development has an imputed value, based on projected cash flow, of $3 million. The actual costs, financing, and split of cash are as follows:

1 Project cost, based on:

Cost of land	$ 300,000
Cost of construction	2,200,000
Total	$2,500,000

2 Required investment is raised:

Purchase and lease of land	300,000
Mortgage (two-thirds imputed project value)	2,000,000
Insurance company equity	200,000
Total	$2,500,000

3 Net cash flow after all expenses, mortgage, and loan payments is estimated to be:

Year 1	Year 2	Year 3	Year 4
$40,000	$50,000	$60,000	$60,000

4 Insurance company is to receive return of 12 percent on its equity first. Then developer is to receive equal amount (both claims are cumulative); finally, remainder is to be split evenly.

5

	Year 1	Year 2	Year 3	Year 4
Net cash flow	$40,000	$50,000	$60,000	$60,000
12 percent of $200,000 to insurance company	24,000	24,000	24,000	24,000
Developer paid	16,000	26,000	30,000	24,000
Developer owed	(8,000)	(6,000)		
Balance to be split:			6,000	12,000
Insurance company			3,000	6,000
Developer			3,000	6,000

From this display, we see that the developer needed his own money to option the land and prepare a submission to lenders. He must also meet any costs above $2,500,000. The insurance company receives the going interest rate for its lease of land and mortgage loan. It then has a priority right to $24,000 a year, and this right accumulates. The developer has a similar accumulating right, but he receives his money only after the insurance company is paid in full. If the net cash flow averages over $48,000 a year, they split the remainder evenly. In the example, the insurance company receives its $24,000 each year. Part of the first year's $24,000 payment to the developer is delayed and accumulates. It is paid off in the second and third years, and the split of overages then begins.

This division of income contrasts with the more traditional one, under which the builder would have bought and leased the land. The building, on the basis of its projected income, would be valued at $3,000,000. The builder would be able to borrow $2,000,000 on a mortgage. His equity in the building would be $1,000,000, based on the increase in income arising from the development process. He would have had to raise the $500,000 difference between the mortgage and the construction cost, but would have had the right to the entire net cash flow.

In many cases, because of cost overruns or delay in receipt of the projected income, lenders have had to step in with more money beyond the initial agreement. In some such cases, after lenders take complete possession, they retain the developer with a management contract. In other cases, the developer's share of any cash flow is cut. In still others, the lender may find another firm to complete and run the project, and the original developer gets nothing.

We have already noted that some developers may be forced into such arrangements because they cannot raise the necessary money in any other way. There are, however, added advantages which might lead developers to seek partners even when they have other alternatives.

1 With a partner, the developer can participate in a larger number of deals. Even if each has a somewhat smaller profit rate, the developer's total return may be far higher.

2 The developer can diversify and thereby lower his or her risks. The risks in all development are so great that developers may be better off even if they have to pay a good deal for diversification.

3 Lenders frequently add a necessary dimension of judgment or knowledge in making decisions. The joint venture may benefit from the local skills of the developer and the wider, broader, national knowledge of the lender.

SUMMARY

New forms of ownership and loans continue to develop. As more people search for real estate investments, they turn increasingly to professional sponsors. Rather than buying the property itself, they buy securities based on real estate.

The advent of real estate in the securities form offers the opportunity to achieve more efficient capital markets for real estate investment. At the same time, numerous problems must be overcome. The listing below indicates some of the areas in which progress is needed:

1 Where the price of the security is supported by the current value of the real estate, properties must have sound underlying economic value.

2 Regulatory consistency at both state and federal levels must be achieved.

3 Real estate securities must be able to compete effectively among themselves and with all other securities in the marketplace for investment dollars. In this regard it should be pointed out that the inconsistency and frequent changes of regulatory guidelines have tended to put real estate securities at a disadvantage vis-à-vis other investment forms.

4 Certain investment characteristics of real estate securities, particularly compensation arrangements, risks and conflicts, liquidity, and after-market questions, must be improved and developed.

5 Disclosure must be investor-oriented, with an emphasis on projections.

Parallel to the growth in real estate activity has been an increased complexity in sale-debt-leasing arrangements. Problems of cash flows, of tax-saving benefits, and of accounting balance sheets and income statements, among others, have led to new forms of agreements as to when debt payments will be required and how responsibility for them will be split. At times what appear to be sales of properties in reality come closer to loans, and vice versa. The investor and lender must look behind the terminology to find the actual economic realities of each proposal.

As lenders have watched developers and builders make large profits which would not have been possible without the funds they advanced, the lenders have become more eager to participate in individual deals. As a result, a number of complex relationships have developed which enable the lender to share in some of the profits. These arrangements vary from options and revenue-sharing agreements to major joint ventures which remain in effect from the initiation phase through the operation phase of some of the country's largest projects.

QUESTIONS AND PROBLEMS

1 Explain the concept of an "investment contract" which results in certain real estate transactions' falling under the law for securities.
2 What are the basic objectives of the securities laws?
3 What are the two basic exemptions under the SEC act?
4 Discuss the general concept of disclosure. What type of information does the seller have to tell the buyer?
5 The Golden Rule Department Store built its building 30 years ago. Its books show the building as almost completely depreciated. What would be some of the advantages of its selling the building and leasing back the right to occupy it?
6 Why has the use of balloon payments increased in borrowing on many income properties?
7 The objective of most developers, it has been said, is to "mortgage out." What does this mean?
8 Describe various forms of equity kickers.
9 Examine the 4-year experience of the joint venture described in this chapter. Assume the developer invested $100,000 of his own money in addition to that furnished by the insurance company and that he pays $30,000 a year on the land lease. Contrast his return on capital in this example with what it would have been if he had received a $2-million mortgage and had had to invest all the remaining required capital himself.
10 What are some advantages to a developer of entering into joint ventures with lenders?

SELECTED REFERENCES FOR PART TWO

Aronsohn, A. J. B., L. R. Kaster, and L. Ratner (eds.): *Joint Ventures in Real Estate* (New York: Practising Law Institute, 1970).

Campbell, K. D.: *Real Estate Trusts: America's Newest Billionaires* (New York: Audit Investment Research, 1971).

Clurman, D.: *The Business Condominium: A New Form of Property Ownership* (New York: Wiley-Interscience, 1973).

—— and E. L. Hebard: *Condominiums and Cooperatives* (New York: Wiley-Interscience, 1970).

Goldstein, C. A. (ed.): *Real Estate Financing: Contemporary Techniques* (New York: Practising Law Institute, 1973).

Mosburg, L. G., Jr.: *Real Estate Syndicate Offerings Law and Practice* (San Francisco: Real Estate Syndication Digest, 1974).

Roulac, S. E. (ed.): *Due Diligence in Real Estate Transactions* (New York: Practising Law Institute, 1974).

———— (ed.): *Real Estate Securities and Syndication: A Workbook* (Chicago: National Association of Real Estate Boards, 1973).

———— (ed.): *Real Estate Securities Regulations Sourcebook* (New York: Practising Law Institute, 1975).

———— : *Real Estate Syndication Digest: Principles and Applications* (San Francisco: Real Estate Syndication Digest, 1972).

Part Three

The Institutional Structure of Mortgage Lending

The institutional structure of real estate lending heavily influences the availability of funds. At times money nearly disappears. At other times it flows with overabundance. What may be only a slight cold and sneezing in the money market can cause pneumonia and near catastrophe in the mortgage market. These movements are the result of the interaction of money. deposit institutions, and lending. Their force is transmitted through a number of specialized institutions. Each plays a unique role. This part explains how they operate and the overall effect of their interactions.

Chapters 10 and 11 show the interrelationships between the flow of funds, the unique character of real estate, and mortgages. They explain the unstable demand for real estate, particularly as it is influenced by and influences mortgage flows. Chapters 12 and 13 describe the mortgage lending institutions and their special features, which are so significant for real estate finance. The importance of various institutions waxes and wanes. New institutions arise to help solve some of the problems borrowers encounter in obtaining money when they need it.

Chapter 10

The Unstable Nature
of Real Estate Financing

Throughout their history, the real estate and building industries have been plagued by extremely wide fluctuations in demand, prices, sales, and volume of construction. Anyone interested in this field should (1) recognize that such fluctuations are certain to occur, (2) understand why they happen, (3) learn how to forecast them, and (4) be prepared to build cyclone cellars in which to wait them out safely.

Records of our bankruptcy and foreclosure courts tell the tale of ventures with excellent long-run prospects which failed because projects were not able to ride out a short-term drop in demand or a sudden decrease in the availability of money. The record shows that failures have hit large, apparently prosperous firms almost as often as those ventures entered into on a shoestring.

Every time interest rates rise rapidly and the availability of mortgage money falls, extreme pressures are exerted on all concerned with real estate investment and finance. In recent periods some of our largest lending institutions have run out of money and capital and have had to be rescued by the government's insuring agencies. Bankruptcy and failure have taken a high toll of builders, contractors, and developers. In each fluctuation, the rate of foreclosures rises. In 1974, for example, many large developers, REITs, and ownership syndicates required aid through the bankruptcy courts. When W. J. Kassuba, a developer, entered the courts and filed for Chapter 11 bankruptcy protection, his assets were said to total over $500 million, including 120 separate properties. There were over 2,200 creditors, among them many of the largest institutional lenders in the United States. The number of projects involved in various stages of construction was close to 50.

FLUCTUATIONS IN REAL ESTATE

Table 10-1 and Figure 11-1 give an idea of the frequency and magnitude of these fluctuations in real estate. While the table reports movements in housing starts, there have been equally sharp fluctuations in the availability of financing, together with major changes in the interest rate or prices charged for loans. Movements in financial availability and in housing starts are closely, although not completely, related.

Between 1947 and 1975, housing starts declined sharply in seven different periods. The frequency, and to some extent the magnitude, of these fluctuations may be increasing. In 1966 starts fell by almost 50 percent, and in 1974 by over 60 percent. While not quite as severe, the five other downturns were nearly as serious. In each collapse of building, a low level of starts prevailed for a 1- or 2-year period.

Sales and prices of existing properties follow similar, but not quite as extreme, movements. Lending on residential mortgages also moves in the same way. Loans made by the four major financial institutions fell by 55 percent and by more than $13 billion from the high to the low quarters in both 1965–1966 and 1969–1970. In 1973–1974 the drop was over $32 billion and more than 50 percent. If corrected for FHLBB advances, the drop was nearly 70 percent. The fall in commitments available for new construction lending was still more drastic. At times almost no new commitments were available.

Fluctuations in interest rates have also been extremely wide. For example, commercial paper rates (the rates on the short-term borrowings of large corporations) rose from under 4 percent in 1972 to over 12 percent in 1974. In earlier periods such increases, followed by roughly similar decreases, were almost as great. While movements in mortgage interest rates were not as extreme, home mortgage rates did rise from 5.4 to 6.8 percent in 1965–1966 and from 7.5 to 10.1 percent between 1972 and 1974. The rise for income properties was still sharper.

Table 10-1 Peaks and Troughs in Housing Start Cycles

(At Seasonally Adjusted Annual Rates)

	Months between high and low	Amount in month, in thousands			Percent decline	Three-month averages			
						In thousands			Percent decline
		High	Low	Difference		High	Low	Difference	
Oct. 1947–Feb. 1949	16	1,036	821	215	−20.8	1,014	846	168	−16.6
Aug. 1950–July 1951	11	1,889	1,154	735	−38.9	1,881	1,182	699	−37.2
Dec. 1954–Mar. 1957	27	1,703	1,068	635	−37.3	1,664	1,080	584	−35.1
Dec. 1958–Dec. 1960	24	1,604	1,041	563	−35.1	1,589	1,148	441	−27.8
Dec. 1965–Oct. 1966	10	1,656	843	813	−49.1	1,522	931	591	−38.8
Jan. 1969–Jan. 1970	12	1,769	1,108	661	−37.4	1,678	1,252	426	−25.4
Oct. 1972–Dec. 1974	26	2,509	868	1,641	−65.4	2,436	988	1,448	−59.4

Source: U.S. Bureau of the Census, *Housing Starts*, Ser. C-20.

This past experience should tell developers, builders, and sellers of real estate that they must expect to encounter an industry depression about every 3.5 years. The demand fluctuations result in both extreme dangers and unusual opportunities for investors and developers. With sufficient knowledge and proper planning, one can avoid the greatest dangers. With better understanding, hard work, and luck, it is possible both to avoid losses and to make sizable profits.

Agreement is virtually unanimous that a major cause of these sharp fluctuations stems from the way in which real estate finance responds to changes in general credit conditions. Why does real estate credit fluctuate? The answer seems to be that fluctuations are due to (1) movements in overall saving and investment, (2) changes in the creation and cancellation of money, (3) the way borrowers and lenders in the general financial markets react, and finally (4) the special responses of mortgage credit to these other changes. We examine each of these four reactions separately. To recognize and predict shifts in the availability of real estate credit, we must understand:

1   The factors causing movements in the overall demand for, and supply of, goods in the economy and, more particularly, those which influence the demand for savings, investment, and spending.

2   The way in which other governmental and monetary policies react to changes in the economy's spending. Particularly, we must consider the way in which the Federal Reserve Board influences the creation of money, the availability of credit, and interest rates.

3   The reaction of credit markets and of borrowing and lending to the fluctuations in the economy and the shifts in monetary and fiscal policy. When these policies shift, credit markets change drastically.

4   The specific responses of real estate financing to the movements of the general credit markets and the flows between financial institutions. These responses put increased pressures on all involved in real estate.

SAVING AND INVESTING; LENDING AND BORROWING

Fluctuations in the availability of funds for real estate are not random events, nor are they brought about through errors on the part of financial institutions or the Federal Reserve. They reflect the results of certain basic decisions which all of us make as consumers or investors, spenders or savers. Savings are income that a household or business firm receives and does not spend. Decisions to spend or save are critical for the economy.

Spending and Saving

Spending is not necessarily limited to current income. Borrowings or past savings can be spent as well. Alternatively, decisions can be made to refrain from spending all current income by saving or repaying past borrowing. Savings by some groups are available to be spent by others on investment goods. It should be emphasized that in this discussion, the term "investment" refers to purchases of physical goods. Purchases of financial assets or common stock are considered financial transactions, not investments. On the whole, families spend less than their income on goods, whether for consumption or investment. Thus they run a surplus. In contrast, businesses as a whole spend and invest more than their current income. Thus they run deficits, or they "dis-save."

Lending and Borrowing

Along with the decisions to invest and to save, individuals and businesses decide how to finance their activities. The cash flows available from income may be augmented by borrowing, or on the other hand, some available funds may be lent to others. While related, decisions as to how to finance spending may be separate and distinct from decisions to save and invest.

Rapid shifts in these decisions lead to the fluctuations in real estate finance and activity noted in the tables and in prior discussions. If the decisions to purchase by spending units exceed the ability of the economy to produce, the sudden increases in demand may bring about sharp run-ups in prices and therefore in inflation. It is these fluctuations in spending, saving, and financing decisions, together with the related reactions of the government, that we must understand in order to grasp what happens in real estate markets.

THE FLOW OF FUNDS

One of the best ways to analyze these decisions, and particularly their potential impact on financial markets, is through the use of the flow-of-funds accounts. These are a special set of national accounts similar to the more familiar GNP (national income and product accounts). They are published quarterly by the Federal Reserve. Table 10-2 is a simplified presentation extracted from these accounts. It is constructed so as to emphasize the principal factors that affect flows through real estate markets.

Table 10-2 is divided into two parts. The top part shows the amounts that each sector of the economy saved and invested in the current year. The bottom part shows the increase in the financial assets of the sectors (the amount of their lending and any changes in their holdings of money) and the increase in their liabilities (their borrowing and the creation of money by banks and the government). In each part there also appears the surplus or deficit statement which makes the part balance.

If we reshape the information, we find that we can construct a table which shows both the source and the uses of funds to a sector and simultaneously the changes in the sector's balance sheet. This is illustrated in Table 10-3.

The first line on each side of this table shows the changes in the balance sheet which result from the current operations of nonfinancial businesses. These firms save and thereby increase their net worth. They also invest in capital goods. From the note to the table, we see that in 1973 their purchases of capital goods exceeded their savings, as they usually do. Nonfinancial businesses ran a deficit of $52 billion on current account.

The second part of Table 10-3 illustrates that in addition to saving and investing, businesses borrow and lend. They purchase, create, and extinguish securities and debt instruments. They may sell a bond to pay off a mortgage. They may borrow on a mortgage, perhaps to buy a building or accumulate money in the bank. Businesses are

Table 10-2 Condensed Summary of Flow of Funds, 1973
(In Billions of Dollars)

	Households	Nonfinancial business	Government	Finance	Rest of world	All sectors
Gross savings:						
Capital consumption allowances	116	93		3		212
Undistributed profits		17		7		24
Other savings	113		−8		1	106
Total	229	110	−8	10	1	342
Gross investment:						
Housing	38	20				58
Structures	3	42		2		47
Consumer durables	130					130
Equipment	3	84		3		90
Inventories		16				16
Net foreign					1	1
Total	174	162	0	5	1	342
Surplus or deficit on current account (S−I)	55	−52	−8	5	0	0
Lending	111	55	40	186	14	406
Increase or decrease in money	13	−1		2	3	17
Total	124	54	40	188	17	423
Borrowing	69	106	44	170	17	406
(Mortgages)	(46)	(27)		(−1)		(72)
Creation of money			4	13		17
Total	69	106	48	183	17	423
Net financial investment or net funds raised	55	−52	−8	5	0	0

Source: Board of Governors of the Federal Reserve System, *Flow of Funds Accounts* (statistical discrepancy distributed), September 1974 supplement.

Table 10-3 Nonfinancial Business 1973 Statement of Sources and Uses of Funds and Balance-Sheet Changes
(In Billions of Dollars)

Uses of funds (change in assets)		Sources of funds (change in liabilities and net worth)	
Investment (change in real assets)	162	Saving (change in net worth)	110
Lending (change in financial assets excluding money)	55	Borrowing (change in liabilities)	106
(Change in money)	$\frac{-1}{216}$		$\overline{216}$

Note: Investment (162) − saving (110) = deficit on current account (52). Borrowing (106) − change in financial assets (55 − 1) = net financial deficit (52).

both major lenders and major borrowers from banks and other financial institutions. In total, however, businesses borrow more than they lend. In fact, they raise (borrow) from other sectors of the economy exactly the amount needed to cover the excess of their investment over saving. Their net borrowing of $52 billion in 1973 exactly covers their deficit on current account, as it must.

The two tables bring out certain significant analytic facts:

1 For the economy as a whole, saving exactly equals investment, and lending equals borrowing. In each case, we are simply looking at two sides of the same coin. A bond is an asset or loan for an insurance company, but it is a debt or borrowing for the issuing corporation.

2 For any household, firm, institution, or sector, the equality need not hold. Some sectors are net savers and lenders; others are net investors and borrowers.

3 There is no exact relationship between changes in the amount of financial and real assets. Individuals can borrow to consume; a business can borrow to cover its losses or to change its financial working capital.

4 On the other hand, the change in the net financial position for any sector exactly equals its net investment or savings. A sector's increase in its net worth can be reflected both in real assets and in a net increase in claims against another sector.

5 A household or business can also, of course, increase its net worth by obtaining claims against someone in its own sector; the table, however, nets out intrasectoral claims.

6 The financial sector or financial institutions play a unique role as intermediaries between savers and investors. Their levels of saving and investment are comparatively unimportant, but their borrowing and lending are extremely significant, exceeding those of any other sector.

7 In addition, the financial sector and the government are where money is created or canceled. Money plays a special role in the entire picture.

Intermediation

Financial institutions serve as skilled intermediaries between those households, businesses, and governments which save and lend and those which borrow and invest.

The share of savings channeled through financial institutions has increased steadily. It is now over 80 percent of the total. The remainder is lent directly in the money and capital markets by corporations and individuals.

There are good reasons why the share of savings channeled through financial institutions has increased. Intermediaries can diversify risks; they can furnish liquidity; they have expertise; they profit from economies of scale; they have long lives. Consequently, an individual is frequently better off paying the financial institution the margin it charges for its services rather than attempting to invest directly. The growth of these institutions has led to more saving, more lending, more borrowing, and more investing.

This same growth, however, has caused problems of instability and inflation. In our economy, spending and saving do not grow smoothly and regularly; they fluctuate. The existence of financial institutions probably increases the violence of these fluctuations and their danger to the economy. The Federal Reserve and other regulatory agencies have been established in an effort to smooth out some of these fluctuations and to reduce their cost to the economy. There are major debates over the degree to which such attempts have been successful. Some believe that any success in stabilizing total demand has been achieved primarily at the expense of greater instability in real estate financing.

Shifts in Spending

The sources of instability are also the dynamic forces leading to change. People's desires and patterns of spending shift. The resulting movements in spending alter levels of output, the methods of production, and prices. Because in our complex economy decisions to spend, to produce, to save, and to invest are made by millions of separate units, there is no guarantee that they will mesh at a desirable level of spending or output. Instead, they may result in either a depressed or an inflationary level of spending. In fact, spending decisions seem to cycle between these opposite states.

In basic economic discussions, these dynamic forces which affect all types of spending are usually illustrated through examples drawn from the field of saving and investment. Since they are also the main sources of instability in real estate, we follow this pattern, but it should be emphasized that similar movements between planned and unplanned, or desired and unintended, spending can and do occur in other spheres as well.

Gross Savings

Funds for real investment arise from the excess in the amounts received by individuals, businesses, or governmental units over the amounts they spend for current consumption. We call this *saving*. Table 10-2 shows that there were $342 billion of saving and investment in our economy in 1973. The figures in the table differ from the more familiar net figures because they include household expenditures on consumer durables and the capital consumption allowances on these durables. Under the more conventional national income accounting, expenditures on consumer durables are all counted as consumption. The table also shows a division of business saving and investment between nonfinancial and financial businesses.

Governments in 1973 ran an $8-billion deficit. This appears in the table as negative saving. Governments appear to do no investing because their purchases of durables and investment goods are not treated as investments. When governments run deficits, they must borrow funds from the market. A deficit means that governments are not saving, but instead require savings made available from the other sectors. During wars and periods of large government deficits, these borrowings create massive pressures either toward high interest rates or for the government to create inflationary money in an attempt to hold rates down. On the other hand, to the extent that governments run a surplus, their funds, whether deposited in financial institutions or used to pay off debts, are available to the loan market and help hold interest rates down.

Gross Investment

The basic fact about investment is that it involves purchases of durable goods. Much of investment is therefore postponable. In some years it is high; in some it is low. In 1973, investment in real estate was $105 billion, or not quite a third of the total. It was divided about 55 percent in residential and 45 percent in commercial and industrial structures. Investment in business equipment and inventories was approximately as large as real estate investment. The largest share of total investment was in consumer durables, primarily automobiles.

When total spending rises too rapidly, demand outruns supply. Prices rise; interest rates rise. More people want to borrow than want to lend. Since borrowing and lending must be equal, some would-be borrowers will be frustrated. Some will not borrow because they decide the interest rates demanded by potential lenders are too high. Others will find funds unavailable. Typically, much of this revision of desires occurs in the area of construction, and particularly in housing.

Desires are also revised through changes in spending and saving decisions. Construction may be cut back if the demand for space falls below the amount produced. Builders end up with an undesired investment; they cannot sell. They lower production, hoping that demand will catch up with supply and that someone will buy their units.

The efforts of the government to influence individual decisions to invest or spend are as important as these decisions themselves. If demand is outrunning supply and prices are rising, the government, through the Federal Reserve, may act to curtail credit and raise interest rates in order to lower demand. Or the government may also use fiscal policy—raise taxes or cut government spending—to lower demand. These governmental measures, interacting with those of private investors and savers, cause building to fluctuate widely.

MONETARY POLICY AND THE FEDERAL RESERVE

Money plays a unique role in the determination of credit flows and spending. However, the importance of money is not at all obvious in Table 10-2. Changes in the amount of money (defined as currency plus demand deposits and depicted by the symbol M_1) were only $17 billion, compared with a $406-billion increase in other types of credit. Yet few dispute the fact that change in the amount of money is one of the most critical factors determining the price (interest rates), the availability, and the type of loans made. In this case, the tail does wag the dog.

The reason for money's importance is that it serves as both our medium of exchange and our standard of economic value. We exchange all goods, services, and financial assets for money. It constitutes a link between the real and financial sides of the market. It is the unit in which debt contracts are written. It is both a source of immediate liquidity and a store of future purchasing power.

Fundamentally, money is a commodity. Like the value of wheat or meat or anything bought and sold, the value of the dollar (the amount of goods it can purchase) rises or falls depending on the amount supplied relative to demand. However, a change in the value of money has a far more pervasive impact than a change in the value of any other commodity. It affects the demand for all other goods as well as their prices. The relationships of money to the markets for both real goods and financial assets are so significant and far-reaching that in the United States, as in almost every other country, the supply of money is a major concern of public policy.

Monetary policy is that policy by which the government influences the economy through changes in bank reserves, money, and credit. In the United States, Congress and the President have entrusted to the Federal Reserve System the duty and authority to establish monetary policy. In formulating monetary policy, decision makers at the Federal Reserve attempt to help the nation reach its economic goals of stability in output, full employment, optimum growth, and no inflation. The Fed must first decide where the economy seems to be headed. Will there be too much or too little spending? Depending on the answer, it selects a target for variables such as money and credit or interest rates. It manipulates a variety of instruments including bank reserves, discount rates, and interest ceilings (regulation Q) so that the monetary variables can hit their target and keep the economy on a desirable path.

If the economy is overbuoyant and excess demand is threatening higher prices and inflation, monetary policy attempts to lower the demand for goods and services. It does this by decreasing the availability of money and credit, which also has the effect of raising the level of interest rates. These movements increase costs to major sectors of the economy. In some cases, available credit may disappear. The burdens of monetary policy are not shared equally. The impacts upon housing, real estate, small businesses, and local governments are far greater than those upon other segments of the economy.

The Federal Reserve does not have complete control of the monetary variables. What happens to money and interest rates depends on what is happening in the economy and in financial markets (especially banks and the Treasury) as well as on what the Fed does. The monetary variables need not move together. At any given time, one may get very different views as to whether monetary policy has turned expansive or restrictive, depending on which measure one uses.

In attempting to move the monetary variables, the Fed uses a selection of monetary tools or instruments through which it creates or cancels money.

Open Market Operations

Monetary policy is implemented chiefly through buying or selling government securities (bills, notes, and bonds). This is called an *open market* operation. (Operations also include foreign currencies.) To stimulate monetary growth, the Open Market Desk of the Federal Reserve in New York bids for government securities in the money market, as other traders do. The Fed pays for its purchases with its own check (or newly printed currency). When the sellers deposit the checks, the accounts at regional Federal Reserve Banks of the member banks receiving the checks are increased; their reserves, consisting of their vault cash and deposits at the Fed, have grown. The Fed has as a new asset the bond it has purchased, and as a new liability the deposit it owes the commercial bank.

This open market operation accomplishes three things:

First, by adding to the demand for securities, it bids up their prices and lowers interest rates. This is illustrated by thinking of a perpetual bond (so that we need not worry about amortizing any discount or premium paid) which has a fixed interest payment of $6 a year. If this bond sells for $100, it yields an annual interest rate of 6 percent, that is, 6/100. If the price rises to $150, it yields an annual interest rate of 4 percent, that is, 6/150. If the price drops to $50, its yield is 12 percent, that is, 6/50.

Second, the open market purchase increases the liquidity of the seller of the bond, who now holds non-interest-yielding money in the form of a deposit instead of an interest-bearing bond. This may either satisfy a changed desire for liquidity or lead the seller to buy more goods or securities.

Finally, it generates an additional Federal Reserve deposit for a commercial bank, increasing the bank's reserves and thereby giving the banking system the power to make more loans and generate more demand deposits. Since the money supply consists of currency and demand deposits, the creation of deposits boosts the total amount of money.

The Discount Rate, Reserve Requirements, Interest, and Credit Controls

Banks can also increase their reserves by borrowing from the Fed, which credits the amount borrowed to their deposit accounts. The interest rate they pay on such borrowings is called the *discount rate*. The discount window is an administered accommodation for use only under special circumstances.

While a move in the discount rate is the most traditional, awesome, and newsworthy instrument in the Federal Reserve's portfolio, it in fact has a minimal real impact, since banks actually borrow very little from the Fed. A move in the discount rate can have a major impact, however, if it is intended to, and does, announce a shift in monetary policy and if it succeeds in changing expectations of future policy.

The level of potential bank credit, the money the reserves will support, can also be shifted if the Federal Reserve changes reserve requirements, or the legal reserve ratio. By regulation, the Fed can set the required reserves at between 7 and 22 percent for demand deposits and 3 and 10 percent for other deposits. When their reserves exceed the percentage required by law, banks can increase their loans or buy securities. When these excess reserves are used up, the banks can no longer generate demand deposits and money until they obtain more reserves.

Compared with open market operations, however, both of these actions, although useful, serve rather minor functions; except for their announcement effects on expectations, they can be neglected in most analysis.

How banks will act to expand deposits cannot be predicted with accuracy. They will be motivated to increase loans and investments to their maximum because they earn nothing on unused excess reserves. On the other hand, no bank wants to lose money as a result of poor investments. Their profits may be higher if they hold idle funds until more profitable opportunities arise.

The maximum or ceiling interest rate that banks can pay on their savings and time deposit liabilities is set by the Federal Reserve under regulation Q. At times, the ceilings may be removed or set so high as to have no effect on bank operations. When the ceilings are below short-term market interest rates, savers who want higher returns will purchase securities rather than make time deposits in banks. As deposits stop growing or fall, so does the credit that banks can make available through loans or investments. Higher ceilings or their removal will, on the other hand, allow time deposits to be attracted.

Selective credit controls limit the amount of credit that banks may make available for certain purposes. As an example, the amount that can be lent to a customer for the purpose of purchasing common stock on credit is set by regulating his or her minimum margin. The required margin is the difference between the market value and maximum legal loan which can be made on a stock, and thus it is the cash a buyer must have as a downpayment. Margin requirements have ranged from 40 to 100 percent; in the latter case banks could not lend at all against such collateral.

Other selective controls have been applied to consumer credit, mortgages, and international lending. These controls limit in various ways credit for specific uses; individually they have a minor effect on total bank credit.

The Monetary Variables

If the Fed decides that demand ought to be restricted, some or all of these instruments will be used to lower the amount of money and credit and to raise interest rates. The movements of these monetary variables will influence the actions of financial institutions. They will have fewer funds to lend and will be more selective in making loans. They will charge higher rates. Furthermore, there may be fewer prospective borrowers. Some people may be unwilling or unable to pay higher interest rates. They may decide that if monetary policy is pressing down demand, this is not a good time to borrow. All these reactions are likely to be especially acute in the mortgage market. As we shall see in the next chapter, the changes in mortgage rates and availability often dominate sales and production of real property.

THE FLOW OF FUNDS THROUGH FINANCIAL INSTITUTIONS

Changes in monetary policy are almost immediately and completely reflected in the flow of funds into and through the major financial institutions. This was shown in Table 2-2. The years of sharp declines in bank and most other deposits (1955, 1957, 1959, 1966, 1969, 1973) are also the years in which the Federal Reserve was using its instruments to curtail the rate of growth in spending.

As banks come under pressure as a result of a lessened availability of reserves, they try to adjust to their new position by selling securities, particularly the short-term government bills and notes which are the banks' main source of liquidity. Banks reduced their holdings of United States government securities in each of the years listed. They also greatly decreased their purchases of other securities.

In order to sell securities, their prices must be marked down, which has the effect of raising their yields. This is also true even if they are only allowed to run off, because then the government must find other lenders to take them. The securities are bought by individuals, corporations, or other financial institutions that find it worthwhile to hold them instead of bank deposits. They pay for their new assets by withdrawing their existing deposits. The banks lose the assets, and their deposits fall as the checks they receive in payment are debited to the purchasers' accounts. Sharp movements in yields on Treasury bills occur when reserves are shifted. Increases in yields spread throughout the markets for securities.

Disintermediation

As yields on many market securities such as United States Treasury bills rise in comparison with those on savings deposits, investors redistribute their funds in favor of the securities offering the higher yield. This process of taking funds out of the financial institutions is known as *disintermediation*, since investors bypass the financial intermediaries to invest their funds directly in the money and bond markets. The consequent drop in all types of deposits is widespread. Deposits in S&Ls did not decline much when money tightened in the 1950s, but since then the situation has changed drastically. The magnitude of fluctuations seems to be increasing for all institutions. These wide swings are closely related to the fact that interest rates are reaching greater heights and experiencing wider movements than has been true in the past.

Such shifts in yields relative to the market and the consequent loss in funds are inherent in the way financial intermediaries operate. They borrow in the short-term market, thus providing the public with the safe, highly liquid assets it desires. But these borrowings from the public are in competition with marketable short-term securities. At the same time that they are borrowing short, institutions lend on long-term assets. Since these turn over slowly, the institutions' earnings are relatively constant even when short-term rates rise. S&Ls cannot raise substantially the rates they offer for deposits every time the Fed moves market rates up. This means that individuals can earn more by buying short-term securities. They do so by withdrawing their deposits. The institutions' ability to compete on a rate basis is handicapped because their earnings are dependent upon long-term loans made in earlier periods at fixed and often lower rates. Savers who are sensitive to differences in yields place their funds directly in the market. They continue to withdraw deposits (disintermediate) until short-term rates again fall. These cyclical variations in deposits have been somewhat exacerbated by federal regulations limiting the amount institutions can pay on deposits. However, the more fundamental problem of the savings institutions lies in their asset structure. They cannot raise the amount they offer even in the absence of regulated ceiling rates because they are unable to increase their earnings as fast as market rates climb.

Money and Lending

We can now summarize the effect of monetary policy on borrowing and lending. When the rate of creation of reserves and money decreases relative to the demand for it:

1   Interest rates rise.
2   Total lending or credit falls.
3   The share of intermediaries or financial institutions in the total declines. A higher proportion of lending is done directly by households and nonfinancial firms.
4   The share of deposit institutions falls by even more.

The impact of shifting monetary policy is a good deal weaker on insurance and pension reserves and other financial institutions than it is on commercial banks and thrift institutions.

These effects are vividly illustrated by the events of 1973 and 1974. Interest rates on federal funds rose from 4 percent in 1972 to over 12 percent in the third quarter of 1974. As a result, the total amount of lending in credit markets between the first quarter of 1973 and the third quarter of 1974 dropped by about 10 percent, or by over $50 billion. The lending by financial institutions fell by 42 percent, or nearly $65 billion. The amount lent by commercial banks and thrift institutions was down 54 percent, or over $90 billion. The share of the deposit institutions in total lending fell from 79 to 48 percent. The share of lending accounted for by other than financial institutions rose from 5.5 to 26.6 percent of total lending.

THE EFFECT ON THE MORTGAGE MARKET

We now come down to the bottom line: the total effect on mortgage lending when monetary reserves expand at a slower rate than demand for them is increasing. We have already seen that the effect is great. It arises from three separate causes:

1   There is less money to lend, and interest rates are higher.
2   Those who traditionally lend on mortgages have a smaller share of whatever funds are available for lending. Even if no change occurs in the willingness of an institution to lend the same percentage of its new funds as previously on mortgages, total mortgage lending still falls sharply.
3   On the whole, institutions are less willing to make mortgage loans. The proportion of residential financing in any growth in assets falls.

Mortgage Lenders Have Fewer Funds

This general situation is reflected in Table 10-4. We see again that in each period of restricted credit, sharp drops occur in mortgage lending. Decreases are especially large for the thrift institutions, whose share of funds available for lending takes the largest cut.

The decline between the first quarter of 1973 and the third quarter of 1974 was the sharpest by far. Total mortgage lending in the period fell by over $30 billion, or over 40 percent. However, we note that between these two periods, federal government funds to the mortgage market rose from $12.1 billion (including FHLB advances) to $29.5 billion. Thus private funds placed in mortgage loans by financial institutions dropped by $49.2 billion, or nearly 80 percent.

The only exceptions to this general picture for private institutions are the LICs and pension and retirement funds. In both 1970 and 1974, their lending increased. This

Table 10-4   High and Low Quarters for Mortgage Lending by Financial Institutions, 1965–1974

(In Billions of Dollars)

	1965 III	1966 IV	1969 I	1970 I	1973 I	1974 III
S&Ls	9.0	1.0	11.8	5.9	35.8	13.5
(FHLB loans to S&Ls)	(.3)	(−1.6)	(2.7)	(4.5)	(5.4)	(9.8)
CBs	6.4	3.3	7.8	2.6	19.4	7.8
LICs	4.8	2.9	2.0	3.0	1.8	5.5
MSBs	4.3	2.9	2.9	.7	5.5	2.1
State agencies and pension funds	1.2	1.5	.3	1.4	.1	.1
REITs	0	0	.2	1.9	4.6	−1.0
Government*	1.0	2.5	3.3	7.2	6.7	19.7
Other financial institutions	1.1	−1.0	.6	−.6	1.1	−4.5
Total	27.8	13.1	28.9	22.1	75.0	43.2

*Includes mortgage pools backing GNMA-guaranteed pass-through securities.
Source: Board of Governors of the Federal Reserve System, *Flow of Funds Accounts.*

occurred because most of their lending is made against commitments to lend in the future issued when markets were easier.

The REITs showed a gain in 1970 at the start of their expansion, but nearly disappeared from the market in 1974. The small financial institutions moved funds from mortgages to other markets in each of the three periods.

The most significant declines, of course, occurred among the thrift institutions and CBs. Excluding the loans made with FHLB advances, we note that the S&Ls and MSBs experienced extremely sharp declines in each of these periods of tight money and disintermediation. Between the top and bottom of 1973–1974, the drop was nearly $30 billion, or over 80 percent.

While most of this decline occurs because the deposit institutions have fewer funds to lend, some of the drop is due to a fall in demand for loans on mortgages caused by much higher interest rates. When the cost of a mortgage rises, demand falls. Numerous studies, however, have concluded that the fall is much greater than can be accounted for by higher interest rates alone. Much of the decrease in lending occurs because fewer funds are available to prospective borrowers on mortgages.

Mortgage Competitiveness Declines

The forces at work causing lenders to shift their funds away from mortgages are diverse. On the whole, mortgages appear to become relatively less profitable as credit tightens. Interest rates on mortgages adjust more slowly than rates on other credit instruments. Falling rates increase the funds available for mortgage borrowers. In periods of rising rates, a greater contraction occurs because lenders find other types of loans more profitable.

Ceilings   Part of this slower adjustment of rates is due to noncompetitive features of the mortgage market. On individual loans for a single house, lenders tend to set quite firm rates. Bargaining or shopping for loans is not common. Furthermore, on the upside, problems arise because of ceilings on mortgage rates imposed by both the federal government and state governments. These ceilings are meant to protect borrowers, but they also decrease availability. The debate over the impact on availability of maximum rates on FHA-VA loans has gone on for over 25 years. While the extent of the problems such ceilings have raised has not been quantified, few believe their impact has been nil.

In recent years, ceilings set by state usury laws which set a limit on interest rates charged have also lowered the competitiveness of mortgage funds among lenders who have other choices. Market rates have exceeded the ceilings set by state regulations. In some cases, adjustments have been possible through use of discounts, but problems arise when lenders fear that their public image is being affected by the large discounts. In other cases, state laws are strict enough to make lending virtually out of the question.

Other Forces Lenders avoid mortgages when ceiling rates are below the market. Even without ceilings, as general interest rates rise, mortgages seem to become relatively less desirable for lenders with alternative choices because of the poorer marketability of mortgages compared with that of bonds, their less certain cash flow, and the greater risk of loss through foreclosure at higher interest rates. All these forces tend to diminish the amount placed in mortgages by lenders who have available choices.

Besides these forces from inside the mortgage market, outside pressure also makes itself felt. The demand for funds by business, which is directly competitive with mortgage lending, intensifies greatly in periods of tight money. Corporations, finding themselves squeezed for funds, seek the necessary financing from their banks and insurance companies. Even if they could pay rates no higher than those on mortgages, they would probably find that their needs were being met even as mortgage lending fell. For sound profit reasons, lenders give preference to regular customers over those like mortgage borrowers who appear at the lender's counter only at rare intervals. Such occasional borrowers tend not to maintain a continuing relationship with the lender. They are less likely to provide profitable business in the future.

Because of the varied factors making mortgages less attractive, it appears logical for lenders who have flexibility in their decisions to put less money into mortgages when money is tight. The diversified lenders—CBs, MSBs, and LICs—seem to follow such lending rules. They decrease the share of mortgages in their total lending when credit tightens.

SUMMARY: WHY INTEREST RATES RISE
AND MORTGAGE FUNDS DRY UP

It is important to review the facts presented in this chapter to make certain that we recognize the relationship between shifts in the flow of funds and easy or tight money for real estate markets. While money may grow either easier or tighter, tight money requires more analysis for real estate. In an easy-money period, funds are readily available. The most important rule for an investor or lender at such times is not to be misled, not to indulge in a euphoric feeling, but to plan for a sudden reversal. Although we have limited our analysis to tight money because of its more serious effects on real estate, all the arguments are reversible.

Increased Demand

At frequent intervals, as a result of individual or collective decisions, the demand for goods, services, and credit in the economy rises. This increase in demand may be reflected in business investment, consumer spending (particularly on automobiles), construction of houses, or government deficits. When such spending surges occur, demand for production starts to outrun the economy's capacity to produce. Prices begin to rise.

When inflation threatens, if capacity and production could expand rapidly enough, there would be no problem. But in such periods our ability to increase output falls far below the rate at which demand expands. It becomes necessary to curtail the demand for goods through government policies, and such a curtailment may be handled in many ways. If it were done by cutting government expenditures, raising taxes, taxing durable expenditures, or taxing or curtailing the availability of credit to spenders outside the housing or property sphere, real estate would not suffer.

In fact, however, because it is easier to use monetary policy than other means, most of the pressure against spending in boom times has traditionally been concentrated in the real estate sphere. It seems to be easier to cut demand by curtailing real property credit than through any alternative action agreeable to the body politic.

When the demand for goods is rising, the change in spending patterns shows up in the flow of funds. Saving decreases; the spending and borrowing of nonfinancial businesses, consumers, and the government increase. In an effort to halt inflationary price rises, either the Federal Reserve fails to accommodate the increased demand for money and credit by holding growth in monetary reserves to prior rates, or it may actually go further and cut back on the reserves supplied. The Fed's objective is to hold the level of purchases in line with the capacity to produce. It tries to force out of the market some of those who can purchase only if they are able to borrow money.

The constant or slower-growing supply of credit, interacting with greater demands, forces up market interest rates. As market rates rise, disintermediation occurs. Rather than accepting only the lower earnings available through deposit institutions, people with savings prefer to invest directly in the credit markets. With their funds drying up, the institutions cut back on their mortgage lending. Other institutions, finding that they can make more profitable loans elsewhere, join them in curtailing real estate credit.

People who want to build or buy properties discover that the interest rates they are asked to pay rise rapidly. At the same time, the availability of mortgage funds falls. People say that no mortgage money is available, but this is not literally true. Some lenders do disappear from the market because of adverse cash flows. However, at some interest rates—perhaps much higher than any we have ever experienced—some additional willingness to lend on mortgages would appear. For most potential borrowers, such a theoretical rate is impossibly high. Usury laws may make lending at these rates illegal. In most cases, moreover, would-be borrowers simply cannot count on earning enough income to pay the high interest rates required to obtain mortgage loans. Potential borrowers fail to get credit and therefore cannot make purchases. The construction and real estate markets find that demand for their products falls drastically. A recession or depression spreads throughout the real property market.

QUESTIONS AND PROBLEMS

1 Do you believe the real estate cycle is regular enough with respect to timing so that you could use history as a guide to the proper timing of an investment?
2 What causes credit for real estate to move up and down so drastically?
3 Does a sector have to save in order to invest? Does the same reasoning hold true for the entire economy?
4 What is the difference between a "financial" and a "real" asset?
5 Must total sources and uses of funds be equal? Discuss the difference between a sector and the economy in this respect.
6 What function do financial intermediaries play in the economy?
7 Why does the Federal Reserve curtail the amount of credit at certain times and cause interest rates to rise?
8 What are some of the things that happen when an open market operation purchases securities?
9 Explain what disintermediation is and why it occurs.
10 Why does a slowdown in the rate at which monetary reserves are created cause mortgage funds to be more difficult to obtain?
11 What is the effect of usury laws on the mortgage market?
12 Residential construction appears more sensitive to movements in financial markets than other types of production. Explain why this is so.
13 What is the effect of unstable mortgage markets on investors?

Chapter 11

Mortgage Flows, Interest Rates, and Inflation

A decline in the availability of mortgage funds and an increase in interest rates are the most critical factors influencing real estate demand, construction, and prices. But they are not the only significant forces. Changes in households, jobs, costs, and government policies also have major impacts. Furthermore, all these changes can create waves of activity in the markets which seem to take on a life of their own.

Major fluctuations occur in the construction of new space. Because of the time it takes to bring new developments to market—the lag between an idea and final occupancy—real estate promoters, developers, and investors frequently overestimate demand or underestimate supply coming on line. If demand has been overestimated and supply expands too fast, vacancies rise, prices and incomes decline, and building activity tapers off. On the other hand, when supply fails to keep up with demand, vacancies disappear, rents and profits rise, profits are high, development booms, and building increases.

In recent years the market has also been buffeted by inflation. If the main effect of inflation were to raise the rents and income from real property, its impact would be extremely favorable. Unfortunately, the situation is more complex. Inflation also raises costs, expenses, uncertainty, and risks, while lowering the availability of funds for financing. Because rents often rise more slowly than costs, net income from property may be squeezed.

Compare Figures 11-1 and 2-2, which show the fluctuations in housing starts and interest rates since 1948. The fact of cycles in both starts and rates stands out even though in the 1970s both climbed to new highs. While interest rates and starts are clearly related, other factors are also at work. To find what drives the real estate cycle, we must understand these market forces and how they interact.

THE DEMAND FOR, AND SUPPLY OF, REAL ESTATE

The sources of demand for different types of real estate are closely related. While at times special factors may dominate the market for houses, land, apartments, commercial space, or other types of property, the underlying demand and supply situations are similar. Because the market for housing and residential space is by far the largest, our knowledge concerning it is more extensive than our knowledge concerning other properties. Therefore, we use housing and residential construction to illustrate how real estate fluctuations occur. The same forces, however, are at work in the many other markets for real property which are discussed in Part Seven.

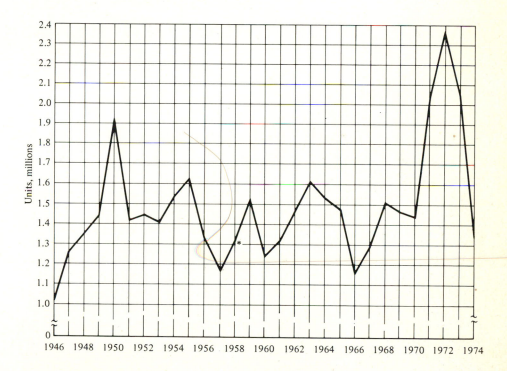

*Count from 1947 through 1958 is for *total private nonfarm* only. Beginning with 1959, the count is for *total private (including farm)*. In 1959, the difference between the two counts was 22,200 units.

Figure 11-1   Housing starts, 1946 to 1974. (*Source: U.S. Department of Commerce.*)

Factors Influencing Residential Construction

That a multitude of factors influence the housing market is obvious from even a cursory examination. The following list presents a fairly typical classification of these forces:

1 Changes in in population
   a Changes in number of persons
   b Changes in age-sex composition
   c Changes in number, type, and size of households
   d Immigration and internal migration
2 Changes in income and employment
   a Total income (past, current, expected)
   b Income distribution
   c Employment and unemployment
3 Consumer actions
   a Consumer tastes and preferences
   b Consumer asset holdings, especially liquid assets and equities in houses
4 Changes in housing prices, costs, and taxes
   a Demand for housing related to its own and other consumer prices
   b Shape of housing cost and supply curves
   c Land use and zoning
   d Income tax treatment of housing costs and income
5 Credit availability and its cost
6 Relationship between occupancy costs and prices of dwellings
   a Real estate taxes and operating expenses
   b Depreciation
   c Cost of equity funds
7 Conditions in the existing housing supply
   a Net replacement demand—demolitions, conversions, and removals
   b Utilization of the housing inventory
      (1) Vacancies
      (2) Intensity of occupancy
   c Prices and rents for existing dwellings
   d Quality and location
8 Special local or regional factors
   a Migration
   b Jobs and income
   c Hurricanes, floods, disasters
9 Reaction to changes in demand
   a Investors' organization and actions
   b Builders' organization and actions
   c Market structure and market information

An Overview of Housing Fluctuations

This list of demand and supply factors contains nothing unusual or unexpected, and yet the interaction of these factors causes major fluctuations and hardships. Builders and real estate men and women go through periods of feast and famine in rapid succession.

Housing starts may increase or decrease by as much as 50 percent in fairly short periods.

In order to understand why these fluctuations take place, two different lines of causation must be examined. First we look at the background of the changes in housing starts or individual dwelling units as measured in Table 10-1. In addition, however, we must look at movements occurring in the average size, quality, and value of each unit. The total amount spent on space is the product of both dimensions: the number of units started times their average value.

Orders to construct new houses come from three basic groups:

1 Individuals who contract for or build houses for their own use.
2 Builders who start houses that they expect to sell to new owner-occupiers. (Some will be sold before construction starts; others are built on "speculation," in the hope that they will sell.)
3 Builders or developers who start apartment houses or rental units.

What determines the number of dwelling units ordered in any period?

The Number of Houses Started   Over any moderately long time span, such as 5 to 10 years, the number of dwellings built is closely related to the basic demand for new units. There are three parts to this demand:

1 Most important is the formation of new households. Every added household requires another house in our total stock.
2 Additional units are needed to replace dwellings removed from the stock for a myriad of reasons—for example, because they are old, worn out, destroyed by fire or flood, or situated in deteriorated neighborhoods.
3 Finally, the number of vacant units must expand roughly at the same rate as the total stock if we are to retain the flexibility that will permit us to move when we want to and find a house we like that meets our needs and ability to pay.

Growth in this basic demand, however, is not immediately reflected in new starts. What effect it has depends upon how it influences the underlying demand and supply situation. There is an extremely large stock of existing dwellings—over 75 million. Most newly formed families and households look first to this stock and its available vacancies to meet their needs. It is in this overall market that demand and supply are matched. The demand for space becomes a demand for new dwellings and new construction only if it cannot be met through existing vacancies. If there is a large surplus of excess space, even though demand is expanding rapidly, it will not show up in new construction. The deficit or surplus in the underlying demand and supply causes rents and selling prices to move up and down. These price movements are the signals watched by developers and builders.

As demand rises, vacancies fall, leading to higher prices and higher rents. Developers and builders compare the expected rents of apartments and prices of sale housing with their developmental costs. These include the costs of construction, what they have to pay to buy and develop land, and how much they are charged for financing. If, after comparison, they find it profitable to build, new houses are started.

If the market worked smoothly and remained always in equilibrium, the stock of houses would grow just fast enough to house the new households, to replace the units removed from the stock, and to bring about the needed vacancies. But the housing market is far from perfect. Prices, rents, and vacancies deviate from their equilibrium for considerable periods of time. Important adjustment lags occur in both supply and demand. Changes in mortgage availability and interest rates cause further large deviations in the rate of starts. Instead of a smooth adjustment to the growth in demand, we find rapid fluctuations. The inventory under construction and of vacant units tends to rise for a period. Then the pressure of excess vacancies moves the rate of starts downward. We end up with a system that first overshoots and then undershoots the movements in basic demand, giving the picture shown in Figure 11-1.

Econometric Studies   There have been hundreds of statistical and econometric studies of the housing market. Basically they all agree with this general description of how the fluctuations occur. Actual starts over an intermediate period are determined by the underlying basic demand. This forms a trend around which other forces drive the year-to-year movements in starts.

In most studies, the availability of mortgage money has the greatest single impact on housing starts. Interest rates are also important. In addition, because rents and prices move somewhat differently from the way costs move, the relationship between these factors is significant. A final important variable is public policy. The amount of money made available directly by governments and by loans by government-sponsored agencies and the amount of subsidy they pay also influence the rise and fall of demand.

In most of these models, the availability of financing, costs related to prices, and public policy lead to the divergence of construction from demand, which in turn causes a change in the number of vacancies. When vacancies become too numerous, they drive down prices and rents and cause housing starts to fall. This means that after a lag, the completion of new units falls as well. The number of units being added to the stock drops below basic demand. Vacancies decrease. Rents and prices rise. Finally the whole cycle starts over again. It is important to recognize, however, that these fluctuations are not regular in shape or timing. While the changes in the vacancy rate should move in a fairly regular path, they can be offset or increased by changes in financing and public policy.

Value or Quality   In addition to the number of units started, the value of each unit built also changes through time. The three primary factors affecting the amount spent per house are the average real income per household, the costs of housing compared with the costs of other goods the family can buy, and the cost and availability of mortgages.

When incomes rise, families typically spend more for their housing. However, the amount they spend will not rise as rapidly as incomes. If a family gets a better buy for other goods, such as cars or recreation, compared with housing, it will often choose to raise the purchases of these other goods and decrease the amount spent on housing. On the other hand, as housing costs rise, families have to spend more to maintain their level of housing standards. Thus increases in costs will raise housing expenditures, but how much depends on what is happening to other prices.

Local Factors   Figure 11-1 shows the actual fluctuations in housing starts for the country as a whole. In any local market the fluctuations are frequently much greater because the same type of movements which influence national demand tend to be far more highly concentrated at the local level. A large apartment complex has little or no effect on the national picture, but it may cause a sharp run-up in local vacancies. Similarly, the closing of a plant and loss of jobs may have little influence on the nation, but it may completely dominate the local housing market. An investor must therefore do more than analyze the national picture. The forecasts of housing which the media carry are concerned primarily with the overall housing market. They are likely to be reflected, but not exactly, in any local market. Investors must be aware of any possible difference. They must stay completely abreast of what is happening to supply and demand in their own localities.

What to Watch for   From this overview the critical factors that must be looked at in attempting to evaluate the demand for a specific property become clear. Most important is the situation regarding recent completions and the amount of space under construction compared with the growth in local demand. Are vacancies increasing? What threat arises from units not yet in the market but already in the development process? What is happening to rents and prices? How do their movements compare with changes in costs?

The local factors must be closely analyzed in the light of the state of the national economy, interest rates, and the flow of deposits into lending institutions. No matter how bright the local picture may be, it can and usually will be overwhelmed if unsatisfactory conditions prevail nationally. A general depression, a shortage of mortgage money, or a sharp rise in the interest rates can offset even the most favorable local demand conditions.

THE BASIC DEMAND FOR NEW HOUSING

Table 11-1 shows where the demand for new housing originated during the 1950s and 1960s, plus that expected for the 1970s. Even though the figures are averages for whole 10-year periods, the table illustrates what has just been said about the housing cycle. During these 30 years, housing starts are shown as about 50 million units. Of this total, new household formation requires about 35 million units, or 70 percent. More than 10 million units are required to replace houses removed from the stock. The actual units removed total more than 15 million, but about a third of them are offset by additions to the stock from mobile homes and public housing, which are not included in the series of private housing starts.

A final demand arises from the growth in vacancies. It may seem strange to show a change in vacancies as part of needed demand, but this is necessary to provide for mobility and choice. Prices and rents adjust to make such vacancies not unprofitable. The costs to carry them are absorbed in the total.

In equilibrium, only from 90 to 92 percent of the stock of dwelling units will be occupied; the other 8 to 10 percent will be vacant. This sounds like a high number of vacancies, but less than 40 percent of them are actually available in the market for

Table 11-1 Disposition of Total Estimated Starts of Private Housing Units in the United States, April 1, 1950–1970, and Projection, 1970–1980

	Annual rate		
Category	1950–1960	1960–1970	Projection 1970–1980
Net additions to households:	978,000	1,040,000	1,500,000
Net removals	308,000	360,000	360,000
Net change in inventory under construction	−20,000	15,000	20,000
Net change in vacancies	214,000	−5,000	260,000
Total private housing starts	1,480,000	1,410,000	2,140,000
Note: Net removals:			
Gross removals	407,000	510,000	620,000
Increase in public housing	(42,500)	(40,000)	(40,000)
Net increase in mobile homes	(56,500)	(110,000)	(220,000)
Total	308,000	360,000	360,000

Source: Based on census data.

those wanting to rent or buy. The remainder are held off the market because they have been sold, because they are dilapidated, or because they are second homes. It is primarily the available vacancies which exert a direct influence on housing starts.

The total demand from vacancies during the period covered by Table 11-1 is estimated at about 5 million. This exceeds a normal 8 to 10 percent of growth in households by about 1.5 million because of the fact that we entered the decade of the 1950s with a severe housing shortage resulting from the failure to build during World War II and the Depression. Once the level of vacancies had returned to normal, the demand from this source fell. The decrease in building from the 1950s to the 1960s was not as great as the drop in demand for vacancies because the other two factors (household formation and net removals) rose, although not strongly. In the 1970s the sharp growth in demand comes mainly from greater household formation. Still it is expected that more than a third of the increase in starts during this decade will be required to provide us with a more desirable level of vacancies.

Household Formation

Increases in the number of households form the largest part of building demand. Builders plan on being able to sell or rent their new units either to newly formed households or to those whom they may attract from existing units. In turn, emptied dwellings attract new households, are filled with families from other units, or perhaps are removed from the market. Any housing unit which fails to attract customers remains vacant.

One cannot assume that new families fill new houses. In fact, the opposite is true. New sales units attract primarily already existing households. Movements within the total stock of houses are complex. It is not possible to relate the need for specific buildings to new or old families. However, when all shifting is completed, one additional dwelling is needed for each added household.

A common error in picturing households and housing demand is to think in terms of the typical family of mother, father, and two or three children. It is simply wrong. In the post-World War II period, households with children have formed only a minor share of household growth. More often new households tend to be couples without children or, more important, units headed by single persons or by other nontypical family types. The widowed grandmother or the pair of young schoolteachers have played as great a role in increasing the need for dwellings as the typical family with children. Yet clearly, these other household types require a different form of housing from the traditional freestanding unit. It is the growth of these other households that has raised the demand for apartment houses so much above former periods.

What primary factors determine the number of households formed in a period? Basic is the growing size of the adult population. Changes in social attitudes and tastes have also increased desires for private dwellings. There has been a tendency for people and families to demand their own rather than shared quarters. This desire for privacy has accelerated in the past 20 years.

Some of the increased demand for greater privacy must be related to higher incomes. Low or falling incomes delay the time at which people marry and cause more to double up (share space). In depressions, more young couples live with their in-laws. As income rises, the number of individuals who can afford to maintain a separate household also expands.

Other factors which influence household formation in unusual periods are comparatively unimportant in normal times. Some households were not formed because of the wartime shortage of space. In theory people may not get married or may not form households if credit is tight or if rents and the prices of houses are high. However, moderate movements in these variables appear not to have much impact on household formation.

In fact, income changes do not seem to have altered demand for houses by more than 50,000 per year in the postwar period. On the other hand, a major depression like that of 1932 would cause a much sharper fall in the demand for houses. There were 300,000 to 400,000 fewer dwelling units required per year as a result of the low incomes of the Great Depression.

The general stability and lack of a great depression in the postwar period have enabled the demographers to do a rather good job of projecting possible household growth for the next 5 or 10 years. On the whole, the growth of demand from households for any period of 5 or 10 years in the future is both the most significant and also the most stable. It is not this underlying demand that causes the real estate cycle.

Net Removals

In addition to units needed to shelter new households, the economy must produce houses to replace those removed from the available stock. Net removals are gross removals minus nonconventional additions to the stock. Table 11-1 shows a surprising fact: Demand from net removals has failed to grow as fast as the stock of housing. In the 1970s, while the total housing stock will average close to 75 million, the expected net removals will total only 360,000 a year. This is less than .5 percent a year—far below what on the surface would seem a logical depreciation rate.

One of the explanations for this failure of net removals to grow is that while total removals have been going up slowly, the effect of this increase on the demand for conventional houses has been offset by the boom in mobile homes. Because they are less expensive and more available in many areas, the number of households making their primary home in mobile units has increased rapidly. (The term "mobile" is perhaps misleading, since the great majority of these units are now in fixed locations and on firm foundations.) The shipments of mobile homes grew from just over 100,000 units a year to nearly 600,000 a year in a single decade. Their growth has led to a new form of real estate investment—the mobile-home park.

Gross Removals

Gross removals arise from demolitions and other losses, such as those from fires, floods, and other disasters. Minor offsets occur when households occupy dwellings in previously nonresidential structures such as hotels and motels. In addition, there are a certain number of conversions and mergers. Conversions are dwellings formed when an existing unit is split to house more families; mergers are the contrasting movements when an extra family moves out. Such shifts in use may reflect alterations of the structure, but more frequently they are merely bookkeeping transactions. They record events such as the rental of some rooms in the house to nonrelatives. During the Depression, conversions or additions made up one of the largest sources of supply. In recent years, they seem to have been offset by mergers.

Demolitions are the most obvious type of removal. They occur because of road building, slum clearance, and the tearing down of units to furnish space for more modern structures. Other dwellings are demolished because they are located outside the main housing stream. For example, when people move from farms or desert small villages, the houses they leave behind stand vacant for awhile and then are eventually demolished. Similar losses have occurred as families have abandoned central cities.

The rate of losses to the stock from these many sources seems to have been growing gradually. During the 1950s, about .7 percent of the housing stock in existence at the beginning of each year was demolished. In recent years the demolition rate seems to have grown to about .9 percent. In addition, of course, the actual number grows somewhat more since these percentages are applicable to a constantly growing stock. Most demolitions are directly related to the size of the housing inventory. A small bulge occurs, however, when new construction is unusually heavy. More rapid movements from rural regions have also increased the rate of losses in the past.

Public Starts and Mobile Homes

The offsets to the gross removals might as readily be treated under a discussion of production. They include new dwellings added to the stock outside the normal channels for private housing construction. The public housing units are paid for by various levels of government and are reported separately. The increase in public housing has remained rather steady over the past decades. It would have risen, but a large number of subsidized units in recent years have been built as private, conventionally started units.

The biggest change in nonconventional production, of course, has come through the net increases in households living in trailers or mobile homes. This part of the supply is hard to project. Production from this source also seems to fluctuate in accordance with the real estate cycle. Our experience with what rates of depreciation, demolition, and obsolescence apply to the existing stock of mobile homes is so slight that we do not yet have a good fix on how large the replacement demand for these units is going to be. The bulk of them have not been in existence long enough to make depreciation and demolition a critical factor. The table assumes that mobile homes will add 220,000 units per year to our housing stock during this decade. This estimate assumes that old ones will be demolished at a quite rapid rate.

Lack of information makes it difficult to explain how or why the categories of net losses vary over time or whether they are related to other fluctuations in housing demand. Some seem to depend on the size of the stock, and some on the number of new families. We would expect the amount of net removals to be higher in boom periods, and we know it will be much lower if there is a severe depression.

The influence of the availability of mortgage credit is also hard to estimate. Cheaper financing increases some types of removals, while it holds down others. Since mobile homes are financed by a type of consumer credit with much higher interest rates than mortgage credit, availability of this financing has been relatively better in periods of tight money. As a result, the actual number of mobile homes used for houses probably has a small contracyclical component. This does not show up in mobile-home shipments, however, because within the period of shipment, large numbers of them move into inventories held by dealers rather than actually becoming part of the housing stock.

VACANCIES

As we have noted, most of the large year-to-year fluctuations in housing starts are caused by rapid changes in the number of vacancies. In certain quarters, inventory changes have taken place at an annual rate of over 500,000 units. Included in the housing inventories are units under construction and those held vacant and available for sale or rent.

Inventories of goods in process are required because of the lag between starts and completions. The number of uncompleted units is determined by the length of the production process and by the changing rate of new starts.

A normal stock of vacant units is needed for new sales and population mobility. An insufficient supply, as in the postwar period, creates a nearly intolerable situation for those requiring different accommodations or wishing to migrate. While individual owners desire no vacancies, the aggregate need is met through prices or rents which make it worthwhile for each to hold his or her share of vacancies in turn. Normal available vacancies should equal between 3.5 and 4.0 percent of the stock. To this must be added about 6.0 to 6.5 percent of the total housing stock for "not-available" vacancies.

Movements of vacancies around this level have been important. Desired and actual vacancies need not be equal. Because of builders' and sellers' errors of optimism and pessimism, additions to the housing stock diverge from final demand. The resulting shortages or overages influence future starts. The reaction of builders to these vacancies depends on the market's organization. There is strong evidence that changes in mortgage availability or terms are among the basic factors causing these unwanted vacancies to fluctuate as they do.

Types of Vacancies

Five major housing submarkets exist: (1) newly constructed single-family houses not yet sold or occupied, (2) previously occupied units being offered for resale, (3) new rental units, (4) previously occupied units offered for rent, and (5) not-available vacancies.

The level of vacancies in one sector may fall temporarily as that in another rises. Builders of new houses attract a surge of buyers by easier credit. New rental units entice tenants from older ones with lures of status or amenities. Then adjustments occur through the price mechanism and the type of new construction started. A feedback causes starts to fall when vacancies rise, and vice versa. Its timing will vary. Vacancies in new houses that are for sale will have an impact on new starts with only a short delay. On the other hand, vacancies in older rental units may not be reflected in lowered starts for several years.

Sales-Type Vacancies   Although information on both total vacancies and their components is increasing rapidly, it is still inadequate. Since 1955, vacancy rates for all sales-type units have varied between .5 and 1.5 percent of all units, or from approximately 250,000 to 850,000 dwellings. For-sale vacancies have increased by as much as 10 percent of starts in critical years.

New sales-type vacancies are the smallest and, under normal circumstances, have the most rapid impact on new starts. Because of carrying costs, any lengthening of the period of sale rapidly erodes the builder's profits. Furthermore, the volume of unsold new units is controlled by limited builders' capital and by the unwillingness of lending agencies to finance additional starts when the builder has a backlog of unsold units.

Vacancies for sale are also found among existing units. Again owners attempt to keep them at a minimum. Most vacancies are due primarily to emergencies, death, foreclosures, or migration. Real estate people advise against vacating a unit prior to its sale because an owner's expenses continue for the empty unit, placing him or her at a disadvantage in bargaining with prospective purchasers.

While vacancies in existing units slow sales and lower prices of competing units, their impact on starts is less immediate than that of vacancies in newly constructed houses. A particular area may experience a local economic disaster, with accompanying high vacancies that will have little or no influence on starts elsewhere. Thus the spatial separation of markets leads to higher total vacancies for the country.

Empty Rental Units   The probability of sizable increases in unwanted vacancies is greater for rental than for sales-type units. The quarterly census surveys indicate that rental vacancies nearly doubled between 1955 and 1961. Moreover, even though rental vacancies rose nearly as fast as new construction, starts continued to expand. In 1961, apartment starts surpassed their previous (1925) peak, while a new postwar peak for rental vacancies was also established.

Between 1961 and 1970 the rate of available rental vacancies fell from 8.7 to 5.3 percent. It then started to rise under the impetus of the boom of the early 1970s. In recent years, about a quarter to a third of vacant rental units have appeared to be located in buildings less than 3 years old. This is equivalent to a 30 to 40 percent vacancy rate for new structures.

Rental vacancies are nearly four times as numerous as vacancies in sales-type units. There are several explanations for these higher vacancy rates: (1) To avoid lowering rents on occupied units, an owner may maximize returns by allowing vacancies to increase rather than by cutting rents. (2) In a market so complex and diverse as rentals, the scarcity of reliable information tends to breed inaction and hence an increase in vacancies. (3) During the first 2 years of operation, delays in renting are normal. The total time for new construction between start and full occupancy covers a 3- to 4-year span, and thus a long period elapses before the vacancies feed back and cause a curtailment of new starts.

Not-Available Vacancies   For a wide variety of reasons, about 60 percent of all vacancies are not available for rent or sale. Some units have been rented or sold and are awaiting their new occupants; others are held in estates; still others are dilapidated and scheduled for demolition.

An important subgroup in this category includes seasonal units—vacation homes or those occupied temporarily by households with primary residences elsewhere. Seasonal units, like second homes, are not available to meet the needs of other households, even though they serve a definite function in our standing stock. It has been thought that with higher income and a greater emphasis on recreation, the percentage of second homes in the total stock and in production ought to rise faster than household growth. But no burst of demand for second homes has occurred. In fact, the 1970 census reported fewer in this category than in 1960. Second homes are one of the possible factors which might raise demand above that shown in the projections. It is an area, of course, where financing may be especially important, since these units are not a necessity. Their growth may also be seriously affected by energy and environmental factors.

Financing and Vacancies

Credit is a major variable influencing the margin by which starts exceed or fall short of final demand. Tightening of credit affects the terms and prices of construction loans, as well as raising the points builders of single-family units must pay for financing. Movements in terms have been sufficient to wipe out all potential profits. For promoters of apartments, availability of credit rather than price has been a critical factor because most often their main concern is to minimize required equities.

The following scenario illustrates the effect of credit terms on starts: When money is easy, builders rush starts. They have more money available, and they pay less for it. With easier terms, they can attract families from existing units. The effect is to increase inventories. Finally the pressure of vacancies builds up. Houses cannot be sold; apartments cannot be rented. Prices fall; foreclosures rise. Lenders are more careful. Less money is available, and the number of starts falls.

THE PRICE AND QUALITY OF NEW CONSTRUCTION

Real estate financing also has a great impact on the size, quality, and price of units constructed.

Most units started today more than meet the basic housing needs of families. They include extra space, extra refinements, extra bathrooms, garages, appliances, and all the other items considered an integral part of our standard of living. The space and quality built into houses have advanced fairly regularly. Values have expanded as households have strived to meet unfilled desires. Prices have risen even faster. The cost per item in houses has increased at the same time as the number and quality of items have risen. While our housing standards are high compared with those of other countries and with past standards, they are still not as high as the average family would like.

It has been possible to raise the amount we pay and to fulfill some of these desires because family incomes and assets have gone up and because the mortgage market, through easier terms, has enabled persons with given incomes to expand the amount of house they can purchase. With both forces operating, capital expenditures have risen rapidly.

The average amount of expenditure per housing start fluctuates with the level of household income, with mortgage terms, and with changes in consumer preferences. A desire for more expensive housing raises the amount of income families allocate to their mortgage payments. While in the postwar period small fluctuations have occasionally caused these factors to fall and housing expenditures to drop temporarily, their general trend has been upward.

As incomes rise, families have more money to spend on discretionary items. Because housing is a necessity, its share of additional income should be expected to be somewhat smaller than it was at prior levels. (Technically, its income elasticity is less than 1.) Since housing needs are met directly after food and clothing needs, minimum housing requirements are taken care of at low incomes. Additional housing expenditures have to compete with demands for all other goods. Accordingly, most past studies have shown that as incomes rise, the amounts spent on housing rise only 60–80 percent as rapidly as other expenditures.

The postwar period has witnessed a certain shift in these relationships. The amount of spending per family for new houses has risen about as fast as income. Demand for better housing rose at the same time incomes increased. The shift in tastes has been attributed to suburban living, higher homeownership rates, a more family-oriented life, and many other factors. Whatever its cause, it resulted in increasing the amount spent on housing faster than expected.

When a family allocates a given sum to housing payments, the amount of house it can buy depends upon the available terms it finds in the mortgage market. The easier the terms, the more mortgage it can carry and the more valuable or larger a house it can purchase. The amount of expenditure per housing unit has moved closely in line with shifting mortgage terms. Longer amortization periods and lower downpayments have brought about the purchase of expensive units. Fluctuating interest rates have caused equivalent rises and falls in the amount of housing purchased.

INFLATION AND HIGH INTEREST RATES

Inflation is frequently considered a major factor making real estate a good investment. This is true. At the same time, however, inflation and the threat of inflation raise interest rates and periodically make it difficult, if not impossible, to borrow money at any feasible rate.

To understand why inflation is both good and bad for real estate, we must recognize the difference between "real interest rates" and "nominal interest rates." Nominal interest rates are simply contract rates in current dollars, with no correction made for any changes which may occur in the purchasing power of the dollar. Real interest rates are nominal rates which have been corrected to take into account any change in the purchasing power (value) of the dollar during the period the loan is outstanding.

Real and Nominal Interest Rates

When we subtract the expected rate of inflation from the contract—nominal—interest rate, we find the real interest rate. For example, assume that a lender is willing to accept a real rate of return of 5 percent to lend money for a year. She expects to lend $100 and get back $105. But if during the year prices rise 5 percent, the $105 she gets back will purchase only the same amount of goods as the $100 she lent. She would receive no real interest even though she had lent her money for a year. If prices rose 8 percent, the amount of goods she could purchase would be 3 percent less than she lent, or she would have a negative real interest rate. If prices were rising at an 8 percent rate, she would have to ask for a 13 percent contract—nominal—rate in order to earn a 5 percent real rate of return and still be compensated for the fact that each dollar she receives will purchase 8 percent less goods.

Real Estate and Purchasing Power

A mortgage loan or contract to lend money provides that a certain number of dollars will be lent and that the borrower will then periodically pay another sum of dollars to the lender for an agreed-upon future period. These payments include both interest on the loan and the repayment of the principal lent originally.

When the loan is made, the lender gives the borrower a certain amount of purchasing power. If prices rise while the loan is outstanding, the dollars the lender receives back will have less purchasing power. The borrower will gain; the lender will lose command over goods and services.

People with capital who expect that prices will rise try to act so as to avoid a loss in purchasing power. One way they may be able to do this is by investing in goods or in real assets such as real estate. Real estate is a major sector in which values are expected to rise when prices rise or purchasing power falls. This occurs because real property produces rents. If these rents can be raised, the level of current income will move up. Rents, or the return to the property, are expected to rise more or less in line with other prices, although often with a lag. If this happens, the owner of a property finds that, to the degree that the rents he charges rise along with the prices of other goods and services, his purchasing power has not declined. He is protected against inflation. The same, of course, is also true for an owner-occupier. His basic cost (that of the house itself), but not taxes and maintenance, is fixed at the price level at which the purchase was made.

Equities and Monetary Assets

Closely related to the idea of real and nominal rates is the relationship between equities and monetary, or dollar-denominated, assets. Mortgages or savings deposits have a definite value in dollars. For this reason they are called *monetary* assets. Real estate and common stocks are called *equities*, or *nonmonetary* assets. Owners of monetary assets are paid interest for the use of their money and for any potential decline in purchasing power. The interest rate must cover both factors.

In contrast, investors in common stock or real estate are owners of real property. No one owes them anything. Their return is not fixed by any contract, but is related to the earnings of the real asset. The earnings or profit on real estate depends upon its future net income and the way in which that income is valued in the market. Total income includes both the current return from the investment and the amount received when the asset is sold. Since neither of these is fixed in terms of money, it is assumed, and history shows, that such returns do tend to increase as the purchasing power of the dollar falls and to decrease when purchasing power rises. However, the relationship is far from exact and may not hold for as many as 5 or 10 years. In the long run, though, ownership of an equity does tend to give an income which varies with price changes and which therefore is a protection against inflation.

Because people with capital can protect themselves against inflation by buying real assets or equities rather than lending out their money, they will agree to lend only if the nominal interest rate they are promised is sufficient to give them the same real rate of return they can expect to receive by investing and holding property themselves. This means that lending contracts must promise a repayment of the principal, a certain real rate of interest, and an additional amount sufficient to offset the expected amount of inflation—that is, the expected fall in purchasing power—or no one will lend money.

The fact that income rises somewhat, but not exactly, with prices raises problems for equity owners when they have to meet specified payments on loans. This is why although in theory, buyers of property in an inflation should be able and willing to pay the high nominal interest rates necessary to correct for the rate of inflation, in practice it does not work out quite that way. The risks to a lender of assuming that everyone will be able to meet higher mortgage payments because of inflation are too great for a normal lender to take. Lenders will agree to make loans to home buyers only on the basis of today's income, not on an income which may at some future time be higher because of inflation. This makes sense. While it may be true that on the average people's incomes will rise with inflation and that they therefore will be able to make higher payments, there will still be a sizable number of individuals for whom inflation will make it harder, not easier, to meet increased payments. In any inflation a fair number of families find that their income does not rise as rapidly as prices. They have to spend more of their budget on food and other necessities, and they have less available to make mortgage payments.

The difficulty of borrowing when nominal rates are high is aggravated in an inflation by the fact that deposit institutions find it harder to lend. They tend to have large portfolios of loans made at preinflation interest rates. As a result, they have trouble attracting funds in competition with lenders who have no money tied up in existing long-term loans. Corporations or borrowers who can adjust their incomes rapidly to the new higher nominal rates can pay higher amounts to attract money. Institutions with funds tied up at lower rates lose deposits. If inflation continues, a whole new system of lending may have to develop to enable loans to be made with high-enough nominal rates to guarantee a real interest rate attractive for lenders.

Uncertainty of Costs and Income

Changing rates of inflation also cause problems because they create uncertainty. In periods of rapidly rising prices, no one can be certain whether future prices will rise as fast, faster, or at slower rates. Uncertainty makes it more difficult to develop real property because such development extends over considerable time. Many firms have spent years planning a new development only to find all their calculations and arrangements washed out by higher costs. After spending 2 years putting together a financing package for $3 million, it is devastating to find that the total of the lowest bids for construction is $4 million and the project cannot move forward.

As with financing, it is not enough to say that if inflation persists, even the higher price will be profitable. A construction loan granted a year ago may not be enough to finish the building if costs move up too rapidly. The builder runs out of money and stops work. Such buildings often seem to stay unfinished for months or years without moving forward to completion. They are in the process of foreclosure, or the builder is waiting for a new source of additional funds.

Furthermore, no one can guarantee that prices and income will continue to rise. Costs might stabilize or rise at a much slower rate. A new building erected on the assumption that rents will rise may be foreclosed before they do. In the case of many office and commercial buildings, lenders will not make funds available until major leases are signed. These leases may not be profitable at new, higher cost levels.

Thus, while the threat of inflation raises the demand for properties and their prices, it is also another principal factor causing the development and production of real property to fluctuate. If rising prices and costs are to make buildings profitable, investors must be able to find money, and at a price they can afford. They must have sufficient capital to hold properties during periods when changing prices cause costs to outrun rents.

SUMMARY: FLUCTUATIONS IN REAL ESTATE DEMAND

The facts and analysis presented in this chapter and the previous one are summarized in Figure 11-2. An understanding of what this figure means and its implications may well constitute the most important knowledge that a real estate investor or lender can acquire. The figure explains why real estate goes through such sharp fluctuations in volume of sales, construction, prices, and profits. Let us examine the flow of information shown in the diagram.

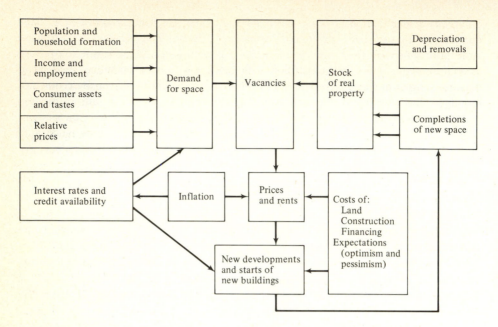

Figure 11-2 Demand and supply: the causes of real estate fluctuations.

Demand for Space   In the upper left-hand sector, we note the primary forces causing shifts in the demand for space: (1) growth in population and households; (2) changes in income and jobs; (3) changes in consumer wealth, liquidity, and tastes; (4) prices of other goods; and (5) interest rates and credit availability. Just as these forces cause the movements in housing demand, they also cause changes in demands for other types of buildings and land. With the exception of interest rates and credit availability, in normal periods most of these factors influencing demand grow in a quite stable manner. Their continued growth gives an underlying strength to real estate markets.

Stock of Real Property   The amount of space available to meet demand comes primarily from existing buildings. In any period this supply is augmented by completions of buildings started previously, and it is reduced by net removals. While the changes in supply tend to be small compared with the total stock (say, 2 to 3 percent in a year), they may be large compared with the growth of demand in a short period such as a year. Many buildings are started when demand is high. They come onto the market in bunches, causing an oversupply. Such gluts compared with new demand are particularly common in a small area such as a city, suburb, or town. Here demand may fluctuate more strongly, and important new construction tends to be concentrated and to come on the market all at once.

Vacancies, Prices, and Rents   The movements in demand and in the stock of space show up in changes in vacancies. In most periods, available vacant space is relatively scarce compared with total stock and overall demand, and this fact causes movements in vacancies to fluctuate widely. When building activity is well above normal or if demand fails to grow, the number of vacancies can shoot up. A 1 percent change in demand or in the stock may mean a 30 percent change in available vacant space. Changes in vacancies affect prices of real estate and rents. Because existing real estate becomes empty and turns over slowly, most prices and rents also adjust only slowly. Prices and rents are also influenced by movements in the costs of land, financing, and construction as well as by the impact of inflation working through change in the general price level.

New Building   Properties are developed and new construction occurs in the expectation of future profits. Thus the basic decisions to develop and build come when a comparison of prices, rents, and costs shows that a profit is probable. All three of these critical decision factors are very unstable. The income from new buildings can rise sharply if demand has outrun new construction. In such periods, buildings coming onto the market are rented or sold rapidly and at inflated prices. Developers and investors enjoy booming profits. On the other hand, a period of too rapid expansion brings about the opposite situation. Buildings take longer than normal to rent or sell. Price concessions must be granted. Profits fall, and foreclosures and bankruptcies rise.

The movements in income and profits are accentuated by swings in the expectations of builders, developers, and investors. A reasonable profit opportunity looked at through rose-colored glasses seems irresistible. Even a poor deal may look good enough to undertake. Developers' optimism is increased by investors only too willing to furnish funds. Developers may have guaranteed profits for themselves even before construction starts. The level of actual building is greater than the underlying situation warrants. When this becomes clear, the market does not simply swing back to normal; it overshoots on the downside. Gradually, because of too little building, profit opportunities again become plentiful. Potentially very successful investments are available. An expansion starts again.

These fluctuations are increased by movements in interest rates and credit availability. A 1 or 2 percent change in interest rates can multiply potential profits 10 or 20 times. Even more significant in ending booms may be the fact that money becomes available only at extremely high—really prohibitive—rates. In 1974 construction loans even to large, well-regarded builders ranged from 15 to 20 percent, with added fees and charges. When mortgage money disappears, development grinds to a halt. Builders and promoters find themselves paying large carrying costs on land and plans which cannot be completed. Available cash flows are used in an attempt to meet commitments for projects whose hoped-for income may be delayed several years.

It is the multiplication or acceleration of shifts in basic demand that creates such severe problems. The closer an operation is to the underlying demand of households, the more moderate are fluctuations. In a typical fluctuation, the total demand for space may vary by only 1 or 2 percent. Average rents and prices may change by very little more. On the other hand, the small changes in underlying demand and supply cause housing starts to fluctuate by 40 percent. Other types of building and development may come to a complete halt until balance is once again regained.

The likelihood that such fluctuations may occur exists in almost all real estate ventures. This is a fundamental reason why certain types of ventures promise very high profits. The high yields are accompanied by a possibility of being completely wiped out. Each investor or lender must decide what risks he or she is willing to take and whether the promised returns are great enough to cover the risks involved. The real property field is broad enough to offer almost anyone the desired mixture of promised yields and risks. Successful investors make certain they get what they are paying for. They avoid risks they cannot afford and investments which do not promise yields commensurate with the underlying risks.

While most of our analysis in these two chapters has been illustrated by data from the housing market, it should be clear that the same factors apply to almost all real estate markets. Major fluctuations in the demand for space—together with a lag in the development of new space, followed frequently by a sudden excess of completed developments—lead to rapid shifts in vacancies, prices, and rents. How these can affect the market is well brought out by the following article—"Downtown, It's a Tenants' Market," by Shirley L. Benzer—from the *New York Times* of August 11, 1974.

When a prominent real estate lawyer asserted recently that "Wall Street is a disaster area," he wasn't refering to the securities markets.

He meant that the commercial office market in New York's financial district has reached the once unheard-of vacancy rate of 11 percent. This means that at least 8 million square feet of office space, out of the 70 million the Real Estate Board of New York estimates is the area's total, is empty. And probably an additional 1.5 million square feet is available for sublease. This adds up to about a dozen typical Manhattan office towers.

Many downtown property owners now spend sleepless nights worrying whether their tenants, whom they once considered to be virtually permanent, will go out of business or move uptown. They are also troubled by the fast-rising prices of fuel oil, labor and repairs.

"The real estate people are in a severe recession, almost a depression," the lawyer said.

Much of downtown's untenanted space is still raw—it has never been occupied. New York's financial center, like many other areas across the country, was overbuilt when business was exploding upward in the nineteen-sixties.

Between 1965 and 1970 about 35 million square feet of new office space was created south of Chambers Street to house the expanding businesses.

In those heady days real estate brokers bought up properties and assembled them into building sites for developers, paying as much as $500 a square foot, even in fringe areas such as South Street and Water Street.

Lewis Rudin, an investment builder, says that the securities industry, anticipating 20-million-share days and the need for more space, prodded the builders on.

"The brokerage houses," he recalls, "were leap-frogging over each other to get prestigious space."

But securities people remember that they were pressured by brokers who showed them floor plans and touted the space as "the last image-building office in town."

Also there are some people who still insist that very persuasive tactics were used to get some tenants to sign leases "at the top of the market," which was about $12 a square foot.

"They were plied with wine, women or whatever was necessary," one real estate man declares. "And a few Wall Street guys woke up to find new Cadillacs in their driveways." But a number of Wall Street houses are now unhappy with their leases.

"We never figured out who signed our lease," the executives at one company complain.

At another big brokerage house, when it came time to re-elect the president, the high cost of the office space and the "vicious, airtight" terms of the lease, worked against him.

In 1970, when some of the buildings were ready for occupancy, the investment business began falling off.

The problem became aggravated about two years later when midtown Manhattan also found it had a lot of empty office space. Midtown landlords started dropping their rents and thus attracted several large investment houses, including Lazard Freres & Co. and Smith, Barney & Co., which moved up from the financial center and brought with them about a dozen large law firms.

More recently the trust departments of several banks, including the Chase Manhattan Bank and the Morgan Guaranty Trust Company, have moved to midtown offices to be closer to their clients and to physically divorce themselves from banking activities.

The New York Stock Exchange reports that 46 of its member firms went out of business last year, while 32 disappeared through mergers or acquisitions. This year, by mid-July, 19 more member firms had gone out of business and seven had been absorbed into other brokerage houses. And Robert H. B. Baldwin of Morgan Stanley & Co. recently predicted that another 100 securities firms could disappear in the coming year.

In the real estate community this means that about 100 securities companies have already, in effect, become competitors of landlords. Since most office leases can be canceled only by bankruptcy many companies that have merged are trying to sublet the space they no longer need.

Then there's the World Trade Center—two gargantuan office towers with more than eight million square feet of space that originally was to be rented only to tenants in international trade.

However, an owner of a nearby building, who feels that the government-sponsored center is competing with private enterprise, charges that "even a tailor can get space there—and he doesn't have to come from Hong Kong."

Building owners are generally incensed that the World Trade Center doesn't pay taxes to the city, as they do. Instead of paying taxes the center makes an annual payment for services. But Harry B. Helmsley, a major real estate owner, says the amount it pays is "criminal."

Mr. Helmsley estimates that privately held property that is assessed equally with the World Trade Center pays the city at least $52-million a year in taxes. Last year the center paid the city $1.5-million, and the most it is ever scheduled to pay is $6-million a year.

Downtown landlords predict that the securities business will eventually expand to absorb some of the excess office space. In the meantime they are trying to draw new tenants into the area, such as foreign and domestic banks, law firms and engineering firms.

To limit their losses over the short term, landlords are signing five-year leases at what is considered the break-even point—$5 to $7.50 a square foot in older buildings and $8.50 to $10 a square foot in new buildings, according to Bertram F. French of Cushman & Wakefield, Inc., renting and managing agents for many downtown office towers. An owner's operating costs, taxes and interest charges in new buildings can range from $7 to $9 a square foot.

Now that it's a tenants' market, landlords are also offering concessions, Frederick K. Marek, a real estate broker with the firm of Julien J. Studley, Inc., says.

"A new tenant might get his moving expenses paid by the owner, or his old lease taken over or a more-than-routine office installation," he explained. An old tenant might get more favorable renewal terms, if the lease is about to expire, simply by mentioning that he's thinking of moving."

Since no one is likely to build in such a market, some of the expensive downtown building sites are now being operated as parking lots to offset the taxes and mortgage interest that can run between $1-million and $2-million a year for an average site.

Lehman Brothers, the investment house, is among the firms that is not going ahead with plans for a new headquarters, although it has already acquired a site at the foot of Broad Street.

Mr. Helmsley is also postponing construction of six million square feet of office space scheduled for Battery Park City, a residential-commercial enclave being developed on the Hudson, adjacent to the financial district.

Sylvan Lawrence, a large property owner in lower Manhattan who is recognized as an expert on real estate in the area, says he is trying to keep out any jackals who might be closing in for a kill. "Nothing's for sale down here," he snaps.

Yet Daniel Rose, a partner in the development company of Rose Associates, has a site on Whitehall Street that he says is available for about $150 a square foot.

Another casualty of the real estate recession appears to be Cushman & Wakefield, the biggest leasing concern in the financial district. The RCA Corporation, which acquired Cushman & Wakefield in 1970 after the banner years downtown, is now trying to divest itself of the company.

On the positive side, real estate people are exulting in the American Express Company's decision to remain in New York and to consolidate its offices in the new building at 2 New York Plaza, which has stood empty for several years.

The structure, which cost about $50 a square foot to build, was recently sold to American Express for $32 a square foot by the estate of the late Sol Atlas and by John McGrath, president of the East New York Savings Bank.

Some detractors call this a game of musical chairs, however, since American Express will be emptying its employees out of two older buildings on lower Broadway and other scattered locations.

But this illustrates a growing trend downtown: Older buildings will be forsaken for the new, now that prices are so competitive.

Some people expect a change in the area's character, to be brought about by Battery Park City and by Manhattan Landing, a mixed-use community planned on the East River. They will house a total of 22,500 families and will bring schools, shopping centers and theaters to the neighborhood.

The housing, which is expected to draw tenants away from some of the deteriorating sections of Brooklyn as well as from other parts of the city, is designed to provide lower Manhattan with its own labor force. Since jobs will be within walking distance, little additional strain on the city's transportation system is expected.

But not all real estate people believe this will be a panacea. Mr. Studley, of the firm bearing his name, suggests that everyone downtown help make the area inviting rather than wait for something to happen.

"Has anyone thought about planting a garden on those vacant lots?" he asks.

QUESTIONS AND PROBLEMS

1 Examine the list of factors influencing residential construction. Pick five of the nine categories and explain how each subfactor would affect construction.
2 What are the basic sources of demand for additional housing starts?
3 Discuss the factors which cause more money to be spent on each new dwelling unit.
4 The number of housing starts in a decade is roughly 50 percent higher than the number of additional households. Why is this so?
5 Vacancies are usually thought of as unwanted and undesirable; yet Table 11-1 shows a demand for new units arising from a vacancy factor. Does this make sense?
6 Some figures for new housing are higher than those in Table 11-1 because they include new mobile homes as part of added housing. Reconstruct Table 11-1 so that it shows total new housing units instead of housing starts.
7 What is the difference between "real" and "nominal" interest rates?
8 Why is real estate thought to be a good hedge against inflation?
9 Under what circumstances does inflation make a piece of real property a poor investment?
10 If the rate of inflation is 10 percent next year, do you think this will be good or bad for those in real estate and related industries?
11 Which would you expect to be more sensitive to credit terms and availability: income properties or single-family homes?
12 Discuss the factors that influence housing supply and demand.
13 Why do markets get "overbuilt"?

Chapter 12

The Big Four
Institutional Lenders

A large amount of activity in real estate markets centers around finding financing. It is not only in periods of tight money that the availability and terms of loans become a preoccupation of investors, brokers, and financiers. At all times, successful operations depend on the ability to find and make good loans under proper conditions. The profits of financial institutions depend on acquiring the loans which fit their needs.

Chapter 2 presented an overview of the mortgage market. Here we describe the various sources of funds in greater detail. For purposes of analysis, we divide lenders into four groups:

1 Most important are the big four institutional lenders; savings and loans (S&Ls), commercial banks (CBs), life insurance companies (LICs), and mutual savings banks (MSBs). They furnish nearly 80 percent of mortgage money.

2 The second largest suppliers of mortgage funds are the various levels of government—federal, state, and local. They hold about 12 percent of total mortgage funds. Their current lending is considerably higher, and they also subsidize many loans made by others.

3 The third primary source of mortgage money is made up of a wide assortment of other financial institutions, nonfinancial corporations, and individuals. These lenders are significant not for the amounts they lend but rather because they make all types of nontraditional, high-risk loans. They make many transactions possible which otherwise could not take place.

4   Finally, there is a group of financial institutions which furnish a rather minor amount of money but which are essential to the current market because they enable many of the others to be active. Included in this category are mortgage banks, mortgage investment trusts (MITs), and public and private mortgage insurance and guarantee programs.

What one can borrow and where depends upon finding a lender. What is lent depends upon the organization and the regulations of the individual institution. This chapter shows what various lenders do, why they do it, and the pressures they face.

Table 12-1 furnishes a broad overview of the major sources of real estate funds. From this table, together with the tables and the description of Chapter 2 and the discussion in this chapter and the following ones, we can obtain a basic understanding of the unique institutional structure of real estate financing.

This chapter examines in detail the four largest real estate lenders—those listed in the first four columns of Table 12-1. Since these large financial institutions do the bulk of real estate financing, they are usually the first approached by most prospective borrowers. In the case of income and specialized properties and for development loans, the approach is often through a mortgage company.

LEGAL REQUIREMENTS

Legal requirements play a significant role in how institutions perform mortgage lending. The most striking fact about them is their tremendous variation. While regulations are becoming more uniform, differences in what institutions are allowed to do are still important.

Legal requirements have developed separately for each type of institution. For CBs and S&Ls, a dual system of chartering and supervision by state and federal authorities exists. State units follow local laws, while national banks and federal S&Ls operate in accordance with their federal charters. Both federal and state units conform to regulations of the federal insuring authorities.

State regulations are especially varied. General statements can be made concerning the regulations which apply to federal units, but each state may establish almost unique regulations in its own jurisdiction. In many states, however, general provisions have been adopted which permit the state's institutions to make any loan allowed to a federal institution doing business in the state. Some state laws are specific, but legislatures attempt to keep them current with the federal acts. However, lags frequently develop as a result of the lack of urgency with which state legislatures may consider changes. In other cases, the state's rules may be far more liberal than those of the federal authorities. Therefore, while in general it is true that rules similar to the federal regulations apply throughout the country, in actuality any particular state may differ vastly from the norm. Rules are in constant flux. S&Ls and MSBs have been pushing for major changes in federal legislation.

MSBs and LICs are chartered only by states, although the MSBs have had laws introduced which would allow federal charters. Again wide variations in regulations exist, depending upon each firm's home state. The rules of LICs have an additional complexity. While regulated primarily by their home state, LICs must comply substan-

Table 12-1 Private Lending Institutions: Real Estate Activity

	S&Ls	CBs	LICs	MSBs	MITs	Mortgage companies	Other
Number	5,400	14,400	1,800	480	200	1,500	Not available
Mortgage loans (in billions)	$270	$140	$90	$75	$15	$12	$60
Regulatory system	Dual: federal and state	Dual: federal and state	Primarily state	Primarily state	Primarily non-regulated	Primarily non-regulated	Primarily non-regulated
Organization	All sizes, local and state	All sizes, local and state	National	Local	National	Local and regional	Local and national
Ownership	Mutual and stock	Stock	Mutual and stock	Mutual	Stock	Stock	Stock
Source of funds	Deposits	Deposits	Insurance reserves and pension funds	Deposits	Equity and short-term borrowing	Equity and short-term borrowing	Equity
Need for liquidity	Moderate	Great	Little	Moderate	Great	Great	Little
Role of real estate lending	80-90%	10-20%	30-40%	65-75%	100%	100%	Small
Preferred types of loans	Single-family: long-term and construction	Construction and long-term; commercial, income, and single-family	Long-term; income properties	Long-term; all types residential and other income	Development; construction; specialized income	All types; as agents or for sale to final lenders	High risk
Typical restrictions (exceptions in all cases)	30-year term; 80% of value—higher on insured; limited nonresidential; no equities	30-year term to 90% of value, but mainly 25-year term and 75% of value; no equities	25-30-year term; usually 75% of value; can purchase equities and joint ventures	25-30-year term; 80-90% of value; no equities	Few restrictions	Few restrictions	Few restrictions

tially with the investment requirements and limitations imposed on local or domestic insurers in any other state where they desire to do business.

Substantial compliance is a technical problem. How restrictive any state's regulations are for an outside firm frequently depends upon the individual company's surplus and the forms of liability it assumes. For most firms, New York State law is paramount. Since New York has traditionally been outstanding in the high quality of its insurance legislation, many other states follow its lead in establishing specific requirements.

Because regulations and traditions differ so much from place to place and because they are in constant flux, general descriptions of market conditions should not be considered necessarily representative of the conditions in specific markets. Rather, the prospective borrower should contact possible lenders to determine whether his or her needs can be satisfied. Knowledge of institutions provides an understanding of why the mortgage market has developed as it has as well as the reasons behind the behavior of particular lenders. Such information provides the background needed to be an effective participant in the mortgage market.

SAVINGS AND LOAN ASSOCIATIONS

As shown in Table 12-1, the largest source of funds to the mortgage market comes from the 5,400 S&Ls. They held over $270 billion in mortgages in 1976, or over 40 percent of the total owned by all financial institutions. Mortgages make up well over 80 percent of their assets. Their only other principal investment is a liquidity reserve composed of cash and United States government securities.

Organization

S&Ls started as primarily local, traditional small-scale organizations, but they have grown steadily in size in the postwar period. Recently the assets of the average (median) association totaled about $16 million. About half of the industry's loans are made by firms with less than $70 million in assets. The $70-million association, which can be considered most typical, has about 14,000 savers and maintains a stock of between 6,000 and 7,000 mortgage loans outstanding at any given time.

The average firm contrasts sharply with the giant holding companies in the S&L field, which may own over $5 billion in assets. More than 40 percent of the industry's volume is accounted for by less than 200 firms, each of which holds over $225 million in assets.

S&Ls are located in every state and in communities of all sizes. Their assets are distributed across the nation fairly evenly in proportion to population and wealth. There is some underrepresentation in the New England and Middle Atlantic states, the principal home of MSBs, and some overrepresentation in California, where the growth of S&Ls and that of the state have reinforced each other.

S&Ls are chartered by both the federal government and the states. The more than 60 percent of the associations that are state-chartered include a large number of very small associations whose depositors are not insured against loss by federal insurance. Federal associations hold more than 55 percent of the assets of all associations. The greatest difference between state and federal associations is probably found in California. That state charters regular stock associations for profit. These firms tend to be the largest, both in the state and in the nation. As a result, in California, the largest S&L state, state-chartered associations hold a much higher percentage of assets than is the case nationally.

Operations

The unique organizational feature of S&Ls is that they exist primarily to gather small deposits of families and individuals, which funds they invest primarily in mortgage loans to help finance homeownership. They specialize in individual home loans. In fact, for maximum tax benefits at least 82 percent of their mortgages must be on residential properties.

Most savings association loans are made directly from their own offices. The bulk of their business is limited to lending within their home state or within 100 miles of their headquarters. While in the past most have had sufficient outlets for their funds locally, at times when deposits were growing rapidly, this restriction has pinched. As a result, regulations now allow associations to participate in or share loans over a wider area. Depending upon a state's regulations, S&Ls can lend from 5 to 25 percent of their portfolio outside their normal lending area.

S&Ls lend for construction purposes, to purchase a house, to refinance an existing loan on a house, to finance improvements on houses, for mortgages on other types of property including land, for mobile homes, and for educational loans.

The strength of S&Ls tends to be in their local market knowledge. As a result, they specialize in loans on existing houses. The proper valuation of such loans often depends on special local circumstances. Because they have neighborhood know-how and can work out arrangements to fit individual needs, they can judge the market more carefully and lend to borrowers whom other types of lenders could not reach. Because of their specialized knowledge, the appraisals of S&Ls tend to be higher, the amount they lend on older homes has been greater, and the period over which the loan must be paid off is longer than for other institutions.

Because this market has been fairly well protected from competition from other lenders, S&Ls have been able to charge somewhat higher interest rates on their loans than the other lending institutions. Typically, also, they seek somewhat higher fees. A fee of 1.5 percent to write the mortgage is not unusual. In addition, their prepayment fees, which may be as large as the interest payable for from 3 months to 1 year, tend to be higher than those of banks, but not necessarily higher than those of insurance companies.

The degree to which associations depart from their traditional pattern of local loans on existing homes depends upon their size, their particular local competitive situations, and their deposit flows. When the demand for funds from their traditional borrowers is adequate, most associations are unwilling to invest in government-underwritten mortgages, with their lower returns and more time-consuming processing.

However, some associations have used the government loan market as a method of adjusting their lending in response to more uneven deposit flows in recent years. When flows have been high, they have been more prone to accept government-underwritten and other special types of loans. They have also participated in shared loans in other areas. As deposit flows have fallen, they have tended to pull back to their preferred market of direct conventional loans serviced by their own staff. Larger associations have also vigorously entered into the tract and multiunit market. They have been aggressive in making loans on land and construction and also the final, permanent loans on new tract units, condominiums, and apartment houses.

Regulations

As the pattern of loans by savings associations has shifted in response to changed market conditions, the restrictiveness of regulations by the Home Loan Bank System and state commissioners has been gradually reduced. Relaxations have allowed higher loan-to-value percentages and longer terms on home loans, plus an increased ability to make loans on commercial property, land, mobile homes, home improvements, and other types of consumer borrowing related to the home.

Although the regulations have been changing at a rapid pace and continue to do so, the general pattern persists. Loans are restricted to a maximum percentage of the appraised value and to specific maturities. How restrictive the regulations are depends on the type of property, on whether there is full amortization of the loan, and on the type of borrower. In addition, while the ability to make loans of riskier types has increased, regulations continue to control the percentage of such loans in the portfolio.

Thus, as a typical pattern, we may examine the required downpayment or its converse, the percentage of loan to value. On government-insured loans, required downpayments are the minimum allowed by the FHA. On mortgages with the top 20–25 percent of loan value guaranteed by a private mortgage insurance company, 95 percent of value can be loaned. On owner-occupied single-family houses in the moderate price range, 90 percent of value can be loaned with up to 30 years to pay. On loans for more expensive owner-occupied houses, the limits are frequently 80 percent of value with 30 years to pay. On other types of property the limits are most likely to be 70 or 75 percent, with amortization required over 25 years. However, in most cases, short-term loans of 2 or 3 years for a smaller percentage of value can be written without amortization.

When we look at the actual loans made, as opposed to the regulations, we find that loans on new houses are most typically for 30 years, with only a small percentage requiring more rapid amortization. Loan-to-value ratios vary from 95 percent down, with the average being close to 80 percent. The high ratios apply primarily to owner-occupied homes with mortgage guarantees (explained in the next chapter). The percentage loaned also depends upon the size of the loan. In 1974 the average size of loan was around $30,000. On existing homes, the average length of the loan tends to be several years less than on a new unit, and the average amount loaned compared with value also tends to be somewhat less.

When we examine the actual portfolios we find that as a whole, S&Ls make about 80 percent of their loans (by value) on one- to four-family houses. Ten percent of their money has gone to apartment houses, and about 10 percent for all other types of loans. Of this last sector, the largest part by far is loaned for commercial properties. While the amount of money being loaned for raw land and its development and for consumer purposes has been increasing rapidly in percentage terms, such loans remain a fairly small part of overall portfolios.

Service Corporations

In 1964 Congress authorized federally chartered S&Ls to invest up to 1 percent of assets in subsidiary service corporations, owned by a single association or by a group of institutions. The powers of these subsidiaries were originally circumscribed to "service" activities such as data processing, property appraisal, and loan credit services. However, service corporation powers were expanded over time, the number of permissible activities was increased, and borrowing limitations were relaxed.

The federal test today permits service corporations to engage in activities "closely related" to housing and S&L operations. In recent years, service corporations have been active in residential and commercial property development, mortgage banking, escrow, trustee and tax services, and low-income-housing construction and urban redevelopment. These activities are either permitted by Federal Home Loan Bank regulation or approved on a case-by-case basis by the Bank Board. Examples of disapproved activities in the past include sponsorship of REITs and ownership of travel and advertising agencies and consumer finance companies.

State guidelines for service corporations usually parallel federal regulations or exceed them, with a few states permitting investment authority up to 3 percent of assets. By 1974, approximately half of all S&Ls had a service corporation investment of some kind. In a highly competitive environment, S&Ls have come to value the diversification and profit potential of the service corporation investment.

COMMERCIAL BANKS

CBs are by far the largest financial intermediaries in terms of both numbers and assets. In 1975 their assets totaled over $900 billion. However, their real estate loans, at close to $140 billion, represented slightly less than 15 percent of their total assets. The importance of banks in real estate lending has risen steadily in the postwar period. In 1945, with total real estate loans of only $4.7 billion, their mortgage lending was the least significant of the four large financial institutions. Now, as a group, banks form the second largest mortgage market.

Moreover, their market impact far surpasses their relative share. They are the largest construction lenders; in addition, they perform many supplemental functions for other originators who make interim loans prior to selling mortgages to final lenders. Furthermore, their sharp year-to-year shifts in commitments to buy mortgages have caused magnified repercussions on yields and terms.

Organization

There are over 14,000 CBs. They vary in size from those with over $60 billion in assets to many with less than $1 million. Spread throughout the nation, they normally lend locally, but in many states, because of branch banking, the concept of local loans almost always encompasses entire metropolitan areas and may include whole states.

The importance of mortgage lending to individual banks varies tremendously. For example, the share of assets of the large money-market banks in New York and Chicago invested in real estate loans has been only about 6 percent. Many of the smaller country banks, however, are usually loaned up to their maximum legal limit.

Their traditional view of themselves as purveyors mainly of short-term credit complicates the role of CBs in the mortgage market. By statute and tradition, they have sought assets more liquid than mortgages as investment outlets for their demand deposits. On the other hand, because mortgages have offered the advantage of high yields for their time deposits, CBs have been particularly active in mortgage lending when such deposits were expanding. Recently their mortgage holdings have averaged about 38 percent of these savings-type deposits.

Banks have also served as originators and servicing agents for mortgages sold in the secondary market. Many banks have been concerned about their position as major local lenders. Unwilling to turn regular customers away, they have felt obligated to make mortgage loans. But when their portfolios of mortgages expanded beyond a sum felt to be reasonable, they sold blocks of these loans. They then continued to service the mortgages for the new purchasers, thus both realizing profits and maintaining customer relations. Since 1972, bank holding companies have become the owners of a majority of the large mortgage companies, while other banks have opened new mortgage companies. This gives banks another entry into the real estate lending sphere.

Operations

The legal lending requirements for banks, particularly nationally chartered banks, have been stricter than those for most other lenders, but these regulations have gradually been liberalized.

Banks play the most significant role in construction lending and in warehousing, or the advancing of interim credit for mortgage and real estate companies. Such loans most closely fit the banks' traditional role as providers of working capital. While many banks take no part in this market, others, including some of the largest, do a heavy volume of interim lending. Several New York money-market banks make participation loans with correspondent banks throughout the country. Without such participation, small, local banks would frequently find that requested construction loans exceeded their legal maximum amount for individual loans.

In the long-term market, banks are a major force in the nonresidential sector. In contrast to savings associations, the law enables them to grant terms on income properties that are as good as, or better than, terms on residential ones. As a result, as much as 40 percent of their long-term portfolio is outside the residential field. Their participation in the conventional single-family market has varied widely.

In the one- to four-family-home category, they are primarily over-the-counter lenders to local customers, competitive in the markets both for existing houses and for new, larger units. They try to preserve good depositor relationships. Recently over half of their volume has been on conventional single-family units.

Banks tend to be somewhat more conservative in their appraising, and therefore to lend a lower ratio of value, than S&Ls. They also usually insist that the loan be amortized over a shorter period. On the other hand, their interest rates, loan fees, and prepayment penalties are normally somewhat less than those charged by S&Ls. Consequently, banks are most often the best place to borrow in the local market for those who do not need a maximum loan or who can meet the higher payments which result from shorter maturities.

About 10 percent of their total outstanding mortgage loans have been FHA-VA, although at times these loans have accounted for as much as 55 percent of their volume. For banks, government-underwritten loans had the important advantage of not having to be counted as part of the mortgage total. However, as the limits on total mortgage holdings have moved up, this factor has become less significant.

Banks' new mortgage commitments depend on available funds, which vary with monetary policy and with their share of savings. Since both these elements have been unstable, CBs' mortgage loans have fluctuated by as much as several hundred percent from year to year.

Regulations

As with S&Ls, the lending regulations for CBs depend upon whether they are chartered by the federal government or by states. Again, the largest number of banks by far are state-chartered. They tend to be the smaller banks, however, so that national banks hold about 60 percent of the assets of all CBs.

On the whole, in the past national banks were more severely restricted in their loans on real estate than state banks were. The regulations limiting national banks in their mortgage lending stemmed from the idea that banks should do primarily commercial lending. The original Federal Reserve Act made no provision for urban mortgages. In 1916 mortgages of 50 percent could be made for 1 year, and in 1927 this was liberalized to 5 years. In 1935 national banks were authorized to make government-insured loans up to the limits established by the FHA. They could also make 60 percent loans lasting 10 years, providing some amortization provisions were included. Full amortization was not necessary, since a so-called balloon payment was authorized at the end of the 10-year period. In 1964 conventional loans of 80 percent were allowed, providing they were fully amortized over 25 years. By 1974 these limits had been raised to 90 percent and 30 years.

In addition to limitations on terms, banks are limited with respect to the amount of their total funds they can place in conventional mortgages. They may lend only up to an amount equal to their capital and surplus or up to 100 percent of their time and savings deposits, whichever is greater. While many large banks do not approach their allowance, this limit, particularly when lower, was the critical factor in determining the mortgage portfolio of many individual banks.

The maximum does not apply to commercial or industrial loans where real estate is offered as an additional security. Mortgages for such purposes are very common. The maximum also does not apply to government-guaranteed or government-insured loans. Government-insured loans can be made outside the CBs' limits of mortgage lending, and this is one of the factors which put these loans at the margin and cause the banks to vary their lending on these securities far more than on conventional mortgages.

The portfolios of the banks are so complex and pressures upon them are so great that constant shifts in policy are not surprising. Banks find large variations both in their flow of available funds and in the relative yields of separate classes of earnings. They react by shifting their investment policies sharply, even in very short periods.

LIFE INSURANCE COMPANIES

LICs, until recently, were the second largest of all financial institutions, in terms of both total assets and mortgage lending. Now, however, their assets are less than those of both the CBs and the S&Ls. We have seen in Table 2-1 that recently, their net mortgage lending has placed them well down on the list of major institutional lenders on real property. In fact, they are now the smallest of the four major financial institutions in current real estate lending, but they rank third in total real estate outstandings.

Even though they are relatively smaller, their importance in the mortgage market remains great. Their holdings of mortgages rose from less than $7 billion at the end of World War II to over $90 billion in 1975. They also hold about $8 billion of real estate equities. The share of mortgages in their total assets climbed from under 15 percent to a maximum of somewhat over 38 percent in 1966. Since then their policy loans, holdings of common stock, and holdings of corporate bonds have increased still more rapidly. Mortgages now represent less than 32 percent of their more than $275 billion in assets. Whereas in the middle 1950s more than 60 percent of the new money received by LICs flowed into the mortgage market, in the 1970s this percentage has fallen to just over 15 percent.

Organization

There are about 1,800 LICs in the United States. They vary in size from small companies to multibillion-dollar ones, with the largest companies holding the bulk of the assets. The large companies, with over $1 billion of life insurance in force, do most of the purchasing of mortgages. In contrast, nearly 1,000 LICs hold few if any mortgages.

LICs are domiciled in every state of the Union. The most popular states for headquarters are Texas, Louisiana, and Arizona, but those with the most assets are in the Northeast. Most companies perform their mortgage operations at their head offices. Some handle all transactions directly. Most use a system of mortgage correspondents spread throughout the country for originations and servicing. A few use their own branches. While most take mortgages anywhere in the country, insurance companies frequently are not represented in small localities.

The bulk of LICs' investment funds are policyholders' reserves. Much life insurance is sold on a level-premium basis. Reserves are accumulated systematically during a policyholder's younger days, when risk of death is less, to build sufficient funds to pay the higher insurance costs expected in later years. These moneys, which require investment, are accumulating at a rate of over $15 billion a year. Mortgages, as a use of these funds, have provided good yields, safety, and practicability and have been relatively easy to obtain.

Operations

Given their basic objectives, LICs attempt to adjust their lending among markets so as to achieve as high a yield as possible. They will lend on mortgages only when expected returns are equal to, or greater than, those obtainable from other investments. Because mortgages have traditionally provided high yields, mortgage loans have been granted up to a point where companies felt constrained by questions of portfolio policies and general risks. In recent years, mortgage investment at between 30 and 35 percent of total assets seems to have been thought of as a proper balance of these risks and yields. But this percentage appears to be falling.

In attempting to balance their yields among types of assets, the LICs as a whole have varied their net annual investment in mortgages by large amounts. Individual companies have found their ability to shift markets highly dependent on how they have organized their mortgage origination process. The larger companies have well-established organizations and correspondents or agents to find and service mortgages throughout the country. Their steady flow of funds requires investment of large sums each year. They make long-run advance commitments. Under these conditions, they have a limited flexibility at any given time. Smaller companies, purchasing loans primarily through headquarters officers, may be in a more responsive position. They can and do vary sharply the percentage of their current flow going into mortgages.

Because LICs work from home offices and find it difficult and costly to control the risks in loans furnished by correspondents and brokers spread throughout the country, they are interested primarily in large loans. The LICs are the biggest lenders on commercial and income properties. They are not restricted to local areas and have had more flexibility in this market than other lenders. Furthermore, since the individual loans on these properties are large, the company can afford the time, effort, and money needed to make certain that the loan is suitable.

The nature of LICs' operations makes it uneconomical for them to compete in most local single-family mortgage markets. In contrast to S&Ls, which lend on older houses in their own localities, LICs tend to restrict their conventional home loans to newer, more expensive units, with a decidedly lower percentage of the total value covered by the loan. They compete in this market by keeping their interest rate below that of other lenders. Still, by its nature this is a limited sphere. These loans appeal primarily to cost-conscious borrowers who have sufficient funds to make fairly high downpayments.

The problems of controlling moderate loans on individual houses over long distances account for the extensive use the LICs have made in the past of FHA-VA guarantees and insurance. In this sphere, the federal agencies' responsibility for underwriting can replace the company's need for more complete inspection of the unit and the borrower. The risk involved is far easier to calculate. Furthermore, government-guaranteed loans are most frequently offered by brokers in volume either as a result of large-scale building operations or because the correspondents are willing to accumulate and process batches of individual loans.

Because government-guaranteed loans are simpler to purchase and because bulk amounts are available, lenders can tailor their purchases more carefully to their needs. LICs can move in and out of the FHA-VA market on the basis of relative yields with far greater ease than is true of the conventional loan market.

Even so, in recent years, because of the large and extremely profitable opportunities in other types of lending, LICs have decreased their mortgage loans on one- to four-family homes. Although they still make loans, in 1974 they acquired less than 1 percent of new mortgages written on these units. Moreover, this amount of loans fell well below the repayments on their outstanding portfolios. As a result, their total amount loaned both on government-guaranteed and government-insured loans and on conventional loans on one- to four-family homes has been decreasing. In contrast, their lending on apartment houses and other types of income properties has remained high. In addition, they have steadily increased their direct ownership of real estate.

Regulations

Because the LICs have more portfolio flexibility than the other major savings institutions, their overall role in the real estate market remains significant. Anyone attempting to find money for a large-scale real estate investment is more likely to deal with an LIC than with any other institution. An LIC uses many of the specialized techniques covered in Chapter 9 to end up either as a participant in the final ownership or as the major final lender with rights to some participation in the profits. The larger companies in particular have been very active in seeking real estate equity investments. They want equities or participation because most of their portfolios remain locked into monetary assets.

Since large LICs sell insurance on a national basis, they traditionally have lent over wide areas and in most markets. Some state insurance regulations place a maximum limit on the total amount of mortgage holdings, usually 40 percent of assets but sometimes more. In addition, as with all other lenders, limits are established on the size of individual mortgages and the total amount that can be granted to one borrower. Such limits are usually related to the total assets or capital of the lender.

A maximum 66⅔ percent loan-to-value ratio has been traditional with LICs. In recent years, this ratio increased to 75 percent and in some cases to 80 percent. None of the limits apply to government-insured or government-guaranteed loans.

Although the laws of most states grant broad lending powers, they do establish various limitations requiring that certain classes of investments or loans not exceed a given ratio to total assets. These ratios are more liberal than those for other financial intermediaries. Common stocks and ownership of real estate for income are examples of authorized investments usually forbidden to others. In addition, most states have general leeway (called "basket") provisions which enable each company to take loans otherwise forbidden up to a specified percentage of its assets or capital.

MUTUAL SAVINGS BANKS

MSBs represent a unique segment of the savings industry. While they are only the fourth in size among the major financial institutions, their role is critical in the states in which they operate. They are concentrated heavily in the Northeast, particularly in New York and Massachusetts. In 1945 their real estate loans totaled about $4 billion. In 1975 they exceeded $75 billion.

There are only about 480 MSBs, or less than 10 percent of the number of S&Ls. Until the 1950s MSBs actually held more assets than the other thrift institutions, but currently they are only about 40 percent as large in total terms as the S&Ls. LICs still hold somewhat more mortgages than MSBs, but the MSBs' mortgage holdings have been growing at a more rapid rate. In addition to being the major lenders in their home states, they have played a significant part in establishing and maintaining a national mortgage market and in helping create the market for mortgage-backed securities.

Organization

As their name implies, these savings banks are mutual organizations founded originally with a decided philanthropic purpose. A principal aim was the promotion of thrift and savings among working people. As a means of achieving their goal, they placed great stress on paying high rates on deposits and also on making funds available to individuals for purchases of homes.

In recent years, however, MSBs have been badly hurt as short-term interest rates have fluctuated in comparison with the rates on longer securities. They were not able to raise their deposit rates as fast as the market. They have been the heaviest losers of funds at times of disintermediation. Furthermore, the right to raise their deposit rates has been taken out of their hands by Congress, which has placed all their deposits under interest rate ceilings.

Their portfolio policy lies between that of the CBs and that of the S&Ls. Their liquidity requirements also fall between the CBs' and the S&Ls', but come closer to those of the S&Ls. Because they have experienced sharp fluctuations in their deposits and because they have some flexibility in their portfolio policy, the amount of any year's savings they have placed in mortgages has varied widely. The mortgage share has moved from 40 percent to over 100 percent in certain of the past 10 years. During the period 1968–1973, between 50 and 55 percent of their asset growth went into real estate loans. However, mortgages still make up over 70 percent of their total assets.

Because of their concentrated geographic area (they exist in only 17 states, and more than 70 percent of their assets are in the top two—New York and Massachusetts), they have expanded far more slowly than the other financial institutions. The existing MSBs have worked hard for a system of national chartering to enable them to spread to other states, but Congress, which must act, has considered this a very controversial topic. The CBs and S&Ls have not wanted added competition. Until the 1950s both the average and the largest MSBs far exceeded equivalent S&Ls in size. In recent years, however, mergers of small S&Ls and the increased size of the large ones, particularly in California, have changed this situation. The largest S&Ls now exceed the largest MSBs in size. There are still far fewer small MSBs, but their average size is now only about four times that of the S&Ls, a decided drop from earlier periods.

Operations

The mortgage operations of MSBs stem directly from their initial purpose and general philosophy. They feel some obligation to promote better housing and welfare in their own cities, but when they lend outside their own boundaries, they are interested primarily in competitive yields and safety.

In their home cities many perform a complete mortgage service. They operate an over-the-counter individual and tract mortgage service, making conventional or insured loans on new and existing houses. They also make construction loans, sell standby commitments, and make loans on multifamily and nonresidential properties.

The percentage of MSBs operating in the national market has not been large, but those in it have been the banks with the highest assets making the largest share of mortgage loans. These banks have concentrated on purchases of large blocks in the secondary market from mortgage companies, CBs, and S&Ls. Their lending outside their own areas usually consists of government-underwritten mortgages. In the past few years, they have also been major buyers of GNMA mortgage-backed securities.

Because their flow of funds has not been as even as that of other lenders and because they have been acutely conscious of competitive yields, MSBs have been in and out of the national market in a rather erratic manner. Mortgage brokers have had to develop special techniques of handling commitments in order to be able to deliver a volume of loans to MSBs in short periods.

About 30 percent of the MSBs' portfolios has been in income properties—divided about equally between apartments and other properties. This proportion reflects the fact that these banks are concentrated in the large Eastern cities, where apartment living has been both traditional and a significant part of the housing market. Over 50 percent of total holdings of one- to four-family-unit loans have been underwritten by the FHA or the VA. Of course their national lending must be of this type, but they have also tended to use government underwriting in their own neighborhoods. The remaining half of their one- to four-family-unit loans, or 30 percent of their portfolios, consists of conventional loans on individual homes.

Regulations

MSBs, as a group, come closest to the S&Ls in their portfolio policies. Since they are entirely state institutions, their regulations differ widely. Their mortgage restrictions are more liberal. They also have a wider choice of other assets.

The single-family-home mortgage can have the highest loan-to-value ratio of all regulated lenders. In the major states, the MSBs can make loans of from 90 to 95 percent of value, depending upon amortization and location. Until approximately 1950, most MSBs were restricted in their mortgage loans to a 50-mile radius or to their home state. Since then they have been able to make or purchase insured or guaranteed loans throughout the country.

MSBs have much greater freedom than S&Ls in purchasing bonds and making small loans. In certain states they may purchase small amounts of stock or other securities. In most cases, however, their investments are carefully circumscribed, usually limited to the legal list of the state's supervisory authority.

SUMMARY

The four largest financial institutions are the major sources for mortgage funds. Regulations allowing them to make riskier loans in terms of lower downpayments, longer amortization periods, mobile-home loans, consumer-type loans, and loans on land have expanded steadily. Even so, their internal dynamics continue to create tensions within the real estate market. At times, the institutions have shifted their real estate lending drastically with respect to both volume and the type of loans they make.

These tensions have increased the importance of other types of financial institutions and have led to major shifts in government programs. In Chapter 16, after we discuss what has been happening, we return to some suggestions concerning how these tensions might be resolved in order to make the relationships between these institutions and the mortgage market more shock-resistant.

QUESTIONS AND PROBLEMS

1   What are the four major lenders on mortgages?
2   If you wanted to borrow on a commercial property, which types of lenders would be most likely to make such a loan?
3   What is the difference between a mutual and a stock company or association?
4   What distinguishes S&Ls from other financial institutions?
5   What is an S&L service corporation?
6   You want to buy a fairly expensive house in a nice section of town. Under what circumstances might you prefer to borrow from a CB rather than an S&L, and vice versa?
7   Discuss the major trends in LICs' participation in real estate markets.
8   Why does the average homeowner not approach an MSB for a home loan?
9   Describe the differences in typical lending by the four major financial institutions on (a) single-family homes, (b) apartment houses, and (c) industrial property.
10 Describe the principal changes which have occurred in the type of loans available on single-family homes over the past 40 years.

Chapter 13

Other Mortgage Institutions

The most interesting real estate deals from the viewpoint of buyers, sellers, investors, and lenders alike are those which require a large amount of ingenuity and creativity. For many sales, finding the financing is a rather routine operation. But others involve problems that call for the most careful analysis and sharp insight. A financing institution must be found that is willing to be convinced the loan it is asked to make will be highly profitable. Skills in putting together financing packages of this type are in great demand and are richly rewarded.

The mortgage lenders discussed in this chapter make creative lending possible. They serve as an interface between the traditional institutions and government lenders and individual borrowers. They are also the source of construction, interim, and special-risk funds.

One such group of lenders performs primarily a facilitating function. They enable the major institutions and the government to operate in a nationwide market which makes money available in areas far from the offices of the final lenders. They accomplish this by serving as originators, servicers, and guarantors of mortgage loans. All these services make the mortgage market more national, more competitive, and easier to enter for both lenders and borrowers. The net result is to reduce the costs of lending.

The three primarily facilitating sets of institutions are (1) the mortgage company, also called the *mortgage bank*; (2) a form of the REIT which specializes in mortgages and is sometimes separated out under the title "mortgage investment trust" (MIT); and (3) the private mortgage guarantee insurance companies, firms which insure loan payments to the ultimate lenders.

In addition, there is a wide variety of firms and individuals which make final, but somewhat specialized, loans. Their importance does not lie in their volume: as we noted, the total volume of all lenders covered in this chapter is less than 15 percent of all lending. Rather, their significance stems from the fact that they often take special risks and furnish money at critical times when it may not be available from the major institutions. The cost to the borrower through many of these lenders tends to be high, reflecting the much higher risks they take. In fact, their major reason for existing is to participate in those parts of the markets where the more traditional lenders cannot or will not operate. Their rates are also high because they are not extremely efficient and because their own costs are high.

MORTGAGE BANKING FIRMS

Mortgage companies form a major part of the correspondent system in real estate lending. They have only a small amount of their own capital to lend, and they do not collect deposits. Their primary activity is to act as correspondents, that is, to find—and frequently to process completely—mortgage loans for institutions which are in other areas of the country or which lack the ability to attract their own customers for loans or to handle the collection process. After placing a mortgage with the final lender, the mortgage bank frequently continues to service the loan for a fee. Servicing consists of collecting sums due on the loan and transmitting them to the final lender. The servicing agent also maintains records and sees that the property is not wasting (deteriorating) and that taxes, insurance, and other payments are kept current. If the account lags or becomes delinquent, the agent seeks to bring it current and may ultimately foreclose for the lender if necessary.

Mortgage banks' holdings of final long-term mortgages are relatively minor, as Table 2-1 brings out. In 1973 and 1974 their net investments in mortgages actually fell by over $4 billion. At the same time, however, they were the third largest makers of initial mortgage loans. In each year they originated and acquired over $13 billion in long-term mortgages, but their repayments or sales averaged $2 billion more than that in each year.

Mortgage companies came into existence because real estate lending must take place at the local level. Loans must be solicited, applications handled, appraisals made, county records checked, and construction inspected in the area where a property is located. Without local correspondents, financial institutions interested in lending outside their own regions would require numerous local offices. It is far more efficient for these functions to be performed by correspondent offices that know their local area and can make and service loans for a large number of national companies, each of which may be located in a different place.

Mortgage companies find and negotiate with prospective borrowers. They check property values and borrowers' credit-worthiness. They handle lending and all the many legal problems during construction to see that money is disbursed properly and that the mortgage is secured legally. Usually they make (or close) the loan in their own name and then sell it to a final lender.

Loans made by mortgage companies can be differentiated into three types:

1   The first type of loan is on new single-family construction. In this market, commitments are usually made to tract builders for a batch of loans, but there may also be agreements with individuals building single homes. The mortgage companies bridge the gap caused by the lag between the start of construction and the final insurance guarantee on insured loans, the actual loan made to the individual borrower, and the purchase of the loan by the final (takeout) lender. A great deal of uncertainty characterizes this period. The builder may not finish construction; eligible buyers may not appear; the final sale may be delayed. An approval of the prospective borrower must be obtained from the insuring or guaranteeing agency. The required daily negotiations between lender and builder cannot be carried on by the distant or ultimate lender.

2   On income properties, the mortgage companies may act primarily as brokers. Since these loans tend to be large, the final lenders can take responsibility for the negotiation of the terms and the disbursement of funds. The mortgage companies, however, know where the money is available. They are approached by developers and by people wanting to buy or sell existing properties. They are able to serve as intermediaries between the prospective borrowers and the lenders.

3   A final type of lending makes money available on existing houses. These are called *spot loans*. They may be brought to the mortgage bank by real estate brokers or through their own local offices. The correspondent business for these and other single-family-unit loans has changed rather drastically over time. Initially, local firms would accept loan applications and process them for submission to insurance companies, which were the primary final lenders. The latter would then decide whether to make the loan. Depending on the market, fees might be paid by the prospective borrower or by the lender.

However, over time the system became more formal. To increase flexibility and to be certain of the availability of funds, mortgage companies usually obtained quarterly or semiannual advance commitments specifying the number and type of loans the final lender would accept. Each tentative loan had to be submitted to the company for final approval. The advance commitment specified the type and amount of loans, locations, size, and the fee that would be paid for origination and for servicing.

Gradually, the mortgage companies moved away from dependence on one or a few insurance companies. They sought correspondent relationships with other institutional lenders such as the MSBs, pension funds, state retirement funds, or college endowments. More recently, the mortgage companies have become the chief correspondents for government agencies. In addition, the companies own an increasing pool of mortgages deposited with trustees against which guaranteed GNMA bonds or other types of mortgage-backed securities are issued.

Mortgage companies also perform a wide variety of functions based upon, and related either closely or generally to, their originating and servicing functions. Since they liquidate foreclosed properties, they usually have property management operations and are often in the real estate brokerage business. Since properties must be insured to the satisfaction of the final lender, they sell insurance. They may operate as advisers to REITs, and in some cases they may specialize in home improvements or other types of consumer finance. They may make second-mortgage loans for their own account or for the account of individuals in their locality, since normally such funds are not available from the big four institutional investors.

Organization

Because mortgage companies are not regulated in any formal way, information about them is less complete than that about other lenders. The Mortgage Bankers' Association of America, with about 750 members, is the main trade association in the field. Most statistics give information only on this group. There may be hundreds of other small or part-time mortgage firms active in various markets. Firms vary in size from Lomas-Nettleton, reputed to be the largest in the country, to one-person part-time activities of real estate brokers. Lomas-Nettleton in 1973 originated over $1.7 billion in mortgages and serviced over $4.4 billion. It also made construction loans, sold casualty insurance, managed an MIT, and performed similar functions. It had about 1,500 employees in 90 offices.

The top 60 mortgage banking firms, a majority of which are subsidiaries of banks or other holding companies, do about half the total volume of the industry. A typical firm would be found near the bottom of this list of 60. It would service a volume of about $350 million in outstanding loans. It would originate about $100 million in loans in a year. To handle this volume would take about 220 employees, about 140 of whom would be engaged directly in mortgage activity. The remaining 80 would be handling insurance, selling real estate, doing property management, and engaging in similar activities. This typical firm would have about $45 million in assets, including interim construction loans and an inventory of completed loans waiting to be delivered to the final takeout lender. Almost all the assets would be financed by funds borrowed from banks against the mortgages pledged as collateral. A typical firm of this size might have about $5 million of its own capital at any time, while it would have outstanding loans of about $40 million.

Very few of even the largest mortgage companies operate on a national basis. Most are local or regional. Even the firms which do operate throughout the country tend to have the great bulk of their business concentrated in three or four states.

Mortgage companies have experienced a period of rapid change and turmoil. The largest ones, which were small, family corporations, have become subsidiaries of holding companies. In addition, their traditional market and procedures have been shifting rapidly. As the Nixon administration attempted to phase the government out of the FHA-VA mortgage insurance and guarantee business, the mortgage banks had to find new spheres for operation. They responded to problems in the market for FHA-VA loans by increasing their activities in both income properties and single-family conventional loans. The latter expansion was helped greatly by the growth of the private mortgage guarantee companies. Both in Congress and in the industry there has been a major debate over the advantages and disadvantages of moving the government completely out of the mortgage insurance sphere.

Changes can be seen in terms of both the type of loans originated in the last few years and the customers to whom loans are sold. Between 1968 and 1973, the percentage of the loans mortgage companies made on single-family units dropped from 70 to 60 percent, and the proportion of these which were conventional (that is, not FHA-VA) rose from 10 to 40 percent. Their construction lending is concentrated primarily outside the single-family market.

The mortgage banking industry services over $110 billion in loans for other investors. In recent years it has originated, on the average, from 15 to 20 percent of all mortgages. However, this amount has varied between 25 percent in 1970 and under 12 percent in 1973. Added to their large share of FHA-VA loans, the mortgage companies traditionally handled from 15 to 20 percent of all construction loans and about the same share of loans for income properties. However, until 1973 the mortgage banks had played a very small role in the conventional one-family-house market, averaging less than 2 percent of originations in this sphere. But in 1973 their share rose to almost 10 percent of this market, although it fell again in 1974.

Similar changes have been reflected in the customers of the mortgage companies. In the prewar and immediate postwar periods, LICs were almost the only customers. However, their share of the mortgage bank business has fallen rather steadily. In the mid-1960s it fell to 50 percent; by 1972 it was less than a third. MSBs were the second largest customer. About a quarter of servicings of mortgage firms were for their accounts, but this share has fallen also. To replace their traditional customers, the mortgage firms have greatly expanded their dealings with government agencies and with S&Ls. Currently more than one-quarter of the loans they service are for the account of, or are for, the mortgage-backed securities of the government agencies.

Another major shift has been in the relationship with S&Ls. In the past the mortgage banks and the S&Ls were primarily competitors. In 1971–1972 and the early part of 1973, however, S&Ls received more funds than they could handle in their own local areas. At the same time, regulations enabled them to buy elsewhere loans guaranteed by private mortgage insurance. They turned to the mortgage banks as a source of available loans ready for purchase at times when they had excess funds. The result was to give the mortgage banking firms a new set of customers. But at the same time, it increased the instability of their business. It also caused them to take much larger, uncovered positions, thereby compounding the risks they faced from changes in interest rates.

Another development is the growing importance of, and interest in, loans on income properties. When loans including participations in the profits or ownership of real estate are sought by investors, mortgage bankers are a good source.

Operations

To round out our picture of what mortgage banks do, it may be worthwhile to summarize how they do it and to point out the current problems which these firms face.

It should be clear that the mortgage banking company's main job is to originate mortgages, that is, to find borrowers, complete the mortgage documents, and make the actual loan with its own funds. When the mortgage loans are closed, they are put together in packages and sold to institutional investors in large blocks, typically $1 million or more. During the life of the mortgage, the mortgage company administers, or services, the loan for the investor. Servicing consists of collecting and accounting for the monthly payments, maintaining an escrow account for payment of property taxes and insurance, examining the property periodically if necessary, and handling delinquencies and foreclosures if they occur. In a foreclosure, the mortgage company takes responsibility for the legal action, sees that the property is put in salable condition, and frequently resells the property.

If the property is to be constructed, in a large number of cases the mortgage company will also handle all the details of the construction financing, the final lender not entering until the permanent loan has been closed.

Commitments

A major shift has occurred in the risks to which mortgage banks are exposed. Formerly—and this is still true in many cases—firms would not lend until they had a commitment from the final lender to take the mortgage at a fixed price. Although generally still available for income properties, individual commitments for single units are harder to obtain than they were in the past. The amount of a single-family-home loan is small compared with that of the normal transaction between a mortgage bank and the final lender. Lenders want to buy a batch of loans at a single time.

A major market for such commitments is maintained by the FNMA and the Federal Home Loan Mortgage Corporation (FHLMC), which periodically auction off their commitments to purchase mortgages at prices determined by sealed bids. If a mortgage company has a stock of these commitments, it can protect itself against interest rate fluctuations and changes in the price of its mortgages while it is accumulating a stock of loans to sell. The protection, however, is far from perfect. Difficulties are caused by the difference between mortgage prices and general interest rates and also by day-to-day shifts between the short- and long-term financial markets, which cause varying movements in rates.

Income

Traditionally, the fees charged for origination in the single-family market were insufficient to cover the actual costs involved. In effect, origination was a loss leader to get the servicing onto the books of the company. The losses incurred in originating the loans were gradually amortized from the amounts received in servicing. Servicing fees typically have ranged from .25 to .5 percent of outstanding balances. In recent years, three-eighths of a percent has been typical.

However, the fact that origination and servicing involve fixed costs complicates the situation. Economies of scale become possible as the size of the individual loan increases and as the number of loans processed by a firm grows. A firm originating either large mortgages or mortgages in a very active market could at least break even on the fees received for origination. On the other hand, the average firm originating mortgages on low- or middle-income houses or in most parts of the country incurred a fair-sized deficit from its origination business because of the high costs involved. Since costs have been rising and origination fees have tended to be fixed, this problem has become more serious. Probably some change from the traditional pricing system is necessary.

Because the actual interest rates on the long-term mortgages were higher than those which had to be paid for short-term money from banks or the commercial paper markets, mortgage companies over most of their history have made a significant part of their profits by carrying (warehousing) the mortgages in stock. In recent years, however, the term structure has altered. As a result, mortgage companies have found themselves paying out more in interest than they receive, which further complicates the unsolved problem of how mortgage companies are to be paid for their services in the future.

The problem can be thought of in more general terms. Throughout our financial structure major questions have arisen as to the value of specialized, in contrast to more general, financial institutions. Mortgage banks are one of the more specialized institutions; their skills lie in the processing and gathering together of mortgage loans and also in their servicing. They have been able to do this work at a lower cost than other institutions. They also made it possible for some semblance of a national mortgage market to appear. They made loans available in regions where there were shortages, while transferring funds from areas of excess savings.

However, their existence depends upon excess funds' being made available by financial institutions. When money is tight in general, such funds disappear. This particular market is hit the hardest by tight money and inflation. Thus the future of the mortgage banking firms is intimately related to the future of the housing market and the mortgage markets as a whole.

The seriousness of these problems can be measured by examining the sources of the mortgage companies' income. About a third of their gross income has come from servicing fees. About 10 percent has been derived from the origination fees paid by the purchasers or sellers of single-family homes. A somewhat larger share (15 percent) has arisen from fees for construction lending and the origination of loans on income properties. Such loans usually have no, or low, servicing fees. In the past, about 20 percent of income came from the interest on the loans made with the firm's own capital or from the spread in interest between what the firm paid its bank and received from its customers. It is this spread, together with profits made on buying mortgages and then selling them at a higher price, that has tended to disappear.

The question is: What will take the place of these fees, and what about the increasing deficits on originations? There remain a wide variety of sources of income: insurance commissions, real estate commissions, property management income, REIT advisory fees, and others, which in the past made up 20–25 percent of the income of the mortgage firms. But the problem persists as to whether a system which depends upon offsetting losses in one sphere with profits in another can remain viable. There is always the probability that specialized firms which do not have to cover losses on some functions will take over the areas that still remain profitable by pricing them in a closer relationship to their true costs.

MORTGAGE INVESTMENT TRUSTS

We have already noted the growth of REITs. We pointed out that one form—the mortgage investment trust—is active primarily in the specialized higher-risk lending activities, including the origination and actual lending for construction, development, and land loans. In contrast to other lenders, almost all the funds of the MITs are heavily concentrated in the most specialized and risky parts of the market. The MITs were a major phenomenon of the early 1970s. They were able to raise over $15 billion in about 3 years. By 1974, the REITs had over $21 billion in assets.

Table 13-1 is a consolidated balance sheet for the largest 172 REITs. It gives an accurate picture of both their lending and their borrowing. In Chapter 8, we commented on the use of leverage and the fact that many trusts speculated on the interest rate term structure. These policies show up clearly in the table's liabilities. The amount of borrowed funds is almost three times the shareholders' equity. Of the borrowings, about two-thirds are in short-term money-market or bank instruments. Most of the rates will fluctuate with the market rates. The short-term borrowings' ratio to equity is more than 2 to 1.

On the asset side, we note that not quite 20 percent of total funds are invested in equities (some of which are properties taken over in foreclosures). About 40 percent of loans are for construction purposes. Other major lending includes loans on land, for development, and for interim or bridge purposes to cover the time gap between construction and the receipt of a loan from a long-term lender. There is also a significant number of junior mortgages. Finally, less than 10 percent of lending at this time was on long-term mortgages.

High Risks and the Hope for High Returns

Because of the high risks involved and the expertise required to maintain such risks within reasonable bounds, the lending markets for land development and construction of tracts, condominiums, motels, shopping centers, office buildings, and industrial parks have traditionally been short of adequate funds. The major financial institutions have not been able to develop the necessary expertise to lend in these markets without engendering far more risks than they or their regulatory agencies considered desirable.

On the other hand, the MITs prided themselves on their ability to take risks. They created and pushed hard most of the newer methods of financing discussed in Chapters 8 and 9. They assumed many of the risks normally borne by the developer and builder. In return, they demanded a share of the entrepreneurial earnings. This has meant that the MITs can be thought of as primarily lenders for development, construction, and other specialized real estate credit needs.

The history of the MITs is still too short to know how successful they will be in finding the proper balance between risks and earnings. They are in the process of trying to recover from their disastrous experiences of 1974, when a high percentage of their loans went into default.

In many states MITs have run into the problem of the usury law. In California, for example, a regulated financial institution can charge a corporation unlimited interest rates, but a nonregulated institution such as an MIT has a 10 percent interest rate ceiling. Ten percent interest was not sufficient to cover their borrowing rates and risks. Fairly typically, they have attempted to charge 3–5 percent above their own borrowing rate. They, in turn, borrowed at 1 or 2 percent above the prime lending rate of the banks—the prime rate being that rate which the banks charge their best customers. Many MITs charged a floating rate—one which rose with the market. But the market

Table 13-1 REIT Industry Balance Sheet

Assets (billions of dollars)	First quarter 1974	Year-end 1973	Liabilities (billions of dollars)	First quarter 1974	Year-end 1973
First mortgages:			Commercial paper	$ 3.38	$ 3.97
Land loans	$ 1.05	$ 1.02	Bank term loans in use	1.88	1.48
Development loans	2.35	2.22			
Construction loans	7.96	7.68	Bank lines in use	5.93	5.02
Completed properties:					
0–10 years	1.43	1.41	Other nonconvertible debt	1.33	1.24
10+ years	1.72	1.57			
			Convertible debt	.74	.70
Junior mortgages:					
Land, development, and construction	.34	.31	Mortgages on owned property	1.55	1.48
Completed properties	.94	.90			
			Other liabilities	.44	.46
Land leasebacks	.52	.51		15.25	14.35
Improved property owned	3.03	2.80			
Cash and other assets	1.78	1.77	Shareholders' equity	5.87	5.84
	$21.12	$20.19		$21.12	$20.19

Source: The statistics are as of the trusts' reporting periods closest to the quarter-end date. For example, the year-end 1973 statistics contain data from REITs for November, December, and January depending upon the trusts' reporting period. The year-end 1973 statistics are based on the published financial reports and questionnaire responses of 172 trusts for the fiscal reporting period closest to December 31, 1973. The first-quarter 1974 statistics are for all REITs (208) of which NAREIT has any record. A number of small organizations which were being operated in the REIT format but which were not filing as REITs for tax purposes were not included in the 208 trusts. The 37 trusts added to the balance-sheet tally between these two quarters (one with $63.1 million in total assets was deleted when it announced it would no longer file as a REIT for tax purposes) have total assets of $208.8 million. Although current balance-sheet data are not available in the case of most of these 37 trusts, they were added to the industry balance sheet for completeness. National Association of Real Estate Investment Trusts.

rates rose so much higher than had been expected that developers' legal or de facto ceilings on what they could pay came into play. Few could afford to pay 18–20 percent plus high fees. In many cases in 1974, MITs found themselves paying out more money to cover their own borrowings from the market than they received on their loans. This occurred even though they still had to absorb the costs of supervision and major risks.

While the rates offered to investors and lenders by the MITs seem high, it is still too early to know whether these rates are higher or lower than one would anticipate for the long run, given the risks they assume and the basic costs of money. Again, the quoted nominal rate they charge and pay their owners and lenders must be carefully analyzed to see how much is real. The nominal rate includes the sum to cover inflation and a factor to cover the risks involved, as well as the real rate of return.

PRIVATE MORTGAGE INSURANCE COMPANIES

The third group of facilitating financial institutions in the mortgage market consists of the private mortgage guarantee insurance companies. They too have experienced a rapid growth. The modern version of this industry started with the founding of the Mortgage Guaranty Insurance Company (now MGIC Investment Corporation) in 1956. Although the number of competitors has increased steadily, MGIC still accounts for about 70 percent of the industry volume.

In 1975, there were 15 such companies with over $25 billion of mortgage insurance in force. In 1973, the industry wrote more than $10 billion in new insurance, a volume roughly equal to the mortgages insured or guaranteed under the FHA-VA programs. These firms would like—and they have strong supporters in their battle—to take over entirely the insurance and guarantee functions which for most of the past 40 years have been handled by the FHA and VA.

Mortgage insurance companies are, as their name implies, primarily insurance companies, although they may also have mortgage subsidiaries which purchase and sell mortgages, invest in mortgages, and issue mortgage-backed securities. A separate insurance policy is written for each mortgage loan covered. By requiring that borrowers buy a policy, mortgage lenders receive insurance against losses from the default of the borrower on the loan. When a borrower defaults, a lender can claim from the insurance company for any unpaid principal, accrued interest, and certain other expenses such as taxes and legal fees which result from a borrower's failure to pay. In case of a default, the insuring company agrees that it will either pay the claim in full (in which case it takes title to the property and arranges for its sale) or pay either a maximum of 20 or 25 percent of the insured loan or the total claimed, whichever is less, depending on the type of policy issued on the original loan. When paid off in this way, the lender retains his or her lien against the property.

Operations

The mortgage insurance companies issue master policies to approved lenders. These master policies indicate that the insurer is willing to do business with the lender covered, in the belief that the lender is qualified. In addition, the policy sets forth the terms and conditions of the individual insurance policies which may be written. MGIC, for example, has over 11,000 such master policies in effect. A lender may obtain such agreements from several mortgage insurance companies, and many do. There is no requirement concerning the number or type of loans submitted for insurance.

An approved lender wanting to obtain insurance on a specific mortgage loan must submit a separate application for each policy. The application must be supported by a copy of the borrower's loan application, a property appraisal report, a written credit report on the borrower, and an affidavit of the borrower's equity. The mortgage insurance company's underwriting unit reviews this material and approves or rejects the application for the specific policy on the individual loan.

Types of Policies

Mortgage insurance companies write many types of policies. Most are on individual houses, although they write policies on commercial buildings as well, and they also guarantee payments of rents on leases. Lease guarantees enable owners of shopping centers to borrow higher amounts from lenders. Policies on home mortgages differ with respect to the allowable ratio of loan to appraised value, the percentage of the claim insured, and the size and term of the insurance premium. Thus a typical insurance policy might cover a case in which the loan is made for 90–95 percent of appraised value, losses up to 25 percent of the loan are covered, and the premium is paid for 1 year. In 1975 the insurance companies charged 1 percent of the loan plus $20 for such a policy. After the first year, the policy could be renewed for a fee of .25 percent of the loan. If premiums were paid for 5 years in advance, the charges for such a policy were 1.75 percent of the loan plus $20. After 5 years additional renewals would cost .25 percent of the unpaid balance per year.

If the loan was 80–90 percent of appraised value and 20 percent of the loan was insured, the charge for a 1-year policy was .5 percent of the loan plus $20. However, renewals still cost .25 percent of the unpaid balance.

Traditionally, most mortgage insurance has been purchased to cover mortgages granted by S&Ls. Such insurance makes it possible for S&Ls to make loans at a higher ratio to selling price than is legal on a noninsured basis. In recent years, the fastest expansion in business of the insurance companies has been with the mortgage companies. They became active customers in 1972, when the FNMA and the FHLMC began to buy conventional private mortgages covered by such insurance. Previously, the FNMA could buy only FHA-VA loans, and the FHLMC bought only from S&Ls.

On the whole, the loss record of the insurance companies has been low. Observers, however, have become concerned periodically because most of the companies have not been in existence long enough to have an actuarily sound record of performance. Their ability to keep losses low depends upon the quality of their underwriting. Some people fear that if competition becomes too great, the pattern experienced in other types of insurance will be repeated, with one or two firms lowering their underwriting standards for competitive purposes. Since the industry is so new, there are also critical questions as to what residual risks remain, as, for example, when mortgage-backed securities are issued based on the mortgages insured by these companies. As in most activities, some lenders and investors tend to be ultraconservative. Others, however, fail to examine the real risks they are assuming with the care which an institution should exercise when it commits fairly sizable segments of its capital based on any insurance policy.

OTHER MORTGAGE LENDERS

In addition to the six financial institutions listed in Table 12-1 and government agencies, numerous other groups lend on real property. While the exact amount of mortgages held by this miscellaneous group is uncertain, most estimates place it at around $60 billion, or between 6 and 8 percent of all mortgage loans. About a third of this total is advanced by corporations and miscellaneous financial institutions, and about two-thirds is held by individuals, trusts, and personal estates.

Corporations and Other Financial Institutions

A tremendous variety of institutions and corporations make real estate loans. One group, the private noninsured pension funds, has over $130 billion in assets. Other groups, such as fire and casualty companies, fraternal life insurance companies, credit unions, foundations, and university endowment and other types of specialized funds, also hold large amounts of assets.

Most of these financial institutions allocate only a small percentage of their assets to mortgage investments. For example, less than 2 percent of the assets of the noninsured pension funds are held in the form of real estate loans. Similar figures apply to the other groups. Because the extent of their participation in the mortgage market is presently small, they are a prime potential market for those trying to develop new sources of mortgage funds. In theory, since they are interested primarily in high yields and have low liquidity needs compared with those of other financial agencies, most of these groups could be a major force in the mortgage market. But in fact, this market has been extremely hard to tap.

The gap between the amount of available funds of these groups and the actual mortgage lending they do is usually attributed to their unfamiliarity, especially in the case of pension fund trustees, with the unique characteristics of the mortgage market. To make it easier for them to put money into mortgages, the mortgage-backed securities (discussed in Chapter 15) have been developed. The theory is that these securities can be purchased in the same way as other types of bonds; therefore, they will be bought by the funds in preference to, or in competition with, the corporate or governmental bond market. In fact, however, the securities backed by mortgages are somewhat more complicated than the others; consequently, this market is still in the process of development.

Nonfinancial Corporations   In addition to the mortgage loans made by financial institutions, a large number of nonfinancial corporations also hold real estate loans. Nonfinancial corporations include all except those engaged primarily in financial activities. These corporations hold mortgages in an amount just about equal to the amount held by the miscellaneous financial organizations.

Nonfinancial corporations have moved into real estate mortgage lending for a variety of reasons. Table 10-2 showed that while nonfinancial businesses as a whole are large net borrowers, they also do a fair amount of lending. Businesses with surpluses often become major lenders, although in the great majority of cases in the short-term markets.

However, some of these corporations have found it worthwhile to make real estate loans in connection with their other corporate business. Thus oil companies have moved into land development, and lumber businesses and a great variety in other industries have felt attracted to the real property field. Frequently these firms make equity and debt capital available. In addition, corporations are sometimes formed to deal specifically in the real estate field. As part of their business, they may make mortgage loans. In particular, many may retain junior liens when they sell part of their real estate holdings. When all these different sources are combined, they add up to total mortgage loans of $8 billion or more.

Again, this sum is fairly minor in the total picture, but it has a much more significant impact in specialized markets such as those for land for development and for income properties. Since these are the areas in which risks are highest and sources of funds are scarcest, even small marginal amounts infused into these markets can make a major difference. Those in the income property market frequently seek out corporate funds as a way of putting together complicated deals.

Funds for Equities   While these miscellaneous corporations have moved slowly into the mortgage market, they have entered the market for ownership of equities more rapidly. Potential high returns, the fact that these corporations need not remain highly liquid, and the fear of inflation are all factors which make equity investments attractive. Pension funds, in particular, have transferred a large share of their investments from the bond to the stock market. As the performance of their stock portfolios failed to meet their expectations, they have sought other equity investments. The real estate market offers an obvious opportunity.

The problem of analysis and management of real estate equities, however, is even more difficult than in the case of mortgages. The funds have been groping toward a solution to their problems. Some have hired in-house staffs. Many have sought participations with developer-managers. Others have put their money into real estate equity funds. Some have used their preferred tax status to buy land and leaseholds under buildings. Others have entered into syndicates.

Most observers believe that in the next decade, the miscellaneous corporations and institutions will be among the most dynamic sectors of the real estate market, for both investment and financing. However, the difficulties of establishing sound procedures for their participation remain formidable.

Individuals

A large number of mortgages are recorded every year in the names of individuals. The average amount for these loans is small, and they are paid off fairly rapidly. The share of individuals in total holdings is about 4 percent—far lower than their importance as measured by new recordings.

Mortgage loans made by individuals tend to be either purchase-money contracts, usually in the form of second, or junior, mortgages taken back when property is sold, or consumer or family loans, providing funds needed for nonhousing purposes but with property utilized as an additional security. However, some wealthy individuals, trusts, and estates are also sources of funds for specialized loans, particularly for land development and income properties.

Although available information on individual loans is spotty, it is quite clear that this is a chaotic and unorganized market. Volume and importance rise and fall contracyclically to the availability of funds from other lenders.

Lacking data, many observers believed that the second-mortgage market was far larger during the 1920s than in recent years. Their belief stemmed from the fact that in the earlier period, conventional lenders required far higher downpayments. Purchases were possible only with second or third loans. When high loan-to-value terms can be granted, junior mortgages would appear to be far less necessary.

Now observers are not as certain that this reasoning is correct. Although second mortgages have almost certainly become far less significant for *new* houses, even in this market tight-money periods show increased junior liens. On the other hand, in the market for *existing* houses, terms on available loans do not seem to have expanded to anywhere near the same degree as those on new homes. Consequently, if they have wanted their properties to be competitive with new houses, sellers of existing houses have been forced to take back junior liens.

There has also been a growing market for junior liens in connection with income properties. In these cases, speculators have been willing to pay exceedingly high rates for second, third, or even higher mortgages. These loans have been thought worthwhile even at these high rates because they sharply increase the leverage and therefore the potential gain, although the risk and possible loss to the owner are also magnified.

SUMMARY

Many of the mortgage institutions described in this chapter either did not exist or were very different in size and function just 20 years ago. Their growth and development reflect the fact that real estate financing remains a most complex sphere of operations.

A buyer's equity remains low in the great majority of cases. The value of a property as a security depends upon the analysis of individual structures, locations, and markets as well as upon credit-worthiness of the borrower and the performance of many acts required to meet individual state laws and regulations.

Mortgage bankers and mortgage insurance companies are specialized institutions established to carry out many tasks necessary in the lending process which would be too expensive if performed by distant lenders. They make lending at a distance feasible.

Mortgage investment trusts have specialized in development, construction, and interim lending. Their functions also demand a high degree of skill and analysis. The existing institutions have far to go before they can solve some of the more urgent problems in this sphere. New opportunities, a constant state of flux, and shifting patterns seem likely to mark the future of these firms, as they have the recent past.

QUESTIONS AND PROBLEMS

1 Describe the functions of a mortgage loan correspondent.
2 Discuss mortgage commitments and their importance to mortgage companies and builders.
3 Discuss the problems and opportunities which face the MITs.

4   Whom does a mortgage guarantee insurance company insure?
5   Explain why the 20 or 25 percent limit on losses is so important to the mortgage guarantee insurance companies. In what way does this create a problem for lenders?
6   Describe the process of obtaining mortgage insurance.
7   Why has it been so difficult for borrowers to obtain loans from pension funds on mortgages?
8   Explain why many investors have bought real estate equities rather than making mortgage loans.
9   What are the primary roles played by the other (than the big four) mortgage institutions?
10   How does a mortgage banker differ from an REIT?
11   Do smaller lending sources make more speculative loans than the major financial institutions? Why?

SELECTED REFERENCES FOR PART THREE

Aldrich, G. H., and Associates: *Report on Real Estate Activities among Major Corporations* (Chicago: Society of Real Estate Appraisers, 1971).

American Bankers Association: *The Commercial Banking Industry* (Englewood Cliffs, N.J.: Prentice-Hall, 1962).

Board of Governors of the Federal Reserve System: *Federal Reserve System: Purposes and Functions* (Washington, 1974).

———: *Introduction to Flow of Funds* (Washington: 1975).

———: *Ways to Moderate Fluctuations in Housing Construction* (Washington: 1972).

Bosworth, D., and J. S. Duesenberry: "A Flow of Funds Model and Its Implications," *Issues in Federal Debt Management*, Federal Reserve Bank of Boston, Conference Series, no. 10, Boston, 1973.

Friend, I., et al.: *Study of the Savings and Loan Industry* (Washington: Federal Home Loan Bank Board, 1969), 4 vols.

Gardner, E. B. (ed.): *Pension Fund Investment Management* (Homewood, Ill.: Irwin, 1970).

Goldfeld, S. M.: *Commercial Bank Behavior and Economic Activity* (Amsterdam: North Holland Publishing Company, 1966).

Graaskamp, J.: "Development and Structure of Mortgage Loan Guarantee Insurance in the United States," *Journal of Risk and Insurance*, 1967.

Gramlich, E. M., and D. M. Jaffee (eds.): *Savings Deposits, Mortgages and Housing: Studies from the FRB-MIT-Penn Model* (Lexington, Mass.: Lexington Books, 1972).

Grebler, L., and S. J. Maisel: "Determinants of Residential Construction: A Review of Present Knowledge," in Commission on Money and Credit, *Impacts of Monetary Policy* (Englewood Cliffs, N.J.: Prentice-Hall, 1963).

Housing and Monetary Policy, Federal Reserve Bank of Boston, Conference Series, no. 4, Boston, 1970.

Jacobs, D. P., L. C. Farwell, and E. H. Neave: *Financial Institutions*, 5th ed. (Homewood, Ill.: Irwin, 1972).

Jones, L. D.: *Investment Policies of Life Insurance Companies* (Boston: Harvard Graduate School of Business, 1968).

Jones, O., and L. Grebler: *The Secondary Mortgage Market: Its Purpose, Performance and Potential* (Los Angeles: University of California Real Estate Research Program, 1961).

Kendall, L. T.: *The Savings and Loan Business* (Englewood Cliffs, N.J.: Prentice-Hall, 1962).

Life Insurance Association: *Life Insurance Companies as Financial Institutions* (Englewood Cliffs, N.J.: Prentice-Hall, 1962).

Maisel, S. J.: "A Theory of Fluctuations in Residential Construction Starts," *American Economic Review*, June 1963.

————: *Managing the Dollar* (New York: Norton, 1973).

National Association of Mutual Savings Banks: *Mutual Savings Banking* (Englewood Cliffs, N.J.: Prentice-Hall, 1962).

Polakoff, M. E., et al.: *Financial Institutions and Markets* (Boston: Houghton Mifflin, 1970).

Rapkin, C., J. R. Ferrari, R. Blood, and G. Milgrim: *The Private Insurance of Home Mortgages* (Philadelphia: University of Pennsylvania, Institute for Environmental Studies, 1967).

Ricks, R. B. (ed.): *National Housing Models* (Lexington, Mass.: Lexington Books, 1973).

Smith, L. B.: *The Postwar Canadian Housing and Residential Mortgage Markets* (Toronto: University of Toronto Press, 1974).

U.S. Congress, Senate Committee on Banking, Currency and Housing: *Study of Mortgage Credit*, 90th Cong., 2d Sess., 1968.

Part Four

Governments and Mortgage Markets

To mitigate the drastic effects on real estate and on the general economy of uneven mortgage flows, the government, starting as far back as the Hoover administration, has introduced an ever-growing variety of mortgage and housing programs, with special agencies to administer them. In recent years, most states have added related programs. The special role of the government is so pervasive that a familiarity with the government programs and how they operate is indispensable to an understanding of real estate finance.

Chapter 14 describes the government programs for subsidizing, insuring, and guaranteeing real estate financing, particularly through HUD, the FHA, and the VA. The government agencies which supply money for real estate loans are discussed in Chapter 15. Most of these are not government departments, but rather are separate agencies with special control, budgetary, and financial relationships to the government. Chapter 16 examines some of the proposals for further improving the way in which the mortgage market operates.

Chapter 14

The Government Programs for Housing Investment and Finance

Housing investment and finance are profoundly affected by programs and institutions established by the federal government and, to an increasing degree, by state and local governments. The government's goals in the real property domain are extremely diverse. At the most general level, the government is attempting to improve the standard of American life. It does this through a variety of programs in planning, development, construction and finance. More specific government goals are (1) to make available to each American family, in the words of the 1949 Housing Act, "a decent house and a suitable living environment" at a price it can afford; (2) to promote stability in the housing industry and thereby to improve stability in the economy as a whole; and (3) to improve the general working of the financial system by assisting the mortgage market, thus avoiding a repetition of the situation in the 1930s, when difficulties in the mortgage market created major problems for the entire financial system.

In a way, many of the government's actions to foster stability and reduce the cost of housing seem ironic. A great deal of the effort and many of the programs are required primarily to offset the depressing effects on housing of governmental action in the monetary and fiscal sphere. As we have seen, probably the most critical problems for real estate markets are the fluctuations in activity and the swings in demand which result from the government's monetary and fiscal policies. If these policies were neutral in their impact, much of the effort expended by the housing agencies could be reduced. The costs of bringing about a better standard of urban life would be far lower.

THE DEPARTMENT OF HOUSING AND URBAN DEVELOPMENT

Although a relatively new Cabinet department, established in 1965, the Department of Housing and Urban Development (HUD) is one of the larger and more pervasive parts of the federal government. The Secretary of HUD is responsible for hundreds of programs, spending about $5 billion every year and assuring billions more of financing. It is rare for one engaged in real estate investment or finance not to have some relationship with a HUD program. For the great majority of builders and developers, the actions of HUD, taken together with the government's monetary and fiscal policies, are key factors determining success or failure.

Most of the programs in which HUD engages as part of its mandate to improve housing and urban life are too specialized to be covered in detail in this book. We examine primarily those programs concerned with housing and real estate finance, while listing others to demonstrate their variety. Specialists will need a greater depth of knowledge concerning the other programs.

HUD has large Washington and regional staffs operating these programs. The administrative and political problems have been immense. Initially many of the programs were handled by separate agencies, each of which tended to develop its own special-interest group. Frequently the passage of housing legislation has depended on achieving compromises between conflicting groups, each interested in different provisions of the legislation. As a result, most observers find a lack of cohesiveness and logic in the overall HUD program and in the way it has been administered.

Recently the government has attempted to decentralize many of the decisions in the urban sphere by giving block grants to states and communities. These do not require as much specific supervision and reporting as the directly administered federal programs. Their aims and functions, however, will continue largely along the same lines. General programs involving real property have included the following.

1   There are programs concerned with the planning, development, and redevelopment of existing communities. HUD gives funds to states and localities to assist them in planning, setting community goals and standards, and managing their development programs. Since 1949 the federal government has granted subsidies and loans to cities to enable them to clear their slums and blighted areas. Most large cities now have sizable areas of land cleared of prior structures. Such land may be sold at a loss for new construction, or it may be used by cities for public purposes. Large cleared areas still in the process of redevelopment can be seen in many localities.

The redevelopment program has been controversial because a good deal of land clearance requires uprooting people who live on the selected sites. Furthermore, frequent claims are made that one part of the city suffers because of redevelopment elsewhere. In response to these and other pressures, HUD inaugurated a number of other programs to assist in the redevelopment and renewal process. There have been model and demonstration city programs. Financial assistance has been available for households and firms displaced by government action. Loans and grants have been available for the rehabilitation of properties, neighborhood facilities and community services have been supported, and code-enforcement programs have been subsidized. The federal government helps people living in slums or depressed and crime-ridden areas to get property insurance that they could not otherwise obtain or afford.

2 HUD also has programs targeted on new communities and on other types of urban problems. It may guarantee loans to cover land acquisiton and loans for the planning and development of new communities. It makes loans and grants for public facilities, particularly in smaller communities, and it makes grants to aid in the development, acquisition, beautification, and preservation of open spaces and lands for parks, recreation, and scenic and historic uses. It has a program which insures urban structures in case of flood losses.

3 HUD deals with the interstate sales of land, particularly land for recreational or retirement communities. These regulations require detailed disclosures at the time of sale. The system of regulation and registration is similar in concept to the systems discussed in connection with the regulation of real estate securities. The regulations assume that if sufficiently detailed information is made available to buyers they can make proper decisions as to whether a purchase meets their needs.

4 The government has a large number of specialized housing programs. (*a*) Some housing finance programs are concerned primarily with increasing the flow of mortgage funds in order to lower their costs and thereby decrease monthly payments. Several of these are aimed at making the secondary market more efficient, thus lowering its costs, and also at inducing more institutions and funds to lend on mortgages. (*b*) Other programs attempt to increase directly available mortgage funds through regulating financial institutions and supporting federal agencies in the housing field. (*c*) In addition to mortgage-market programs, direct payments or subsidies to owners, builders, renters, and lenders on housing units are made in an attempt to increase the amount of housing.

SECONDARY MORTGAGE MARKETS

Secondary mortgage markets are those in which existing mortgages are bought and sold. Here lenders desiring to invest additional money can find mortgages available for purchase. Lenders desiring more cash can sell loans already in their portfolio, at what they hope is close to their true value.

The growth of insured or guaranteed loans has been of major assistance in making possible increased sales of mortgages to numerous institutions. Before the government's programs come into existence, mortgages suffered as an investment vehicle because they were primarily local devices with limited liquidity. Even the actual loan instruments differed tremendously from one area to another. No basic procedures existed for transmitting information on a national scale as to what was happening in a local market.

Before the creation of the FHA, every mortgage sold in the secondary market had to be handled on an individual basis. The lender had to check carefully the security as well as the borrower. Even so, risks were high. The foreclosure experience of the early 1930s demonstrated that traditional mortgage lending techniques were not suitable for their tasks.

The ability to sell existing loans is important to give liquidity to the mortgage market. Unless a loan can be resold without a large loss from current market rates, lenders are locked into their portfolios, and the number who can lend on mortgages is reduced. Only those who know they will not need to obtain funds through selling a mortgage will tie up their money. In contrast, when a true secondary market exists, lenders can sell out of their portfolios; this added liquidity tends to increase the amount of money which lenders are willing to make available in any market. The secondary market in mortgages has not been liquid. In times of monetary ease, someone wanting to sell a mortgage could find buyers. At other times buyers would virtually disappear. This problem of an uncertain market for future sales has caused major difficulties for builders and mortgage bankers. Traditionally, these groups have had only limited working capital. Yet little money is available on construction mortgages unless the person lending is assured that a final source of funds—a takeout loan—will be available at the time a house is completed and sold. Most purchasers need a mortgage to pay for a house. Unless loans are available, builders are not able to sell their newly constructed units. Therefore, short-term lenders such as banks or REITs want to see a firm commitment that someone will lend to the ultimate purchaser before they are willing to advance construction funds.

The problem of liquidity in the secondary market still exists. The market is quite thin and disorganized. Even though units can be traded, volume remains small. Currently, however, a national computer network called Amminet (automated mortgage-market information network) exists, which makes it possible for many of the largest holders of mortgages to offer them for purchase or sale to other major mortgage lenders. Chapter 2 also noted that a futures market for mortgage certificates guaranteed by the Government National Mortgage Association (GNMA) was started on the Chicago Board of Trade in 1975.

While these are steps toward a hoped-for improvement in the secondary mortgage market, the degree of success they may bring remains uncertain.

The government programs have been successful in other ways in bringing about major improvements in mortgage lending practices: (1) They have made it possible to make moderate-sized loans on individual houses in distant areas. (2) The federal agencies' underwriting replaces a lender's need for complete inspection of the unit and the borrower. The risk involved is easier to calculate. (3) Furthermore, because correspondents are willing to accumulate and process together batches of individual loans, government-insured loans are usually offered by brokers in a volume sufficient for large institutions. (4) The existence of the federal programs has led to the removal of state restrictions on terms and areas of lending for mortgages. The mortgage has become a more standard commodity which can be traded over wide areas and purchased by lenders having no knowledge whatsoever of the security underlying the mortgage or the basic credit reliability of the borrower.

THE MORTGAGE PROGRAMS OF THE
FHA AND THE VA

The establishment of the FHA in 1934 constituted one of the earliest and most important attempts to improve the secondary mortgage market. Ten years later the loan guarantee program of the VA was added. For purposes of analysis we can group both together, as has generally been done in the market.

The FHA and the VA, with a few exceptions, do not lend money or build houses.

They act as insurers or guarantors of repayments from borrowers to the approved private lenders who make the funds available.

Goals

By insuring or guaranteeing the lenders against the loss of principal on their loans, the FHA-VA programs have sought to meet two major goals. One is that already discussed: the development of a national mortgage market. The aim has been to make it possible for lenders throughout the country to make loans on houses in areas far from their institutional base.

A second goal is to "encourage improvement in housing standards and conditions." One way to do this is to decrease the share of current income required by owners or renters to make payments on a particular house. In addition, the FHA has taken more interest than other lenders in the quality of construction and the location of houses it has insured.

The desire to improve housing conditions has also led to the use of the program to promote the construction of houses which Congress felt would otherwise not have been built. Under major defense and war housing programs, the government assumed risks and additional costs of building in nonstable areas and in areas which had previously lacked standard housing and financing conditions. The concept of special aid has expanded to include housing for low-income groups, housing in urban renewal areas, housing for the elderly, cooperatives and condominiums, nursing homes, and major long-tern loans for rehabilitation and home improvements.

The two separate goals have caused a dichotomy of interests in the FHA programs. Following the first line, some have conceived of the programs primarily as methods of improving the private mortgage market. In their view, mortgage insurance was to be self-supporting; the government was simply to guarantee against catastrophic losses caused by events beyond the control of private insurers.

The other line stresses the public features of the government's programs. Its proponents have insisted that the government ought not to be involved in any program whose standards fall below acceptable levels of public policy. These pressures led the FHA to set higher building, neighborhood, and environmental standards on houses eligible for its insurance than the minimum levels set by market practice. These same reasons also led the FHA to move earlier and with greater vigor than others to insist on equal opportunity and nondiscrimination in the sale or rental of the housing on which it insured loans.

With the growth of private mortgage insurance, the special assistance and subsidy programs of the FHA have made up an increasing share of the total. Insurance of normal risks has tended to shift to the private market. To counteract this tendency and widen their market, mortgage companies have lobbied strongly for a separation of the normal mortgage insurance functions of the FHA from its special-assistance functions. They want a government-sponsored agency similar to the Federal National Mortgage Association (FNMA) to take over the less risky insurance functions from the FHA.

In contrast to the confusion over what the FHA was to accomplish, the program for guaranteeing veterans' mortgages has always been thought of principally as a veterans' benefit. It has not been expected to pay its own way. Even so, at some periods of its history, outside observers have felt that the VA was concerned more with the impact of its program on housing starts and builders' volume than with the needs of individual veterans.

Volume

The proportion of all housing covered by FHA-VA programs has varied greatly. At some times the relative advantages of these programs have been large. At other times they have dwindled, particularly in periods when interest rate ceilings set on insured loans fell below the market. The FHA share has also depended upon the percentage of total housing being built in multifamily units. Except for a period immediately following World War II, when the FHA was dominant in the multifamily field, the share of government insurance programs covering income properties has tended to be small. However, in 1974, because of rental subsidy programs, about 40 percent of newly issued mortgages on multifamily units were insured by the FHA.

HUD estimates that in 1973 and 1974 about 12 percent of newly built residential units were insured by mortgages under the FHA-VA programs. Many of these loans covered houses built under the various special-assistance and central-city programs. The FHA percentage of nonsubsidized new construction was small. In contrast, in 1950 and 1954 the government programs accounted for nearly half of all housing starts and for more than half of new dwellings carrying mortgages. Until the recent drop in volume, a normal share of the market for the FHA-VA programs seemd to be about 30 to 40 percent.

In 1975, reflecting this past size, nearly 30 percent of all residential mortgage loans outstanding were still government-underwritten. This, however, was a considerable drop from the peak reached in 1955, when these loans totaled over 45 percent of outstanding mortgages. Although the importance of the federal programs for most of the housing market has diminished, they remain significant, especially for the special-assistance or other high-risk programs, for housing of low- and moderate-income families, and in certain regions.

Costs of Housing and Mortgage Terms

The basic thrust of the FHA programs has been to expand the housing market by making possible lower downpayments, lower interest rates, and longer periods of amortization. Chapter 4 and Tables 4-1 and 4-2 show how lowering downpayments and lengthening amortization periods expand the market for homeownership. We saw that as a result of the FHA-VA programs and their influence on other types of mortgage lending, the downpayment is no longer a serious hurdle for most potential homeowners wanting to buy moderately priced houses.

On the other hand, success in expanding the market through decreasing monthly payments has not been as great. Initially the FHA-VA programs made it possible for most families with a fully employed wage earner to buy a house if they so desired. However, housing costs and property taxes have risen faster than income. Furthermore, the interest rates on mortgages have doubled. Because the interest factor is so significant when rates are high, many families with moderate incomes once again find they cannot buy a new house. They could make the downpayment, but they cannot meet the monthly payments.

Types of FHA-VA Programs

A lengthy description of the types of programs available from the FHA and the VA is not worthwhile because they change so frequently. It is useful, however, for those concerned with lending and investing to understand the basic principles of the government insurance and guarantee programs and to recognize how the individual programs tend to differ. Programs vary in accordance with the type and amount of risks they insure; with the procedures required for obtaining the insurance or guarantee; and, finally, with the amount and form of the payment received by the lender in case the borrower defaults on the loan.

A convenient classification divides the programs into:

  1   Property improvement and mobile-home loans (FHA Title 1)
  2   Traditional mortgage insurance (parts of FHA Title 2)
  3   The VA guarantee programs
  4   High-risk, partially subsidized insurance programs (parts of FHA Title 2)
  5   Programs that subsidize the costs of mortgage insurance, of construction, of renting, or of interest rates
  6   Coinsurance programs proposed in 1975

Property Improvement and Mobile-Home Loans: FHA Title 1

Unlike other programs, loans for modernization or home improvement do not depend on mortgages for their security; rather, they are in the nature of personal or consumer loans. Frequently a mortgage already exists. Therefore, the notes for these loans are usually not recorded or made liens against the property.

Modernization and improvement loans are limited in amount ($10,000 on a single-family home since 1974) and in time (approximately 7 years). Interest rates vary with the size and period of the loan. Maximum rates are subject to regulation and have varied between 8.83 and 12.00 percent.

The charge for this insurance is .5 percent per year. The FHA collects this sum and pools it to make the necessary payments to lenders in cases of loss. Within the very broad limits set by the FHA, the actual terms with respect to credit requirements and income depend upon the lender. Under this program, lenders are coinsurers with the FHA, which sets up an insurance reserve for each participating lender. The amount in the reserve is increased by 10 percent of each new loan made. Claims paid are subtracted from the reserve balance.

If a loan defaults, the FHA agrees to pay the lender 90 percent of the loss in cash. The reserve is not like that for many types of consumer loans, where the seller eventually will get a payment from the reserve if no losses occur. In this case the reserve simply reverts to the FHA. After 2.5 years, the reserve is decreased by 15 percent a year.

Title 1 loans are also available for purchases of mobile homes which meet FHA standards. The insurance procedure is the same, based upon a pooling of reserves and coinsurance, but in this case the length of the loan can be approximately 15 years, and the amount is larger.

FHA MUTUAL MORTGAGE INSURANCE

Although now diminished in size and scope, mutual mortgage insurance follows the original concept of the FHA. It is important to understand its procedures because mutual mortgage insurance is the father both of the special-assistance high-risk government programs which have since proliferated and of modern private mortgage insurance.

Initially, the concept of FHA insurance was similar to that of commercial fire or life insurance. The FHA was to pay its own way through mutual insurance funds, but the government agreed to make up certain losses if catastrophes caused the funds to be inadequate. Insurance policies written during a time period (such as a year) were pooled together. The losses from any loans which went bad in that pool were originally charged against the pool. However, losses exceeding the amounts available in a particular fund could be covered through a reinsurance fund which received a certain percentage from the many funds established. If the insurance experience in any fund was favorable—that is, if the payments for losses on insurance contracts written did not completely utilize the fund—the mortgagor could receive a partial refund of previous premiums when making the final mortgage payment, and the insurance was extinguished.

The most important program of this type has been Section 203(b), insuring mortgages on owner-occupied property. Another important section has been 207, covering traditionally built multifamily rental units.

To protect its insurance funds, the FHA establishes procedures and standards for insuring loans. It examines (underwrites) each loan to make certain it meets FHA standards and contains no extraordinary risks. Approved lenders apply for FHA commitments to insure particular loans which are to be closed under specific conditions. The conditions include forms to be used, title regulations, and FHA approval of the eligibility of the property and borrower. Conditional commitments are granted for a specific property with prospective terms, but with an unknown mortgagor. Firm commitments are issued upon approval of the eligible borrower.

With a firm commitment, the mortgagee can advance the money and close the loan. If all the terms of the commitment are met, the FHA issues an insurance contract specifying the fees to be paid and listing the conditions under which the lender will be reimbursed for losses and the manner of reimbursement.

The FHA charges a commitment fee, other initial processing charges, and an insurance premium of .5 percent per year on the unpaid balances. The fees have varied over time, depending upon the FHA costs of underwriting.

Requirements

An examination of some of the factors which the FHA considers in its underwriting offers a good picture of how the program actually works:

1 The FHA is concerned with the qualifications of the mortgage lender. A borrower must deal with an FHA-approved lender. This means that the mortgagee must meet certain criteria. The FHA wants to be sure that the lender can properly process and service insured loans.

2   The amount of insurance and the eligibility of a loan depend upon its purpose. Thus the FHA insures only loans which fit into specified categories. Unless a loan meets these criteria, it will not be insured. Except for Title 1, the FHA will not insure a second mortgage, nor will it insure a first-mortgage loan if a second mortgage exists or is required to make the purchase possible.

The percentage of a loan insured depends upon occupancy. Normally, a larger percentage will be insured if the building is to be owner-occupied. If the loan is on a newly constructed house, the percentage of the mortgage insured will be less for houses not inspected by the FHA during construction. It is assumed that such inspections reduce risks. The major part of the FHA program has been the insurance of low-downpayment loans for newly constructed moderate-income housing.

3   The FHA has strict maximum requirements relating the amount of a loan on a house to the appraised value or actual selling cost of the dwelling unit. Under amendments to the act in 1974, the FHA was willing to insure 97 percent of the first $25,000 of appraised value or acquisition cost, whichever is less; 90 percent of the next $10,000; and 80 percent of a final $10,000. Thus the maximum loan insured on a single-family house would be $41,250, and, in fact, the mortgage loan cannot exceed this amount. As a result, every dollar of cost over $45,000 for a house bought with an FHA-insured mortgage must be met by an additional dollar in the downpayment. No further uninsured loan can be taken out. A buyer must find cash to cover the difference between the selling price and the maximum insurance available for the loan.

4   The FHA is concerned with the design, construction, neighborhood, and livability of the houses it insures. No loans will be insured unless they meet the particular minimum criteria established for each title (type) of loan. Even if the minimum criteria are met, the amount of insurance granted depends on how good the FHA judges these features to be. Judgment is based upon the FHA's view of the long-run interest of the buyer and the housing market with respect to design.

5   The FHA sets minimum amortization payments. Under Title 203(b), the principal traditional program, a loan must normally be paid off in 30 years or three-quarters of the remaining economic life of a property, whichever is less. The 30-year limit may be extended to 35 years if the mortgagor's income is so low that he or she could not meet the payments for the 30-year-term loan and if the property was constructed subject to FHA or VA inspection. Under other titles and programs, the maximum term of a loan can vary from 20 to 40 years, depending upon the type of property securing the insured loan.

6   The FHA establishes maximum interest rates and fees for each insured loan. This has been one of the most controversial parts of the FHA program. When the maximums are much below market rates, lenders will not make FHA-VA loans, and this source of money disappears. On the other hand, the ceilings have tended to hold down escalation of rates in certain periods. The presidential commissions examining this question have urged that a dual system be tried. Loans meeting certain criteria would be freed of the ceilings.

7   As part of the individual loan underwriting procedure, a great deal of emphasis is placed on the borrower's expected ability to meet the loan payments. Loans are insured only for eligible borrowers who meet specific credit standards. Except in particular circumstances, borrowers cannot be above 62 years of age. The required mortgage payments and other housing expenses must fall within prescribed ratios to the borrower's current and prospective income.

8   The FHA requires that certain relationships be established between the borrower and the lender in each insured transaction. Thus it requires a particular form or forms for the mortgage and the note covering the loan. On new construction, builders must warrant their work. The seller must not discriminate by sex, color, or religion. The borrower must be informed of the FHA appraised value before the sale is completed.

Claims for Reimbursement

Even though care is taken with loans, a sizable number do go into default. At this point the insurance contract begins to pay off. Lenders must inform the insuring office within 60 days after default and periodically thereafter. Within a year of default, lenders must acquire title by some means, or they must institute foreclosure procedures.

To secure the insurance benefits, the mortgagee must be able to deliver title to the FHA within 30 days after acquisition with the property free of waste (loss of value due to undermaintenance). Upon delivery of title, the insured lender may collect from the mortgage insurance fund either cash or negotiable debentures with interest and principal guaranteed by the United States government.

Insurance claims are divided. Payment is made immediately for the entire unpaid principal balance of the mortgage plus amounts for such things as taxes, assessments, insurance, part of foreclosure costs, and costs necessary for protecting, preserving, or operating the property.

In addition, the mortgagee receives a contingent-claim certificate to cover the difference between the initial payment and the total necessary expenses. The contingent claims cover the remaining foreclosure costs, unpaid interest, and repairs necessary to restore the property to proper condition. The amount received on this claim will depend on the housing market and the cost of sale. When a property is sold, the Federal Housing Commissioner calculates total costs. If the net receipts exceed all these costs, the difference is used to pay as much as possible of the certificate of claim.

Coinsurance

In 1975, HUD proposed regulations for a new coinsurance program providing a 90/10 sharing by HUD and the originating lender, respectively, of net losses incurred on coinsured loans. These loans are of the type insured under Title 203(b), but under coinsurance, the lender is responsible for credit underwriting, property appraisal, and disposition. In return, the lender receives an origination fee, and the lender's liability is limited to a 5-year period, after which the loan reverts to 100 percent FHA insurance. While somewhat similar to coinsurance under Title 1 loans, the new program provides that the lender may receive a portion of any excess reserves built up over the 5 years, depending on actual loss experience. A portfolio stop-loss provision limits total lender exposure on mortgages originated and coinsured within each calendar year to 1 percent of the total principal amount of such mortgages. Finally, secondary purchasers of coinsured loans are fully protected by recourse to the originator through repurchase or substitution or, in the event of nonperformance by the originator, to the FHA for full recovery.

VETERANS ADMINISTRATION

The system of mortgage guarantee set up by the Veterans Readjustment Benefits Act of 1944 and the Veterans Housing Act of 1970 runs roughly parallel to that of the FHA insurance. A fundamental difference, of course, is that the VA program is only for eligible veterans. While in most periods more loans have been insured under the FHA program than under that of the VA, in recent years the VA guarantee has actually been the more significant factor in the market for nonsubsidized, non-high-risk market loans.

To enable the veteran to purchase a better-quality house, or one with more reasonable terms than might otherwise be available, Congress has agreed to guarantee lenders against some or all of the losses that may arise as a result of the added risks assumed when veterans are granted better mortgage terms than those prevailing in the market. As with FHA loans, the government (except in a small number of cases) does not put up the money, but simply guarantees the lender against certain types of losses.

Requirements

The terms of the VA and the FHA have been roughly similar with respect to the eight criteria just listed and discussed in connection with the FHA. However, there are some significant differences. The VA specifies that the full amount of a loan is eligible for guarantee if it does not exceed the reasonable value of the property as determined by the administrator. This allows loans to be 100 percent of the price; that is, no downpayments are needed. In fact, the majority of loans made require no downpayment. In addition, there is no limit (except the lender's risk) on the size of loan guaranteed.

Borrower requirements also parallel those of the FHA, but with the obvious difference that the borrower must be a veteran eligible for the loan guarantee benefits. Specific eligibility is determined by the VA in accordance with acts of Congress. The loan-to-income ratios required by the VA tend not to be as strict as those of the FHA. Limits are established by the individual lender, who is charged with being prudent so that the burden on a veteran borrower will not be too great. There is no minimum downpayment requirement, and the maximum period of amortization is 30 years.

Claims

The form of the guarantee differs somewhat from that of FHA loans. The VA guarantees mortgage lenders against losses up to specified limits. In 1974 the maximum guarantee cover was moved up to 60 percent of the amount of the loan, to a maximum of $17,500. Thus on a $10,000 loan the maximum loss paid by the VA was $6,000. On a $40,000 loan it would be $17,500.

The VA guarantee declines pro rata with payments on the loan. To illustrate, assume that the lender has received $5,000 in payments on a $10,000 loan. At this point the guarantee still covers 60 percent, but only of the outstanding $5,000. If the VA had to make good on its guarantee, the lender would not be reimbursed for any loss over $3,000. If the lender's loss were $4,000, for example, the VA would pay $3,000, and the lender would be responsible for the remaining $1,000 loss.

There is no charge to the veteran for the guarantee. Since it has no continuing insurance premiums to collect, the VA does not establish accounts with lenders, as the FHA does. Once it has issued a guarantee, it retains no continuing relation to the loan. It steps in only in case of default. Lenders service the accounts; if a default occurs, they must notify the VA. Since the guarantee is a form of veteran benefit, the VA has rather liberal default requirements, the purpose of which is to aid the veteran. Lenders can use extra time in attempting to cure a default. They can also modify or extend the terms of a loan if this will help the veteran.

When all efforts to cure a default have failed, lenders may file a claim for the full amount of the guarantee. All expenses of lenders, including interest, may be reimbursed, providing these do not exceed the amount of the VA guarantee.

If the buyer of a house is eligible as a veteran, borrowing with the use of the VA guarantee has several advantages. The cost of mortgage insurance is saved, and there is no minimum downpayment or maximum size of loan. How much will be loaned and how much cash will be required are worked out in individual negotiations between the buyer and the lender. Depending upon prevailing conditions in the local housing market, terms may be somewhat more flexible. The VA gives greater consideration than other loan insurers to the veteran's needs and problems in making a determination of such factors as authorized income limits and credit-worthiness and in allowing forbearance when payments are missed. All these benefits stem from the basic fact that the VA is established to aid its clients (individual veterans) to buy and maintain their own homes. Therefore, it need not, and does not, follow market practices too closely.

THE GOVERNMENT HOUSING SUBSIDY PROGRAMS

While the FHA-VA programs have been extremely successful in expanding the mortgage market and in broadening the number of people who could buy houses, they left out many low-income families and special groups, such as the aged, who could not afford standard housing. As a result, one of the most widely accepted, yet most vehemently debated, concepts in the real estate field developed: the idea that the housing expenses of some families should be subsidized by the government. Basically our political system has assumed that through the technique of direct or indirect government subsidies, we ought to facilitate homeownership, assure a decent minimum standard of living, attempt to offset some of the destabilizing impacts of monetary and fiscal policy on housing construction, and perhaps offer equal living opportunities to people of different racial and income backgrounds.

The total amount of these subsidies has been greatly expanded through what seemed originally like a rather unimportant exemption and available deduction in our income tax system. The provision that payments for mortgage interest and property taxes could be deducted and the rental equivalent of equity in our homes could be excluded made homeownership cheaper. Although in theory families at all income levels could take advantage of these benefits, tax subsidies tend to rise as a family's income increases.

By 1975 the federal government was spending around $15 billion a year on housing subsidies. Of this amount, $11 billion to 13 billion went to high-income groups through their right to deduct housing expenses from the federal income tax. About $3 billion went to low-income groups whose housing expenditures were subsidized directly. In addition, sizable subsidies went to the federal mortgage lending agencies discussed in the next chapter.

The question of subsidies through the tax system is taken up in Chapter 21. Here, we want to examine some of the basic features of the subsidies to low-income groups and the debates surrounding them. While the form varies tremendously, certain basic features are significant in every housing subsidy system. The general concepts, developed over time, apply to most of the low-income subsidy programs.

We illustrate these factors by examining some of the regulations which apply to a particular program called FHA Title 235 and to the program which replaced it, Section 8 of the Housing and Community Development Act of 1974. Until terminated, FHA 235 was one of the most active programs of the federal government. It falls into both of two separate categories: the FHA high-risk program and the direct subsidy program.

As a result of a great deal of debate and criticism of the form of the subsidy, the rules and regulations for Section 8 are far less structured than those for Title 235, and they give HUD substantially more freedom over costs and payments. However, it is easier to understand the basic concepts of, and the controversy over, the subsidy by examining the 235 program because it is clearer and at the same time is fairly typical of most other subsidy programs. It should be noted that these regulations were in effect for the original low-income 235 program and not for the moderate-income 235 program which was inaugurated in 1975. This later program was devised to provide for somewhat higher income groups. Its regulations were drawn to offer smaller interest rate subsidies and to require much higher initial payments.

Eligibility   Which family or unit is eligible for a subsidy depends upon (1) the costs of standard housing in a locality and (2) comparison with average incomes in that locality. Usually an absolute limit is put on the cost of the subsidized unit or the amount of a loan that will be given to a family, nonprofit association, or local housing authority seeking a subsidy. Under FHA Title 235 the limit was $18,000 (later $21,600) for a single-family unit, but this limit could be increased. It was raised by $3,000 in certified high-cost areas. Another $3,000 could be added to the loan if the family contained five or more persons and the house had four or more bedrooms.

There has been a constant pressure to raise program limits as the cost of standard housing has gone up. Certain programs had limits set so low that they could be used only in very low cost areas. Frequently those limits meant that some of the better programs could not be brought into the central cities, where a large part of the housing problem exists.

To avoid some of this problem, Section 8 limits rents on assisted units to 10 percent (20 percent in special circumstances) above the fair market value of each type of unit in each general locality as established by HUD.

Amount of Subsidy   The amount of subsidy given to a family or to the builder or owner of a building varies with a family's income, the locality, and family size. To qualify for a program, a family's income must fall into a certain range. There is a maximum income level above which it is assumed that no subsidy is required. In addition, most programs will not accept a family whose income is so low that it cannot meet the minimum payments required over and above the subsidies made available by the federal government.

Again using the 235 program as an illustration, in determining what costs must be met, the government considers the total required monthly payments to own or rent a new standard housing unit. Such payments must cover interest, amortization, taxes, insurance, and mortgage insurance premiums. The necessary monthly payments are compared with a sum equal to 20 percent of a family's adjusted gross income. However, the authorized income level is increased depending on the number in the family and the number of minor children. For instance, in a particular city under the 235 program, a two-person family with income over $5,400 could not qualify. On the other hand, a family with six minor children could qualify even with an income of $8,775. The difference depends on the allowed exclusions based upon family size. In addition, 5 percent of the earnings of adults, all earnings of minor children, and nonrecurring income are excluded.

In Section 8, the Secretary of HUD was granted the right to specify maximum required nonsubsidized monthly payments which the family had to pay—between 15 and 25 percent of the family's income, with the percentage set to depend upon factors such as those just discussed.

Percentage of Eligibles   While in theory all families falling into the income brackets for which subsidies were available could qualify, in fact the percentage of eligible families has been greatly limited by the amount of funds made available. As a result, those who did qualify could be thought of as having won a gift or lottery by almost a random process. One of the major criticisms of the program has been that of two similar families, one would receive a very large subsidy, while the other would receive nothing. Under Section 8, all families with a gross income at least 20 percent below an area's medium income are eligible.

Form of Subsidy   In most cases the subsidy covers the difference between the market cost, or economic cost of living in a particular house, and the share of that cost which the program assumes the family should carry. Under the FHA 235 program the actual costs are compared with a sum equal to 20 percent of the family's adjusted gross income. HUD would pay the lender an interest subsidy for that amount of the mortgage payment exceeding the 20 percent limit. The amount paid to the lender as an interest subsidy is the difference between the monthly payment on the mortgage and 20 percent of the borrower's income level. In the case of 235, the maximum HUD subsidy cannot lower the interest rate paid by the borrower below 1 percent, no matter how low his or her adjusted gross income.

In cases of subsidies of local housing authorities, the HUD subsidy can cover all capital payments, for both interest and amortization, on the property. The actual amount a family must pay from its income can run anywhere from 5 to 25 percent, depending on the particular program. In other words, the amount of a subsidy, while based on the difference between economic rents and family income, also depends on the particular program under which a family qualifies.

Minimum Payments   In order to qualify as many people as possible, downpayments have been kept to a minimum, and maximum amortization periods have been used. Under 235, a very low income family was required to pay only $200 down. However, the required downpayment would rise to 3 percent of the appraised value if a family's income exceeded the income limits set for public housing in the community by more than 35 percent.

Similarly, the term of the loan could be increased from 30 to 35 or even 40 years if lengthening the amortization period made it possible to qualify a family otherwise ineligible because the required payments over the shorter term would be too high.

No matter what the actual term of the loan, the subsidy is calculated as if the amortization were made over a 40-year period. Most of the programs subsidizing local housing authorities are required to use a minimum 40-year amortization. By lowering current loan payments as far as possible, the number of eligible families is maximized, and the current budget cost of subsidies is minimized.

The Government and the Lender   When the maximum interest rate authorized for a program is below the market, private lenders will not put up money. When this occurs, as explained in the discussion of the GNMA programs, the government steps in and becomes an indirect lender. The government purchases the loan at an agreed-upon price from the mortgage broker or other lender who made it initially. The original lender processes the loan to profit from the origination and servicing fees. HUD, by buying the loan, agrees to accept a below-market interest rate. If it then sells to the FNMA, it recoups most of its payment. The difference or loss on the loan is in addition to the interest subsidy payments that the government makes monthly on the mortgage.

Types of Programs

The subsidy programs have developed along two lines. One was a direct outgrowth of the basic FHA concept of creating more eligible homeowners by reducing required downpayments and monthly payments. The government attempted to increase the number of eligible persons still more by assuming additional risks. To the extent that Congress appropriates public funds to cover such excess risks rather than having the homeowner pay these costs, the owner is aided through a subsidy.

A second line of development comprises a whole group of programs based upon government funds, direct loans, and direct subsidies.

FHA High-Risk Programs   The earliest example of government assumption of additional risks to increase the supply of housing occurred in the 1940s. At that time, in order to increase the supply of defense and war housing, the government set up special FHA programs for which the standards, particularly with respect to costs, were lower than those for the mutual mortgage insurance programs. The government was willing to guarantee that it would make up any insurance losses in order to be certain that building would take place in areas considered too unstable for normal FHA insurance and also in areas which had previously lacked standard housing and financing.

Gradually the concept of special aid through FHA high-risk programs expanded to include loans to marginal groups or others who needed special assistance but who could not qualify under normal lending standards. Periodically Congress has changed the terms, conditions, and interest rates of mortgages for these programs which the FHA could insure. The objective has been to improve the housing conditions of particular groups when Congress believed special aids were necessary. The FHA compilation of insurable loans shows over 40 different types of mortgages covered. Except for the few initial standard-type programs, almost all of them insure exceptional risks, covering, for example, homes for disaster victims, rehabilitation housing, homes for servicemen and servicewomen, homes in outlying areas and in urban renewal areas, experimental housing, and housing for the elderly.

The general techniques in all these cases are similar. Congress determines that to help a particular group afford housing, special terms or interest rates are necessary. The better the terms and the lower the interest rates, the more easily a group at a given income level can afford a particular level of housing. Easier terms authorized have included a zero or only a $200 downpayment, amortization periods up to 40 years, and interest rates as low as 1 percent.

Since such terms increase the FHA's risk, Congress authorizes a special title and a special insurance fund for each program. In effect, Congress agrees to pay for any losses for these titles from future appropriations, if necessary. The amount of losses will depend upon how well the programs are managed and how closely the established terms approach market ones. Many programs may be self-supporting; others may require large subsidies. The point to recognize is that Congress, with much popular support but also with a great deal of political opposition and many battles, has determined that such special programs are a proper use of the FHA organization and insuring function.

Special-Assistance Plans and the Tandem Plan   One special feature of the high-risk programs has led to another form of special assistance. This additional program is handled by the GNMA, described in the next chapter.

Lenders are often unwilling to make loans for these high-risk programs, even with the FHA's guarantee of payment of the principal. Uncertainty as to possible delays in processing, amortization periods extending so far into the future that they become undesirable, and similar features make these mortgages unsalable even with insurance. The programs would fail unless the government furnished a market. This is one of the tasks of the GNMA ("Ginnie Mae"). It purchases loans which appear uneconomic to the private market. It covers its costs either by being able to borrow at lower rates than private lenders or by using appropriated federal government funds.

Mortgages are originated by lenders and mortgage bankers in the normal manner. If they had to be sold in the private market, their prices would be marked down, and the lender would take a loss. Instead, the lender is able to sell them to the GNMA for the amount loaned. The GNMA collects the monthly payments on the mortgages, but they are less than private lenders demand for such loans.

The Tandem Plan   The "tandem plan" is a related program by which the GNMA subsidizes part of the interest rates of particular borrowers. When interest rates have been exceptionally high and housing starts have been declining, this plan has been used to lower the rates paid by borrowers. It is a form of subsidy to the families who can obtain such loans.

The operating basis of the tandem plan is the fact that changes in interest rates are translated directly into the price of mortgages. Thus a 7.75 percent 30-year-term mortgage which is expected to be paid off in 12 years will sell for $91.36 per $100 of principal if current market rates for equivalent mortgages are 9 percent. Under the tandem plan, with market rates at 9 percent, the GNMA may issue a commitment to buy at par (100), a 7.75 percent mortgage on a project or unit for which such special assistance is authorized. At the same time, the FNMA issues a commitment to the GNMA to buy the mortgage at the market rate ($91.36). When the mortgage is sold to the FNMA, Ginnie Mae absorbs the loss between the par price it paid the originator of the mortgage and the lower market price it receives from the FNMA, in this case $8.64 per $100 of loan. The GNMA has also recouped its funds by sales of mortgage-backed securities to the Federal Financing Bank.

The object of the tandem plan is to show a lower rate of expenditures from the federal budget than would be shown if the GNMA bought and continued to hold the mortgage. The GNMA buys its mortgages with appropriated funds. Without the sale to the FNMA or the Federal Financing Bank, the budget would show an expenditure equal to the entire mortgage loan. The government would hold a new asset—the mortgage—but under traditional government budget accounting, no credit is gained from added assets. Instead, the whole sum paid for the mortgage shows as an increase in the deficit and the public debt.

Under the tandem plan, when the asset is sold to the FNMA, funds are received to offset most of the original expenditure. The budget records as an expenditure only the difference between what the GNMA pays to buy the mortgage and what it receives from the FNMA—in the example above, $8.64 per $100 of mortgage. While in a private accounting sense the government is no better off, the administration in office gets credit for a better budget performance.

Public Low-rent Housing   One of the earliest direct subsidy programs was the low-rent public housing program authorized by the United States Housing Act of 1937. Under this scheme, HUD provides financial and technical assistance to local housing authorities, which plan, build, and operate low-rent public housing projects. A local housing authority can obtain its units in various ways: It can build new projects, rehabilitate existing structures, purchase units from builders ("turnkey" method), or lease units from private owners.

In each case the dwellings are rented to low-income families at a rent below the market or economic rent. The difference between actual costs and those paid by the tenant is covered by a subsidy from the federal government, the state, or the local agency. The federal subsidy consists of annual federal contributions made to cover the debt service on the bonds of the local authority. These bonds, which are tax-exempt, are issued to cover the necessary capital costs for the acquisition of the public housing.

Senior Citizen Housing (Direct Loans)   Another type of subsidy applies in projects built by nonprofit, cooperative, or limited-profit sponsors for rent either to those aged 62 years and older or to the handicapped. In these cases the government makes loans for 50 years at 3 percent interest. Again, the difference between the monthly payments required on such a loan and those which would be required by the market is a subsidy to those who meet the law's requirements and are able to rent units in these projects.

Interest Supplements on Home Mortgages   Under various programs, the best known of which have been those under Sections 235 and 236 of the National Housing Act, HUD makes monthly payments to lenders to reduce owners' interest costs. Buyers must qualify for the subsidy and have the mortgage insured by the FHA. The interest costs may be reduced to as low as 1 percent.

As we have seen, in these as in the other programs, the amount homeowners must pay is based on a percentage of their income. In most of the programs, persons being subsidized must pay between 20 and 25 percent of their income for housing expenses. The remainder of the actual costs of living in the home is subsidized by HUD through meeting part of the mortgage payment. The specific income requirements and the amount of the subsidy are established separately for each locality.

Leasing of Low-rent Housing   Section 8 of the Housing and Community Development Act of 1974 greatly expanded and gave primary emphasis to the subsidy programs previously incorporated under Section 23 of the Housing Act of 1937. It authorized HUD either directly or through contracts with local authorities to subsidize rents in privately owned and operated dwelling units. This section pays the difference between the rents private owners are authorized to charge and the rents low-income families can afford. The program aims at using the existing housing stock or the ability of the private market to produce lower-priced houses than public bodies could. It also has sought to avoid the concentration of low-income families in large projects.

The basic procedures follow those of most other subsidy programs. The federal government, through HUD, enters into a contract to subsidize rents on a given number of units. These dwellings are then rented to low-income families who would not be able to pay the amount required by the market from their existing income. The difference is paid to the owner through an assistance payment. The purpose is to enable such families to rent a dwelling unit meeting normal housing standards, but to leave them with enough income for other expenditures.

Housing Allowances   In the 1930s, the National Association of Real Estate Boards (now the National Association of Realtors) advocated the idea of paying housing allowances directly to low-income families to use as they wish for some of the rent of a standard housing unit. This idea has become increasingly popular and is now accepted as a useful one by most housing economists. Again, such housing allowances are set so as to make up the difference between a fixed percentage (such as 25 percent) of the family's income and the general rental level of standard houses in the locality. The purpose of the allowance is to make the greatest possible use of existing housing units while enabling families to choose the houses they desire.

There is fairly solid evidence that subsidies made directly to low-income families buy more housing services per dollar spent than subsidies tied to new construction. A question has been raised, however: If these allowances were widespread, would they raise the level of rents so high that most of the value of the subsidy would go to landlords rather than to those in need of the housing assistance? If rents rose to a much higher level, it would be particularly unfair and expensive for those who do not receive the housing assistance.

A few experiments have been aimed at discovering whether supply will be increased adequately if the subsidy is not related directly to a new unit. While there are some indications that it can work (through so-called filtering), disagreement over this question is still great.

SUMMARY: SOME UNANSWERED QUESTIONS

The subject of the desirability of housing subsidies has been vehemently debated for over 40 years, with little indication that a decision will soon be forthcoming. In fact, it is interesting that England, which had one of the earliest and largest of the subsidy programs, in recent years has completely shifted its concept of a proper program from one extreme to the other.

The following are some of the critical unanswered questions:

1   Who should qualify for the programs? Here the debate arises over the very large sums given to high- and moderate-income families, compared with the low subsidies which go to the poor. Even more important, there appears to be little logic and fairness in selecting the poor who receive subsidies. Many are eligible, but only a few actually benefit.

2   How large should the subsidy be, and how often should it be recomputed? The problem of amount is a serious one and is closely related to the question of who should qualify. The tendency in recent years has been to recompute the subsidy as a family's income changes. This is not always the case, however. Under several of the mortgage subsidy programs, such as the tandem plan, a family that gets a mortgage at a lower-than-market interest rate will continue to be subsidized no matter how wealthy it later becomes.

3   Back-door financing? The problem of the amount of subsidy is related to the source of the funds. On the whole, the tendency by the government has been to disguise the cost of housing subsidies in the budget. There has been a great deal of back-door financing, that is, the use of programs that do not require appropriations, even though the government makes a subsidy available. One of the major reasons for the emphasis placed upon mortgage programs is that the amount of appropriations required and chargeable to any given year's budget tends to be low compared with the actual housing constructed. Tax exemption has been widely used for the same reason.

4   How should the programs be managed? This question again has been controversial. Over time, major responsibility has been taken by HUD and by state and local authorities. In addition, attempts have been made to use nonprofit associations and profit-making corporations. Responsibilities have been shifted back and forth among these various groups, depending upon the amount of dissatisfaction with the existing program. Such changes continue to be made as new problems and opportunities arise.

5   Should the subsidy programs be tied to new construction? Most programs have required that a unit be newly constructed to qualify for subsidies in the low-income programs. It has been argued that unless housing allowances are tied directly to increases in supply, their effect is to raise demand further and therefore to raise prices and rents. It is argued that the market would not bring down housing prices in a normal manner because the time lags in construction are so large. It has also been claimed that builders, landlords, and unions, seeing higher prices, would demand an increase in their incomes, and therefore the higher prices would be reflected almost at once in higher costs. As a result, any subsidies not tied to construction would not aid those being subsidized. In fact, others in the housing market whose incomes were not being subsidized would be penalized, since they also would be forced to pay the higher costs.

These problems are still unsolved. Economists who stress the efficiency of free markets and their ability to adjust believe that better methods are available than tying the subsidy to new construction. On the other hand, those who emphasize the unusual features of the housing market are not willing to give up the tie to new construction.

6   In addition to arguments over whether subsidies should apply only to new construction, major problems have arisen because many programs have grouped those receiving the subsidies into large projects. Under the traditional public housing programs, large numbers of poverty-stricken families have been brought together in single neighborhoods. Since families that are poor have many other problems besides bad housing, the result has been a concentration in certain localities of problem families, bringing in their wake severe problems of health, crime, and education to these project areas. Experience has produced general agreement that the housing programs need to break down rather than increase the tendency of problem families to concentrate in specific areas. The neighborhood costs of existing concentrations have been too high.

QUESTIONS AND PROBLEMS

1   List five programs administered by HUD and briefly describe their purpose and the techniques used.

2   What is the secondary mortgage market, and what role does it play in housing finance?

3   What are the major improvements in mortgage financing which resulted from the FHA-VA programs?

4   Why do you think the volume of FHA-insured mortgage lending dropped sharply?

5   Describe six requirements which must be met before the FHA will agree to insure a mortgage loan. What is the logic of each?

6   Contrast the downpayment and limits of insurance or guarantee of the FHA and VA programs.

7   Describe the techniques and requirements used by the FHA coinsurance program.

8   How does HUD determine the level of income which makes a family ineligible for a housing subsidy in your community? How is the amount of subsidy determined?

9   Explain how the GNMA tandem plan works.

10   Some people speak of public housing programs as "low-cost." Others immediately point out that this is incorrect—that they are low-rent or low-income programs. Discuss.

11   What are some of the major problems in the current attempts by the government to assist low-income families to improve their housing?

12   Contrast the FHA home insurance program with private mortgage insurance.

13   What should be the federal housing policy?

Chapter 15

Government Sources of Funds

In addition to the indirect effects exerted by official programs on housing through the mortgage insurance, guarantee, and subsidy programs, governments are very important direct sources of mortgage money. In 1974 more than 37 percent of the net money flowing into the residential mortgage market came from government agencies. This represents the net amount of mortgage acquisitions made by these agencies. Their total impact diverged from this total, however, because of two offsetting factors: (1) The funds for the government mortgage securities backed by pools of mortgages come from other lenders, and (2) more than $7 billion of the increased lending shown under S&Ls was made possible through funds lent to the associations by the Federal Home Loan Bank System (FHLBS).

When the Federal Home Loan Bank Board (FHLBB) advances are added to the purchasing and guaranteeing of pools of residential mortgages by all government units, the government's share of residential lending in 1974 was about half of the total. In the weakest months in the private market, its share was over 60 percent of the total. (See Table 10-4.)

The principal federal government agencies in the mortgage field are the FNMA, the FHLBS, and the Federal Land Bank. Other major federal agencies include the GNMA, the Farmers Home Administration (FMHA), the VA, and several older departments which do some lending on real estate. In addition to HUD's major direct lending role, loans are also bought by the General Services Administration; the Department of Health, Education, and Welfare; and the Small Business Administration.

Sponsored Agencies

The first three agencies listed above are called *sponsored agencies*, while others are typical government agencies. What is the difference between these two types? We noted that a substantial effort has been mounted to make money available for mortgage lending without requiring government appropriations or direct lending by the government of its own funds (back-door financing). Housing-market specialists have felt that if the mortgage agencies could be removed from the government budget, they would be more flexible in their lending programs.

When agencies are included in the budget, their lending tends to be curtailed in periods when government spending or deficit is of concern. Such periods have often coincided with the greatest shortage of mortgage funds. As a result, government agencies have tended to operate in a manner opposite to that which would enable them to perform their housing function. They lent less when they should have been lending more. To counteract this tendency, several of the agencies have been removed from the budget and have become government-sponsored agencies.

What is the difference? It depends on who puts up the capital for the agency and who is responsible for the debt. The government-sponsored agencies attempt to raise capital from private investors and lenders. Furthermore, the government disclaims ultimate responsibility for their debt.

However, the market clearly believes that the government has an implied and very strong commitment to step in and pay the debt if necessary. In most crisis situations the sponsored agencies have the right, when in need, to borrow certain sums directly from the Treasury. The market assumes that the government supervises the agencies closely enough to make certain either that they will be able to meet required payments through this ability to borrow from the Treasury or that the amount they can borrow from the government will be increased in time of need. The following discussion of the FNMA describes the organization and operation of a typical sponsored agency.

THE FEDERAL NATIONAL MORTGAGE ASSOCIATION

The largest, and in some ways the most interesting, of the federally sponsored credit agencies is the Federal National Mortgage Association. More commonly known as the FNMA (or "Fannie Mae"), it was established by Congress in 1938 to set an example for private lenders of how to operate in the secondary mortgage market. For its first 30 years, while it performed valuable functions, the FNMA's example was not followed. In the last few years, however, some of its concepts appear to be spreading to private firms.

The FNMA has had four major functions: (1) It has established procedures to demonstrate that mortgages can be successfully bought and sold in the secondary market, (2) it has acted to provide needed liquidity to the market at critical times, (3) it has established a successful market for future commitments when other lenders have been out of the market, and (4) it has increased the total flow of money to the mortgage market by issuing its own notes and bonds to attract new funds. In 1974 it increased its mortgage purchases by more than $5 billion and held over $30 billion of mortgages in its portfolio.

The Organization of the FNMA

As we have noted, the FNMA is a federally sponsored agency, but not a federal agency. Its common stock and other securities are owned by private individuals and organizations. It has a 15-member board of directors—5 appointed by the federal government and 10 elected by the stockholders. Its common stock, which is bought and sold on the New York Stock Exchange, has been subject to sharp speculative rises and falls.

While the FNMA's management is similar to that of other private corporations, the election of its president is subject to approval by the President of the United States, who may also remove him. In its operations, the management must walk a fine line between its responsibilities to the American public, because of its special charter and special borrowing and tax advantages, and its responsibilities to its private owners. The Secretary of HUD retains general regulatory powers to see that the FNMA fulfills its public responsibilities. He is charged with ensuring that the FNMA's actions are consistent with the general economic policy of the government and that it does not neglect the low- and moderate-income housing markets. In addition, the FNMA retains its responsibilities for innovations and policies to improve operations of the secondary market.

FNMA securities are closer to those of the federal government than to those of a private corporation. In most cases, they are eligible for purchase in accounts which must hold government securities. They have the indirect backing of the United States Treasury. The corporation pays federal taxes on its profits, but it is exempt from certain state taxes.

On the other hand, at times the FNMA has seemed concerned more with the traditional corporate functions of increasing its profits and maximizing the price of its common stock in the market than with its public responsibilities. The shift from its status as a federal agency to that of a federally sponsored agency removed it from the federal budget, from the limits imposed by civil service on salaries of its personnel, and from similar controls on its operations. There is a general agreement that the efficiency of its operations has improved, but debate over how well it is performing its public functions breaks out intermittently, particularly when mortgage money is short.

The Sale of Mortgage Commitments

A major change in FNMA operations occurred in 1968. At that time its new president, Raymond Lapin, revamped the method by which the FNMA issues its commitments. Replacing the semiarbitrary system of setting the prices at which the FNMA would buy mortgages, a mechanism was set up based on market prices established through public auctions.[1]

---

[1]The new system was based on a series of recommendations by this book's senior author, Sherman J. Maisel.

Until that time, the FNMA periodically announced that it would purchase mortgages at fixed prices based on the location of the underlying property, the amount of downpayment, and the face interest rate. These prices never quite matched actual movements in the market. As a result, at times no mortgages were traded. At other times the FNMA would be overwhelmed by offers. When this occurred, it rationed its commitments either by slowing down administrative action, by requiring that applicants queue up in a waiting line, or by setting arbitrary limits on the size of loans that would be purchased. Since these limits were often lower than those required for loans in many cities or regions, the program could not be used in large sections of the country.

The Auction System   The FNMA auction system recognizes that one of the corporation's main functions is to furnish builders, mortgage bankers, and other lenders with the firm future commitments they need to operate. At the same time it recognizes that mortgage prices shift constantly as the availability of money for mortgages and long-term interest rates varies.

Prior commitments are important in the secondary market. Mortgage bankers make commitments to lend money to builders and sellers of houses at agreed-upon interest rates when sales are made. The mortgage company runs two risks when it grants such commitments:

1   It may not find a buyer for the inventory of mortgages it accumulates. Since its own capital is limited, the firm cannot fulfill its commitments unless someone with adequate funds agrees to take the purchased mortgages off its hands. Someone will always buy mortgages if the price is lowered enough, but having to accept less money than it loaned would soon break the mortgage bank.

2   Interest rates may rise. A rise in interest rates means a fall in the price of a mortgage. A mortgage company with outstanding commitments will have to buy mortgages at prices above the current market and then sell them with serious losses.

How does the FNMA commitment process work? The FNMA agrees to auction off its commitments at regular intervals. The amount of commitments issued changes somewhat depending on demand. The length of potential commitments has also varied. Initially, commitments at differing rates were issued for mortgages to be delivered within 3, 6, or (on new construction) 12 months. More recently, the FNMA has auctioned standard 4-month commitments and has established prices at which it would sell 12-month commitments for new construction.

How does this auction actually operate? The FNMA announces a specific date for an auction. Bidders must be approved FNMA dealers who are eligible to service the loans sold to the FNMA. Bidders specify the price and the service fee they will accept if they can deliver a group of loans to the FNMA. In effect, they agree to a net interest rate for these mortgages. The FNMA accepts the bids that give the highest net interest yield, which is the same as agreeing to buy the lowest-priced mortgages offered.

The Commitment   The FNMA specifies a fee which successful bidders must pay for each commitment. This fee is not refundable. On the other hand, holders of commitments need not deliver any mortgages. When they have a batch of mortgages ready to deliver, if they can get a higher price elsewhere, they will. They use the commitment to protect their inventories against the losses they would sustain if mortgage prices fell. It also ensures them and their lenders that they have guaranteed buyers for their portfolios. They may turn their inventories over several times against a particular commitment.

If interest rates fall, mortgage prices will rise, and holders of commitments will not use their commitments. If interest rates rise, they will deliver to the FNMA. The FNMA experiences adverse selection. If mortgage prices rise, it will get no deliveries against its commitments. If prices fall, deliveries will be made at interest rates below the current market. It must set its fees to cover the fact that even though prices at which it will buy mortgages are set in a free market, the FNMA, rather than the mortgage seller, is taking the risk of future price changes.

When lenders deliver mortgages to the FNMA, they receive the agreed-upon price. Normally they will continue to service loans on a monthly basis under their agreement with the FNMA.

One of the initial concepts of the FNMA was that it would be primarily an intermittent source of funds. It would buy mortgages when money was tight and sell seasoned mortgages when funds from investors were ample. Although some sales have been made in accordance with this precept, most of the time pressures to increase the availability of mortgage funds have been great. Rarely does a period appear to be a good one for the FNMA to sell mortgages and reduce available investor funds. As a result, the FNMA has become primarily another form of intermediate financial institution. It facilitites the movement of funds from the money and bond markets to the mortgage market. It issues its own securities consisting of commercial paper, notes, and bonds. It uses these funds to invest in mortgages.

THE FEDERAL HOME LOAN BANK SYSTEM

The FHLBS is a mixture of federal agencies and federally sponsored agencies. Since 1932, when it was established as a credit reserve system for thrift and home-financing institutions, its functions have changed and expanded. It is now concerned, among other things, with how and where S&Ls operate, the issuance of deposit insurance to these institutions, the channeling of funds to S&Ls from other financial markets, the furnishing of a secondary market for mortgages, and, in some cases, direct subsidies to borrowers.

The structure of the system is complex. At the top are several official federal government agencies headed by the same three people wearing different hats. The main agency is the FHLB Board, consisting of three members appointed by the President with the advice and consent of the Senate. These three people also operate as the Federal Savings and Loan Insurance Corporation (FSLIC) and the Federal Home Loan Mortgage Corporation (FHLMC). The nation is divided into 12 regions, each containing a Federal Home Loan Bank. These banks are quasigovernmental agencies. Their stock is owned by their member S&Ls, which elect a majority of their directors. Their presidents (who are not government employees) are elected by the individual banks' directors with the consent of the FHLBB. Each of these presidents—as, for example, the president of the FHL Bank of San Francisco, the largest—has certain responsibilities to his members and directors. Each is expected, however, always to keep the public interest paramount.

There are approximately 4,700 members of the System. Almost all are S&Ls. MSBs and LICs are eligible for membership, but few have joined.

Chartering, Insurance, and Regulation of S&Ls

A great deal of the effort of the FHLBB is concerned with establishing and maintaining a strong thrift system. The Board charters federal S&Ls and approves their conversions, mergers, and branches. It issues deposit insurance. It regulates state-chartered S&Ls that are insured by the FSLIC, and it approves S&L holding companies and S&L service companies. It regulates the types of loans S&Ls can make and the amount of specific types of assets which can be held in any association's portfolio. It sets maximum interest rates by type of deposits. It examines individual associations to see that they are complying with the regulations. If an association is not sound, the FSLIC may rescue it or force it out of business.

The Board operates through a series of carrots and sticks. Associations may need advances, or they may want to change locations, to branch, or to merge. If associations are acting improperly, they may be ordered to cease and desist from continuing certain activities. Federal S&Ls have been required to be mutual associations with no private stockholders. Some state-chartered associations are stock, or for-profit, corporations, while others are mutuals. The FHLBB has been pushing a program which allows conversion of some associations from mutual to stock ownership.

The Federal Savings and Loan Insurance Corporation

The FSLIC operates in much the same way as the more familiar FDIC. All federal associations must have their accounts insured. State-chartered associations may be insured if they qualify. A surprisingly large number—but mainly small associations—remain uninsured. The size of an individual's account covered by insurance has been upgraded steadily. In 1974, it was raised again to $40,000.

Occasionally debates have erupted as to the relative advantages and safety of the FDIC and the FSLIC. Initially there was fear that the reserves of the FSLIC—based on premiums paid by members—might not be adequate to cover large losses. In the 1960s reserves reached 2 percent of covered assets. In emergencies, the corporation can also borrow from the Treasury. Since losses have not been large, even during severe contractions in inflows of funds to S&Ls, the fear that the corporation's reserves might be inadequate seems to have disappeared.

There have also been arguments over possible delays in payments to depositors from the FSLIC. In theory, in some states an S&L facing a run on deposits could delay payments of withdrawals to match the rate at which money flowed in. In fact, since the FSLIC's support of S&Ls in trouble has been extremely flexible, such fears have also almost disappeared. In the great majority of cases, the corporation has kept associations in business by advancing necessary sums or merging them with sounder associations. Furthermore, the liquidity problems of associations have been mitigated by the willingness of the Home Loan Banks to advance large sums to associations losing deposits.

Federal Home Loan Bank Advances

The third main function of the FHLBS, and the one for which it was primarily established, is to act as a major secondary source of funds for its member associations. The FHL Banks borrow in the money and bond markets on consolidated notes and bonds, issued with maturities ranging from a few days to over 10 years. This money is loaned to associations to meet unexpected withdrawal demands, to provide seasonal liquidity, and to cushion the shock of a slowdown in deposits as money markets have tightened while commitments to lend have had to be met.

The availability of short-term loans is important when a local crisis creates a sudden need for funds for a member institution. Since most assets are in mortgages which are hard to liquidate, the availability of another source of money means that an institution has time to accumulate cash through its normal flow of funds and through additional sales. Short-term loans for seasonal purposes increase the amount of mortgages the members can hold. If they had to hold cash to meet a normal seasonal withdrawal pattern, they could make fewer loans. Under the present system, associations can plan to meet these seasonal needs through borrowing.

Advances can also be made on a long-term basis of up to 10 years. They increase the money available to the whole mortgage market and particularly to localities where the need for money outruns local savings. In a typical year, half or more of the member associations have been borrowers from the FHL Banks. The amount of advances has been growing steadily. In 1974 more than $10 billion was lent, while the maximum outstanding at one time was over $21 billion.

Short-term loans to members can be based on the notes of the individual borrowing institution. Long-term advances require specific collateral, usually in the form of a pledge of particular first-mortgage loans held by the member. The amount of borrowing is limited in rather complex ways. In effect, the ability to get funds from the banks depends on the institution's own capital, the amount of its withdrawable accounts, and the amount of stock it holds in its regional FHL Bank.

The funds made available to the FHL Banks come from three sources. Member associations are required to purchase capital stock. As their second source of funds, the FHL Banks accept deposits from their members, on which they pay a small interest rate, which varies among regions. These deposits are primarily liquidity reserves. The final and most important source of funds arises from the ability of the FHL Banks to issue consolidated obligations of bonds, notes, or certificates in the general money market. These instruments are secured by the capital of the banks, the notes of their members, and the underlying mortgages. In effect, this technique makes it possible for the System to attract money into mortgages that could not or would not buy mortgages directly. A bank or insurance company will buy these notes in competition with other bonds even if its own mortgage portfolio is filled. As a result, the total money available to the mortgage market is greater than it would otherwise be.

This ability to attract additional funds is an important accomplishment of the System. It also acts to widen the geographic distribution of mortgage funds. Most borrowing by the FHL Banks is done in areas with ample money supplies, while their advances to members tend to go to areas of shortages.

The improved liquidity for emergencies and the ability to meet seasonal fluctuations are also significant plus factors. Member associations can put more money into mortgages than would otherwise be possible. The pooling of the liquidity reserves of all members results in decreased costs and more strength for each individual institution.

The Federal Home Loan Mortgage Corporation

The Emergency Home Finance Act of 1970 authorized the establishment of the FHLMC (nicknamed "Freddie Mac"). The S&L industry desired an agency competitive to the FNMA, which they felt was dominated by builders and mortgage bankers. Furthermore, they wanted a secondary market established for conventional mortgages equivalent to that maintained for FHA-VA mortgages by the FNMA. At that time, the FNMA acted as a secondary market only for government-issued or government-guaranteed loans.

As noted previously, the directors of the FHLMC are the three members of the FHLBB. Capital comes from the FHL Banks. The corporation engages in a wide variety of secondary market operations. It buys and sells mortgages and, in addition, will participate (buy part of a mortgage) with member S&Ls.

The basic operations of the FHLMC are similar to those described for the FNMA. S&Ls and mortgage bankers accumulate during a month or several months a portfolio of eligible loans, which they then arrange to sell to the FHLMC. The original lenders retain the servicing under contract from the FHLMC. They earn money in the form of fees for originating the loans and from portfolio gains or losses based on interest rate changes. By selling loans from their portfolios, they obtain funds to make new loans.

The FHLMC obtains its money by issuing notes and bonds or by selling securities backed by a specific portfolio of mortgages. It makes a profit or loss depending on the spread between the interest it receives on its mortgages and what it pays to borrow. The rate the FHLMC pays to borrow is less than that paid by borrowers on mortgages because the securities it issues are more marketable. Its borrowing rates are also lower because the FHLMC is a government-sponsored agency. In addition, it sells its securities to small lenders, pension funds, and others who do not have the staff to check, analyze, and account for individual mortgages. Such lenders accept a lower rate than they would on mortgages because they are saved time, risk, and effort.

FEDERAL LAND BANKS

Most people have never heard of the Federal Land Banks. Yet they are by far the largest lenders on farms and therefore on land in general in the United States. They hold about half of all farm mortgages. The banks were established by the Federal Farm Loan Act of 1916 and now operate in accordance with the Farm Credit Act of 1971. The Land Banks are a federally sponsored agency operating generally very much like the FHLBS. They are, however, closely tied in with the federal intermediate credit banks and banks for cooperatives, the other parts of the Farm Credit System.

Mortgage loans on farms, ranches, rural houses, and farm-related businesses are made by the Federal Land Banks through 578 local federal land bank associations. Loans have a maximum term of 40 years and a maximum loan-to-value ratio of 85 percent. Borrowers must become members of their local land bank association through the purchase of stock equal to 5 percent of their loans. When a loan is repaid, the stock can be sold back to the association.

The funds for the mortgages are raised in the market by sales of consolidated issues of the 12 Federal Land Banks. These securities sell at the favorable rate the market establishes for the federally sponsored agencies. The actual interest rate charged the borrower on a mortgage is variable, changing in accordance with the total cost of money to the Land Banks. Repayments are frequently rescheduled, depending upon the exigencies of the farm markets.

THE GOVERNMENT NATIONAL MORTGAGE ASSOCIATION

We have already discussed the Government National Mortgage Association, also called the GNMA or "Ginnie Mae," in connection with some of the direct subsidy programs of HUD. Ginnie Mae is a daughter of Fannie Mae, the issue of a 1968 reorganization. Unlike the FNMA, it is an official federal agency. Its president is an assistant secretary of HUD. In terms of budget, spending, personnel, control, and similar factors, it operates as part of the government, directly responsible to the Secretary of HUD. The 1968 act transferred various special government programs from the FNMA to the GNMA. As a result, the GNMA holds directly a number of mortgages. These are loans made to aid special governmental programs.

We saw in the last chapter that such loans are still being made under the tandem plan and special-assistance plans. However, in the majority of cases, the GNMA does not retain these mortgages in its portfolio. Rather, it sells them to the FNMA, absorbing the loss on the mortgages in the current year's budget.

Guaranteed Mortgage-backed Securities

A recent program of the GNMA has become its most prominent. This is the guaranteeing of securities backed by mortgages and sold through the private bond market. How does this program work? We have noted that mortgage-backed securities are an indirect way of borrowing money on mortgages from lenders who would rather hold a simpler and more marketable instrument than a large number of individual mortgages. The GNMA guarantees the timely payment of the principal and interest on private securities backed by a pool of mortgages. By this guarantee, the securities become equivalent in safety to government bonds.

An FHA-approved mortgagee with the right to service for the GNMA can originate a mortgage-backed security. The originator must meet certain minimum-net-worth tests. The major originators have been mortgage bankers, and the FNMA and the FHLMC, but other lenders have also used the program. They apply to the GNMA for a guarantee of securities to be issued against a pool of at least $1 million in mortgages. The mortgages must basically be similar with respect to terms, types, and rates. At the time of guarantee, they can be no older than 1 year. The securities are registered and are issued in the denominations requested by the purchaser. If sold, they are reregistered, and new denominations may be issued. Most of the securities issued, except by government agencies, have taken the form of so-called pass-through securities. The pass-through feature refers to the fact that every month, each holder receives his or her proportionate share of the collections received from the mortgage pool. This includes scheduled principal and interest, plus any prepayments and proceeds from mortgage liquidations. Since prepayments may occur in pass-through securities, the length of time the security will be outstanding and its rate of payment will vary.

Lenders who receive the commitment they requested from the GNMA transmit the pool of eligible mortgages with all necessary related documents to a designated custodian. This must be a fiduciary regulated by a federal or state agency that also meets GNMA standards. The custodian certifies the receipt of the mortgages and the supporting documents. In turn, the GNMA guarantees the securities based on the particular mortgage pool and sends them back to the issuer.

The GNMA charges an annual fee for its guarantee. This is used to cover any losses it may incur if it has to make good on its guarantee because the funds from the mortgages are not collected according to schedule or because the originator fails. The originator sells the mortgage-backed securities but continues to service the loans. The securities may be sold directly by their initiators, but many are sold through major investment banking houses. Several underwriting and brokerage firms maintain a market in GNMA mortgage-backed securities. They quote current prices when requested.

The securities are meant to appeal to lenders who want to invest in mortgages but who are not equipped to handle the problems of servicing individual mortgages or even of handling them through correspondents. By using GNMA mortgage-backed securities, buyers sacrifice some interest compared with what they would receive if they purchased mortgages directly. A pass-through instrument does not relieve buyers of the uncertainty, inherent in mortgages, of when repayment will occur. They run the same risk of changes in interest rates associated with regular mortgages. On the other hand, they own a security guaranteed by the federal government. Its marketability is not as good as that of a government bond, but it is far better than that of mortgages. The security also is equivalent to individual mortgages with respect to some of the tax advantages which mortgages carry for lenders.

The rapid rate of growth of these securities shows that they fill a definite place in the investment strategy and portfolio of investors. Institutions purchasing GNMA securities gain the tax breaks. They gain higher interest rates. They have a more diversified portfolio. They also reduce their administrative burden. The FHLMC also issues securities called guaranteed mortgage certificates. However, while these are backed by a pool of mortgages, they are really bonds with mortgages as collateral. Their terms and repayment are not related to the underlying mortgages.

FARMERS HOME ADMINISTRATION

Much of the lending on rural houses is done by the FMHA, a direct agency of the government similar to the GNMA. To qualify for a loan or subsidy from the FMHA, a homeowner must choose a house in a rural political subdivision of less than 10,000 population and must have been rejected for regular financing by a bank or other mortgage lending institution. The size of the program has expanded rapidly. Yearly volume of new loans has exceeded $2 billion.

The FMHA operation is called an *insured loan program*, but in reality it is a direct loan program, with the funds from which lending takes place being replenished by FMHA-issued fully guaranteed government securities backed by a pool of mortgage notes. Loans are made and serviced through over 1,700 local offices. The loans are made at below-market interest rates. In addition, depending on their income, borrowers may also receive a direct interest subsidy much as they do under the FHA 235 program. Downpayments may be nominal, and the maximum amortization period is 33 years. Loans may be made for new construction, to purchase existing homes, or for major improvements.

The government-backed FMHA securities resemble somewhat those of the GNMA. However, rather than using the complicated GNMA pass-through system, which the FMHA has employed on some securities, most notes are issued for fixed periods. Thus they are virtually identical to Treasury securities. However, because they are less marketable, they carry higher interest rates, the result of the cost of keeping them out of the budget. The difference between what the FMHA costs and what it receives from the borrowers is made up by congressional appropriations.

OTHER FEDERAL AGENCIES

While the bulk of lending on real property is handled by the agencies already described, other federal agencies have made loans on real property in the past and probably will in the future. Some of the subsidy programs of HUD are based on direct lending from the department itself. This has been true of some forms of housing for the elderly, of college housing, and of rehabilitation loans, for example. Similarly, while the great bulk of the VA's work has been guaranteeing mortgages, under certain programs the VA lends directly to veterans in areas where others would not lend at the terms set on VA mortgages. The VA and the FHA continue to carry loans on houses on which they have already foreclosed and paid the claims of the lender and which they have subsequently sold in the market in an attempt to recoup.

The Small Business Administration makes loans at rates below those available from other lenders in areas hit by disasters. Other parts of the government are concerned with different types of buildings. When structures are not being built in the spheres of their concern, such as educational buildings or hospitals for the Department of Health, Education, and Welfare, funds may be made available directly by the department, and mortgages or liens will be retained. While in recent years most of these programs have not been large, the total of outstanding loans in these various categories comes to several billion dollars.

STATE AND LOCAL GOVERNMENT CREDIT AGENCIES

Over 40 state and local government units have been established to administer public mortgage credit and housing assistance programs. This is one of the fastest-growing parts of the market. Many of them use funds obtained by borrowing on tax-exempt municipal securities. Tax-exempt securities sell at lower interest rates than those subject to federal income taxation, and these lower rates have been passed through to borrowers.

Some, such as the New York State Urban Development Corporation (UDC), have had a great deal of freedom to plan and expedite major programs made up of nonsubsidized, federally subsidized, and state-subsidized housing. However, because of a default and general problems in the market for state and local bonds, the UDC and other similar agencies have been forced to curtail many activities.

In addition, many state governments have established agencies to purchase mortgage loans from private financial institutions in need of greater liquidity. These agencies operate as secondary market facilities in the same way as the federal government agencies in the field. They provide supplementary support to local residential mortgage markets.

Cal-Vet   The oldest of the state programs is that of the California Department of Veterans Affairs, Division of Farm and Home Purchases. This program was established in 1921 and has been active ever since. A brief description of its operations gives some idea of the way in which these programs work.

The Cal-Vet program uses funds obtained by the issuance of state of California bonds. Since these bonds not only are exempt from federal and state income taxes but also have the full faith and credit of the state pledged for their repayment, they carry among the lowest interest rates available.

Eligible veterans can apply to the department either to purchase existing homes or to have homes built. The dwellings must meet the appraised value set by the department plus various standards of the types discussed in connection with the FHA. The actual units are purchased by the state, which then sells them to the veteran under a contract of sale. The department also sells both hazard insurance and mortgage life insurance to the owners at rates which, based upon the state's mass purchasing ability, are extremely low.

In practice, the loans are made primarily to the upper income groups among veterans because the amount of the loan is limited. (The amount has changed over time, but recently it was $20,000.) Because these limits usually have not been sufficient to pay fully for an adequate house, large downpayments have been required. Frequently there has also been a long waiting period for the loans. As a result, only those veterans who had a good deal of cash of their own and who could afford to wait were able to use the program.

Since the program has enabled veterans to borrow money at a considerably lower rate than they could have obtained in the open market, it has been extremely popular among those aided. The people of the state have looked on the program as a form of veterans' benefit similar to veterans' bonuses paid in other states.

Low-Rent Programs   Many states have authorities which aid in the building of low-rent housing. These programs may either supplement or run side by side with those of the Federal Public Housing Administration.

In these and other programs to reduce the costs of lower-income and middle-income housing, states have attempted to minimize appropriations from their own tax funds. Again, this has been done through the relending of money which the state has been able to raise on its own lower-rate bonds. Also, states have often granted various types of property tax exemptions to either the developers of property or the buyers.

The types of problems raised by the state and local programs are completely analogous to those raised with respect to the federal programs discussed at the end of the last chapter. Major doubts center around who actually benefits from the programs. More specifically, it has been asked whether it is useful to have a small number of families benefit greatly, while the largest number of citizens in almost identical income and status groups do not benefit at all.

SUMMARY: RESULTS

While the housing programs remain in flux and under constant debate, there is general agreement that, particularly in the mortgage field, a record of solid accomplishments can be claimed. What results have past programs achieved?

1   There has been a notable decline in home mortgage interest rates in relation to other long-term debt instruments. Because all interest rates have increased sharply, these improvements are frequently overlooked. An examination of relative spreads, however, shows that over the past 10 to 20 years, mortgage rates have risen by 1.5 to 2 percent less than other long-term rates. Furthermore, while in the past some parts of the country paid far higher rates than others, regional differences have almost disappeared.

Such improvement results directly from the standardization of mortgage instruments and the growth of a national mortgage market. The programs of mortgage insurance and guarantees have made the mortgage a more standard commodity and have removed legal restrictions against national lending. Lending on a larger scale has also reduced the costs of raising capital. Such reductions have been even greater when the government's credit has been used.

2   There has been a sizable increase in low-downpayment mortgages—those with a high loan-to-value ratio. This has tremendously increased the number of potential purchasers of homes. Low downpayments have been made possible by longer amortization periods. A family with a given income can afford a higher loan with a low downpayment because of the smaller required monthly payments for each dollar borrowed. Although much higher nominal interest rates have cut into this advantage, still the benefits gained from a combination of low downpayments and longer amortizations have expanded homeownership dramatically. The percentage of owner-occupied houses increased from 44 percent in 1940 to 63 percent in 1975.

3   Housing standards have improved. The government programs have insisted that properties meet minimum standards. In addition, the reduced monthly payments have enabled a family to afford more house with a given amount of income. The expansion of ownership has improved housing maintenance. "Do-it-yourself" saves a great deal of money over hiring skilled workers who charge high wage rates. While programs such as urban renewal have been subject to bitter attack and although major urban ills remain, progress has been considerable.

4   A moderate number of low-income persons (particularly families with only a female head, families with a large number of children, and the elderly) have been furnished heavily subsidized units of varying quality.

5   On the other hand, instability in real estate markets has not lessened; rather, it has probably increased. However, without the government programs, the situation probably would be far worse. Despite the fact that instability and inflation have put all financial markets under great pressure, the government programs have kept minimum levels of funds flowing into housing.

QUESTIONS AND PROBLEMS

1 Why did the United States government shift from the use of regular government agencies to government-sponsored agencies in the housing field?
2 Describe the main operations of the FNMA.
3 Do you think there may be a conflict between the responsibility of the president of the FNMA to his stockholders and to the President of the United States, who approves his election? Give your reasons.
4 Describe some of the principal functions of the members of the FHLBB.
5 There have been major debates as to whether the sponsored agencies should buy only government-insured or government-guaranteed mortgages or should also purchase those carrying private mortgage guarantee insurance. What are the arguments on both sides?
6 Explain the objectives of the GNMA mortgage-backed security program and how it works.
7 What is the difference between the FHA and the FMHA?
8 Why do you feel that state and local government housing credit agencies have expanded?
9 Why are there so many sources of government funds? Would it be better to have just one agency?
10 Why are governments needed as sources of mortgage money?
11 How do activities of government lenders affect private-sector sources of loans?

Chapter 16

Changing the Mortgage Market and Financial Institutions

Few are satisfied with the way the mortgage market has operated in recent years. When funds have been short and rates high, loud demands for change and improvements have come from those interested in mortgages. Numerous and varied solutions have been offered, including proposals for substantial changes in the structure and regulation of our major financial institutions, improvements in mortgages and their markets, additional subsidies to borrowers or lenders, and penalties on other credit users.

Each time the market has experienced a fluctuation in interest rates and available funds, there has been an accompanying shift in how those in the market have viewed the future. Predictions of impending disaster have alternated with predictions of constant growth and profitability. Is there logic behind these hopes and fears?

Actually, there seem to be two separate fears. The first is that there will be a permanent lack of money for mortgage loans. In every period of tight money, the available funds for mortgages have been sharply curtailed. During such periods, fears have been expressed that the problem would be of long duration and that unless special steps were taken, there would be a perennial shortage of money for housing and other real property development.

The second fear is that financial institutions—particularly the thrift institutions, which have funded the bulk of mortgage lending—will not be able to adjust to modern conditions. As instability has become more pervasive, thrift institutions have had a harder time retaining their deposits and their general position in the financial world. It is feared that a basic structural problem is inherent in their organization and that they will not be able to stay abreast of modern developments in financial markets. If these trends continue, and particularly if the extent of instability in financial markets persists, the thrift institutions may either fall by the wayside or be reduced to playing a more minor role. If this occurs, it is not clear who would take their place as mortgage lenders and where mortgage money would be found.

In trying to analyze these problems, we first consider the general question of the supply of, and demand for, mortgage funds; then we look at the peculiar situation of the thrift institutions. Finally, we discuss some of the proposals to bring greater flexibility into the mortgage field.

THE FUTURE SUPPLY OF, AND DEMAND FOR, MORTGAGE FUNDS

The best answer to those who express the fears outlined above seems to be that while disaster may strike, it is not inevitable. Most observers believe that if inflation can be controlled, there should be no long-run shortage of mortgage money. The dangers are that (1) we will fail to control inflation, (2) we will delay necessary changes in financial institutions, and (3) we may fail to solve the problem of poverty, with its tremendous impacts on our housing standards.

Clearly, all these dangers are real. Institutions resist change. If they lack sufficient flexibility, pressures on existing markets and institutions will continue to recur. However, such pressures need not cause an adverse mortgage market. The demand for and supply of mortgage money can intersect at real rates of interest not far different from those of the past. Such possibilities become evident from an examination of long-run projections of the flow of funds.

The Flow of Funds Again

In Chapter 10 we used the flow-of-funds accounts to analyze fluctuations in the short-run demand for, and supply of, mortgages. These accounts can be used to understand long-run trends as well. Looking ahead for the next 10 years, we find that the same necessary identities will prevail: The real supply of savings has to equal investment and the total amount of lending will equal the amount borrowed. But as in current analysis, this necessary identity may be beside the point. What we want to know is whether the necessary equality will occur at interest rates and with adequate funds to ensure a socially desirable level of housing. We want to know whether existing trends and institutions will enable the financial system to meet national goals or whether major program changes will be necessary.

More specifically, we can ask whether existing trends will so limit the availability of mortgage funds and raise their costs so high that either the production of real property will be below current levels or production will fail to expand as rapidly as desirable. Will families have to pay so much for mortgage loans that the demand for housing will be cut back to the point where production will be inadequate? Will high costs of money and low production force moderate-income families to pay more than is socially desirable for their shelter?

To determine whether the long-run supply of mortgage funds will be satisfactory requires both (1) a projection of the desired amount of construction and (2) a value judgment as to what reasonable share of their income families should pay for shelter. The debates of the past 40 years will continue. Has the rate of construction of new housing units and rehabilitation of old ones been rapid enough to meet standards of socially acceptable living? Governments are subsidizing the shelter costs of many families. Will projected interest rates be such that the number and amounts of subsidies will have to be increased? If increased subsidies are required, what form should they take, and who should pay for them? Are there programs that can lower the costs and increase the availability of mortgages by improving the market rather than by increasing subsidies?

All these factors influence the expected demand for mortgage funds. When a proper level of lending has been estimated, it must be compared with expected supplies. The level of savings and the total flow of funds can be projected. If existing trends continue, mortgage borrowers will receive a certain share of these flows. This share can be expanded if mortgage borrowers pay higher rates than other potential borrowers or if institutional changes occur which increase the competitive position of mortgage borrowers. The question we face is whether action should be taken to enhance this competitive position and, if so, what form it should take.

The Demand for Construction and for Mortgages

When we examine past trends in saving and investing and in borrowing and lending, no insoluble problems appear. The desired level of investment in housing and other real estate projected for the next 10 years is not out of line with past trends. Nor is there any obvious reason why the supply of, or demand for, savings should alter radically. Most 10-year flow-of-funds projections show only minor shifts in the real rate of interest.

We cannot be as optimistic with respect to how borrowing and lending will take place. Our thrift institutions are in a state of flux. Basic alterations in their form and regulations may be necessary. Still, when we recognize what dynamic movements have occurred, such changes do not seem impossible to achieve.

Investment   This view of long-run trends starts with a projection of the amount of investment in housing believed desirable. There is rather general agreement that if, between 1971 and 1980, housing starts average between 1.9 million and 2.1 million units a year, if .1 million to .2 million units are rehabilitated per year, and if the number of mobile homes increases by .4 to .6 million units a year, the housing stock will be improving at an adequate rate. In addition, while the real costs of each unit are expected to grow compared with the real costs of other products and services, the relative increase is not expected to be unreasonable.

An adequate rate of housing construction can be compared with the projected increase in the gross national product that comes about as a result of a growing labor force and increasing productivity. The desired level of housing investment can be achieved if housing takes between 3.6 and 3.8 percent of the GNP. If housing were to reach this share of the GNP, quite an expansion in building would be required compared with the situation in the final years of the 1960s. But housing would not need to take as high a share of production as it took in the early 1960s. Indeed, its share of the GNP would be less than it was for the entire decade of the 1960s.

Saving   An examination of trends among the other claims against production reveals no obvious reason why such a level of real investment in housing and related construction should cause any difficulties. Private saving from 1959 to 1970 averaged 15.8 percent of the GNP. In addition to paying for all private investment, this amount of saving sufficed to cover sizable government deficits and a fair amount of foreign investment.

Most analysts believe that if the demand for investment does rise, rather small changes in saving—mere fractions of a percent of the GNP—and only small fractions of possible government surpluses or deficits will be sufficient to fund such increases. While problems may arise because the government fails to adopt proper policies, nothing basic in our economy points to the probability that desired savings will not adequately fund desired real estate investment.

More or less the same statement can be made about the level of borrowing and lending. If the economy is in general balance, any drastic change in the general credit situation would be unexpected. It is true that major changes in either government policy or financial institutions or a flight from savings due to a more rapid inflation could drastically alter the existing balance. But without such movements, we should expect borrowing and lending also to expand about in line with the GNP. This would be particularly true if government deficit financing were more restrained than in the past decade.

TRENDS IN THE SHARE OF MORTGAGES IN TOTAL CREDIT

Still, questions remain: Are other forces at work which lessen the chances that mortgage credit will continue to receive its customary share of total credit? Even if no decline occurs, can the situation be improved? Are there actions which could lower the interest rates that mortgage borrowers will have to pay?

The share of total borrowing on mortgages required to support an adequate level of housing seems about equal to its share for the whole decade of the 1960s. While a good deal higher than in the late 1960s, the mortgage share of lending would be considerably less than it was in 1972 and 1973. The problem is not one of having to find funds for a greatly expanded mortgage demand. Rather, it is one of maintaining mortgages' share of existing lending while increasing the stability of this lending.

The critical problem seems to be the difficulties that major institutional lenders have in maintaining their mortgage flows in the face of widely fluctuating interest rates and a growing gap between real and nominal rates. The deposit institutions continue primarily to borrow short and lend long. Solution of their problems and those of the mortgage market requires greater stability in interest rates, methods of smoothing deposit flows, and ways of improving the competitive position of mortgages.

Numerous solutions for these problems have been suggested. Among the most widely debated are:

1   Removing interest rate ceilings on deposits
2   Giving thrift institutions broader powers to accept more types of liabilities, including demand deposits, and to purchase other assets and make nonmortgage loans

3 Introducing variable rate or purchasing-power-indexed mortgages
4 Altering the form and amount of tax subsidies
5 Giving mortgages a preferred status among the loans of other institutions
6 Using taxes to lower the demand for funds from lenders competitive to mortgage lenders
7 Increasing the role of federally sponsored agencies
8 Indexing or correcting the purchasing power of savings accounts
9 Continuing to improve the mortgage market

Ceilings on Interest Paid on Deposits

The federal government, using its control over the chartering and insuring of deposits in financial institutions, has imposed maximum interest rate ceilings on time and saving deposits through regulation Q of the Federal Reserve and related regulations of the FDIC and the FSLIC.

These regulations are aimed at decreasing the competition for deposits. It is assumed that if savers are paid interest rates below those which would be set in a free, competitive market, lending institutions will charge mortgage borrowers somewhat less. Many, however, believe that the lower rates paid to savers simply raise the profits of the financial institutions at the expense of small savers. In addition, when the gap between the ceilings and market rates becomes wide, instability is greatly increased by funds flowing out of the financial institutions.

President Nixon, both directly and through his Commission on Financial Structure and Regulation (the Hunt Commission), urged that after an interim period designed to give the thrift institutions a chance to adjust to a new competitive situation, the ceiling regulations (except on demand deposits) be dropped. President Ford readopted these suggestions. The resulting debates clarified many underlying factors: (1) Under the existing regulations, the thrift institutions cannot compete in tight-money periods with CBs and other lenders for funds; (2) many savers are willing to accept lower rates on deposits because their safety is guaranteed by the federal government; (3) ceiling rates serve, therefore, to transfer to borrowers from depositors part of the lower rates which result from federal insurance; (4) if instability increases, the value of this existing aid to mortgages is highly doubtful; and (5) it might be better to subsidize mortgages without lowering the return on savings to small depositors.

While most observers feel that some system better than interest rate ceilings can be devised, it is unclear whether a system without regulations would be more or less stable than the current one. There is also great uncertainty as to who would gain, who would lose, and what costs would result from removing ceilings. This uncertainty, together with the great likelihood that any changes would decrease returns to some politically well-entrenched groups, makes negotiation of an agreement on what modifications should be enacted extremely difficult.

Broader Powers for Thrift Institutions

In addition to suggesting changes in ceilings as part of its solution to the problems, the Hunt Commission advocated that thrift institutions be given more and broader powers to accept a greater variety of deposits and other liabilities and also to make loans to more types of potential borrowers. Heretofore, regulations over their lending, as well as income tax laws which increase the profitability of holding mortgages, have limited the lending of the S&Ls primarily to mortgages.

The Hunt Commission advocated allowing thrift institutions to offer checking accounts for households and nonbusiness entities. It favored wider lending and investment powers, including the right to make consumer loans and to invest in real estate and equities. All such powers would be subject both to specific limits and to a general "leeway" authorization. The Commission urged that the special regulations restricting loans outside the residential mortgage field be eliminated and that lenders instead be given special tax credits for making mortgage loans.

The Hunt Commission's recommendations and similar ones have been both highly praised and sharply attacked. A great deal of the controversy has been based on the views of different individuals and institutions as to the effect of the proposed changes on their own profitability. Some of the debate has concerned the more general question of whether our existing system of specialized institutions with limited competition and regulated lending has become outmoded.

Many with a special interest in borrowing on mortgages take the position that if the existing preferred access to household savings were removed, the total amount of mortgage funds would fall, their cost would rise, and their availability might be no less cyclical. Others believe that the present system cannot continue without major changes. They foresee a continuous erosion of the role of thrift institutions, greater and greater volatility in available funds, a system with less than maximum efficiency, and a transfer of income from small savers to borrowers on mortgages, many of whom may be wealthy.

In 1973, the Federal Reserve and the FHLBB attempted to move part of the way toward a removal of deposit rate ceilings by taking off the ceiling on time deposits of 4 years or more. The outcry from those in the thrift and housing industries was so great that Congress, with very little opposition, passed a law requiring that the ceilings be reestablished.

VARIABLE RATE MORTGAGES

The introduction of a variable rate mortgage is another suggested approach to assuring more mortgage money for thrift institutions. If mortgages of this type are to be widely used, federal as well as many state laws and regulations will have to be changed. Variable rate mortgages are not too common in the United States, but are widely used in England, Canada, and other countries. They are, however, used here for mortgages of the Federal Land Banks, the Cal-Vet, and other official programs. They have been adopted by some of the largest thrift institutions.

Variable rate mortgages are ones in which the contract interest rate is movable. Either it changes in accordance with some predetermined relationship to a market interest rate, to the lender's cost of funds, or to a purchasing-power or consumer price index, or interest rates may be subject to a periodic renegotiation. There are three different types of variable interest rate mortgages. In each, a change in the mortgage interest rate is triggered by the movement of some outside index. The interest owed on the mortgage moves with the index.

1 In the first type, if it is agreed that loan payments should vary, the monthly payments will be adjusted by the amount necessary for the increased interest payments to cover the added interest costs.

2 In the second type, a variable maturity loan, the monthly payments remain the same. However, the amount of each payment which is applied to the amortization of the principal increases or decreases by the same amount as, but in the direction opposite to, the change in the interest payment.

3 In the third type, if rates move beyond a certain point, a new agreement as to interest rates may be negotiated between the borrower and the lender. If no new rate can be agreed on, the loan may be called.

As a numerical example, assume a 25-year 8 percent mortgage with a monthly payment for interest and amortization of $7.72 per $1,000 of mortgage. At the end of a year, the index has fallen by more than 1 percent. In that case, the contract calls for a reduction of 1 percent in the interest rate to be paid. With a variable payment mortgage, new payments against the remaining principal of $987 will be recalculated at the new 7 percent rate. Instead of $7.72 per $1,000, the required monthly payment would become $7.08. With a variable maturity mortgage, monthly payments would remain at $7.72 per $1,000 of mortgage, but a larger share would be credited to the principal. The mortgage would be paid off in under 20 years instead of the remaining 24.

Of course, if market rates rose, the opposite would happen. The borrower would either have to pay more per month or have to pay for a longer period. If rates rose enough so that interest charges exceeded the monthly payment, the borrower would actually be adding to his or her debt rather than repaying part of the principal. The amount owed would increase. Such a situation is not illogical if we assume that when the property was sold, the entire principal could be paid off.

The Why of Variable Rates Why do many people feel that variable rate mortgages should be used more widely in the United States? Advocates believe that such mortgages will (1) stabilize the deposit flows to depository institutions and thus enable them to maintain their mortgage lending, (2) decrease average interest rates on mortgages, and (3) allow a more equitable division of income between borrowers and lenders.

Deposit institutions lose funds when they cannot compete with the market. If the income they receive from interest rates on mortgages moved more or less with market rates, they would be able to change the rates they pay their depositors in accordance with market movements. This would mean that their inflows and outflows of deposits and, it is hoped, their loans would be more stable. It would be a useful change, doing away with a great deal of the current instability. However, for this change to occur, the existing interest rate ceilings on deposits at institutions would have to be removed, and the institutions would actually have to change their deposit rates in competition with the market.

Mortgages now carry a considerable interest rate risk (their prices will change drastically as interest rates change) because of their long life and because they bear fixed interest rates. The risk must be borne by borrowers. It becomes part of the interest rate they are charged. To the degree that variable rate mortgages succeed in reducing this interest rate risk, their charges should be lower than those on fixed rate mortgages.

Among the three types of variable rate mortgages, the variable maturity mortgage seems more advantageous than the variable payment mortgage because it removes the risk to borrowers of having to increase their monthly payments even though they have no added income with which to make the larger payments. Variable rates and payments have been used more and more frequently on income properties. Often they are based upon the actual cash flow of a property.

But people ask: What about the risk that the principal will not be paid off rapidly enough unless the amount of the payment changes? Unless we assume that interest rate rises are most likely to be caused by inflation, the slower payment on principal may pose a danger. If we can make such an assumption, the inflation which increases the interest rates should also raise the value of the property used as security. As a result, risks would not increase.

In the past, some uses of variable rate mortgages have seemed unfair because borrowers had little protection and frequently were not aware of the implications of their contracts. California law (1970) seems to solve many of these problems. It requires (1) that the method of downward and upward adjustments be identical, (2) that rates change no more often than twice a year, (3) that the maximum rate change in any six months be .25 percent, (4) that the borrower have the right to pay off the loan within 90 days of any rate increase, and (5) that there be full disclosure. The law fails to specify which rate should be used for adjustment. The market rate on Treasury notes of either 3 to 5 or 5 to 7 years seems logical and equitable. The FHLBB has regulations similar to those of California, discussed above.

It seems probable that if the difficulties of thrift institutions get worse, the push for changes in existing regulations and toward variable rate mortgages will intensify rapidly. The entire experience of regulations shows that if the law lags too far behind what is occurring in the market and what is economically necessary, the laws and regulations will be circumvented. Some people will put money abroad; others will change the basic forms of their savings; others will buy variable rate corporate bonds. As a result, both the deposit institutions and the mortgage market will suffer.

TAXES AND SUBSIDIES

Many suggestions for improving mortgage flows depend upon either enlarging the present system of tax subsidies to savers or mortgage lenders or—taking the opposite tack—penalizing competitive users of credit by means of taxes. Almost all such proposals would affect in some way both the stability and the secular availability of mortgage flows.

One set of proposals, for example, would eliminate or delay income taxes on interest received on deposits. The amount of tax benefit could vary with the size of the deposit, with its length, or with the income of the depositor. Clearly, in all these cases there are major problems of equity. It is difficult to shape a politically acceptable proposal which spreads its benefits equally among the population rather than concentrating them among the wealthier families who do the bulk of the saving.

Other proposals would continue or increase the tax benefits given to mortgage lenders. There have also been suggestions that the existing subsidies to lending institutions through the government-sponsored agencies be raised. These additional tax benefits or credits would, it is hoped, induce institutions to increase the share of their loans made to housing.

It has also been suggested by certain members of Congress and their staffs that rather than going the benefit route, financial institutions be penalized if they fail to make sufficient mortgage loans. Laws have been proposed that all financial institutions which benefit from federal laws, whether through taxes, insurance, or chartering, be required to invest a certain share of their assets in residential mortgages. The amount would vary by type of institution, but those failing to meet the quota set by Congress would be penalized.

Other proposals look to the competition which takes funds out of the mortgage market. It is known, for example, that when money markets are tightest, large corporations and large borrowers tend to get a considerably larger share of the flow of funds than they do in normal periods. It has been suggested that in such times, mortgage lending could be aided by imposing penalties on other users of credit. A tax could be placed either on additional borrowing or on competitive investments. The assumption is that these penalties or taxes would be imposed in an inflationary situation, when the total amount of borrowing and investing is too high.

Other controversial proposals include increasing the direct subsidies from the government either to purchasers of real estate or to mortgage borrowers. Many argue that direct subsidies are a more efficient method of stimulating housing than indirect subsidies, tax benefits or credits, or the regulation of institutional lending. In theory, giving a direct subsidy to the person who wants help is more efficient than giving indirect subsidies through institutions or intermediaries. It is also clear, however, that the existing complex situation has many built-in supporters. For example, income tax reformers have found that the tax subsidy to homeowners is one of the most intractable to deal with. There is a tendency in this, as in other programs, not to rock the boat. Maintaining the status quo prevents many battles.

These debates are part of more general arguments over whether the variety of tax and subsidy programs lowers the normal efficiency of our financial markets. Some believe that any changes in taxes or regulations are likely to be harmful. Proponents of reform argue that existing taxes and our institutions in their present form do not appear to be working well. Problems are persistent, especially those of instability and inflation. Under our current system, the real estate field seems to feel most of the impact and makes most of the sacrifices when it comes to fighting booms. Advocates of change believe that new techniques would spread the burden of fighting booms more evenly than is now the case. While conceding that the new proposals would create problems, they believe that these problems would not be as great as the ones that now pervade the field.

The continued expansion of the federally sponsored agencies is due to the fact that they have shown themselves to be capable of dealing with these problems in a somewhat less controversial manner than many other institutions. They are a new form of intermediation between the financial and mortgage markets. Subsidies to them raise fewer questions than subsidies to private institutions. On the other hand, their borrowing is in partial competition with that of the thrift institutions. The priority to be given them in comparison with other techniques can be determined only in the overall context of what is proper and fair to borrowers as opposed to savers, what is proper and fair to builders in comparison with lenders, and what priority should be given to housing in our national goals.

In general, people's views on what type of changes might make sense seem to depend on their analysis of what actually happens now, as well as their analysis of how a financial market completely divorced from regulation would work. Those who believe that our financial markets are functioning well now and are distributing credit equitably and efficiently oppose any change, except possibly doing away with interest rate ceilings and specialized institutions.

On the other hand, those who believe that the existing system is inefficient and unfair say we can do better. They believe that the market can be improved if taxes and regulations are reshaped. They also fear what may happen if we simply abolish all existing regulations. They point out that the present system was constructed to solve problems of intolerable instability which arose in unregulated financial markets. They fear that a drastic change in existing institutions would either increase the total instability in our economy or else cause the share of mortgages in total lending to fall sharply both in periods of tight money and also over time.

CORRECTING THE PURCHASING POWER OF SAVINGS ACCOUNTS

To improve the volume and equity of the flows to savings and to mortgages, it has been proposed that savings institutions be authorized to offer accounts with a guaranteed purchasing power for up to $10,000 of each individual's savings. These indexed savings accounts would guarantee to pay as a minimum the real rate of interest (say, 3 percent) plus any change in the consumer price index over the previous 12 months.

The institution would have to pay any nominal interest rates between 3 and 8 percent. However, if the nominal rate (the real rate, 3 percent, plus the change in the Consumer Price Index) went over 8 percent, all added required sums to correct for the purchasing-power drop would be paid by the government as a tax credit or refund on the subsequent year's income tax.

This proposal was aimed at assuring each family that a minimum level of savings would be protected against inflation. It would improve the competitive position of savings institutions, since people would know they would not lose in an inflation. It would decrease disintermediation, stabilize mortgage flows, and end part of the pressure on housing.

If inflation went over 5 percent, it would increase government transfers. The higher the inflation, the more the government would have to pay. On the other hand, these expenses would merely partially offset the increased income and profit the government makes from inflation.

IMPROVEMENT IN THE MORTGAGE MARKET

There is little disagreement that if the efficiency of the mortgage market can be improved, costs will come down. We have seen that the considerable improvements already made have brought down mortgage rates compared with those on bonds and other long-term instruments. There still seems to be a fair distance to go, however.

If the various states adopted more uniform mortgage and foreclosure laws and if better appraisal standards permitted us to classify conventional mortgages more properly into relative risk classes, we would take a big step forward.

It is still true that there are probably more institutions that do not make mortgage loans than institutions that do. Among those institutions making loans on mortgages, real property still has a low priority compared with other investment areas. In tight-money situations, when these lenders are offered other types of loans, they substitute for mortgages partially because of the lack of standardization of risks in the mortgage market.

Another possible type of change would make mortgages more flexible. The sizable equities that owners build up in their homes should be a low-cost source of funds for making home improvements, for supplementing the retirement incomes of elderly persons. or even for securing consumer loans. But in fact "open-ending," as the use of the mortgage for supplemental lending is called, has proved to be very difficult. Usually the interest rate on the follow-up loan should be different from that granted initially because market rates change. The priority of the lien for this added money may differ from that of the initial loan. All these considerations lead to new and expensive title searches and other added costs. As a result, until new laws, regulations, and procedures are put into effect, this entire lending sphere, with its many potentialities, will remain negligible.

Moreover, past attempts to persuade states to adopt model real estate lending laws have not been very successful. In many states the mortgage remains an expensive instrument to use in borrowing. Achieving greater marketability through the establishment of more uniform standards and a broader national market seems a logical goal. Even limited progress along these lines could be most helpful.

SUMMARY

There is no necessity for mortgage flow to remain depressed in the 1970s. The proportion of saving and lending needed to finance an adequate level of housing is no larger now than it was in the 1960s. However, the ability of housing to compete for this share of total funds is closely related to the share of savings which the thrift institutions can attract.

Institutions run into difficulties when short-term rates approach long-term ones and when inflation increases nominal rates. The danger that such periods will recur at intervals in the future is great enough to lead many people to believe that substantial modifications in the way institutions operate are called for. Most of the proposals for change are controversial:

1   Broader powers for attracting funds and lending might increase the institutions' total loans, but not necessarily their housing loans, and might cause rates to rise even further.

2   Variable rate mortgages would enable institutions to compete, but only if borrowers agreed to accept such mortgages.

3 Tax exemptions or other forms of subsidy would also work, but questions arise as to who would get the subsidies, how they would be controlled, and whether the groups aided would be the most deserving ones among all other claimants of public funds.

4 Even minor improvements in the legal and regulatory structure of mortgages turn out to be harder to negotiate than one would expect.

QUESTIONS AND PROBLEMS

1 What are some of the long-run problems of the mortgage market?

2 Explain why interest movements are more significant in mortgage markets than in others.

3 Do you believe that there will be a shortage of mortgage money in the years 1980 to 1985? Why?

4 Which three of the suggested methods of aiding the mortgage market seem to make the most sense? Which suggestions do you feel might be counterproductive?

5 What are the good and bad features of government controls over maximum interest rates which financial institutions can pay depositors?

6 Do you think all borrowers on residential mortgages should be subsidized? Do you think any should be? Where would you draw the line between those who get such subsidies and those who do not?

7 Would variable rates be more or less attractive to borrowers? Why?

8 What are the reasons for adopting regulations leading to more competitive financial markets? Why should the existing regulations be preserved?

9 Should those who invest in mortgages be given special incentives over those who make other investments?

SELECTED REFERENCES FOR PART FOUR

Aaron, H. J.: *Shelter and Subsidies: Who Benefits from Federal Housing Policies?* (Washington: Brookings, 1972).

Break, G. F., et al.: *Federal Credit Agencies* (Englewood Cliffs, N.J.: Prentice-Hall, 1963).

A California Housing Program: 1975 (San Francisco: San Francisco Development Fund, 1975).

Cohn, R., and S. Fischer: *An Analysis of Alternative Non-Standard Mortgages,* M.I.T., The Sloan School, Mortgage Study Report, no. 5, Cambridge, Mass., 1974.

Financing the Nation's Housing Needs (New York: Committee for Economic Development, 1973).

Friend, I., et al.: *Study of the Savings and Loan Industry* (Washington: Federal Home Loan Bank Board, 1969), (4 vols.).

Gramlich, E. M., and D. M. Jaffee (eds.): *Savings Deposits, Mortgages and Housing: Studies from the FRG-MIT-Penn Model* (Lexington, Mass.: Lexington Books, 1972).

Grebler, L.: *The Future of Thrift Institutions* (Danville, Ill.: Joint Savings and Mutual Savings Banks Exchange Groups, 1969).

Housing and Monetary Policy, Federal Reserve Bank of Boston, Conference Series, no. 4, Boston, 1970.

Morris, P. R.: *State Housing Finance Agencies* (Lexington, Mass.: Lexington Books, 1974).

Policies for a More Competitive Financial System, Federal Reserve Bank of Boston, Conference Series, no. 8, Boston, 1972.

Sametz, A. W. (ed.): *Cyclical and Growth Problems Facing the Savings and Loan Industry* (New York: New York University Graduate School of Business Administration, 1968).

Solomon, A. P.: *Housing the Urban Poor: A Critical Analysis of Federal Housing Policy* (Cambridge, Mass.: M.I.T., 1974).

U.S. Commission on Financial Structure and Regulation: *Report* (the Hunt Report) (1971).

U.S. Commission on Mortgage Interest Rates: *Report* (1969).

U.S. National Commission on Urban Problems: *Report* (1968).

U.S. President's Committee on Urban Housing: *Report* (1968).

Part Five

Managing Risks: Appraisal and Valuation

How much lending institutions can lend depends upon their ability to attract money and frequently upon government actions. Each lender, however, must decide when to lend, to whom loans should be made, and the maximum safe amount for each mortgage. This part analyzes the decisions lenders must make. It describes the risks inherent in any loan and the methods by which lenders seek to keep losses from these risks at a minimum.

Chapter 17 introduces the problem of risk in both lending and investing. The formal concepts and the language employed appear to be more complex than is the case in actual use. Although many lenders and investors will be satisfied with an intuitive grasp of the major risk factors, the use of more formal procedures is spreading rapidly. How risks of individual loans are controlled by lenders is explained in Chapter 18. Careful valuation and good appraisals are a key factor in keeping losses low. Unfortunately, the process often breaks down. Periods of exuberance and overoptimism lead to careless analysis and major errors, the consequences of which, as we have seen, can be severe. Chapter 19 shows how institutions get into trouble when they fail to analyze their total or portfolio risks. It outlines the techniques needed to minimize the risk of major losses.

Chapter 17

The Lending Decision and Profit Planning

We have seen that financial institutions play a crucial role in determining the amount of funds available for real estate investment. The supply of funds depends both upon the flows within financial markets and upon the decisions of thousands of separate lenders. Each must decide whether or not to make millions of individual loans to borrowers and at what interest rates and terms. What are the factors which govern good lending decisions?

Safety and liquidity are usually ranked first among the factors influencing a firm's willingness to lend. As fiduciary institutions entrusted with funds by thousands of individuals, lenders are required by both law and tradition to give utmost priority among all operating criteria to the safe return of these funds. Therefore, a decision to buy more mortgages or to buy any individual mortgage must be weighed in the light of the lender's ability to repay deposited funds.

The second factor to be considered is the relative profitability of a given mortgage in comparison with other potential investments. Mortgages bear a certain interest rate and may yield additional sums through fees or discounts allowed from their face value. On the other hand, they engender operating costs, carry risks of loss, and may create a tax liability. When these factors are weighed together, a net yield can be calculated. Does this potential yield make it worthwhile to make the loan on real property, or would a bond or equity investment be preferable? Perhaps the decision may be to hold cash or liquid assets, on the assumption that a more profitable mortgage may be offered in the future.

These various considerations may result in a go-slow decision for mortgages as a whole, or they may result simply in an increase in individual selectivity, which will have the same effect. More stringent conditions will be likely if the firm is close to its legal or traditional limit for mortgage lending.

In this chapter we examine the general factors that influence lending decisions. In the following two chapters we discuss the actual lending and management techniques which successful lenders use in an attempt to keep their risks at a reasonable level.

MORTGAGES AND RISKS

The risks which a lender faces can be divided into two types:

1 Losses on individual loans due either to a random series of events or to a poor selection of loans (poor underwriting)
2 Losses due to improper management of the firm's portfolio, including losses resulting from (*a*) lack of diversification, (*b*) interest rate or money rate changes, (*c*) illiquidity, and (*d*) price changes or the failure of a firm to protect itself against inflation

Risks

In the technical financial literature, risk is usually defined in terms of the possible variability of future returns from an asset. Risk is inherent in equity purchases of real estate, common stock, and other assets. Real estate purchases or construction loans have usually promised rates of return far above those being offered at the same time on bonds or saving certificates. A major part of the differences in promised yields, however, may be required to compensate lenders or buyers for the fact that they have no assurance that the promised return will be paid.

For purchases of equities, the distribution of risks is a two-way street. Outcomes may be above or below the expected return. In boom or speculative periods the analysis of promised returns tends to be optimistic, and probabilities are great that the expected yields will not be achieved. The opposite is true in periods of crisis or when confidence is low. Successful investors accurately judge the degree of market optimism or pessimism. They make their own evaluations of real risks and adjust promised profits more closely to reality.

In real estate lending the same considerations apply. A lender chooses a portfolio of assets and a structure of liabilities with a view to achieving a proper trade-off between potential profits and losses. The amount of risk assumed will differ from person to person and from firm to firm, depending on how risk-averse the individual or the company is. Law and tradition operate to make most regulated financial institutions avoid high risks. To understand the way risk is handled and analyzed, we must become familiar with certain basic concepts.

Probabilities of Returns   Any real estate loan or investment decision is based upon a forecast of the future. Usually we estimate the return or yield we expect to receive from the loan as a single figure, or point estimate. Thus in the case presented in Table 17-1, we would usually speak of a 10 percent rate of return. This is actually the best or most likely forecast. However, we are always conscious of the fact that the future is uncertain. The chances are often slim that the return from an investment will be exactly as forecast.

In recent years investment analysis has increasingly attempted to take the factor of uncertain returns into account. This is done by analyzing situations in which estimates can be made of the probabilities of the particular event's occurring. Most of us are familiar with the concept of probabilities and the ability that it gives us to make statements about uncertain events.

For example, the dice player about to roll cannot say exactly what point or number will come up. However, because the probabilities of each number are known, odds can be given for or against any number. If the dice are honest, the odds can be calculated exactly.

In the case of betting on a football or basketball game, odds are also calculated. In these cases, however, the odds are not exact, but result from the estimates of informed observers. Additional information—concerning the health of a star quarterback, for example—can cause significant shifts in the odds.

Risks and probabilities in real estate come far closer to the model of a football pool than to that of a dice game or a roulette wheel. The analysts do not know what will actually happen, but they are willing to state their beliefs as to the probabilities of future outcomes. A probability is simply the chance of an event's occurring. Thus, on an honest die, the odds that a 5 will turn up on any roll are 1 in 6, or there is a probability of 16⅔ per 100. Similarly, the probability that a head will turn up when we flip an honest coin is .5, or 50 out of 100.

When future events are cloaked in uncertainty, we attach probabilities to their actual occurrence. Forecasters or lenders can specify how likely they believe any outcome to be by drawing up a "probability distribution" and by attaching a probability or likelihood coefficient to each possible outcome. Probabilities are coefficients less than 1 which together must add to 1.

Case 1 in Table 17-1 represents the probability distribution that a life insurance lender might apply to a joint venture. The loan is made at a rate of 10 percent, and the lender believes the probability is 30 percent that he will receive exactly this interest. Because there is a kicker, the lender believes that he may actually receive a 20 percent return, but this possible return has a probability of only 10 percent. He places the same probability on the loan's going bad and returning only 2 percent, with other probabilities falling between.

Expected Rate of Return   From a probability distribution such as Table 17-1, the expected rate of return can be calculated. This is a weighted average of all possible rates of return. Each possible rate is multiplied by its probability coefficient, as in the first three columns of the table. The resulting products are totaled to get the expected rate of return—the 10 percent at the bottom of the third column. While 10 percent is the expected rate and the one used in most decision processes, we see that the odds in case 1 are only 3 out of 10 that it will be the actual outcome. To repeat, the expected rate of return is the weighted average of all possible outcomes.

Table 17-1   Probabilities of Returns

Possible rate of return, %		Probability of possible rate of return		Expected rate of return, %	Deviation of possible from expected, %	Deviation squared		Deviation squared times probability
				Case I				
2	×	.1	=	.2	−8.0	64	=	6.4
6	×	.1	=	.6	−4.0	16	=	1.6
8	×	.2	=	1.6	−2.0	4	=	.8
10	×	.3	=	3.0	0	0	=	0
13	×	.2	=	2.6	3.0	9	=	1.8
20	×	.1	=	2.0	10.0	100	=	10.0
		1.0		10.0	Variance of return		=	20.6%

Standard deviation = $\sqrt{20.6\%}$ = 4.47%

				Case 2				
0	×	.5	=	0	−10.0	100		50.0
20	×	.5	=	10.0	10.0	100		50.0
		1.0		10.0	Variance of return		=	100.0%

Standard deviation = $\sqrt{100\%}$ = 10%

Measuring Risks under Uncertainty   We can now define risk in a more technical manner. It is a measure of the dispersion or spread of possible returns from the expected future returns. It is the "variance" or the "standard deviation" of the probability distribution, or a measure of how "tight" the distribution is.

The last three columns of Table 17-1 show a calculation of the variance and standard deviation. The variance is a weighted average of the squares of the deviations of all possible rates of return from the expected rate of return. Thus in case 1, the 2 percent possible return deviates by 8 percent from the expected rate of 10 percent. This deviation is squared and multiplied by its probability. It contributes 6.4 percent—almost one-third —to the total variance of 20.6 percent. The other contributions are calculated in the same way. The standard deviation (often called *sigma*) is merely the square root of the variance, or approximately 4.47 percent in the example.

To understand the concept of risks, let us assume a different probability distribution for the same property, shown as case 2 in Table 17-1. Suppose that instead of the probabilities in case 1, the company believed that the venture would do either very well or very poorly—that the chances were 50 percent that it would default with a zero return and 50 percent that it would return 20 percent. In this case the expected rate of return is still 10 percent. The variance, however, is now 100, and the standard deviation is 10 percent.

Figure 17-1 presents another example of investments with differing risks. It reflects two properties, each of which has an expected present value of $25,000. They have, however, very different risks. We see that there is only a very small chance that venture A will lose any money, nor is there much chance that it will make a great deal. In the case

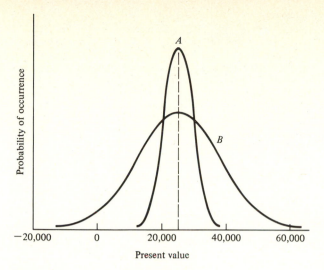

Figure 17-1 Comparison of risks.

of venture B, however, the estimators show odds that are far from negligible that the property may lose $15,000 or make $60,000 at the assumed discount rates.

If offered a choice between two properties, one with a probability distribution like that of case 1 or venture A and the other with a probability distribution like that of case 2 or venture B, most people would choose the first. In both cases the rate of return is the same, but the risk in the first case is less. By making such offers in the market, we might find out how risk-averse people are. In Table 17-1, for example, some might pick the second case if it had an expected rate of return of 12 percent instead of 10 percent to make up for the fact that its standard deviation is more than twice as large. For others, the necessary added returns might have to increase to 15 percent or even more because the chances of getting no return are 50 percent, which is too high for many investors.

A Decision Tree for Probable Outcomes

Other ways have been developed for taking uncertainties into account when knowledge-able people are willing to make informed guesses as to probable outcomes. One method, known as the "decision-tree" procedure, has been used in lending decisions and also for bidding on contracts, for making investments, and for dealing with large-scale developments. While it requires more work than is worthwhile for most decisions, it gives a good deal of insight into how to think about the effects of different possible outcomes. As computers become more common in real estate and lending offices, the use of such techniques will grow.

Figure 17-2 is a decision tree. We illustrate the decision-tree method using an example introduced by Bruce Ricks.[1]

An investor is offered as a sale-leaseback a building with a net-net lease. The

[1]R. B. Ricks, *Recent Trends in Institutional Real Estate Investment* (Berkeley: University of California, Center for Real Estate and Urban Economics, 1963).

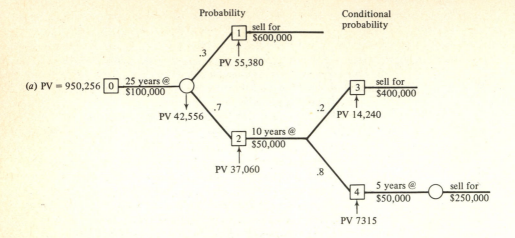

(b) 1 $100,000 for 25 years + $600,000 at 25th year
  3 $100,000 for 25 years + $50,000 for 10 years + $400,000 at 35th year
  4 $100,000 for 25 years + $50,000 for 10 years + $50,000 for 5 years + $250,000 at 40th year

(c) 1 $100,000 (9.0770) + $600,000 (.0923)   = 963,080 [(.3)   = (.30)] = 288,924
  3 $100,000 (9.0770) + $50,000 (.5672) + (400,000) (.0356) = 950,300 [(.7) (.2) = (.14)] = 133,042
  4 $100,000 (9.0770) + $50,000 (.7020) + (250,000) (.0023) = 943,375 [(.7) (.8) = (.56)] = 528,290
                                                                                                      1.0   950,256

Figure 17-2 A decision tree for real estate investments.

offering price of the building is $1,000,000. The lease states that the tenant will pay $100,000 in rent for each of the next 25 years. At the end of 25 years he will have several options open to him:

  1 He can give up the building. If the lease is not renewed, the reversion value or sales price of the building at the end of the twenty-fifth year is estimated at $600,000.
  2 He can renew the lease for another 10 years at a rent of $50,000 per year. The investor's advisers tell him they believe the chances that the lease will be renewed are 70 percent, or .7. If the tenant takes the option to renew the lease, he has a second renewal option at the end of the next 10 years.
  3 He can again refuse to renew, in which case the reversion value of the building at the end of 35 years is estimated to be $400,000.
  4 The tenant can take a second renewal option for 5 years, again at $50,000 a year. The reversion value at the end of this second option, or 40 years, is estimated to be $250,000. The advisers say that if the tenant takes the first renewal option, the probabilities are 80 percent, or .8, that he will take the second option and renew.

  This information is diagramed in Figure 17-2. No matter which options are taken, the investor will receive the $100,000 in rent for each of the next 25 years. At that time, the tenant makes a decision. The probabilities are .3 that he will take the top branch and give up the lease. In this case we have the numbers shown as line 1 in Figure 17-2b. This line shows the income from the lease for 25 years plus the reversion at the end of 25 years.

If the tenant decides to renew (.7 probability), we follow the lower branch. This means that the tenant will pay $50,000 for each of the next 10 years and that in the thirty-fifth year another decision must be made. The probabilities are .2 that the top fork of the branch, ③, will be followed—the lease will not be renewed. The value to the owner if the tenant follows this branch is shown as line 3 in Figure 17-2*b*. Finally, if a decision is made to renew the second time, the bottom branch is followed, with the results to the owner summarized in line 4.

There are at least two ways for the investor to calculate the present value of this entire tree. Upon investigating the credit risks of the company and other potential investments, the investor (insurance company, pension fund, etc.) decides to use a 10 percent discount factor or desired rate of return. (See Chapter 6 for the specific techniques.) Figure 17-2*c* shows one procedure for calculation.

First, the present value of branch ① is calculated. The present value of a 10 percent ordinary annuity for 25 years has an interest factor of 9.0770. This is multiplied by the $100,000 annual rent. Similarly, the value of the reversion at the end of 25 years is calculated. The present value of a property worth $600,000 in 25 years when discounted at 10 percent is $55,380. These two values are added together to give $963,080 as the present value of path number ① as shown in Figure 17-2*c*.

This branch has a .3 probability of occurring. Therefore, it contributes .3 times its value to the investor's estimate of the present value of the entire offer.

Next, the values of branches ③ and ④ are calculated in the same way. Branch ③ has a present value of $950,300. What are the odds that it will be the final path? Here we have a case of conditional probabilities. If the first renewal occurs, the odds are .2 that the lease will not be renewed at the second option. Therefore, the probability of the middle path, ③, is found by multiplying its conditional probability of .2 by the probability that the tenant will have taken up the first option to renew (.7). Thus the chances that the present value of the middle path will occur are .7 × .2, or .14.

Similarly, we find that the chances that the investment will follow the lowest path, or path ④, are .7 × .8, or .56. The probabilities that the tenant will follow one of the three options exhaust all possibilities. They add to 1, as they must.

We see that in Figure 17-2*c*, when the three possible paths with their probabilities are weighted, the present value of the offer is $950,256. Since this is less than the asking price of $1,000,000, the company would not buy the building unless the offer were renegotiated.

We could also have calculated the present value by rolling back down the decision tree. Thus we see:

1 At decision point ①, the present value of the first choice that the tenant will not renew is $55,380. The chances that this path will be followed are .3.

2 The present value of the choice at decision point ③ is $14,240. Its value times its probability of .2 is added to the present value at point ④ of $7,315 times its probability, plus the present value of the rent from years 25 to 35. Adding these three weighted factors together gives a present value for the choice at point ② of $37,060.

3 We now find the value at the time of the first decision to renew. It is .7 × $37,060 + .3 × $55,380 = $42,556.

4   When the value of that decision is added to the present value for the initial 25-year lease, which is $907,700, we again find that the present value of the entire offer is $950,256.

This second technique emphasizes the time value of money and the relatively small impact of the far future on present values when we have a discount rate as high as 10 percent. For example, we see that the present value of the reversion of the property which is expected to sell for $400,000 in 35 years is only $14,240. The reversion value at the end of 40 years has a present value of only $575.

Because values fall so rapidly, the decision-tree approach is far more useful when considering a sequence of decisions only a few years out than when considering decisions that are as far in the future as the ones in this example. It would be logical to use this technique for long leases only if there was a sharp fall in discount values back to the neighborhood of 5 or 6 percent, as was the case in the late 1940s.

CORRELATIONS BETWEEN RISKS

One of the advantages of decision trees and measures of the variances of risks is that they call attention to the need to consider possible events both over time and in relation to the entire portfolio of an institution. Lenders and investors must be concerned with more than the risks of individual loans. They must base their decisions on how risks or potential profits of the entire institution will be affected by their choices. The risks to an institution are not a simple averaging of the risks of individual loans. Rather, the institution's risks, or portfolio risks, depend both on the risks or variances of individual loans and on how these loans relate to one another. Portfolio risks depend on the covariance or correlation between loans. What is the likelihood that they might all go bad at the same time?

The losses on different properties, loans, or decisions may vary considerably with events in the economy and financial markets. Thus in a depression the rate of return on GNMA debentures is likely to increase, while loans to land developers are likely to show no income and large losses. The opposite will be true in a boom. The relationship or correlation between these real estate assets is said to be negative. On the other hand, loans on land and for construction are likely to be positively correlated. Their chances of loss and gain rise and fall together.

An investor who includes a variety of assets is diversifying his or her portfolio. The process of diversification may, but need not, lower the total risk. What occurs will depend on the type of correlation that exists between the investor's assets and liabilities with respect to how they react to major changes in the economy, in money markets, and in real estate markets.

1   Most real estate assets have positively correlated risks. As a result, a simple diversification through the addition of more such assets may do little to reduce risks. This was the experience of REITs in 1974.

2   Some properties are nearly uncorrelated in their risks. Adding a number of them to a portfolio tends to reduce its overall risk. Thus a portfolio of home mortgages built up over time and including scattered locations has a fairly low overall risk because, except under extreme conditions, most loans will not default at the same time.

3 Some assets, as in the example of land loans and GNMA debentures, have a negative correlation. Adding both to a portfolio will reduce its total risks. If in doing so, lenders can increase their average expected rate of return without increasing their risk, they will be better off. Their expected profits will rise without adding any risk. They should take any action which will increase their profits within the limits of their desired risks.

In considering how to plan what risks should be accepted, lenders must recognize that while the penalties of assuming too many poor risks are all too obvious, avoiding them altogether is impossible. The best that firms can do is to make the most judicious selection among risks so as to minimize the threat of loss while maximizing the net yield which will remain after paying for the probable losses from loans which do not return their expected yields.

In planning profit and risk strategies, it is useful to divide the problem into considerations of (1) individual loans or properties and (2) overall or portfolio considerations.

Risks from Underwriting and Random Individual Losses

When we examine a portfolio of individual loans, we find that some losses will occur for nonsystematic or random reasons. Each individual loan runs a basic hazard of loss. Insofar as this is random, it is similar to an actuarial or insurable risk, the probabilities of which can be fairly well calculated. In fact, losses of this type can be insured against through policies with the FHA or mortgage guarantee insurance companies.

Other losses, however, will tend to move together. They will occur as a result of systematic factors in the operation of the firm, the firm's choice of loans, or what is happening in the economy.

Conceptually, it is not hard to distinguish the types of losses from one another. Consider any portfolio of mortgages with properly made loans. The borrowers have assumed contracts which they can meet, and there is a reasonable expectation that they will desire to fulfill their loan commitments. The lending process was error-free, and the economy continues on an even keel. But even with all these conditions prevailing, some delinquencies, foreclosures, and losses will develop, simply because of the random occurrence of normal events, which, while not predictable for any single loan, can be predicted for an entire class.

What are some of these events to which every group of loans is exposed but against which they cannot be protected by better lending practices?

Most important are various family troubles or catastrophes. Every time there is a divorce, separation, serious illness, or death, payments on the mortgage are likely to be endangered. Losses will result from delayed payments. In especially serious cases, the family may have to move out of its home. Whether a forced sale causes a loss depends on the state of the market and on how soon the trouble occurs after the mortgage has been granted.

Similarly, responsible workers or business people may suddenly experience a sharp drop in income or even lose their jobs, sharply curtailing their ability to meet loan payments and causing consequent losses to lenders.

Finally, the value of individual properties may fluctuate as a result of shifts in neighborhoods, changes in tastes, or even physical disasters not fully protected against. Any of these may lead to a cessation in payments and to foreclosures with losses. Income properties are also subject to losses of this nature.

In all these cases, the only way to avoid losses would be to stop all normal lending. While they cannot be forecast, with a sufficiently large and diversified mortgage portfolio, such losses can be estimated and covered by reserves established for that purpose.

Experience shows that these reserves need not be large, but this holds true only if the loans are made or underwritten properly. In addition to the above-listed random causes, many losses occur because lenders fail to do a good underwriting job. As a result of market pressures, enthusiasm, or carelessness, firms find that substantial errors arise in underwriting. The purpose of mortgage risk analysis is to ensure that loans are properly classified so that the risk each contains can be recognized. However, this requires that the job of risk analysis be done properly. Careless or ill-advised lending will increase potential losses.

Chapter 18 analyzes some of the techniques a firm can use to improve its underwriting and avoid losses in this first category of risks.

Portfolio Risks

Besides the risks inherent in individual loans, lending always carries a threat to the safety or solvency of the entire institution. Positive correlation between the risks in a portfolio may cause losses to mushroom, and the entire institution may be threatened. Portfolio risks are often confused with the risk of random individual losses just described, but the random losses do not in themselves threaten the institution. No one worries too much about occasional losses in individual cases; they are the normal risks of any business. What causes serious concern is the threat to the safety of the institution which would result if whole classes of loans were subject to a large, simultaneous run of losses or foreclosures. The portfolio risk is based on the possibility that groups of loans will go bad together, in contrast to the first type of risk, in which individual failures to pay occur more or less randomly and can be absorbed by reserves.

Various forces cause portfolio risks over and above the simple summation of the risks of losses on individual loans. The possibility is always present that a national economic catastrophe like that of the 1930s will destroy both the ability of large numbers of borrowers to pay and the desire of others to purchase. Another type of threat to a portfolio of local loans is the danger that a major local industry may close down. Individual institutions may overload themselves with loans of a particular type. Too great a concentration on a single builder, a new subdivision, or a special type of tract house could jeopardize the safety of the entire institution in case of a sudden loss of value.

Depressions and Recessions   Historically, the most important type of risk has been that related to major economic movements that affect the entire national income and alter the ability to pay for buildings, the prices that various types of property realize in the market, the costs or charges applicable to real estate, and the interest rate.

The most obvious danger is that another major economic depression like that of

1929 to 1932 will occur. That depression caused enormous losses in most mortgage portfolios. It wiped out large numbers of lending institutions. As the level of income fell, individuals found it harder and harder to meet their mortgage payments. Because the market for foreclosed property was so poor and because houses deteriorated more rapidly in lenders' hands than in those of the owners, lenders frequently found that it did not pay to foreclose.

A related possibility is that the real estate market as a whole or particular parts of it may go through a major depression separate and distinct from one in the overall economy. Specific depressions and losses are particularly likely to occur in individual submarkets, such as those for hotels, apartment houses, and office buildings, or in individual cities or suburbs. Submarkets can meet with disasters because of overbuilding or collapses of local demand.

The discussion in the next chapter shows large fluctuations in delinquencies, foreclosures, and losses on mortgages. There is a tendency for lenders and others to be overinfluenced by recent experience. Major errors of both optimism and pessimism occur. It is far safer to base decisions on a longer view of lending, including the experience of the 1930s along with that of 1974–1975.

Since problems are compounded when local markets experience unusually high unemployment, large national lenders enjoy important advantages in absorbing losses in submarkets. To them such losses appear comparable to random individual risks. A lender who has a small percentage of loans in any submarket will not be hurt badly if the submarket deteriorates. On the other hand, an institution that, because of laws or poor management, has concentrated loans in a single area assumes much heavier risks.

Interest Rate Movements   Bad loans are not the only source of portfolio risks. A firm can also become bankrupt if it loses large sums when the price or value of its mortgages changes. Several times we have discussed the fact that when current market interest rates change, the value of mortgages with a fixed interest rate contract also shifts. As interest rates rise, the value or selling price of the mortgage falls.

In such periods an investor who has to sell a mortgage will receive a reduced price. This is one reason why mortgage bankers seek commitments from Fannie Mae. If interest rates rise, they are still able to deliver mortgages at a price agreed upon in the auction.

To some extent, institutions are partially protected against drops in prices of their assets by the fact that the regulating agencies do not require that mortgages be carried at market prices. The mortgages and other investments of a financial institution are frequently carried at their book value—the price paid for them by the institution—rather than the price they would fetch in the market. If the institution continues to hold the loan, it need not charge a loss against its reserves or equity. However, this rule is only a partial protection. The yield received by the institution will be lower than that earned by investments being made currently. If the institution has to borrow or pay market rates for its deposits, it will be penalized in comparison with those firms able to invest at current market rates.

This risk of a decline in market value due to an increase in market interest rates is called, as we have seen, the *interest rate*, *money rate*, or *price* risk. Such risks are particularly common in the mortgage market, partly because loans are lengthy, and partly because by regulation in some cases and tradition in others, borrowers may be allowed to pay off their loans with small or no penalties. This means, again, that the lender has adverse selection. If the value of a mortgage falls because of an increase in interest rates, it will not be paid off, but will remain in the lender's portfolio. On the other hand, if the value of a mortgage rises, borrowers may prepay their loans, and lenders may find themselves with cash which they will now have to invest at the current lower market interest rates.

Liquidity   The inability to get payment when the lender requires money illustrates a third type of portfolio risk in mortgages: their potential lack of liquidity. The *liquidity risk* is the possibility that extra costs may be generated if part of the mortgage portfolio must be sold in order to obtain a larger-than-normal flow of funds.

This risk is increased by the fact that most lending institutions borrow short and lend long. They gather their funds through short-term deposits. If market rates rise above deposit rates, there can be a sudden rush of funds from the institution. This is called *disintermediation* because savers or holders of funds invest their money directly rather than through a financial intermediary. When money flows out, the entire portfolio must be examined to see where cash can be raised at the most reasonable rates. If the mortgage portfolio cannot free sufficient funds to meet the institution's needs except at an excessive cost, a further risk is incurred.

Losses from portfolio risks may be increased by the fact that if a class of loans goes bad and many foreclosures occur simultaneously, the properties may have to be liquidated or handled outside normal channels. The history of the 1930s shows that, except where major lending errors were made, with adequate time the security gained from the property is sufficient to repay most of the outstanding debt. This ability to sell the property if the borrower fails to meet the contract is one of the popular features of mortgage lending. On the other hand, if many loans go bad at the same time, sales of property do not offer the lender the same opportunity to collect. When lenders' portfolios are cluttered with slow payments, foreclosures, and other problems, they may have to sacrifice properties rather than give the market a chance to absorb them at nondistress prices. As a result, additional losses are suffered in liquidation that would not have occurred if the same loans could have been handled through routine procedures.

Such handling of losses threatens the institution's solvency. If capital reserves are wiped out, distress liquidation may require the whole organization to be closed. When major portions of the portfolio go bad, risks to the organization's existence rise astronomically. In determining its investment policy, the institution must either protect against this risk directly or recognize that the face or promised mortgage yields must be reduced by the potential losses which can result from the need to liquidate part of the mortgage portfolio to obtain cash.

Inflation   A final type of portfolio risk is due to inflation. Changes in prices and purchasing power alter the value of a portfolio. Portfolios held entirely in monetary or dollar-denominated assets experience a drop in real values along with the purchasing power of the dollar. Other assets such as equities or those with equity features may over time, but not necessarily over a period of a few years, have a more stable real value.

Chapter 19 discusses the techniques which successful managements use to protect themselves against the great dangers arising in the portfolio sphere.

NET YIELD ON MORTGAGES

We have noted that risk is a primary factor determining the lending of financial institutions. A second essential factor is a loan's net yield. Whether a mortgage loan is made will depend upon the decision of the lender as to whether the mortgage will increase his profits more than the utilization of the funds in other ways. Because knowledge of both costs and income is far from exact, decisions are less scientific than is sometimes claimed. In many cases decisions are based on rules of thumb as to what percentage of funds should go into mortgages in contrast to other loans, or they may be based upon the concept that certain types of funds should go into mortgages. In recent years, however, lenders have paid increasing attention to the actual profitability of individual loans.

In this process, lenders must estimate both the costs of making a loan and the income they expect to receive from it. In turn, costs are divided into the amount which must be paid for the money loaned and those costs arising from operating the business and making and servicing individual loans. Income is derived both from the interest rate charged on the loan and from fees and discounts, or points. At the same time, part of the income must go into reserves to pay for actual or potential losses, and part goes to pay the government's taxes on income.

Because the relationships between these factors are complex, it is difficult to determine specific costs and actual income. However, to arrive at logical decisions, a firm must possess enough knowledge of these factors to be able to make at least minimal estimates and projections.

COSTS

While in many ways the problems of measuring costs for mortgage lending are similar to those of measuring costs for other economic activities, a few special features are worthy of note. On the whole, lenders tend not to be very exact in their cost allocations. They find it difficult to assign specific costs to particular activities within a firm. Lenders enjoy important economies of scale; that is, costs fall with volume. Because it costs small lenders more both to originate and to service loans, if they are to make a profit, they must offset their higher costs either by being especially sharp or by having better-than-average knowledge of their markets and giving superior service.

Cost Analysis

One of the difficulties of measuring costs is that, traditionally, financial institutions have not shown several types on their books. They have tended to operate on close to a cash basis, writing off costs which should be spread over a longer period and failing to take into account other costs. Examples can be found in the costs of portfolio acquisitions, depreciation, and changes in market values of mortgages. All these are frequently not included in accounts or are dealt with in such an arbitrary manner that they provide little knowledge helpful for future action. As an example, many accounting systems charge off currently all the expenses of obtaining a loan portfolio. However, sales of mortgage companies and of groups of loans show that additions to a portfolio have an immediate value which will be realized in the future. Loans placed on the books contribute to profits as they continue in existence. Some of these profits can be cashed by selling the loan.

Costs engendered in obtaining these loans should, for the purposes of earnings analysis, be considered as charges against future rather than current income because they will pay off in the future. Such allocations to the future are common in the insurance field, where financial analysts usually show 20 to 50 percent of the value of unearned premium reserves as part of the firm's value. Current changes in these reserves are taken into income. Increases in a mortgage loan portfolio are equivalent to these unearned premiums. The costs of obtaining them have been paid out, but income from them will flow in during the future. The rights to service loan portfolios have sold for from 1 to 2 percent of their face amount. This is one measure of values created when loans are originated.

For the purposes of cost analysis, in addition to treating items differently, the firm must restructure a considerable amount of its data. The accounting records must be adjusted to reflect true alternative costs and revenues, not simply those shown on the books. The expense and income accounts must be regrouped so that they will be in a more logical form for necessary decisions. Financial accounting divides costs into those for interest and other payments for money, on the one hand, and those for operating expenses, on the other. Cost-volume analysis requires the further division of operating expenses in accordance with the time period over which they can be influenced.

Examining mortgage lenders today, one notes a striking increase in their awareness of these problems and their ability to handle them. When we first wrote on these topics in the early 1960s, only the most skilled and advanced firms utilized these concepts. Since then the planning and budgeting functions have become large and significant. Constantly increasing competition, plus the shock of numerous outside pressures, convinced managements that they could remain profitable only if they developed more specific information and more formal decision-making processes.

Economies of Scale

Many studies have shown that costs decrease as lenders expand in size. The rate of decrease slows down as the lender gets larger and larger. Thus a lender who services loans of $10 million will find his cost per dollar of loan to be between 85 and 90 percent of that of a lender who does only a $1-million business. To get an equivalent saving by further expansion, the lender's volume would have to rise to $100 million. At that point, he would have benefited from most economies of scale, although another small decrease in costs per loan may occur for firms servicing over $1 billion in loans.

Some costs, however, are a function of the number of loans rather than of total volume. As a result, the cost per dollar falls with the amount of each loan. Efficient servicing agencies estimate that it costs from $30 to $35 a year to service an average home loan. This works out to a cost of 3 percent to service a loan with an outstanding balance of $1,000, while the cost of servicing a loan with an outstanding balance of $70,000 is less than .05 percent.

This economy of size is one of the traditional reasons why large loans on commercial or other buildings have had slightly lower interest rates than home loans, even though their risk is actually greater. The lower cost of servicing such loans has been passed on to the borrower. Another reason why such rates are lower is that they are in a more competitive market. Many lenders are not equipped to seek out and service all the loans they need or want at a particular time. These larger loans can be brought to them for direct negotiations and acceptance or rejection. As a result, borrowers with large loans may find bidding for them more competitive.

Cost of Money to Be Lent

Lenders' major variable cost is the amount paid for the money which the firm lends out. This may run 80 percent or more of gross operating income. Two factors influence the firm's cost of money.

First, the movements of total demand, supply, and government policy in the overall money market determine the average interest rate on such money-market items as Treasury notes and on long-term government, corporate, and municipal bonds. Most institutions can buy other assets or lend in the other money markets. As a result, the going rate in all lending markets is competitive with mortgages and must enter into the analysis of the variable costs of money.

Second, most financial institutions have a more direct control over their money costs through their own policies in paying for, and attracting, savings. The analysis of the cost of savings is similar to the analysis of the cost of lending. Institutions have certain fixed and variable costs in their saving operations. They also face a competitive situation in the savings market. They can alter both the rates they offer for funds and the advertising and other expenditures they make to attract them.

Joint Costs

In the typical financial institution many costs are joint; that is, they are paid out for services which apply to both the saving and lending operations or to several types of investment services. Some investment officers supervise both the bond and mortgage portfolios. Some executives administer both deposit and lending services. A new, expensive building or a series of community advertisements will attract both depositors and borrowers.

In addition, loans, deposits, and other sources of income may be interrelated. A loan that otherwise would not pay for itself may be worthwhile because it brings a firm prestige, goodwill, or a good customer or because it results in improvement to the community.

As an example, a few LICs have related their mortgage loans to the sale of insurance. They recognize that if the mortgage brings in a customer who otherwise would not buy insurance, some of the usual cost of selling can be credited to the mortgage. A lower yield can therefore be accepted than would otherwise be the case. The borrower-customer can get more attractive terms by entering into both bargains.

Other cases exist of lending institutions' engaging in more than one line of business. If problems of conflict of interest and of monopoly pressures can be avoided, certain types of tie-in sales may be profitable. For example, a mortgage company with escrow, title, and insurance affiliates may be able to accept lower fees for the mortgage itself.

Still more prevalent is the recognition of the impact of loans on an institution's public image and also on its own welfare through strengthening the community. Mortgages on churches may be unprofitable in and of themselves, but if they attract depositors and borrowers, their advantages may offset their basic intrinsic problems.

Most deposit institutions recognize that they depend for their funds on their locality. As a result, the more they can help local firms and local business activity, the better off they will be. They may therefore lend in their own markets at somewhat lower rates than required for equivalent loans elsewhere. They properly recognize that by helping their community, they are helping themselves.

COMPETITION

Both the cost of funds and the amount of income a firm receives for its loans depend upon its competition. The markets, however, are far from perfect. A wide variety of rates and services may be paid for funds, while similar differences are found on the income side.

On the funds side, the degree of competition from other institutions varies greatly by location, by type of savers, and by size of account, among other factors. On the lending side, differences stem from the type of property and its location and from the time at which people are seeking loans or are making deposits. The markets are sufficiently imperfect and complex for a lender to be able to develop both a marketing and a pricing strategy.

Lenders can compete by cutting prices, by improving the terms of their loans, or by adopting nonprice techniques such as more advertising or added services. Firms choose strategies in accordance with their particular strengths and weaknesses. Since the legal and portfolio needs of different institutions vary widely, each lender can plan a multivariable strategy. Lenders must be certain to protect the areas where they meet the most competition, while taking advantage of the ones in which their strength is concentrated.

To illustrate, in most areas S&Ls find far more competition for FHA- and VA-guaranteed loans than for conventional ones, since the government-guaranteed loans can be bid for by mortgage companies and sold in the national market. Similarly, insurance companies may actively solicit loans for higher-priced units and apartment houses but not for smaller or cheaper dwellings. Banks may be actively in, or primarily out of, the local market depending on available funds. For older homes, competition may exist primarily among S&Ls.

The knowledge of what others are doing is an important factor in setting one's own rates. Because national lenders find it harder to shift rates to meet local competition, their rates are a known factor which can be treated as such by others when making pricing decisions. Local firms can react more immediately and concretely to changing quotations. Their current situation with respect to funds and need for loans and their probable reactions must be given more weight in setting policy than the situation and reactions of national lenders.

Lenders increase their flexibility by altering their fees, discounts, and services before they change interest rates. Two reasons for this policy are that interest rate changes (1) may cause reactions among borrowers with outstanding loans and (2) may more easily be met by competitors. Since loans are so different, it is often possible to tailor yields through the fee structure without upsetting the market or one's competitors.

Altering services or using nonprice competition may also make more sense in many cases than changing rates. Experience in other marketing areas makes it clear that some customers can be attracted primarily on a price basis, while others respond to a different set of stimuli. It is almost always a mistake, however, to assume that putting all one's efforts into one type of competition will give the best results. Discount houses expanded rapidly because department stores neglected price-conscious families. Lenders cannot afford to neglect any method of competition simply because in the past they have been successful with one particular approach.

The strategies of nonprice competition are as varied as the elements they deal with. Institutions attract borrowers and depositors by their advertising, by their locations and offices, by the speed with which they act, by the number of solicitors they hire, by their gifts, by their public image, and by activities in civic and social groups.

INCOME

The bulk of income originates in the interest rate charged on loans and in the fee structure. In firms which sell various services, however, income may be generated through a loan's impact in these other areas rather than directly.

The interest rate cannot be considered by itself. The net yield is the important factor. This means that all the offsets to income already discussed must enter into the analysis. The rate must be adjusted for differential risks, for the effect of the loan's terms on liquidity, and for additional costs that can be related directly to the individual mortgage. Only when all these elements have been taken into account can the true income from a loan be calculated.

Some types of loans have heavy charges directly related to them. For example, in construction lending, the firm needs personnel to inspect the plan, check the documents, watch the progress of construction, and make certain that funds paid out go to the individual claimants so that mechanic's liens will not occur. These requirements reduce the potential income from the loan. Similar needs exist for handling property improvement loans, for land development loans, and for alteration and repair loans. The costs differ by type of loan, and so do the potential yields.

One way to attempt to offset these additional costs is through a fee schedule for special loans. Fees may also be charged on regular mortgages to cover the cost of placing the loan on the books. These fees are a significant part of income. Changes in their amounts are important in keeping the firm competitive.

Because the initial costs of originating a loan may be quite high, they reduce the profitability of the mortgage for its first several years if no fee is charged. On the other hand, fees and their related premiums and discounts allow income to shift without the necessity of altering the quoted interest rate. Because interest rates are usually quoted in even increments of .25 or .5 percent, any change in the rate has a large impact on both the firm's income and the borrower's payments. Fee charges of 1, 2, and 3 percent for loans add three additional steps in the interest rate structure in between the usual .25 percent steps that most firms quote.

It is also true that changes in fees may constitute a better means of competition than interest rate movements do. Fee shading is more difficult for competitors to match. Fees also allow the firm to shape its charges more exactly to the individual loan. If risk or cost analysis indicates that a loan is particularly advantageous, the borrower may be offered a premium. On the other hand, if the risks or costs are unusually high, the loan may still be worthwhile if sufficient fees can be collected to equalize the net income.

TAXES

The final factor in calculating net yield is taxes. We have commented on the significant role that taxes and potential tax subsidies play in investment decisions. This is particularly true for mortgage lending. Because of the sizable risks that mortgage loans contain, one must think of current interest receipts as partly a net yield and partly a payment to compensate for future losses. Such a theory leads to the establishment of bad-debt reserves. These reserves contain receipts put aside from income to compensate for possible future losses.

Unfortunately, there is no way to predict future losses accurately; such predictions can be no more than estimates. This impreciseness, which is of primary concern to management and supervisory agencies, is also of interest to the income tax collector. Money placed in a bad-debt reserve authorized by the IRS is usually not subject to income taxes unless and until it is transferred out of the reserve and is returned to the current income account.

If the bad-debt reserves exceed actual losses, a firm has two types of potential tax savings. Most importantly, the excess amount in the reserve establishes what is loosely called a ''tax-free loan'' from the government. When they must be declared as current income, earnings subject to tax are cut in half (assuming a 50 percent tax rate). For every $1,000 earned, only $500 remains after taxes to reinvest in the firm. In contrast, income transferred to the bad-debt reserve pays no tax. All of it is available for reinvestment. A company desiring to build up its available funds is saved taxes on that part of income credited to an authorized bad-debt reserve. However, to the extent that this credit to the reserve exceeds actual future requirements, it is really part of current earnings or income. The existence of the reserve gives a tax saving. The amount of this saving is retained for the present by the firm. Even if it must pay equivalent taxes at some future time, in the interim the sums can be used profitably by the institution.

A second possible saving exists if it is assumed that tax rates will be lower in the future. If the rate is lower at the time the reserves are carried to earnings, an additional saving will be realized.

Authorized Reserves

For many years, because they could reduce any potential earnings by a transfer to loss reserves, MSBs, S&Ls, and LICs paid minimal income taxes. This is no longer the case.

MSBs and S&Ls now work under a complex formula of authorized reserves. In effect, they have to calculate their normal income subject to tax. In this calculation they can take credit for routine expenses, including interest or dividends on share accounts or deposits. They can then transfer a percentage of the remaining otherwise taxable income to a bad-debt reserve against their mortgages. This nontaxable transfer is authorized providing that it does not raise the reserve against mortgages to more than 6 percent of loans and providing that total reserves are not above 12 percent of savings. This percentage authorized for transfer was 45 percent of taxable income in 1975, to be reduced to 40 percent by 1979. The Hunt Commission and others have proposed that this special tax treatment of reserves be replaced by a special tax credit based upon an institution's lending on housing.

Insurance companies now are taxed on a ratio derived from earnings required on their reserves over total earnings. Various adjustments are made for types of earnings and for general expenses. The formulas are extremely complex and vary from firm to firm.

The net effect of these changes in the tax law is to cause the taxability of mortgage earnings to vary from year to year within the same institution, among institutions in the same year, and among assets at separate times. The relative tax rates for mortgages will fluctuate depending on recent losses and on previously accumulated reserves. The calculation of comparative net yields raises still more difficult problems because the variables are so numerous. The net impact of taxes on decisions appears somewhat less than in former periods. However, it still is a factor that must enter into earnings analysis. At times it may still be the decisive factor determining whether an institution should expand its mortgage portfolio in comparison with other potential investments.

SUMMARY

In deciding how much to lend on mortgages or in other markets, lenders must consider both their risks and their potential profits. Risks develop from underwriting or individual losses and from portfolio problems. The yield on a mortgage depends on the costs involved, on the prices charged (and therefore on the income received), and on the taxes which must be paid against income.

QUESTIONS AND PROBLEMS

1   It is often said that once a loan is made, things can only get worse. Explain.
2   A lender is offered a loan that has a 20 percent chance of paying 6 percent, a 40 percent chance of paying 9 percent, a 20 percent chance of paying 10 percent, and a 20 percent chance of paying 12 percent. What is the expected yield?
3   If the lender in question 2 is risk-averse, should he take the loan described or a loan paying a sure 8.5 percent?
4   How can lending risks be minimized?
5   What does the concept of risk mean as applied to real estate lending?
6   Distinguish underwriting risks from portfolio risks.
7   Is loan servicing a profit item or just a necessary administrative burden?
8   Examine Figure 17-2. Assume that because of inflation you feel each estimated sale price for the building should be doubled. How much difference would this make for the estimated present value?
9   Discuss the different types of risks which can cause portfolio losses. Which would you think is the greatest danger?
10   Why should the IRS limit the amount of authorized bad-debt reserves?

Chapter 18

The Control of Individual Risks: Appraisal and Valuation

Few things are more discouraging to lenders than the need to foreclose on a mortgage. They are threatened by a potential loss. A customer is likely to be suffering and may become bitter. The community and any regulatory agency involved will become concerned if the number of foreclosures rises to any degree. While delinquencies are not as disturbing, they too can be costly. They require extra work and effort. In almost any lending operation, handling a small percentage of problem loans will be nearly as costly as servicing a large number of routine cases.

But not all delinquencies and foreclosures can be avoided. Some are an inevitable accompaniment to all lending. Lenders must attempt to reduce individual risks of loss or added costs to the best of their ability. They also want to be sure that if they accept certain risks, they do so knowingly and are adequately compensated for their effort.

Lenders work to avoid losses in four ways:

1 Most important is risk management, which analyzes and attempts to estimate the risks involved before a loan is granted. A sound loan processing procedure is required to ensure that each loan application is carefully analyzed and that its risks are properly evaluated.

2 Next there must be an efficient program of loan supervision. After a loan is made, costs and losses can be reduced by means of a program which guards against delinquencies, which cures as fast as possible the delinquencies and defaults that do occur, and which liquidates with minimum losses loans that cannot be cured.

3   In some cases, a careful weighing for added income compared with the risks assumed is called for. Not all risks can or should be avoided. Many can be more than offset by higher interest rates or added fees. This, however, requires a proper program of loan evaluation and supervision. REITs, for example, stressed their ability to gain extra income by a proper management of risk. Many, however, failed to establish the necessary procedures to make certain that the added income was really high enough to offset the increased risks.

4   Finally, it is possible to insure against the added risk. Many real estate lenders find that, rather than establishing their own risk analysis units, they may be better off using FHA-VA or private mortgage insurance or GNMA mortgage-backed securities. Because there are important economies of scale in risk evaluation and supervision, smaller lenders may find that it pays to compensate others for these services.

LOSSES ON LOANS

In the last chapter, we discussed risks as the variance of the expected rate of return. Many real estate lenders, however, when considering individual loans, are far more concerned with possible losses. In addition, since the great majority of loans still carry a maximum rate rather than a variable one, in estimating the risk of loans, lenders consider only the probability of loss. They define risk as the difference between the contract and the expected rate of return. Lenders can also consider risk as the amount of reserve required as a charge against gross income to offset probable losses from failures by borrowers to pay loans as agreed.

With home loans or other frequently made loans, the probabilities of loss may be calculated on an actuarial or statistical basis. Such calculations are made by the FHA and insurance firms. Most lenders, however, use a more subjective estimate of risk.

Some costs arise from the additional administration required to collect on loans which cannot be handled normally. Servicing costs rise if a family runs into difficulties and fails to meet regular payments. Loans may have to be renegotiated with forgiveness of interest, extension of the payment period, or similar changes in the contract.

More serious costs arise if the property must be taken over when payments cease. Losses from this source will equal the difference between the amount of net return received on liquidation of the property and the outstanding loan. This difference will depend on how much was lent originally and how much has been paid off; on changes in the value of the property due to movements either in the market or in prices in general; and on such factors as the costs of foreclosure, maintenance and administration, and selling the property.

The number and percentage of delinquencies have grown rapidly over the past 10 years, particularly in comparison with the situation in the 1950s. The number of foreclosures has also increased, but not by much more than proportionately to the number of mortgages outstanding.

According to reports submitted to the Mortgage Bankers Association, the rate of delinquencies on one- to four-family-home mortgages doubled in the past decade. While in the 1950s a rate between 2 and 2.5 percent was normal for delinquencies of 30 days or more, in the fourth quarters of 1972, 1973, and 1974, rates stood well above 4.5

percent. For delinquencies of 2 months or more, it rose steadily from about .5 percent to over 1.25 percent. While rates vary by type of mortgage and type of lender, this general picture is not untypical of all lenders.

The picture for foreclosures is roughly similar. The Great Depression of the 1930s caused the delinquency and foreclosure rates to shoot very high. In 1933 there were over 250,000 foreclosures, or more than 4 percent of mortgages outstanding. The demoralization of the market was so complete that many believe that without moratorium laws and the active intervention of the Home Owners Loan Corporation, which took mortgages in danger of foreclosure off the hands of lending institutions, the number of foreclosures might have been three or four times greater in 1934 and 1935 than it actually was.

The number of foreclosures decreased sharply in the postwar boom market. In the 1950s there were under 50,000 a year, or less than .2 percent of outstanding mortgages. By 1964 the number exceeded 100,000, or about .5 percent of outstanding mortgages. Since then there have been between 100,000 and 140,000 foreclosures a year, or between .4 and .5 percent of outstandings.

Rates for some types of mortgages and in some states have been much higher. FHA single-family-home mortgage foreclosure rates have reached 1.2 percent of outstandings in some years, while foreclosures of multifamily or income-type projects have been as high as 2.5 times above the average. In Florida the cumulative rate of foreclosures on one-family-home mortgages for the period 1935 to 1972 was 11.23 percent, while in the District of Columbia for the same period it was 1.34 percent.

In 1974 and 1975, some of the largest REITs went into technical default in their own loan agreements because so many of the mortgages they held became delinquent. Most of these were development mortgages or mortgages on income properties. An REIT was fortunate if no more than 10 percent of its loans failed to meet interest and amortization payments. In many cases the number of mortgages delinquent more than 60 days rose well over 60 percent. Foreclosures also became commonplace.

Amounts of Losses on Foreclosures

The rate of foreclosures is only one measure of the risks involved in mortgage lending. Even more significant is the total amount lost on each foreclosure.

After foreclosure, depending on the state's foreclosure and redemption laws, title may pass to an outside buyer or to the lender. If the lender holds the title, he can then sell the property, taking as much time as he believes advantageous, given his estimate of future markets. For example, the FHA retains ownership of foreclosed properties for an average of 2 to 3 years, but individual properties may be retained for as long as 10 years.

There are four sources of costs to the lender from foreclosures: (1) the amount of the unpaid mortgage debt; (2) the cost of foreclosure and the cost of fixing up and repairing the building, if necessary; (3) the costs of maintaining the building during the period it is for sale, as well as the actual cost of sale; and (4) the costs of interest not received on the debt from the time of first delinquency until the new owner takes possession.

All these costs have been rising rapidly. For example, the FHA estimates that in the last half of 1973, it lost about $8,000 on each house it sold, not counting lost interest. While the figures are not exact, the average foreclosed mortgage was probably about $17,500. The average unit sold netted the FHA roughly $12,000. If we add the various costs, we can estimate that the house sold for $5,500 less than the mortgage, the out-of-pocket costs of holding were about $2,500, and lost interest was probably about $3,500. Thus on a foreclosure of $17,500 the total loss, including foregone interest, was roughly $11,500, or 65 percent of the mortgage that went bad.

This loss ratio is about double the percentage losses experienced a decade earlier. Clearly, losses of this magnitude make it worthwhile for lenders to expend a great deal of effort on risk analysis and to make certain either that they insure their losses elsewhere or that they include a sufficient charge in their rates to offset the actual risks they assume.

AVOIDING LOSSES

In every program of risk management, attention must be paid first to the analysis of individual loans. The basic causes of the types of delinquencies and foreclosures likely to strike any loan must be understood. In addition to knowing what dangers exist, every firm needs a sound processing procedure to ensure that each loan application is carefully analyzed and that its risks are evaluated in accordance with these procedures. Only then can the decision be made as to whether a prospective loan qualifies and is worth making.

Previous studies of mortgage experiences list 15 to 20 separate factors in any given loan which will cause its risks to deviate from the average. An examination of these factors and their impact on the probability of losses is vital to potential lenders or borrowers. An understanding of real estate financing requires that participants in a loan recognize what probable losses they are engendering when some features are included rather than others.

The basic factors influencing risks can be divided into four general categories. Each lender must be sure that all these individual factors are properly weighed. The following list contains many of the most important items. It is not complete, however, since new causes of delinquency and default may develop, while other forces may be at work in particular situations. Each lender must add personal experience to this framework.

1   Loan characteristics
    a   Mortgage terms
        (1)   Amortization provisions
        (2)   Loan-to-value ratio
        (3)   Existence of junior liens
    b   Interest rate
    c   Type of loan
2   Borrower's characteristics
    a   Ownership and occupancy
    b   Income
        (1)   Income-expense ratio

    (2) Occupation
    (3) Credit rating
  c Family status
  d Transfer of title
3 Property characteristics
  a Type
  b Price
  c Design
  d Age
  e Location
4 Portfolio characteristics
  a Concentration by age
  b Concentration by location
  c Concentration by type
  d Interest rates
  e Liquidity

A firm formulates a program to control risks by developing procedures to handle the potential losses. All lenders must establish correct lending criteria and exercise careful control of the entire loan process. They can accomplish these goals by means of well-planned standard operating procedures. Such procedures are typically entrusted to a loan department, which then becomes responsible for the proper handling of all applications. It makes recommendations concerning whether a loan should be granted, whether the terms requested should be modified, or whether the application should be rejected. In most financial institutions, the final responsibility for lending is entrusted to a loan committee. In a well-functioning operation, however, most of the real responsibility is delegated to individual lending officers. The committee takes up and approves most loans in a routine manner. It concerns itself mainly with the largest or with particularly unusual loans.

Formal procedures ensure the inclusion of all necessary information. They establish individual responsibility. The reasons for the granting of a specific loan are recorded in a single place. Weak loans that have not lived up to expectations may be reevaluated to see why they went wrong and what lessons might be learned from them.

The Loan Application

What are the ingredients of a well-operating standard procedure? First comes a set of standard forms used throughout the organization. They include forms for loan applications, for interviews, for appraisal reports, for credit reporting, for the final risk evaluation, for the loan recommendation, and for the loan approval.

The forms are accompanied by either verbal or written instructions to make certain that all are dealt with properly. Depending on the size of the organization, step-by-step processing will follow either formal or informal procedures. Finally, the procedures include the bases to be used for the lending decision and a technique for future reevaluations.

While many lenders have utilized primarily informal procedures in the past, such techniques are rapidly going out of use. Because of their many advantages, formal written procedures are taking their place. In the first place, they ensure that no important steps are left out of the lending process. Second, fixed routines tend to limit personal variations and ensure more complete agreement with the overall organizational goals. While many loans may still be exceptions to general policies, formal procedures make more certain that logic and sure reasoning will be applied in the granting of the variances; they are less likely to result from mere whims. Finally, the recording of the facts and reasoning behind the loans makes possible the process of reevaluation. In attempting to find what went wrong in the initial analysis of a poor loan, it is very frustrating to encounter only a simple notation of "granted" in the file.

The loan application and the borrower's interview supplement each other. They serve (1) to welcome prospective borrowers, (2) to aid them in making their financial decisions, (3) to obtain preliminary offers to borrow subject to further negotiations, (4) to obtain part of the information necessary for evaluating loans and servicing them if granted, (5) to inform prospective borrowers of lending and servicing procedures, and (6) to screen out unlikely applicants in order to save unnecessary efforts.

The application starts with a statement of the amount of loan requested and the proposed terms of repayment. The application is a preliminary offer of a contract by the prospective borrower. As in many real estate transactions, it may be accepted, rejected, or met by a counteroffer from the lender. Final terms may require substantial negotiations.

The second section of the application contains information on the real property which will form the security for the loan. First comes a legal description of the land. For a house the description is fairly compact, being concerned mainly with location, price, size, year built, and structural characteristics.

For an income property far more facts are needed. Because their importance is greater, locational factors need expansion. The description of the improvements must also be in greater detail. Financial and operating statements are needed so that the ability of the property to earn the required payments can be calculated. Other important facts may be attached, such as a list of leases showing terms and tenants.

The final section of the application contains information about the borrower. Included are statements concerning family status, employment, previous employment, and assets and liabilities. For an income property, the form requests information about both the corporation making the application—balance sheets, etc.—and its principal owners. Applications must be signed, and the credit and other information contained therein certified as true.

Completed application forms containing the basic information needed by the lender will be checked and supplemented by credit and appraisal reports. However, applications are important because they contain applicants' personal statements concerning the loan they want and their certification as to their own credit-worthiness and the condition of the physical security.

The Loan Interview

Interviews may occur before or after receipt of the loan application. Many people shop for loans from several sources. They must be treated courteously. Frequently, however, no formal application follows. In other cases, the preliminary interview makes it clear that the applicant will not qualify for a loan. Such clients should be discouraged as soon as possible from making a formal application.

The interview is extremely important in the lending process. Its nature will depend on the size of the firm and its type of operations. Usually loan officers with the responsibility of analyzing the loan and recommending on it also handle the interviews. They may specialize by type of loan, or they may deal with all sorts. The larger the loan or the more complex it is, the higher in the organization's structure the interview and final negotiations will take place. As the complexity of the loan application and its attachments increases (for example, when a loan on a new shopping center is being proposed, rather than a single-house loan on an existing structure), more skill and training are required of the interviewer.

The interviewer is a salesperson, a public relations expert, and a lending analyst. The interview serves as a screening device to prevent unnecessary paperwork. Acceptance of applications for loans that are sure to be refused causes wasted effort and ill will. On the other hand, unsatisfactory prospective borrowers must be turned away without losing their respect or friendship.

Interviewers can serve as valuable sources of education for borrowers. In explaining the logic behind the information required on the application, they can aid prospective borrowers in making a proper decision as to what financial obligations to incur. Frequently families are attracted to a house and attempt to borrow far more than they can repay. The interviewer must explain why everyone will be better off if this is not done.

Interviewers can also ease future servicing of loans. They can explain the firm's procedures. They can stress the need for promptness, while pointing out that borrowers should take the initiative and seek out the lender if any problems develop. If borrowers know what they are expected to do and why, future relations will be more cordial.

All these other duties, however, merely supplement the interviewer's main function of obtaining as much information as possible in order to judge the prospective borrower's credit-worthiness. The loan officer must gather from the applicant all the specific details necessary for a proper evaluation. Part of this information is furnished on the application form. However, the information which the interviewer gathers from informal discussion and the give-and-take of questions and answers may be still more significant.

Loan repayments depend partly on the borrower's desires, partly on the likelihood of his or her income's continuing, and partly on family relations. Since judgment of these factors tends to be subjective, evaluation of the same data by different interviewers may vary greatly. The skilled loan officer has the best judgment in these spheres.

Interviewers must also be negotiators. They must recognize during the discussion what prospective terms are likely to be unsatisfactory and where changes might be made to minimize future risk. During the interview process, they can probe to find out whether the borrower is willing and able to make changes in critical items. It is frequently much easier to negotiate differences before they are put down in black and white.

When the conference is finished, the loan application and the interviewer's notes should contain the information necessary for the further processing of the loan. Unsatisfactory requests should have been withdrawn. At the end of an interview, loan officers should be able to indicate whether a loan will probably be granted, but they must also be careful to point out that they do not have the final responsibility. Additional information will be obtained from the credit and appraisal reports. The loan committee will base its decision partly on the interview and partly on added facts, but the firm's portfolio position will also enter into the final decision.

BORROWER AND LOAN CHARACTERISTICS

Significant differences exist between risks on owner-occupied properties and those held for income purposes. The likelihood of a loss on an owner-occupied unit is tied more closely to the borrower than to the property.

With an owner-occupier, personal income and assets play a significant role in determining losses. As long as they are adequate, the property is not likely to be tested as to market value. Normally, stable persons who are good credit risks and meet with no misfortune will not stop payments on their own homes even if the value of their equity becomes negative for short periods. When they run into temporary difficulties, payments may continue if they have assets to draw upon.

This situation holds for income properties only when the debt service on a property is a minor share of the borrower's total income. For example, with plants, stores, and similar units where a fiscally sound corporation is on the note or the lease, debts will continue to be paid even if the particular location does not live up to expectations. Consequently, much risk evaluation of income properties such as shopping centers and office buildings has been based primarily on the financial statement of the lessor rather than on an adequate income analysis of the property. Lenders have tried to assure repayment by insisting that good names be on sufficient leases to carry the financing.

On the other hand, properties such as apartment houses, small shopping centers, and individual stores are normally not in a position where leases can carry the loan. They are often owned by real estate corporations or syndicates whose only asset is the property under loan. Each property must stand on its own feet. If the income does not meet the financial costs, foreclosure or voluntary transfer of the property to the lender is inevitable. Clearly, the risks involved in loans on this latter type of property are considerably greater than in the former cases.

The analysis of borrower characteristics for owner-occupied properties and their relationship to the terms of proposed loans attempts to estimate and control the possibility that the mortgagor will fail to fulfill the loan contract. The lender aims to choose borrowers who have the ability and the desire to protect their ownership. The evaluation must consider both intangible and tangible factors. Is the borrower a person of character? How does he or she view the responsibility that being the signer of a note entails? Other influences will include the borrower's motivation, family life, health, and future prospects, in addition to such specific factors as income, assets, and liabilities.

The facts on the loan application regarding income, employment, and balance sheet are basic sources of data. They are checked by the judgment of the interviewer and by the character and financial facts shown on a credit report. Each supplements the other. The skilled interviewer verifies the application and elicits additional consequential facts.

Credit reports, usually obtained from organized credit agencies, record the amount of credit previously obtained by borrowers and the promptness of payment. They also reveal significant factors such as reputation, mobility, assets, and any litigation, unpaid claims, or bankruptcy.

Credit Characteristics of Mortgagor

The first factors rated are basic attitudes of the borrower such as honesty, integrity, and judgment. If any are unsuitable, the probability of default is high.

Borrowers' past payment records are assumed to measure their character and attitude toward debts. If credit reports show a long record of delinquencies or slow pays, the chances are great that the mortgage loan will be treated in a similar fashion.

Studies of defaulted loans have shown that divorce and broken homes are a significant cause of foreclosures. Risks of divorce are high for newlyweds who are very young. The mortgagor with an established family is a better risk than the single person. Finally, the analyst should consider the borrower's history in financial management. Serious past errors in judgment, whether in conducting business matters or in contracting personal debts, raise questions of ability, whereas a successful record of personal saving with growing assets evidences the probability of continued success. This is true even if the assets are drawn down for the house purchase and therefore are not available for offsetting risks in and of themselves.

Adequacy of Income

While character and motivation are vital, few loans are made if there is doubt about a borrower's credit-worthiness. For this reason, the income of the owner-occupier is the most important single factor determining whether or not foreclosure takes place. About 40 percent or more of foreclosures occur because the owner's income has fallen. Some differences can be predicted at the time the loan is made. Risks are higher for lower-income families, for those who assume a higher-than-normal ratio of housing expense to income, and for those who have jobs or businesses less stable than the average.

The record indicates that some sharp falls in income must be considered as random or normal risks. Every family has some likelihood of experiencing an income drop. On the other hand, certain occupations, such as those of self-employed business people and manual workers, have above-normal instability. Since unemployment and business losses are the two largest causes of foreclosures, in these cases the risks of loss must be greater.

Some families are poor credit risks for other reasons which can be ascertained through careful investigation. A family may make a habit of overextending itself. Even if a family has not overextended itself in the past, the risk will be increased if the mortgage loan raises its required payments too high. The ratio of expense to income is important. It becomes even more significant when future expenses are poorly forecast. Rising taxes, high maintenance on older houses, and unexpected repairs on new units all raise the expense-income ratio and frequently bring about higher foreclosure rates.

The usual method for measuring adequacy of income is to set up rules of thumb relating mortgage payments (principal, interest, insurance, and property taxes) or total housing expenses (mortgage payments, maintenance and repair, utilities, and heating) to a family's projected income. According to common rules of thumb used by lenders, mortgage payments should not exceed 20 or 25 percent of normal income; in other words, a borrower's ratio of monthly income to monthly mortgage payment should be 5 to 1 or 4 to 1.

Many lenders follow rules of thumb which require higher ratios to income, the larger the loan. Such rules reflect the well-documented fact that people with higher incomes usually pay a lower share of their income for housing, but they do not reflect ability to pay. In actuality, many other factors besides the simple ratios must be considered. Other assets and other unusual expenses are the most important of such influences. Past high housing expenses successfully met are obviously significant also. With inflation and higher interest rates, all rules of thumb may allow higher payments in the future.

The FHA considers total housing expenses rather than merely mortgage payments. Heat and utilities vary greatly from one part of the country to another. They allow total expenses to be 35 percent of income, and even up to 50 percent if proper justifications can be made.

Stability of Effective Income

In addition to the amount of a family's income, the prospects that it will be maintained must be considered. This means that occupation, length of present employment, type of job, and sources of secondary income are important. The longer a person has been employed in a stable industry, the greater the chances that income will continue. For the self-employed with a history of job mobility, frequent unemployment, or seasonal or unskilled work, there is an increased danger of future income loss.

The question of evaluating secondary income, such as that from moonlighting or a wife's or children's employment, has become controversial in recent years. The traditional attitude has been that wives may become pregnant and stop working. Second jobs held for long periods become tiresome. Children marry and move away. If the mortgage payment requires the additional income from any such source, trouble is likely to result. Secondary income is, however, a valid source for clearing up other outstanding obligations, such as auto or furniture installment payments. With such money available, the danger of defaulting on these short-run debts is much less.

In recent periods, however, it has appeared that some lending officers were making such judgments in an arbitrary manner. They were giving little or no credit for a wife's income, even though she had held a job for a long time or gave every indication of continuing to work. In some cases, it was clear that arbitrariness amounted to discrimination against women. As pressure has built up and as Congress has enacted laws against discrimination on the basis of sex, lenders have become aware of the problem and have acted to make certain that their rules and decisions are based on sound facts and judgment and are not arbitrarily discriminatory.

Mortgage Terms and Motivation

Next to income, the most important factor in loss control is the borrower's motivation. Lenders must ensure that borrowers will be sufficiently motivated to continue making payments even if difficulties arise with the property or if its price becomes temporarily depressed.

A borrower is assumed to be more highly motivated to continue making payments if a loan is on his or her permanent home bought willingly in a normal market. Those buying for future sale, to save rent in a tight market, or for part-time use show a greater tendency to default.

Too high a loan-to-value ratio, maximum amortization periods, and the existence of junior liens are three additional factors, besides failure to maintain sufficient income and a poor attitude toward debts, that cause most delinquencies and defaults. Risks of loan defaults are greatest in a loan's first few years. During this period no type of amortization arrangement or generally acceptable loan-to-value ratios seem adequate to protect basically poor loans. However, if a loan survives the first danger period, risks are reduced as an owner's equity rises.

Mortgage terms significantly influence risk because they determine the purchaser's equity and the relationship between the loan and the property value. The lender wants borrowers with sufficient equity either to make it worth their while to continue to meet the payments or to permit the property to be sold for more than the outstanding loan. If equity is negative or close to zero, the borrower may not go to the trouble and expense of trying to sell the property. The owner may also milk the property, making minimal or no payments while gathering income or occupying the unit.

The lender's risk may rise because of the borrower's low original downpayment, because of physical depreciation or obsolescence, or because a fall in the price level causes the property's value to decline faster than the rate of amortization of the loan.

Previous studies show that foreclosures and losses do rise as downpayments fall. They also demonstrate that lenders are not protected purely by their own loan-to-value ratios. A low downpayment resulting from a junior mortgage increases considerably the risk of loss to the holder of a first mortgage, even though the value of the loan is far below the initial selling price.

Income Properties

Most of the above discussion has had to do with loans to be used for the purchase of a one- to four-family house to be occupied by the borrower or to be put to his or her own use. The analysis is based on making as sure as possible that the owner will want and will be able to make the required payments.

Income properties call for an entirely different method of analysis. Primarily, the risks revolve around the possibility that the cash flow or income from the property will be inadequate to meet the required payments. The analysis presented here is primarily in terms of expected income during the period of the loan and follows the analysis given in the chapters which specifically treat investment in income properties.

PROPERTY CHARACTERISTICS
AND THEIR APPRAISAL

In addition to careful analysis of the borrower's characteristics and their relationship to the necessary payments on a loan, the control of losses requires a systematic examination of the property on which a loan is to be made.

For several reasons, the real property underlying the mortgage loan constitutes a basic source of its security. In the first place, if the value of the property exceeds the loan balance, the borrower will want to retain ownership. Even when the borrower cannot maintain payments, he or she will take the responsibility of selling the property or transferring ownership. The lender will be saved much turmoil and extra expense. Second, if payments are not made, the property's value will determine what can be obtained when it is sold after foreclosure. If the property is worth enough, the lender will suffer no loss.

Property Type and Risks

The form of ownership and use of a property are important determinants of the degree of risk involved in a loan. Fluctuations in the market tend to be much greater for certain properties than for others. Overbuilding, undue optimism, and lack of careful controls are far more common in connection with income properties than individual homes. Past studies of mortgage foreclosures show that defaults on income properties tend to be two to three times as common as defaults on single-family homes. In some years of the postwar period, foreclosure rates on income properties ran as high as 10 times those on single-family homes. Also, of course, because loans on income properties tend to be much larger, risks are more concentrated.

Risks related to the price of a property are not well defined. They rise rapidly if an error occurs in appraising the true value. Market price, if not based on an efficient, knowledgeable, well-operating market, may diverge sharply from the true market value. If such gaps are not caught in the appraisal process, the loan may be based on an inflated price, and the dangers of loss are multiplied.

Losses are more probable also if the design is substandard. By "design" is meant the property's physical characteristics, livability, visual appeal, continuing usefulness for its particular functions, and ease of maintenance. Properties that fail to compete with buildings erected later often experience defaults on their loans. Good design determines whether values can be maintained.

The quality of construction is significant. Buildings that have been skimped on with respect to structural features can compete only when they are new and in tight markets. In competitive situations, their values fall. Physical characteristics also determine future operating and maintenance costs. Rising operating costs have been a serious cause of foreclosures, as homeowners find that they have insufficient income to meet the new expenses or that the net yield of income properties is eaten into by maintenance and repairs.

Age

For owner-occupied homes, there is little evidence that risks vary with age of property. There is, however, an indication that mortgages on new homes in tracts are riskier than individual mortgages, whether on new or older units. This is partly because new areas tend to be unstable, with a fairly high initial turnover. Any errors that have crept into the design or construction will make it hard to resell those units, which can be expected to reappear fairly rapidly on the market.

It is also highly probable that the processing of loans on homes in tracts will be less rigorous than the processing of individual loans. The prospective borrower has the strong support of the builder in qualifying for a loan. This support may take the form of advice on how to qualify, pressure on the lending officer, or outright chicanery. Whichever applies, mass sales and processing of loans increase the lender's danger.

Location

Location may refer either to the geographic area—the city, suburb, metropolitan area, state, or similar unit—or to the particular site within the general area.

The geographic area is important because as the economy develops, some areas are passed by. They may decline sharply, while others grow at a rate far above average. Loans in expanding areas will be more secure. Losses in a declining area may be heavy. In addition to growth, differences in taxes and foreclosure procedures and costs may have a significant impact on risks.

For residential property, long lists exist of specific locational factors that significantly influence consumers' decisions. These include the general attractiveness of the site, location with respect to public services and transportation, general tax rates, school systems, and status in general. As these factors vary, the amount of risk shifts.

For income properties, location becomes the paramount factor. A unit in a declining market will have falling income and will lack ability to meet mortgage payments. In this sphere, the type of locational analysis depends upon the particular kind of property involved. Retail locations compete with one another and with new shopping centers. Office buildings change in desirability and status. Warehouses are affected by transportation patterns. In each of these cases, the appraiser must select a method of analysis related to the specific problems. The lending officer must check the appraiser's reasoning, holding in mind the history of overoptimism which has occasionally besmirched the past record of appraisals of income property.

Natural physical features, design, and zoning or protective covenants are the chief factors which influence the physical attractiveness of neighborhoods. The higher value of view sites, waterscapes, wooded areas, and sites with similar features is familiar. The opposite impact of flood dangers, airport noises, or slide areas is as obvious. The design of streets, landscaping, and the placement of houses can enhance or detract from the natural values. Dreary, monotonous neighborhoods suffer. Inharmonious land uses, such as factories or garages, are a danger. So are large numbers of houses whose design is becoming obsolete. Since loan risks depend upon the development of land uses, zoning and other controls over land use are important.

Values rise when more people want to live in an area. The quality of schools and the area's reputation are critical variables for families. Other types of civic buildings are also important for families and other groups. Transportation usually implies freeways and parking, but other forms also have an impact, and mass transit is becoming increasingly significant. The further a house is from transportation, stores, and other facilities, the more time and money must be spent on driving.

Recent studies show high rates of movement, delinquencies, and foreclosures due to unexpected increases in costs of insurance, utilities, and taxes. Many newly created suburban communities have found themselves in an intolerable situation because of extreme demands on limited school facilities. Taxes skyrocket. Families move out to better districts or have to sell when they find their required tax escrows rising. Wise lenders recognize these dangers. Their neighborhood analyses carefully estimate any unusual demands on public facilities.

TRADITIONAL APPRAISAL METHODS

Appraisal is the process of estimating the current value of a property. This estimate is the start of a calculation through which lenders can predict their risk. They can ascertain the current relationship of the proposed loan to the property's value and the owner's equity. Such an appraisal is important legally. Almost all fiduciary institutions are restricted by law and regulation to loans of no more than a certain percent of value. If the appraisal is perfunctory or inaccurate, the lender may violate the law.

The risk of future loss depends not only on the current relationship of the debt to the property's value but also on future relationships. The lender must be concerned with the gap between the outstanding loan and the property's value during the entire period that the loan is outstanding. This gap will widen or narrow from its initial amount depending on whether the rate of amortization exceeds the rate of depreciation. Lenders must therefore use the appraisal as a basis for estimating the future pattern of depreciation. They must compare the projected amount and timing of losses in value through depreciation with the amortization schedule and the owner's initial equity in order to estimate the minimum equity the owner will hold at any future date.

In this chapter we discuss primarily traditional appraisals as they are used by lenders for evaluating risk. We must recognize, however, the importance of appraisals in the entire investment procedure. A great deal of the final part of this book, which describes investment analysis, is actually a discussion of more sophisticated appraisal techniques as they are currently employed by major investors and lenders.

Because the appraisal process is so central to lending activities, the art of appraising has expanded rapidly in recent years. Several professional societies, a number of journals, and many books exist in the field. The literature is large and replete with many arguments concerning the meaning of value, the purpose of the appraisal, and similar problems. It must be recognized that many of these arguments apply primarily to unusual cases or are essays attempting to improve the knowledge and skills of the individual appraiser.

The results of an appraisal are usually communicated in a report or in a letter giving an opinion as to value. The appraiser presents the results of his or her research and explains how the conclusion was reached. The sometimes wide discrepancies still existing among individual appraisals of a single property are often a source of concern. While appraisals have long been the subject of controversy and criticism, the amount of active debate has escalated. Fraudulent appraisals contributed to the problems of mortgage bonds in the 1920s. The recent difficulties experienced by REITs and public syndications involved questionable price-value relationships.

It is recognized that the large differences between appraisals of a property occur partly because the act of appraising remains as much an art as a science and partly because appraisers do not agree on what value they are attempting to estimate. Moreover, many believe that the problems arise from the fact that traditional appraisal methods allow considerable opportunities to "juggle the numbers." The implicit approaches underlying traditional appraisal methods do not adequately show how the appraiser reached the valuation decision. They make replication by other appraisers very difficult.

Value

Appraisals provide an indication of the market value of a specific property. The term ''value'' can assume many meanings. Indeed, appraisal theoreticians trace in detail the origins of various concepts of value and debate at length its most appropriate definition. A list of at least 20 different concepts of value is not uncommon.

Many appraisers feel that when they are hired by sellers, they should arrive at different estimates of value from the ones they calculate when they are hired by purchasers or lenders. Many others believe that such ideas of divergent values are wrong. They hold that a single value exists and should be estimated. Each user of this estimate can then adjust it for his or her own purposes. Since neither point of view is completely accepted, divergent estimates for the same property exist. Each user of an appraisal should be aware of what it is based on and what information it is attempting to convey. Since so many factors influence values and since values are used for so many purposes, it appears preferable to consider the relevant range of values rather than a single figure. This range then becomes part of the decision-making process for all concerned.

Definition of Value Probably the most widely accepted definition of market value, or fair market value, is that used by the courts:

> The highest price estimated in terms of money which a property will bring if exposed for sale in the open market, allowing a reasonable time to find a purchaser who buys with knowledge of all the uses to which it is adapted and for which it is capable of being used.

Other definitions extend this one by stipulating (1) that the seller must also have full knowledge of current and potential uses and (2) that neither party is acting under duress. The FHLBB qualifies its definition with the phrase: ''Providing the purchaser receives a warranty deed and takes advantage of typical financing and providing the seller receives all cash.'' Essentially, these definitions seek to describe a normal transaction free of special circumstances.

The appraisal literature agrees that value is the present worth of future benefits to typical users and investors arising out of ownership. Thus market value reflects the combined judgments as to the present value of future benefits. This point can also be expressed by saying that a purchaser of an income property buys a stream of future benefits, including both income over time and the residual value at the time the investment is ended.

Different analysts and investors have varying expectations as to the level and timing of the economic benefits that can be expected from a property. Different appraisers and investors also have separate expectations as to what a reasonable or satisfactory return may be. Both these factors suggest that it is not at all surprising to find different values expressed for the same property. In a sense, value, like beauty, is in the eye of the beholder.

Because this is true, it is helpful to know the basic assumptions an appraiser uses. Indeed, the more precisely one can evaluate a set of assumptions and compare them with another appraisal, the better the lending or investment decision will be. In practice, however, because the key assumptions are often "under water," as opposed to being out in the open, it is frequently difficult to evaluate the reasoning the appraiser used in reaching his or her ultimate decision. Consequently, many critics of the appraisal process believe it is susceptible to a good deal of behind-the-scenes manipulation.

The Appraisal Process

The valuation process attempts to assemble all the elements affecting the present and future economic benefits of a property and to judge the amount people are, and will be, willing to pay for these benefits. Depending upon the existing data, the appraiser will use primarily one of three approaches: (1) the market data, or market comparison, approach; (2) the cost approach; or (3) the income capitalization approach. Appraisers usually place most reliance upon the method which makes use of the best available data. If they have adequate comparisons, most of their estimates will be based upon market information. However, for income properties, this information will be filtered through a complex valuation process. Appraisers will use the other approaches to check their conclusions and, in certain cases, to set outside limits to their estimates of value.

Market Comparison   The market data, or market comparison, method bases its estimate of value on recent actual purchase prices and on the current offers and asking prices for properties comparable to the one under appraisal. The problem of finding recent equivalent prices may be great. Adjustments frequently have to be made to allow for time variations and for the inclusion or exclusion of specific factors such as size, style, and location.

A series of actual prices is quite a firm base for value, even though it is no guarantee of future values. However, in either highly exhilarated or depressed markets, the going price may differ from value. Allowances must also be made for special influences on the buyer and seller, such as motivation, market knowledge and skills, and financing. Not every sale meets the value criteria of knowledgeable buyers and sellers entering freely into contracts with no duress.

Difficulties also arise in finding the necessary market data and in determining how the necessary adjustments should be made. A good model for these adjustments would require an accurate identification of the crucial variables which influence value, as well as enough information to be statistically reliable. While constructing a model of market behavior for single-family homes with common characteristics is not too difficult, in larger investment properties major problems arise. The differences between one property and another and the discrepancies in the data available for them make a simple market comparison model difficult to apply. Even so, market information is basic to the other approaches also.

The Cost Approach   Under the cost approach (also called the *replacement-cost* or *reproduction-cost* approach) to the appraisal process, the appraiser estimates the cost of reproducing the improvements on the subject property in terms of today's costs of building materials and supplies. Since it is impossible to estimate the cost to reproduce land, the land value is derived by a market comparison with selling prices for similar sites in the area.

The replacement-cost approach is particularly suitable for new buildings. It operates on the theory that no buyer should pay more than the current cost of a substitute property. Actual replacement costs of a new structure are calculated. Numerous methods exist for calculating such costs, ranging from a detailed analysis of the specific proposed construction to procedures based on much looser techniques, such as average costs per square or cubic foot. To the replacement cost must be added the market value of the site and other costs engendered in the construction and property transfer process.

For existing buildings, the replacement cost must be reduced by an estimate of accrued depreciation. The usefulness of this approach is sharply reduced by the need to subtract depreciation, which creates greater inaccuracies as the age of a building increases. Much depreciation is caused by obsolescence rather than by physical wear. The measurement of the actual value lost as a result of time is almost impossible except through some use of the market data process. No technique except actual comparisons can measure what has really happened.

Other problems are caused by underimprovement or overimprovement of the property, by which is meant that improper amounts have been put into the structure in relation to its basic use. As an example, gold-plated bathtubs may be expensive and have a high replacement cost, and yet they have little value to the average home purchaser. Even a complete and itemized bill for construction of a new unit may give too high a value if it contains features for which the average buyer will not bid.

Another major criticism applies to the idea that replacement cost sets the upper limit on value, since on its face this contradicts the basic objective of the development business. Developers create assets whose value in the market exceeds the cost of producing them. The importance of the entrepreneurial and creative functions is hard to include in a reproduction-cost estimate; yet for many loans, the purpose of the appraisal is to ascertain what the property will be worth when it is built and operating.

Income Capitalization   Under the income capitalization approach, the appraiser estimates a project's probable income and then selects a capitalization rate based on the type of property and its location. Finally, the appraiser translates the expected income stream into an estimate of value by the process of capitalization. As shown on page 97, a capitalized value is found by dividing the projected income figure by the capitalization rate deemed appropriate. Thus a property with an indicated income of $8,000 is appraised at $80,000 if the capitalization rate is 10 percent ($8,000/.10 = $80,000).

Because of the deficiencies in the two other traditional appraisal methods and because the capitalization approach comes closest to the way in which investors evaluate investment property, many appraisers prefer the income capitalization approach. If the appraisal is for an investment decision, this approach clearly seems the most appropriate. Indeed, the definition of value as the present worth of rights to the future benefits arising from ownership argues for the supremacy of the income capitalization approach.

Estimating Income The appraiser starts by projecting the expected annual income for the property for the entire period of the appraisal. To do this, the scheduled gross revenue is estimated, and losses from vacancies and collections are subtracted to obtain the effective gross revenue. The appraiser next estimates operating expenses and subtracts them from effective revenue to get an estimate of operating or net income. This net income is standardized for the entire appraisal period.

The process of estimating income and expenses is identical to that used in investment analysis. We discuss it in detail in Part Six. A point to note, however, is that the estimate of net income, which is the final input to a traditional appraisal, is only the first step in a modern estimate of value through investment analysis.

Selecting a Capitalization Rate The appraiser next selects a capitalization rate. On pages 97 to 100, in discussing the concept of capitalization, we pointed out that rates vary depending on the handling of the problem of recapture of value lost with the passage of time. Which recapture theory is adopted makes a considerable difference in the rate actually applied. In addition, rates vary from period to period and from building to building, depending on such factors as current interest rates, type of building, and risks. Again, several methods are commonly used to estimate a capitalization rate:

1 The most common is the comparison method. The appraiser seeks to find comparable properties which have recently sold and for which he can obtain actual incomes and prices. Using his judgment as to how these other buildings and the one he is appraising differ with respect to various relevant factors and risks, he adjusts the rates exhibited by them in arriving at his own rate. Many brokers and investors commonly derive and use such rates in a very simplified form.

Often they use the *gross income multiplier*, which is simply the price of a building divided by its gross revenue or rent roll, as shown in Table 18-1. This table shows the selling prices, gross revenues, and gross income multipliers for five buildings which sold recently in a neighborhood.

Depending on how comparable he believed each building to be, the appraiser would use this information to select a multiplier for the building he was appraising. He would multiply its estimated revenue by the multiplier to get an estimated value. Thus if the gross revenue for the building under appraisal were $12,000 and he selected a multiplier of 7, he would appraise the building as worth $84,000.

Table 18-1   Income Multipliers

Price	Gross revenue	Gross income multiplier	Net income	Net income multiplier
$ 75,000	$12,000	6.3	$ 4,800	15.6
110,000	16,000	6.9	9,380	11.7
85,000	11,000	7.7	6,500	13.0
120,000	20,000	6.0	11,700	10.3
83,000	12,000	6.9	7,200	11.5

The gross income multiplier is a rather crude rule-of-thumb technique since it implies that the chief factor in a property's fair market value is its gross rents. This assumption ignores many other factors that influence income. For example, we would expect multipliers to vary depending on whether an apartment was in a walk-up or in a building with elevators, whether it was furnished or unfurnished, or whether it was old or new.

A *capitalization rate* or a *net income multiplier* similar to the gross income multiplier can easily be determined. It is clear that operating expenses vary from building to building over time, as operating results do. Consequently, many appraisals are based on the capitalization of net income rather than gross income. An estimate of a capitalization rate is found by dividing the net operating income by the property's selling price. (To this must be added a factor for recapture if that is believed necessary.) The net income multiplier is found by dividing the property's price by the net income. Thus the net income multiplier is the reciprocal of the capitalization rate.

Again referring to Table 18-1, we find that net incomes range between 40 and 60 percent of the gross revenues, depending on the property. An average property in the table, correcting for differences, shows a net revenue of $7,916 and an average price of $95,000. The capitalization rate is 7,916/95,000 = 8.333%. The net income multiplier is 95,000/7,916 = 12. The two rates are reciprocals, as defined, since 1/12 = 8.333%.

If the net operating income of the subject property were $6,500, its value would be appraised as $78,000 because, by the net income multiplier, 12 × $6,500 = $78,000; or, by the capitalization process, $6,500/.08333 = $78,000. As a matter of interest, the net income multiplier is equivalent to the "price-earnings multiple" used in appraising common stock values.

The problem with such income capitalizations is that they do not take account of other significant factors influencing the value of the property, such as financing, tax benefits, or changes over time in any of the factors determining net income. While appraisers can use their judgment in adjusting the rates to correct for such factors, as soon as they do so it becomes very difficult for them to specify exactly which changed assumption caused a certain shift in value. They can show the effect on value of separate assumptions, but it is hard to decide which assumption is more logical or more probable.

2 Another method of deriving capitalization rates is to estimate the return an investor would require to make the investment. The necessary return is built up from a risk-free investment. Thus the buildup might be as follows:

Interest rate of risk-free government bonds	6.25
Payment for lack of liquidity	1.50
Payment for investment management	.75
Payment for risks of price changes	1.25
Capitalization rate	9.75

The capitalization rate on separate properties would vary with risks and management costs. Thus a relatively safe property with few management problems would have a lower capitalization rate than a slum property.

3 A third technique is to examine the costs of each slice (tranche) of available financing. For example, an investor might be able to borrow 60 percent on a first mortgage at 10 percent, and 25 percent on a second mortgage at 14 percent, while investing the final 15 percent from his or her own equity funds with a desired return of 12 percent. The capitalization rate would then be calculated as:

First mortgage	60% at .10 =	6.0%
Second mortgage	25% at .14 =	3.5%
Equity	15% at .12 =	1.8%
Total		11.3%

4   The most sophisticated traditional capitalization method is the Ellwood version. The primary contribution of this method is that it takes into account the impact that financing terms can have on value and the positive or negative changes in annual operating results as well as terminal value. The various combinations of mortgage terms, operating results, and terminal-value changes are incorporated into Ellwood tables which facilitate the appraisal process. These tables still require calculations which many appraisers find difficult if not actually confusing. As a result, a simplified version of the tables is available which makes the Ellwood method much easier to apply. The Ellwood method is essentially a rather rigid, pretax present-value method.

The capitalization rates the analyst selects must be based on his own assessments of probable operating expenses. If he accepts the figures of others at face value, he may well find substantial inconsistencies between the approach he is taking to value his subject property and the approaches used by others in the comparable properties for which he has gathered information. Each appraiser may be employing a different approach to derive the particular capitalization rate that he or she uses.

In effect, the requirement of appraisals is a necessary but not a sufficient condition for lenders to control their risks. The appraisals form a basis on which risk can be calculated, but they do not remove it. Furthermore, because appraisals are so subjective, one of the remaining elements of risk described in the next chapter is the fact that the appraisals will be biased (in the statistical sense) so as to lead to an acceptance of too many bad risks. In 1974 and 1975 many major real estate institutions defaulted on their own loans as a result of too many poor appraisals.

REGRESSION ANALYSIS

Increasingly sophisticated analysis of risks has recently been undertaken with the use of computer programs and regression analysis. These programs enable a management to spot appraisals or proposed loans which seem out of line. The individual cases can then be examined in greater detail and either rejected or renegotiated to require a larger downpayment or a higher interest rate to compensate for the greater risk.

The basic technique used for these programs is that of multiple-regression programs. These computer programs enable the firm to calculate or purchase a regression or predicting equation from past data on sales or loans. What the computer does is to calculate mathematically the best relationship between a dependent variable and a number of independent variables. Thus if the price of houses depends on their size, number of bathrooms, and age, the regression shows how much the dependent variable (the price of the house) will change for each unit movement in any or all of the independent variables. The program also calculates the amount of dispersion or variance in the historical data around the average predicted price. As a simplified illustration, we might say the house (call it P) depends on, or is a function of, the size (SF), the number of bathrooms (B), and its age (A); that is, P = f(SF, B, A).

The actual equation calculated by the computer might show that the price of the house was equal to 25.50 times the number of square feet (SF) in it, plus 1,500 for each bathroom (B), minus 700 for each year of age (A). Thus the regression equation would be

Price in dollars = 25.50SF + 1,500B − 700A

If a house had 1,200 square feet of space, contained two bathrooms, and was 3 years old, these factors would be substituted in the regression equation, which would then be solved to obtain an expected price of $31,500, or

25.50(1,200) + 1,500(2) − 700(3) = $31,500 = price

While the determination of what form the regression equation should take is somewhat complex, depending on one's model or theory of the market, once a good or proper equation has been found, its use in practice is quite straightforward. The estimated price or other dependent variable can be found by a clerk with a hand calculator in a few minutes. Two examples of how such equations can be used follow.

Price Regressions   The regression with three independent variables was a simplified one for illustration purposes. In fact, a good estimating equation for housing prices can be obtained by the use of eight independent variables. Multiple listing services, appraisers, assessors, and lenders frequently have records of the prices at which houses have sold in the market plus the special features of each house sold. The following facts are listed and fed into the computer for each house in the sample of sales made in the past 3 years:

Price in dollars (P).
Square feet of floor space (S).
Hundreds of square feet of lot size (LS).
A construction-cost index (cost).
Number of bathrooms (B).
Existence of air conditioning (C)—code 1 if present; otherwise, code 0.
Quality of construction (Q). Code into 5 classes—lowest is 1; highest is 5.
Type of garage (G). Code 0 for none; code 1 for one-car; code 2 for two-car.
Age of house in years (A).

In the process of developing the estimating equation, better results are obtained if floor space and construction costs are multiplied together before the regression is run. Their product is given the symbol SF. When the sample of sales within the past 3 years is run through the computer, a regression equation of the following type and values is estimated:

$$Price\ (P)\ =\ .21SF\ +\ 18LS\ +\ 1200B\ +\ 900C\ +\ 450Q\ +\ 400G\ -\ 800A$$

A customer asks an S&L to make a loan of $24,800, or 80 percent of price, based on a selling price of $31,000 for a house which has 1,100 square feet, is on a lot of 8,000 square feet, has two bathrooms, is not air-conditioned, is of quality class 3, has a single-car garage, and is 10 years old. The construction-cost index is 130. From the data furnished on the loan application, a clerk fills in the estimating equation as follows:

$$P\ =\ .21(1,100)(130)\ +\ 18(80)\ +\ 1,200(2)\ +\ 900(0)\ +\ 450(3)\ +\ 400(1)\ -\ 800(10)$$

$$= 30,030 + 1,440 + 2,400 + 0 + 1,350 + 400 - 8,000$$
$$= \$27,620$$

The S&L has a rule of not questioning for loan valuation purposes selling prices which do not exceed the estimated price by more than $1,500. When the equation was estimated, 80 percent of loans offered fell within that range, and experience has confirmed this distribution. In this case, the selling price is $31,000, compared with an estimated price from the equation of $27,620. The loan is turned over to a senior officer, who will determine the reason for the difference and will decide whether the S&L should accept the extra risk of a loan which would be 90 percent rather than 80 percent of the selling price predicted by the equation.

Risk Regressions   Instead of estimating expected prices, some institutions use regressions to signal loans which may involve more than a normal risk because of the attributes of the borrower. Thus a regression equation may be calibrated on the basis of a bank's past loans which have become delinquent by 90 days or more or which have actually gone into default. The type of variables included would be ratio of debt service to income of borrower, loan-to-value ratio of the loan, number of wage earners in the family, age and occupation of the family head, and amount of other debts owed by the borrower.

Again, the regression equations may be used in several ways. A lender might accept without further investigation all borrowers whose estimating equation gives a risk index of 1.0 or lower. The lender might decide that all potential borrowers with a risk index above 1.0 would require a more detailed analysis. Furthermore, borrowers with a risk index between 1.1 and 1.2 would be charged an extra quarter of a point annual interest on their mortgages, and those with a risk index between 1.2 and 1.3 would be charged an extra half point. Those with a risk index over 1.3 would be automatically rejected no matter what the added investigation showed.

It should be recognized that the risk indexes are based on statistics and past data and therefore measure probabilities rather than any certainty that errors or losses will not occur. Wide experience in consumer lending, however, does show that objective regression analysis can be of tremendous aid to lending officers. Their skills and judgment are checked against actual past experience by the regression technique. The combination of the regression equation and the lender's skill leads to lower risks and lower losses.

SUMMARY

Risks are controlled by managing them. The loan application and interview are used to screen out potential problems and to obtain further information needed to analyze both the borrower and the property which is to secure the loan. Individual risks depend on the characteristics of the loan, the borrower, and the property. The borrower is qualified through a credit check and analysis. The property is appraised. The loan may be tailored to fit the results of the appraisal and the borrower's ability to pay.

While there have been great improvements in risk analysis both for borrowers and for properties, we must recognize that a good deal of subjective judgment is still required. Those doing the rating tend to be carried away by optimism or pessimism. When everything is booming, the prospects for almost any property look good. It is at such times that the role of management in maintaining proper standards becomes especially critical.

QUESTIONS AND PROBLEMS

1   In evaluating a loan application, is the property or the borrower more important?
2   Is there only one appraised value for a specific property?
3   Should the appraisal be implicit or explicit in approach?
4   What are the three traditional approaches to value? Should each be used for every appraisal?
5   What are the various capitalization rates and methods that can be used?
6   How are capitalization rates derived?
7   Does the use of regression analysis ensure that the indicated appraisal value is the true value of a property?
8   What amounts will a lender save if it is possible to get a deed transferring a property rather than obtaining it through foreclosure? What losses will the lender still be faced with?
9   Explain how various characteristics of the borrower affect the risk in a loan.
10 Which of the basic factors influencing risks would you expect to affect the value estimated in an appraisal?

Chapter 19

The Management of Portfolio Risks

From the start of World War II to the mid-1960s, failure and bankruptcy of large financial institutions seemed to be a thing of the past. Forced liquidations were unusual, even for small institutions. But beginning in 1965, several large commercial banks, savings and loan associations, mortgage banks, and mortgage investment trusts were forced to close. While in most of these cases problems arose from poor underwriting of individual loans, the actual failures resulted from a poor or nonexistent portfolio policy. These institutions met disaster because they overconcentrated their lending in particular lines, in loans with inadequate liquidity, or in loans with long-term fixed interest rates whose values plummeted as market interest rates rose.

These losses underline the point that preoccupation with individual loans will not solve a lender's problems of risk management. The total composition of a firm's portfolio may lead to additional dangers. If many loans go bad simultaneously, the institution's solvency will be endangered. If the lender needs a substantial amount of cash that can be obtained only at high costs, the firm will face a crisis of liquidity. If interest rates shift suddenly, the firm may have sizable capital gains or losses.

In addition to lowering losses on individual loans, risk management has a second major goal—to obtain an overall portfolio composition that will minimize the dangers of insolvency and illiquidity. This attention to the overall composition of loans as distinct from their individual analysis is spoken of as the *management of portfolio risks*.

Preventative policies include careful regard for diversification, the planning of cash flows and liquidity, and the establishment and maintenance of sufficient reserves. The failure or near collapse of institutions almost always appears to result from unsuccessful efforts in one of these spheres.

PORTFOLIO POLICIES

Management decisions as to the distribution of total holdings among various types and maturities of loans and investments constitute portfolio policy. Frequently this policy is implicit rather than explicit. Many institutions have paid little attention to the need for a portfolio policy and the reasons for adopting one. In other institutions, especially in well-managed ones, it is recognized that each change in economic conditions, in the money market, or in the competitive situation requires a reexamination of, and perhaps a shift in, portfolio policy.

Each firm's decisions are limited by its charter and supervisory body. Almost all state and federal regulations put specific bounds on the type and amount of mortgages an institution can hold. In addition, the policy adopted will have to reflect the firm's type, size, and geographic location. How and where a bank or an insurance company invests are conditioned by the amount of funds it receives, where its office is located, and the particular business it is in.

Every fiduciary institution recognizes a special relationship to its depositors, or clients. When it accepts funds from a large number of individuals, a trustee type of relationship results. The managers must pay particular attention to the firm's safety and liquidity. To be successful and perform their entire task, however, they must also give considerable weight to the potential returns of different forms of investment.

Objectives

Most advisers recommend that the first step in the development of any portfolio policy be a clear statement of the goals to be achieved. Why is the firm making certain types of loans? What does it hope to achieve by changing its mortgage policy? What weight should be given in any change to the needs and desires of depositors, potential borrowers, the management, or stockholders?

After the firm states its goals, procedures must be established for the management of its portfolio to achieve them. These plans specify such matters as how the necessary decisions will be made, who will take the responsibility, and how often the policy will be reconsidered. The program must specify the type of decisions with respect to assets that a policy review must include. It also must establish the criteria for making these decisions.

Many types of criteria might be used to define a firm's goals. It does little good to have too simple a statement of policy, such as that there will be an attempt to maximize profits or net yields. Situations are too complex. A more operational set of criteria is necessary. Those responsible must have guidance as to what types of action the management believes will be of greatest help in reaching the overall goals. These would include the amount of expansion or contraction of lending desired, particular types of loans to be sought, and types of risks to be avoided or accepted.

It is necessary in establishing the criteria to recognize the impact on the long-run success of the firm of such factors as rate of growth or leadership in new techniques and markets. Because it increases scale, may lower unit overhead costs, may have tax advantages, and could lead to greater diversification, growth has often been selected as a goal in and of itself. Another aspect is a consideration of the amount of risks, particularly with respect to possible portfolio losses, that the firm will accept.

When it changes its portfolio, a firm must decide whether to move with the industry average or to strike off by itself and hope to be an innovator and industry leader. On the one hand, the firm may aim to stay near the industry's norm with respect to timing, types of assets, and profitability. The advantage of attempting to steer by the industry's norm is that a management is less likely to incur criticism. If something goes wrong, everyone in the industry will suffer together. The excuse that the management did only what the industry thought proper will usually be accepted as a sufficient explanation. However, management decisions are increasingly being held to higher levels of accountability. Further, following the industry may not avoid bankruptcy or other dire results such as occurred in the 1930s. It also will not allow the management to profit from its own ability.

On the other hand, policy may stress innovations and an attempt to choose the most profitable paths. The firm can carefully examine the market, relative risks and yields, and future prospects. Then the management can use its analytic skills to search out the best solutions. It can hunt for new opportunities, pockets in the yield curves, and better operations. Such a goal may yield high potential profits, but also higher risks.

A mixed strategy might call for a policy of constantly searching for more profitable paths but moving only partway down them away from the industry's norms. The firm establishes as its goal that of being a limited innovator. It will use its skills but not take unusual risks.

Types of Policy Decisions

Having determined its goals, the lender must adopt a specific program to select the policies which will achieve its objectives. Both the goals and the program should be in writing so that they will be logical and clear to all in responsible positions. The programs should be described in broad general terms, but they must also show in detail which decisions must be made and how often each specific decision criterion should be reviewed.

The decisions should consist of agreements to expand or contract particular classes of assets. After the general lines of movement have been established, the program's implementation will be up to the individual lending officers. Which assets will be purchased at any time will depend upon several different factors.

First consideration should be given to the type of asset. How much money should the firm place in mortgages, bonds, consumer loans, stocks, or other assets? Within each of these categories, how much should go to particular subcategories? For example, how much of the money allotted to mortgages should go into one-family residences, multifamily residences, income property, or raw land?

Another important determination relates to the quality distribution of assets. In times of easy money, mortgage portfolios show a tendency to fill with lower-quality loans. Offers that would be rejected in normal circumstances are taken because money is so available. A policy statement with respect to quality should point out to lending officers the likelihood that such tendencies may occur. It should specify how far the firm is willing to go to generate additional business and what compensating advantages should be sought.

RISKS AND PROFITABILITY

The theory of risk analysis is more advanced than the practice. However, the subject is so significant that analysts should have a clear understanding of what is involved. The problem is to structure both the liabilities and the assets of a firm so as to yield the maximum profits within a risk profile which has been carefully considered and properly determined. Each type of asset as well as each liability, such as a loan, a bond, a deposit, or stock, contains a different degree of risk.

The problem of the firm is to fit them together. In most cases, difficulties arise when a large number of the assets turn out to be positively correlated in their reaction to movements in the economy or in money-market rates. The portfolio risks of a firm will not decrease unless a deliberate effort is made to select a portfolio policy which calls for diversifying among assets and liabilities with low risk correlations.

Five different sources of portfolio problems are (1) overconcentration, (2) lack of liquidity, (3) too large an interest rate risk, (4) losses from inflation, and (5) inadequate reserves.

A portfolio policy starts with a balancing of the risks and returns within each of these categories. The risks involved in the loan portfolio are examined from every angle. Which loans are most vulnerable in a depression? Which assets offer potential liquidity? Which do not? What about inflation?

If the risks appear too high, a plan to reduce them must be worked out. This frequently means calculating alternative costs for dealing with a problem. Some loans might be sold. New funds might be used to increase liquidity. A program can be formulated to protect against inflation. Every part of the program must be weighed against the others. The object is to reduce risks with a minimum cut in profits or to increase profits with a minimum rise in risk.

However, unless the objectives are laid out clearly, they will rarely be achieved. It is possible to reduce risks. But unless they enter specifically into the planning of the firm, experience shows that they may climb rapidly to dangerous levels. The following sections discuss some of the critical factors which enter into a proper determination of profitability and risk.

THE LOAN PORTFOLIO

The careful underwriting of each individual loan serves to reduce some of the risk. Under normal circumstances, when loans deteriorate as a result of random individual mishaps, the total number of loans in the portfolio determines the amount of risk. As in many insurance situations, the larger the number of loans, the smaller the total risk.

The chances that an unusually high percentage will go bad in any period decrease with the size of the portfolio.

The law of large numbers leading to decreased risks applies, however, only if no correlation exists between the loans which could cause many of them to go bad simultaneously. In contrast, if loans are of a similar type, portfolio risk is greater because all may react in a uniformly unsatisfactory manner to the same outside forces. If a city is hit by an earthquake, the closing of a military base, or a large excess of apartment houses, many loans may simultaneously be affected adversely.

Diversification of loans attempts to minimize such correlation, or covariance. There may be diversification with respect to time of lending, areas, neighborhoods or regions, types of properties and individuals, or any of a number of other possible bases of classification.

Risks incurred in individual loans are much greater in some years than in others, partially because a loan's success in its first 5 years is heavily influenced by the state of the economy. When incomes and housing prices are rising, only the poorest of loans will not succeed. On the other hand, even mild recessions or periods of stable building costs lead to foreclosures of loans that otherwise would be bailed out by a voluntary transfer of the property.

Risk analysis shows that it is dangerous for a portfolio to contain too many loans issued at the same period. Loans processed together in time are governed by the same underwriting and appraisal views and principles. There is usually a tendency to depend too much on recent experiences. A class of loans that has been profitable may be pushed to the limit. When incomes are rising and jobs are plentiful, predictions of future income may be too high. Clustering in time may increase the danger from an economic downturn because, under normal amortization procedures, a large body of young loans will not have had much of their principal repaid.

Over and above the danger of market changes, new loans have a higher risk than older ones. With younger loans, as opposed to mature ones, it is more likely that the property or borrower will have hidden defects that will show up with time. Furthermore, the newer the loan, the less the reduction in principal. The borrower has a smaller equity and less interest in maintaining payments. Most loans experience the largest losses in their second or third year.

The risk manager must clearly recognize that high correlations in time sharply increase the amount of portfolio risk. A group of loans with a normal age distribution will be far safer than a collection of new loans made under fairly uniform economic and underwriting conditions.

Area of Lending

Regulations commonly require institutions to limit their mortgage loans to local areas, often defined as within 50 or 100 miles of their home office or the state in which they are located. Because lenders have the most knowledge of local conditions, it is assumed that they can make safer loans in their own neighborhoods than elsewhere.

Although better knowledge may lower individual underwriting risks, area limitations may decrease total safety by curtailing diversification. Experience proves that the smaller the area, the greater the risks that its entire property market will go bad. The pressures on whole regions, such as West Virginia, defense communities, and other special-purpose locations, are common knowledge. Still more common is the experience of towns which have enjoyed a boom and then suffered a sharp drop as a result of the closing of a military base or major defense plant. Even in Los Angeles, a small area found itself with several thousand unsold houses when the defense picture changed. In such situations, a large percentage of the properties in a town lose value simultaneously. Any institution with a high proportion of its portfolio concentrated in loans on a few locations within an area obviously faces greatly increased risks.

Types of Property and Individuals

Lenders frequently find that for a period, certain types of loans may be far more profitable than others. A savings association which financed John Smith when he was a small contractor may keep his account as he grows bigger and more and more successful. It may feel extremely lucky to have such an outstanding, profitable account. In many such situations, however, the association suddenly finds that the borrower has gone bankrupt and that its losses may run to several million dollars.

Similarly, in times of rapidly rising land prices, shortages of rental units, or expanding tourist traffic, special loans on raw land, apartments, or motels may yield excellent results. Suddenly prices level off, the boom ends, or overbuilding becomes obvious. Firms heavily concentrated in what they thought were fine loans take heavy losses.

While regulations unfortunately create concentration within areas, they usually attempt to limit concentration in other types of risk. They require diversification by type of loan and individual. Such compulsory diversification may look better on paper than it is in fact. It may not meet the problem of covariances of risks on loans all made at the same time. Correlations can exist between many seemingly different types of loans if all rest on the same basic premises. It is such covariances that must be avoided through proper risk management. Lending officers must do more than comply with the letter of regulations. They must recognize the intent and logic of these regulations and make certain that true diversification is protecting the firm against the possibility that many loans will go bad at the same time. They must avoid the excess losses created by having to liquidate a large number of loans in a short period.

PLANNING FOR LIQUIDITY

Liquidity has been defined as the ability to obtain cash when needed without incurring high costs or other risks. In the regulations affecting particular institutions, it also is frequently defined in very specific terms such as cash, Treasury bills, or other short-term assets, certain ratios of which to total resources may be fixed by law. The need for liquidity arises because most financial institutions, either contractually or by custom, agree to make available to their depositors funds entrusted to them on demand or upon short notice.

Even when, as with savings accounts, delays could be required, institutions are loath to demand such notices. Failure to pay on demand would shake major premises on which recent saving expansions have been based. The average family looks upon savings institutions as proper places to hold liquid assets, on the assumption that their money will be rapidly available in case of emergency.

The management of liquidity takes several paths. It goes beyond the relatively simple decisions as to what percentage of the firm's liabilities should be held in cash or quick assets. Four different possibilities arise in planning for liquidity:

1   Liquidity can be protected by forecasts of, and controls over, the normal flow of funds growing out of individual deposits and withdrawals, normal loan amortization and repayments, and the need to pay out moneys on existing commitments. The use of certificates or time deposits with fixed dates of maturity can improve management in this category.

2   Liquidity can be attained by borrowing cash.

3   Money can be made available by shifting loans to other lenders. What would be the cost of transferring or selling a mortgage in case of need? Such costs, differing among types of loans, must be considered in estimating each one's risk and net yield.

4   The costs of liquidity can be lowered by protecting against so-called interest risk. There is the danger that even though a loan may be easily marketable, it will have to be sold at a financial sacrifice because of changes in the money market. Because mortgage loans are made at fixed rates, their value shifts with changes in the going rate of interest. While losses may be considerable, gains are less likely. The lender cannot call the loan if interest rates rise, but because most loans specify that they can be refinanced or paid off (often with some penalty), the borrower may return the money if rates fall.

Cash-Flow Analysis

Most lending institutions are devoting more time to protecting their liquidity by forecasts of their flow of cash. Depending on the type of institution, such forecasts are made daily, weekly, or monthly. They cover different periods such as tomorrow, the next week or month, or periods up to 2 years in length.

In these forecasts, factors affecting cash flow which are analyzed and projected may be divided into as few as 5 or 6 or expanded to 20 or more, on both the gain and loss sides. The number of items predicted depends on the type of institution, the complexity of its operations, and the excellence of its management.

The importance of cash-flow analysis has received much greater attention as a result of the frequent periods of disintermediation from deposit institutions which have occurred in the postwar period. Insurance companies have experienced similar problems through an expansion of policy loans.

Periods of sharp withdrawals have followed local economic distress and major periods of scare buying. Primarily, however, they have occurred when market interest rates on short-term securities have moved above the rates paid by financial institutions.

For a particular firm, the extent and impact of such losses depend on the degree of diversity found among the institution's depositors. What share is owned by large, knowledgeable depositors? What share is held by employees in a cyclical industry? The individual making cash forecasts must know his or her own firm, its market peculiarities, and the pressures upon it. Many forces can create a concentrated cash drain. Risks are multiplied because the same forces which cause faster withdrawals are likely to slow deposits. One cannot depend on normal inflows to offset outflows occurring because of these special factors.

Cash flows are also influenced by rates of amortization, interest earnings, and interest payments. Although they have a heavy seasonal component, these factors form the more stable part of the cash-flow estimate. The amount of amortization depends upon the structure of the loan portfolio. Usually it does not change sharply in short periods. Under level-payment plans for interest and amortization, the percentage of payment going to amortization rises with the age of the loan. High payments against principal may give significant stability to the total flow.

Advance payments on mortgages are another source of funds that varies greatly. They depend on the rate at which houses are resold. Sales, in turn, are dependent on economic conditions. In periods of tight money or rising interest rates, when firms would like to get their money back faster, an opposite movement is probable. Tight money and high rates make it worthwhile for borrowers not to refinance. In addition, properties are sold subject to existing mortgages, thus cutting off a normal flow of advance repayments.

The outflow of mortgage loans against previous commitments is another difficult area of forecasting; however, careful analysis can help greatly here. The backlog of outstanding commitments may suddenly cause a firm a good deal of distress. The percentage of commitments taken up by borrowers varies with changing interest rates. The fluctuating rate at which commitments are used can work to the lender's disadvantage. If the money market eases or if borrowers are offered better terms elsewhere, they will not use the commitment. On the other hand, with a tightening market and rising rates, the percentage of commitments actually used increases. Lenders can avoid some of these difficulties by charging for advance commitments. To be profitable, the rate they charge must more than offset the risk of losses resulting from shifts in interest rates.

Borrowing on Mortgages

One of the methods through which lenders obtain additional liquidity is by borrowing against the mortgage portfolio. Such borrowing may be done to meet day-to-day requirements for operating capital or to cover emergency requirements for funds which arise through errors in the projection of cash flows or unforeseen withdrawals. Still other borrowing, on either a temporary or a permanent basis, aims at meeting heavy demands in certain markets by bringing in funds from elsewhere.

We have already noted that the FHL Banks are one principal source of such borrowing. Savings associations have found the FHLB System a major source of liquidity. It has been a significant source of funds to meet seasonal requirements. In order to increase the amount they could lend over and above their own resources, many associations have remained steadily in debt to the FHL Banks. Finally, most firms plan to use the banks as a rapid source of liquidity in case of sudden need. The existence of this backing plays an enormous role in day-to-day operations. Without it, the individual institutions would have to carry much greater liquidity.

Mortgage Warehousing

Most other lenders have not borrowed to the same extent on their mortgage portfolios. When they have, their chief method has been through so-called mortgage warehousing at CBs. In warehousing arrangements, a CB extends short-term credits to a mortgage company or savings bank on a note, with a group of mortgages serving as general security for the note. In another technique, the original lender sells individual loans to a CB with an agreement to repurchase the mortgages within a stated time period.

Most warehousing is used by mortgage companies to obtain working capital for their day-to-day operations. These organizations make construction and individual mortgage loans to their clients. However, the ultimate lenders, such as the FNMA or purchasers of a GNMA-guaranteed security, delay payment to the mortgage company until a fully satisfactory group of loans can be delivered, most frequently after receipt of the FHA insurance or VA guarantee.

During the period in which money has been paid to the builder or seller but before the mortgage company has received its payment from the final lender, it requires interim financing. CBs lend mortgage companies operating capital on notes against their total assets, which include primarily the partially completed loans in their portfolios. When correspondents take final delivery of the individual mortgages, the payments they make to the mortgage companies are used to liquidate the bank loans.

The specific techniques of warehousing require the mortgage companies to pledge particular assets behind their notes. Such questions as transfer of title, escrow accounts, and checking of construction by the banks depend upon a company's financial stability, its past record, and the experience of the CBs with it and with other mortgage lenders.

Warehousing of mortgages to meet unusual cash drains or in anticipation of future cash flows is not as common, but it does occur. At times, MSBs and LICs have miscalculated their cash flow because of an uneven takedown of commitments or because of a sudden demand for cash. Rather than sell permanently some assets, they have preferred to borrow on part of their portfolio. Such techniques have also been adopted by some savings banks as the normal procedure for meeting seasonal surges in their fund requirements.

Normally warehousing takes place through the pledging of individual mortgages against a note. Sales of specific loans to CBs with a repurchase agreement are not as common, but they have some definite advantages. In such cases, the borrowers' balance sheets need not show a debt to the bank, even though their repurchase contracts have the same effect.

In all warehousing, the CB attempts to retain the maximum degree of security by obtaining the right to foreclose on the final property if necessary. In the vast majority of cases, however, it expects that the loan will be repaid through the normal operation of the mortgage company. Individual loans must be taken over only if the mortgage company runs into difficulties.

Sales of Participations

A final technique of borrowing against a mortgage portfolio is through the use of mortgage participations, by which is meant the sale of a share of an individual loan to another lender. The buyer pays the seller for his or her share and becomes the legal owner of whatever share was purchased. Again the objective may be to obtain either working capital or long-term funds. The principal type of short-period participation occurs when a savings bank sells 80 or 90 percent participation in mortgages in its portfolio to a CB. Usually there is an agreement to repurchase.

Normally in these cases, the servicing remains with the original lender. The CBs are paid fees in accordance with commercial loans rather than mortgage rates. The lines of credit are extinguished either seasonally or when the brief period of need has passed.

In contrast, savings associations sell large numbers of participations on a permanent basis in order to increase the lending they can do in their own market. As an example, a California association may agree to sell a 50 percent participation in each of 100 mortgages to an Ohio association. Each firm is a legal owner of one-half of each loan. They share the risks. Because California has needed more savings than are available, mortgage interest rates have been higher there than in Ohio. The participation agreement leads to increased interest for the Ohio firm, more money to lend in California, and more diversification for both associations.

Typically in such agreements, the originating association keeps all or most of the initial fees received for making the loan. It also retains part of the interest payment as a fee—say, .5 percent of the outstanding balance—for servicing the loan. Both associations share equally in amortization, repayments, and any losses.

A Secondary Market

Sales of assets are another major source of liquidity. Most institutions hold governments or other liquid assets as a first source of additional funds. Such assets are normally short-term assets, to avoid the problem of having to take capital losses which arise when interest rates shift in the long-term market. If, however, more funds are required than can be made available from these first lines of defense, mortgages may have to be sold.

We have seen the steady improvement in the secondary mortgage market due to a great deal of government effort. However, we also noted the differentiation between the true secondary market, where lenders desiring more cash can sell loans already in their portfolio—at what they hope will be close to their true value—and other transactions also spoken of as secondary-market operations, such as the insuring or guaranteeing of mortgages and the sale of mortgages by agents to correspondents.

Currently, lenders such as mortgage companies can make loans either against outstanding commitments or for their own risk, with the expectation that when they have gathered together a sufficient batch, these loans can be sold. To be sold, such loans must usually be insured or guaranteed. S&Ls also sell participations to other S&Ls from newly made loans or from their portfolios. Sales of income property loans are also frequently made against specific commitments. Still, it is very difficult for most lenders to find buyers for any number of noninsured conventional mortgages in their portfolios.

However, the market has improved over the years. Prices of existing mortgages are more uniform. They adjust more rapidly to movements in general interest rates. Selling costs have declined. Some added lenders, such as pension funds and small financial institutions, have entered the market.

We have noted that these improvements have wiped out some of the large geographic differences in mortgage interest rates and that the net yield on mortgages is closer to that on other instruments. As a result, liquidity for mortgages has improved.

PROTECTING AGAINST INTEREST RATE RISKS

The fact that mortgage loans last for long periods means that three separate adjustments must be made in the gross interest rates, or yields on mortgages, that do not apply to the interest rate on shorter, more liquid loans. These three factors—the income risk on longer loans, the term of the loan, and the inclusion of rights to repay sums in advance—are all features that the bond and other money markets recognize require higher charges. Since all these features are contained in mortgages, they should be acknowledged and allowed for in calculating net returns.

Interest Rate Movements

Figure 19-1 shows the prices at which a standard mortgage would have sold as a result of changes in current market interest rates. These movements in value may be considered typical of the quarter-to-quarter changes which affected an average existing mortgage portfolio because of interest movements. The figure does not consider the impact on value of seasoning or similar influences. At the height of mortgage interest rates in 1974, a specific mortgage would have had a capital value nearly 40 percent less than at the peak of its value in 1951. Declines of as much as 5.5 percent in value occurred between adjacent quarters.

If existing portfolios had had to be liquidated or if lenders had been required to value their mortgages at actual market worth, many institutions might have been in considerable difficulty. The movements in capital value in some periods would have more than offset operating profits.

Chapter 6 explained in detail why the value of existing mortgages alters when market interest rates change. The current value of any loan is the discounted stream of future interest and amortization payments. When the market shifts, the new interest rate requires that discounting take place at a new rate. This causes a shift in the mortgage's current value. No one will offer more for it than could be obtained by current lending. If the mortgage has to be sold, the price offered will be based upon the current present value, not the face interest payments.

Calculation of the present value of a loan is complicated somewhat by the fact that the date the mortgage may be expected to be paid off will vary depending upon how its face interest rate compares with the current market. Thus Figure 19-1 is based on the assumption that 30-year mortgages will, on the average, be repaid by the end of 12 years. However, the actual fall in value may be greater than assumed. Loans which carry an interest rate below the market and those for long terms have a smaller probability of advance repayment. Experiences of repayments based on rising prices for properties cannot be extrapolated as an estimate of average lengths in other periods. In cases where prices have fallen or not gone up, it may be worth paying a higher interest rate in order to get out more funds in cash. Lenders in theory can increase their protection somewhat against loans being assumed by new borrowers simply because they have favorable terms. They can include acceleration clauses to require that loans be repaid if a property is sold.

The Term Structure of Interest Rates

The term of the loan is another significant factor affecting its true yield. In normal times, borrowers must pay higher interest or premiums on loans for longer periods.

This fact, often neglected in the mortgage market, is a basic part of the structure of the bond market. For example, in the municipal bond market, there have been frequent periods in the past when rates for loans rose by an average of 5 basis points, or .05 percent in interest payments, for each year of additional length. Twenty-five-year bonds have carried interest rates that ranged from 25 to 75 percent higher than those for one-year bonds.

The reason for this rising rate has been analyzed according to what is called the *term structure of interest rates*. The existence of rising rates in many periods is clearer, however, than the reasons for them. The most common theoretical explanation of a rising yield curve is that lenders expect higher short-term rates in the future. Another explanation of the increases is the assumption that lenders believe that the risk on any loan rises with the length of its maturity. Such a risk premium may exist in fact, but in theory it is not necessary. A more probable reason is that there are more savers who desire to hold near money or very liquid assets than savers who want to have a guaranteed interest rate on loans extending far into the future.

A desire for liquidity is not universal. Insurance companies, for example, enter into contracts in which they guarantee certain rates of interest on their policy reserves for long periods. As a result, these companies want to ensure a rate on their assets that extends as far into the future as their outstanding commitments. However, while they and some other savers desire long-term assets, statistically more savers seem to want short-period loans. Such a surplus of demand for short-term assets can lead to the term structure of rates characterized by a rise with length to maturity.

Since the existing term structure means that borrowers pay more for longer loans, mortgages should also carry a higher interest rate, the longer the period of amortization. Mortgages with equal monthly payments will have varying amounts going each month to interest and principal depending upon the amortization period. For a mortgage with an 8 percent interest rate and payments spread over 20 years, the average period for which the principal is outstanding is about 13 years. In contrast, in the case of a similar loan amortized over 30 years, the funds will be loaned out on an average for about 22 years.

While particular market conditions will cause differences in the rates charged for loans with these two different lengths, a rather sharp rise in the term structure can mean that the longer loan should be charged about .75 percent more in annual interest rates than the shorter one. The specific amount charged for the longer loan should rise with the average rate of interest and with the likelihood that advance repayments will be delayed.

Prepayment Privileges

A final consideration affecting the interest yield depends on whether the note of mortgage is closed or open. A closed loan cannot be prepaid without a penalty; an open one can. Modern mortgages usually allow prepayments, but only with a prepayment penalty that decreases depending on the length of time the mortgage has been in existence.

When interest rates have risen, however, lenders not only have allowed prepayments but also have offered bonuses for them. To illustrate, in 1974 some lenders were offering discounts of 5 to 20 percent for full or partial repayments. A typical letter from an S&L told a customer that it would accept $12,800 in full payment for an outstanding loan of $15,000. Furthermore, if the borrower could not pay the full amount, the S&L would reduce the balance by $117 for every $100 in excess of current payments received on the debt in any month. Such offers reflected the fact that the existing mortgage carried an interest rate of 5.5 percent, while the S&L was turning away borrowers offering higher than 10 percent for new loans.

Such bonuses were made necessary by the fact that in the absence of a variable rate agreement, the lender cannot require the borrower to pay higher interest rates after the original agreement has been made. On the other hand, with an open mortgage or one with a low prepayment penalty, the borrower can renegotiate or obtain a mortgage at a lower rate elsewhere.

This ability to renegotiate is exactly equivalent to the call feature on a bond. Thus is also has a recognized value. A callable, or optional, bond allows borrowers to refinance and save interest if rates fall. Furthermore, lenders risk having to liquidate their investment and find another in a period that may not be as favorable. Uncertainty of maturity, added to that of the length of the term, increases the uncertainty of most mortgages.

Since the mortgage market has not given proper consideration to this feature, we must turn to the bond market to obtain an estimate of the value of this call privilege.

Studies of the bond market have compared similarly rated bonds with and without call privileges. A bond which could not be paid off for a minimum of 5 years was worth 15 basis points more than one that could be paid off at any time. A 10-year deferment was worth 25 extra points. In effect this means that an open mortgage, that is, a mortgage without a prepayment penalty, probably should be considered to have a .25 percent lower interest yield than a closed one.

It can be seen that in comparing the potential yields of different mortgages or of mortgages as compared with bonds, it is necessary to estimate the various income risks, costs of the term structure, and costs of potential calls if a useful comparison is to be possible. Many of these differences might be neglected if it were not for the problem of liquidity. The risks and costs of these features are due to the potential need to sell mortgages or reinvest funds in the future. The better the job an institution can do in estimating its flow of funds, the greater the ease with which it can borrow against its portfolio; and the higher the efficiency of the secondary market, the lower the risks and costs in these factors which differentiate mortgages.

INFLATION: PRICE CHANGES

Chapter 11 discussed the problem encountered by lenders in protecting their portfolios against changes in purchasing power. Not only are most lenders interested in getting back the number of dollars they lend, but they usually also want returned roughly the same purchasing power or command over goods.

In some ways, inflation is not an immediate threat to financial institutions, since both their assets and their liabilities are stated in dollars. Therefore, the purchasing power of both sides moves together. The danger arises from the probability that savers will not continue to entrust their funds to an institution which keeps paying them back in dollars of a reduced value. In addition, a significant part of the liabilities of many institutions is made up of capital belonging to their owners. The management needs to protect the purchasing power of these investments to stay competitive with other corporations which do offer such protection.

An Inflationary Premium

One way in which lenders can attempt to protect themselves against rising prices is to add an inflationary premium to their interest charge in order to compensate themselves for the reduced ability to purchase with the funds returned. The required risk premium is equal to the expected percent change in prices.

For example, suppose the real rate of interest is 5 percent. A lender is willing to make a mortgage loan at 5 percent for 30 years provided he gets back his principal at the end of the period and provided all transactions are in real terms, that is, provided both his interest and principal are paid back to him in purchasing power equal to that which prevailed at the time the loan was made. He believes prices will rise at a compound rate of 3 percent a year. How much will he have to charge to compensate for this expected inflation? The answer is that he will be protected if he receives the real rate he desires (5 percent) plus the expected percent change per year in prices (3 percent). In other words, if he receives 8 percent a year, he will earn a real rate of roughly 5 percent and will be compensated for the fall in value of both his interest payments and his principal.

It surprises many to learn that with a 3 percent inflation rate, after 30 years the purchasing power of a $1,000 principal payment will be equal to only about 400 of today's dollars. It seems unlikely that an extra 3 percent a year could make up the difference between $400 and $1,000. However, those who think back to our discussion of compounding will recognize that the protection arises from the fact that the lender can reinvest the extra 3 percent interest each year, and this sum grows at a compound rate. Thus while the purchasing power of the lender's $1,000 falls to $970 at the end of the first year, reinvestment of the $30 inflation premium will yield $1,030 in principal. After 30 years the principal will have grown enough so that even though each dollar is worth only 40 cents in today's terms, the value of the compounded principal will have grown to roughly $2,500—a total equivalent to $1,000 in today's purchasing power. (The example is not exact because it only roughly accounts for changes in the purchasing power of the annual interest. It also assumes, as most yield tables do, the ability to keep reinvesting at an 8 percent interest rate.)

Such attempts to protect against inflation are, of course, one of the causes of high nominal interest rates. The demand for loans is high among borrowers who believe they will be able to repay in less valuable dollars. At the same time, lenders demand higher interest rates to protect themselves against the risk of falling purchasing power for their money.

Indexing

Adding a premium to the interest rate is not the only way of reducing the risks of price changes. In many countries, mortgages are written in terms of purchasing power. A

$1,000 loan has a 5 percent rate of interest. If prices rise 5 percent in a year, an equal percent is added to the real rate so that the interest rate paid in that year will be 10 percent. If prices rise another 3 percent the next year, the rate charged will fall back to 8 percent. (Note that changes in the rate are not cumulative. An addition in a year equivalent to the price change for that year corrects for the fall in the purchasing power of the outstanding principal.) Such so-called indexed (from the purchasing-power index) loans have the advantage of removing a great deal of uncertainty. Loans and interest payments are made in terms of constant purchasing power. There is less need to try to guess where prices are going.

The use of variable rates on mortgages serves a similar purpose. If market interest rates move with price changes, a variable rate mortgage will automatically include the interest rate premiums necessary to protect against inflation.

Diversification

Finally, lenders can attempt to protect themselves by holding a broad spectrum of assets rather than merely those denominated in dollars. No one can be certain whether interest rates at any period include the total risk premium needed to compensate for future inflation. The knowledge, fears, and expectations of borrowers and lenders differ. The ability to find other assets which are protected against inflation also varies. As rates of price changes move widely, our ability to judge the future accurately decreases. Successful investments may be influenced more by luck than by skill. If prices move up and down erratically, protection against such risks requires a diversified group of assets which will react in opposite ways to price changes.

This attempt to find diversified assets explains the eagerness, discussed in Chapter 9, with which financial institutions have sought equity investments and "kickers" whose returns would increase with the price level. Many institutions, however, have been limited in the amount of funds they can place in equities. These regulations originate in the recognition of one type of risk in equities—the safety of principal. However, they neglect a type of portfolio risk—the maintenance of purchasing power.

Institutions such as pension funds which are governed by the "prudent-man rule" rather than by specific regulations have become one of the major markets for real estate. A solution to this problem for other institutions depends on what changes take place in the overall regulations which apply to them.

RESERVES

The final task of risk management is the establishment of adequate reserves. When reserves are discussed, they are usually thought of as required primarily because of the existence of risky assets. Examinations of institutions that have failed in recent years, however, indicate that embezzlement or defalcation on the part of officers can also be a major cause of failure. Reserves, therefore, are also required in addition to bonding and insurance in order to cover malfeasance and other failures of employees to perform their duties properly.

The discussion in this chapter and prior ones should have made clear the shortcomings in the widely held idea that reserves should simply be a fixed share of an institution's assets. The risk that a firm faces varies with many more factors than the mere existence of assets.

In the first place, each type of individual asset has a separate risk attached to it. Loans on raw land or income properties carry two to three times the risk of loans on single-family houses. The risk falls fairly rapidly with the age of the loan. The whole concept of mortgage risk rating, whether done formally or informally, indicates that firms can increase or decrease their potential losses as they see fit.

In risk management, a significant problem arises because an individual firm must recognize that it has to be concerned with the variance of losses in addition to their average. Any individual firm has a certain probability of being above or below the average losses for a group of firms. With respect to the random element in losses, the distribution around this average should be a fairly normal curve. Recognizing this fact, an institution can properly estimate its probable cost of risks and net yields by assuming that such random losses will occur. To protect itself by reserves, however, it must consider the possibility that its losses will be near the extremes of the normal curve.

In addition to the individual random elements, however, reserves are also required to handle the problem of portfolio risks. The amount of portfolio risk is partly a function of the size of the firm. With proper management, the larger the firm, the smaller the probable variance around the average will be. All other factors being the same, small firms need considerably larger (in percent) reserves than large firms.

The risks of the small firm are still greater because it is more likely to suffer from nonrandom risks. Any errors in mortgage risk analysis are likely to have a relatively greater impact on a small organization than on a large one. Diversification is harder to manage, particularly with respect to regional dangers. To protect itself, the small firm must be far more aware of the perils of too much lending in any specific area, to any individual or firm, or on any one type of property.

The additional problems raised by liquidity can be handled partly by reserves, but they can also be managed through planning. Thus government-insured loans have a greater access to the secondary mortgage market than conventional loans. There are other possible arrangements that can make it easier to sell some mortgages, thereby reducing dependence on liquidity reserves. The need for reserves can also be lowered by a better distribution of loans by amortization period and a better forecasting of the flow of funds.

SUMMARY

Risks depend on the overall portfolio composition as well as on the probability of losses on individual loans. Diversification reduces a firm's risk because it reduces the likelihood that many loans will go bad simultaneously as a result of the same cause. If it leads to the inclusion of equities, it also offers some protection against changes in purchasing power.

Liquidity, or the ability to get cash rapidly, also calls for special planning. It is affected by the firm's flow of funds and by its ability to convert existing assets into cash. Secondary markets are important in enabling mortgage lenders to increase their liquidity.

Mortgages can also be dangerous because they are monetary assets with fixed interest rates extending well into the future. Firms can protect themselves against such risks by variable rates, by sufficiently high risk premiums, and by the inclusion of equities in their portfolios.

QUESTIONS AND PROBLEMS

1 In developing an investment policy, is it acceptable for management to do what everyone else appears to be doing?
2 What are the major sources of portfolio problems?
3 Discuss the investment theory "Put all your eggs in one basket and watch it like a hawk" in the context of portfolio diversification.
4 How can liquidity problems be protected against?
5 In an inflationary period, would a borrower probably have to pay a higher rate if the loan were "indexed" or if it were written on a fixed rate basis?
6 How can a portfolio of loans be diversified to reduce risk?
7 What do we mean when we say that many mortgage lenders "play both sides of the market"?
8 Explain why the price of an existing mortgage changes as interest rates rise or fall.
9 The term structure of interest rates is also spoken of as the slope of the interest curve. What is meant by these expressions? Find out what typical slopes have looked like in recent years.
10 Why is an open mortgage worth more to a borrower than a closed one?

SELECTED REFERENCES FOR PART FIVE

The Appraisal of Real Estate (Chicago: American Institute of Real Estate Appraisers, 1973).

Cooper, J. R.: *Real Estate Investment Analysis* (Lexington, Mass.: Lexington Books, 1974).

Fama, E. F., and M. H. Miller: *The Theory of Finance* (New York: Holt, 1972).

Fisher, D.: *Money and Banking* (Homewood, Ill.: Irwin, 1971).

Guttentag, J. M., and P. Cagen: *Essays on Interest Rates* (New York: National Bureau of Economic Research, 1969, 1971), vols. 1 and 2.

Herzog, J. P., and J. S. Early: *Home Mortgage Delinquency and Foreclosure* (New York: National Bureau of Economic Research, 1970).

Kinnard, W. N., Jr.: *Income Property Valuation* (Lexington, Mass.: Lexington Books, 1971).

Malkiel, B. G.: *The Term Structure of Interest Rates: Theory, Empirical Evidence, and Applications* (New York: McCaleb-Seiler, 1970).

Markowitz, H. M.: *Portfolio Selection: Efficient Diversification of Investments*, 2d ed. (New York: Wiley, 1971).

Rapkin, C., J. R. Ferrari, R. Blood, and G. Milgrim: *The Private Insurance of Home Mortgages* (Philadelphia: University of Pennsylvania, Institute for Environmental Studies, 1967).

Ratcliff, R. U.: *Valuation for Real Estate Decisions* (Santa Cruz, Calif.: Democrat Press, 1972).

Ricks, R. B.: *Recent Trends in Institutional Real Estate Investment* (Berkeley: University of California, Center for Real Estate and Urban Economics, 1964).

Ring, A. A.: *The Valuation of Real Estate* (Englewood Cliffs, N.J.: Prentice-Hall, 1970).

Robinson, R. I., and D. Wrightsman: *Financial Markets: The Accumulation and Allocation of Wealth* (New York: McGraw-Hill, 1974).

Roulac, S. E.: *Real Estate Venture Analysis 1974* (New York: Practising Law Institute, 1974).

Sharpe, W. F.: *Portfolio Theory and Capital Markets* (New York: McGraw-Hill, 1970).

Walters, D. W.: *Real Estate Computerization* (Berkeley: University of California, Center for
    Real Estate and Urban Economics, 1971).

Wendt, P. F.: *Real Estate Appraisal: Review and Outlook* (Athens: University of Georgia Press,
    1974).

Weston, J. F., and E. F. Brigham: *Essentials of Managerial Finance*, 3d ed. (Hinsdale, Ill.:
    Dryden, 1974).

U.S. Department of Housing and Urban Development: *Valuation Analysis for Home Mortgage
    Insurance: A HUD Handbook* (1973).

U.S. Housing and Home Finance Agency: *Mortgage Foreclosures in Six Metropolitan Areas*
    (1964).

Part Six

Investment Decisions

Previous parts have concentrated on the importance of real estate financing and decisions which must be made by lenders. The last two parts are concerned with the decisions which must be made by investors. What makes a property profitable? How can potential profits be compared for different investments? What should an investor consider when making decisions? When does it pay to invest?

Chapter 20 deals with the variety of measures used in investment analysis. The factor which has been at the heart of much real estate investment—tax shelters and other considerations—is discussed in Chapter 21. Chapter 22 explains how an investment property can be analyzed over its entire history. There are three principal phases of the investment cycle. Each affects an investment's profitability and desirability. In Chapter 23, we turn our attention to economic and environmental impact studies. The need for facts continues to grow at a rapid pace as more and more groups come to have a say in decisions concerning what form development may take. Because real estate investments last so far into the future, many of the assumptions entering into investment decisions may be wrong. Investors are developing techniques which enable them to see how sensitive their expected profits or losses may be to incorrect projections.

Chapter 20

Investment Analysis in Real Estate

Investment decisions range from snap judgments based on a hunch or a tip to careful evaluations based on months of skilled staff work and vast quantities of data. Most fall in between these extremes. In many cases, investors lack the time, money, or skills to do an adequate job of analysis. But even in the face of hasty or skimpy research, investors who possess a basic understanding of what good analysis should include—those who know which variables are significant—seem to exercise greater judgment and make better decisions. Even though they include the relevant factors only intuitively, their guesses and hunches are better because they know what to look for. They are not flying completely blind.

This chapter introduces the factors which enter into investment decisions. It discusses both what is needed in the investment process and some of the many measures used to compare and evaluate alternative investment possibilities.

STEPS IN THE ANALYSIS OF A REAL ESTATE INVESTMENT

Table 20-1 shows in broad detail the analytic process for a typical investment decision. There are three stages. Each may be repeated several times. If the initial projections appear unsatisfactory, plans or assumptions are changed to see how they affect the final results.

Table 20-1   The Investment Decision

	Phase I		
	Investment cycle		
	Origination	**Operations**	**Termination**
Projections of cash flow and after-tax income	The investment	Scheduled gross revenue	Net sales price
	Tax structure	Effective revenues	Taxable income
	Financing	Operating expense	Tax on sales income
	Total investment	Operating income	Use of funds
	After-tax investment	Debt service	Loans
	Sources of funds	Tax effects	
	Estimated return schedule		
	Cash flow	Cash flow	Cash flow
	Tax effect	Tax effect	Tax effect
	Total current benefit	Total current benefit	Total current benefit
	Phase II		
Measuring profitability and rates of return	Calculation of profitability and rate-of-return estimates Estimate of risks and sensitivity		
	Phase III		
The investment decision	Decision to purchase, negotiate, or reject: Adjust costs Increase potential income Alter financing Reallocate risks		

1   The first phase in the investment decision consists of a projection of the cash flow and after-tax income. This requires research—frequently in the field—to develop complete financial projections over the entire investment cycle. Forecasts are made of revenues, vacancies, and operating expenses by category. Mortgage terms and depreciation schedules are determined. An estimate is made of possible sales prices at different times in the future.

The tax effects of various possibilities must be estimated. Frequently this includes a plan to structure financial and other expenditures in such a way as to achieve the optimum after-tax results.

2   The second phase converts the projected income statement into a measure or measures of profitability together with an estimate of the risks involved. Investors have many competing opportunities. They must weigh them with respect to one another and with respect to risk-corrected returns. One of the primary advantages of real estate investment is that of leverage—the opportunity to use other people's money. The degree of leverage is a major factor determining the degree of risk involved. It can be manipulated to meet individual needs and desires.

Many investments continue to be based on inadequate analysis and unsophisticated techniques. Rules of thumb give a quick reading on a particular situation, but they furnish insufficient insight for making important investment decisions. Because so many do place undue reliance on simplistic approaches, the opportunity exists to achieve significant competitive advantages by using more sophisticated decision-making methods.

   3 The final phase is the actual investment decision or, more frequently, a decision to replan or renegotiate. Some investments such as securities or syndications are offered at fixed prices. In these cases, a decision will be made either to buy or to refuse in order to hold funds elsewhere.

   Many offers, however, include an opportunity to alter the contents of the package. The price or the financing details may be subject to negotiation. For proposed developments, the entire contents may be replanned. A suitable projection of benefits and risks makes such alterations possible. The answer need not be "yes" or "no." Aware investors have enough knowledge to be able to reshape the package to fit their needs.

COMPONENTS OF REAL ESTATE RETURN

To see how money is made in real estate investing, it is helpful to recognize the basic components of expected returns. For real estate properties, as for other investments, there is an initial commitment of funds. Next, as a result of operations, a flow of cash or income occurs. Finally, when the investment is terminated—or when it reverts—it is hoped that there will be an additional cash flow based on the sale of the property or a refinancing.

   Real estate returns depend upon five separate factors:

   1 The amount invested
   2 The amount, cost, and conditions of financing available
   3 The amount of revenues and expenses, or net income
   4 The final value or selling price of an investment
   5 The tax effects of the investment

   In Chapter 4 and throughout the intervening chapters, we have stressed the significance of leverage, or the relationship between the amount invested and the cost and conditions under which financing can be found. We have emphasized that decisions as to equity and debt create major profit possibilities.

   High profits can ensue if the amount of money invested is low compared with the total cost of a property, if large jumps occur in the net cash flow or investment yields, if the amount (multiplier) people are willing to pay for a given cash flow increases, or—best of all possible worlds—if all these occur together. Making certain that all these events do take place is the art of successful real estate investment.

Leverage, Services, and "Soft Dollars"

Profits are calculated on the effective amount invested over the period of ownership. Many real estate holdings require only a small investment. Owners frequently buy properties with very little of their own money. Some may borrow a great deal of the total cost (leverage). Others may acquire ownership rights in exchange for noncash services such as those furnished by a promoter, developer, broker, lawyer, or architect. Some may invest with money that otherwise would have to be paid in income taxes (soft dollars). When the amount of equity required for an investment is low, large percentage gains are possible. As a corollary, a large amount of property can be owned and controlled for not much cash.

Net Income

Net cash income is the difference between cash receipts and payments to others. Since with real property, net income is usually only a small part of the total, any increase in gross income with lesser changes in expenses will cause a large percentage rise in returns. Not untypically, a creative new owner might find a property with $100,000 in gross income and $98,000 in expenses. If, through better management and new ideas, this owner could raise the amount collected in rents to $125,000, while expenses went up only to $105,000 (not an unlikely change), actual net income would be multiplied tenfold. Returns would rise by 1,000 percent, as shown by:

$$\text{Net income} = \text{gross income} - \text{expenses}$$

$$\frac{\text{Final net income}}{\text{Initial net income}} \times 100 = \text{percent increase in income}$$

$$\frac{\$125,000 - \$105,000}{\$100,000 - \$\ 98,000} = \frac{\$20,000}{\$\ 2,000} \times 100 = 1,000\%$$

Risks   Yields are high on real property because risks are great. In the previous example, if expenses increased to $105,000 but income rose to only $103,000 (again, not an improbable change), a net profit would be turned into a loss. Sharp swings from profits to losses are frequent. Many factors can cause such shifts. Rents and other income are subject to cyclical fluctuations. Buildings or whole neighborhoods deteriorate or become obsolete. Wage and other costs rise. Competition intensifies. Interest rates, taxes, and other financial costs may shoot up.

Usually several claims on the operative income take precedence over those of the investors. These include debt service on the mortgage, reserves, and sponsor compensation. Some in the industry like to call the amount remaining after these have been taken care of "cash available for distribution."

The Final Selling Price, or Appreciation and Equity Buildup

Cash proceeds from a sale or from refinancing can be an important component of the yield on a property. An increase in cash realized at the termination of an investment over and above the initial equity investment can occur in several ways.

First, amortization of the mortgage debt on the property leads to a lower debt and an increase in the owner's share of the value. This is called *equity buildup*, and it can be an important component of return.

Second, if the operating income is improved over what was projected at the time of acquisition, the property will be worth more.

Third, the gross or net multiplier by which income is multiplied to give the sales price can rise. This can mean a higher sales price with a constant or even reduced income. If, in addition, an increase in income is multiplied by an increased multiplier, appreciation may be large.

As an example, assume that an investor has a property yielding a net income of $5,000 a year, for which she paid $25,000; that is, the net income multiplier and the price-earnings ratio are 5:

$$\text{Income multiplier} = \text{price-earnings ratio} = \frac{\text{price}}{\text{income}} = \frac{\$25,000}{\$\ 5,000} = 5$$

Obviously, she would profit greatly if she could find someone willing to pay her $10 for each dollar of this income. The property would sell for $50,000 ($5,000 × 10 = $50,000). Many large profits are due to changes of this kind in the income multiplier of properties. Depending on how much of her own money she used to purchase the property, her profit could run from several hundred to several thousand percent.

Some of such changes arise from shifting views of real estate as an investment. Inflations and depressions cause rapid moves in income multipliers. Threats of—or actual—tax changes may also have major consequences. When interest rates move, price-earnings ratios in the stock market shift. Repercussions will be felt in the related capitalization rates in the real estate market.

In addition to those changes in capitalization rates due to market forces, other movements can be brought about by owners. Investors may reduce the risk of income fluctuations or future shifts in selling prices. They may increase a property's market-ability. They may widen its appeal to those with a more favorable tax status. All actions of this type greatly alter income multipliers and are a source of large profits or losses.

Fourth, inflation must be included, although it is not really an independent factor. When prices rise, operating incomes should grow accordingly. In addition, expectations of further inflation should increase the net income multiplier. Inflation has an independent effect only if it is unanticipated. In that case, it should increase the rate at which a property appreciates.

Appreciation and equity buildup are both deferred and conditional returns. They are deferred in the sense that they are available only when a property is sold or re-financed. Their receipt may be further delayed if at the time of sale, secondary financing is involved. We have seen that when the expected rate of return is high, future income does not have a great impact on present values. Thus a dollar of appreciation to be received 10 years from now is worth only about 16 cents if the rate of return is 20 percent. Furthermore, given the risks associated with any investment in today's dynamic and uncertain business environment, we have few guarantees that present values will not change dramatically, nor is the direction of change at all certain.

Tax Considerations

Tax considerations often play an important role in real estate investments and must be included in all cash-flow and income analysis.

1   An investor may be able to acquire property with funds that are all or par-tially tax-deductible and thereby pay fewer taxes. Such tax savings reduce the effective costs of an investment.

2   In addition, the cash flow from operations may be sheltered from taxes as a result of depreciation allowances. (These concepts are explained in Chapter 21.) Cash income received without a tax obligation has a multiplied value.

3 Furthermore, in some cases the tax losses exceed the property's cash flow and thus shelter other income as well. This again increases the total return.

4 Finally, at the time of sale the increase in value may be taxed at a capital gains rate which is lower than that applicable to ordinary income.

To recapitulate: Investors make money by buying properties with good potential operating incomes. They may increase both their risks and their returns by using borrowed money and paying for it at a rate below the rate of return on the property. Favorable tax consequences may be sought by buying with largely tax-deductible dollars, by sheltering cash flow and possibly other income from taxes, and by paying the lower capital gains rates at sale. During the period in which an investor owns a property, he or she hopes the operating income will increase. If the property is sold at a price based on a more favorable capitalization rate, profits will be raised still more.

While all these possibilities exist, they do not necessarily make an investment logical. Investors should seek properties on which returns will be acceptable without the need of advantageous financing arrangements, tax structuring, operating income improvements, and gains resulting from a shift in capitalization rates. Investors will be far safer if they depend on a sound projection of a good operating income at the time they invest. If, in addition to a favorable income outlook, all the other factors turn out to be combined in a single deal, the returns may be spectacular.

THE CASH-FLOW AND AFTER-TAX STATEMENT

Investment analysis depends upon projecting the amount of money which will have to be invested, the amount of money which will be received back, and the timing of expenditures and receipts and upon analyzing the risks that the projections will be wrong. This means that an investor needs a basic statement of future outlays and income.

Good investment decisions require the best and fullest possible projections to show the complete cash-flow and tax consequences for the proposed investments. Such projections are called *pro forma financial statements*. A pro forma statement in accounting is an estimated or illustrative income statement, in contrast to one reporting actual facts.

Table 20-2 outlines the type of information an investor would like to have in order to make a sound decision. The projection and analysis of such financial statements are at the heart of all real estate investment. We discuss some of the problems of obtaining these data and their analysis through case examples in Chapters 22 and 23. These show both how the statements can be prepared and how they are handled in the best-managed enterprises. The amount of actual time and effort expended in preparing such tables varies greatly depending on the size and complexity of a particular commitment. In smaller and less important investments, many shortcuts may be taken. This will also be true of firms with unskilled management or ones that are out to sell regardless of the value to the buyer. On the other hand, in a large number of complex developments, the actual analysis and data collected far surpass those presented in the outline.

Some critics argue that reliable projections are difficult, if not impossible, to make. Good projections require collecting a fair amount of data. While difficult, this can be accomplished, and it is worthwhile. Good analysts believe that they can make more accurate predictions for real estate investments than can be produced by those fore-

Table 20-2 Income Statements

Origination	Operations	Termination
Investment schedule:	Scheduled gross revenues	Gross selling price
Land	Minus vacancy and collection	Minus selling costs
Building	loss	Net sales price
Personal property	Effective gross revenue	
Financial payments		Total investment
Organizational expenses	Minus operating expenses	
Acquisition costs	Operating income	Minus depreciation
Reserves and working capital		Tax basis at sale
Total investment	Minus venture administration	
	Minus sponsor's participation	Taxable income:
Minus tax effects	Cash flow before debt ser-	Recapture
After-tax investment	vice and reserves	Capital gain
		Total
Financial aspects:	Minus debt service	
Mortgages	Minus reserves	Capital gains tax
Annual debt service	Cash flow before taxes	Recapture tax
Downpayment sources		Total tax due
	Cash flow before debt service	
	and reserves	Proceeds of sale:
	Minus interest	Net sales price
	Minus depreciation	Minus tax
	Taxable income	Minus mortgages
		Net cash flow on
	Tax effect (for specific effec-	sale
	tive tax bracket)	
	Plus cash flow before taxes	
	Total current benefit	

casting corporate earnings or future stock market prices. However, in this as in other financial fields, what may be possible far exceeds what is commonly done.

Investment Cycle

The form of the statements in Table 20-2 is based on the belief that real estate ventures can best be evaluated in terms of the full investment cycle. This cycle consists of three phases: origination of the venture, its management and operations, and its termination, including disposition of the property. Because the financial and tax consequences of the factors that enter into a deal are both subtle and complex, a decision which neglects them and uses only part of the relevant information may well be erroneous. Each part of the cycle contains information necessary for a proper analysis of the others and for the final decision. This is why careful analysts will base their final opinions only on a careful study of the whole cycle.

Origination The origination phase includes planning and organizing both the entity which will own and operate the property and the buying or developing of the property itself. As the first column of Table 20-2 shows, numerous factors affect the amount of investment and actual funds required from the investors.

First in time, an estimate of the cost of the project must be developed, based on its design if it is to be a new construction or on the purchase price if an existing building is being offered. Various other costs must also be estimated, as shown in the table. A second type of decision involves the tax structuring of the entity. The next chapter deals with these problems in detail; however, the actual tax effects, and therefore the net after-tax investment, will vary greatly depending on how they are dealt with.

The final, and for many purposes the most important, set of decisions deals with financing. These decisions take into consideration the source of funds; the number and type of mortgages (as well as the funds available from investors and promoters); the rate at which the funds are to be available; and, finally, the annual constant (or the amount of debt service and the leverage) which will have to be met throughout the life of the investment.

In accordance with the specific decisions made with respect to these items, the analyst carries over from the origination schedule information as to total investment, financing, depreciation allowances, and the tax structure.

Operations   The operations phase involves management of both the property and the venture. Special considerations that merit attention are listed in the income statement found in the second column of Table 20-2. The critical factors of this statement include scheduled gross revenues, effective gross revenues, operating expenses and income, debt service, the tax effect, and cash flow before and after taxes.

As with other businesses, an income property requires management and working capital. While some investors manage both the venture (the overall financial and tax aspects and dividend and other payments) and the actual property, more and more owners look to outside organizations for these services. Fees will have to be paid for managing both the property and the venture or for managing either. Often there will be an incentive compensation arrangement, called a *sponsor participation*.

The bottom line of the financial statement shows the total current benefit the owners may expect from operations. This line will vary for each year of the investment.

Termination   The final phase of the investment involves the disposition of the property and the dissolution of the venture. Usually properties are disposed of in one of three ways:

1   An outright sale occurs, in which the new buyer pays cash and either assumes the existing mortgage or arranges new financing.
2   The venture agrees to provide some of the financing by accepting part of its payment in the form of a note or mortgage.
3   The property is exchanged for another property.

The critical parts of the income statement for termination, as shown in the third column of Table 20-2, include the sales price, the calculation of taxable income, the question of whether a monetary claim or another property carries into a further phase, and the determination of the net cash flow to the owners from this phase.

If either an exchange or financing from the owners is used to sell the property, the investment cycle will continue. The venture does not terminate; rather, a new estimate must be made for the new form of operations, and a final statement of the eventual termination must be estimated.

Rate-of-Return Schedule

The bottom lines showing both the cash flow and the tax benefits for each year and each part of the investment cycle must be transferred to a rate-of-return schedule, as outlined in Chapter 6. Table 20-3 is a sample of such a schedule. This final schedule is the critical one for determining the potential profitability of the venture and making the final investment decision. The preparation of this schedule completes the first phase of the investment process.

Table 20-3 Example of Pro Forma Summary Financial Statements

Investment, 1975

Price of building	$1,000,000
Minus mortgage	900,000
Downpayment	$ 100,000
Points on mortgage	27,000
Initial expenses and reserves	51,000
Total equity	$ 178,000
Prepaid interest	81,748
Minus tax benefits	54,374
After-tax investment (total current benefit)	$ 205,374

Operating statement

	(Net operating income) Cash flow before debt service (1)	Cash flow before reserves (2)	(Total current benefit) Cash flow after taxes (3)	Cash flow after taxes plus equity buildup (4)
1976	$88,000	$81,851	$79,851	$86,000
1977	89,760	1,863	39,305	46,031
1978	91,300	3,403	37,070	44,426
1979	93,500	5,603	36,294	44,341
1980	95,150	7,253	36,426	45,227
1981	97,350	9,453	45,063	54,690
Average per year	$92,510	$18,238	$45,668	$53,453

Cash flow at termination, 1981

Selling price	$1,062,000
Net sales price	998,280
Cash flow	$ 154,986
After-tax cash flow	21,516

Because initial payments may be paid in over an extended period (staged) and because the termination phase may extend for several years if a debt or exchange property is accepted in partial payment, the rate-of-return schedule may show both outlays and incomes from each phase in several years. This is illustrated in the schematic presentation shown below.

Income in Pro Forma Statements

Phase	Years									
	1	2	3	4	5	6	7	8	9	10
Origination	x	x	x							
Operations		x	x	x	x	x	x			
Termination							x	x	x	x

The property analyzed in Table 20-3 is simpler. The investment and final benefits occur in single years. They are not spread out.

CALCULATIONS OF PROFITABILITY

When investors examine a proposed real estate investment, they want to know whether it is likely to give them the profit they want and whether it will present a better use of their funds than they could expect from putting their money *elsewhere*. Every real estate investment is competitive with other real estate ventures and with short-term money-market assets, long-term financial assets, and other equity investments. The problem of investment analysis is to make a successful choice from among all available opportunities.

Indexes of Profitability

Ventures of different sizes, duration, and character are offered to investors. Real estate analysis constructs measures of profitability which summarize these different factors for each investment. With a given measure, an investor can compare alternative investments in order to choose the most profitable one. In recent years there has been a steady increase in the sophistication with which real estate investors have approached this problem of developing profitability measures.

The desirability of an investment depends on many different things. All must be estimated by making projections of the future. For owner-occupied properties there are flows of rental services from the available space, future expenditures, and an expected receipt of cash at time of sale. For income properties there is also cash flow, plus certain tax benefits, plus potential income at termination. The analysis of the profitability of a purchase requires balancing these expected benefits against the initial and all future money payments. The usefulness of a measure depends on both the soundness of its underlying theory and its ease of application.

Profitability analysis consists of translating pro forma income statements, such as Table 20-3, for all three phases of the investment cycle into profitability indexes which can be compared with one another and with past investment experience. With the advent of the computer, many possible indexes can be calculated, each based on a different set of assumptions as to the future. In fact, separate indexes are often calculated for a wide number of assumptions about the economy. Separate calculations are also made using different assumptions as to when the investment will be sold. When taxes play a significant role, profitability may be extremely sensitive to when a property is sold because allowable depreciation and expected capital gains may differ widely over time.

Risks

Calculations of profitability indexes alone are not sufficient for a complete investment analysis. In addition to its expected profitability, each venture has a degree of risk attached to it. The risk includes the possibility that it will fail and that some or all of the investor's funds will be lost or, on the other hand, the possibility that the project will be far more successful than its initial projection. How great the risk is and what probabilities there are of a very high return may play as large a part in the selection of a venture by an investor as the most probable or expected profit. Some investors want to trade potential profits for safety, while others may be willing to take much higher risks if there is some possibility of tremendous gains.

Furthermore, the type of risks and what they depend on can play an important role in an investor's overall strategy. When he puts together his entire investment portfolio, he will often find that he can reduce his total risks by spreading his investments over different types of ventures and by putting funds into markets which are expected to react in different ways depending on what is happening in the economy to cause changes in the expected profits.

Opportunities for Improvement

A potential investor should expect a good deal more from investment analysis than simply a comparison of profitabilities and risk. When many real estate ventures are analyzed, it often appears that one or two factors are especially critical for their success. When in an analysis this becomes clear, investors can increase their efforts to make certain that the critical assumptions are sound and that the conditions surrounding the investment are made as favorable as possible. They need not be satisfied with the initial analysis. They can greatly improve their prospects by focusing on key variables. The investment analysis should aid investors in determining which are the most significant factors and what possibilities exist for their improvement.

THE MORE TRADITIONAL MEASURES

The development of the field of investment has seen a rapid increase in the number of available measures of profitability. In the construction of these measures, there is usually a trade-off between simplicity of calculation and understanding and the total volume of information furnished. Each investor can decide whether minimal information obtainable through simple procedures will suffice or whether he or she desires more complete information requiring greater effort to put together as well as to use and understand.

Free and Clear Return

One of the simplest measures of profitability is the free and clear rate of return. This is defined as the net operating income (that is, before debt service) divided by the total purchase price (equity plus all mortgages). In most cases the estimates are based on a simple average expected return over a number of years. As an example, the property discussed in Table 20-3 shows an average net operating income of $92,510 (column 1) and a $1,078,000 purchase price ($178,000 equity + $900,000 mortgage debt). This means it would have an 8.6 percent free and clear return, calculated as follows:

$$\frac{\$92,510}{\$1,078,000} = 8.6\%$$

Broker's Equity Return

Broker's equity return is defined as the actual cash-flow return to the investor divided by his equity investment. This definition is frequently used in brokers' offices to describe a particular property. In examining such offers it must be recognized that a rate of return on an equity will vary greatly depending on how the cash flow and the equity are defined. Thus, for the expected cash flow, the following different calculations may be used:

Cash flow
Cash flow plus after-tax effects
Cash flow plus after-tax effects plus equity buildup
Cash flow plus after-tax effects plus equity buildup plus appreciation

Similarly, for the equity investment the definition could include:

The difference between the quoted price and the nominal mortgage
The initial equity required, including such other items as points on the mortgage, underwriting commissions, and legal fees
The original cash downpayment, including such other items as prepaid interest, underwriting commissions, and legal fees adjusted for the tax effect of the deductible items

Many other definitions of cash flow and equity investment could be added to these lists and may be encountered in particular offers.

To illustrate the impact of alternative definitions, Table 20-4 shows different measures of broker's equity return based on the information in Table 20-3. In column 1 of Table 20-4 we show cash flows or dollar benefits averaged for the 6 years of the ownership. The first row shows the cash flow before reserves, or the average from column 2 of Table 20-3. The second row shows the cash flow plus the tax effects. The third row adds, to the cash flow plus tax effects, the payments on principal or equity buildup, column 4 of Table 20-3. Finally, the fourth row adds to the cash flow and tax effects the actual appreciation shown after its tax effects also. This adds to the average cash flow from operations the cash flow from termination shown in the lower portion of Table 20-3, also averaged over the 6-year holding period. It differs from the previous row by including the actual estimated appreciation after taxes, which is less than the payments on mortgage principal.

Column 2 of Table 20-4 shows at the top the amount of the equity, assuming that no prepaid interest is paid, but including the actual downpayment, the various costs to purchase, and the points paid on the mortgage. The remaining figures in the column are the calculated broker's equity return. To avoid the problem of the prepayment of interest and its return, the broker's equity return for this column is figured only for cash flows and benefits in the years 1977 to 1981. Column 3 adds to the downpayment the pre-

Table 20-4   Example of Broker's Equity Return

	Cash-flow benefit in dollars (1)	Percent return on downpayment of $178,000* (2)	Percent return on downpayment and prepayment of $259,748 (3)	Percent return on after-tax downpayment and prepayment of $205,374 (4)
Cash flow before reserves	$18,238	3.1	7.0	8.9
Cash flow plus tax effect	45,668	21.8	17.6	22.2
Cash flow plus tax effect plus equity buildup	53,453	26.4	20.6	26.0
Cash flow plus tax effect plus actual appreciation	49,254	24.2	19.0	24.0

*Calculated on data for 1977–1981 only.

payment of interest, while column 4 gives credit for the tax shelter achieved with the prepayment of interest.

We see that the figure used for the downpayment can vary from $178,000 to approximately $260,000, while the cash flow can range from $18,000 to $53,000 per year depending on which definition is used. Again, depending on how the individual figures are combined, the estimate of the broker's equity return is seen to vary from 3.1 to 26.4 percent.

Obviously, none of these figures is totally correct. Each contains different information that may be more or less useful to the prospective investor. More important, however, the investor who receives an offer with the broker's equity return calculated and who uses it for comparisons with other properties must be sure that the figure is calculated in the same manner for the alternative investments. Since the object of a profitability figure is to allow such comparisons, major errors will occur if the definitions are not identical for the properties being compared. Great caution should be taken in using these measures to avoid being misled by them.

Payback Period

The payback period for an investment is the number of years required to recover the original cash investment. It is the ratio of the initial investment to the annual cash flows for the recovery period. The payback period will depend on whether tax effects are taken into account. For example, from Table 20-4, if we take the actual cash investment and cash flow, we find that the payback-period estimate is

$$\frac{259,748}{18,238} = 14.2 \text{ years}$$

On the other hand, if we consider the tax-shelter effects, we find

$$\frac{205,374}{45,668} = 4.4 \text{ years}$$

Both calculations are approximate because there are slight differences in the annual returns. The tremendous difference between the two, however, makes clear the major effect on real estate investments of considering the amount of tax shelter.

The payback method usefully identifies the period of time over which invested funds are at risk. However, investors are interested in receiving a return or profit beyond the mere recovery of their investment. Using the criterion that one should choose investments with the shortest payback period, it is possible to select an investment that brings back the invested funds rapidly but leads to no profit. This criterion can lead to the rejection of an investment which has a slower payback but which generates substantial profits through continued payments that extend well beyond the payback of the initial investment.

Appraisal

In Chapter 18 we discussed appraisal as a basic method of valuation used in real estate investment. In effect, it too is a profitability index, but one that asks a somewhat different question from the ones posed by most of the other measures. Appraisal asks: Given the projected cash flow of a property, what is its present value? As we saw, this value is found by capitalizing the expected cash flow on the basis of a selected capitalization rate. The rate selected must reflect the risks of the projected flow as well as the rate of return which an average or a specific investor expects to earn on his or her property.

We have seen from Tables 20-3 and 20-4 that the rate of return will vary greatly depending on how one defines the cash flow. It will also vary with the question of recapture, payments on the debt, and tax benefits to the investor. Usually appraisals take account of very few of these factors. They look at the property more as a security from the point of view of the lender. They consider primarily the capitalization of the net operating income of the property and its expected net selling price.

Returning to Table 20-3, we see that during the 6 years of the sample property, its net operating income is expected to average approximately $92,510 a year, and its net selling price is expected to be about $1,000,000. Using a capitalization rate of 10 percent, these estimates give a current value of around $965,000. At a capitalization rate of 9 percent, the present value is slightly over $1,000,000.

The use of appraisal seems to be far more practical from the point of view of lenders or property tax appraisers than from that of potential investors. Investors are far more concerned with how much money they must put up, their leverage, their after-tax benefits, and their risks. Trying to incorporate these in the capitalization rate creates a number of difficulties. Seldom can the actual risks or their causes be made explicit. Instead, they are incorporated in the overall capitalization rate. Many investors would prefer that their problems and questions be made explicit and brought out specifically in the process of investment analysis.

PRESENT-VALUE MEASURES OF RETURN

We have criticized the techniques of profitability measurement discussed so far because they do not furnish the investor with a measure of profitability that is accurate enough to be used in investment analysis and actual investment decisions. What factors would a better index contain? Among other things, an improved measure would do the following:

1 Include the amount, timing, and full tax consequences of the initial investment.
2 Take account of all cash flows from operations over the entire life of the investment.
3 Consider all tax effects, both tax shelter and tax liability, over the entire life of the investment.
4 Account for the cash proceeds (or obligations, as the case may be) from the expected sale. All tax considerations should be taken into account, including the capital gains tax as well as the ordinary income tax on the recapture of any excess of accelerated depreciation.
5 Recognize the time value of money.
6 Express the return as an index that permits comparison of projects. It is desirable for projects involving different amounts of invested capital, separate tax consequences, and a variety of termination dates to be readily comparable.
7 Incorporate relative risks and potential rewards in the index.

Pro forma financial statements, such as Table 20-3, enable us to take into account the amount, timing, and full tax consequences of all cash flows over the full life of the investment. More sophisticated methods of analysis use these data while also introducing the time value of money. They express the expected returns in the form of indexes to permit comparisons. They also allow risks to be incorporated into the investment decisions.

In Chapter 6 we discussed the concept of the time value of money and the calculations of present values and internal rates of return based on the discounting of future payments. These concepts enable us to calculate two different types of profitability indexes. Both types are used, with some analysts preferring one, and some the other.

Important for each is the selection of an appropriate discount factor or cutoff point for internal rates of return. The selection by an investor will involve a process similar to that utilized in picking capitalization rates. The rate of return will depend on such factors as what similar properties are earning, the investor's objectives and strategy, current interest rates, economic conditions, and the degree of risk involved.

Calculating the Indexes

In Table 20-5, the actual calculations of profitability indexes from the data of Table 20-3 are illustrated. It is assumed that after careful study, the investor has selected 12 percent as the desired discount factor and cutoff point for internal rates of return.

Present Value Column 1 of Table 20-5 lists the total benefits from Table 20-3. The initial cash outlay is the after-tax investment. The cash flow is that which includes tax benefits (column 3 of Table 20-3), with the after-tax cash flow from termination added in for 1981. The 12 percent discount factor for each year is multiplied by each year's cash flow to get its present value, shown in column 3 of Table 20-5.

When these are added together, we note that the benefit stream from this investment has a positive cash flow of $1,107. An investor would find that he would receive an after-tax yield of over 12 percent on his investment.

Profitability Index   The present-value data are frequently translated into an index form by dividing the present values of all positive flows by all negative flows. Assuming a cash outlay only in the first year, this benefit-cost ratio can also be considered as the present value of future returns over the initial cash outlay.

An actual calculation is shown in the middle portion of Table 20-5. The positive present values of column 3 (upper portion of the table) are added together and then divided by the initial cash outlay. The ratio or profitability index is 1.005. This again reflects the fact that the investment is profitable at a 12 percent discount rate. An index below 1 would mean that the investment would not be earning 12 percent.

The profitability index (PI) can be used to compare different investments, but it runs into problems if the cash outlays are of different sizes. Thus we would normally select an investment with a PI of 1.2 over one with an index of 1.1. But what if the first one was a property with an outlay of $10,000, while the second had an outlay of $50,000? We can easily calculate that the dollar profit in the first case is $2,000, while in the second it is $5,000. In both cases these profits are over and above the 12 percent return on the investment. In such cases, the choice will depend on the investor's capital position and general investment strategy rather than on a simple comparison of the profitability indexes.

Table 20-5   Profitability Measures

		Present value	
Year	Total benefits (1)	Discount factor (12%) (2)	Present value (3)
1975	(−$205,374)	1.0000	(−$205,374)
1976	$ 79,851	.8929	$ 71,299
1977	39,305	.7972	31,334
1978	37,070	.7118	26,386
1979	36,294	.6355	23,065
1980	36,426	.5674	20,668
1981	66,579	.5066	33,729
Total	$ 90,551		+$ 1,107

Profitability index

Profitability index (PI) $= \dfrac{\text{present value of positive payments}}{\text{present value of negative payments}}$

$$= \frac{206,481}{205,374} = 1.005$$

Internal rate of return

$$205,374 = \frac{79,851}{(1 + i)} + \frac{39,305}{(1 + i)^2} + \frac{37,070}{(1 + i)^3} + \frac{36,294}{(1 + i)^4} + \frac{36,426}{(1 + i)^5} + \frac{66,579}{(1 + i)^6}$$

Internal rate of return $= i = 12.21\%$

Internal Rate of Return We saw in Chapter 6 that the calculation of the internal rate of return is another way of using the time value of money in calculating yields. Instead of selecting a particular discount factor, an investor can ask: Given the required cash outlays and expected cash flows, what discount factor would cause the investment and the future stream of benefits to be equal?

Table 20-5 presents the calculation of the internal rate of return for this case. The discount factor which makes the present positive and negative values of column 1 (upper portion of the table) exactly equal is 12.21 percent. The investor can compare the potential rate of return on this investment with the potential rates of others. In such comparisons, it is necessary to adjust for relative risks.

Comparison of Present Value and Internal Rate of Return

Arguments often arise as to whether it is better to compare present values or internal rates of return. In most cases, it makes no difference. A comparison of two properties using either method will lead to the identical choice. Thus in Table 20-5, both the profitability index based on present values and that based on the 12.2 percent internal rate of return indicate that the investment is worthwhile.

However, occasionally differences will be found. The two indexes can lead to opposing conclusions, particularly if the cash flows are uneven and the internal rate of return turns out to be considerably removed from the discount factor used in present-value calculations.

Thus it is possible to have a project with a present value of $18,000 at a discount rate of 10 percent and an internal rate of return of 20 percent, while another project might have a $10,000 present value at a 10 percent discount rate but with a 25 percent rate of return.

If we could choose only one, which should it be—the property with the higher present value or that with the higher internal rate of return? To decide, we must recognize what causes this difference. It is the same problem encountered in the selection of different capitalization rates, noted on page 99.

The internal-rate-of-return calculation assumes that the cash flow received in any year can be reinvested at the calculated rate of return until the end of the investment. The present-value procedure, on the other hand, implies either that the funds received as cash flow will be used elsewhere at the then-existing market rate or that if they are reinvested in the project, it will be at the discount rate initially used for calculating the present value.

Thus where a conflict arises, the present-value procedure assumes that the reinvestment would be at 10 percent for both projects, whereas when the internal rate of return is calculated, it would be at 20 percent for one and 25 percent for the other. The fact that flows are uneven and arise at different periods in the future causes the conflict, with the two criteria suggesting opposite choices.

Which method is best for an investor depends greatly on his or her assumption as to which rate is more likely to apply at the time of reinvestment. Many observers believe that this reinvestment factor makes the present-value calculations preferable. They consider it less likely that an internal rate of return calculated now will continue unchanged in the future than that an investor will maintain his or her current rate of discount.

Furthermore, in the present-value technique, individuals use their own particular cost of capital. As a result, calculations may show that it will pay them to switch investments, whereas if the internal-rate-of-return calculation is used, they might not recognize an opportunity for greater profit. For example, an investor with a very high discount factor might find that an investment will have a positive present value for only a few years. At that point it could be sold to another investor with a lower discount factor. The sale would be worthwhile to both—the profitability index would show at that point a negative present value for one and a positive present value for the other. Meanwhile, the internal rate of return from the property would be the same for both investors.

A major advantage of the internal rate of return, on the other hand, is that it does not require that a discount rate be specified in advance. The rate of return arises in the course of the investment analysis of each project. Because the indexes are comparable, it is simpler to compare the internal rates of return for all possible projects. Furthermore, while the problems of uneven rates of flow and reinvestment are theoretically significant, they can be solved rather easily through various additional computer calculations.

SUMMARY

The heart of real estate investment analysis is the projection of pro forma financial statements. These are required for each phase of the investment cycle. Assumptions as to the buildup of equity can loom large in estimating profits. Because taxes are so significant in real estate ventures, they must also be included.

The pro forma statements must be translated into statements of potential profits or yields. Many methods have been devised for this purpose. Among the more traditional ones are those involving free and clear return, broker's equity return, payback period, and appraisals. In using these methods, it must be remembered that they are very sensitive to slightly different definitions; they also tend to ignore the time value of money, and in averaging over years, they may wash out possibly significant factors.

Most modern investment analysis uses either the present-value or the internal-rate-of-return concept in calculating potential profits and yields. While some experts believe strongly in the advantages of one over the other, in most cases both will lead to similar decisions. These measures allow specific inclusion of an investor's individual tax situation and the value of money to him. They can be simplified by shortcuts to the point where they are no harder to calculate than the earlier methods. Of course, the more shortcuts are used, the greater the danger of missing information.

QUESTIONS AND PROBLEMS

1 What are the deficiencies of traditional profitability measures such as broker's equity return?
2 Why is the investment life cycle concept preferred over looking at just one year?
3 What characteristics should a profitability measure have?
4 Describe the component elements of the investment life cycle.
5 Some investors think that to make an investment decision all they need do is select the right profitability measure and compute the return. Discuss.

6 What are the principal factors which influence the amount of cash received when a property is sold?
7 What is a pro forma financial statement?
8 Explain what is meant by the payback period for an investment.
9 Explain the major differences between the use of internal rate of return and present-value calculations in determining the desirability of an investment.
10 A property costs $300,000. After all tax considerations, it returns $50,000 a year for 5 years, and returns $200,000 upon sale at the end of the sixth year. Assuming a 12 percent discount factor, what is its present value?

Chapter 21

Tax Considerations

Tax considerations are important in most investments; in real estate investment they are often paramount. No astute real estate investor makes decisions without a careful analysis of all tax implications. Some investments that look unattractive on initial analysis are quite appealing when seen on an after-tax basis. On the other hand, some good pretax returns are substantially diluted when taxes are taken into account. Real estate investments that offer a "tax shelter" or "tax saving" may possess sharply increased profitability. Because they allow a real estate investor to take tax deductions today in exchange for future tax obligations, he or she profits from an increased current cash flow (the net cash difference between revenues and expenses currently available for spending or other investment). Since money available today is worth more than the same amount of money in the future, the profits from tax shelters are real, especially when interest rates or yields are high. Furthermore, if the future obligation can be shifted to a lower tax bracket, profits may be further enhanced.

Tax laws and tax rulings are changed frequently. Rates and deductions are restructured. Investors must both understand the general theories of tax impacts on real estate values and be able to relate these general concepts to recent and prospective changes in the tax system. As new tax proposals are adopted, they change the value of a property to specific individuals and consequently the demand for properties and the prices at which they sell. The mere consideration of tax proposals by Congress or the IRS will influence present values depending on how the proposed changes would affect the factors discussed in this chapter.

For these reasons, a special study of tax consequences is an integral part of investment analysis. Tax impacts on profitability are affected by decisions (frequently called *elections*) that must be made in planning for each phase of the investment cycle. However, the actual impact of taxes will vary among individuals depending on their personal tax situation. For this reason, the financial flows shown in Table 22-2 carefully differentiate between cash flows, taxable income, and total tax benefits.

TAX SAVINGS

Tax savings depend upon careful tax planning (structuring). They can be gained in several spheres:

1 Some payments on investments may be tax-deductible, thus reducing the investor's current tax liability and lowering the effective cost of the investment. For example, if an investor with a 50 percent effective tax acquires a $100,000 property with a $20,000 cash payment, all of which is tax-deductible, the effective after-tax cost of buying the property is only $10,000.

2 Because cash received from an investment may not be immediately taxable, an investor has more money available to invest or spend elsewhere. A piece of real estate pays $1,000 in current tax-sheltered income. Investors in a 40 percent bracket retain this $1,000, whereas they would have only $600 left if they had had to pay taxes on a $1,000 receipt.

3 On occasion not only will the actual cash income from the property be sheltered, but so will income from other sources. Thus a property may have a $1,000 cash flow and a $2,000 tax loss. The $1,000 in cash from the property is sheltered from taxes, and the unused additional tax loss of $1,000 shelters an equal amount of other income. The 40 percent tax-bracket investor saves $800 in taxes.

However, it must be constantly held in mind that current tax deductions which exceed actual losses in economic value may become taxable income later. Real estate investors do not avoid income taxes; they shift the time of payment. This deferral of payment is valuable since investors have the use of their funds during that period. If an investor's tax bracket is lower when the tax must be paid, an additional benefit is realized.

Cash Flows and Taxable Income

A tax shelter exists when current cash flow exceeds taxable income. Depreciation is what makes a shelter possible. *Depreciation* is the deduction from accounting income for the possible loss in value of a property from wear and tear, time, and obsolescence. It serves to allocate the cost of an asset over its useful life. The depreciation deduction is a bookkeeping expense that reduces the taxable income but not the cash flow.

The tax deductions can be enhanced by the use of borrowed money. The tax law permits the owner of a property to take depreciation on the total investment including that part paid for with borrowed funds as well as that paid for with his own money.

Thus an investor may receive cumulative deductions equal to several times his initial equity investment.

The amount of tax shelter can be found by comparing the flows of cash and taxable income. This is illustrated in Table 21-1.

Table 21-1 shows a property with $1,000 in cash revenue; $400 in cash operating expense; payments on debt service of $500, including $400 in interest and $100 for principal; and a depreciation allowance of $450. The cash flow is $100; the taxable income is a negative, or minus $250.

The significant differences between the columns are in the treatment of the depreciation allowance and the principal payments. The taxable income is reduced by depreciation, which in theory reflects that portion of an asset used up in the period. Because the depreciation deduction is a bookkeeping expense and does not reduce the cash income, it is possible, as shown in Table 21-1, to have simultaneously a negative taxable income and a positive cash flow.

On the other hand, principal payments to amortize the outstanding debt have the opposite effect of depreciation: they reduce the cash income but do not reduce taxable income. Just as depreciation is a noncash but a tax expense (lowering taxable compared with cash income), principal payments can be thought of as a cash but a nontax income item (lowering cash compared with taxable income). Of course, the principal payments build up the investor's equity position, and when the property is sold or refinanced, part or all of them may be realized (thus the derivation of the term "equity buildup"). Still, the immediate effect of principal payments is that taxable income is not lowered, while the cash income needed to pay the resulting tax liability is reduced.

The relationship between cash and taxable income depends on how depreciation compares with the principal payment. Frequently the base for depreciation will approximate the mortgage indebtedness. Both figures are often in the range of 70–80 percent of the total purchase price. Further, there may be a similarity between the building's anticipated useful life and the term of the mortgage. In such cases the critical consideration is the timing of these noncash expense and income items, since over time their totals will be roughly equal.

Table 21-1   Comparison of Cash and Tax Income Statements

	Cash flow	Tax flow
Revenue	$1,000	$1,000
Operating expense	−400	−400
Operating income	$ 600	$ 600
Mortgage payments:		
Interest	−400	−400
Principal	−100	
Cash flow	$ 100	
Depreciation		−450
Taxable income		$ −250

TAX RATE

How much one has to pay in taxes, or preferably saves, depends on the amount of taxable income, the legal form of ownership, and the tax rate. Corporation tax rates have been 20 percent on the first $25,000 of income and 48 percent on all income above $25,000. Partnerships and REITs are not tax-paying entities. Instead, income from them, as well as from individual ownerships, is included in an investor's personal income tax return.

An individual's tax depends on total gross income, number of dependents, and amount of personal deductions. Additional benefits are offered to special classes of people, including the blind and those over age 65. Most taxpayers, however, will use a tax table such as that in Table 21-2, which is for a married couple filing a joint return.

The calculation of one's tax liability is a two-step process. One finds the amount of tax that applies at the bottom of his or her particular income bracket. The bracket also has an indicated tax rate which is applied to the amount by which the taxpayer's income exceeds the base level for that bracket. For example, consider an income of $33,000. Table 21-2 shows the tax liability to be $8,660 plus 42 percent of the amount over the $32,000 base level of this bracket. Thus on the $1,000 incremental income above $32,000, the tax is $420 (42 percent of $1,000), for a total tax liability of $9,080 ($8,660 + $420).

These rates apply to the taxpayer's ordinary income. When income results from a capital gain, taxes are calculated at the lower capital gains rate. For a corporation, the maximum capital gains rate is 30 percent. For individuals, capital gains are reduced by 50 percent before the appropriate ordinary income rate is applied. Furthermore, there is an alternative computation. If an individual's total capital gains in any year do not exceed $50,000, the maximum rate is 25 percent of the capital gains.

Under the 1969 Tax Reform Act, there is a minimum tax of 10 percent on "tax-preference" items in excess of a statutory exemption. For real estate investors, the primary tax-preference items are (1) the excess of accelerated depreciation over straight-line depreciation and (2) one-half of the excess of net long-term capital gains over net short-term capital losses. As a practical matter, the minimum tax is not significant for most investors. However, revisions in the minimum tax are probable since it has failed to ensure that all taxpayers pay a seemingly reasonable portion of their income in taxes.

Effective Tax Rate   A dangerous tendency exists for promoters and investors alike to talk in abstract terms such as the "50 percent tax bracket," when in fact such a rate may be totally inapplicable to the particular investor. Tax planning should be based on the tax rates that actually apply for a specific investment and investor. The "myth" of the 50 percent bracket must be recognized, and generalization must not be substituted for analysis of the facts in specific situations.

The effective tax rate is the average amount of a taxpayer's income paid as income taxes. The effective marginal tax rate for an investment is the average amount that would be paid in taxes for the brackets sheltered by the investment, *not* the marginal tax rate for the top part alone. The effective rate is the critical one in analyzing tax

Table 21-2   Tax Rate Table

Rate Table for Married Individuals Filing Joint Returns and Certain Surviving Spouses*

Taxable income				Tax	On excess
Over	Not over	Pay	+	rate, %	over
	$ 1,000			14	
$ 1,000	2,000	$ 140		15	$ 1,000
2,000	3,000	290		16	2,000
3,000	4,000	450		17	3,000
4,000	8,000	620		19	4,000
8,000	12,000	1,380		22	8,000
12,000	16,000	2,260		25	12,000
16,000	20,000	3,260		28	16,000
20,000	24,000	4,380		32	20,000
24,000	28,000	5,660		36	24,000
28,000	32,000	7,100		39	28,000
32,000	36,000	8,660		42	32,000
36,000	40,000	10,340		45	36,000
40,000	44,000	12,140		48	40,000
44,000	52,000	14,060		50	44,000
52,000	64,000	18,060		53	52,000
64,000	76,000	24,420		55	64,000
76,000	88,000	31,020		58	76,000
88,000	100,000	37,980		60	88,000
100,000	120,000	45,180		62	100,000
120,000	140,000	57,580		64	120,000
140,000	160,000	70,380		66	140,000
160,000	180,000	83,580		68	160,000
180,000	200,000	97,180		69	180,000
200,000	300,000	110,980		70	200,000
300,000	400,000	180,980		70	300,000
400,000		250,980		70	400,000

*Applies for a qualified surviving widow or widower in the first two years after the year in which the spouse died.

deductions. Specifically, many investors as well as promoters and salespeople incorrectly use their top marginal tax bracket to calculate the value of a potential tax saving. By way of illustration, consider the taxpayer with a $33,000 income. Although the *marginal* rate on his incremental income is 42 percent, as shown in Table 21-2, his total tax liability of $9,080 gives an *effective* tax rate of 27.5 percent. The effective marginal rate for a $20,000 tax deduction arising from a real estate investment would be 32 percent, or $6,400, whereas someone using 42 percent for his or her calculations would expect a saving of $8,400. The possible true savings resulting from tax deductions are large, but caution should be used not to exaggerate them.

THE ORIGINATION PHASE

Each part of the investment cycle has unique tax characteristics. Effective planning can minimize tax costs and maximize tax savings, thereby increasing the overall return on investment.

Legal Form of Ownership

A critical decision to be made during the origination phase is how the venture should be structured for tax purposes. This includes a decision as to the legal form of ownership. The amount of tax depends on the type of legal entity holding title to a property. In certain cases investors pay taxes twice on distributions. Such forms of ownership are called *double-taxation entities*. Corporations are usually double-taxation entities. Chapter 7 discussed the various choices of ownership. It appears that in most cases, investors can gain by using a limited partnership—with flow-through accounting—for real estate ventures. However, when this choice is made, care must be taken to differentiate the partnership from a corporation and to ensure that it is not treated as an association and taxed as such.

Development and Acquisition

Other decisions to be made during the origination phase concern the valuable opportunities to realize tax savings which arise when developing and acquiring real estate. One important decision concerns whether various payments made in developing property are (1) to be expensed and deducted for tax purposes in the period they are incurred or (2) to be capitalized and thereby added to the cost of the physical improvements which for tax purposes are written off over time.

A closely related decision is whether the taxpayer elects a cash basis or an accrual method of accounting. Under cash accounting, income and expenses are recognized when received or paid. Under accrual accounting, adjustments are made to relate the timing of revenue to that of the expenses incurred to produce it.

Expenditure items that may be either expensed or capitalized consist primarily of financing charges (interest, points, and commitment fees) and taxes (property, payroll, and, in some states, sales taxes on the purchase of materials and supplies). A difficult question often arises as to whether other costs, particularly overhead items, are "period" expenses and therefore deductible or expenditures that should be capitalized. Since the guidelines and interpretations in these as in other tax areas are ever-changing, expert advice is an absolute necessity.

Prepaid Interest   Prepaid financial items (that is, points and interest) are popular means of enhancing the tax-shelter aspects of an investment. With the exception of certain restrictions on excess investment interest, interest paid on debt is deductible in determining income tax liability. As we saw earlier, when part of a cash payment to purchase real estate is classified as tax-deductible prepaid interest, the resulting tax saving reduces the effective cost of making the investment.

Prior to the autumn of 1968, many real estate ventures deducted up to 5 years of prepaid interest when purchasing a property. Then, revenue ruling 68-643 reduced the allowable prepaid interest to the amount for the balance of the current year plus 12 months of the next year, provided no material distortion of income results. Up until this ruling, investors frequently purchased properties with totally soft—that is, tax-deductible—dollars.

Organizational Expenses   The deductibility for tax purposes of expenses incurred in organizing a venture is also subject to debate. Generally, these items are not deductible for tax purposes in the year they are paid. Instead, they are included in the basis of the property. At the time of sale, they reduce the amount of taxable gain otherwise due.

Some attorneys and accountants are of the opinion that the cost of organizing a venture can be amortized over its expected life. Such a tax election would increase the tax deductions during the operating phase of the cycle.

Sponsors of some offerings have sought to increase front-end tax deductions by prepaying various operating expenses, such as management fees or land lease payments. The IRS has been almost totally successful in the courts in disallowing such deductions.

TAXES DURING OPERATIONS

During the operations phase, the tax liability is calculated by subtracting from revenues the total of operating expenses, interest on the mortgage, and authorized depreciation. We have seen that principal repayments are not deductible as an expense, but are a "noncash" income item. Investors do not have them as current cash income; yet they must include them as part of their taxable income.

Generally in the early years of an investment the detrimental tax effects of principal payments are more than offset by depreciation deductions. However, since in most circumstances principal payments increase and depreciation deductions decrease each year, eventually noncash income exceeds noncash expense. The tax liability becomes larger than the cash flow from operations. Known as the *crossover point*, this is the best time, many investors believe, to sell the property and acquire a new one with more favorable tax characteristics.

Depreciation

The allocation of the cost of property to periods in which it provides economic value is accomplished through the accounting mechanism of "depreciation." The depreciation method selected determines the amount of tax deductions available.

The calculation of the amount of depreciation depends upon (1) the depreciable basis (that is, the value of the improvement to be depreciated); (2) the depreciation method; (3) the useful life (number of years over which depreciation is spread); and (4) the salvage value, if any. There are three primary depreciation methods.

Straight-Line Method   Annual depreciation is calculated by dividing the depreciable basis by the years of useful life. Thus a $50,000 building (after excluding the land, a nondepreciable asset) with a 20-year life would be depreciated at a rate of 5 percent, or $2,500 per year.

Declining Balance   In this technique, the amount of depreciation taken each year is subtracted from the remaining or adjusted basis before computing the following year's depreciation, and so the same depreciation rate applies to a smaller or declining balance each year.

The IRS allows the use of "accelerated depreciation" in certain cases. This means that the deductions are greater (accelerated) than those which could be taken under the straight-line method. The percentage factor applied to the straight-line rate is usually 125 percent, 150 percent, or 200 percent. For the building with a $50,000 basis and a 20-year life, and using a 200 percent (or double-declining) balance, the first year's depreciation would be 10 percent (200 percent × .05), or $5,000. At the start of the second year, the adjusted basis or balance has declined to $45,000, or 90 percent of the basis. Depreciation would be $4,500, which is 10 percent of the reduced balance, or 9 percent of the original basis (90 percent × 200 percent × .05), and so on.

Sum of the Year's Digits   Under this procedure (which is rarely used, however), the firm is allowed to charge off a percentage based upon the length of time a building has been depreciated compared with its total life. The annual depreciation factor is a fraction that has as a numerator (the top) the remaining years of useful life for the asset and as a denominator (the bottom) the sum of the year's digits. Thus for a 10-year asset, the depreciation factor for the first year is 10/55 (55 = 10, 9, 8, 7, 6, 5, 4, 3, 2, 1); for the second year, 9/55; and so on. For a 20-year asset, the first-year factor would be 20/210 (210 = 20, 19, 18, ..., 3, 2, 1).

Accelerated Depreciation

Accelerated depreciation is used because the difference between the authorized deduction and the lower straight-line method increases the tax shelter. The amount of non-taxable cash flow, for example, in our $50,000 case rises from $2,500 to $5,000 in the first year if we use the double-declining method. The difference is less in the second year, and eventually the rate based on the declining balance will fall below the straight-line rate. (In these and similar cases, it may be possible to switch to the straight-line method when that becomes advantageous.) We shall also see shortly that this accelerated depreciation may, through the "recapture" provision, cause some of the gain upon sale to be taxed at a higher rate than would otherwise apply.

The 1969 Tax Reform Act authorized the use of the following depreciation methods:

For new residential buildings—accelerated methods including 200 percent of the straight-line and sum-of-the-year's-digits rates

For used residential buildings (provided they have more than 20 years of remaining life)—accelerated methods limited to 125 percent of the straight-line rate

For new nonresidential buildings—accelerated depreciation limited to 150 percent of the straight-line rate

For used nonresidential buildings—straight-line rate only

Certain special conditions apply to the selection of the depreciation methods for FHA low-income housing properties.

Useful Life

For a given depreciation method, the shorter the useful life, the larger the depreciation deduction. Guidelines concerning useful lives as suggested by the IRS are shown in Table 21-3. In practice, the useful life selected for depreciation purposes is often shorter than that indicated by the guidelines. Two justifications are frequently given. First, it is often claimed that the quality of construction for the property is inferior to

Table 21-3   Useful Lives of Depreciable Assets*

Depreciable assets	Years
Apartments	40
Banks	50
Dwellings	45
Factories	45
Farm buildings	25
Garages	45
Hotels	40
Loft buildings	50
Machine shops	45
Office buildings	45
Stores	50
Theaters	40
Warehouses	60

*Based on IRS revenue procedure 62-21, *Guidelines for Depreciation*.

the standard utilized by the IRS. Second, it is argued that while the property may have a *physical* life equal to that suggested in the IRS guidelines, its actual *economic* life is substantially less. Changing market forces and shifting demand patterns make it unlikely that a specific asset will experience an extraordinarily long economic life.

Components

One means of reducing useful life for tax purposes is through component depreciation, whereby individual parts of the property are depreciated. With the component method, certain elements, such as carpets, drapes, utilities, and the roof, are depreciated over relatively short periods of time, while the basic building shell is depreciated over a somewhat longer time period than it would be otherwise. Component depreciation bunches a greater proportion of the total depreciation into the early years and in effect leads to a form of accelerated depreciation.

   The impact of alternative depreciation methods is best conveyed by means of an illustration. Assume the following:

1   A building costing $100,000, with a 30-year useful life and no salvage value
2   Components of the building (useful life) as follows:
   $10,000—furniture, stoves, and carpets (7 years)
   $15,000—roof (10 years)
   $10,000—air conditioning (10 years)
   $15,000—doors and woodwork (15 years)
   $50,000—structure, studs, floor, etc. (30 years)

Column 1 of Table 21-4 shows the allowance for the building under the straight-line method. The remaining columns show the straight-line method applied to the components. The depreciation deductions are almost twice as great for the component method. If the component method is combined with accelerated depreciation, even

Table 21-4   Component Depreciation

Year	For complete structure (1)	Components Furniture (2)	Roof (3)	Air conditioning (4)	Doors (5)	Structure (6)	Total (7)
1	3,333	1,429	1,500	1,000	1,000	1,667	6,596
2	3,333	1,429	1,500	1,000	1,000	1,667	6,596
3	3,333	1,429	1,500	1,000	1,000	1,667	6,596
4	3,333	1,429	1,500	1,000	1,000	1,667	6,596
5	3,333	1,429	1,500	1,000	1,000	1,667	6,596
6	3,333	1,429	1,500	1,000	1,000	1,667	6,596
7	3,333	1,429	1,500	1,000	1,000	1,667	6,596
8	3,333	0	1,500	1,000	1,000	1,667	5,167
9	3,333	0	1,500	1,000	1,000	1,667	5,167
10	3,333	0	1,500	1,000	1,000	1,667	5,167
Total	33,330	10,003	15,000	10,000	10,000	16,667	61,673

faster writeoffs will result. But where component depreciation is used, the IRS will insist upon a longer life for the shell; i.e., perhaps 50 to 60 years for the shell of an apartment building.

TAXES UPON TERMINATION

When property is sold or exchanged, the resultant gain or loss may be classified as either a capital or an ordinary gain or loss. Since the tax on capital gains is usually much less than that on ordinary income, it is advantageous for the seller to be able to qualify for the capital gains treatment and the lower tax rate. In addition, at the time of termination it is sometimes possible for the seller to delay tax payments by exchanging the property, selling it on installments, or (if it is an owner-occupied unit) taking other necessary action.

While the exact definition of a capital asset eligible for capital gains treatment is complex, as a rule real property qualifies if it is held for long-term investment purposes or if it is used in the taxpayer's trade or business and is not held as part of an inventory of properties that are primarily for sale.

Capital Gains Tax

In planning to hold their potential tax liabilities from a sale to a minimum and to keep their cash flow as high as possible, taxpayers would like to have as small a taxable income as possible without reducing the real benefits from a sale. At the same time, they would like to ensure that the largest possible portion of their gains is taxed at the capital gains rate. To do so, they must avoid the recapture clause of the law and also avoid being classified as dealers, in contrast to investors.

The Adjusted Basis   The amount of the taxable gain is calculated by subtracting the basis from the net proceeds from the sale. While there are certain exceptions, the *basis* for capital gains in most cases is the initial purchase price or cost to the taxpayer, less the accumulated depreciation deductions to date, plus all costs incurred to originate the investment that have not previously been deducted. Thus, while certain costs are not includable in the basis for depreciation and therefore cannot be expensed over the holding period of the investment, they can be included in the basis for capital gains. In this way they serve to reduce the tax liability at sale.

The net proceeds from the sale amount to the gross proceeds minus the costs involved in effecting the transaction, such as brokerage commissions and advertising and legal fees. An example of the calculation of the tax due upon sale is shown in Table 21-5. The first calculation is that of the adjusted tax basis. We see a property bought for $1,000,000 with $51,000 of initial costs that were not included in the base for depreciation. This is reduced by the accumulated depreciation deductions of $503,300, to give an adjusted tax basis of $547,700.

Next the net sales price is calculated. It is the gross sales price of $1,062,000 less selling costs, giving the net sales price of approximately $998,000. The adjusted tax basis is subtracted from this figure to give the final taxable income of $450,580.

To find the actual tax, it is necessary to figure the amount subject to the capital gains tax and the amount subject to recapture, which is taxable at the taxpayer's ordinary bracket. The seller must subtract the amount due on the mortgage and the amount due in taxes to get the net cash flow, the $21,516 in Tables 21-5 and 22-6.

Recapture The tax law provides that in certain cases, some of the gains from a sale that would otherwise be paid at a lower—the capital gains—rate may at times be lost because of the recapture provision. This specifies that the portion of the gain upon sale of a property which arises from the difference or excess between accelerated and normal depreciation may be taxed at the ordinary income tax rate rather than at the capital gains tax rate.

If the property is sold within 100 months of purchase, the entire amount of the gain based on the accelerated depreciation in excess of straight-line depreciation will be taxed as ordinary income. If the property is sold 200 or more months following purchase, recapture does not apply.

For residential property, if the sale falls between 100 and 200 months of purchase, the amount of the excess depreciation subject to recapture is reduced by 1 percent per month for each month beyond 100 months.

Thus, in the table, the property is an apartment house sold at the end of 72 months (the entire example is explained on page 380 in Chapter 22). The amount of excess depreciation is $83,300, all of which must be paid for at the ordinary income tax rate. If the property had been sold instead at the end of 10 years, or 120 months, and if the amount of excess depreciation were the same, the amount subject to recapture would be reduced by 20 percent (120 − 100), or by $16,660. This amount would be subtracted from the income taxable at ordinary rates and would be added to the remainder taxable at the capital gains rate.

Possible Cash Deficit Since both the tax and the outstanding mortgage balance must be paid off from the proceeds of the sale, there may actually be a negative cash flow at that time. The fact that depreciation deductions generally accumulate at a more

Table 21-5 Taxes upon Termination

Adjusted basis:		
Purchase price		$1,000,000
Plus organization costs:		
Legal and accounting fees	$17,000	
Reserves	10,000	
Underwriting commissions	24,000	51,000
		1,051,000
Less accumulated depreciation deductions		503,300
Adjusted tax basis		$ 547,700
Gross sales price		$1,062,000
Less selling costs:		
Brokerage commission	$47,720	
Advertising	7,000	
Legal fees	9,000	63,720
Net sales price		998,280
Less adjusted tax basis		547,700
Taxable income		$ 450,580
Recapture		83,300
Capital gains		367,280
Capital gains tax (25%)		91,820
Tax on recapture (50%)		41,650
Total tax due		133,470
Mortgage outstanding		853,294
Cash from sale		154,986
Less tax due		133,470
Cash flow		$ 21,516

rapid rate than mortgage amortization payments serves to reduce substantially the cash available for paying the tax obligations. Indeed, where high-leverage financing is utilized, unless the selling price has appreciated greatly over the purchase price, chances are good that the after-tax cash proceeds from the sale may be negative.

Many investors are surprised to find that they have an unanticipated tax liability when investments go awry. A mortgage foreclosure, for example, may require a payment of income taxes because the amount owed on the mortgage exceeds the adjusted tax basis. Such a condition frequently prevails in highly leveraged new construction projects if aggressive depreciation policies have been followed. In such instances, investors not only lose their equity in the property but also incur a tax liability based upon the difference between the foreclosed debt and the adjusted basis. Where recapture of accelerated depreciation is due, some of this liability may be at ordinary income tax rates. As another example, in the event of an involuntary conversion of an owner's property, such as destruction by fire or the taking of it through condemnation, any gain realized is also taxable. However, in such cases the tax can be deferred if the proceeds are reinvested in a similar property. The taxable gain is limited to any excess proceeds not reinvested.

Dealer or Investor

Finally, a seller will try to ensure that he or she is not taxed at ordinary rates by virtue of being classified as a dealer. Sales of real property by a dealer are taxed at ordinary income rates, while sales by an investor qualify for the lower capital gains rates. The term ''dealer'' refers to one who holds property in an inventory of properties that are primarily for sale. An ''investor,'' on the other hand, holds property for long-term investment purposes or uses the property for trade or business. Whether a specific property is held primarily for investment or as inventory awaiting sale turns on whether the owner's primary business is that of ''dealing'' in real estate and on whether the owner has engaged in ''dealer-oriented'' activities such as major improvements and promotional activities. A person with a real estate license and office, one who completes transactions frequently, and someone engaged primarily in building or developing are all likely to be classified as dealers rather than investors. However, the determination is based on the actual facts of a specific situation.

Furthermore, ''once a dealer'' does not imply ''always a dealer.'' A dealer may assume a passive investor position, such as buying an interest in a limited partnership organized by a general partner with whom he or she is not affiliated, and thereby qualify for capital gains treatment on that investment, assuming the venture is not involved in dealer-oriented activities.

Selling Land   A difficult question is raised where the sale of the property is not to one buyer but is in multiple units (lots or parcels) to many buyers. Here, the question is whether this represents (1) the orderly liquidation of an investment or (2) the process of selling from an inventory held for sale in the ordinary course of business. For large parcels of land, the sale of subdivided individual lots may well be a more economical way of disposing of the property than seeking to sell it as a whole. Whether such a transaction is treated as ordinary income or capital gain depends on such factors as the number of units, the size of the parcel, the length of the holding period, and the amount of improvement and sales activity. How the property was acquired can be significant as well; for example, acquisition through inheritance is favorable for capital gains treatment.

DELAYING THE TAX LIABILITY

We know that because of the time value of money, it is often advantageous to delay the period in which a tax must be paid. This delay is particularly worthwhile for those who believe that their payments will be in a lower bracket in some future period. Thus people with an unusually high income in one year often try to delay their tax liabilities to a future year. On the other hand, if a person is afraid that his or her tax rates will be higher in the future, the possible increase in taxes will have to be measured against the time value of money.

We have mentioned that there are three primary ways in which the tax liabilities on capital gains at time of sale can be delayed. We shall discuss them briefly.

Installment Sales

If sellers do not receive all cash at the time of sale but provide some financing for the buyer, it is possible to defer the tax liability. If no more than 30 percent of the selling price is paid in cash, sellers may qualify for "installment sales accounting" to the degree that they accept a note, or "paper," rather than cash. This allows them to pay their tax liability on a basis proportionate to the schedule on which they receive their cash.

The basic procedure for calculating tax liability using the installment sales accounting method is as follows:

1 Determine eligibility by verifying that cash in the year of sale does not exceed 30 percent of total selling price.

2 Calculate the taxable gain on sale.

3 Calculate the "contract price" (that is, total proceeds from sale—sum of cash and all debt obligations running from buyer to seller). The regulations guard against attempts to claim interest on the unpaid debt as capital gains.

4 The amount of gain to be recognized each year is determined by multiplying the ratio of the total taxable gain to the total contract price by the amount of cash to be received in that year.

As an example, consider an investor who sells her property for $100,000. She receives $10,000 in cash and a $20,000 second mortgage, while a $70,000 outstanding first mortgage remains in effect. Assume that her capital gain is $20,000. In this example, since less than 30 percent of the price is in cash, the seller may report on an installment basis. If she does so, then two-thirds of each payment she receives in the future must be reported as a capital gain. Two-thirds is the ratio between the gain and $30,000 (the $10,000 cash plus the $20,000 second mortgage) she is to receive over time. Thus she reports a gain of $6,667, or two-thirds of the initial cash payment, and she must also report for tax purposes two-thirds of each principal payment she is paid on the second mortgage as it is received.

It should be emphasized that the installment sales accounting election must be made in the year of the sale. It is the tax rate in effect in each year for the individual's tax bracket that applies when the income is received.

Tax-deferred Exchange

A specialized technique intended to minimize taxes is the tax-deferred exchange, whereby the owner of one property exchanges it for another property. In fact, three-party exchanges are often used. On occasion there may be five, six, or even more participants in an exchange. Such transactions require creativity, technical proficiency, and careful documentation. They are complex and call for special study and analysis.

To qualify as a tax-deferred exchange, the properties involved must be of a "like kind," although it should be noted that "like kind" has a broad definition encompassing essentially all real property. An exchange must truly be an exchange, planned in advance and so designated, and not a "label" applied after the fact.

Tax-deferred exchanges are a specialized and complex disposition technique. By means of such transactions, owners can exchange their equity in one property for equity in another without paying taxes. But these transactions are not "tax-free," as many real estate people incorrectly describe them, since the tax liability will be paid eventually either on a future sale or out of the owner's estate. The fact that the owner's basis for depreciation is limited to that of his or her earlier property suggests the critical importance of careful tax planning. For owners of properties with a relatively low basis substantially below market value, on which a sale would trigger a large tax liability, exchange may be a useful technique. However, they may find that they should not trade for properties with large favorable depreciation characteristics, since they will not be able to utilize these depreciation characteristics to their full potential. Instead, they may benefit more, contrary to normal circumstances, by using this equity to acquire high-cash-flow income properties with only limited depreciation possibilities.

Of special importance in evaluating the desirability of a tax-deferred exchange is the *boot*. The boot is cash or other property received in addition to the property being exchanged tax-free. Who gives the boot and who receives it are extremely important because the boot enters into the new tax basis. A person giving boot can add it to the previous basis of the property he gave in exchange to determine his new basis. For example, a man who owns an apartment house with a market value of $80,000 and a cost basis of $30,000 exchanges this building for an apartment house with a market value of $90,000, giving his building plus $10,000 in cash. The investor finds that the basis of his newly acquired building is (1) the $10,000 cash boot given and (2) the $30,000 cost basis of the building he traded. His new cost basis is the sum of these two, or $40,000.

Let us examine the situation for the other party in the trade. He traded a $90,000 building with a cost basis of $50,000. He received in return a building worth $80,000 and a $10,000 boot in the form of cash to equal the market value of his building. If he had received all cash, he would have had a $40,000 capital gain. Instead, only the $10,000 in cash received is a recognized capital gain for which he is taxed. He maintains the same cost basis of $50,000 on his new building. This basis would be reduced by the cash received, except for the fact that he pays an immediate capital gains tax on this sum.

Sale of Principal Residence

Normally, a person realizing a gain on the sale of property must pay a tax. However, for primary residences the tax may be deferred if the seller buys and occupies another residence within a specified period before or after the sale. Some additional time is allowed if a new house is being built. The cost of the new residence must equal or exceed the adjusted sales price of the old home.

The gain not taxed is subtracted from the cost of the new residence, thereby lowering its basis. As a result, the tax may be continued to be deferred as long as the taxpayer continues to purchase another residence each time he or she sells and meets other qualifications. But eventually the gain may have to be realized. When the purchase price of a new house is less than the price of the old one, the gain taxed in the year of sale may be held to the difference between the cost of the new residence and the adjusted sales price of the old one.

TAX STRUCTURING

A variety of aggressive and creative techniques are used to maximize the tax-shelter advantages of a particular investment. Categories of tax-structuring techniques include (1) maximizing front-end writeoffs, (2) increasing the amount of depreciation deductions, and (3) creating tax characteristics so that one group of investors receives extra tax deductions in exchange for giving a second group more cash flow.

Front-End Tax Writeoffs

Front-end tax writeoffs (that is, payments chargeable for tax purposes against current income) can result from the prepayment of interest and/or points. The purpose of the payments is to increase the amount of tax shelter, thereby reducing the cash flow from the investor's pocket needed for the investment. Since traditional lenders are seldom very flexible, prepayments have usually been against secondary financing, such as wraparound mortgages. When the lender is also the seller, the deductibility of such payment may be questioned by the IRS.

Of more concern is the tendency, resulting from attempts to gain maximum front-end tax deductions, for deals to be structured in ways that violate fundamental economic logic. The combination of excessive prepayments, inflated wraparound mortgages, and sale-leaseback arrangements can cause excessive prices to be paid. The cash advanced goes to pay artificial "deductible" charges rather than building up equity for the owners. Furthermore, paying an expense before it is otherwise due involves a "present-value" penalty, since money that could be earning a return is given up. In considering prepayments, frequently there is a failure to weigh the possible gains in the overall after-tax return against any increased risks for the whole venture.

Staging The front-end deductibility of an investment can be enhanced by "staging" investor capital contributions. This means that payments of the equity are made in stages; that is, they are spread over different time periods. Staging generally is used in new construction ventures. The next chapter discusses the methods of staging in some detail.

Operations Deductions

Deductions to reduce taxable income and increase the tax shelter during operations are achieved by altering depreciation and interest expenses. Some wraparound mortgages have been structured so that debt-service payments consist entirely of interest, generally at rates above the market. This is an increase in real costs, and so tax advantages are gained at the expense of the ultimate proceeds from the sale. Frequently, because of low amortization, the mortgage balance may so exceed the basis at sale that investors must use not only the proceeds from sale but also cash out of their own pockets to pay the tax liability. Furthermore, as such ventures often employ very high debt ratios, the break-even point may approach or even exceed 100 percent occupancy. The full significance of this precarious balance may not be appreciated by investors. At times the implications are hidden and deferred through the use of a short-term sale-leaseback, under which the debt service and expenses and a specified cash distribution are guaranteed for several years. At times, the guarantee is paid for simply out of a premium using the investor's own money.

Depreciation deductions have been enhanced by aggressive assumptions regarding useful lives and by componentization. Problems have arisen, however, since cash flows may be sharply reduced when the assumed useful life of the improvements has passed and depreciation ends; at the same time, non-tax-deductible amortization may be steadily increasing. Investors may have to pay the resulting tax liabilities from funds other than those generated by the property.

Disproportionate Allocation

Disproportionate allocation is another way in which some ventures have enhanced their tax-shelter appeal. Under such arrangements, special classes of shares are designed to receive a particular component of the return. Such arrangements are often known as *A and B share syndications*. Their object is to separate the tax and cash-flow benefits and to sell each independently. One group of investors receives its return primarily in the form of high annual cash distributions. They give up their rights to immediate tax deductions to the second group. The split makes sense primarily if the marginal tax rates for the two groups are very different.

Unless a valid and legitimate economic justification exists for the proposed allocation, the IRS is likely to contest it. In practice, developing a valid economic justification has proved to be relatively difficult.

One method of establishing A and B shares has been to create two partnerships. The A partnership owns the property and leases it to the B partnership for a rent just sufficient to meet the mortgage payments. The A investors receive no current cash flow. Their return consists essentially of the tax deductions arising from depreciation and the right to a possible future capital gain. The B partnership operates the building. Its investors enjoy a high cash return but little or no tax shelter and no participation in property-value increases.

In a variation of this approach, the B partnership owns the land and leases it to the A partnership, which owns the leasehold improvements. The A group gets the benefits of tax deductions arising from depreciation. Another form involves one partnership but two different classifications of owners, with the cash flow and the tax benefits allocated between the two groups.

A futher variation on the A-B concept involves the use of subordinated debentures issued by the partnership or other owning entity. Similar to a corporate bond, the debenture is a debt instrument whose claim to the partnership's property is subordinated to that of all mortgages. Some debentures have incorporated redemption and conversion features as well. Because the rights and privileges associated with debentures tend to be clearer than those relating to other debt instruments and because they avoid certain conflict problems, their use is less likely to be challenged than other approaches to disproportionate allocation.

AN EXAMPLE OF AN INVESTMENT FOR TAX SHELTER ONLY

Tables 21-6, 21-7, and 21-8 present a summary example of an investment made primarily for tax-shelter purposes. This example is typical of many syndicate offerings

Table 21-6 Projected Income and Cash Flow (Henley Townhouse Manor)

Year	Total income	Operating expenses	Mortgage interest and insurance premium	Depreciation and amortization	Taxable income (loss)	Cumulative taxable income (loss)	Payments on mortgage principal	Replacement fund payments and interest thereon	Cash flow
1971		$ 11,042		$ 32,478	($43,520)	($43,520)			*
1972	$117,627	151,981	$ 13,478	117,107	(164,939)	(208,459)	$ 822		$ 7,968*
1973	301,985	107,755	161,331	153,397	(120,498)	(328,957)	10,242	$ 8,327	14,330
1974	302,271	107,755	160,538	141,306	(107,328)	(436,285)	10,982	8,666	14,330
1975	302,567	107,755	159,687	131,042	(95,917)	(532,202)	11,776	9,019	14,330
1976	302,873	107,755	158,775	122,194	(85,851)	(618,053)	12,627	9,386	14,330
1977	303,190	107,755	157,797	115,557	(77,919)	(695,972)	13,539	9,769	14,330
1978	303,518	107,755	156,747	110,614	(71,598)	(767,570)	14,519	10,167	14,330
1979	303,856	107,755	155,622	105,862	(65,383)	(832,953)	15,568	10,581	14,330
1980	302,927	107,755	154,416	104,774	(64,018)	(896,971)	16,694	9,732	14,330
1981	301,930	107,755	153,122	101,857	(60,804)	(957,775)	17,901	8,822	14,330
1982	302,197	107,755	151,735	94,100	(51,393)	(1,009,168)	19,195	9,182	14,330
1983	302,471	107,755	150,249	87,873	(43,406)	(1,052,574)	20,581	9,556	14,330
1984	302,753	107,755	148,654	82,891	(36,547)	(1,089,121)	22,069	9,945	14,330
1985	303,044	107,755	146,943	79,025	(30,679)	(1,119,800)	23,666	10,350	14,330
1986	303,343	107,755	145,110	75,996	(25,518)	(1,145,318)	25,376	10,772	14,330
1987	303,650	107,755	143,143	72,967	(20,215)	(1,165,533)	27,211	11,211	14,330
1988	302,278	107,755	141,035	77,890	(24,402)	(1,189,935)	29,178	9,980	14,330
1989	300,810	107,755	138,774	80,198	(25,917)	(1,215,852)	31,287	8,664	14,330
1990	301,001	107,755	136,350	72,591	(15,695)	(1,231,547)	33,549	9,017	14,330
1991	301,193	107,755	133,751	66,129	(6,442)	(1,237,989)	35,973	9,384	14,330
1992	300,702	107,755	130,964	56,877	5,106	(1,232,883)	38,574	9,079	14,330

*The cash-flow deficit in 1971 will be funded from mortgage proceeds and capital contributions. The cash flow available for distribution in 1972 is from operations after final endorsement. This projection is dependent on future events and may be significantly affected by changes in economic and other circumstances.

Table 21-7 Taxable Income and Cash Flow, 1976 (Henley Townhouse Manor)

	Cash flow	Tax return
Total income	$302,873	$302,873
Operating expense	107,755	107,755
Mortgage interest and insurance	158,775	158,775
Mortgage amortization	12,627	
Replacement fund deposit	9,386	
Depreciation		122,194
Total expenses	$288,543	$388,724
Cash flow	14,330	
Taxable income		(−$85,851)

made in 1970 and 1971. They consisted of limited partnerships which invested in FHA Section 236 new developments. These apartments had HUD subsidy contracts which guaranteed the majority of mortgage interest, thereby allowing the apartments to be rented at lower rents.[1] In this example, total funds to complete the development are estimated at about $2.5 million. The limited partners contribute $310,000 in capital, most of which is paid to the developers as a profit and risk allowance for their efforts.

The FHA insures a 40-year mortgage for $2,156,000. It calculates the initial equity investment as approximately $240,000 and allows a 6 percent return on this sum, or $14,400 a year. In contrast, when the tax benefits are figured in, the actual returns are calculated to average somewhat more than $41,000 per year over and above the developers' initial normal profit for their efforts. In place of a 6 percent return (which might be reduced by depreciation), the limited partners, according to the projections, receive a return of somewhat over 20 percent a year.

The entire difference between 6 and 20 percent, and therefore the appeal of this type of investment, lies in the tax benefits, as shown in the tables. Table 21-7 displays a typical year—1976. In that year, the authorized depreciation (a noncash item) exceeds the two cash (nontax) items of mortgage amortization and replacement fund deposits by $100,181. If we assume that the partners are all in a 50 percent bracket, they benefit to the extent of the $14,330 actual cash flow plus $42,925 in tax shelter (one-half of the $85,851 reported tax loss). Their total benefit for that year is $57,255.

Table 21-8 shows how this works out for the individual investor. He puts up $31,000, divided into equal payments in each of three years. His maximum cash return is $1,361 in any year. On the other hand, his tax shelter goes as high as $15,670 in 1972. For the entire period, his cash flow is projected as $27,977, and his estimated income tax savings from sheltering current income are $58,563.

As is shown in the note to Table 21-8, however, some of this tax saving is only deferred. The example assumes that the investor can sell his share for $1 at the end of the period; that is, at that time the building will have a value equal to the outstanding mortgage. On this assumption, the investor's books will show a $114,101 capital gain

---

[1]For complete details of this case, see S. E. Roulac, *Case Studies in Property Development* (Menlo Park, Calif.: Property Press, 1973), pp. 233–252.

Table 21-8 Projected Results for Investment of $31,000† (Henley Townhouse Manor)

Year	Cash flow	Taxable income (loss)	Estimated income tax savings (Approximate federal income tax bracket 50%)	Benefits generated (Approximate federal income tax bracket 50%)	Cumulative cash on hand after recovery of investment (Approximate federal income tax bracket 50%)
1 1971	—	($4,134)	$ 2,067	$ 2,067	($8,266)*
2 1972	$ 757	(15,670)	7,835	8,592	(10,007)*
3 1973	1,361	(11,447)	5,724	7,085	(13,256)*
4 1974	1,361	(10,196)	5,098	6,459	(6,797)*
5 1975	1,361	(9,112)	4,556	5,917	(880)*
6 1976	1,361	(8,156)	4,078	5,439	4,559
7 1977	1,361	(7,402)	3,701	5,062	9,621
8 1978	1,361	(6,802)	3,401	4,762	14,383
9 1979	1,361	(6,211)	3,106	4,467	18,850
10 1980	1,361	(6,082)	3,041	4,402	23,252
11 1981	1,361	(5,776)	2,888	4,249	27,501
12 1982	1,361	(4,882)	2,441	3,802	31,303
13 1983	1,361	(4,124)	2,062	3,423	34,726
14 1984	1,361	(3,472)	1,736	3,097	37,823
15 1985	1,361	(2,915)	1,458	2,819	40,642
16 1986	1,361	(2,424)	1,212	2,573	43,215
17 1987	1,361	(1,920)	960	2,321	45,536
18 1988	1,361	(2,318)	1,159	2,520	48,056
19 1989	1,361	(2,462)	1,231	2,592	50,648
20 1990	1,361	(1,491)	746	2,107	52,755
21 1991	1,361	(612)	306	1,667	54,422
22 1992	1,361	485	(243)	1,118	55,540
Total	$27,977	($117,123)	$58,563	$86,540	

*Represents unrecovered investment.

†Payable in August 1971, June 1972, and February 1973.

Note: Effective payback period:

First installment	1 year, 8 months
Second installment	2 years, 3 months
Third installment	3 years, 2 months

Assuming the sale of a partnership interest for $1 more than the unpaid balance of the mortgage at the end of year 22, the cash needed per unit of investment to pay the capital gains tax is $34,229 for a 50% tax bracket limited partner computed as shown at the right.

Tax losses—years 1–22	$117,123
Cash flow—years 1–22	27,977
Proceeds of sale (sales price less mortgage balance)	1
	145,101
Less cost of investments	31,000
Capital gain	114,101
Capital gains tax at 30% rate	34,230
Less proceeds of sale	1
Cash required to pay capital gains tax resulting from sale at end of year 22	$ 34,229

373

at the time of sale, and he will have to pay a $34,230 capital gains tax, assuming his effective ordinary tax bracket is raised to 60 percent because of the gain.

His actual rate of return will depend on assumptions as to other matters such as a possible preference tax, his real tax brackets, what interest rates are assumed on money set aside to pay the capital gains, and similar matters. In practice, however, such limited partnerships have been sold on the basis of a projected rate of return of well over 20 percent a year.

TAX REFORM

The tax law governing real estate investment is in a constant state of flux. New cases, new rulings, and new interpretations are continually reshaping and redefining the tax law. Additionally, congressional legislation, some of major significance and some not, periodically sets down new rules. At this writing the last major tax legislation was the Tax Reform Act of 1969. Considerable "accrued momentum" exists for tax reform. Much of the stimulus comes from the highly publicized cases of very wealthy individuals who pay only nominal taxes or none at all. Prominent among the vehicles for this tax avoidance have been various tax-shelter investments, including real estate. We do not want to guess what form tax reform may actually take. Rather, we want to point out the reasoning behind various approaches to changes in the law and regulations.

A specific example is the April 30, 1973, Treasury Department announcement of its "Limitations on Artificial Accounting Loss" proposals, popularly known as "LAL." According to the announcement, LAL "is designed to eliminate 'tax shelters' which have introduced substantial distortions into the income tax system." LAL is not intended to affect the professional, but rather the outsider who buys into the industry in search of tax losses. The announcement proclaimed: "The income tax system can successfully continue to be used as a means to provide major incentives to serve vital maximum goals."

The primary targets of LAL are preopening construction costs (in the form of interest, tax, and fees) plus so-called tax-shelter tax losses arising from accelerated depreciation when used to shelter other income, as shown in Table 21-8. In essence, LAL aimed at halting the use of deductions in excess of cash flow to offset income tax liability arising elsewhere. The resulting modified form of pass-through accounting is similar to the taxation characteristics of the REIT, where tax-free cash flow can be distributed, but tax losses cannot be utilized to offset other income.

Under the LAL proposals an investor in multifamily residential properties could use the tax losses resulting from accelerated depreciation from one investment only to offset income from another such property. Investors in nonresidential property, however, could utilize the losses due to accelerated depreciation only to offset income from properties in the same "unit." As with any proposal, various important elements were undefined, such as whether "unit" refers to contiguous properties or to properties owned in common by a large fund.

Under LAL, if all or a portion of the accelerated depreciation deductions in excess of straight line would cause a taxable loss that could not be used currently, such excess accelerated depreciation could be deferred until such time as it could be utilized. Thus, while investors would not be denied the opportunity to utilize accelerated depreciation, much of its appeal would be eliminated by LAL.

Many other tax-reform changes besides LAL have been proposed. Some, such as increasing the amount of the minimum tax or eliminating the lower taxes available on capital gains, would affect all investors, including those in real estate. Other proposals are aimed more directly at real estate. Among these are proposals that would prohibit any accelerated depreciation, limit the amount of total depreciation deductions that could be taken, and deny the opportunity to include the mortgage indebtedness in calculating the depreciation base. One has merely to review the particular advantageous tax characteristics available to the real estate owner to identify potential targets of tax-reform proponents.

In evaluating the relative merits of various tax-reform proposals, it is important to remember that few other business sectors carry the heavy tax burden that real estate does in the form of the property tax. Some experts hold that the effect of the property tax is equivalent to a sales tax on real property of between 10 and 25 percent. Indeed, a strong argument can be made that the perceived "tax loopholes" that favor real estate are, in actual fact, needed to offset the effects of the property tax.

If the special tax characteristics of real estate were removed, the effect would be to reduce the return to investors, to increase the costs to consumers of space, or to reduce the compensation of those providing services to real estate enterprise. To the extent that investors now make "extraordinary" returns which would be eliminated by tax reform, the costs of space would be unaffected. This apparently is the assumption on which many tax-reform proposals are based. But experience has shown that real estate investors as a group do not enjoy returns sufficiently better than those available elsewhere to enable them to absorb a significant reduction in the value of their investment. The problem of tax reform is how to remove the inequities favoring some, while retaining necessary incentives which may well be close to the average which has prevailed.

SUMMARY

Real estate decisions must be carefully evaluated in terms of their tax consequences. In some instances, there are opportunities for forward planning that can enhance the overall return. In other situations, where such flexibility is not available, full knowledge of the tax implications of the contemplated transaction will result in more informed judgments.

Investors should be cautious and differentiate between marginal and effective tax rates on any proposals. It is important to give careful consideration to the relevant tax and business factors in selecting the legal form of ownership in which title to the property will be held.

The tax consequences of a specific venture should be studied over the full investment cycle. Certain tax deductions may be achieved in developing and acquiring property, while creative structuring may accomplish a more favorable allocation of the tax and economic benefits of a property between different investor groups. It is important to recognize that different options, each with unique tax consequences, are available in terminating the investments.

Because the tax law undergoes a constant process of change and revision, it is essential to have the latest information and to consult knowledgeable professionals for interpretation of complex issues.

QUESTIONS AND PROBLEMS

1 What is the significance of the difference between marginal and effective tax rates?
2 What is meant by "soft-dollar financing"?
3 Depreciation is often called a "noncash expense." Explain.
4 What factors determine the amount of depreciation deductions?
5 What considerations influence the amount of tax liability due on disposition of a property?
6 How can disproportionate allocation of the economic and tax benefits of real estate investment be achieved?
7 What is accelerated depreciation, and why do owners use it?
8 An investor sells a property for $200,000. He receives $10,000 in cash and accepts a $40,000 second mortgage above the existing $150,000 first mortgage. His total capital gain is $30,000. How much capital gain must he report in this first year?
9 Explain the operation of the tax deferral available to one who sells and purchases a principal residence.
10 Explain how certain income properties that never report anything except operating losses for tax purposes can still be sensible investments.

Chapter 22

Development of the Financial Statement

Identifying profitable real estate investments requires both careful projections and skilled planning to maximize possible income while minimizing risks. Chapter 20 explained how to measure profitability. In Table 20-3 we presented pro forma financial statements, but we delayed detailed analysis of them until after a discussion of the crucial tax factors. In this chapter we examine in more detail the significant forces and decisions which influence the financial viability and profitability of a real estate investment.

THE ORIGINATION PHASE

Chapters 5 and 18 discussed questions asked by lenders of developers or prospective owners seeking mortgage loans. In the origination phase of a venture, a developer or promoter must also plan how the venture will be owned and how the property will be operated. If the project is for development alone, the venture will end when construction is completed and the property is sold. If an existing property is to be purchased, most effort will be devoted to planning the venture and obtaining the necessary financing. If an income property is to be both developed and held, all aspects of the operation must be considered together.

The planning of the venture, in contrast to the physical planning of the actual property, is concerned primarily with raising the necessary funds and structuring the investors' risks and tax benefits. Some money will be raised as equity and some as debt. The relationship between the two determines the leverage and the potential risk-reward ratios. The planning of the venture must also deal with the form of ownership, how the equity will be raised, and the timing of the equity contributions.

In the case of new developments, developers must gather front money and arrange for the construction and permanent loans. They will need funds to bridge the gaps during construction and for reserves against untoward events during the start-up period, particularly for losses that may occur if full occupancy is delayed. For an existing project, the critical factors are the purchase price and how that will be funded.

Equity Funds

Because the risks of equity holders drop drastically when promoters obtain a final financing commitment, the ability to raise equity funds shoots up at that time. It becomes far easier for promoters to sell part of a project to others. If they have the financing arranged and, in effect, have the approval of hard-nosed outsiders of the basic development plan, they can expect to receive enough funds to ensure them a fair percentage of their total profits. In many cases, promoters will gain their profit by selling a large share of the equity, while retaining a mangement contract or other form of participation which enables them to share in the profits both during operations and at termination. The Empire State Building case illustrates a type of program in which such sharing occurred.

The amount of equity funds to be raised by promoters depends on the conditions set by lenders, who seek maximum security for their loans. It also depends on what writeup, or increase in value, the promoter or developer gets credit for as a result of the development process. If the estimated increase in the value of the property is large, the promoter will not have to bring in much money. The loan may cover all the actual expenses. The writeup on the value of the land or the expected increase in the value of the total project over and above the owner's actual out-of-pocket costs forms part of his or her equity. An owner whose financing covers 100 percent of the costs is said to have "mortgaged out."

Previous chapters have discussed ways in which developers raise equity capital. They can form a joint venture with a major lender or pension fund; they can syndicate the venture through either a public offering or an offering to a limited group of friends and acquaintances; they may sell the project to an investor; or they may issue securities. The chapter on taxes discussed factors which help determine the decisions made in this area. At this stage of the development, promoters have a good deal more to promise and to show to potential investors. At this point, too, investors may still gain important tax benefits which would be lost if they held off their investments until the actual completion of the project.

Staging   One way of looking at these tax benefits is through the concept of "staging," a term indicating that the new investors or buyers will not necessarily put up all their money at one time. Rather, they may contract to invest a certain sum but to put up the money at three or four different times (or stages), usually when the development reaches certain fixed points at which more capital is needed.

Three basic reasons for the use of staging are (1) the time value of money, (2) a desire to minimize risks, and (3) a hope for added tax benefits.

1 Most active real estate developers and investors place a very high value on cash. They have more opportunities to invest than they have funds available. This has become increasingly true as the process of development has slowed down and as their money has been spread over more potential investments. They do not want to put any money into a venture until absolutely necessary. They have better uses for the funds elsewhere. They want the stages to be set so that money is not called for until it is required by the progress of the development.

2 Staging is also used to reduce the risks of the person putting in the equity by increasing the developer's incentive to achieve efficiency and minimize cash needs. One way in which the buyer can reduce the risk is to put up funds only as the seller achieves certain predetermined objectives. Some typical stages of the purchase might be (*a*) when an actual general contract on a fixed bid is awarded, (*b*) when the property is completed, (*c*) when enough tenants have signed leases to equal the break-even point or to achieve a certain stabilized rent roll, and (*d*) when a given profit level has been reached.

Clearly, the more conditions introduced into the purchase agreement, the less risk the purchaser takes and, therefore, the higher the price that must be paid and the lower the expected profits. As an example, if the amount of the payment due at a stage depends on the operating results and if the early operating results are good, the amount to be paid will be higher.

3 Many investors seek to achieve maximum tax benefits. To the extent that they obtain a tax shelter, they purchase with fewer of their own after-tax dollars. In the origination stage, some initial expenses are tax-deductible, while others are not. Frequently during this stage an attempt is made to assign to the equity investors the payments with tax benefits, while planning to pay for most of the remainder from the loans.

Origination Expenses

Other important requirements for funds at the time of origination are definitely not tax-deductible and therefore require hard dollars. Among them are organizational expenses such as legal fees, accounting costs, consulting fees, costs of selling the securities, and other costs such as those of underwriting commissions for brokers who bring investors into the venture. Reserves and working capital are also needed to handle unexpected costs and also the possibility—or even probability—that it will take a building longer than expected to achieve its initial tenancy and occupancy rate. During the rent-up period, a negative cash flow is common.

Furthermore, during operations, particularly of commercial buildings, rents may drop below expenses when one or two major tenants leave. There can also be unanticipated maintenance expenses. The probabilities of such negative cash flows are sufficiently great that most lenders require borrowers to set aside funds for adequate reserves. Even if lenders do not so insist, attempting to operate a venture without them may greatly increase its risks. Such reserves, however, are not an expense when they are set up and therefore cannot be deducted from taxable income.

Similarly, costs such as brokerage commissions, title fees, escrow fees, and others directly related to acquisition must be capitalized and included in the depreciable base of the property. They are not tax-deductible when paid, but can be deductible over the period used for depreciating improvements. However, if land represents a significant portion of the total purchase price, a proportionate share of the acquisition costs may have to be allocated to the land and therefore will not be depreciable.

All the decisions made during the initial analysis have a major impact on a venture's success. They are carried through to the pro forma financial statements. They become part of the critical profit analysis to determine whether the venture will work. Moreover, at the early stage of the venture, decisions tend to be flexible. Therefore, they are among the major elements that can be altered and negotiated in order to reduce the risks and increase the prospects for profits.

ILLUSTRATIVE CASE EXAMPLE

The pro forma statements in this chapter, which were summarized in Table 20-3, are based on a new apartment building offered as a partnership in 1975. The offering price is $1,000,000, including the cost of construction and the builder's and promoter's profits. The $1,000,000 is allocated as follows: $100,000 to the land; $300,000 to personal property, with an estimated 6-year life; and $600,000 to the building shell, with an estimated 30-year life. The property is financed with a loan for $900,000 at a 9 percent interest rate for 30 years, or a 9.66 percent constant rate to service the debt.

The property is projected to generate revenue of $160,000 in 1976, and it is anticipated that the revenue will increase 2 percent each year. Vacancies are estimated to be 5 percent of the scheduled gross revenue; operating expenses are projected at 40 percent of the scheduled gross revenue. Each year $3,000 will be set aside, in addition, for operating and contingency reserves. These reserves will all be spent on refurbishing the property in the year prior to sale. It is assumed that the transaction will be closed December 31, 1975, and that full tenancy will be effective January 1, 1976. The property will be held for 6 years and sold at the end of that time for a price that is 6.25 times the scheduled gross revenues. The proposed selling price has the identical relationship to gross revenues as the terms of purchase do. Investors are assumed to be in a 50 percent effective tax bracket.

Investment at Origination

Table 22-1 shows the actual investment choices made, their cash costs, their potential tax benefits, and their after-tax effects. A $900,000 mortgage has been offered on the building requiring a payment of 3 points, or $27,000. While the downpayment is stated as $100,000, the actual cash required to buy the building is $127,000. Of this sum, $27,000 is an expense for tax purposes, permitting a tax shelter to be obtained. Thus the investors' taxes are $13,500 less than they would otherwise be. Their after-tax downpayment is $113,500.

In addition to the downpayment, various expenses must be met in establishing the partnership. These total $51,000 and include selling expenses and organization fees plus initial reserves. None are deductible for tax purposes. They are capitalized and become part of the total basis of the corporation. They thus affect the profit at the time of sale. The figure shows a total required equity of $178,000, or $164,500 after the tax benefit.

Table 22-1   Investment at Origination

Description	Amount	Tax effect	After-tax investment
Price of building	$1,000,000		
Less mortgage	900,000		
Downpayment	$ 100,000		$100,000
Plus points	27,000	13,500	13,500
Actual downpayment	$ 127,000	$13,500	$113,500
Selling expenses	25,000		25,000
Organization fees	16,000		16,000
Reserves	10,000		10,000
Required equity	$ 178,000	$13,500	$164,000
Prepaid interest	81,748	40,874	40,874
Total money raised	$ 259,748	$54,374	$205,374

Prepaid Interest   Prepaid interest is listed separately in the table. Whether it is worthwhile to prepay interest depends on the expected effective tax bracket of the investors in the year the interest must be paid, the effect of the prepayment on the terms of the mortgage, and the time value of money.

In this case, the interest payment is moved from 1976 to 1975, thus increasing the tax shelter in the year of origination at the expense of the first year of operations. The effect actually lowers the expected yield. Prepayment makes sense only if it results in better terms on the mortgage or if the investors expect a good deal higher income in 1975 than in 1976.

With the prepaid interest, the total money which must be raised is $259,748, or $205,374 after the tax-shelter effects. The latter amount was used as the initial cost in the profitability estimates in Chapter 20.

THE OPERATING PHASE

Table 22-2 illustrates the development of the pro forma statement for the operating phase of the investment. There are four vital sections in the income statement:

1   Cash before debt service, or operating income. This cash flow determines whether the lender gets paid or foreclosure occurs, as well as the cash available for all other purposes.

2   Cash flow before reserves or cash flow before taxes. The priority claim against operating income is the debt payment. This must be met if the venture is to be viable. To underscore the importance of reserves—which are, however, voluntary uses of the venture's funds during operations—we include payments in and out of reserves in this section.

3   Taxable income. The amount of taxable income, or in this case tax loss, depends on operating income and the amount of depreciation. Taxable income will often be negative even though there is a positive flow of cash to the investors.

4   The current benefit. In addition to receiving a net cash flow, investors may benefit from the ability to shelter other income and thus pay less in current taxes. The

Table 22-2 Income Statement

	1976	1977	1978	1979	1980	1981
Scheduled gross revenue	$160,000	$163,200	$166,000	$170,000	$173,000	$177,000
Less vacancies and collection loss (5%)	8,000	8,160	8,300	8,500	8,650	8,850
Effective gross revenue	$152,000	$155,040	$157,700	$161,500	$164,350	$168,150
Less operating expense (40%)	64,000	65,280	66,400	68,000	69,200	70,800
Cash before debt service (operating income)	$ 88,000	$ 89,760	$ 91,300	$ 93,500	$ 95,150	$ 97,350
Less principal	6,149	6,726	7,356	8,047	8,801	9,627
Interest*	0	81,171	80,541	79,850	79,096	78,270
Debt service	$ 6,149	$ 87,897	$ 87,897	$ 87,897	$ 87,897	$ 87,897
Cash flow before reserves	$ 81,851	$ 1,863	$ 3,403	$ 5,603	$ 7,253	$ 9,453
Less reserves	3,000	1,863	3,403	3,734	3,000	3,000
Net cash flow before taxes	$ 78,851	0	0	$ 1,869	$ 4,253	$ 6,453
Cash before debt service and reserves	88,000	89,760	91,300	93,500	95,150	97,350
Less depreciation	90,000	87,200	84,900	82,500	80,400	78,300
Less interest	0	81,171	80,541	79,850	79,096	78,270
Less maintenance in year of sale†			0	0	0	18,000
Taxable income	($2,000)	($78,611)	($74,141)	($68,850)	($64,346)	($77,220)
Tax effect (for 50% effective brackets)	1,000	39,305	37,070	34,425	32,173	38,610
Net cash flow	78,851	0	0	1,869	4,253	6,453
Total current benefit	$ 79,851	$ 39,305	$ 37,070	$ 36,294	$ 36,426	$ 45,063

*Prepaid for first year.
†Funded from reserves of $3,000 each year.

benefit varies with the amount of tax losses, the ability to have losses flow through to the investors, and an investor's effective tax rate.

Each of these parts of the statement must be projected separately. The value of the statement depends on the completeness of the underlying analysis and the accuracy of the projections.

Cash Flow before Debt Service

For many purposes, the first five lines in the income statement are the most important. They show the expected annual cash flow before debt service. This cash flow is the basic factor in determining both the income during ownership and the future selling price. However, an investor is interested in more than the average annual flow. How much it rises and falls may also be vital. If the flow drops below the scheduled debt service, the investor will have to make up the difference from other funds, or the property will go into default. This danger, of course, explains why potential lenders examine this line with such care. An adequate and stable cash flow determines both the value of the underlying security and the protection available for the lender against the added costs from default and foreclosure.

Revenues   Operating income and cash flow are directly tied to revenues. The effective revenue—the amount actually expected to be collected—is the critical factor. However, it is useful to compare the scheduled revenues and the expected effective revenues in order to identify the reasons for the gap between them.

The scheduled rent level depends on the amount of space and the rent that the market is expected to pay for each unit of space. The estimate of what rents can be charged to keep vacancies at a desirable level requires an economic analysis of the particular rental market, as discussed in Chapter 23.

Investors must set rent schedules so as to achieve a proper balance between rents and vacancies. They are interested in obtaining the maximum effective revenue. All other factors being equal, occupancy rates will be higher when rents are lower. Two schools of thought exist as to what policy should be pursued regarding the trade-off inherent in rental policy. Some owners are very disturbed if there are any vacancies at all; others get upset with their property managers when occupancy is 100 percent, believing this indicates that rents are too low.

The decision as to this trade-off between rent levels and expected vacancies determines the allowance necessary for vacancy and collection losses, which is the difference between scheduled and effective revenues. Most should arise from vacancies alone. Collection losses, caused by failure of the property owner to collect rents from tenants, can be minimized by procedures to screen prospective tenants and by careful controls in following up on those who are late in paying their rent.

In Table 22-2, the vacancy factor is estimated at 5 percent of scheduled gross revenue. Although this figure is often used in the industry, it should be emphasized that such a generalization is not applicable in many cases. Whether 5 percent or some other figure should be used depends on the analysis of the actual market as well as on the decision as to what rent level should be set. Each market has particular characteristics, and each separate property has a unique relationship to the market. The actual determination of the projection for vacancies is derived from the same market analysis used to determine the scheduled gross revenue.

In the table, revenues are projected as increasing at 2 percent a year. This projection depends on the expected rate of inflation, the fact that buildings depreciate, and the fact that the ability to charge top rents decreases as other, newer apartments are built. In recent years a 2 percent expected rental increase might be considered conservative, but it is possible to include alternative assumptions in the income projections. We can also measure the degree of sensitivity of the projections to the separate assumptions while measuring the risks an investor takes.

Operating Expenses   Operating expenses are the costs of servicing the tenants and managing and maintaining the property. A listing of representative operating expenses is contained in Table 22-3; however, generally there are far fewer relevant expense categories. A more typical grouping for projections would include on-site management, off-site management, utilities, property taxes, maintenance, and miscellaneous.

Some expenses, such as property taxes and insurance costs, are almost entirely out of the control of the management. Other prices, such as those for supplies, services, payroll, and utilities, will not be controllable, but the management may be able to keep total costs down, depending upon the efficiency with which materials are used and the skill of the on-site supervisory performance.

In projecting operating expenses, practitioners frequently use ratios to simplify the work. While expense ratios can provide an effective screening device to determine whether the pro forma presentation appears reasonable and the property worth analyzing at greater length, caution must be exercised in using them. Many factors enter into expense ratios. It is unwise to base estimates on other properties unless one is certain of all the underlying factors.

The following are among the factors which influence the level of expense ratios: the age of the building, whether it is furnished or unfurnished, the extent of landscaping and recreational facilities, whether children are allowed, the amount of property taxes, whether utilities are included in the rent, the size of the complex, the regional location of the project, and the time of year. As an example of the variances in these

Table 22-3 Representative Operating Expenses

Supplies	On-site management
Services	Off-site management
Miscellaneous operating expenses	Other administrative expenses
Insurance	Interior painting and decorating
Real estate taxes	Exterior painting and decorating
Other taxes	Maintenance and repairs (internal and external)
Payroll expenses	Gardening
Payroll taxes and benefits	Elevator maintenance
Electricity	Pool service
Gas (excluding heating fuel)	Trash removal
Water	Advertising
Heating fuel	Rental commissions

ratios, a recent study of operating experiences for a large number of apartments in Los Angeles, San Jose, and San Francisco found that the average expense ratio varied from 52 percent of scheduled rents in Los Angeles to 34 percent of scheduled rents in San Jose, with San Francisco falling between at 43 percent. In San Jose property taxes and utilities made up more than 60 percent of the total expenses, while in Los Angeles they were only 40 percent of the total. Clearly, in considering expense ratios, some data will tend to be more reliable than others. An accurate projection of operating expenses, particularly for new projects, will require field research and an analysis of the relevant economic data.

For Table 22-2, operating expenses are assumed simply to be 40 percent of the scheduled gross revenue and to change at the same rate as gross revenue. They increase from $64,000 in 1976 to $70,800 in 1981.

Available Cash   When operating expenses are subtracted from the effective revenue, the result is the cash available to meet debt service and other needs.

In the case of Table 22-2, cash increases from $88,000 to $97,350 during the course of the 6 years. This result is based on the assumption that both revenues and expenses will rise at the same percentage rate rather than by the same dollar amount. This is an example of leverage. Since there is a gap between the two, if they increase at similar percentage rates, the gap, or amount available for other purposes, will widen.

In this case, the projected cash flow must be based on an economic analysis of the property. In many cases projections will arise from actual operating statements. The operating statements must be examined carefully and not accepted at face value. Many management techniques can be used to manipulate both the revenues and expenses. Temporary special leases to fill the property, postponement of needed maintenance, and use of materials which will not last all have the effect of producing a temporary jump in the apparent revenue from the property. Their total effect, however, may well be just the opposite, with revenues falling sharply when the artificial influences can no longer be used.

Cash Flow before Taxes

Rows 6 through 11 of Table 22-2 show the derivation of the net cash flow before taxes. The size of this sum is important because it provides a clue to the property's ability to carry its debt burden.

Debt Service   The debt service is simply a statement of the constant, or the annual payments due on the debt. The constant is divided into different amounts of principal and interest each year. In this case the property is to be financed with a loan of $900,000 at 9 percent interest to be paid off over 30 years. This results in a 9.66 percent anual constant to service the debt, or required payments each year of $87,897.

The cash flow before reserves is derived by subtracting the debt service from the net operating income. Because interest is calculated on the unpaid balance of the principal, which decreases each year, the amount of the debt service going to interest payments also decreases annually.

No interest is due in 1976 because the first year's interest is prepaid as part of the initial purchase. The debt service in the first year is only slightly over $6,000. The cash flow before reserves in 1976 is increased because of the large prepayment of interest. Thus in 1976 the cash flow before reserves is $81,851, whereas in 1977 it is only $1,863.

Again, the cash flow before reserves shows the significant impact of operating leverage. The debt service remains constant, and so the total increase in cash flows through to the investors. The net cash flow becomes a larger percentage of the total year by year.

Reserves An income property, like a manufacturing company, requires cash or working balances beyond the amount spent in purchasing its production facilities. Cash is needed to cover the gaps in time between when money is spent and when the associated revenue is received. In addition, cash is needed for major maintenance and refurbishment, since such expenditures often exceed the funds made available by a year's operations. Finally, cash provides a hedge against contingencies and unanticipated emergencies which may drain funds from the company.

An income property can be thought of as an independent, self-contained business. Its operating income depends directly on the availability of reserves to maintain the property at the standard necessary to support the desired rent levels and to meet debt payments if there should be a drop in revenues. Inadequate reserves may cause property conditions to deteriorate, resulting ultimately in reduced revenues, higher operating costs, and lower proceeds from eventual sale.

The amount of reserve needed depends on market forces, management's pricing and tenancy policies, the tenant profile, and physical factors related directly to the specific property. In a soft rental market, more reserves are needed than when demand is strong. Management's initial rent-up policy will affect reserve requirements, since more funds will be needed if management holds out for top-dollar rents rather than seeking to achieve a rapid rent-up with the possibility of raising rents later.

The type of tenant is also directly related to the amount of wear and tear. Property with children normally needs more maintenance expenditures than one limited to retired senior citizens. Similarly, furnished apartment units require more replacement expenditures than unfurnished ones. Physical characteristics of the property affecting reserve requirements include its age; the extent and quality of the amenities furnished in each individual apartment, such as dishwasher, garbage disposals, air-conditioning units, carpets, and drapes; the overall quality of construction; the amount and quality of landscaping; how much deferred maintenance exists; and the amount and nature of recreational facilities, such as game rooms, gymnasiums, tennis courts, and swimming pools.

Again, because the characteristics and conditions of individual properties vary so widely, the appropriate level of reserves should be determined by a specific analysis for each separate property. This will involve an assessment of its remaining useful life and the projected amount that will have to be spent for each component of the property at the date of its expected replacement.

Possible economies of scale in maintenance and replacement must be carefully evaluated in determining their actual timing. As an example, while there may be a saving in purchasing all the dishwashers at one time, such potential savings must be offset against the advantages of making replacements for such units when the apartment is vacant. There can be substantial variance in the amount of expenditures required from reserves from year to year. The probability of a surprise expenditure can be minimized by careful advance planning.

The tax deductibility of reserves and working capital is contingent upon when such reserves are expended, not upon when they are placed in reserve. To the extent that reserves initially funded at the time of the purchase of the property are expended during its operation, they may be directly deductible. However, if they are spent for assets that will last and be of benefit to the venture over a period longer than the immediate operating period, the purchases would be capitalized and depreciated at the appropriate rates.

For the property in Table 22-2, an addition of $3,000 a year to reserves is planned. However, we note that in the second year of operations, the amount of available cash is expected to be less than the desirable increase in reserves. For this reason, higher amounts are projected to be added to the reserves for the two following years to make up for the shortfall. The actual cash flow after debt-service payments and set-asides for reserves is zero for 1977 and 1978.

Annual Current Benefit

The cash-flow figures apply to any investor. They are of major concern for any lender and are a measure of potential risk. However, they alone are not sufficient for an individual to estimate the actual profitability or benefit he or she will derive from owning a property. The net benefit will depend, in addition, on how much of the total income is subject to tax, or the amount of any tax shelter that may be obtained, as well as on the person's actual tax bracket. Therefore, the next step in projecting the total benefit from ownership of the property is to determine its annual taxable income.

Depreciation In calculating taxable income, a critical factor is the depreciation deduction. As we saw in Chapter 21, the amount of authorized depreciation depends on the value of the property, on the rate of authorized depreciation, and on whether accelerated depreciation can be used.

Table 22-4 shows the projected depreciation for the sample property. As noted, the building is valued at $900,000, of which $600,000 is allocated to the shell, and $300,000 to personal property available for more rapid depreciation.

Table 22-4 Depreciation Schedule

Year	Personal property	Building double declining balance	Total
1974	$ 50,000	$ 40,000	$ 90,000
1975	50,000	37,200	87,200
1976	50,000	34,900	84,900
1977	50,000	32,500	82,500
1978	50,000	30,400	80,400
1979	50,000	28,300	78,300
	$300,000	$203,300	$503,300

No depreciation can be taken on the land. The building shell has an estimated 30-year life, but the $3\frac{1}{3}$ percent rate is accelerated by the use of the double-declining-balance procedure. As a result, in the first year depreciation at a $6\frac{2}{3}$ percent rate is taken. When this is multiplied by the $600,000 base, the depreciation deduction in 1976 is estimated at $40,000. The same $6\frac{2}{3}$ percent rate times the undepreciated balance of $560,000 at the start of the second year gives approximately $37,200 (the figures have been rounded) for the building shell in the second year.

The remaining property is depreciated on a straight-line basis over a 6-year estimated life. This gives an annual depreciation deduction of $16\frac{2}{3}$ percent of its $300,000 value. Thus the annual depreciation for this part of the project is $50,000.

The total expected depreciation for each year is shown in Table 22-4. The total is carried to Table 22-2, where it is shown as depreciation (row 13). Because of the double-declining-balance feature, the amount of the depreciation deduction available each year falls steadily.

Taxable Income   Since taxable income differs from the net cash flow because of the existence of depreciation (a noncash expense) and of payments on principal (a cash expense which cannot be deducted for tax purposes), there are two ways of calculating taxable income:

1   Taxable income equals cash before debt service minus depreciation and minus interest payments. Examine the fourth column for the year 1979 in Table 20-2. In that year we see:

Cash flow before debt service	$93,500
Less depreciation	82,500
Less interest	79,850
Net loss for tax purposes	(−$68,850)

This is the sum available as a tax shelter for other income.

2   Taxable income equals the cash flow after debt service plus amortization minus depreciation. We can calculate the same loss by using this second relationship:

Net cash flow after debt service, before taxes	$ 5,603
Plus amortization of principal	8,047
Minus depreciation	82,500
Same tax loss	(−$68,850)

In the example, in the year 1981 taxable income is further reduced by the amount of $18,000, which must be spent for maintenance and repairs in the year of the sale. This $18,000 was accumulated from the setting aside of $3,000 each year into reserves. These funds were part of taxable income in each of those years, but when they are actually expended, they become an expense and a deduction for tax purposes.

As we look across the columns in Table 22-2 and the calculations of taxable income, the movements we see are fairly typical. Inflation or other appreciation causes the revenue from the property to increase year by year. More cash is available to the owners. At the same time, the amount of depreciation falls every year because of the use of the declining-balance method. Amortization rises year by year, and the outstanding debt falls. Less of the debt service goes for interest. As a result, the amount of taxable income increases yearly—or, as in this case, the amount of tax shelter drops in each successive year.

Any drastic fall in the depreciation allowance causes a sharp change in the available tax shelter. Because a 6-year estimated life is used for all except the building's shell, such a change is projected for this property at the end of the sixth year. The authorized depreciation deductions fall by $50,000 in the seventh year. As a result, if the projection were carried out to the year 1983, this property would begin to show a positive taxable income.

We usually think of having a positive taxable income as the whole purpose of owning a property, but we recognize that in reality this is only partially true. To calculate his or her total benefits from ownership, the investor must take into account cash flow, the effects of taxation, and the final change in value. In this case, as in many others, the tax effects may be the most critical. For this reason, the sharp drop in depreciation is likely to force a decision as to whether the property should be offered for sale.

Tax Effects   The calculation of the income statement through the projection of taxable income is the same for each individual, but the actual current benefits will differ greatly depending on the size of the owner's income and the effective tax from which it is being sheltered. For the purpose of Table 22-2, we have assumed that the partners have enough other income so that, on the average, they will reduce the taxes they owe by 50 percent for each dollar of deduction carried through from the real estate venture to their individual tax returns.

To point up the significance of the 50 percent figure, let us assume that this property is held by a single investor. In that case, at 1975 tax rates, a married couple filing a joint return would have to have had about $85,000 in taxable income from other sources, after they had used all their other deductions and exemptions, in order to achieve the 50 percent tax benefit shown in the figure. If this property were owned by a couple whose income was only $50,000 after all deductions and exemptions, the tax benefit they would receive from ownership, instead of 50 percent, would be less than half of that shown in the table. The actual benefits would fall far below those estimated on the pro forma statement.

But the calculation of a 50 percent benefit would be approximately correct if the property were owned by a partnership of 10 couples, each of whom held one-tenth of the ownership, and if each of them had a taxable income of about $50,000. These differences arise because ownership of a large building by a single individual gives him such a large tax deduction that his effective tax savings are well below 50 percent unless he starts with a very large income from other sources. These critical differences underline the importance of examining the investor's actual effective tax bracket before attempting to say what tax benefits would accrue.

In the example, however, since it is assumed that each partner has an effective 50 percent bracket for the total amount of the shelter, the amount of tax benefit is derived by multiplying the taxable income by .5. Since the taxable income is negative in each year illustrated, the owners can use the total tax loss as a deduction to shelter other income. Each reduces other taxes by one-half of the annual negative taxable income shown in Table 22-2. Thus the tax benefit in 1976 is $1,000, and in 1977 it is $39,305.

Total current benefits depend on how much cash investors receive from the property as well as on the amount of tax loss. The benefits are summarized in the bottom row of Table 22-2. Actually, the greatest return is in the first year, when tax losses are at a minimum. In that year, the nontaxable net cash flow from the property is $78,851. This reflects the low debt service required in the first year. No interest is being paid because it was all prepaid in the previous year. In reality, the owners are merely receiving back their prior interest payment. In contrast, in 1975, they had a tax benefit to the extent of one-half of the prepaid interest, which, as shown in Table 22-1, lowered the amount of after-tax investment.

No net cash flow occurs in 1977 and 1978. The small net revenue goes into the reserve fund of the venture; it is not paid out. In the remaining years, the net cash flow rises, while the tax effect falls. Because the tax-shelter effect declines more rapidly than the cash increases, the total current benefit from the property declines slightly every year until the last.

BENEFITS AT TIME OF SALE

Finally, we need to calculate the benefits to be received at the termination phase—the time of sale, exchange, or refinancing of the property. The benefits depend on what price the property can be sold for. This is a function of the operating income the property is earning, available financing, and the specific tax benefits that the next buyer can expect. These in turn are influenced by how good the management has been, what has happened to the price level and to business in general, and the current level of interest rates. Because all these depend on projections, we shall see in the next chapter the importance of techniques of estimating the likely price under different conditions.

One point is clear: Because of the tax laws, depreciation for the new owner will not be as large. On the other hand, at the time the building is sold, its current income is a known quantity rather than a projection from a market analysis. The fact that the building has tenants and that it has an effective revenue schedule and known expenses reduces the risks for the second purchaser. For the case illustration, we assume that the various factors are offsetting and that the property will again sell at 6.25 times its scheduled gross revenue for the sixth year of its life, 1981.

In this example, we assume a sale of the property. Many offers of investment, however, use an assumption that the property can be refinanced. These offers project appreciation of the property as well as an equity buildup. They are extremely dependent on future costs and availability of financing. The profitability of refinancing will also depend greatly on whether accelerated depreciation has been used.

In Table 22-5, we see that the expected selling price is $1,062,000, which is 6.25 times the gross revenue of $177,000. Selling costs of 6 percent, or $63,720, are assumed. They reduce the gross to a net sales price of $998,280.

Taxes on Sales

The largest expenses at the time of sale will be the taxes which must be paid. During the ownership of the property, the tax deductions and tax shelter give the partners the

Table 22-5 Pro Forma Termination Statement

Gross sales price	$1,062,000
Less selling costs (6%)	63,720
Net sales price	$ 998,280
Tax basis	547,700
Taxable income	$ 450,580
Recapture	83,300
Capital gain	367,280
Capital gains tax (25%)	91,820
Recapture tax	41,650
Total tax due	$ 133,470
Cash from sale	144,986
Less total tax due	133,470
	$ 11,516
Plus original reserves	10,000
Net cash flow on sale	$ 21,516

benefit of time value; they receive more income currently, even though they are aware that they may have to pay a higher tax in the future. During the ownership period, a great deal of the cash flow, plus other income, is sheltered, but at the time of sale a final reckoning must be reached. The tax to be paid upon termination will depend on the rate of the capital gains tax, the amount of recapture or that part of the gain subject to ordinary tax, and the possibility that some of the capital gains may be subject to the minimum tax, or tax on preferences.

If the tax is high enough, as we saw in Chapter 21, it may be delayed by terminating the ownership through an exchange. The fact that taxes frequently have been high is one reason why exchanges have been a booming business for real estate brokers.

Capital Gains   In estimating the amount of tax due, we again note that the actual amount depends on the effective tax bracket of the partners. The situation is similar to the problem of estimating the tax bracket in figuring the tax benefits during the period of operations. If the capital gain is a large amount, it will automatically raise the bracket at which taxes will be paid. Thus in Table 22-5, we calculate the capital gains tax on the assumption that the property is owned by many partners and that the total capital gain for each partner in the year of sale will not exceed $50,000. Clearly, if the property were owned by a single individual, the size of the capital gain would be so large that unless this person had many losses in the year of sale from other properties or from common stock, the effective rate that he or she would have to pay on the capital gain would be at least 33 percent. However, as long as only half of the gain need be reported as income, the effective rate cannot exceed half of the top bracket rate.

Taxable income is derived by subtracting the tax basis from the net sales price. The adjusted tax basis is the purchase price plus capitalized but nondepreciated organization costs, less the total of depreciation deductions. Table 21-5 shows the calculation of the tax basis for our case property. This actual tax basis of $547,700 is carried through to Table 22-5. Subtracting this amount from the net sales price gives a taxable income of $450,580.

How this amount is divided between income subject to ordinary tax and income taxable at the capital gains rate depends on how much accelerated depreciation has been taken and on the length of time the building has been owned. For this illustration, we calculated the split on page 364 in Chapter 21. The result we saw was that $83,300 is subject to recapture, to be taxed at the ordinary rate, while the remainder is a capital gain, of which only half is included in taxable income. These figures, again, are shown in Table 22-5.

The total tax due is found by applying the assumed 50 percent effective rate for each partner to one-half the capital gain (that is, one-half the expected capital gain), to find an indicated capital gains tax of $91,820. Again, assuming that the tax bracket for the amount subject to normal taxes will be 50 percent, we find that the tax on the recapture sector is $41,650. Adding the two together, we arrive at a total tax due of $133,470. Again, this is assuming that none of the partners will have more than $50,000 in capital gains during the year and very little other income. If the property were held by a single investor, the tax payments would be at least $160,000.

Net Cash Flow on Sale

Finally we come to the matter of keenest interest: How much money do the owners of the property receive at the time of sale? This is found for the subject property by subtracting the outstanding mortgage balance of $853,294 (the original mortgage principal of $900,000 less the accumulated sum of the six annual principal payments) from the net sales price of $998,280. The cash received at time of sale, after paying selling costs, is $144,986. Subtracting from this the total tax which must be paid yields a net cash payment from the sale of $11,516.

In addition, at the time the venture was started, $10,000 of the amount put up by the buyers went into reserves. Under the assumptions of Table 22-2, none of these reserves were required during the course of operations. Sufficient additional reserves were accumulated during operations to meet the cost of refurbishing, which process is completely reflected in the operating income statements. Consequently, at the time of sale the $10,000 invested initially can be repaid to the partners. Thus the net cash flow at time of sale is estimated to be $21,516.

SUMMARY

Calculations and projections made for the three phases of the investment cycle—origination, operations, and termination—enable the analyst to draw up the combined cash-flow statement, which is the basis for calculations of the potential profitability of the investment. Together with the combined pro forma financial statements for each period, it will be the basis of the negotiations for the purchase of the property.

The current costs and benefits during each of the three phases of the investment cycle for the case property are summarized in Table 22-6. While, as we saw in Chapter 20, this table is fundamental to the final decision, it is not enough as it stands. It must be translated into an estimate of potential profits and risk.

Table 22-6 Total Current Benefits

Year	Origination	Operations	Termination	Totals
1975	($205,374)			($205,374)
1976		$79,851		79,851
1977		39,305		39,305
1978		37,040		37,040
1979		36,294		36,294
1980		36,426		36,426
1981		45,063	$21,516	66,579

The analysis of the prospective returns of the investment should be based on the full investment cycle and should take into consideration all tax consequences and all financing effects. Use of the complete cycle requires the analyst to develop information for the entire life of the proposed venture. This requirement is one of the major advantages of the investment-cycle approach. It forces explicit awareness of many factors that otherwise might be considered only implicitly or else disregarded. Even if no ultimate sale is contemplated, placing a terminal value at some point in time shows what anticipated future benefits can be expected when the investment is completed. The value of this factor, depending on how far it is in the future, may play an important role in the entire investment.

The investment-cycle approach to analyzing real estate ventures will lead to better investment decisions. It must be recognized, however, that the results of the analysis will be only as reliable as the quality of the basic information and the assumptions which enter into the projections. Each of these must be carefully checked to make certain that it is as sound as possible.

QUESTIONS AND PROBLEMS

1 Describe two different methods of computing taxable income.
2 What is the reason for staging investment contributions?
3 In planning a real estate investment, the downpayment paid to the seller is the number that is used in evaluating its potential return. Discuss.
4 Knowledgeable real estate investors find that after looking at a couple of deals, they have a good idea of what operating expenses are likely to be. Discuss.
5 Why are reserves necessary?
6 Discuss the concept of an optimum rent level in contrast to a maximum one.
7 Discuss the advantages and disadvantages of using cash flow or current benefit in evaluating a proposed real estate investment.
8 Using the pro forma financial statements in this chapter, explain how a tax shelter is advantageous even if some of the tax break will be recaptured.
9 What answer would you give to someone attempting to sell you a property who said that no one can possibly get the information needed to prepare proper pro forma statements?
10 How would the benefit of the property described in this chapter differ if it were owned by one individual rather than a ten-member partnership?

Economic Studies and Risk Analysis

Chapters 20 and 22 explained how prospective investors use financial information to create profitability statements which can be used to compare projects and accept or reject ventures. Since these statements and their analyses are only as good as the information which underlies them, more and more effort is being put into improving their quality. In the case of a large project involving the expenditure of substantial sums, investors and lenders frequently demand an independent economic study of the proposed venture. Related studies may also be required by governments before they will approve either a proposed land use or a possible sale of securities.

Either as part of the economic studies or as part of investment analysis, more attention is also being paid to the probability that the projections will be wrong. Investors want to know what may go wrong and how their investment will be affected.

This chapter deals with economic and feasibility studies, environmental impact studies, and sensitivity studies of risks based on uncertainty.

ECONOMIC AND FEASIBILITY STUDIES

The feasibility of a project is of critical concern to both the promoter and the investor. An economic study and an investment analysis are necessary for decision purposes and to justify each participant's involvement. Studies serve to explain a venture to interested parties. If they are based on an independent third-party view, they can be far more effective than a promoter's own presentation. Use of a third party implies that some expertise has been incorporated into the planning and conceptualization of the project in addition to that of the developer. However, the degree to which this is true depends on the responsibility of the outside expert. His or her work and reputation must be checked, not simply taken for granted.

The analysis of feasibility from the point of view of investors is roughly similar for both new developments and existing property. They want to know whether to buy or sell, whether they will gain more profit from the venture than they could elsewhere, and whether it makes sense to convert land to a new use. A maxim of real estate investing holds that the key to success is buying right. If investors overpay for a property or commit funds to a development project lacking in economic justification, they find themselves behind from the start.

A new development project poses a more complex investment decision than an existing property, where there are fewer uncertainties. A going project already has actual financial statements. They need only to be checked out and possibly modified in the light of potential economic movements. An economic study for a new development must provide the basis for defining the project. Both the opportunity and the need exist to evaluate the plans, the requirement for funds, and the probability of success. These studies can be the basis for suggesting revisions which can bring about improvements.

Equity investors are on a constant hunt for the best prospects. They want studies which find the areas with the best opportunities. Then they are interested in identifying the best locations within those areas, and finally they want to evaluate particular situations.

In contrast, lending institutions react primarily to specific proposals. They want to verify to their own satisfaction that the property will generate adequate cash to provide the necessary security for a loan. Potential lenders are interested mainly in an economic study which will furnish them an indication of the possible risk they are taking with a specific loan or the range of comfort they may expect.

For both the investor and the lender, the projections of the income statement and the timing of the cash flows, as well as the risk, will depend on both overall economic factors and the specific market conditions of the individual venture. An economic study must take both into account.

Types of Questions

The focus of economic studies from both the investor's and the lender's perspective is the expected future return. Will the property enjoy a competitive price-value relationship so that those committing resources can expect an adequate rate of return?

The price-value relationship depends on whether the project satisfies user needs at competitive rates. Only to the extent that a project meets the demands of the market will it be satisfactory in the long run. However, in the short run, because of market imperfections and because some people invest or lend out of ignorance, projects that lack intrinsic value may generate attractive financial returns for their promoters.

The economic study of primary interest to the investor is that which underlies the pro forma financial statements and leads to the appraisal of investment value. As we have noted, the primary focus of those who put up the money centers on cash flow—the difference between the revenues and operating expenses. Consequently, the emphasis of economic analysis must be on determining such probable cash flows. Of necessity, these are predictions from the existing facts, with all the dangers and potential errors of projections into the future.

The object of studies is to provide prospective investors and lenders with a projection for each element of the financial statement over the full investment cycle. This approach contrasts with the traditional appraisal, which is based on a single normalized operating statement. The appraisal estimates changes in the levels of rents, vacancies, and operating expenses, as well as the ultimate selling price. It then reflects most of these data in a single capitalization rate. The advantage of the financial-statement approach is that it is explicit rather than implicit. It shows the specific factors that are expected to change values or the rate of return, rather than averaging them into a single capitalization rate.

Most economic studies, however, furnish something other than a basic financial analysis. They are shaped so as to answer questions such as the following:

1   Where is the best market and particular site for a development?
2   What is the best use for a specific site?
3   How should a project be planned to give it the greatest chance of success with respect to such elements as (a) what price should be sought for apartment units or stores, (b) what pace of development should be followed, and (c) what rate of absorption should the market be expected to supply?

These questions, as well as specific projections of revenues and expenses, are answered by an analysis of the supply and demand situation at individual sites. Such analysis leads to estimates of what the market wants, how much it will pay, and how the demand for a property will react over time. Cost data are obtained from operating reports of similar property. They, too, are projected on the basis of past trends and forecasts of general economic conditions.

Types of Studies

While the study for investment analysis is the most important, many different types of economic studies are made for a variety of purposes, intended users, and specific situations. All have certain common elements, but the basic data may be shaped in different ways according to the predominant purpose. Among the names used for various types of economic studies are the following:

Investment analysis
Highest- and best-use study
Land-utilization study
Site-selection study
Market study
Market research
Marketability study
Compatibility study
Feasibility study
Appraisal

Reuse appraisal
Economic analysis
Economic research
Projections
Economic base study
Environmental impact study
Economic impact study

As their names imply, because the reports are aimed at different audiences, they tend to vary in their analytic procedures. This means that each study must be carefully planned before it starts so that it can best answer the specific questions required of it.

STUDIES FOR THE PUBLIC

The last two types of study on the list are becoming more and more important in the development process. They attempt to answer questions of public concern.

Whereas in earlier times developers were almost universally welcome and found public approvals easy to obtain, the situation has changed in recent years. Today the developer may encounter significant resistance based on stringent standards and often led by opponents organized to fight a proposed project. The public is interested in a project's effect on the physical environment, in its economic impact, and in the degree to which it conforms to established planning standards. Environmental impact reports are required by law for all public projects. Many states require them for private projects as well. Such studies aim at reporting the potential effects of converting land to a new use.

In addition to the promoter and the investors, interested parties in a land conversion include (1) local governments, (2) adjacent landowners, and (3) the general public.

1 Local government jurisdictions want to know about the economic impact of a project on their municipal finances, especially with regard to schools, sewer systems, and water supply. In many communities, numerous governmental agencies have jurisdiction over a proposed use. Even though requirements may be overlapping and even conflicting, promoters must gain approval of each one if they are to proceed.

2 The owners of adjacent land want to know whether a proposed use will benefit or harm their property. While in many cases a new use enhances such values, in other circumstances adjacent landowners find that the value of their properties has decreased. For this reason they want a study that will enable them to scrutinize carefully the proposed new use.

3 The general public is becoming more and more involved in land-use decisions. Many groups concerned with the livability of their environment take an active role in determining whether a project should be authorized. If they are not satisfied, they frequently go to court, which leads to long and costly delays or, in many cases, to the abandonment of projects which fail to gain their support.

Environmental Impact Report

Environmental impact reports (EIRs) are required to assess the impact of a proposed land use on the public interest. Studies that consider only the economic and not the physical consequences of a change are known as *economic impact reports*.

The term "environment" is broad. Included in the natural environment are geology, soils, hydrology, groundwater, vegetation, wildlife, fisheries, climatology, and meteorology. Of particular concern is the presence of any rare or endangered plant or animal species. The human or cultural environment includes the present use of the land, transportation systems, municipal services and utilities, demographic factors, socioeconomic factors, agriculture, historic factors, recreation facilities, visual and aesthetic elements, noise elements, air quality, and areas of unique interest or beauty.

In the past, many municipalities aggressively campaigned for development in the belief that it would increase their tax revenues more than their costs. Owners of the land also reaped large gains. But today, local communities are increasingly coming to the conclusion that the economic impact of new developments is more likely to be negative than positive. Consequently, developments which were once sought after are now resisted. A conflict arises with those owners seeking developmental profits.

Most communities have master plans laying out a general framework of expected land uses. Each new proposal for a conversion of land use is examined to see how its use and density conform to the master plan. For instance, a proposal to construct an industrial plant in a residential area would be rejected as nonconforming.

However, use is not the sole criterion. Density standards, measured in terms of either the number of residential units or, for commercial use, floor-area ratios, are often applied. Thus if an area shown in a plan is restricted to houses with minimum lot sizes of .75 acre, a proposal for townhouses involving densities of eight units per acre would probably be opposed as nonconforming. In some cities ordinances also specify the height and bulk of proposed structures. Moreover, developers increasingly find that the definition of conformity is not confined to objective standards alone. More and more communities are applying subjective criteria to distinguish conforming uses from those which are nonconforming.

Although to many the contents of the environmental impact report are somewhat of a mystery, the information that government officials most often ask for is data of the sort that developers themselves take into account in their own project planning. However, the divergent points of view of government officials and developers may well result in a different emphasis and orientation.

Table 23-1, which shows the suggested guidelines for a draft environmental impact report of the Department of City Planning of the City and County of San Francisco, gives an insight into the possible contents of such a document. A project must be described in terms of its location and its technical, economic, and environmental characteristics. The environmental setting of the project must be described, especially in terms of the type, intensity, and scale of surrounding land uses, as well as in terms of the region's population characteristics. Specific information is to be furnished on the direct and indirect effects of the project on the individual elements of the environment shown in the table. The effect on each element is to be rated on a scale of 0 to 3, with 3 being most substantial, and 0 meaning no effect. When a rating is higher than 0, it must be explained. Ratings of 2 or 3 must be explained in considerable detail. Alternatives to the proposed project, including no project at all, are to be discussed and evaluated.

This report is considered a draft. In actual fact, the environmental report in final form is often produced by the appropriate government agency itself. It is based on the

Table 23-1 Conditions of the Environment Susceptible to Influence and Change

(To Be Evaluated in Terms of Their Short-Term and Long-Term
Potential Adverse Effects)

Land
1 Landforms and unique physical features, such as bays, tidelands, beaches, lakes, hills, and slopes
2 Soil stability, compaction and settling, and susceptibility to earthquake damage
3 Erosion and sedimentation
4 Alteration of ground contours

Water
5 Drainage and runoff
6 Surface, ground, bay, and ocean water

Air
7 Quality, in terms of gases, chemicals, smoke, dust, or particulate matter, clarity, and odor
8 Microclimate, in terms of temperature, wind, moisture, and precipitation

Plant and animal life
9 Trees, shrubs, and ground cover
10 Mammals, birds, reptiles, amphibians, fish, shellfish, insects, and other invertebrates
11 Rare or endangered plant species or plant communities
12 Rare or endangered animal species or habitat for such species

Land use
13 Residential, commercial, industrial, or public uses
14 Structures, above or below the ground
15 Pattern, scale, and character of the neighborhood
16 Physical division or disruption of the neighborhood or community
17 Recreational facilities

Population
18 Density and distribution
19 Economic, ethnic, racial, and age characteristics
20 Displacement and relocation
21 Congestion and crowding

Services and utilities
22 Public schools and educational facilities
23 Police and fire protection
24 Health facilities
25 Water and electric power systems
26 Sewage systems
27 Solid waste disposal

Transportation and circulation systems (public and private)
28 Capacity of existing systems
29 Effect on surroundings from changes in systems

Cultural facilities and aesthetics
30 Historical or archaeological sites
31 Unique or uncommon structures
32 Scenic views or vistas
33 Open space or natural qualities, including landscaping

Source: Department of City Planning, City and County of San Francisco.

Table 23-1 Conditions of the Environment Susceptible to Influence and Change (*continued*)

Health and safety
34   Noise levels and vibrations (on-site and off-site)
35   Construction hazards
36   Earthquake hazards
37   Hazards to general health, safety, and welfare
38   Use or disposal of potentially hazardous materials

Objectives of the city
39   Master plan of the city
40   Neighborhood plans
41   Economic stability
42   Employment
43   Services
44   Housing quality

Other (specify)

_____

_____

_____

information supplied by the sponsor of the project applying for approval, plus additional material worked up by the government. The sponsor must bear the major costs of the research effort, which can range from a few thousand dollars to several hundred thousand dollars, depending on the type of project. In the San Francisco case, all consultants contributing to the report must be identified. Additional information may have to be provided to meet the needs of the final report.

PROJECTING DEMAND

The mandatory public studies are usually developed only after the promoter has put together his own studies for the needed investment analysis. The projection of revenues and expenses in the financial statements depends on the demand and supply situation for the particular project.

The types of information needed for projecting revenues and expenses differ depending on whether it is expected that land will go into single-family homes, apartments, commercial property, or industrial use.

The economic study moves from general considerations to specific ones. Depending on the size of a project, it may start with the economic and demographic profile of the entire area, including population, employment, and income. More important than the absolute numbers are their trends and composition. Thus for a housing study, the number and formation rate of households are of particular concern. Attention is given to the general quality of local services, including schools as well as medical, recreational, and shopping facilities. The objective of this part of the study is to develop projections of the anticipated general demand and the probable supply over time.

In projecting demand, it is not enough merely to extrapolate from past experience. Rather, the focus must be on what generates demand. More specifically, the analyst must ask: Where will the demand for the specific site come from? What factors will cause people to want to live in this area as opposed to living elsewhere? Where will they work? How strong is the employment base? Will there be adequate transportation to enable people to commute to work? Will the incomes available be high enough to support the type of housing contemplated?

Sources of Data

The answers to many of the questions needed to project demand can be found in information frequently available in the public domain. The starting point for demographic information is the United States census. Conducted every 10 years, the census is a comprehensive survey of the country's economic and demographic characteristics. Additionally, more specialized studies are made at other times.

Census data cover virtually all political units of the nation, as well as statistical areas down to a city block. Table 23-2 gives an indication of the range and detail of coverage for population and housing characteristics included in the 1970 census.

Traditionally, census data have been available in the form of printed reports, but now most are obtainable on computer tapes. Known as *summary tapes*, they allow the user virtually unlimited flexibility in designating the combinations and cross-tabulations of census data for a particular area. They can be used to give a planner detailed information on selected areas, even those defined merely as a specific distance surrounding the property being evaluated.

Many other federal and state government agencies also publish statistical data. For example, traffic counts for specific roads are available from state highway departments. The state tax collector publishes retail sales figures by type of business and location. The human resources office tabulates employment by occupation. Particularly useful are county and city planning departments, since they maintain records on the dollar volume of building starts, vacancy factors, and the like. A number of banks publish local data through their economics departments. Often information on vacancies can be obtained from the post office or from utility companies. In addition, numerous private organizations publish research services or make available special studies.

Field Studies

Despite all these sources of data, people who are preparing studies often find that the specific information they want has not been tabulated. Moreover, the accuracy of what they find may be suspect. This means not only that careful analysis is required but also that the general data must be supplemented by fieldwork. This is almost always true with respect to obtaining specific details pertaining to a particular venture. Obtaining such information usually involves interviews with property managers, owners, tenants, brokers, bankers, and others knowledgeable about the market being studied. Where appropriate, a formal consumer behavior survey, involving either personal or telephone interviews, may be utilized.

While details of the type required often prove difficult and frustrating to obtain, they

Table 23-2 Content and Coverage Comparison, 1960–1970

(Sample Percentages for Population and Housing Items Included in the 1970 Census in Comparison with the Items in the 1960 Census)

Population	1960	1970	Housing items	1960	1970
Relationship to head of household	100%	100%	Number of units at this address	–%	100%[f]
Color or race	100	100	Telephone	25	100[g]
Age (month and year of birth)	100	100	Access to unit	100	100
Sex	100	100	Kitchen or cooking facilities	100	
Marital status	100	100	Complete kitchen facilities		100
			Condition of housing unit	100	
State or county of birth	25	20	Rooms	100	100
Years of school completed	25	20	Water supply	100	100
Number of children ever born	25	20	Flush toilet	100	100
Employment status	25	20	Bathtub or shower	100	100
Hours worked last week	25	20	Basement	25	100
Weeks worked last year	25	20	Tenure	100	100
Last year in which worked	25	20	Commercial establishment on property	100	100
Occupation, industry, and class of worker	25	20	Value	100	100
Activity 5 years ago		20	Contract rent	100	
Income last year:			Vacancy status	100	100
Wage and salary income	25	20	Months vacant	25	100
Self-employment income	25	20[a]	Components of gross rent	25	20
Other income	25	20[b]	Heating equipment	25	20
Country of birth of parents	25	15	Year structure built	25	20
Mother tongue	25	15	Number of units in structure and whether a trailer	20	20
Year moved into this house	25	15	Farm residence (acreage and sales of farm products)	25	20
Place of residence 5 years ago	25	15[c]	Land used for farming	25	
School or college enrollment (public or private)	25	15			
Veteran status	25	15	Source of water	20	
Place of work	25	15[d]	Sewage disposal	20	
Means of transportation to work	25	15	Bathrooms	20	5

Item		
Mexican or Spanish origin or descent		5
Citizenship		5
Year of immigration		5
When married	25	5[e]
Vocational training completed		5
Presence and duration of disability		5
Occupation industry 5 years ago		5
Air conditioning	5	5
Automobiles	20	15
Stories, elevator in structure	20	5
Fuel—heating, cooking, water heating	5	5
Bedrooms	5	5
Clothes washing machine	5	5
Clothes dryer	5	5
Dishwasher		5
Home food freezer	5	5
Television	5	5
Radio	5	5
Second home		5

[a] Single item in 1960; two-way separation in 1970 by farm and nonfarm income.
[b] Single item in 1960; three-way separation in 1970 by social security, public welfare, and all other receipts.
[c] This item is also in the 5 percent sample but limited to state residence 5 years ago.
[d] Street address included in 1970.
[e] In 1960, whether married more than once and date of first marriage; in 1970, also includes whether first marriage ended by death of spouse.
[f] Collected primarily for coverage check purposes.
[g] Required on 100 percent for field follow-up purposes.

are vital for many decisions. Since the real estate investment and finance decisions are based on the expected cash flow and returns derived from projections of operating results, such projections must realistically reflect actual market conditions.

PROJECTING SUPPLY

Information on the probable level and strength of demand is meaningful only when set against data on supply. Supply estimates start with the quality and quantity of the existing space inventory. The inventory may decline as a result of demolitions following from condemnation or removal to make way for new development, as well as because of voluntary removals by owners who elect not to make their space available.

The inventory is increased by new construction activity. This means that a projection of supply must include a forecast of the level of building permits and new construction starts. Forecasts must consider the availability of sites for future construction in light of their suitability in terms of such factors as zoning, size, shape, topography, soil conditions, location, and access. At times natural barriers, such as mountains or water, limit the land available for future development or make it necessary for construction to be located on land some distance away. Such findings are especially important in the analysis of a specific site.

Real estate markets are very particularized. It can be highly misleading to rely on statistics for a large area or even on some of the broader statistics for a local area. As an example, while a region may have a very low vacancy rate, the rate in a specific neighborhood can be quite high. Or it may work out that in a neighborhood with a 20 percent overall vacancy factor, investigation will reveal that the units standing vacant are not what the market wants. A project which is designed at the right price for families with children or which is of a size particularly suited for unmarried people might have a spectacular demand if it supplies a hitherto unfilled need. It is the particular factors which enter into and surround each site that make specific investigations so important as a basis for projected financial flows. However, because gathering such information is costly, care should be exercised to concentrate available funds on acquiring the critical data needed for decisions.

Effective Rent Levels

The projection of demand and supply will culminate in a very specific outline of the type of units expected to meet with assured demand over the life of the project. Thus the separate demands for townhouses, garden apartments, and highrises will be analyzed. The examination of other properties in the neighborhood will show what type is most in demand and at what rents. The projection will show the expected rents for each type of unit which might be built as well as the vacancy rate to be expected at the optimum level.

Operating Costs

The economic study will give the actual costs being experienced by various types of projects. The ratio of maintenance, heat, operating personnel, and other expenses will be contrasted by type of unit. Each will differ depending on the land use being projected.

When the revenues and expenses are put together for different uses, the developer will be able to choose the one that seems most suitable. On the basis of this choice, even more detailed statements will be worked out for use in planning and also as the underlying analysis for lenders and other prospective investors.

The economic studies culminate in sets of pro forma financial statements, loan applications, security prospectuses, and similar reports, together with their supporting data. Their specific form and detail depend on their prospective use. Their value depends on how well they have caught the shifting forces of supply and demand, and how carefully these forces have been projected into the future.

UNCERTAINTY AND RISK

Improving the accuracy of pro forma financial statements through good economic studies is one way investors can reduce their uncertainty and risk. But the possibilities of error are still great. Every potential error is a source of risk for investors. If the cash flow drops below the amount required for debt service and reserves turn out to be inadequate, the entire equity may be lost. On the other hand, if an inflation occurs or if the property remains fully occupied at rents above those projected, the existence of favorable leverage may raise the actual return far above that projected.

In Chapter 17 we discussed several formal ways in which investors might handle the problem of uncertainty. Some investors attempt to estimate the degree of uncertainty or risk of individual properties by a formal procedure and use their estimates to adjust the discount factor.

More often, such adjustments are made in an ad hoc manner. The expected cash flow is cut, or the discount rate is increased. Thus an investor who compares two ventures and feels that one is riskier may arbitrarily reduce the expected cash flow or benefit by 10 or 20 percent. The investor would then accept a proposal only if the present value or rate of return on this venture after such a downward adjustment remained as high as, or higher than, that on an alternative.

Similarly, an investor facing two offers, one of which seemed riskier, might calculate their present values using a 10 percent discount factor for the less risky offer and a 15 percent discount factor for the one that seemed to carry more risk. The investor would then accept whichever ended up with the higher profitability index. This same type of procedure is followed when capitalization rates are altered in traditional appraisals.

Analysis by Monte Carlo Simulations

Another growing technique used to assist investors in making decisions under uncertainty is computer simulation. Many computer software packages are available which permit sophisticated analysis of the risks involved in particular investments. Many large real estate brokers and many consultants have access to these packages and to computers. As a result, they can compute and make available a great deal of data with respect to any specific investment proposal.

The basic idea behind a Monte Carlo simulation is that it makes it possible for an investor to see what might occur under a variety of possible conditions. The simulation shows possible earnings under different assumptions as to future cash flows and relevant pro forma financial statements. This technique enables an investor to see how sensitive estimates of value and of profits are to possible errors made in putting the projections together. On the basis of the picture it paints of the risks involved, the investor can decide whether they are so great as to make the venture unattractive.

The simulation programs start with pro forma financial flows like those we have been discussing. The analyst decides which projections or lines in the statement are most likely to be in error and consequently to cause major differences in the estimated value of the investment.

To illustrate, investors would probably be concerned about whether the rent schedules shown in the financial statements will actually be achieved. They might also feel, as a result of past experience, that projected vacancy levels can be badly underestimated or that operating costs may grow faster than expected. If all these conditions were to materialize, they would affect the projected sales price as well, since it is based on a multiple of the rent schedule. Monte Carlo simulations allow the investor to make alternative assumptions as to each of these major factors in the projection and to see how these added factors change the expected yields and profits.

Estimating the Probability of Changes   After selecting the variables for which the initial projections are most likely to err, the analyst next must decide on the form that changes are likely to take:

1   While computers can handle any type of information, analysts commonly specify the expected probability distributions in order to avoid having to construct a large number of tables for each of the variables. They specify the distributions in terms of the expected variance around the average or mean. Thus one might specify that the rent schedule was expected to rise by 2 percent a year and that the standard deviation of this estimate was 1 percent. In nontechnical terms, this would mean that in approximately 68 percent of the cases, the actual increase in revenues in a year would fall within a range of 1 to 3 percent. In 95 percent of the cases, the range of increases would be between 0 and 4 percent.

2   In some cases, a simple distribution cannot carry enough information. For example, in the case of many apartment buildings, vacancies are projected at an average 5 percent a year. We know, however, that vacancies cannot fall below zero and might run as high as 50 percent or more. Therefore, the analyst, in putting in a distribution for vacancies, would probably want to use a skewed distribution—one which, even though it used 5 percent as an average, would give a greater chance for 10 percent vacancies to occur than for zero vacancies.

3   Analysts also need to specify the degree of dependency or correlation between the movements of their different factors. Thus if they assume that changes in operating costs are directly related to movements in revenues, they might continue to use a similar rule.

4   Since revenues may depend on the degree of inflation and since inflation usually persists for several years or more, analysts might want to specify a form of time dependence. They would not assume that what happens in any one year is independent of what happened the previous year. Thus they might say that if revenues went up 3 percent in a year, the change in revenues in the following year would not be between 1 and 3 percent, but would be more likely to fall between 2 and 4 percent. This would be a form of time dependence, or correlation over time.

On the basis of their analysis of the probable errors to be found in the projections and how they are related to one another and related over time, analysts will specify a set of distributions for each of the variables with which they are concerned. They might specify distributions for the effective rent schedule, operating expenses, the vacancy rate, and the final selling price.

A Monte Carlo Simulation   Given these assumed distributions, the computer is set to work. It is told to create a large number of pro forma financial statements of the types shown in Tables 20-2 and 22-2. It does this by picking for each year to be studied a number at random for each of the variables in which errors are likely from the probability distributions the analyst has furnished.

Thus for 1978 the computer would pick a new estimate of the rent schedule, a new vacancy factor, a new operating expense, and the selling price if the property were sold in that year or later. Using the previous assumptions for taxes and the discount factor, it would then calculate either a new estimate of present values or a new estimate of the internal rate of return. The computer would rapidly make similar calculations for anywhere from 10 to 30 cases, in each case picking different numbers from the probability distributions in accordance with the rules laid down by the analyst.

Figure 23-1 shows the possible distributions of the estimated present values of the property or the estimated internal rates of return based on 30 computer runs of the type described. (In the normal case, the computer will draw the charts desired.)

Figure 23-1a shows the number of cases falling in each present-value class. This might be the distribution of present values based on an assumed discount factor of 10 percent with the property to be sold at the end of 8 years. The average expected present value appears to be close to $20,000, but a few of the computer runs show that with a string of unfavorable events, losses are possible.

In Figure 23-1b estimated rates of return are shown, but other profit measures could be used. Based on 30 sets of computer selections from the probability distributions supplied by the analyst, this chart is a cumulative probability distribution. It shows the odds calculated from the different runs that the rate of return would fall above or below a particular rate of return. Thus in this case, the different runs seem to show that the expected rate of return will be between 12 and 14 percent. (This is where the cumulative probability becomes .5.) On the other hand, the chances of a negative rate of return seem to be less than 10 percent. No combinations of selected possibilities gave returns worse than a negative 5 percent, and none better than a plus 30 percent.

Figure 23-2 presents similar information, but for each possible year from 1 to 15 that the property might be held. The solid line shows the expected rates of return based on the average assumptions used in the original case. However, the returns are calculated not for just the 6-year holding period but for any number of years from 1 to 15. The dotted lines immediately above and below the solid line are drawn one standard deviation from the average. They mark the boundary within which 68 percent of the simulations fell in any year. The dashed lines, drawn two standard deviations from the solid line, form the boundary within which 95 percent of the 30 simulated cases fell in each year.

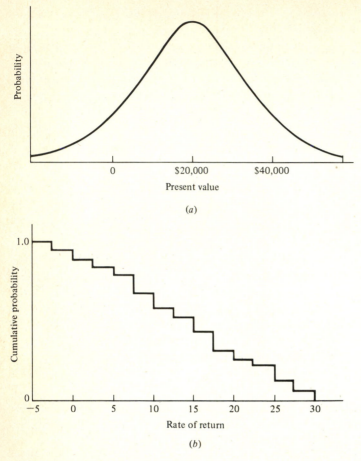

Figure 23-1 Distribution of possible rates of return and present values projected from Monte Carlo simulations.

The lines are simply another way of picturing the results of the simulation. They show how far the expected rate of return might vary from the most likely case, given the probable errors in the projections the analysts think might occur.

Using the Charts The two figures together give an indication of the type of information computers can furnish. Everyone familiar with computer output is aware that there are likely to be too many, not too few, data when a problem is being analyzed. What the computer does in this case is to calculate the present value or internal rate of return of a number of probable situations. The probabilities depend directly in a mathematical manner on the assumptions given to the computer by the analyst.

The information in the figures can be used by the analyst in many ways. For example, from Figure 23-2 he can choose the year when the property is most likely to have its highest overall profit rate. The analyst can also see what dangers may arise if the property is held for too long or too short a time.

In this case we see that there is only a slight difference in the expected rate of return

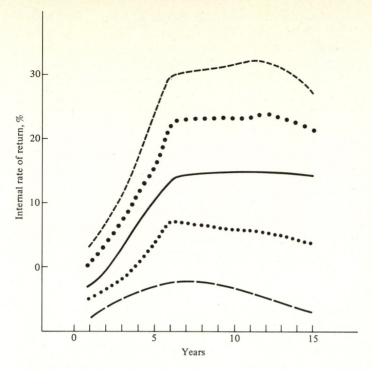

Figure 23-2 Projected movements of rates of return related to possible movements in factors determining a property's income.

for holding periods of anywhere between 6 and 11 years. This information is valuable for calculating risks. We know that because high interest rates and recessions come frequently, it may not be possible to sell a property advantageously in a single year or two. The figure, however, indicates that nothing in the underlying structure of this venture leads to the expectation that a higher yield would prevail for only a brief period. An investor is not likely to be penalized if it becomes necessary to hold the property for 2 or 3 extra years.

Both figures give other indications of risk. Thus from Figure 23-2 we can see that if the property is held for a basic period of 6 to 10 years, even though on the average it will have a positive rate of return, this is far from a certainty. In about 40 percent of the cases, the rate of return either will be negative or will fall under a desired 10 percent.

Similar information is shown in Figure 23-1. Looking at Figure 23-1a—the distribution of expected present values in the eighth year—we note that the distribution is somewhat skewed toward present values below the average. This is because of the possibility—built into the program—that vacancies will be much higher than the average expected 5 percent.

Figure 23-1b enables us to read off immediately the probabilities that the venture will actually lose money or that it will make a large amount. We can then determine, for example, if it turned out that money is likely to be lost in 20 percent of the cases, whether the average rate of return is high enough to make it worthwhile accepting this risk.

Other, similar distributions can be used for the same purpose. For example, the computer, instead of being asked to chart the internal rates of return or present values, could be asked to chart cash flows. These are derived in the simulation during the construction of the financial statements. From a distribution of estimated cash flows, one can estimate in what percentage of cases the reserves set up as part of the venture would not be adequate, thus incurring the danger of foreclosure. Such simulations allow another approach to risk bearing and decision making. For example, an investor might specify that she was not interested in any venture with more than 5 percent probability that a negative cash flow would continue for more than 2 years. Such a stipulation would stem from her unwillingness to be wiped out, no matter how great the expected gain might be on the average.

It is worth reemphasizing that the simulation does not add any information to that which the analyst puts into the computer. What it does is to calculate the risks inherent in his assumptions and in the way in which the venture is financed and put together. It shows how sensitive the pro forma statements are to the underlying assumptions. This type of sensitivity analysis is very difficult to perform analytically. It is much simpler with a system of trial runs using different assumptions, which the computer does so easily.

SUMMARY

Economic studies aim at improving the decision-making information for investors and lenders or other interested parties. The studies are careful projections of demand for, and supply of, space based on as complete an analysis as is economic or feasible. Information about the area and the neighborhood is used to project specific costs and revenues and also to examine alternative land uses and designs.

The growing public concern with land use has led to a demand that even more complete studies be prepared for public decision makers. An environmental impact statement may be considered typical of growing requirements in this sphere.

Risks arise in any investment because of the probability that events will not conform exactly to what has been predicted. Different techniques can be used to introduce the concepts of risk and uncertainty into decisions. One useful technique consists in analyzing the sensitivity of the expected yield to unexpected events. With computers and Monte Carlo simulations, such an analysis becomes relatively simple.

QUESTIONS AND PROBLEMS

1 How can a computer be used for sensitivity analysis?
2 What parties are interested in the findings and conclusions of economic studies?
3 What type of economic study is becoming more important in the development process?
4 Why are economic studies required?
5 What should be considered in an environmental impact report?
6 Explain the relationship between an economic study and the pro forma financial statements.
7 The friction engendered between citizen groups and developers over some environmental impact studies is often due to fear of economic impacts. Discuss.

8   Observers believe that in recent years, more errors have been made in forecasting costs than in forecasting supply and demand. Do you agree? Explain.

9   What are some of the critical assumptions whose effects you would want to analyze by sensitivity analysis?

SELECTED REFERENCES FOR PART SIX

Aronsohn, A. J.: *Partnership Income Taxes*, 4th ed. (New York: Practising Law Institute, 1974).

Downs, J. C., Jr.: *Principles of Real Estate Management*, 10th ed. (Chicago: Institute of Real Estate Management, 1970).

Graaskamp, J. A.: *A Guide to Feasibility Analysis* (Chicago: Society of Real Estate Appraisers, 1970).

Income and Expense Analysis (Chicago: Institute of Real Estate Management, annually).

Isard, W.: *An Introduction to Regional Science* (Englewood Cliffs, N.J.: Prentice-Hall, 1975).

Jobs, People and Land: Bay Area Simulation Study (Berkeley: University of California, Center for Real Estate and Urban Economics, 1968).

Journal of Real Estate Taxation (Boston: Warren, Gorham & Lamont, quarterly).

Kane, B. J., Jr.: *A Systematic Guide to Supermarket Location Analysis* (New York: Fairchild Publications, 1966).

McCoy, J. O., et al.: *Federal Taxes Affecting Real Estate*, 3d ed. (Chicago: National Institute of Farm and Land Brokers, 1970).

McNulty, J. K.: *Federal Income Taxation of Individuals* (St. Paul, Minn.: West Publishing Co., 1972).

Office Building Expense Ratios (Chicago: Office Building and Management Association, annually).

Pellatt, P. G. K.: "The Analysis of Real Estate Investments under Uncertainty," *The Journal of Finance,* May 1972.

Pyhrr, S. A.: "A Computer Simulation Model to Measure the Risk in Real Estate Investment," *The Real Estate Appraiser*, May–June 1973.

Ricks, R. D, and H. Friedman: "Federal Taxes and Real Estate Investment Decisions," *Proceedings, 1968*, The National Tax Association.

Robinson, G. J.: *Federal Income Taxation of Real Estate* (Boston: Warren, Gorham & Lamont, 1973).

Roulac, S. E.: "Life Cycle of a Real Estate Investment," *Real Estate Review*, Fall 1974.

_____: "Sophisticated Investment Analysis Helps Structure, Measure True Profitability," *Apartment Construction News,* April 1973.

_____: "Truth in Real Estate Reporting," *Real Estate Review,* Spring 1973.

Seldin, M., and R. H. Swesnik: *Real Estate Investment Strategy* (New York: Wiley-Interscience, 1970).

Urban Land Institute: *Dollars and Cents of Shopping Centers* (Washington: 1963).

Walters, D. W.: *Real Estate Computerization* (Berkeley: University of California, Center for Real Estate and Urban Economics, 1971).

Warren, R. L.: *Studying Your Community* (New York: Free Press, 1965).

Wendt, P. E., and A. R. Cerf: *Real Estate Investment Analysis and Taxation* (New York: McGraw-Hill, 1969).

Willis, A. B.: *Willis on Partnership Taxation* (New York: McGraw-Hill, 1971).

Part Seven

An Investment Strategy

Real estate investments can take several forms. Successful investors match their needs and desires to the specific features of each venture. They improve their profits by planning their investment strategy and then doing the analysis necessary to select the best properties. Many investors have been sadly disappointed when ventures sold as guaranteed protection against inflation and certain to return high gains turned out poorly. Such failures occur either because investors buy ventures that are far more risky than they realize or because they fail to take even elementary precautions to ensure that they will receive fair value for their money.

Chapter 24 describes how to plan an investment strategy. How much money should go into real estate, and what types should be selected? In Chapter 25 we discuss the choices facing a family or firm looking for space. Should it rent or buy, and how should this decision be made? The advantages of investing in real estate securities are analyzed in Chapter 26. What types are available? How should people choose the ones best suited to their own investment strategies? Chapter 27 describes the features unique to each type of property. What characteristics shape the risks and profits associated with each? The final selection of a real estate portfolio is dealt with in Chapter 28. How does planning help achieve investors' goals and increase their returns?

Chapter 24

The Strategy of
Real Estate Investment

Forecasting and measuring a property's profitability are only part of an investment decision. Investors face many different types of choices. Deciding on how to approach them can be thought of as the selection of an investment strategy. The knowledge required for selecting the best strategy is important for individual investors. It also plays a major role in the actions of brokers, lenders, and others concerned with the real estate process.

Like practitioners in any field, many investors have depended in the past on intuitive knowledge and a gambler's instinct. Many tended to be either great successes or disastrous failures, frequently fluctuating from one extreme to the other. As knowledge has increased, however, more successful real estate investors have been able to hang onto their profits. They have been able to outperform others because they carefully plan and effectively execute an investment strategy. While strategic planning is important to any enterprise, it is of particular concern in real estate investing because the process is so complex.

We have discussed the complexities of analysis in real estate financing and investment. The investor faces numerous choices. Any particular deal may encompass a number of separate and distinct possible investment positions, each with very differing potentials for risks and profits.

Investors with a considered investment strategy can approach the decision process in an orderly manner. By means of advance planning, they eliminate many possible actions inappropriate to their particular needs and objectives. When an opportunity presents itself, they are in a position to make an informed decision. Without an investment strategy, investors often find themselves with no clear course of action. Investment results suffer from a haphazard, uncoordinated, unplanned, nondiscriminating approach.

Planning an investment strategy centers around answering the questions of why, how, and when to invest. The many unique investment characteristics of real estate must match the characteristics of the individual investor. What should one look at in deciding his or her own strategy? The following factors are important:

1   The investor's existing wealth, assets, and income

2   The risks the investor is willing to take to achieve high, average, or low but safe rates of return

3   The investor's talent for investment analysis and management and the amount of time he or she can devote to these activities

4   The investor's ability to utilize property to meet his or her own space needs

5   The parts of the industry that the investor believes have the best prospects

6   Whether the investor wants to invest in real property through common stock, REITs, other securities, partnerships, or a personal, individual ownership

7   At what point in the real estate cycle the investor wants to enter and in what type of properties

After clarifying his own views on each of these topics, the investor can then pick investments that meet his personal needs and desires.

INVESTOR CHARACTERISTICS AND OBJECTIVES

The amount to be invested in real estate and the form of return desired are a function of the investor's wealth, other assets, and income. These factors determine the usefulness of tax shelters and various forms that returns can take. The investor's personality and attitudes are important in determining how much risk or diversification should be sought. The time the investor has available to hunt for and manage investments, together with his or her skills and ability along these lines, is another critical influence on strategy. A property that is useful to a person who can manage and maintain it might be an actual liability to someone else.

The fact that a buyer can be found for almost any property does not mean that every investor should consider investing in each property. The appropriate type of venture is different for each investor, depending upon his or her own position and objectives.

Wealth, Assets, and Income as Determinants of the Amount of Investment

Real estate investments can be made for any amount between $100 and $100,000,000. How much to invest in any single venture and how much to invest in real estate as a whole depend on an investor's circumstances, preferences, objectives, and other assets.

Of major import is the investor's financial position. What is his or her net worth? What is it likely to be in the future? What holdings does the investor have now? How much is in cash, and how much in other forms of liquidity? Some investors raise their funds primarily by saving out of current income. Others have an unused ability to borrow money which they can invest if they so desire. Many people have existing investment portfolios which they hope to improve by shifting some into, or out of, the real estate field. A person with a fair amount of existing assets will find it much easier to invest than one who must accumulate investable funds from income after providing for necessary expenses and existing obligations. In each case, however, a decision must be made as to how much will be available for new investments.

After a minimum of security has been assured, potential investors must decide how to divide their funds. For this purpose each possible investment offers different degrees of risks and rewards. Most investors prefer to diversify in order to reduce their risks, allocating some funds for liquidity, some for common stocks, some for bonds and mortgages, and some for real estate.

A particular real estate investment strategy makes sense only when it is related to other parts of an investor's portfolio. Each sector should reinforce the others by offering features otherwise lacking in the portfolio. Real estate as an investment offers a tax shelter, a potential inflationary hedge, and large possibilities for leverage. Leverage can bring about high potential returns with high risks. In deciding how much of their assets to place in real estate, investors must decide which of these features they most desire and how these can be related to their other holdings.

Form of Return

After investors decide, on the basis of their financial position, how much to invest, they must determine in what form they want to achieve their return. Real estate investments return their yield in three forms: cash flow, tax shelter, and capital gains. Cash flow and tax effect are realized each year. Equity buildup and appreciation, which lead to capital gains, occur over time, but they can be realized only when the mortgage is refinanced or the property is sold.

Returns may be spread evenly over time or concentrated in a particular time period. Some investors need current cash income. Others are interested primarily in obtaining a tax shelter to offset other income subject to a high tax rate. For similar reasons, some investors may be concerned chiefly with deferred cash and hoped-for capital gain. Each specific investment situation tends to emphasize a different element of the return. Unless, as part of their strategy, investors consider in advance what difference the form of return makes to them, they will be at a disadvantage in responding to the investment opportunities that are offered.

Tax Shelter

As discussed earlier, taxes often are very important in real estate investments. Consequently, investment decisions must be based on an investor's present tax rate and also on that projected over the life of the venture. Although complaining about how much one has to pay in taxes seems to be a favorite American pastime, a high tax bracket is often the generating force of a real estate deal. Investors in high tax brackets are in the best position to take advantage of tax deductions arising from depreciation and interest. Unless there is a need for a tax shelter, many investments make little sense.

The differential impact of the tax shelters separates potential investors and determines what type of properties they may be interested in. Thus nonprofit organizations which are tax-exempt entities should normally avoid investments where a major portion of the return must be realized in the form of tax savings. Similar considerations apply in the case of retired individuals and others in a relatively low tax bracket.

Corporations face a somewhat different tax problem. While a property may generate substantial tax losses that will lower a company's tax payments, such tax losses also reduce its reportable earnings. As a result, most publicly held corporations cannot afford to pay as much for a tax shelter as an individual can. This holds true even when the corporation is in a higher tax bracket. The reason, most simply, is that the Wall Street financial community does not value tax losses in the same way an individual does in measuring an investment. The results of the investment are translated to the company's income statement as a loss. This shows as a reduction in overall income from other activities and lowers its reported accounting earnings during the tax-shelter period. The net effect tends to be that the price of the stock of the corporation is reduced compared with that of the stock of other companies whose real income may actually be less. Real estate firms have complained for years about the accounting rules under which they must operate, believing that their stock prices are being penalized, compared with the situation that would obtain if they could report their potential returns under a different set of accounting rules.

Risk and Diversification

The investor's attitude toward risk is a third factor of great importance. Many investors are attracted to real estate primarily because of its high leverage and the possibility of extremely high returns, despite the probability of large losses. Other investors find such risks completely incompatible with either their personalities or their investment objectives.

An investor's risk posture is revealed by the degree to which he or she is willing (1) to concentrate assets in one or a few properties and (2) to borrow personally to finance an investment program. Some people avoid real estate investments because such investments are large and may require a high concentration in one or a few ventures, which can be adversely affected by location, luck, or forces impossible to foresee.

The problem of borrowing is that if the investor uses sizable personal borrowings, a loss or drop in the cash flow in one investment could have a disastrous domino effect on his overall portfolio. However, assuming that properties are financed on nonrecourse terms—the lender or seller having recourse only to the property and not to the borrower—losses on a highly leveraged property will not automatically affect the balance of the investor's portfolio. Such a property would have a high break-even point, and the possibility of a negative cash flow would be increased, but if the investor does not need to meet the negative cash flow from other sources, he or she will lose merely the single property and not necessarily the whole portfolio.

An investor's tax bracket and risk tolerance are somewhat interrelated. Because additional borrowing generates more interest and depreciation writeoffs, investors in higher tax brackets can often utilize higher leverage more advantageously than investors in lower tax brackets. But it must be emphasized again that this type of tax consideration too frequently has led to poor investment decisions. The investment must stand on its own feet if it is to be a successful tax shelter or general investment.

Investors, in assuming risks, must also take into account the possibilities of diversification. A portfolio of many risky investments may have a lower overall risk than would be indicated by a simple addition of the dangers involved in the individual ventures. This, however, is true only to the extent that the different properties are subject to contradictory forces. Too often this is not the case. Diversification can lower real estate risks to the extent that the dangers arise from factors specific to a particular property, such as location, style, and management. However, investors often find that while they have bought several properties, these are of the same type, were produced in the same period, and involve the same general concepts. In such cases, risks are reduced only slightly. Even if enough differentiation is achieved to minimize the above risk factors, the investor must be aware that even many diverse types of real estate investment will be similarly affected by the business cycle and tight money. In choosing an investment strategy, the investor should be careful not to be fooled by seeming diversification which, in actuality, does not exist.

Time and Talent

An investor's personal circumstances are a fourth characteristic influencing an investment strategy. A family's situation determines what kind of housing it needs, as well as how much time it has available to devote to investment activities. Because finding, evaluating, and managing real estate investments are time-consuming and expensive processes, it is critical for investors to assess carefully the amount of time and effort they can devote to managing the investments. If several members of a family want to be involved in the investment program, the kinds of situations that can be considered may be very different.

Available time is often the most important factor in determining whether a particular type of investment is likely to be profitable. For example, a great deal of the return for a certain property may actually be in the form of payments for management or for labor personally applied. Men and women who have plenty of time or who want an avocation different from their regular jobs may find extremely good investments in the area of the small apartment or older house. They will be paid, but probably at a rather low hourly rate, for time that they would otherwise waste or for work which they find pleasant, not onerous. The availability of a real estate investment turns what would otherwise be wasted time into a higher income.

On the other hand, investors must carefully examine the circumstances surrounding their employment, as these too can be important in formulating an investment strategy. The factor of how long a person will remain in a location is one of the most critical variables in making a "buy or rent" decision concerning a home. Similarly, someone who is likely to be transferred on short notice would find it imprudent to own a portfolio of local properties requiring continuing attention. Those who must travel extensively or who work exceedingly long hours may find themselves with little time available to supervise and administer their investments.

Finally, investors must critically assess their own resources in terms of time and expertise to compete in the real estate investment business. An individual investor's competition, to a large extent, will come from those who devote their full time and energies to their investment programs.

While the real estate investment business has been characterized by a notable lack of professionalism, this state of affairs seems to be rapidly changing. More and more key decision makers have gone on to advanced study in business, law, planning, and related disciplines. They may have varied experience, and many have undertaken extensive continuing education programs. Rarely does the individual investor operating alone have equivalent sophistication and knowledge.

Effective property management is fundamental to successful investment results. Except on a small scale, it is difficult to do well with only part-time involvement. Indeed, many urban housing problems, such as landlord-tenant relations and lack of maintenance, frequently are traceable to part-time involvement on the part of the owner of the property.

For all these reasons, investors must determine whether they have the time, expertise, and inclination for real estate decision making and management activities. What are the probabilities that an individual will be able to originate, evaluate, and manage good investment opportunities? Those who lack the necessary skills and ability must seek other forms of investment, not dependent upon their own direct ownership and management.

RATE OF RETURN

A further consideration, which in some ways encompasses many others, is the decision as to what rate of return to seek for a given investment. It is vital to any sound strategy that the decision on the rate of return be made logically and with a recognition that no series of investments can promise higher-than-normal rates of return, except as pay for services rendered. Investors operate in very competitive markets which tend to ensure that payments are equal to the basic return on capital plus any skills and efforts which are put into a project. Returns that are abnormal depend upon special skills, the taking of higher risks, or luck.

Competition for Investments

Those involved in the real estate business, especially those in selling positions, tend to make unrealistic claims about returns that can reasonably be achieved from real estate investments. These claims are prima facie in conflict with basic economic theory. The real rate of return on any investment, corrected for risk, effort, and special features, is related more directly to the overall rate of return on all investments in the economy than it is to the particular type of investment to which funds are committed. Investor funds tend to move from less attractive to more attractive investment opportunities.

Supply and demand have a significant impact on the allocation of capital among various types of investment. To the extent that one specific type, such as real estate, enjoys a greater return than other investment opportunities, capital will be diverted to it from other areas. This infusion of new capital to the area which started out at a higher level causes the returns available from this class of investment to decline. Indeed, the very success of any particular investment opportunity means that over time it will move to a return more closely approaching the average available among all investments.

While some studies show high rates of return to common stocks or to real estate, there is no proof that these returns over long periods are higher than would be expected, given the risk or pay for other factors which may be included in the estimated rates of return. Furthermore, the average rates of return tend to be somewhat lower than most people have in mind when they invest in real estate or in common stocks.

Estimated Returns

We have a great deal of information about how investors have fared in the stock market, but only a minimum number of studies of returns in real estate. Over a sweep of 50 or 60 years, common stocks seem to have earned about 8 to 10 percent on a pretax basis.

In any period such as 1 or 2 years—or even 5 or 10—these averages have not prevailed. In 10-year periods from the mid-1950s to the mid-1960s, investors in common stocks earned 14 percent on the average. In some shorter periods they earned far more. On the other hand, in the decades ending in 1974 and 1975, returns were far less, ranging around zero for 10 years, depending on the specific date picked. In several years, they were sharply negative.

Is it logical to assume that over time, real returns of real estate investors cannot differ greatly from real returns of investors in common stock? To many people, this concept of an average rate of return seems contrary to everyday experience. We know that many people have made large sums investing in real estate. Returns of 50 or 100 percent, based on a few years of land speculation or ownership of certain types of income properties, have been realized by many. Insurance companies and pension funds rushed into real estate in the late 1960s, assuming they could earn 15 to 25 percent on their entire portfolios. How do such returns jibe with the idea that over time, and given an average investor, the rate of return on all investments must be related to that on all others as determined by a general competitive market? What are the factors that may make real estate returns as a whole, or for certain categories, appear higher than the average, whether taken over shorter or longer periods?

Achieving High Reported Rates

Even though real estate does not pay returns out of the ordinary when corrected for special factors, it may still form a valuable part of many investment portfolios. It is valuable to those who, because of their asset positions, tax brackets, or special skills, can earn extraordinary returns.

However, a danger is ever present. Those who fail to make certain that they profit from the way in which an investment meshes with their own position are likely to receive a real rate of return lower than they would in other investments. Investors who are not careful pay for special characteristics which they cannot use. As a result, they waste money and lower their real rate of return. On the other hand, if they match their needs carefully to their real estate investments, they can profit—perhaps handsomely.

What are the special factors enabling a real estate investor to earn above-average returns even in a competitive market? We have already commented on many of them in our analysis of the investment decision. When we examine returns in real estate which are above average, we find that they are related to the following types of investment action. In each case the specified action of the investor serves to increase his or her rate of return over what would be expected from the yield on an average investment.

1   The risks of the market and management costs are reduced because a family or firm invests in a property for its own use. It profits by retaining the risk premium which the market must pay.

2   The investor has picked a property with above-normal risks. The real return may be high also if the investor succeeds in reducing the risks of his or her own portfolio by a proper diversification.

3   The investor is in a tax bracket that makes it possible to profit from the fact that the government tax subsidies return more than the marginal rate set by the competitive market.

4   The investor has exceptional entrepreneurial skills and is being paid for this above-average ability.

5   The investor has accumulated knowledge and an analytic ability to pick projects which, on the average, stand out and pay added returns.

6   The owner spends his or her own time performing management tasks, making repairs, and taking care of maintenance work and similar jobs. The pay received for these efforts is included in the owner's stated rate of return.

7   The rate of return is high simply as a matter of luck. The distribution of real estate returns around the normal is even wider than it is in the stock market. One could expect, by throwing a few darts or making random choices, to hit a certain number of real estate investments with unusually high or low returns. Some appear as big winners; others, as big losers. On the other hand, when all these random elements are averaged out, the returns no longer appear abnormally high or low.

8   The investor is being paid for giving up liquidity.

9   The investor, because of the amount of capital he or she controls, has invested in a unit costing more than one which can be purchased by the average investor.

10   The investor is a successful forecaster of the real estate cycle. He invests near the start of rising markets and is not caught in an overextended position when the market falls.

When we put all these factors together, it may well be, as some preliminary research by the authors indicates, that an after-tax rate of return on real estate investments somewhat above that of common stocks is reasonable.

A more interesting theory, which has not been proved but which many familiar with the real estate market believe to be the case, is that in real estate investments, item 5 in the above list may be especially significant. There may be a very positive payoff for specialized investment analysis.

A large amount of empirical and theoretical research suggests that individual stock prices move in a random manner and are not susceptible to specialized investment analysis. The competition among analysts means that stock prices rapidly reflect the general state of knowledge. There is no proof that, over time, any large institutional investors do better than would be expected as a result of random movements about the average.

In contrast, because so few resources have been devoted to a systematic study of real estate performance, as opposed to stock and bond research, those engaged in specialized analysis of real estate investments may currently receive an above-average return. It may be possible with careful analysis to assemble properties or a portfolio with smaller, not larger, fluctuations in rates of return compared not only with an average of real properties but also with an average of all equities.

This, then, is the investment problem that individuals face. Certain characteristics of their jobs, their knowledge, their assets, their taxes, or other factors make it possible for them to boost their real returns (corrected for risks) above the average by developing a proper strategy. But it is not simply by investing in real estate that they will achieve their goal. They do it by investing in a proper selection of real estate assets.

RENT OR BUY?

The most common real estate investment decision concerns how a person, family, or firm should acquire the space it needs for its own use. A family can buy or rent its home; a company may lease or own its office or production facilities.

Most persons maintain permanent residences which they own or rent for an extended period. How often they move is a critical factor in determining whether it is better to own or rent.

In addition to the main residence, at one time or another most households have secondary housing requirements. They may need overnight housing on trips or holidays. People who regularly vacation in a specific area may own a second home. Others, however, usually stay in transient housing facilities, including hotels, motels, campgrounds, and the like.

Businesses' space needs parallel those of households in many ways. Businesses maintain home "bases" in the form of corporate headquarters, a manufacturing facility, service headquarters, and distribution facilities. Businesses, moreover, often utilize multiple bases, with corporate facilities in many locations throughout the country and even the world.

In some markets, particularly when the household or company is on a very tight budget, the need to find new space presents a major problem. The search can be frustrating, time-consuming, and often discouraging. The ideal house never seems to be available; what is available seems to be overpriced. Furthermore, moves from one base to another are all too often made under pressure. Timing of the transition is often crucial. A family moving to a new area must take care not to interrupt its income. In the same way, a corporation must locate new space without disrupting its basic flow of business. But in spite of possible troublesome aspects, a need for space may often involve an investment opportunity. A company or a household can, with adequate planning, often exploit this need to its own advantage.

For many families housing has been a preferred and most successful investment. With ever-rising construction costs and land prices, many houses have grown in value with time. Such increased values have depended upon the houses' being well con-structed, well designed, well maintained, and desirably located. Careful buyers can select houses with these characteristics. When buyers are not under inordinate pressure, they can enjoy the advantage of waiting for the right deal.

Businesses, too, are in this same situation of having to decide whether to rent or buy their space, but in either case the fact that they need space and can pay for it gives them a powerful position in the investment market.

Most real estate investments depend for their success on the willingness of someone to pay for occupying space. Families or companies looking for space generate the necessary market for a property. They are the source of the space demand eagerly being sought by all real estate owners. Their problem is to decide whether they can best use their power through renting or through buying. The next chapter analyzes many of the factors determining which decision will be best at what times, for, as in all investment decisions, timing is critical in these markets.

INVESTORS OR FURNISHERS OF SERVICES?

The real estate industry is composed of two broad categories: (1) those who provide services to the industry and also those who act as processors and (2) those who invest in real property. The latter commit their funds to direct investment positions. The former process land and buildings and supply other types of services. The broad group of industries related to real property includes real estate brokerage, property development, construction, mortgage financing, appraisal and feasibility consultation, insurance, property management, and the sale of building materials.

While there is often a high covariance of economic movements among the investors and those furnishing services, this is not always the case. At certain times economic conditions which may aid the processor are adverse to the interests of investors. When new building activity is high, processors do well, since there is a high level of demand for their services; however, a high volume of building causes substantial additions to supply. The new supply-demand relationship determines the revenue stream and therefore the income of investors. If supply rises too rapidly, investors find themselves in trouble. Conversely, when the level of building activity drops, investors may benefit because fewer additions are made to the supply. As a result, investors' revenue per unit may rise, and they can capitalize on the favorable supply-demand relationships. Thus both processors and investors can expect to be influenced by the cyclical swings of the building business, but the movements in overall supply and demand may well be less in sales and in some other types of services than in construction.

TYPES OF INVESTMENT POSITION

Another way of looking at investment strategy is to recognize that there is more than one way to invest in real estate. The most basic decision is whether the investor wants to be a lender (and thus be in the position of owning debt with real estate as a security) or to become an equity owner.

The debt position assures some predictability and stability of income as well as the security of principal. Returns have been high compared with those of other debt instruments, but liquidity has been low and risks rather great, compared with liquidity and risks associated with other forms of debt.

The equity owner, of course, carries all the risks and potential rewards that we have just discussed. These can, however, again be varied depending on what form the equity position takes. Investments in the common stocks of real estate groups are similar to those in other common stocks. However, movements in stocks of firms related to real estate have a basic relationship to underlying movements in real property itself. As a result, those with a good understanding of real estate financing and investment practices can reach a more informed decision as to what to expect from the entire category of such stocks.

Direct Ownership One form of equity position, whether through personal investment or through a firm, is to own property directly. This is by far the most common type of investment, and much of it is for owner occupancy. In addition, however, some people own directly and manage various types of income property. In this case the equity carries with it both the right and perhaps the headaches of another job. The owner receives income as a manager and perhaps as one who furnishes construction or maintenance services.

Small Syndicate The form of ownership closest to single, individual, direct ownership is ownership by a group of friends or acquaintances who get together in a joint venture to own or develop a property. This was the traditional form of joint venture. The advantages are the ability to gauge one's partners and the possibility of finding an investment tailored to one's own needs. The disadvantages are the almost complete lack of liquidity in such situations; usually if one has to sell, purchase will be made by one of the other partners or by a mutual friend.

Securities By far the largest increase in investments in recent years has come through the purchase of publicly issued securities in real estate programs. The most common form has been the limited partnership, since, as we have seen, this type of entity can pass through the tax-shelter advantages of real estate.

Securities in this form have tended to be somewhat more liquid than the small syndicates, but other questions arise. Chapter 26 deals at length with some of the major issues which must be faced when a decision is made to invest in real estate in this form.

Common Stock We have already noted that much investment in the real estate industry is done simply through the stock market. Many types of real estate processors have sold stock to the public. In addition, there is a limited number of firms specializing in real estate property ownership which have issued stocks. A problem here has been the difficulty of passing through the tax advantages of real estate ownership, as well as the fact that the market has been unwilling to bend its standard accounting procedures to take account of the normal differences in the flow of funds through real estate firms.

REITs The final type of position is probably the easiest to assume—that is, through an REIT. In our extended discussion of them, we saw that one can find REITs investing primarily in equities, some with large and some with minimal leverage; REITs which invest primarily in long-term mortgages; and REITs which specialize in construction and other development financing. It is this last group which met with such disastrous results in 1974 and 1975.

THE LAND-USE CYCLE AND TYPES OF
REAL PROPERTY USE

How a property reacts to major economic trends is a basic feature determining its investment suitability. Real estate values vary with a property's stage of development and its characteristics. For analytic purposes, we may consider investment opportunities in real estate in terms of five phases through which property may pass: undeveloped, predeveloped, developed, declining, and redeveloped. Deciding where in this cycle to buy and what type of property to select is another important part of formulating an investment strategy.

Undeveloped Land

In its raw, or undeveloped, stage, land derives its value from the commodities or services it produces. It is a resource for food, raw materials, or recreation.

Predeveloped Land

The value of predeveloped land depends on its future development potential. It may still be used for agricultural or extractive purposes, but its price is now determined by its anticipated contribution to an integrated economic enterprise represented by a completed and functioning property. We saw in Chapter 5 that this stage offers both the highest risks and the greatest potential returns. If the land is developed successfully, the percentage increase in equity and profits can be huge.

Developed Properties

Developed properties represent space in which people carry out the many activities of their daily lives: (1) Residential real estate provides space for basic shelter; among the higher-income groups, it may also be symbolic of a certain way of life. (2) Commercial real estate is space where people sell goods and services. (3) In office buildings people administer the various functions of society. (4) In industrial real estate, goods are manufactured. (5) Finally, there are a number of special uses for real estate. These, together with land, are the types of property analyzed in Chapter 27.

In the developed phase, land and buildings are inseparable as far as their use and basic values are concerned. Although land may be owned and financed separately, its value is tied to the economic activity of the space it supports. The owner of the building pays the landowner from the revenue generated by the whole package, which determines their joint value. To the extent that land is owned separately from improvements, it is generally in a priority position, with first claim on income. In such cases, land is considered to be the most stable and least risky of investments in property.

Whereas in earlier stages owners and their agents are relatively passive, in the developed part of the cycle they are very active, in both off-site management endeavors and on-site physical activities. Successful property investment depends not only on all the economic, political, and social forces that impinge upon real property but also on the many management activities which maintain and increase the revenues after a property has been built.

Declining Properties

Over time, most properties suffer a decline in value as a result of changing economic conditions, shifting patterns of land use, physical deterioration, and functional obsolescence. They may become substandard and eventually be abandoned or redeveloped.

Regional Change   Economic and political forces cause the prosperity of regions to rise and fall. New technological development stimulates the expansion of some companies and the decline of others. Conditions which made an area a center of economic activity may no longer exist. Many cities that were among the largest at the beginning of the century have lost population and economic values. Transportation innovations make some regions more desirable and others less so. Government spending decisions create activities in certain areas, while causing sharp reductions elsewhere. For the investor, the critical factor is that a region's economic health has an important impact on property values within it.

Neighborhood Change   Land-use patterns shift; neighborhood conditions change. Highly desirable parts of town become less so. The center of business activity may move. When neighboring properties are not adequately maintained, a property suffers. If the highway is rerouted, a property that once enjoyed a prime location may become virtually inaccessible. While land-use patterns affect a specific property's value, most investors can exert little influence over their nature or direction.

Aging   Many wonder how buildings can be abandoned in the face of shortages of space, especially of housing. Buildings decline in value because their qualities compare unfavorably with those of competing properties. Older apartment buildings may lack elevators, custom bathrooms, kitchen appointments such as dishwashers and garbage disposals, and the full recreational facilities offered by new apartment complexes.

When a building's condition deteriorates, turnover rises. The new tenants tend to have lower incomes and more limited opportunities. When a building falls into a state of disrepair, the cost of holding it may outrun the revenues it can generate. In the face of negative cash flows, owners may abandon the properties to the tax rolls, with the city eventually acquiring ownership by virtue of its priority tax revenue claim.

If such conditions persist and are unchecked in an area, the neighborhood may become a slum. The operating costs compared with revenues for properties in many central cities are so high that buildings have to be abandoned. The boarded-up, unoccupied buildings are a blight on the urban scene.

Substandard Units   A significant share of the nation's housing stock may decline into substandard condition. Such a decline is a prelude to boarding up and to either destruction or redevelopment. While in some cases rents charged accurately reflect the value of the space, for other low-priced properties rents may be excessive, indicative of either a shortage of space or the fact that run-down conditions in dilapidated buildings may generate extremely high management and operating costs. In some cities where rent control laws keep rents below actual costs, landlords are faced with extremely difficult choices.

Tight housing markets combined with disadvantageous bargaining power on the part of tenants may make it possible for unscrupulous landlords to "milk" properties by charging excessive rents and providing inadequate or nonexistent management and maintenance. In such situations, owners seek to get the maximum cash flow over a short time period, abandoning the property when faced with the necessity of major expenditures to bring the building up to the housing code.

Landlord-tenant relations in run-down properties tend to be stormy. There is usually high turnover. Both residents and outsiders may literally destroy the property, breaking windows, knocking holes in the walls, and tearing out kitchen and bathroom fixtures. Needless to say, such destruction and vandalism raise operating costs.

In the current social and political climate, there is mounting opposition to slumlord practices that exploit the poor. Representation of tenants' interests has rapidly grown stronger, and it is likely that slumlords will come under increasing pressure to provide decent housing at reasonable rents. Unfortunately, the pressures caused by slumlord profiteering have spilled over into the legitimate market, often subjecting conscientious landlords to unrealistic tenant demands and resulting in a decline in maintenance and services, and even in abandonment of properties.

Redeveloped Land

The final investment phase for real property is redevelopment. As the term suggests, properties undergo new development activity. Large-scale activities, such as the redevelopment of entire areas, are often described as urban renewal projects. More frequent, especially in the 1970s, is the refurbishment and major rehabilitation of specific properties. If a structure is in a state of extreme disrepair or suffers from such advanced obsolescence that rehabilitation is not feasible, the existing improvements may be razed and the property returned to a predeveloped land stage.

Refurbishing a run-down building can be a particularly interesting investment opportunity. Frequently the property can be acquired for its land value only, with the physical improvements obtained at no cost. Some properties can even be acquired for less than the land value, since the owners avoid the cost of tearing down or moving existing structures. But if the existing structure is sound, all it may need is some upkeep, refurbishment, and repair.

The market for rehabilitating properties has tended to be a very specialized one. The ability to envision a new use for a building or to see that a building is in a good-enough location and has a basically sound-enough structure so that rehabilitation will pay is a skill not given to many. On the other hand, those who have either the entrepreneurial ability or the time, managerial skill, or actual craftsmanship to do the basic work frequently find that rehabilitation is an excellent use of their time and energy.

The advantage of rehabilitation is many cases is that it can be performed by individuals with a minimum amount of capital. They build up their equity through their own labor. As the equity increases, they frequently find that they can get financing, take some of their equity out, and use the funds to rehabilitate another unit.

SUMMARY

Developing a sound investment strategy requires making some specific decisions. On the basis of their own needs, wealth, desires, time, skill, and other characteristics, investors must determine:

1 How much money to invest in real estate as against other types of investment.

2 What form of return to seek. Investors may desire a tax shelter, capital gains, or maximum current income.

3 What type of risks to assume. Returns are related to risk. Is the investor willing to seek maximum gains through high leverage? Will he or she risk everything on a property? Can risks be reduced through diversification?

4 What role to play. Will the investor buy property for his or her own personal use, manage properties, or be primarily a passive or silent partner?

5 What rate of return to seek. Investors should plan to realize more than they would on common stocks, but how much more will depend on the risk they take and on the time they devote to analysis and their ability along these lines.

6 Whether to invest in real property or in other businesses related to properties. Property can be owned directly or with others or through securities or common stocks. An investor must choose from among these different options.

7 What strategy to adopt. Strategies differ depending on where in the real estate cycle an investment is made and on the type of property purchased. Each has a particular advantage or disadvantage for a given investor.

QUESTIONS AND PROBLEMS

1 It has been said that the motives of real estate industry participants are in conflict with those of real estate investors. Discuss.

2 Is it reasonable to expect that real estate investments will consistently outperform common stock investments?

3 What are the choices that must be made once one has decided to invest in real estate?

4 The use of real property is said to experience a life cycle similar to that of consumer products. Discuss.

5 Should an investor have a specific strategy, or would he do better to respond to particular opportunities as they present themselves?

6 It can be asserted that a firm can achieve a higher return from a real estate investment if it occupies the space itself. Why is this so?

7 Real estate investors are found more frequently among those in high tax brackets than among those in low ones. Does this reflect more than the simple fact that people in high tax brackets are usually the most wealthy?

8 Of the many factors which may cause reported rates of return on real estate to exceed those of other investments, which do you think are most important?

9 Discuss the advantages and disadvantages of different methods of participating in real estate investments.

10 Do you think real estate investments are riskier than other types of investments? Why or why not?

Chapter 25

Investing in Property for One's Own Use

What kind of building to occupy is one of the most important economic decisions faced by every family, household, and firm. It is not an economic decision alone; its consequences are far broader. The quality of the living environment has a direct impact on the quality of life of a household; similarly, the ability of a firm to generate adequate net revenues is greatly affected by the quality of the working environment.

Both households and firms must occupy space. Thus their space decisions focus not on whether to occupy space but on the amount, location, and quality of the space and on the terms under which it will be occupied. Both financial and nonfinancial variables are significant. Whether a move is made or not, a decision is reached, even if it is to stay put.

A purchase of space to occupy for one's own use is by far the most common real estate investment made by households and firms. Each one faces a "rent or buy" option. A majority of households and a strong minority of firms decide to buy. This chapter explains why.

People who buy do so because they have a wider choice and can better satisfy their space needs. Buying turns out to be a good investment because owners, in supplying their own demand, cut out the middleman and reduce the costs of risk and management. Buying is made still more attractive for many by government assistance through special tax and mortgage regulations and subsidies. Purchasers seize the opportunity presented by their own space demands.

The actual timing of the specific decision to become an owner rather than a renter will depend on economic and financial conditions, the owner's or firm's personal needs, mortgage availability, and what units are actually available for occupancy when a need arises. The list of considerations influencing a user's decision can be overwhelming.

In this chapter we first describe some noneconomic considerations in the search decision and then the economic factors which determine whether it pays to rent or buy. We use a representative family to illustrate the decisions, but the same types of factors must be analyzed by firms, other types of households, or those interested in buying a property to own and manage.

HOW TO SEARCH FOR SPACE

While buying a house has been greatly simplified, it remains a complicated transaction, probably more complex than is commonly recognized. The complexity lies not only in the legal and financial steps involved but also in the variety of choices that must be made simultaneously.

Since services are provided only at fixed locations, the choice of a house also comprises a package of environmental factors. House sites include a mixture of status, access, convenience, municipal services, and job opportunities. Owning a house in the central core may mean saving the cost of an extra car. The social reputation of some areas is higher than that of others. The schools in various locations may differ markedly. Services such as water supply, police and fire protection, and sewage disposal also vary widely, even in a single metropolitan area.

People often begin to search for new space because they are dissatisfied with what they have. A change in circumstances alters space needs. Family compositions change. Rising incomes mean that families can improve their housing standards. If children leave home, space needs may shrink.

Similar decisions face corporations. Their business may expand or contract. They may decide to manufacture more and make less use of suppliers. They may decentralize to regions or concentrate more functions in the home office. They may feel that a new type of space would give them a new image and better marketing results.

A Decision Model

When space needs arise, listing of the purposes the new space should serve can be extremely useful. Too often space decisions reflect an unorganized approach on the part of the user. If, instead, a formal decision model is established, the potential buyer can consider explicitly rather than implicitly each of the considerations that should bear on the decision.

Such a model can be used to evaluate all opportunities, including rent and buy situations and building or making do with available space. A conscious specification of preferences enables the decision maker to identify what is and what is not wanted. These specifications can be compared with what is available. Search is shortened by eliminating the majority of "available" space, thus allowing concentration on the few possibilities that most closely conform to the model's profile.

Although a variety of decision models can be used, in practice a simple list of criteria, with weights assigned to each according to its relative importance, works well. The searcher starts by listing what he wants in a space and how important each factor is to him. He can then rate each property brought to his attention to see how it compares with his desires. After a number of tries, key factors are almost automatically recognized. A good buy becomes obvious when it appears.

Decision Criteria

A list of criteria can be divided into classes depending on their importance and function.

Essentials Certain criteria will be listed as essential, thereby establishing minimum standards. Included as necessary might be the number of square feet and rooms in a house. Minimum standards might be set for heat, the electrical system, and the kitchen. Some families might specify a particular location or a maximum commuting distance. An upper limit to cost, of both downpayment and monthly expenses, would also be commonly included in this category.

Desirables The necessary criteria are usually further qualified by desirable features. For instance, 20 percent added to the minimum essential space would be desirable; so would an extra room. Other considerations of this type might include such factors as parks, libraries, schools, nearby shopping, public transportation, landscaping, outside appearance, storage space, a view, a garage, and play space. Certain families, of course, would classify some of these items as essential rather than desirable.

Prohibitions Just as some conditions must be met, the existence of others will rule a space out of consideration. Nearby factories, certain locations, price, and a second story are examples of features which could cause some people to reject particular offers.

Negatives Just as some items may be desirable but not essential, some may be negative but not prohibitive. Costs, both current and projected, might be found in this category. A high property tax might be offset by a good mortgage.

Scoring and Buying

The use of essential and prohibitive conditions simplifies the search. Scoring each desirable and negative item permits properties to be compared and offers to be made. Comparisons are useful in preparation for the bargaining process which normally accompanies each offer.

The markets for space are somewhat imperfect, with great differences between units. Decisions, especially when a family is buying a house, are greatly influenced by intangible considerations reflecting personal tastes and desires which may cause a house to have much greater appeal to some than to others. Because the emotional factor is so strong, a listing of criteria may save a family from making a major error.

Experience shows that when the right house comes along, there may not be time for a prolonged assessment and agonizing appraisal. For a distinctive and attractive house, a prospective buyer may have to make an on-the-spot decision. Experience with the use of a simple decision model shows that the buyer can rapidly become aware of the values and of what is being offered at what prices. When the right unit comes along, a decision to buy is easier if this existing knowledge has already been organized, ready to use in making a rapid decision.

THE COST OF OWNERSHIP

Because the cash costs, as differentiated from the real costs, of ownership usually exceed those of renting, careful evaluation of the full economic implications of the use decision must be made. Higher-than-expected housing or space costs often mean that a budget must be curtailed elsewhere. Tax factors are so important in real estate decisions that analysis of the relative merits of rent and buy options requires a consideration of the full investment cycle. Owners in higher tax brackets enjoy substantial tax advantages since many costs are deductible, a benefit lost to renters. These tax benefits are more pronounced for housing than for nonresidential space. Indeed, once all tax consequences are considered, those in higher brackets often find that their effective cost of housing is substantially lower than their actual cash payments. However, moderate-income families may find that taking the standard deduction for income taxes saves them more time and money than itemizing. They gain nothing from the potential tax benefits. In this section we consider the impact that changing economic conditions have on the costs of homeownership by examining recent experiences and projecting them into the future.

Projected Costs

Although when a person buys a house it is impossible to tell exactly how much homeownership will really cost, the factors which determine future payments and costs are few in number and well worth considering in detail. Table 25-1 shows these factors as they appeared to a representative purchaser of a house insured with an FHA mortgage in 1960 and as they actually worked out for those who bought in 1960 and sold in 1970; it also gives the same projections made for a similar family in 1974.

In examining this table, we find that it is easiest to consider and project costs in six different categories:

   1 The acquisition, or capital, cost of buying a house is most significant because its size directly determines many of the necessary outlays and actual costs. The acquisition cost is the purchase price plus the closing, financing, and other costs which must be paid before title is passed.

   2 Initial expenditures reflect the amount the owner must pay in cash at the time the house is bought. The difference between initial expenditures and the acquisition cost is covered by a mortgage on which monthly payments must be made.

   3 Annual cash costs are the payments which must be made monthly, primarily to cover the mortgage but also including taxes, insurance, and maintenance.

   4 When a house is sold, the owner is likely to receive back a certain amount of cash. The receipts on sale depend on the actual selling price and expenses.

Table 25-1   Costs of Owning a Home for 10 Years

| | 1960–1970 | | 1974 |
	Projection	Actual	Projection
Acquisition, or capital, cost:			
Purchase price	$14,700	$14,700	$29,200
Closing costs	300	300	800
Total	$15,000	$15,000	$30,000
Initial expenditures:			
Downpayment	1,060	1,060	1,170
Closing costs	300	300	800
Total	$ 1,360	$ 1,360	$ 1,970
Annual cash costs (10-year average):			
Interest and mortgage insurance	790	790	2,530
Amortization	230	230	300
Real estate taxes	190	280	800
Maintenance and insurance	165	180	400
Total	$ 1,375	$ 1,480	$ 4,030
Receipts on sale:			
Return of downpayment	1,060	1,060	1,170
Return of amortization	2,300	2,300	3,000
Appreciation or depreciation		3,000	6,000
Less selling costs	(1,200)	(1,800)	(3,600)
Total	$ 2,160	$ 4,560	$ 6,570
Estimated actual annual costs (10-year average):			
Interest on mortgage	790	790	2,530
Interest on equity	90	165	350
Real estate taxes and maintenance costs	350	460	1,200
Amortization of selling and closing costs	150	210	440
Appreciation		(300)	(600)
Total	$ 1,385	$ 1,325	$ 3,920
Income tax saving	(270)	(310)	(920)
	$ 1,115	$ 1,015	$ 3,000

5   The actual annual costs to own differ from the annual costs paid during ownership because they include allocations per year of the difference between the initial expenditures and the receipts at the time of sale. They also include a loss of interest on the equity money tied up in the property.

6   The actual annual costs will also be influenced by a family's income tax bracket and whether it must pay a capital gains tax at the time the house is sold.

Acquisition, or Capital, Cost   In Table 25-1, the purchase price of the house is $14,700 in 1960 and $29,200 in 1974. While most housing expenditures are a function of the amount initially invested, the relationship between initial costs and expenses is not exact. Houses purchased for the same price will experience different patterns of taxes, maintenance, and resale value.

While the typical purchase price of a new house nearly doubled between 1960 and 1974, it would be hard to find many basic differences between two typical houses built in those years. A 1974 house was about 10 percent larger, but its lot was smaller by a third. Almost all the differences in prices can be accounted for by changes in the price of developed land and by higher construction costs.

The incidental costs required to close the deal, including title insurance, mortgage fees, and similar items, more than doubled during this period. Part of this rise was, of course, directly caused by the larger size of the transaction in dollars.

Initial Expenditures   The differences in downpayments make it clear how this hurdle eased during this period. The required downpayment went up only $100, even though the purchase price virtually doubled. In 1960, the buyer received a mortgage of $13,640. The interest rate was 5.75 percent plus .5 percent mortgage insurance, and the mortgage was payable over 30 years.

In 1974 the mortgage was $28,030, but the interest rate was 9 percent, and the mortgage insurance was .5 percent. It, too, was payable over 30 years.

Annual Cash Costs   A person who is about to buy a house must estimate what it will cost each year to live in it. Even if the prospective buyer fails to do so, the lender will make the calculations, since lenders are concerned that borrowers not assume too heavy a load.

The largest share of the prospective annual financial outlays depends on the size of the mortgage, the interest rate, and the period of amortization. While mortgage payments are set at the time of purchase and stay at a fixed level, as we saw in Chapter 4, the actual percentage going to interest and to amortization changes each month. In Table 25-1 we show averages of each for the 10 years following the purchase.

Real estate taxes, maintenance costs, and costs of insurance must be estimated, and here variations will occur depending on the locality, what is happening to its assessments and tax rates, and the condition of the house and expected costs of maintenance. The figures shown in the table are based on FHA averages for new houses of the indicated price.

The difference in annual cash costs between the 1960 and 1974 projections is startling. While the cost of the house has doubled, the amount that must be paid out in annual payments has virtually tripled. Most of the difference is accounted for by the much higher interest rates. The percentage increase in real estate taxes, however, is even higher. The other items have changed generally only in proportion to the purchase price.

Annual Actual Costs   To estimate what it will actually cost to live in a house, it is not enough to know what amounts will be paid out upon purchase and monthly thereafter. Financial outlays differ from actual annual costs. The top half of the table shows the actual financial outlays that will have to be made. For many families, this is the critical factor, since unless these payments can be made, they cannot contract for the purchase. On the other hand, many people want to know what the real cost of living in a house will be. They want a projection of actual costs to help them decide whether to own and how expensive a house to buy. Real costs will differ from the initial and annual cash payments depending on how much cash is received above what is owed on the mortgage when the house is sold. This, in turn, is contingent on what happens to the housing market and on the length of time between the purchase and sale of the house.

Receipts on Sale Changes in the price of a house depend on how good a buy was made originally, on what happens to the specific house and its locality, and on inflation. For most of the postwar period, homeowners have experienced very favorable trends. Increases in the general price level, and especially in land prices, have been so large that they have more than offset the physical depreciation and obsolescence of the structures. As a result, most people who have sold houses have found that their values have appreciated rather than depreciated.

Unfortunately, however, the overall effect of rising prices has not been felt evenly in all periods or in all localities. Some houses have depreciated in value because of their locality. In other cases, houses purchased just prior to tight-money periods have been affected by a fall in general demand. In such periods, even though building costs rose, the sale value of existing houses did not rise.

The first two lines under "Receipts on sale" in the table indicate that during this postwar period, most prospective owners assumed that they would get back their initial downpayment and also an amount equivalent to the amortization of their mortgage. This means that they expected actually to sell the house for at least what they paid for it.

The third item is appreciation or depreciation. In 1960 most families probably assumed that they would do well to sell their house after 10 years for the price they paid, and the projection shows no appreciation or depreciation. In fact, however, the selling price of a house built in 1960 increased at a rate of about 2 percent a year. This meant that a family that purchased a house for $15,000 in 1960 could have sold it in 1970 for approximately $18,000. The family would have received back upon sale not only their downpayment and amortization but also a $3,000 appreciation. In the 1974 projection, it is assumed that the buyer takes this past experience into account. Even though he recognizes that an end to inflation could cause the value of his house to fall, he expects to gain the same 2 percent increase in value per year that he could have in the past. He therefore expects to sell his house for $6,000 more than he paid for it.

Selling Costs The last major cost the homeowner must pay is that of selling the property. This charge becomes most important if a family moves within a short period. Selling costs run from 8 to 10 percent of the price. Included are agents' fees, title and attorney charges, fees or points on the mortgage, and escrow and stamp fees, plus the risks of having to redecorate or to hold a unit vacant while a sale is being made. Selling costs have increased somewhat during the period, both because transaction amounts are larger and because the specific percent charged has gone up. We note that in 1960, the family estimated it would have to pay $1,200 upon sale, while this amount has risen to $3,600 in the 1974 projection. At times mortgage fees paid by the seller could add $1,500 or more to this sum.

The high costs of turning over a property mean that a family that must move within a year or so after purchase finds its costs much higher than expected. In fact, we can calculate from the table that if a house is sold at the end of only 1 year, actual costs will be just about double the projected annual costs. The longer one has to amortize selling and closing costs, the less impact they will have. On this basis, one can generalize that a family expecting to occupy a house for less than 3 years will probably be better off renting than buying.

The time at which transfer costs are offset by possible appreciation probably comes somewhere in the 3- to 5-year interval. However, the range in time can be considerable. Fortunate families experiencing a rapid appreciation in the value of their house can sell for enough to more than offset selling costs in a shorter period, while less lucky ones may lose compared with the projection or compared with the cost of renting, even if they occupy their house for a considerable period.

Estimated Actual Annual Costs   Most actual ownership costs depend directly on the annual cash payments. Thus the interest on the mortgage, real estate taxes, and maintenance charges are actual costs of ownership. On the other hand, the downpayment and the amortization payments on the mortgage are current financial outlays which, it is hoped, will be returned. Consequently, they are not actual costs. The fact that they have been paid, however, means that the owner has put equity into the house. The lost interest on this equity should be estimated as one of the actual costs of ownership. Again we note how large the difference in projected actual costs is between the 1960 and 1974 projections. Some of this gap is the difference in interest rates in the two periods. Some arises from the final two items under "Estimated actual annual costs" in Table 25-1, or the difference between the initial expenditures and what is received from the sale. We have seen that these differences are determined by the actual costs of transfer or selling and closing costs as well as by the amount of appreciation or depreciation that takes place. The 1960 projection assumed that because the house would be sold for what it cost, the owner would not be able to offset the selling and closing costs by appreciation. Even though the 1974 owner projects a 2 percent appreciation, he estimates that he will pay three times as much per year to live in a house selling for twice as much with perhaps 10 to 20 percent more value to him.

Taxes   The final item in the table under "Estimated actual annual costs" is a possible income tax saving. This also varies significantly among individuals. Income tax savings are the amount which owners do not have to pay to the IRS because they incur certain costs. These savings may range from 0 to 50 percent or more of interest (both real and imputed) and property tax payments, depending on the family's tax bracket and on whether expenses are itemized. With payments at the level shown, it almost always pays to itemize.

The income tax saving shown in the table is based on a 25 percent tax bracket. The higher one's marginal tax bracket, the more important this saving becomes. For many families in moderate to high income brackets, it is the most critical factor in making a housing decision. This potential saving has been one of the fundamental facts leading people to buy apartments rather than continuing to rent them, as was generally the case in the past.

The table does not show the potential offset to the tax saving which can arise from having to pay a capital gains tax on the amount of appreciation. Whether such a tax will have to be paid depends on whether, and how soon, a family buys another house following the sale of their original property. As we saw, under current tax law, when homeowners sell their personal residence, they are exempt from taxation on the gain associated with that sale if the proceeds of such sale are reinvested in another residence within 1 year, providing the new purchase is equal in cost to the sale. Families in the elderly category receive still more generous treatment.

The Record of the 1960s

The projections for 1960 and 1974 are the best available at the time of purchase. Now that the 1960s have passed, it is possible to have a retrospective view of what actually happened to a family buying the typical FHA house in 1960. We note, in fact, that the estimated actual annual cost at the end of the 10 years was very close to the estimate of the beginning. It averaged about $60, or 5 percent a year less than initially projected.

The close relationship is due to the fact that so many costs are fixed when the purchase price is determined and the interest and amortization payments for the mortgage are agreed upon. These costs run between 60 and 70 percent of the total.

We see from a comparison between the two columns that the purchasers in 1960 underestimated four factors: real estate taxes, maintenance and insurance, appreciation, and selling costs. All were higher, but fortunately the increase in the value of the house was sufficient to more than offset both the increased operating expenses and the fact that it cost somewhat more to sell the house at the end of the decade than originally estimated.

For the 1974 projection, one of these factors—namely, greater appreciation—has already been included. If taxes and maintenance costs rise faster, inflation would have to be somewhat higher than estimated for the projection to work out.

Another way of looking at ownership costs is to note that on the basis of the lower interest rates and the 2 percent a year increase in value during the decade, a family was able to live in an owned home from 1960 to 1970 for a total actual expense of about 9 percent of its value per year, less any tax benefits that they gained. For the decade beginning in 1974, with a 9 percent mortgage the family's housing costs are projected at about 13 percent per year of the purchase price, less any tax benefits. Annual actual costs have risen with the percentage increase in interest rates. In addition, the base against which these higher costs are applied (the purchase price) is doubled. These two factors together mean that the average family had to pay almost three times as much per year in actual housing costs in 1974 as a similarly situated family had to pay in 1960.

MORTGAGES AND HOMEOWNERSHIP

Chapter 4 described the important role mortgages play in homeownership. Because of the high cost of houses relative to family resources, without mortgages most families could not become homeowners. Furthermore, small changes in mortgage terms have a large impact on the number of families who can buy in any period.

Mortgages enable a family to use leverage in becoming investors. Every family making a housing decision must decide how much to borrow or what leverage to use. On the theory that their incomes will most probably improve over time, many households "overbuy" in relation to their immediate incomes, anticipating that in a few years they will be able to handle comfortably mortgage payments that initially represent a real strain. If a household purchases a home appropriate to its current resources and if its income subsequently rises, it may find itself occupying a house of lower quality than it likes. The family must buy a new house and move if it is to upgrade its housing. Since moving entails substantial costs, including transaction costs and the cost of the physical move itself, as well as time and disruption, a family may be better off pursuing a strategy that minimizes the number of required moves.

Those knowledgeable in personal finance observe that using a mortgage to achieve homeownership represents a form of forced savings and investment. If the house increases in value over time, the initial downpayment will represent an excellent investment. At the same time, the principal payments on the mortgage increase the household's equity in the house.

Extended Mortgage Terms

One frequently hears arguments that borrowers should pay as much down and select as short an amortization period as they can manage. One reason given for this view is that the risk of default is less with a higher downpayment. Those who offer this advice seem to be confused as to what is good for the lender and what is good for the borrower. We saw that the lender's risks may rise perceptibly if the borrower's equity is too small. If the borrower is forced to default with a low equity, the lender is likely to suffer a larger loss. This risk applies primarily to the downpayment, however. The impact of longer amortization periods is not as clear, although risks may increase for loans beyond 25 years in length. The borrower's risks and dangers may be the opposite of the lender's. If some unfortunate event occurs or if a house turns out to be a bad buy, the lower the borrower's equity, the less his or her loss will be.

A second argument used to urge borrowers not to lengthen the term of their mortgage is still weaker: It is that the longer the term of the mortgage, the higher will be the percentage of interest in the total payments. Thus a constant-payment loan of $1,000 at 9 percent interest amortized over 30 years will include about $1,896 in interest payments, whereas the same loan paid off in 15 years will include only $826 in interest charges. The two interest payments are compared, and it is assumed that the smaller interest payments are clearly preferable.

This argument misses the whole concept of lending and borrowing. It should never be used by a lender because the same logic would lead to the conclusion that no household should ever borrow. A cash payment avoids all interest charges. People borrow because they can use the money and because they feel the satisfaction gained from the loan is greater than its cost. Interest is the cost of borrowing. No one should waste the services of other people's money if it is not needed. On the other hand, if the larger loan greatly improves a family's housing standards or if the money is needed for other purposes, the larger the loan, the better off the family will be.

The family's real costs include a return on its equity. Building up equity reduces interest paid, but at the cost of interest foregone. Most consumer advisers believe that families should borrow on mortgages rather than elsewhere. Clearly no advantage is gained from saving 9 percent interest by making larger monthly payments on a mortgage if it means paying 16 percent on an auto loan. Since their house is the best security most families own, borrowing on a mortgage will result in lower interest costs than borrowing in any other way.

Liquidity and Leverage

Another aspect of borrowing a maximum sum on good security is that of liquidity, which applies to many individual investments in addition to houses. The argument is sometimes advanced in favor of higher downpayments that you decrease your monthly payments and therefore your risk. The truth of the contention depends on whether compulsory saving is necessary. What would the individual do with the money not put into a downpayment? If he dissipated it foolishly, his payments would be higher, and he would have little to show for them. If he invested the amount not put into a downpayment in his business or in some other enterprise, he might earn a return higher than the mortgage rate, although such a strategy may increase his risks.

On the other hand, if he kept this sum as a liquid reserve, he would decrease his risks while incurring only low or negative costs, depending on money's value to him. Risks would be less, for in most families the danger in mortgage payments is not one of falling slightly below the amount needed each month but, rather, one of being unable to pay anything for some interval. A man who lost his job would find that the difference in monthly payments resulting from a 20-year instead of a 30-year amortization period would not help much in meeting his payment needs.

A mortgage has another advantage to the average family. It is usually a debt which can be extinguished at will, and it is therefore another form of liquidity. Most modern mortgages are drawn up with the interest rate fixed for their entire period. Usually the debtor can prepay them with only a negligible penalty. (Warning: some carry heavy prepayment penalties.) Although the debt can be retired, the debtor, as a rule, cannot be forced to pay it off in advance.

If the interest rate rises, the borrower has a bargain; he or she is paying less than the going rate on the debt. If the interest rate falls, the borrower may be able to refinance the mortgage and start again at the new, lower rate. This is one of the few circumstances in which an individual can gain as a debtor. Many have profited in this manner by the swings in interest rates. In a similar way, an unwary individual may lose on bonds. Corporations often have the right, either completely or within stated limits, to determine when a bond should be paid off. The holder of the bond loses if interest rates rise. If they fall, the corporation can gain by calling and paying off the bond.

Homeowners with a large mortgage are also employing leverage. Their downpayment gives them the ability to control a very large asset—their house. They may give up $1,000 in bonds, deposits, or stocks for owhership of a $30,000 asset. Whether they gain from their leverage depends, as we have seen, on the length of time they hold their asset and on what happens to housing prices in the interim. Their investment may work out well or poorly. The average family, however, can in this manner buy an asset which will protect a large portion of its housing expenses from inflation. This has been an important factor in making homeownership so popular.

THE FIRM'S DECISION

It is clear that a set of decisions and economic factors similar to that faced by individuals confronts firms which must decide whether to rent or buy. They need to find space which meets their particular needs. Choices will differ greatly depending on how important location and status are to the marketing concept of individual businesses.

Economic criteria for firms and families are almost identical. A higher cost may have to be paid for a rental unit. Most critical, however, is whether in fact a real choice exists—whether suitable space is actually available in both categories. Also important are how much the firm will have to pay from its capital to buy and what dangers will be encountered if it must move at an awkward time.

Sometimes a firm has little choice. It may find that to occupy space in a certain office district or shopping center, it will have to rent. For other locations or for special-purpose buildings, investors may demand so much risk protection in rents that the firm must buy or else not find a property.

For many firms, the expected return on capital and the increased risk of bankruptcy due to leverage dominate the decision. Capital-short firms find renting far simpler than trying to raise the capital to buy. Others seeking investments find none better or safer than becoming their own landlord.

In other cases, the danger of having to move may be the dominant factor. A firm can build up a vast amount of patronage and goodwill in a certain location. As a tenant, it fears the possibility of having to pay much higher rent when its lease is up or of losing its market if forced to move.

PERSONAL USE OF INVESTMENT PROPERTY

Another form of personal use of property is that of owning and managing it oneself. This form of investment has many advantages. Owners, in effect, run the property as their business, on either a full-time or part-time basis. They gain a job with income, and they control their own management results without depending on others.

Many real estate investors get their start by owning residential property on a small scale. A family might buy a duplex and live in one unit while renting out the other. Such investments are strictly do-it-yourself, "Mom and Pop" operations. The buyers of these units envision reducing their own rent and building up an equity over time. Since there is considerable demand to own such units, often the cash flow is negligible or nonexistent. But because of generally increasing price levels, it has been possible to trade up over time into a larger unit by using both the appreciation and the equity achieved by paying down the mortgage. With added equity, the duplex may be disposed of, and a four-plex property acquired. After a time, this might be exchanged for perhaps a ten-unit property. Many large real estate portfolios have started out in such a fashion.

Where investment and use objectives are combined, owners are investing their "sweat equity" into the project as well as their capital. Maximum returns from such a strategy can be achieved by buying properties whose values can be increased. Such properties have usually been neglected by their previous owners. New paint and general repairs are needed. By making such improvements and putting in new cabinets, modernizing kitchen and bathrooms, and converting a large house into flats and installing separate entrances, the revenue stream can be built up. Such strategies work best when the owner is active as a contractor, laborer, maintenance supervisor, property manager, rental agent, bookkeeper, or whatever else is needed.

Generally, the ''fixer-upper'' strategy is most profitable where aggressive leverage is employed. Because investors start with limited capital, unless they achieve substantial leverage, they must wait a long time before they have created enough value to warrant obtaining a larger unit.

Some investors prefer to concentrate on one building, trading over time for larger and larger properties. Others prefer to build a portfolio of many small units. Indeed, many real estate investors specialize in owning a number of single-family homes which they rent out. Eventually, when the investor develops an adequate operating base of capital, he or she can take a longer-term orientation, perhaps electing a more conservative strategy that concentrates on better properties and employs lower leverage with higher downpayments to reduce risks.

Investors starting as owner-managers may be so successful that they can own a home of their own rather than continuing to live in the building. Indeed, to the extent that investors are successful enough to afford this option, the question of whether to continue to live in an apartment is an important one. Investors who continue to serve as on-site managers find their lives filled with constant interruptions and 3 A.M. phone calls from tenants complaining that their toilet does not work, for example. If investors are successful enough and so inclined, they can insulate themselves from these aggravations.

On the other hand, some couples, upon retirement, may move the opposite way. They sell their home and use their capital to buy a small apartment or motel. They want the job as manager to supplement their retirement income. Not only are the aggravations and distractions recognized as part of the job, but they may also constitute a welcome new social outlet.

As suggested earlier, residential investment is the most popular form of real estate investment. Consequently, there is a large pool of potential purchasers for small properties. The economic characteristics of residential investment properties vary significantly with size. The larger the property, the better the return that can be achieved. Investors with larger amounts of money can buy not only bigger properties but also smaller ones. As there is more competition for the smaller properties, their prices get bid up and the cash flow is depressed. Further, the investor should recognize that many people are willing to invest their ''sweat equity'' into managing and improving properties. Unless investors are so motivated, they are likely to find themselves at a disadvantage.

The price of a property reflects the perceptions of the buyer and seller regarding its future operating performance as well as their respective rate-of-return criteria. Investors may see properties they would like to buy snapped up by others who are willing to accept a lower rate of return or who are more optimistic about their probable operating results. More knowledgeable investors may find that the relative lack of sophistication of many people active in the small residential property investment field works to their disadvantage. Competitors less discriminating in what they will pay for properties often bid up the prices to unrealistic levels. The investor may decide not to make such properties part of his or her strategy because most appear overpriced.

SUMMARY

The most common type of investment is purchasing a property for one's own use. Some purchases are forced on the buyer because no satisfactory rental choices exist. Many, however, are made because of real potential savings. Owner-occupiers or managers save paying others for work they do not need or are willing to do themselves. Risks are reduced when supply and demand are directly matched. A family can hedge against future inflation and rises in prices and rents by using leverage and a relatively small amount of its own capital.

Risks arise primarily from making a poor purchase, from changes in income which make it impossible to carry the debt contracted for, or from the necessity to sell the property too soon. Even though markets for owner use are better than those for many other types of real estate, they become illiquid when demand or financing dries up. In addition, transaction costs are high. Tax deductions lower the costs for many, but standard deductions have reduced this advantage for many others.

As in other types of investment, there is no sure thing. Careful financial and economic projections should be made. At the same time, one must recognize that there is real value inherent in the various emotional satisfactions that grow out of owning a home or property that matches closely one's desires and needs.

QUESTIONS AND PROBLEMS

1 Because every residential house is unique, prospective purchasers must look at as many houses as they can to find the one that best fits their needs. Discuss.
2 Why are people motivated to own houses as opposed to renting them?
3 Why is the effective cost of housing often different from the sum of its cash payments?
4 How have the costs of homeownership changed since 1960?
5 Why do some people decide to rent instead of buy housing?
6 Most families who shift from renting to owning increase their monthly cash housing expenses. Why does this happen?
7 An elderly couple are likely to find that they do not save on income taxes as a result of owning. Even so, they may be better off owning. Discuss.
8 Many people (especially purchasers of condominiums) have complained in recent years that their cash costs of owning were much higher than they had been led to believe when they bought. What are the major causes of such increased costs?
9 Booklets on homeownership sometimes contain statements such as, "A house with a $50,000 initial price will cost $145,000 if you buy it with a 30-year mortgage and $91,300 if you buy it with a 15-year mortgage." Explain why such statements are logical or illogical.
10 What are some of the principal advantages and disadvantages of personal use and management of a real estate property?

Chapter 26

Investing in
Real Estate Securities

After buying a property primarily for their own use, most investors who want to put money in real estate do so by purchasing securities. They must decide whether the securities should be common stocks or joint ventures. A number of common stocks of firms which derive a large part of their income from real estate are traded on the major stock exchanges. Even more are traded over the counter. Joint ventures are currently offered by all types of sponsors, promoters, and potential partners.

The major advantage of common stocks in contrast to joint-venture securities is that they are more liquid. A quoted price exists at all times. Moderate amounts can be sold at prices close to the market. The markets tend to be more professional. There are many actual and potential buyers and sellers. In addition, the amount of published financial information is extensive for many of these firms and is normally subject to SEC reporting regulations and supervision. Comparability is quite good.

Joint ventures, in contrast, are bought primarily either by people who can profit from their tax-shelter features or by investors who feel that by sacrificing liquidity or by properly calculating risks, they can obtain a higher return. They may frequently sacrifice knowledge as well, putting faith in the promoter. In certain local situations, however, investors may find that they can do a better analytic job on a proposed partnership offer than they can with common stocks—for example, when they are sure that they have all the information they need and all the information available to other insiders.

Deciding among types of securities, like choosing the type of investment, will depend on investors' overall strategy. How much time and effort are they willing to put into analysis? How large are their assets, and what is their tax bracket? What are their needs for liquidity and income?

INVESTING IN REAL ESTATE COMMON STOCKS

In choosing from among common stocks related to real estate, it is possible to establish various classifications. Frequently, of course, they are overlapping. Firms do not engage in a single activity; many are multiline. Still, firms engaged in different real estate activities carry different dangers and react uniquely to market forces. An investor seeking a diversified portfolio should divide firms into separate categories and select stocks from several of the basic types available.

One approach is to divide firms into the following classifications:

1 Primarily builders and developers
2 Suppliers of construction materials
3 S&Ls and other financial intermediaries
4 Service organizations, including mortgage guarantee firms and mortgage bankers
5 Owners of real property
6 REITs

The Combination of Stock Market and Real Estate Risks

Most investors are well aware of J. P. Morgan's famous dictum that the one thing certain about the stock market is that it will fluctuate. In the same way, the one thing certain about stocks based upon real estate is that they will fluctuate even more. The basic movements in the general level of stock prices are amplified in real estate stocks by the fact that the profits and losses of these firms vary far more than the average.

This greater amplification of movement or increased risk is a major reason why returns on real estate stocks will be greater than the average (although not necessarily higher if a cost is assigned to the greater risks). Because of high risks, the number of investors who choose real estate stocks is only a small part of the total. Holdings of these stocks by major institutions tend to be small.

It follows that if real estate firms are to attract investors, their stocks must offer special benefits. Those who can fit these stocks into their investment portfolios will gain in comparison with their holdings of other stock which may offer them features that they do not need. Again the critical factor in determining an investment strategy is to differentiate among types of investment in order to get the best potential trade-off between rate of return and other stock features.

Prices of stocks depend not only on economic considerations but also on investors' perception of the "market." Adam Smith described his book *The Money Game,* the best-selling chronicle of the investment business, as "a book about image and reality and identity and anxiety and money." The stock market adjusts very quickly to changes in national mood and attitude. Prices can move sharply upward on good news or plummet quickly on bad. Vacillations in stock market prices tend to be greater than those in the economy generally.

Throughout this book we have emphasized the unstable nature of real estate markets. In recent years fluctuations in interest rates and in credit availability have increased with magnified impacts on the mortgage market. In turn, these movements have been reflected in sharply fluctuating housing starts and in real estate markets in general.

Because of the fluctuations and because the stock market tends to exaggerate the significance of positive and negative trends, price movements in real estate stocks vacillate more sharply than common stocks generally. As an example, in 1974, a year in which common stocks suffered from generally poor performance, 19 of the 20 biggest losers were real estate stocks. This overreaction effect is shown in Figure 26-1, which compares the *House and Home* real estate stock index to the Standard and Poor's Index of 500 stocks.

Builders and Developers

In classifying stock, one finds that the degree of stability in the price of a firm's stock is related to how closely its activities and earnings are tied to new construction. Thus we should expect builders and developers to be among those with the most violent movements in earnings because they are almost completely dependent upon the housing cycle.

Until recently, few builders and developers were publicly owned. Those which were publicly owned concentrated primarily on commercial construction for a fee. Home building was dominated by small companies. Few had the volume of operations

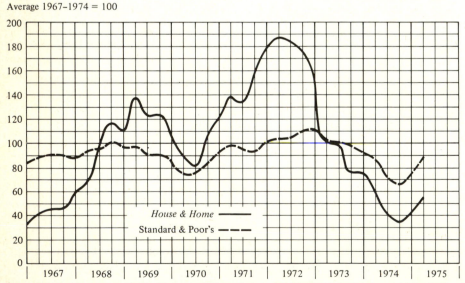

Average 1967–1974 = 100

Figure 26-1   Movements in the House and Home Index of 25 Real Estate Stocks and Standard and Poor's Combined Index of 500 stocks, 1967–1975.

or managerial depth required of a public company. Changing conditions prompted many developers to build larger organizations. Increasingly, the larger producers sought money from the public capital market.

The builders expanded to overcome the vagaries of the building cycle and to reduce costs. Economies of scale were anticipated through more effective management, more sensitive planning, less costly and more reliable financing, and better coordination of the overall process. The larger central staffs and higher overhead needed to provide these services required a large volume of business in a number of different markets to support them.

The strategy of serving multiple markets reduces the overall adverse impact of a specific project. But the success of this strategy hinges on being able to retain profitable volume in many markets, even in the face of an overall decline in housing activity. While in earlier market declines a number of large builders were able to maintain or even improve their profitability, in 1974 few were able to do so.

Many of the large builders of the middle to late 1960s were acquired by major public corporations. Many firms were attracted by the then high profitability of real estate and construction. The 1969 survey of corporate earnings performance by First National City Bank showed a return on net worth of 14.9 percent for construction firms and 14.6 percent for real estate firms, as compared with 10.4 percent for all companies.

Companies whose businesses were characterized by a high cash flow and low growth rates, such as the steel industry, saw housing as an excellent growth opportunity. Similarly, large corporations whose expansion possibilities in their traditional field were limited because of the possible antitrust problems saw an attractive opportunity in the housing sector, with its low degree of economic concentration.

Many firms thought that the increasing attention to urban problems and environmental concerns, as well as indications that a larger share of the federal budget would be directed to these areas, represented exciting future markets. Companies selling materials and products to the building industry saw a chance both to stimulate their own sales and to learn more about their products, as well as to achieve a degree of vertical integration. Other companies became involved in housing and development when they thought they saw the possibility of an imaginative transfer of competencies gained from providing goods and services in other industries.

The overall record of publicly held producers has been poor. Many corporations engaged in housing played "creative accounting" in an effort to pad earnings and increase share values. Indeed, in certain cases the primary motives of corporations appeared to have been to make their book earnings, as opposed to their real earnings, look good. In an attempt to limit the extent of creative financing, both the SEC and the American Institute of Certified Public Accountants have taken strong steps to eliminate past abuses.

Suppliers of Building Materials

There are many different types of suppliers of building materials. Included are firms furnishing basic structural components, such as Weyerhauser; manufacturers of insulation products, such as Owens-Corning Fiberglas; manufacturers of interior floor coverings, such as Armstrong Cork; and suppliers of kitchen appliances, such as General Electric.

In many cases the earnings and stock prices of these firms do not react as violently as those of other so-called real estate stocks. In fact, the average stock for construction material firms moves with only slightly greater amplitude than the market as a whole. This reflects the fact that many of these firms sell as much of their product for maintenance, repairs, and rehabilitation as they do for new construction; in some cases they sell even more. These follow-on markets are more stable. In addition, the fact that many of them have greater actual control over their selling prices helps to improve their stock's performance.

S&Ls and Other Financial Intermediaries

The stock actions of the S&Ls are more closely related to movements in the real estate cycle than those of the many major financial intermediaries we have discussed in earlier chapters. It should, of course, be kept in mind that many of the principal lenders in the S&Ls, LICs, and MSBs remain mutual institutions and therefore do not have stock available for investors.

The volume of existing loans for S&Ls does not alter drastically. In fact, in each recession year their actual assets have increased. Only in rare months and for a minority of firms has there been a time in the postwar period when their total assets have run down.

This, however, has not solved their problem because their current flow of funds and their new loans do fluctuate greatly. They are in the unfortunate position of having most of their assets carrying past interest rates, whereas their inflow and outflow of current savings depend upon the gap between their regulated rates, earnings, and current short-term interest rates. As a result, when short-term rates have risen rapidly, they have been squeezed. Receiving only a minor current inflow of savings, they have had to halt most new loan commitments and borrow money from the FHL Banks to meet their existing commitments. Since they borrow this money at high short-term market rates, there is a decided squeeze upon their earnings and their stock prices.

Facilitators

There is a great variety of facilitators and service organizations for real estate markets. They include mortgage bankers, real estate brokers, and consulting firms. Other specialized companies such as the FNMA and the mortgage guarantee insurance firms also provide special services that facilitate transactions and provide additional liquidity to real estate markets.

Again, one might expect that firms of this type would not react as severely to the housing cycle as builders and developers. These firms have a large volume of continuing business generated by past services which does not decrease along with new construction. For example, mortgage bankers did well in prior recessions because their servicing became a larger share of their total volume and because they were not losing money by placing current business on the books. Similarly, mortgage insurance companies continue to collect on insurance written in the past even though their new volume falls.

Such anticyclical behavior, however, is possible only to the extent that these firms have not engaged in activities which are closely related to interest rates, or the price of money, or are dependent entirely on new construction. In fact, in the 1974 recession many of these firms found their net revenues suffering greatly, even though the actual volume of their total business did not fall or, in many cases, continued to expand. This arose from the fact that much of their revenue turned out to be related to interest rate movements and stock prices rather than merely to the volume of their total business.

It may well be that with the experience of 1974–1975 behind them, these firms will pay more attention to the interest rate risks they are assuming. If they are successful, we would expect that the fluctuations in their revenues, and therefore in their stock prices, might become less over time.

Property Owners

There is a large number of firms whose incomes depend in whole or in part upon their ownership or operation of properties rather than upon the current production of real estate. How well they do in comparison with others depends upon the supply and demand situation in their particular part of the market.

Real Estate Equities   A number of public corporations exist solely to invest in real estate equities. Some started out as developers and elected not to continue to build new properties, but to hold and manage what they had developed. Others were formed through consolidations of a number of real estate partnerships into a single corporate entity. In spite of the double-taxation status of corporate ownership, several have performed well. Their results have varied with their leverage and the risks they have taken.

Hotels   Ownership of stocks of companies in the hotel industry affords the investor a means of participating directly in a particular type of property ownership. Although basic real estate considerations, including location, competing properties, and market support, are critical for success, the hotel business, more than any other property type, is highly dependent upon operations as opposed to property considerations. Firms in industries providing leisure services have experienced among the most drastic fluctuations of any on the stock exchange.

Supplementary Holdings   Some companies, by the nature of their primary businesses, have major real estate holdings. Frequently, however, these holdings are still supplementary, and the stock prices of such companies are dominated by their major activities. Firms in this category include railroads, forest product firms, and companies involved in mineral and oil exploration.

REITs

Finally we come to the most publicized of the real estate common stocks, the REITs. They have already been discussed at length. As noted, it is important to differentiate the mortgage trusts, which engage in lending activities, from those trusts which make direct equity investments. Yet since a trust may elect a number of investment policies, some take on hybrid characteristics, making it difficult to distinguish and differentiate between them.

In the early 1970s aggressive mortgage trusts leveraged themselves highly by borrowing funds short and lending them long. Given favorable relationships between the cost of their money and what they could make on their investments, these REITs initially seemed to do well. However, with money borrowed on short-term loans for commitments to long-term mortgages or equity positions, their adjustments were severe because increases in borrowing costs could not be offset by higher revenues. The situation became still worse as lenders refused to renew their credit lines and insisted that loans be repaid. When these conditions were combined with the inability to collect on loans, the effect on stock prices was disastrous.

When they were growing and doing well, REITs were able to sell new shares at prices above book value. This achieved a "contradilution" effect, increasing the book value of the initial shareholders. But when the REITs encountered trouble, their prices fell well below book value, a relationship the opposite of that which prevailed in earlier years. The investment community became disenchanted with, and lost confidence in, the earnings and financial statements reported by many REITs.

Even though equity real estate trusts are significantly different from mortgage trusts, many investors fail to draw a sharp distinction between the two. At the same time, because equity REITs are dependent upon the supply and demand for their properties and upon the cost of mortgage borrowing, they have had their own problem properties and general difficulties. Consequently, the equity trusts suffered sharp price declines as well. This result again seems to support the thesis that the stock market often tends to respond more on the basis of psychology than of economic reality.

PICKING THE PROPER STOCKS

In Chapter 24, we listed nine factors that might make real estate a good investment for an individual, though recognizing that most returns on investments are competitive and cannot vary too much from the average. Many of these points apply specifically to a selection of real estate stocks. So does the general point that a successful strategy requires the choice of stocks for a portfolio that fit the investor's needs. All successful investors make certain that they pay only for what they need and that they get what they pay for.

Accepting the general view of how the stock market works, there are three major reasons for an investor to select real estate stocks:

1   The investor picks these stocks as part of an overall strategy of diversification.

2   The particular stocks have valuable features which make them worth more to the individual investor than they are to the market as a whole.

3   Contrary to what many students of the market believe, the investor feels that he or she can do a better-than-average job of analyzing stocks and will be paid for, and profit from, this analytic ability.

Diversification

Studies show that it does not take a very large, diversified portfolio to obtain a rate of return approximately equal to all stocks based on price changes and dividends. Some investors pick real estate stocks as part of an overall diversification program, particularly those who are willing to accept a diversified portfolio with above-average risks and returns. They choose stocks with a high probability of fluctuations and, as a result, increase their yield. Because some real estate equities move somewhat differently from the way other widely fluctuating stocks do, they have a significant role in a strategy of holding but diversifying among volatile stocks.

Matching Stocks to an Investor's Need

Other features that can make it worthwhile for individuals to put their money into real estate stocks stem from the fact that they can match their needs to particular stocks. People who can afford greater risks and lower liquidity will receive a higher rate of return from real estate stocks. This type of return may best fit the needs of those in certain age and income brackets.

Through a judicious selection of stocks, an investor can determine what share of current income is to be in capital gains, in taxable income, or in tax-free distributions. Real estate stocks have more features of this type than the other shares in the markets.

Another opportunity lies in taking a special position with respect to one's expectations of long-run inflation. There is a great deal of uncertainty as to how future inflations will affect stock prices. On the other hand, it appears logical that a highly leveraged position in which the interest rate on the debt is fixed should work out better in times of inflation. The average investor has a hard time finding a good inflationary hedge. The heavily leveraged position of some real estate stocks makes them superior as an inflationary hedge to stocks as a whole.

Better Analysis and Timing

Some people may do better by specializing in the stocks of one industry, particularly if they work in the industry and can acquire a special feel for its problems and opportunities. Good analysts believe that they can increase their returns by proper timing of buy-sell decisions. Their analysis may depend on an accurate projection of profits and losses of individual stocks or on a better-than-average projection of cyclical movements.

Many people engaged in a specific industry have a better sense of the problems of its markets than the average person. As a result they believe that they can do a better job of analysis of specific stocks. By following a few stocks related to their other business activities, they hope to be able to predict temporary earnings, gains, or losses and to convert them into profitable market trades. Such successes are especially likely when the market overreacts to a particularly good or bad event and they can take a somewhat longer view.

Perhaps a more logical hope is to be able to do well in forecasting the cyclical movements in real estate. Anyone who can improve on the average forecast of the cycle has a potential source of profits. This follows from the fact that real estate stocks fluctuate more in amplitude than the market as a whole.

Those with the ability to forecast the real estate cycle can go in and out of real estate stocks and even ''short'' them in order to make their gains. Investors who feel fairly certain of their timing but who nonetheless believe that one should maintain a rather fully invested position can still gain by moving from real estate stocks to less volatile ones at the right time and then reversing their position. For instance, assume that when the market rises from 90 to 110, a typical real estate stock moves from 80 to 120. A similar enhanced amplitude occurs on a downward movement. Given this pattern, an investor would like to shift from other stocks to real estate shares near the bottom of a cycle and then shift back near the top.

With this type of program, the investor's timing need not be as good as if he decided to get out of the stock market completely. Assume that when the real estate stock reaches 120, he shifts over to an average stock. If the market falls, he will be relatively better off than he would have been if he had retained his previous position. His loss will be reduced. On the other hand, if the market goes up another 20, he will be better off than if he had taken a cash position, even though he will not gain as much as he would have if he had retained his position in real estate stocks. Some experts argue that the hope of profiting from better analyses and timing is illusory. They believe that large institutional investors can hire experts with such knowledge. The resulting competition among the institutions causes the returns on real estate stocks, as on all, to adjust to the competitive situation. Others feel that there is still a profit possibility for the knowledgeable individual. They believe institutions become too hidebound, particularly in spheres such as real estate. Those with better information make unusual gains.

This possibility for gain will be particularly likely when a person has a better understanding than the average investor of the accounting complexities of particular real estate shares. Previous chapters have shown how in many periods, real estate returns based on standard accounting principles differ considerably from the real economic rate of return. The reported income statement may show a significantly different timing of earned income than occurs in fact.

Analysts who understand what is involved in such movements can base their investments on their own analyses, which are more accurate than the market's. While it may take a considerable length of time for such situations to work out, they may be extremely profitable. This type of stock situation is avoided by most financial analysts and investing institutions. Only in rare cases are they interested in situations which require more than a year or two to become obvious.

The same factors which make it worthwhile for investors to place individual real estate stocks in a portfolio may make it even more worthwhile for them to purchase shares in joint ventures.

SELECTING A JOINT VENTURE OR SYNDICATE

Syndication has been one of the most rapidly growing forms of real estate investment. The reasons for this growth are convenience, promotion, and economic advantages.

Small Size Participations in syndicates have been available in units with minimum investments ranging from $2,000 to $10,000. They have been sold like stock. Purchasers wanting to invest in real estate have found available a convenient ownership form that does not require all the time, effort, and knowledge usually needed to purchase real property. The small size of the typical unit means that investors can purchase a portfolio of several different investments without having a great deal of capital.

Promotion   For many years the life insurance industry has stressed the fact that insurance is sold, not bought. Millions of Americans carry life insurance, but very few have ever walked into an office and asked for a policy. People buy because they are approached by salesmen, who make a profit from selling insurance.

The same basic statement can be made about investments in real estate syndications. While some people with a well-thought-through investment strategy have sought out syndicators and have made it known that they were in the market for units, this is not the typical case. People have invested in real estate joint ventures because they have been approached by promoters and salesmen. The promoters and salesmen are active because they profit by selling the units. Without the profit arising from the sales efforts, any growth in syndication would probably have occurred very differently.

Economic Advantages   While syndications have been primarily sold, not bought, the selling has been possible because syndications do have a genuine underlying economic advantage. When people want to invest in real estate, a syndication may well be a logical form. The primary economic advantages are of four types:

Syndicates and joint ventures are single-tax entities.
Expertise and independent judgment are available.
There are important economies of scale.
Diversification and greater staying power can be obtained.

1   The tax-shelter advantage of joint ventures has been covered fully. It has been the primary factor used by promoters and salesmen. Without the tax shelter, it is probable that real estate syndication would remain a fairly small-scale, local enterprise appealing primarily to groups of friends and acquaintances.

2   One of the major promises of syndication is that by purchasing a small investment, one becomes a partner with skilled real estate operators. While this frequently is not the case, it can occur. Many of the nation's largest and most prominent real estate professionals utilize joint-venture relationships extensively. An individual who properly selects his or her investment can become a partner with some of the major financial institutions or most prominent real estate entrepreneurs.

Clearly, the possibility of obtaining such expertise is critical for many potential investors who simply do not have the time or skills to analyze individual properties. They can put their time to better use by analyzing their potential partners and then putting their trust in the expertise of the promoters they decide to invest with.

3   Another major advantage of the joint-venture relationship is the opportunity to realize economies of scale in buying and managing properties.

Small properties, even if they can be bought at a good price, are at a competitive disadvantage to larger properties. Their operating expenses are proportionately greater. Recreational facilities and special features are higher on a per-unit basis. Property management—for both the on-site resident manager and the off-site executive manager—is more efficient and cheaper when spread over a larger number of units.

The same type of scale economies applies to acquisition activities. Costs of evaluating the market area, arranging financing, negotiating purchase terms, and obtaining legal documentation do not vary directly with the size of a property. Similar analysis and work are required for each purchase, regardless of size. The relative costs of these activities, again, are greater for small properties.

4   Through joint-venture relationships investors can achieve improved diversification. The partnership can buy multiple properties, thereby lessening dependence on any one property. The problem of risks tied to a particular location or property type, which plagues individual purchasers of real estate, can be avoided. Similarly, it may be easier for a partnership to raise and maintain the reserves necessary to avoid a complete failure due to temporarily impeded cash flows. The amount of reserves for a number of properties will be proportionately less if the properties have sufficient diversification. As a result, the risks through partnerships may be considerably less than those through investment in one or two properties.

While diversification may reduce the likelihood of substantial loss, the very fact of ownership of multiple properties means that an outstanding performance by a single property may be diluted by that of other, less successful investments. Thus, while the risk of downside loss is lowered, the upside potential may also be restricted.

PICKING A SYNDICATE

Some joint ventures have been good; some have been disastrous. This means that careful analysis is necessary if one expects to obtain profitable results. It is not the buying of a joint venture that is important; rather, the facts of the specific syndicate will determine its success or failure. Many investors have found themselves with unsuitable syndicate securities which they picked because of insufficient analysis and a lack of knowledge of how this market works. What are the factors that should be examined in considering any individual offer? Experience show that four types of factors should be looked at carefully:

1   The type of joint venture
2   The financial analysis of the offer
3   The sponsor and his record
4   The partnership agreement

Type of Joint Venture

In picking a syndicate, various possibilities arise as to the type of joint venture: (1) Investments can be made through a private or public partnership; (2) the investment can be in single or multiple properties; and (3) if purchased through a public offering, the document making the offer may identify the specific property or properties to be purchased, or it may leave the selection of the properties to the sponsor after the partnership has been formed. Since these types of ventures exist side by side, there are obvious advantages and disadvantages to each.

Private or Public   The private joint venture is often based on a single property purchased by a limited group of friends or acquaintances or clients of an investment counselor. Its prime drawbacks are likely to stem from its small size, its ties to a particular location, and a danger of poor management and lack of expertise.

On the other hand, while it is certainly possible to misjudge, in many cases one can put greater trust in local friends or acquaintances. A local broker may know a property or neighborhood so well that his analysis and management skills are far superior to what would be offered by a firm which might rate much higher in most other situations. In addition, there are likely to be considerable cost savings in the private venture. There is a greater certainty that the price of the property has not been inflated. The promoter's profits tend to be considerably less.

Even more important may be the probability of a greater congruence of interests between investors and promoters. In many private ventures, promoters are active investors themselves. Their profits, or rate of return, will be somewhat greater than those of the silent partners, but their gains will be realized only if the promotion is successful. In contrast, in many public offerings, promoters, and particularly the salesmen, may make their profit simply from the successful sale of the units.

The major problem in investing in private ventures is simply that of finding available units. Except through luck, it may take a great deal of time and effort to find neighbors or friends who have the necessary expertise, are active in the real estate business, and are willing to engage in partnerships. As a result, even though investors may want to become part of a private venture, the possibility of finding one which fits their needs may be so low that they decide to engage in other forms of partnership.

Single or Multiple Properties   When examining public offerings, investors sometimes find that an offer is for a partnership in a single property. In other cases an investment fund is established which will purchase several different properties. What are the relative advantages of this choice?

Proponents of the single-property form prefer the investment theory of "putting all your eggs in one basket and watching it like a hawk." They feel that better analysis is possible for a single, specified property. The promoter will have to furnish the information required for an investment analysis. Investors who have the proper skills can determine for themselves whether a specific property seems like a good investment. They can rate the offering compared with all their other investment opportunities.

The single-property syndicate gives the investor a better opportunity to select an investment that most closely matches his or her own objectives and to participate in a partnership with others who share similar goals. With only one property involved, it is easier to package and structure an investment to emphasize cash flow, tax shelter, or some other objective. Multiple-property funds, in their search for diversification, may mix properties that serve different investor objectives.

Those who prefer multiple-property funds stress primarily economies of scale and of diversification. In larger partnerships fixed costs can be spread over more investment dollars. There will be savings in management, a better use of reserves, and perhaps greater expertise.

One clear possibility of saving is in the registration process, which is both time-consuming and expensive. Assuming that the minimum cost of a registration with the

SEC is $50,000, it makes sense to seek fewer registrations and to raise more money per syndication. Rather than undertaking a number of single-property syndications in a year, major syndicators find it more desirable to do an extended offering of a substantial size.

With the possibility of buying several properties, promoters may find it easier to match their marketing operations to the results. They may offer a multiple-property syndicate, with the option of buying one, two, or any number of properties, depending on the actual number of investments sold. This form of syndication combines flexibility in raising money with the advantages of specified properties. Such an approach, however, requires that the syndicator have the financial strength and dexterity to effect an alternative use for any properties contracted for if he fails to raise the required amount of investment dollars.

Nonspecified Assets   Finally, while some syndications specify the type of property or the specific property that will be considered for investment, others—the nonspecified-asset fund, the blind pool, or the blank-check fund—state simply that the sponsors will purchase properties with the funds raised. The investor must rely solely on a general statement of the fund's objectives. Clearly, in these cases investors cannot evaluate the investment quality of the real estate itself, since there is no information on any particular property.

Conflicts arise in timing the property purchase to the availability of money. It is difficult to retain the right to acquire a property while complying with government requirements and completing the mechanics of the offering. If the scheduling is not precise or if unexpected delays are encountered, deals may be lost. The property's price for the specified fund may include a premium charged by the seller because he or she has to agree to take the property off the market for a prolonged period while the sale of the investment units is in process. In the blank-check fund these difficulties are avoided because the general partner has a larger degree of freedom in timing the acquisition of properties.

Other timing problems arise because in the nonspecified fund, the actual amount of capital to be raised is uncertain. The fund may end up with too little or too much equity capital for the type of portfolio it has promised. This, again, is a problem of scale. Unlike common stocks, which are divided into extremely small fractional interests, real estate ownership requires large units. The cash required for a parcel of prime real estate, even with mortgages, may be substantial. The general partner of a nonspecified fund obligated to invest a pool of capital in real estate may find his or her potential selection limited. When buying a small number of properties, it is difficult to allocate one's available funds on an optimum basis. Some blind pools seem to acquire less desirable properties simply to make the numbers add up. In other cases the sellers are able to demand high prices when they realize that there is a sum of money waiting to be invested.

Above all, there is the problem that individual investors in the blind pool may end up with investments that do not necessarily serve their own particular objectives. The investment policies of the blind pool usually allow substantial latitude. There appears to be a tendency to turn to "boiler plate" in the preparation of such prospectuses and to insert a series of standard phrases that are devoid of essential meaning. While more general investment policies facilitate the accumulation of diversified properties and allow flexibility to the general partner, the investor may find the ultimate portfolio not to his or her liking. A particular case in point is the unknown and uncertain amount of income tax deductibility in the year of the investment. With a specified property, investors know exactly what they are buying and how it fits their tax-shelter needs.

Financial Analysis of a Venture

One of the most important parts of choosing a venture is the financial analysis. How good a job can be done depends upon the type of offering. For example, a blind pool probably will give virtually no information useful for financial analysis since even the promoters are not aware of what types of costs and income can be expected.

On the other hand, a prospectus for the purchase of a single property will contain the projections of the promoters. In certain cases, there is a record that can be looked up, as when one considers purchasing an investment unit from an existing holder. This will also be true if the form of venture is to be that of an REIT or an existing real estate corporation, where financial statements of past operations can be obtained.

In all these cases care must be taken to adjust the past data. The difference between an accounting statement meeting accepted practices and a statement most useful for economic decisions must be recognized. Still, it will frequently be true that the advantages of having some sort of financial data available are so great that this will determine the type of investment for many investors. They will stick with offerings for which they can make a financial analysis, as opposed to proposals that make far more attractive promises but for which checking the promises is far more difficult.

What sort of information can one expect to find in a prospectus? What should one look for? The specific projections of the promoter are most important. While these will often be impossible to check directly, they can be checked against the market and against similar information on other properties. For example, if most apartment houses in the area show 40 percent of gross revenue required for operating expenses and the prospectus estimates that the proposed unit will require only 20 percent of its revenue for operating expenses, something would appear to be wrong. Either revenues have been overestimated or costs have been underestimated. It may be that the particular project is so very unusual that its costs will be far different from those of all others, but again, experience and the theory of competition say that this is unlikely to happen.

Similarly, if most apartments in the area sell at six times gross revenue and the proposal states that the venture will cost eight times revenue, more complete information is called for. Why is the syndicate paying a third more for the property in terms of price-revenue relationships than is being paid for others surrounding it? Again, the chances that a property is so unusual as to be worth a third more are not great, although it might turn out in a careful checking of the venture that this type of multiplier does make sense.

A simple reading of the prospectus will frequently raise questions and point up danger signals. A comparison with other, similar projects may show that the promoter is loading costs onto the venture. If management fees, brokerage charges, legal fees, and other costs run a good deal higher than costs for similar ventures, the investor obviously should ask what he or she is getting for these higher costs. They reduce the potential return unless they buy unusual services.

While it is a more complex task, careful investors find it worthwhile to redo the pro forma financial statements of the prospectus in the form shown in Chapters 20 and 22. Simply writing down, in a more logical form, the information furnished often makes it obvious that some critical assumptions are questionable. In other cases, it will rapidly appear that the promoters are defining rate of return in such a way as to increase greatly the promised, although not the real, rate of return.

Table 20-4 showed that the reported rate of return can easily vary by 300 percent or more, depending upon what figures are taken from the same financial statement. Obviously, reconstructing the data to show what is really promised can greatly aid investors. They would naturally tend to choose a venture that they think offers a 25 percent rate of return rather than others offering only 10 or 12 percent. When ventures are compared in identical form, it may well turn out that a unit that is promising less actually is offering more.

EVALUATING THE SPONSOR

In many cases a choice has to be made between a financial analysis and one's estimate of the sponsor's ability and probability of performing. This is a critical dichotomy which is hard to resolve. Should investors place most of their faith in the financial analysis or in the sponsor's background and promises? Clearly, the answer depends upon getting the maximum information about each, recognizing the problem, and determining on the basis of the knowledge available which should be given the greater weight. A tremendous promise in terms of financial data is worthless if it comes from a self-serving or even potentially embezzling sponsor. On the other hand, a careful sponsor with a very good track record may feel that it is unnecessary to make extravagant promises to obtain investors. Such sponsors are careful about protecting their reputations; they would rather exceed their promises than never fulfill them.

Since an investment depends so completely on the sponsor, it is important to evaluate four salient elements:

1 His track record
2 His organization
3 His credit standing
4 His record with respect to cutting corners

Track Record

Ultimately, an investor in a syndicate is buying management. The ability to achieve one's projections and handle the inevitable problems is an essential of successful management. Because most investors encounter a sponsor in his money-raising capacity, they tend to make investment decisions on the basis of the sponsor's marketing rather than management abilities, which are hard to judge at this stage.

As noted previously, a real estate investment should be thought of as a separate business entity requiring an ongoing management. Consequently, the management's ability and its financial record are of particular concern. The investor should note how long the sponsor has been in business, how well capitalized the business is, and the motives and objectives of the sponsor, the management, and the owners. The investor should consider the sponsor's experience in terms of the number of deals he has been involved in, the number and type of properties he has acquired, the extent of investors with whom he has been involved, the size of offerings, and the location of properties.

The sponsor's track record reports the results of his previous deals. The investor should not look for an unblemished record, but rather for solid, overall performance. Indeed, sponsors with significant experience who claim never to have made a bad deal either are misrepresenting the truth or are destined to encounter difficulties soon. Since uncontrollable factors influence real estate markets, sponsors should not be expected to have perfect vision.

In evaluating the track record, it must be recognized that many techniques can be used to enhance the current year's results or defer recognition of a bad deal. Accounting principles leave a great deal of flexibility in reporting results. Consequently, a short track record must be given far less weight than one extending well back into the past.

In evaluating a track record, the investor should determine precisely what type of real estate ventures the sponsor has offered. Expertise in a local market and in specific property types is not necessarily transferable to new markets and property types. An investor will want to know whether the sponsor has emphasized conservative, economically justified real estate ventures or whether previous deals relied primarily on tax gimmickry. Similarly, experience with investments such as commercial credit-sale-leasebacks does not necessarily prepare a sponsor for the different management tasks related to an apartment building.

Organization

The experience, education, and organizational depth of the sponsor's management team must also be evaluated. Some companies have strong organizations of several talented executives, while others are merely one-person operations. It is clear that risks are greater if a firm is totally dependent on one individual.

In evaluating a record, one wants to know whether it was achieved by the current team or by those who have departed. Managers knowledgeable in real estate matters are in short supply. Because the real estate business is essentially entrepreneurial and attracts individuals who aspire someday to run their own companies, the existence of a competent management team is no guarantee that it can be retained.

There is an old saying that in most cases, knowledgeable and sophisticated managers who *can* be hired are not worth hiring. Because of other attractive opportunities, the price of a competent, trained staff always appears to be too high. Thus a good management team usually has to be developed rather than hired.

Individual managers should be evaluated in terms of their experience—in business, and in real estate particularly—as well as their education. While traditionally, formal educational preparation has not been thought of as particularly important in real estate, increasing professionalism and sophistication of the business suggest that individuals who have not had preparation in modern management and analytic techniques may well be at a disadvantage.

Consideration of a sponsor's professional reputation is part of the process of evaluation of his organization. How well known is he? Is he active in his trade and professional association? In evaluating the sponsor, the investor should be cautious of stories that may be written about the sponsor's organization. Many of these are verbatim reproductions of laudatory press releases prepared by the sponsor's public relations representative.

Often, much can be learned about a company by considering the quality of its professional advisers, including those doing legal, accounting, appraisal, and general consulting work. Does the sponsor work with the most knowledgeable and highly regarded advisers, or does he try to economize in this area? Further, an investor might explore how the advisers are actually used. Some sponsors maintain prominent firms on retainer, paying them primarily for their name without having them do any work. Obviously the sponsor hopes to achieve a marketing advantage by being able to point to this prominent firm as his adviser. In this regard the investor will want to know whether the advisers really work in an advisory capacity or merely act to endorse what the sponsor has decided to do.

Some sponsors utilize a so-called independent advisory board. This group may be represented as actively evaluating prospective investments and reviewing the sponsor's overall operations. In a sense, it is often presented as being very similar to a board of directors. Usually the advisory board will be composed of a number of prominent, widely known individuals. The critical question is whether these individuals have any knowledge or experience directly transferable to the investment at hand and whether they are actually asked to provide any meaningful contribution to the investment.

A useful means of getting an insight into the sponsor's management ability and posture is to visit his offices. The size of the sponsor's organization should be consistent with the scale of his operations. If he has too heavy an overhead in lavishly furnished, expensive space and if the atmosphere is intended more for marketing impression than organizational efficiency, this will ultimately be paid for by the investor. If the sponsor and members of his organization pursue a particularly extravagant life-style, unless they are of independent means, the investor is paying for this as well. While these cautionary comments are not meant to imply that an overly frugal, low-budget approach is necessarily best, investors should think carefully about whether they would be more comfortable with a performance-minded, as opposed to a promotion-minded, sponsor.

The record-keeping problems of real estate ventures are complex, and they can be difficult and baffling. Too frequently, sponsors have marginal or even inadequate accounting systems. Not only are tax returns late in being prepared, but also the actual status of the properties may be unavailable, or even unknown. Indeed, sponsors who lack high-quality, reliable accounting information will be totally incapable of effectively managing the program's investment.

Credit Standing

The credit standing of a sponsor not only measures his past success or failure but also is a sign of his ability to bring a proposed venture to a successful conclusion.

Information on a sponsor's financial position can be obtained from Dun and

Bradstreet ratings, major creditors, and the like. Investors might want to contact past investors to ask their opinions. Further, they should investigate whether the sponsor has previously filed for bankruptcy, gone through a financial reorganization, or encountered other financial difficulties. Some promoters have had repeated disappointing—if not disastrous—results, and yet they continue to attract new investors. In fact, too many prominent institutions fail to make even the most rudimentary investigations into the previous dealings of developers and sponsors. They put their faith in the security of the property, only to find that they take losses as a result of human failures.

Sponsors often cite letters from bankers attesting to their financial stability and volume of business. Frequently such letters indicate that the company has maintained "mid-six-figure" balances over periods of time, for example. By its very nature, any significant real estate transaction involves the escrowing of large amounts of money. These are the situations frequently referred to in the bankers' letters. Thus it is important that the investor investigate carefully the true circumstances of all representations made, rather than taking them at face value.

The risks in many ventures will be much smaller when sponsors have adequate capital of their own. The ultimate success of an investment depends upon the sponsor's ability to fund the offering. An investor who is considering an investment at year-end for the purpose of achieving tax shelter wants to know that the sponsor will in fact meet the deadline. Similarly, an investor considering a nonspecified property fund for diversification will want to be sure that the sponsor can raise enough money to acquire a diversified group of properties.

Credit standing is also an index of the ability of a sponsor to raise money when things begin to go wrong, as they frequently do. The concept of "staying power" appears throughout the joint-venture analysis. Staying power can be built into individual ventures, but frequently it is not. It is at these times that the financial, or credit, standing of the sponsor may make the difference between a rapid foreclosure and a granting of sufficient time to work out problems.

Cutting Corners

There are many opportunities in joint ventures for sponsors to cut corners. They can slight important needs; they can place their own interests above those of their partners; they may engage in true conflicts of interest; they may badly puff, or overstate, the true situation; they may just be careless or inept.

Conflicts of Interest   Investors should look into a sponsor's other activities. If the company only puts together investment ventures, the pressure to put together a new deal may conflict with impartial judgment. Full-time syndicators must make new offerings on a regular basis in order to stay in business. Thus, even at times when it is inappropriate to buy a property, full-time syndicators must put out deals to cover their overhead. While national companies have a broader market in which to search and therefore can reduce these risks somewhat, major problems in real estate syndication have resulted from pressure to put out deals to meet the sponsor's overhead.

An investor should evaluate the sponsor's other activities as they relate to the subject offering. Does the sponsor propose to manage the property and engage in self-dealing by providing insurance and other services to the venture? Sponsors who possess good property management talent will often do a better job for investors by managing the property themselves, but all too often real estate ventures are organized to create a vehicle to provide fees and commissions for other segments of a sponsor's business. The investor should investigate potential conflicts and be wary of self-dealing by the sponsor that would be adverse to the investor's own interest.

New development projects where the developer will concurrently be the general partner are almost always fraught with potential conflicts of interest. These must be weighed against some very attractive features of ventures of this type. Assuming that an equitable sharing arrangement is structured and that the development is a successful one, the investor is likely to do better in such projects than in others where the developer and general partner are separate parties. At the same time, though, the fiduciary obligation of general partners is put to a severe test. They must balance their own desire for profit from the development of the property with their responsibility to serve the investors' interests. Thus such projects should be evaluated with extra care, particularly in light of the significant risks associated with new construction.

Registration   In selling investments, some sponsors suggest that because an offering has been registered with a securities regulatory body, the investor can be confident that it has met a test of at least a minimum level of quality. While regulatory agencies review offerings, their criteria have no necessary relationship to an investment's quality. In fact, some of the most fraudulent and least desirable real estate offerings have been public registrations cleared by public regulatory agencies.

When considering a private placement offering, the investor should be concerned about whether the sponsor has adequately satisfied the requirements for a private placement. As discussed earlier on pages 135 to 138, strict standards apply to determining what is a private placement and what is not. If a sponsor makes an offering under the guise of a private placement exemption which in fact turns out to be public, investors can demand rescission—the refund of their money plus an annual return thereon.

While individual investors might find the opportunity to ask for a rescission attractive, they must recognize that if they have that opportunity, so do all the other investors. If rescission is demanded, the pressure on the sponsor may be too great for him to handle. Consequently, investors may find that request for recission, even where the deal is a very good one, has a very detrimental effect on the sponsor and thus ultimately on the deal itself.

Acquisitions   A sponsor's philosophy concerning, and approach to, the acquisition process are particularly important. Research and experience indicate that the amount of resources committed by sponsors to the acquisition process varies dramatically. Some sponsors undertake a diligent investigation of properties. Others are irresponsibly casual in their approach. In fact, the executives of one large real estate company claim they never visit the properties they acquire.

Those sponsors whose visits to the property consist of flying into town, taking a cab to the property, inspecting an apartment or two, and then returning to the airport are not doing a significantly better job. As emphasized earlier, successful investment decisions are the result of detailed, painstaking fieldwork. Reliable information is not obtained in a short period of time or a matter of hours.

The availability of sponsors' detailed documentation of the acquisition process is a measure of their acquisition confidence and capability. Investors should expect sponsors to have undertaken the detailed type of analysis described in earlier chapters. The data a sponsor generates should be evaluated in terms of the most sophisticated profitability measures. Further, extensive sensitivity analysis should be undertaken to evaluate the impact of all the alternative outcomes on the investment results.

Sponsors who assert that sophisticated financial techniques are inappropriate for real estate investment decisions are really saying that they do not understand these techniques and their advantages. In the majority of circumstances, such ignorance on the part of the sponsor is reason enough to avoid his deal.

THE PARTNERSHIP AGREEMENT

The fourth factor which must be analyzed is the legal relationship between the investor and the promoter; this is set forth in the partnership agreement. Two basic parts of the agreement specify (1) the legal relationship between the investor and the general partner, as well as the powers of the investor, and (2) the amount of compensation to be received by the promoter and general partner.

The Legal Basis

Since most joint ventures are sold on the advantages of a limited partnership, it is essential that the contracts be drawn so that this objective is not frustrated. It is necessary that the partnership certificate be approved and recorded in the appropriate jurisdiction. The agreement must expressly preclude involvement by individual limited partners in the ongoing management decisions. Investors are interested in making certain that they obtain honest results and tax benefits without being exposed to additional liability.

While limited partners can have no voice in the management, they should be kept completely informed by required reports. They should have the right to replace the general partner, dissolve the partnership, and probably approve of major changes in the financing and sales of properties. Investors want to make certain of their recourses in case they become dissatisfied with the performance or conduct of a promoter. Their rights are covered in stipulations concerning how meetings are to be called, form requirements, and rules of replacement. The agreement will also specify the provisions under which investments can be transferred and repurchased.

Assessments

Another important question is that of assessments. Both the syndicator and investors are inviting trouble by entering into an agreement that is silent on this point. Essentially, an assessment is a charge levied against the partners for additional contributions. The various approaches in the partnership agreement to the issue of assessments can be categorized as follows:

1   A stipulation of mandatory assessments
2   A stipulation of no assessments
3   A provision that partners may loan funds to the partnership or a provision that additional limited partnership interests may be sold, with the existing limited partners having the right of first refusal

The decision as to which of these provisions is best for the investor depends on his or her financial position and reasons for entering the syndicate. In effect, the choice is between risking a partnership which lacks staying power because it cannot raise funds at critical times and entering a partnership which may require more funds from the investor. Most small investors will probably find that they are better off with the stipulation of no required assessments, but with provisions that additional funds can be raised either through loans or through the sale of additional partnership interests.

Compensation

The sharing of the profits and losses of the venture is of particular concern. While it is essential that the sponsor have an attractive-enough deal so that he is sufficiently motivated on the investors' behalf, it is important that the deal not be so favorable to the sponsor that not enough is left for the investors. The problem is to achieve a fair balance of sponsor incentive and investor return.

A number of arguments indicate that the sponsor's compensation should be higher than the traditional payment to a securities underwriter. Because most real estate offerings are relatively small compared with mutual funds and corporate security issues, the legal and organization costs are significantly greater relative to the money raised. Because investors' knowledge of real estate investments is substantially less than their knowledge of other securities, marketing costs are greater.

Promoters of real estate investments also incur higher costs in identifying, evaluating, and selecting properties than securities underwriters do. Compensation to sponsors must be high because of the many properties they evaluate and reject for each one that they package and offer. The search for appropriate investments is conducted in a market characterized by highly imperfect information, in contrast to the more ready availability of information on Wall Street.

Brokers' Fees   In many cases, compensation to promoters is achieved by paying them as real estate brokers or by paying them a percentage of total assets. These forms of compensation can lead to latent conflicts of interest. It is important that the difference between a real estate broker and a sponsor representing the investors be recognized. Because sponsors perform a very different function from that of brokers, they should not be compensated on a similar basis. The broker represents the seller and seeks to find the best buyer. The sponsor represents the buyer and seeks to find the best real estate parcel. The responsibility of sponsors, furthermore, is a continuing and ongoing one. They must exert their best efforts for the investors in order to achieve a maximum return.

In their fiduciary role, sponsors have a staff of acquisition specialists who negotiate directly with the seller to buy properties on a net basis. Since the real estate brokerage agency function is incompatible with the sponsor's fiduciary responsibility, the real estate commission should be discouraged as a form of compensation. Some sponsors seek to avoid this conflict by stipulating that the venture will pay the commission, not the seller. Such an arrangement is at best contrived; at worst, it could cause the venture to pay two real estate commissions on the same property.

Percentage of Assets   The second form of compensation, based on a percentage of gross assets, may tempt sponsors to increase gross assets, and therefore their pay, (1) by paying too high a price for property purchased; (2) by buying properties with maximum leverage and so increasing the financial risk; or (3) by failing to provide adequate depreciation and operating reserves.

The financial benefits that may tempt sponsors to leverage property purchases excessively or to set up inadequate reserves follow from the fact that, all other things being equal, the more funds invested in high-leverage situations, the greater the sponsor's compensation. Thus for a given sum of money raised from investors, shifting the downpayment from 20 to 10 percent doubles the sponsor's compensation by doubling the assets purchased. If assets can be purchased with downpayments of 5 percent, the promoter may receive as front-end compensation an amount in excess of the funds collected and invested.

Allocations   The allocation of profits and distributions is a matter of such importance that the partnership agreement must be specific as to proportion, priority, conditions, and timing of distributions to the limited partners and the general partner. The object should be to find methods of compensation that motivate the promoter and general partner to serve best the interests of the limited partners.

A reasonable form of front-end compensation is a simple fee equal to a percentage of the money raised. Such a fee basis reduces the temptation to acquire properties for prices or terms that may not be in the best interests of the investors. Similarly, rather than scheduling a property management fee equal to a fixed percentage of the gross revenues, it is preferable to stipulate that the general partner will receive a certain amount of the cash available for distribution after a base return has been distributed to the limited partners and that the general partner is then to receive an additional percentage of the remaining cash.

While all kinds of compensation agreements can be found, a type which is not untypical and which seems fair provides that general partners be compensated for their expenses up to a certain amount, perhaps with an inflation adjustment, and that after reimbursement for their services they share both in current income and in any capital gains that may be made from the property. The specific percentages allowed will depend upon the point at which the sharing begins. If the investors are to get all funds up to a specified return, such as 8 or 10 percent a year, and are to receive the first X percent of capital gains, then the percentage of the remainder going to the general partner may be as high as 20 or 25 percent.

In all agreements of this type it is vital that the definition of profits, income, revenues, prices, assets, etc., be very specific. Many partnership agreements leave a great deal to be desired in terms of the amount of interpretation that is necessary after the partnership has actually been established.

It is generally agreed that in making decisions, investors should be less concerned about the amount of compensation to a sponsor than about what they themselves stand to get out of the venture. Top talent may command premium compensation. As the adage goes, ''Don't worry about what I make—compare what you get with your other opportunities.'' This, however, makes sense only if the goals of the sponsors and the investors are similar. The object is to motivate the sponsor to maximize the investors' return. Such motivation does not exist where the sponsor earns substantial profits merely by originating the deal and then has only limited compensation for ongoing management responsibilities.

The preferred approach involves a reasonable fee for putting together the venture and then substantial incentive compensation dependent upon the investor's first realizing a preferred return. Such a compensation arrangement was utilized in the Empire State Building Associates venture, described in Chapter 8, and this investment has seemed to be quite successful for both the promoters and the investors.

SUMMARY

Many people will find that they can secure the real estate equities they desire by purchasing securities. Common stocks are liquid. They are easily obtained. There is a great deal of published information about most of them. They tend to share the major advantages and disadvantages of stocks in general. However, they are more volatile and have a greater return than other stocks. They vary a good deal in their attributes depending on what sector of real estate they are based upon. Many have features which result in low tax payments, but under accepted accounting principles these usually yield low reported profits compared with profits in other industries.

Real estate syndicates have been sold primarily on the strength of their ability to shelter other income from taxes. They may be small shares in single or multiple properties. Depending on the type of fund being offered, the specific properties and their investment analysis may or may not be known to the investor before he or she joins a venture.

Most of the success of any investment depends on the sponsor. If the sponsor offers poor management or skims the cream from the deal, the investor is likely to lose, no matter how good the venture appears on the surface. The sponsor must have the experience and ability needed to handle extremely complex problems. In addition, the venture's agreement must be detailed so that the duties and responsibilities of the general and limited partners are explicit. Sponsors' compensation should be so structured that their profits depend upon profits for the investors and not primarily on their ability to sell syndicate shares.

QUESTIONS AND PROBLEMS

1 It is well known that the prices of common stocks fluctuate. What is the behavior of real estate stocks relative to that of common stocks generally?
2 What has been the track record of publicly held developers?
3 An REIT is organized and sells shares for $20 each. The funds are successfully invested, dividends of $2.50 are paid, and the shares subsequently trade at $40. An equal number of shares are sold at the $40 price. Discuss the key relationships here and the terms for this phenomenon.

4 In the previous question, what is the average book value per share? If the shares subsequently trade at $8 per share, what is the probable reason?

5 What are the implications of the concept of "economies of scale" as regards the investment approach for the individual investor?

6 Many people believe that the performance of real estate stocks in 1974 was far worse than would normally be expected. Discuss.

7 What are the arguments for and against the view that, even without inside information, some people can outperform the market by analyzing and investing in a specialized group of stocks such as those of firms related to real estate?

8 Would you prefer to invest in a local syndicate or in one managed by a large national firm? Why?

9 Discuss the favorable and unfavorable aspects of making an investment in a syndicate on the basis of its financial statements, in contrast to the reputation of its sponsor.

10 What are the major features to be considered in evaluating a partnership agreement?

Chapter 27

Property Types and Characteristics

Although every real estate investment is unique, different property classifications share certain common characteristics. When the economic characteristics of the various property types are understood, better investment decisions can be made. Investors are interested in how the basic and specialized features of each property relate to their own investment strategy. What are the specifics which have the greatest influence on a property's practicality for a particular portfolio?

Real estate values derive from the functions served by a property. Real estate investment is not so much an investment in the tangible attributes of real property as it is an investment in business activity. The investor who buys a property buys a series of anticipated economic benefits. Indeed, each investment can be thought of as an individual business with distinctive operating economics. The better an investor understands the economics of the property he or she is acquiring, the better the chance that the investment decision will be successful.

The variety of possible types of investments is so great that even the most experienced investor can easily be overwhelmed by their profusion. For this reason, a simple system of classification for the purpose of comparison serves an extremely useful function. Such a technique of comparison is illustrated in the foldout table entitled Characteristics of Property Types.

For each type of property we show the function performed, its primary investment characteristics, some typical factors of ownership, and the primary economic characteristics which determine its value and how it is likely to change over time.

We discuss these property types under the headings of land, residential properties, and nonresidential properties. Investors typically approach property in this way. In Table 5-3, we listed some of the features which influence the return on an investment and which must be considered by both the potential investor and the lender. In this chapter, after a brief discussion of some of the significant factors which differ among property types, we expand the description of the special features, problems, and opportunities associated with some of them.

In any real estate investment the price asked for a property is premised upon certain assumptions regarding people's behavior and their attitudes toward real estate spaces. A price generally reflects how many people want to use the space and what they will pay for it. Some factors that affect these patterns can be controlled—for example, by utilizing advertising promotion to attract people and by employing effective management to motivate them to continue patronizing the property. Other factors, such as general economic conditions and employment patterns, are beyond the immediate control of the owner. If people decide not to use a space because it does not appeal to them, because it is poorly managed, or because it lacks access or adequate transportation, the investment will be unsuccessful. Thus the behavioral expectations implicit in all real estate investment play a critical role in determining ultimate success.

LAND

If purchases of properties for personal use are excluded, land is the most active sphere for real estate speculation and investment. Because land includes that used for farming and for other raw-material production, more money is invested in it than in any other category of income property. Its annual sales are also the highest. It offers the largest potential gains and losses.

Land is attractive as an investment because it is limited in amount. Spectacular profits have been made by many investors in land. But although profits of 50 to 100 percent over a 3- or 4-year period have not been uncommon, the price of most land depends directly on the value of the product it produces. Values have fluctuated primarily with agricultural prices and productivity, and therefore average gains have been limited.

While land is fixed in amount, a great deal of it is available for development. Successful development in most cases is the point at which the largest gains are made. It follows that success in land investment requires the ability to forecast both the time at which land will move into the predeveloped stage and the time at which it will pass through this stage to successful development. Land prices usually jump in the few years just before land is converted to urban use. In addition, successful developers are well paid for the risks they take. If forecasting has been poor and no actual development occurs, profits depend—as the saying goes—on finding another "sucker," someone who will pay to hold the land even though it will not generate adequate revenues to be profitable for him either.

Land can be purchased by anyone and in almost any amount to fit the individual's own wealth or income. The smaller the investment unit, the faster acreage costs rise. Financing is difficult to obtain except through the seller. Holding costs tend to be high, with a negative cash flow in many cases. On the other hand, land being used for agricultural or recreational purposes may create sufficient revenue to carry itself, but usually with little or no income on invested equity.

Land can provide a good tax shelter, and land in use has served as an inflationary hedge. Thus it may be an attractive investment for those concerned primarily with future income. On the other hand, land investments tend to be highly illiquid and to involve substantial transaction costs for both buyer and seller. The fact that land has a negative current cash flow limits the holding period if the transaction is to be profitable.

All these factors make the matter of proper timing and forecasting critical. Because so many mishaps occur, the actual profits on individual transactions which are successful must be extremely high to offset all the failures. It is not clear whether in fact they do so. Many people are attracted to land speculation as to a lottery. They should know that they are paying much more than the expected value of the ticket (land), but they buy the ticket in the hope of making a large killing.

Because of the way the market works, land investors must identify their objectives carefully. They need to focus on when they expect values to change, the probable range in the time horizon, and what is a tolerable level of risk. It is especially important to determine the amount of money to be tied up in a project. Delays, both in market responses and then in approvals for development, can greatly extend holding periods and increase costs. Potential rewards must be carefully evaluated in the context of the risk assumed.

Generally, a successful land investment depends upon a particular key event. Examples of such key events are the opening of a new plant which creates additional employment and need for housing and the completion of a major highway or transportation system which makes a previously inaccessible area convenient. Developments by other owners may also help.

Investors must attempt to identify the key event that will spell success for their land investment. They must assess carefully when (and if) it will occur and what impact it will have. Because land investment is a speculation, contingency plans are necessary.

Undeveloped Land

Most land is undeveloped. While in some instances urban growth will, in time, cause the land to be in demand, much undeveloped land lacks convenient access to population centers. Other characteristics of a tract may also preclude its development. An unfavorable climate, excessively steep terrain, or inadequate soil conditions all diminish commercial usefulness. Further, substantial amounts of land dedicated to public use for parks or preserves or to streets and highways are also unavailable for development.

Table 27-1 presents a simple classification of undeveloped land. Properties may serve as raw material for a production process or for food, energy, materials, or recreation, or they may be held for financial and speculative purposes. In many uses

pping centers	Office buildings	Industrial property
goods, distribution cen- tunity for concentrated xperience	Personal services, administration and management of economic and social systems	Conversion of raw materials, pro- duction of manufactured goods, labor, land and capital meet here
good	Average	Average to high
ium	Low	Low
	Average	Poor
	Average	High
ood if leases are strong	Relatively good if leases are strong	Very hard to sell unless there is strong long-term lease
dependent upon major store as anchor tenant designated percentage gned	Financed often on a floor-ceiling arrangement whereby additional increments of financing depend on threshold levels of leasing being achieved	Financing depends on credit rat- ing, often owned by occupant; if not, financing will depend on credit rating of lessee
to be owned by larger ncluding corporations, insurance companies	Tend more to be owned by larger investors including corporations, REITs, and insurance companies	Often owned by users; otherwise, REITs and other institutional in- vestors
er investment proper- e, but tend to become	Come in all sizes, but a number are very large and require substantial capital	Tend to be medium-sized to larger units
es constant promotion n to maintenance and action	Average to low	Relatively low, although negotiat- ing leases can be very time-con- suming
cularly in negotiating conducting promotions	Average, though lease negotiation requires high level of sophistication and expertise	Average to high; lease negotiation can be particularly complex
management econo- ger centers; can enjoy on activities	Size tends to be of less concern, although it can effect certain sav- ings	Manufacturing trend to larger facili- ties, although many businesses require modest amount of space
ds (particularly heavy uburbs); small busi- chain stores	White-collar workers, administra- tors and managers, large and small businesses	Blue-collar workers, managers, large and small corporations
leases	1- to 10-year or longer leases	Lifetime down to short-term
density, general eco- ditions, spending pat- nce of demand "mag- al attraction to bring nter)	Economy, politics, social modes, communications technology, size of work force, work technologies (space per worker, equipment per worker)	Economic conditions, business cycles in specific industry, foreign trade and tariffs, raw-material availability, technological devel- opments, land-use laws
ilability, competitors' of demand potential, -store location deci- housing development, onditions, government	Corporate location decisions, fi- nancing availability, government decision (i.e., locating new facili- ties), corporate "image" decision, space utilization patterns, business climate, removal of space from market, movement in direction of "urban" downtown	Land-use controls, pollution regu- lations, technological obsoles- cence, changing manufacturing or service orientation of economy, conversion of space to alternative uses, removal of industrial space from market
assessment policies, vailability (specialized programs), land-use	Restrictions on convertibility to condominiums, property tax as- sessment policies, financing avail- ability (specialized government programs)	Property tax assessment policies, financing availability (specialized government programs), land-use regulations, pollution emission standards

Characteristics of Property Types

ents	Existing apartments	Hotel and motel	Individual, strip, commercial, and small office properties	
menities, and	Shelter, housing, amenities, and living environment	Protection for travelers, home away from home for travelers, a communications related property	Exchange goods; distribution centers; personal services; administration and management	Exch ters; shop
	Reasonable	Possibly high	Average to good	Avera
	Low to medium	Medium to high	Low to medium	Low
	Good	Good	Low	Avera
	Average	High	Average to high	Low
maller units	Generally good for smaller units	Harder to sell because of operating risks	Low to average	Relat
al financing, e for devel-	70 to 80% financing available from conventional sources; seller often carries back secondary financing	Financing dependent upon previous operating record and strength of management	70 to 80% conventional sources; seller may often provide secondary financing	Finar depar as we of lea
including artnerships	All types of owners, including many individuals and partnerships	By operating companies or when owned by individuals or partnerships, generally leased to an operating company	Smaller investors, individuals, small groups	Tend inves REIT
somewhat apartments	All sizes; tend to be many small units available	Range from "Mom and Pop" operations to very large units	Moderate	Some ties a larger
l rent-up; going oper-	Average, except that "problems" can make excessive time demands	Excessive; a 24-hour operation requiring constant attention	Average to high, particularly where leases are of shorter term	High; and a tenan
	Average	High; the constant client contact and continual turnover, combined with diverse array of services provided, require broad knowledge	Average	High, lease
s realized	Substantial economies realized with larger units	Trend to larger units is more efficient for operations	Low, unless multiple properties owned	Subst mies joint
ls of mod- ho choose ually rents g unit)	Families and individuals of moderate means or those who choose not to own a home	Individuals, families, travelers, business	Households, small businesses, chain stores, white-collar workers	All ho usag nesse
iums, and	Month to month, some year leases, condominiums and cooperatives	Overnight, weekly	1-year to long-term leases	1 to 5
family for- and eco- le modes, ed	Population increases, family formation rates, social and economic changes	General economic conditions, recreation and leisure trends, transportation availability and pricing, special events (conventions, conferences, expositions)	Population levels, transportation access and technology, parking, competition	Popu nomi terns net" peopl
ng stock emnation, r new fi- oval pro- nt, special FHA sub- g allow-	Removals from housing stock by demolition or condemnation, political environment, conversions to other use (condominiums), conversions from other uses (e.g., hotels), supply of new units	Removal of space of existing units from market; conversion of existing units to alternative uses; perceived demand; financing availability; land-use regulations; conference, convention, and exposition demand	Land or lot availability, existence of commercial "strip," local government attitude toward transportation and strip development	Capit perce depa sions econo regula
miniums, t policies, pecialized land-use	Restrictions on convertibility to condominiums, property tax assessment policies, financing availability (specialized government programs)	Restrictions on convertibility to condominiums, property tax assessment policies, financing availability (specialized government programs), land-use regulations	Zoning, building codes, willingness to supply services, traffic control	Prope finan gover regula

	Agricultural and undeveloped land	Predeveloped land	New apar
unction	Agricultural, forest, and mineral production; recreation	Held for investment and speculation on successful development	Shelter, housing, a living environment
vestment characteristics:			
Cash flow	Low (or negative)	Negative	Low to medium
Tax shelter	Low	Low	High
Inflation hedge	Good	Good	Good
Operating risk	High	High	High
Liquidity	Relatively illiquid	Generally hard to sell	Generally good for s
Mortgage financing	Financing primarily by sellers and specialized government programs	Financing almost exclusively available from seller; favorable financing terms reflected in higher selling price	70 to 80% convention with land lease possib oper to "mortgage ou
vnership characteristics:			
Owner's equity	Generally owned by user with increasing tendency to investment by institutional investors and partnerships	Owned primarily by individuals, partnerships, and large corporations	All types of owners many individuals and
Size	Can be bought in all sizes, but meaningful operating economies require substantial holdings	Can be of any size	All sizes; tend to be larger than existing
Management time required	Heavy; constant supervision required if in use	Low, although it is essential that important developments be monitored, but when disposition occurs, substantial management time could be required	Extensive for initia average to heavy for or ations
Management expertise required	Very high; timing of paramount importance	Moderate, although ability to interpret—and influence—political and economic trends is important	Average
Economies of size	With the trend to use of more advanced technology and larger capital-intensive equipment, large land holdings advantageous	Large acreage can represent substantial economies of scale	Substantial economi with larger units
:onomic characteristics:			
Users	Farmers, ranchers, individuals, corporations	Large corporations, individual speculators	Families and individu erate means or those not to own a home (u for more than an exist
Term of use	Lifetime down to yearly leases	1 to 5 years	Year leases, condom cooperatives to lifetime
Demand influences	Population levels, food and other consumption levels, technology, transportation systems	Population trends, general economic conditions, land-use controls, transportation systems, availability of money for development, government programs (new communities financing)	Population increases, mation rates, social nomic changes, life-st amenity packages offe
Supply influences	Water availability, transportation access, removals due to development activity, fertility and soil conditions, scenic or other recreational possibilities	Land-use regulations, conversion to developed status, establishment of parks and natural preserves, regional growth patterns, density and sprawl trends, volume of land promotion activity	Removals from hou by demolition or con availability of money nancing, land-use ap cess, political environm government programs sidized housing, hou ances)
Government controls	Crop subsidy programs, formal financing programs, land-use controls	Land-use controls, restrictions on marketing practices	Restrictions on conc property tax assessma financing availability (government programs regulations

Table 27-1   Undeveloped-Land Uses

Unused—natural state	Natural resources—raw materials
Public	Mining:
Private	Ores
	Minerals
Agricultural	Power:
Crops:	Fossil fuels:
Tree crops:	Oil
Timber—forestry	Gas
Fruit	Coal
Vine crops	Steam—geysers
Row crops:	Water
Grain	**Recreational**
Vegetable	
Ranch:	**Speculative**
Grazing animals	Holding
Foraging animals	Subdivided
Production:	Lot sales
Dairies	
Furs	

land is financially self-sustaining. However, to the extent that excess depletion of natural resources occurs, there is, of course, an ecological and societal cost.

Generally, little speculative value is associated with most land in raw-material use. Large gains occur primarily as a result of a change in land's use to one with increased revenues. Sometimes a production use of land is intended only for an interim period until further development is deemed feasible. In other instances, a raw-material use of land represents its highest and best use, and it will remain in the undeveloped stage for the foreseeable future.

Predeveloped Land

The predeveloped phase of land covers the several years immediately before development. The investment concept during this phase centers around finding property where future development can be envisioned, but before the development prospects are so widely known as to bid up the price. Profits accrue to those with the best vision and forecasting ability or to those who can influence the future development. Holding land over this interim period often involves a form of "land banking."

Land in the predeveloped phase may be for sale because its owners are not sophisticated investors, because they have to sell for personal reasons, or because they want to sell to ensure a profit. While some land in this situation is purchased by future developers who also act as land speculators, a great deal is available for others. Most developers treat land as a raw material similar to lumber, bricks, mortar, and the like. When developers are ready to begin building, and not before, they buy their land just as they buy their building materials.

As the process unfolds, the party owning the land determines when to seek development and what type to undertake. The value of the land will depend on the use and on what the market is willing to pay for it. If the chances for success are uncertain, a developer will expect a greater return. If there is a known and strong demand, a developer will pay a premium price. In the former instance, the developer's own efforts will be most influential in creating whatever profits are made, whereas in the second case market conditions assure the profits.

It is expensive to hold land. Property taxes and insurance must be paid, as well as debt service. Knowledgeable land investors maintain that a price appreciation of between 15 and 20 percent per year is required to make land investment in the predevelopment phase worthwhile. It is clear that such increases can be obtained only in the few years just before development.

Investors must be cautious in relying on other sales as evidence that the asking price for a land parcel is reasonable. In many cases land sells back and forth from one speculator to another. Since the transactions are highly leveraged, with little cash involved, the selling prices may not be representative of an all-cash sale. In fact, some properties have been in the "predeveloped" phase for years and years and have gone through many owners. Indeed, where land prices have been bid to levels that make their subsequent development uneconomic, it can be said that the highest and best use of such land is merely for speculation.

Changes in land use require government approvals including subdivision regulations, zoning, environmental impact standards, and the like. Since there has been increasing opposition to development activity, investors must proceed cautiously and evaluate carefully the probability of securing the approvals necessary to implement the conversion which will determine the land's ultimate value. In the end, behavioral factors often become more important than economic conditions in determining the ultimate success of an investment.

The concept of a "path of progress" is often used to forecast the possibility of a significant development. Potential land investments are represented as being in the path of progress. In fact, according to many land promoters, just about every potential land investment is directly in the path of progress. Apparently the path follows a very winding and circuitous route, or it may be so wide that every property is included in it. In any event, investors should ignore hucksterism. They must weigh the economic factors being relied upon to cause the price of land to rise and the behavioral factors being relied upon to permit the intended conversion.

Subdivision of Land with Poor Prospects

Some unscrupulous promoters have made questionable profits by selling undeveloped and basically undevelopable land that they represent to prospective purchasers as having an exciting investment potential. Promoters acquire unused land for a relatively low price (perhaps $100 per acre or so), subdivide it into many individual lots with perhaps two or three lots to the acre, mount an aggressive promotional campaign, and then sell the land for several thousand dollars per lot.

Purchasers are told that buying such lots will enable them to achieve financial independence. In perhaps a majority of such cases the promises and representations are fraudulent, since the lot's only value—and a dubious value at that—is for use by the owner, not as an investment for future gain. The lot buyers have paid highly inflated retail prices for their land.

Speculative lots, in contrast to speculative large parcels, have investment value only if the space can be used for residential, recreational, or other such purposes. But because most prospective developers buy large parcels at wholesale, they need not and will not pay a retail price for single lots. Thus investors in speculative lots either must find another individual to buy or must bet that the wholesale value of the land, which immediately prior to their purchase was only a hundred dollars or so per acre, will increase enough so that they can sell it to a builder and recoup the retail price they paid plus a profit.

In the usual case, the holding cost of the property—15 percent per year is not unusual—and the transaction cost of reselling it are such that lot purchasers can never hope to make a profit or even recoup their purchase price in a subsequent sale unless they can find a similar "investor." More often than not, the sadder—but, one hopes, wiser—investor defaults on the payments. This allows the developer to take the lot back and sell it again.

It should be emphasized that such land schemes, which in recent years have proliferated in Florida, Texas, New Mexico, and California, have been made possible primarily by misleading advertising and deceptive selling tactics. Indeed, very few people would ever buy such lots if they had access to, and allowed themselves to believe, the facts behind the promotion. Increasingly, stringent regulatory guidelines are making it more and more difficult for land-sale promoters to commit fraud and to destroy the future usability of a property by splitting it into numerous small parcels that will be almost impossible to recombine for comprehensive development.

Comprehensive Development

There is an increasing tendency to plan development projects that integrate multiple uses. Thus a highrise structure might combine residential, office, and commercial space in one building. More and more, large residential developments include some commercial and office space. In recent years increased attention has been devoted to new community development. In some instances this involves a major rehabilitation project. In others it features the creation of a complete new community. Indeed, some observers call these comprehensive developments the ultimate real estate investment.

Generally, three types of new communities exist:

1 The "new town in town," as its name suggests, is created within the confines of an existing city. An example is the new community on Roosevelt Island, located in the middle of the East River, opposite midtown Manhattan.

2 The "satellite" new town is located adjacent to a major metropolitan area, where many of its residents will work. Although such communities have their own identity, they may be highly dependent in an economic sense on their larger neighbor.

3 The third category of new community is the "frontier" development, which is physically separated from existing major metropolitan areas and thus requires much greater self-sufficiency.

In the industrial era, most new communities were "company towns" whose "demand generator" was the employment created by the company—generally in a manufacturing or extractive industry. Such communities were often "frontier" in that they were relatively isolated from other development. Today, however, most new communities are oriented primarily to housing and tend to be located adjacent to a major metropolitan area.

By their nature, new communities involve a very long time horizon, extending 15 years, 20 years, or longer. This characteristic requires all parties involved to place particular importance on careful planning—economic, social, and financial. It requires the recognition of the significance of the timing of costs, revenues, government development, and immigration patterns. Because of massive capital requirements, investment in new communities is effectively restricted to large financial institutions, corporations, or syndicates. In some cases, individual lots are sold on speculation, but such a form of marketing is likely to be inefficient and to lower the prospects for a successful community.

As with all real estate investment, careful economic analysis is of great importance. While some new communities, such as the "experimental prototype community of tomorrow" (known as EPCOT) being developed adjacent to Disney World in Florida, can create their own demand solely by virtue of their existence, most have to be based on their ability to meet a specific housing need or provide enough employment to attract people. Indeed, the question of whether the development should focus on housing or employment is analogous to that of whether the chicken or the egg came first. Without employment, there is not likely to be any demand for housing. But without housing, companies will be reluctant to locate new offices and plants within the community. Like many critical aspects of real estate development, this question requires careful negotiation.

Finally, investors in new communities must carefully consider the "market" and the projected penetration rate. The analysis used to support a new community project often turns out to be based on dubious assumptions. As an example, one project was represented as requiring only a 1 percent penetration of the market in order to be successful. Although such a statistic may not be unreasonable on its face, a more careful examination of the assumptions underlying this "analysis" revealed that the market was defined as the entire Eastern seaboard. Some of the so-called new communities are nothing more than lot-sale operations in fancily named suburbs. The earlier caveat with regard to lot sales can apply equally well to many "new community" operations.

Risk Analysis

Because the risks in land speculation and development are so great, it is a logical sphere for risk analysis. Many of the probabilities of loss are sequential. A successful project must surmount a large number of hurdles, each with an appreciable chance of failure. Investors should adjust the value they assign to the projected payout of a successful project to reflect the probabilities of these possible failures. This point can be illustrated by a simple application of the decision-tree analysis.

Consider a project in which there is a 1 in 10 chance of market failure and a 9 in 10 chance of market success. A decision-tree representation would appear as follows:

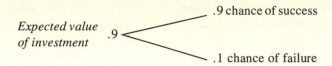

Expected value of investment .9

.9 chance of success

.1 chance of failure

If the payoff for successful completion of the project were $1,000, the expected value, adjusted for the probabilities of success or failure, would be $900. If costs to the developer were less than this figure, he or she would make a profit. If costs exceeded this amount, the developer would lose.

This, however, is a simplified illustration. In reality, the development and construction process involves numerous steps, each of which has its own set of probabilities. Clearly, more important than the probability of successfully completing one phase of activity is the cumulative probability of negotiating the entire sequence of events. This can be illustrated by assuming a project involving three sequential events—successful obtaining of land approval, financing, and marketing. Each of these events has a 90 percent chance of success and a 10 percent chance of failure. The decision-tree representation for this series appears as follows:

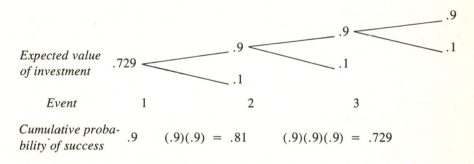

While the chance of completing event 1 and obtaining governmental approvals is .9, the chance of getting by event 2 is .81, and that of getting by event 3 is .729, making the total odds less than 3 in 4.

The risks in development have been growing. Additional decision points have increased the chances of failure, particularly because of the complexities the developer must now cope with in the land-use approval process. Consider the consequences of adding an additional event or of changing the odds on one event or on all events. In the example above, the probability of success for each event is .9, and the cumulative probability for three events is .729, but if a fourth event is added with the same 90 percent probability of success, the probability for the project as a whole becomes only .656. If the probability of success for the fourth event were only .8, the cumulative probability would drop to .583. If the probability of success for each event were .8, the cumulative probability for three events would be .512, and for four events it would be .410. Clearly, increasing the odds of failure and adding additional events with some possibility of failure greatly lowers the cumulative probability for overall success.

Given the many component elements of the development and construction process, it is not surprising that the chances of disappointment along the way are great. Yet developers must make enough profit on their successful projects to offset the costs incurred on those which are not successful. These developments in turn influence the profitability and desirability of land speculation. The final value of the land may be extremely high, but if most of the value reflects simply the costs of reaching the final development, as well as the costs of money lost on unsuccessful developments and on unsuccessful land speculations, the investor in land will achieve a far lower return than appears to be the case when only the profit on a development which has successfully cleared all hurdles is taken into account.

RESIDENTIAL PROPERTIES

Table 27-2 gives an indication of the many different types of investments in residential properties. This sphere is the most important for real estate investors interested in developed properties. Even excluding owner-occupied units, an investor is more likely to purchase a residential income property than any other type.

Because of its importance in the field, most of the special features of investing in residential properties have already been covered in this book. Chapters 5, 7, 20, 22, and 25 dealt with major problems of investment analysis for residential properties. At this point we summarize in extremely brief form some of the critical factors presented in these chapters, while adding information on a few types of residential real estate not so commonly considered by potential investors.

Table 27-2 Residential-Property Uses

Permanent	Transient
Primary residence:	Hotel
Houses	Motel
Apartments:	Recreation:
In-law apartments	Resort
Multiplexes (duplexes to six-unit buildings)	Spa
Flats (one unit per floor)	Condominiums
Garden apartments (lower than four	Convalescent
stories)	
Elevator buildings	
Highrises	
Townhouses	
Condominiums	
Cooperatives	
Mobile homes	
Houseboats	
Nursing homes	
Secondary residence (second homes):	
Cabins	
Condominiums	
Mobile homes	

Residential Investments

While it requires great oversimplification, we can summarize under seven headings many of the points already made concerning residential properties and detailed in the foldout table.

1 Investments in residential properties are readily available. There is an active market for them in most cities. They come in all sizes and fit all pockets. Investors can choose the amount of money they want to place in their investments, the scale of operations they are interested in, and their potential risks. Liquidity is good for real properties. On the other hand, because demand is greater for small units and investments that are low in equity, the rate of return tends to rise with the size of the operation.

2 Investors can expend as much or as little of their own time and effort as they wish. Small units are usually feasible only when managed by their owners. Frequently they will not pay unless the owners serve as handymen and do a fair percentage of the maintenance themselves. Many people like this type of activity. When they buy small units, they get a job in addition to an investment. On the other hand, while larger units can be managed by owners, the owners can, if they desire, turn them over to management companies, which will take complete responsibility.

3 Most residential investments are available with a great deal of leverage. Mortgages run from 70 to 95 percent of the price. First mortgages are often available with amortization periods of 20 to 35 years. The required payments on second or purchase-money mortgages depend upon price and individual bargaining.

4 Most residential properties carry a large potential tax shelter. Congress has voted special tax subsidies for owners of residential properties. The tax shelters are higher for new properties and those designed for low-income families, but they are substantial in almost all cases.

5 Because the tax shelter is high, prices are bid up. As a result, the cash flow tends to be relatively low compared with that of many other investments.

6 A critical question in determining the actual yield is how large capital gains may be. If values appreciate with inflation, many residential investments which would otherwise be only fair will turn out to be good. Thus these properties make good investments for people who are seeking an inflation hedge and who feel certain that rents will go up with the price level and that both will continue to rise rapidly in the future.

7 Finding a good residential investment depends primarily upon an accurate investment analysis. The return is contingent on a correct projection of future rents and operating costs. These, in turn, depend on such factors as location, design, construction, and management. An advantage for the average investor is that there is a great deal of information available on properties of this type. So many units are rented and sold that, without too much effort, a person can become fairly expert in the economics of investments in these properties in his or her own area. This same information can also be used in analyzing offers of syndicates and common stocks where the company is investing primarily in residential properties.

SPECIAL TYPES OF RESIDENTIAL UNITS

In the past decade there has been a great deal of investment activity in mobile homes, hotels and motels, and other residential-recreational properties. These spheres have had their ups and downs, probably even more than other types of real estate investment. They are, however, well worth considering by one who hopes to become an active investor.

Mobile Homes

In the past 20 years mobile homes have become an important part of our stock of new housing. Economic analysis shows that the price and costs of mobile-home ownership fall somewhere between those of ownership of a conventional house and a car, as do the marketing and financing. Some features of both the housing and the auto industries come to light when we examine the decision concerning whether to continue to rent, to buy a conventional house, or to buy a mobile home.

The mobile home got its name from the fact that the units were originally trailers pulled behind cars and designed to provide temporary secondary housing. Until shortly after World War II there were only a few permanent trailer parks; most mobile homes were clearly intended to provide temporary, as opposed to permanent, housing.

In the intervening years mobile homes have increased in size and luxury. Many of them now approach conventional tract housing in quality, features, and dimensions. They do, however, lack weight and solidity, and how their real depreciation will compare is unknown. Mobile homes are built in a factory and transported to a site on wheels. Once located in the mobile-home park, the unit is put on blocks, or even a block foundation, and the wheels are usually removed.

The production of mobile homes has increased markedly over the last two decades, to the point where such units now represent approximately 20 percent of the annual additions to the nation's housing stock. The primary stimulant to the growth of mobile-home volume has been their relatively low price. Their expansion has been facilitated by improved financing; formerly it was almost impossible to get long-term mortgage financing on mobile homes. Another factor favoring mobile homes is that they tend to be classified as personal property for taxation purposes, thereby enjoying a much lower tax rate than they would if they were taxed as real property.

Today, the vast majority of lower-priced freestanding housing units are mobile homes. While industry proponents maintain that for the same dollar, higher-quality housing can be obtained in a mobile than in a conventionally constructed home, some critics have been outspoken in citing deficiencies in mobile homes. Indeed, because construction standards for mobile homes are less demanding than those which apply to conventional houses, the mobile home may deteriorate far more rapidly. Consequently, the owner of a mobile home cannot expect the price appreciation that has been achieved with conventional houses.

Mobile-Home Parks   The high volume of mobile-home production has created a strong demand for places to "park" the units. Indeed, during the period of rapidly expanding production, the demand for space in mobile-home parks exceeded the supply. Such conditions stimulated the development of additional mobile-home parks. As often happens in real estate markets, conditions of oversupply developed, with some new parks suffering from heavy vacancy rates.

A major source of profit in mobile-home parks is the selling of new mobile homes. Indeed, many claim that the successful "tenanting" of a new mobile-home park is highly dependent upon the sales of new homes. For this and other reasons, many parks are managed by their owners, who also sell new and used units, but parks can also be purchased to be run by hired managers.

Initially the investment emphasis in parks was as a form of land speculation. The park was thought of as a method of deriving the carrying costs for land in the path of development. Some investors still view mobile-home parks as such interim land uses. However, in recent years the ratio of improvements to total value has increased greatly. As potential tenants have demanded more recreational facilities, better landscaping, and better lighting and hygienic arrangements, the cost of actual investments has become many times greater than that of the land. Since most of this additional investment can be depreciated at comparatively rapid rates, the parks have now succeeded in interesting those who seek rapid tax writeoffs and tax shelters.

Because selecting a home requires a major decision, most parks take longer to fill up than new apartment houses. But when fully occupied, they tend to generate somewhat higher cash flows. Since the process of moving out of a mobile-home park is more complex and more expensive than the process of moving out of conventional rental housing, once a quality mobile-home park is tenanted, it tends to stay occupied as long as it is well managed. Indeed, some parks require that tenants who want to move sell their units to new tenants before doing so. In cases such as this, a mobile home may render a family relatively immobile.

Temporary Residential Units

Hotels and motels are temporary residential facilities. In this sense they are a "home away from home." Reasons for being away from home include business, pleasure, or a transitional status between one home and another. Indeed, some people are in a continuous transitional status and occupy such facilities on a more or less permanent basis.

Some hotels offer apartments for longer-term occupancy. They may cater exclusively to tenants who prefer hotel conveniences, including daily maid service, front-desk messages, dry cleaning, and barber and beauty shops. At the same time, certain luxury apartment buildings provide services similar to those offered by hotels. In fact, some properties are accurately described as apartment hotels.

Retired persons no longer interested in maintaining a separate home represent a big market for hotel rooms. The advantages of social activities, prepared meals, and available medical care are appealing to senior citizens. Several properties previously unsuccessful as transient hotels have been successfully operated as permanent housing oriented toward senior citizens.

Hotels and motels serve families on vacations as well as traveling business people. Many depend for their profits on a substantial convention business. Frequently, companies will rent hotel facilities for special meetings. On occasion, hotel facilities are used to provide temporary office space. Certain illicit businesses use hotel facilities on a regular basis.

The critical success factors for hotels and motels are location, size, and management. Many which formerly enjoyed brisk business have found themselves at a severe disadvantage when a highway was relocated away from their front door. Smaller motels have been facing increasing difficulties in competing because they are unable to offer the facilities of larger hotels and also cannot take advantage of economies of scale and management. Further, the large chains with hotel facilities throughout the country offering central reservation services have a significant competitive advantage.

In 1973 there were 8,798 motor hotels with a total of 1,008,124 rooms in the continental United States, according to the Helmsley-Spear Hospitality Division annual census. For purposes of the survey, a motor hotel was defined to include any property with transient facilities, open more than half of the year, containing at least 50 guest units as well as adequate on-site parking, and built or completely refurbished since 1945. The number of motor-hotel properties represented a 94 percent increase over the 1965 level, and the number of units was up 134 percent. The average property had 115 units, reflecting the continuing trend toward larger motels.

Industry observers believe that the rapid expansion in recent years has not been warranted by market demand. Indeed, increasing costs of building force room rates higher and higher. Many facilities are finding it difficult to obtain these rates. Consequently, a certain number of existing units will suffer financial difficulties, and many new units will not go ahead as planned.

It should be recognized that a hotel or motel, unless rented on a long-term lease, requires more active management than many other property types. More personnel are involved, maintenance and cleaning are required more often, and the scope and extent of services offered are broader. Because stays are of short duration, management is continuously seeking new business. At the same time, because travel is an easily postponable item, a dip in the economy or an increase in travel costs can have a sharp adverse impact on motel revenues and profits.

Recreational Real Estate

The shorter workweek and projected higher discretionary incomes have led to rising expectations for more leisure and a boom in recreational real estate.

Some resort properties are hotels and motels that cater exclusively to vacationers. Frequently, special rates are offered to groups that schedule meetings of trade associations or educational courses in a resort environment. A number of individuals have second homes in the mountains, on lakes, or at beaches.

While many second homes have been built individually by their owners, in recent times there has been an increasing trend for second homes to be part of large projects, similar in concept to single-family tract-home developments or planned-unit developments. Indeed, many land-sale programs are based on the prospects of second homes' being built and the promise that substantial profits will be realized by lot purchasers. As noted earlier, such promises may well be illusory.

While most recreational property must be considered primarily a luxury expenditure, some has turned out to be an excellent investment. When the owners are not using the property, it can be leased at favorable rates. If the property is well located, often sizable gains can be realized when it is sold.

User-oriented Securities An interesting new concept in recreational real estate offering both user rights and potential investment returns is that of user-oriented securities. These can take various forms. The first, and most prevalent, involves specific ownership, usually in condominium form, of a particular unit or room in a property which is essentially identical to a second home but which is offered for rent when not being used by the owner. Income that results from short-term rentals may be a secondary consideration. Alternatively, the condominium with investment characteristics will arrange a pool of rental units with a marketing campaign to rent the unit in the owner's absence. In some situations the unit is for rent only at the owner's request, while in others strict limitations are imposed on the use by the owner. Clearly, in the latter instance the prospects for an attractive return on investment are greater.

A second form is the so-called time-share arrangement, whereby a purchaser gains user rights to a specific property for a particular period of time on a recurring basis. In essence, the buyer acquires a long-term lease for some fraction of a year. Thus he or she might acquire rights to use a specific condominium for the first two weeks of every July. Such arrangements may or may not have investment characteristics.

A third form of user-oriented securities involves a partnership holding title to the real estate with the individual investors being granted rights to use the facilities owned by the partnership. The partnership may own one property or a portfolio of properties, with investors having the right to different kinds of resort facilities such as skiing, water-oriented activities, or a golf course.

NONRESIDENTIAL PROPERTIES

Nonresidential improved properties make up the final sector of real estate investments. While they do not bulk as large in total value as residential properties, they tend to be much larger in terms of individual units and to be more expensive. Table 27-3 gives some indication of the variety of investment possibilities. Each separate item tends to have unique investment qualities.

It is the nonresidential properties that seem to shape the character of most cities. Their skylines are determined by the office buildings which form the center of the metropolitan area. Together with major department stores, these highrise office buildings have been the backbone of the central city. Because of the concentration of people, their land values have far exceeded all others. As properties of this type have shifted their location, new housing areas have been located to gain access to the employment and shopping opportunities provided by the new commercial and office building areas.

In the postwar period, a major battle occurred between centralization and decentralization of commercial and office space. Some cities experienced a rapid growth in office buildings and a moderate growth of hotels and retail outlets in their downtowns. In more cases, there has been limited growth of office space downtown, accompanied by a major transfer of shopping to the suburbs. Finally, some cities, despite intensive civic efforts aimed at maintaining the key role of the downtown, have experienced near disasters. More and more activities have moved away from the downtown areas, which have been left with dilapidated and substandard buildings.

Table 27-3   Nonresidential-Property Uses

Commercial property	Special-purpose property
Downtown:	Entertainment:
Stores	Theaters
Malls	Museums
Merchandise market	Bowling alleys
Suburban and fringe:	Arenas
Strip commercial:	Recreation:
Stores	Buildings
Fast food	Complexes
Gas station	Convention centers
Supermarket	Parking:
Shopping centers:	Lots
Neighborhood center	Single-level buildings
Community center	Multilevel buildings
Regional center	**Other**
Office property (personal services and administration)	Schools
City offices:	Hospitals
Highrise	Churches
Street-oriented	Islands
Professional centers:	Foreign
Medical	Exotic
Law	
Trade-center agglomeration	
Storefront	
Suburban offices	
Plant offices	
Condominiums	
Industrial property	
Production:	
Extractive operations	
Processing raw materials	
Manufacturing:	
Light:	
Lofts	
Street level	
Heavy:	
Clean	
Dirty	
Assembling	
Distribution and storage:	
Warehouse	
Research and development	

Recently, similar rapid changes have afflicted the outlying areas. Shopping centers and buildings built in the postwar period stand empty or have seen a steady deterioration in their activity and type of use.

Stores and Shopping Centers

Commercial property for consumer sales has traditionally been the backbone of most cities. This property includes all the space in which people meet face to face to buy and sell goods and services. It ranges from hamburger stands and gas stations to large department stores and regional shopping centers.

The glamour associated with commercial space, as well as much of the literature on the subject, has been concentrated on shopping centers. In contrast, typical investors will find that most available offers deal with individual stores in downtown areas or along strip developments. The larger properties and the major shopping centers tend to be purchased by syndicates or real estate corporations, frequently with the major tenants as participants.

The foldout table separates the analysis of shopping centers from individual and strip properties. "Strips" are the buildings lining most highways and arteries leading into more concentrated shopping sectors. The investment factors can be differentiated quite clearly between the two types, although there is great variety within each type.

Investments in stores and shopping centers are available in all sizes and amounts. When a property has a long lease, management is negligible. On the other hand, many individual properties as well as large centers require an active management to obtain tenants and customers and to maintain the property's income. Management is available for hire, at a fee.

The risks and rate of return also vary greatly, again depending on the type of tenant and the length of the lease. Some store properties with long leases to national tenants are among the safest of all income properties, while some small units are in constant trouble. Financing is usually good, but again it depends on the unit and the tenant. Except for buildings with long leases, liquidity (or the ability to receive the units' value rapidly without a high transaction cost) is low.

Tax and inflation shelters are average to low. The supply of, and demand for, space can fluctuate widely. In addition, while units with leases providing for overages—higher rent payments as dollar volume rises—were thought to be excellent inflationary hedges, many have not worked out as hoped for. Competition and excess supply have kept many overages at a low or nonexistent level.

Individual Stores   The typical smaller building is often owned by the firm occupying it. There are major economies when a firm owns its own building. In addition, it need not worry that it will be held up for higher rents if it succeeds in building up a great deal of goodwill and recognition related to its particular building.

Investments in shops vary greatly in size as well as in potential returns and risks. They range all the way from purchases of properties with leasebacks to major firms, in which the return is more attuned to a bond than anything else, to purchases of marginal stores, where the return frequently depends on successful rehabilitation.

The variance of returns has also been tremendous. Some commercial properties and shopping centers have been extremely successful; others have been disasters. Changes in styles and shopping habits have led to obsolescence and extreme depreciation in many commercial properties. Even new shopping centers, which have frequently been sold on the promise that with inflation they would achieve higher payments for rents as sales increased with prices, have often had disappointing results. The inflation has occurred, and average unit sales have gone up, but the total volume and rents of individual centers have not increased because of a tremendous expansion in their number. Competition has been keen. Major tenants, upon whom the success of large centers depends, have demanded that they be compensated for their drawing power through extremely favorable leases. At the same time the rapid increase in new centers has taken sales from older units. As these centers have lost volume, the problems of keeping them filled and of maintaining them at a decent level have multiplied. Many have become worthless.

The key to the analysis of stores is the fact that their value depends on the volume of sales they can generate and the cost of attracting customers. Sales depend on the number of customers and their incomes. Shopping has followed the customers to the suburbs. The use of the automobile has brought about a decided alteration in shopping habits. Parking and locations related to freeways or other highways have been critical factors for many stores.

Individual retail stores are generally freestanding, part of a string development, or part of a central downtown area. Location is of prime importance for retail space with respect to access, parking, and particularly "image" and "prestige." In this regard, the land use in the immediately adjacent area is of particular importance. Knowledge-able retailers prefer to be located close to their main competitors. They feel that the concentration of stores serves as a magnet to pull many more shoppers than would come if the store were isolated.

The retail shopping core in the central business district is a "shopping center" in the literal sense. Such downtown shopping areas usually reflect a lack of coordination and integration. Prestige women's clothing stores may be set immediately alongside a discount appliance store.

Shopping Centers   The term "shopping center" today has grown to mean a very specialized type of retail shopping facility. Generally, the construction of the stores is concurrent or phased over time, the total center is built according to an integrated plan, the entire shopping facility is under one management and ownership, and the specific types of stores are planned and controlled.

Shopping centers fall into three categories—neighborhood, community, and regional—according to the market they serve, their size, and the number and size of their major tenants. As a rule of thumb, a neighborhood center would have up to 50,000 square feet of retail space, and a community center between 50,000 and 200,000 square feet of retail space, with the regional center being larger. Usually, the regional center has at least two major anchor tenants, such as Sears, Montgomery Ward, Macy's, or Penney's. Increasingly, the large centers are built as enclosed malls with year-round climate control. Frequently, major office complexes, reflecting an extension of the trend of multiple uses in one structure, include several floors of underground shopping space as well.

The key to a successful shopping center is having strong anchor tenants, for they are the magnets that attract the shoppers, who, once there, will patronize the smaller stores as well. Recognizing their own importance, anchor tenants aggressively negotiate their lease terms. Generally, they will pay lower rent than the minor tenants. And in some cases, where the anchor tenant is particularly strong and the developer is highly motivated to include it in the center, the anchor tenant may own its own space on very favorable terms.

The majority of shopping-center leases feature a fixed rent for the space with owner participation in "overages" once sales reach a designated level. Depending on the terms of the lease, the amount of the overage participation may escalate over time, or there may be a ceiling on the amount of additional rent that can be paid as overages.

The shopping-center business is highly competitive. Although a new center may complement an existing one (for instance, if it is located immediately adjacent with a large parking area separating the two centers), in most cases a new center will have an adverse competitive impact that results in a split market. New centers with more modern design and construction have caused many older centers to become obsolete. Because of the competitive nature of centers, it is easy for overbuilding to take place. In such cases it is extremely difficult to rent the space. When vacancies occur, they tend to have a very depressing effect on the property, since no one likes to see a center with empty stores.

Errors in measuring potential sales have been made because too much stress has been placed on the mere size of the center and its commuting distance. More recently, it has been recognized that a family's marketing decision may be extremely complex. Management has become particularly important in successfully attracting customers. Shopping centers often devote considerable resources to special events aimed at bringing people to the center. The mix of shops offered and the reputation of the major tenants, as well as their advertising efforts, also can be extremely important.

As the high risks connected with shopping space have become more evident, the investment advantages have deteriorated. Loans are based on minimum rents from tenants, particularly those with national names and assumed credit-worthiness. A number of major national retail chains have become bankrupt. Tenants are no longer willing to sign for long leases because of competitive risks. Loan terms have consequently become less favorable, and the cash flow to investors has diminished.

In many situations the tax shelter is not great. A fair percentage of the total value is frequently the nondepreciable land. As a result, depreciation is less than in many other types of properties. Because of greater competition, capital gains which inflation seemed to promise have not been achieved.

Office Buildings

The term "office building" usually brings to mind an image of the Empire State Building, the Sears Tower, the World Trade Center, or the equivalent skyscraper (usually the First National Bank) in one's hometown. Such structures are competitive office buildings, planned with space to rent to a succession of large or small tenants. But office buildings includes many other types, ranging from small structures of perhaps a few thousand square feet to massive ones of more than a million square feet, from garden office complexes in the suburbs to central-city highrises, and from specialized uses such as medical buildings to multipurpose buildings. Office space may be found on the upper floors of shopping buildings above the retail selling space. There are many single-occupancy buildings, owned and occupied by a single firm or by a unit of the government. Most business districts have a telephone building, a utility building, and one or more insurance companies with large downtown headquarters.

Single-occupancy units are even more common in the outskirts. They may be at a company's plant, in an industrial park, or simply off by themselves with plenty of parking. Similar structures are built on a competitive basis. Most common are professional buildings, often built by two or three doctors for their own use. Some are larger structures housing the offices of a number of doctors and dentists. Small competitive buildings for salespeople, business services, or numerous other groups are also found.

From the foldout table we note that many of the investment characteristics of office buildings are like those of stores. In fact, in strip or individual properties, the same unit may shift back and forth from one use to the other. On the other hand, multioccupancy buildings are in some ways closer to apartment units than to other investments. They require constant active management and have a high ratio of current costs to revenue. As with stores, marketability, financing, and risks depend upon the length of the leases, which tend to be shorter than those for stores.

There are all types of opportunities available for investment, but the larger units tend to go to joint ventures. They are financed by major insurance companies and other large lenders. Frequently the amount of financing is related to the level of rent achievements. If units cannot be rented, expensive standby or interim loans may be necessary.

The new office building field has been one of the most active areas for "creative financing" and for joint ventures or participations with the lender. Since large office buildings require substantial capital, their development is dependent on this financing. Because lenders require that a minimum amount of the space be leased as a condition for granting financing, a major anchor tenant can become particularly important. The developer may face delicate negotiations in balancing construction costs and financing commitments while simultaneously seeking to persuade a variety of prospective tenants to commit to leases.

Smaller buildings, however, and particularly rehabilitations and conversions of units, are handled by individual investors. This type of property is a particular area for the real estate brokers in many communities. Although the occupants of office space are usually tenants, ownership of one's own space is common in many single-occupancy units. In recent years there has been increasing interest in commercial condominiums, in which users own the space that they occupy. The condominium concept is especially attractive to professionals such as doctors and lawyers as well as to certain closely held small businesses.

Since a high percentage of total property costs is often in land, tax shelters are not great. Any inflationary protection tends to lag because of many longer leases, while rents on shorter leases can be raised only gradually, even though considerable increases take place in taxes and operating expenses. Risks are high because of the tendency for supply and demand to get out of phase.

An office building or area will often cater to a specific industry group, such as international trade, or to a particular profession. In fact, many cities are characterized by whole districts that feature a particular trade, such as wholesale marts or the garment or jewelry industry.

The office building market is highly competitive. The time horizon for planning is a long one. The competitive nature of the market, combined with the long time horizon, leads to cyclical conditions of overbuilding and underbuilding. During times of easy money and business optimism, considerable new office space will be built. But when economic conditions change, the owners may find themselves sitting with nearly empty buildings, as occurred in New York City in the early 1970s.

Typically the demand for office space in an area expands rapidly, but then tends to slow down and may even contract. At the same time, because a considerable length of time is required to plan and build a new building, supply lags behind. The high demand calls forth a large volume of space. When it appears on the market, vacancies shoot up. Rents remain stable, but concessions are necessary to attract new tenants. Tenants are attracted by the prestige of a building, its location, and particularly its services, rather than by price. Tenants dislike moving, and there is a considerable cost involved in changing. Since space costs are not an important item for many firms, they will not be influenced by minor differences in rents. The market is not price-elastic.

Frequently developers will have to take over space vacated by the tenants they attract. They plan to sublet it themselves at a later date. When money is easily available and lenders are competing for mortgages, speculative office buildings can be financed without substantial preleasing commitments. While this aids the developer, it can imply significant risks. The financial planning must give careful attention to the leasing rate as well as the cost that will be involved in special tenant improvements.

Several factors that have contributed to the growth in office space suggest that continuing demand will be generated. Increasing orientation of the economy to service employment means that more companies will need office, as opposed to industrial, space. Further, there has been a trend toward increasing floor space per employee. Specialized office equipment also requires more and more space. A particularly rapid growth sector has been the government, which is essentially a service industry with major office space demands.

During periods of strong economic conditions companies seek to upgrade their facilities and their image by moving from older space and acquiring prestige office locations. Further, expanding projections of companies' space needs for the future have caused some to stockpile for these expected needs by occupying a small portion of a building today, while renting to minor tenants. The expectation is that in future years, perhaps two decades hence, it will require the vast majority of the building.

It is rare that an office building can be successful standing alone; it needs to have both support facilities and other compatible buildings in the immediate area. If developers take the initiative to embark on a project where none has gone before, they run the risk that no one will follow. But if they wait until development is well under way, they may find that the prospects for renting space have been picked over and that they are left in a soft market with substantial vacancies. Indeed, many foreclosures have occurred when developers tried to add just one more project to an already saturated market.

A successful prestige office building can be a highly lucrative investment. Companies will willingly pay premium rates at levels disproportionately above those for other, less desirable space. But the potential high returns are accompanied by very real risks. In this, as in so many other types of real estate investment, extremely large profits are gained on purchases made at the right time. When timing is wrong, investments may be mediocre to poor.

Industrial Property

Industrial real estate houses manufacturing activity and provides storage for products, materials, and inventory. It can range from steel mills, manufacturing plants, loft buildings for the garment trade, and large warehouses to the newly popular "mini-warehouses." Because industrial real estate uses tend to congregate together, a recent trend has been toward industrial parks with attractive landscaping, certain common facilities, and other amenities that serve many companies.

An effective way of categorizing industrial real estate is according to whether the space is being used for storage or processing. If it is being used for processing, is the manufacturing activity light or heavy, clean or dirty?

Originally, industrial properties were located in the central core of cities, usually adjacent to water—rivers, lakes, or bays—to take advantage of natural transportation. Transportation access still plays an important role, but now the major emphasis is on rail, highway, and in some cases airport access. More and more, industrial space is being located away from the center of the city.

Investment opportunities tend to be in joint ventures, such as in these industrial or warehouse parks; in long-term leases to major tenants; or in marginal properties.

The industrial real estate field tends to be more specialized, with fewer lenders and fewer investors, and far narrower than the field for other real estate properties.

Industrial property that is fully leased with a strong base commands a premium price, but buildings without tenants may be priced at a substantial discount below their replacement value. Consequently, in buying and selling industrial real estate, timing is the key to success. Unless the property is being sold to a buyer who intends to occupy it himself, the availability of a tenant becomes crucial. For this reason firms that specialize in both renting and selling such properties have a decided advantage.

In most industrial properties the building is a large part of the total package. As a result, they tend to have a high rate of depreciation. This means that the tax-shelter aspect is one of the most significant factors in the investment analysis. It is also the reason why many large corporations are willing to rent their plants on a long-term lease basis. In effect, by selling the advantages of the tax shelter to owners in high tax brackets, these companies find they can raise capital at lower rates than they can through borrowing the money and owning their own plants. These companies also prefer to rent rather than own the space they occupy because they can usually make a higher return by using the capital in the business than by investing it in real estate and because depreciation deductions have a detrimental impact on the income statement.

Because industrial development can often mean a substantial boost to the local employment base, some communities aggressively seek new industry development. Incentives may include favorable rates on bond financing, good plant sites, and low property tax rates. Increasingly, however, vocal "no growth" advocates have caused many cities not only to rescind their inducements intended to attract new industries but also to go even further and erect outright barriers to industrial expansion.

Most industrial property is special-purpose in that it includes machinery or has a particular layout designed for a specific type of industry. This means that it is expensive to convert to other tenants and uses.

Many industrial properties are leased to a single tenant. Such arrangements imply very different management responsibilities from those which obtain where there are multiple tenants, as in an apartment project. Because the owner is dealing with industrial enterprises, the rent will generally be a fairly small percentage of the company's total budget. Consequently, changes in the cost of business space tend to have less impact on the financial position of tenants than changes in rates for residential space do. At the same time, the tenant is likely to be more professional in decisions regarding contracting for the use of space. If the market is soft, he or she will likely drive a much harder bargain than a residential tenant might. But companies seeking industrial space generally have relatively fewer options than individuals seeking apartments. Risks arise because of the rapid turnover and failure rate of small industrial companies.

Special-Purpose Properties

The final section of Table 27-3 lists a number of miscellaneous properties which we can think of as special-purpose. Because of their design and construction, these properties tend to have little use or to be very expensive to revamp for purposes other than those for which they were built. In most cases, the success of the building depends upon the success of the business operated within it. Except for parking structures, it is difficult to separate the analysis of the property from the firm operating it.

The table shows examples of buildings in the entertainment field, but there are also hospitals, schools, and various other specialized buildings. A constant need exists for properties of these types. Financing is hard to get, but because an underlying demand exists, successfully completed projects pay large returns.

Because of their high risks, higher-than-ordinary rents can be expected from successfully occupied special-purpose properties. But the danger of overbuilding seems to be particularly great. For example, a certain market area may support a specialized entertainment facility, but the addition of a second operation may cause both to encounter financial difficulties. Because these facilities tend to reflect quick responses to apparent demands, the risk is that supply will expand too rapidly. Movie theaters, tennis clubs, bowling alleys—all forms of entertainment—seem to have gone through this type of cycle.

Parking facilities, including lots, single-level garages, and multilevel structures, are essential to central-city areas and for properties with uses involving heavy traffic patterns. Unless the parking facility has multiple stories or a conversion to a higher use is made, it will represent a land-intensive use with limited benefits beyond immediate cash income. In this sense, many parking facilities represent an interim land use.

The value of the parking structure is dependent upon people's desires to patronize stores and facilities in its immediate neighborhood. While technological innovation in the form of rapid transit may alter demand, in such circumstances the property would most probably be worth more as a building site. Besides the charge for parking, factors critical to success include turnover rates and the existence of evening and weekend business.

The number of possible special-purpose properties is too large to deal with each individually. The general lines of analysis laid out for the previous cases apply to them also. There must be a careful projection of the market plus a specific estimate of income and operating costs. This can then be translated into an effective net income. On the basis of knowledge of mortgage terms available for these properties, tax consequences, and risks, these projected returns can be capitalized into an estimate of value.

The estimate of value becomes the basis for attempting to get the necessary financing. If money can be raised, the project can proceed. As in all such cases, two types of success are possible. The first is based on convincing prospects that a line of reasoning is sound, that a demand exists, and that a profit will be forthcoming if the project is built. If investors are available, a promoter will make a profit. The second type of success is measured by the actual market results after the project is in operation. The possibilities of true profits, as opposed to merely promoter's profits, will depend upon how good a job of analysis and risk estimation has been performed.

SUMMARY

An examination of real properties brings out their tremendous variety. Something will be available to match almost any investor's needs. The foldout table shows a useful way to consider what types of properties might fit a particular investment strategy. For this purpose it outlines both typical owner and investment characteristics as well as significant influences on demand and supply.

Investment in land, except when it is paying for itself as part of an ongoing producing operation, is probably the riskiest of all. Consequently, a successful venture returns the highest gains. Successful timing, to minimize costs of holding land while its value rises, is the prime force in profitable gains. Successful developers also reap large incomes.

Residential properties make up the largest number of investments in developed real estate. There is great variety in terms of sizes, shapes, degree of required management, and potential for analysis and use of personal skills. Almost everyone can find a property that meets his or her needs. How profitable such an investment will be compared with other possibilities depends on how well the property's cost and revenues have been projected. Losses occur when people overpay—because they fail to calculate investment value properly—or because the projections turn out to be wrong.

Nonresidential properties offer the greatest returns to firms or individuals purchasing for their own use or to those with the time and capital to become skilled professionals or semiprofessionals. These are major spheres for the activities of syndicates and REITs. The high risks and high returns of individual properties place a premium on diversification across several types of properties or several markets.

QUESTIONS AND PROBLEMS

1. The most important factor in the majority of investments in land is "timing." Explain why this is so.
2. While the greatest increases in land values depend on development, some investors believe it worthwhile to hold land that will never be developed. What will changes in the value of such land depend on?

3. Explain what problems must be overcome and why the odds have been against successful investments in individual lots in many speculative developments selling lots to individuals. What situations can make such investments worthwhile?

4. Illustrate the fact that the more decision points there are which have success probabilities below 100 percent, the less the chances for success.

5. It is easier for the average investor to judge the value of a residential property than any other type. Why is this so? What would you consider the three most significant advantages of investing in a residential income property?

6. Many motels are individually owned and operated as franchises from a major chain. Explain the advantages of franchising in an industry such as motels.

7. Many large stores have dropped in value by 80–100 percent in the past 20 years. What type of changes can cause such rapid movements in value?

8. Some of the most creative real estate investments in recent years have been in the redevelopment of commercial space. List some of the features that have made possible one or two such successful developments in your community.

9. Explain the concept of reducing a company's cost of space by selling the advantages its building may provide as a tax shelter.

10. Pick two or three different types of investors. Examine the foldout table and use it to explain why they would be better off investing in certain types of property and avoiding other specific types.

Chapter 28

Planning a Real Estate Portfolio

The final test of an investment strategy is the actual portfolio of investments that results. It may be the product of a careful plan, or it may reflect merely what an investor happened to acquire over time. A rational portfolio reflects the intelligent implementation of a well planned, internally consistent investment strategy.

The final parts of this book have covered many points that ought to be considered in planning a well-thought-through portfolio. This chapter brings many of these concepts together in summary form.

Formulating a strategy for a real estate portfolio is complicated. Numerous variables are involved. Several alternative strategies may make sense. Basic to any strategy is the requirement that the plan be consistent with the resources and objectives of the organization or individual in question. We have seen the important role that an investor's characteristics play in influencing the investment that he or she should appropriately consider. The individual's investment objectives further narrow the choice. In essence, investors must match their characteristics with those of each security or property, while at the same time structuring their portfolios so that the characteristics of each investment complement those of every other one.

THE PORTFOLIO PLAN

There is no single perfect portfolio. A portfolio must be tailored to the individual investor, varying with his or her economic and family circumstances, job, personality, knowledge, and wants.

In planning a portfolio, investors should recognize what a mix of investments does and what it costs. They have to decide whether they want to put all their eggs in one or a few baskets or spread them over many. Those who decide to split their investments reduce their risk of a major error, but also their chances of extraordinary gains. Significant diversification may make it impossible to achieve a proper economic scale. It may also mean that the investor cannot devote enough time to key decisions.

Many investors will decide to restrict themselves to investments in common stocks and property for their own use even though they believe in the necessity of holding real estate to obtain a well-balanced portfolio. They can place stocks with a high real estate content in their portfolios. They may feel that because of a lack of time and the much greater availability of information on stocks and their much higher liquidity, they need not be concerned with other types of property.

On the other hand, those with more money, those who want the maximum amount of leverage to meet their ultimate goals, or those who feel that in their tax bracket they need a large amount of tax shelter will clearly choose the ownership of properties or joint-venture securities.

Ensuring Profits

Another determinant of investors' choices is how reliable they believe their investment analysis to be. Can they do a good-enough job of analysis to lower their risks? One of the major advantages of real estate to informed investors is that, through careful analysis, they may be able to estimate their probable returns more completely than in other investment spheres. By means of astute management investors can also ensure a better flow of revenues. Their profits are not entirely dependent on others.

However, the degree to which it is possible to control and estimate risks depends on an investor's situation:

1 Owner-occupiers are in a very special position to reduce their risks; thus the rate of return in buying a property they will occupy may be large. Investors who do not occupy a property must rent it to others. They must ask for a much higher return to cover their greater risks.

2 Participants in the industry, such as brokers or developers, are also in a special situation. They see enough opportunities to find good buys that meet their own portfolio requirements. People active in real estate sales are well aware that while the market is comparatively good, at frequent intervals offers appear which, because of special circumstances, are far better and more attractive deals than the average. These tend to be the key to many successful investments.

3 Many individuals can, on a full-time or part-time basis, devote enough time and effort to the analysis of individual properties so that they gain sufficient knowledge to pick a portfolio with above-average returns. This is not simple, however, and requires more than an occasional foray into the market.

4 Others recognize that although they cannot depend on their own expertise, their personal situation may enable them to take advantage of other factors, such as a tax shelter or an inflation hedge, which will boost their returns above those earned by the ordinary investor.

5 While many discussions place considerable emphasis on diversification, this reduces only one specific type of risk—that of an individual venture going bad because of its own inherent weakness. Diversification of real estate properties may do little to decrease the risk from overall economic or financial occurrences.

More important than general diversification is that which meets the needs of a specific investor. Thus we have constantly stressed the importance to analysis of the tax consequences in real estate. Because the tax situation is so important, a given investment is worth far more to some individuals than to others. Similarly, factors such as leverage and liquidity will have far different import to different people. Some investors pay a premium to avoid a situation with high leverage, while others pay a premium to gain it.

Because of these wide variations in portfolio requirements, the particular factors related to each type of investment and property play a different role for every investor. The foldout table contains our summary in an extremely limited form of some of the key features of the various types of properties. This table shows the strategic considerations which vary with particular investment property types. Bringing together much of the information about properties, the table makes it possible to illustrate how different investors can select certain property types for their own portfolios. As illustrated by the table, when analyzing a property an investor should consider:

1 The function of a property type—its purpose and reason for existence.

2 The investment characteristics of the property type. What about cash flow, tax shelter, inflation hedge, risk, liquidity, and financing?

3 The characteristics of owners. How much equity is required? Who normally buys? What amount of management time and skills is required? Are there important economies of scale?

4 The economic characteristics determining values. Who are the users? How long are typical leases? What are the major factors influencing demand and supply? Is the government a critical factor?

In working with the table, it must be recognized that it is a simplification based on approximations and generalizations. The suggested relationships do not hold in every case. Rather, this format is intended to provide a starting point for individual investors to differentiate among the characteristics of properties in developing the portfolio that meets their needs.

INVESTOR CHARACTERISTICS

A feel for the problem of making the choices for a proper portfolio and an understanding of the content of the foldout table may be acquired by planning portfolios for different types of potential investors. This exercise makes it clear why each investor must consider his or her own special circumstances.

Young Family

One type of portfolio can be planned for the young family in an adequate salary bracket but with limited capital. For example, assume that a young man with a family has $25,000 available for investments. His salary covers living needs, but is not high enough for any savings beyond life insurance. Any additional wealth or buildup of assets will depend on the results of his $25,000 investment.

This investor can afford to take some risks. He is interested in using leverage because the consequences of a loss in capital are not critical. At the same time, a sizable gain will ensure a higher standard of living in the future. Such investors can spare little time or effort to put into managing a property. They would find a tax shelter useful, but its value would not be as great to them as to someone in a high marginal tax bracket. Therefore, they should not overpay by investing in a property whose value is set by investors in high tax brackets. Instead they should choose properties for capital appreciation and an inflation hedge.

What would a real estate portfolio look like for an investor of this type?

Clearly, the first item would probably be the purchase of a home. In this way the family gets a maximum amount of leverage. Mortgages tend to be high; downpayments may be as low as 5 or 10 percent. The tax shelter which the house provides is large and of maximum usefulness because it can easily be reported on the income tax. The family gains a built-in inflationary protection against rising rents; the largest share of its housing costs will be fixed as long as it continues to live in the same house. At the same time it has a chance for the capital gains arising from amortization of its mortgage. If housing costs and prices continue to rise as they have in the past, it can expect some additional capital appreciation.

The main risk associated with buying a home centers around the fact that transaction costs are high and liquidity is poor. If the family is forced to sell the house within the first few years after purchase, it may suffer a loss. On the other hand, if the family does not have to move, it can expect to get a relatively high return from this investment. Chapter 25 showed why the purchase of a house makes good sense for the average family that can live in it long enough and can find a house that meets its needs.

What about funds available for additional investment? An examination of the foldout table seems to show that this type of family is probably best off investing in either an existing apartment house or some kind of commercial shopping property. It may find that it can best make such an investment through buying units in a syndicate or through an equity REIT or real estate corporation. The latter two are relatively liquid investments, and they probably provide some diversification. Purchasing a security seems to be an adequate solution for such a family with limited capital and little time to devote to its own investments. For most securities, the family can find the necessary information readily available, particularly if the security is a listed common stock.

Existing apartment houses may also make sense as investments because they carry chances for capital gains and act as an inflationary hedge, both of which are important to this type of investor.

Investments in apartments made through purchasing common stocks are comparatively liquid. Their prices vary with both the stock market and the real estate market, but in an emergency they can be sold rapidly and cash can be obtained. A unit purchased in a syndicate will be hard to cash in if such a need arises.

Retired Couple

What kind of portfolio makes sense for a couple who are about to retire and who have $100,000 they can invest in real estate securities or property? It is clear that most investors in this situation are not interested in taking high risks for high returns. They want a large cash flow because they need income. They should not pay for leverage or a tax shelter. They want protection against inflation, fearing that unless they have a number of assets with income that will rise with prices, they may find themselves in the situation of too many retired couples who are badly squeezed by inflation.

An obvious investment possibility, again, is the ownership of their own home. On the other hand, if they shrink from the problems of maintenance or if they plan to travel, they may well find that ownership of a condominium is preferable. With either type of ownership, they will secure the advantages of maximum leverage, minimum risks, and the certainty that a major part of their budget will be guaranteed against inflation.

The retired couple should avoid investments that emphasize tax shelter and are characterized by high risks. Rather, after providing for adequate liquidity, they should concentrate on investment programs offering good current income as well as an inflation hedge.

However, many people in this situation have extra time on their hands and could manage and even maintain properties. Thus this couple might find that an attractive investment would be a small existing apartment building. In this case, too, they would be guaranteeing their future rent; they would be paid for the time they put into managing the building and even for making repairs or performing janitorial services. They would also have an investment with a low tax shelter, and so they would not be competing with high-income investors. Their main problems would be the keen competition for this type of investment from others in similar circumstances and the danger of placing too much of their capital in a single investment that could go bad.

COMPLEMENTARY PROPERTIES

With regard to logical investments for other types of investors, an examination of the foldout table brings out the fact that various property types complement one another in individual portfolios. For example:

1   A new apartment house returns much of its benefits through the tax shelter of existing income. An investor who cannot use its available tax shelter will have paid too much for the other benefits it returns.

2   On the other hand, an investor in a ground lease is purchasing primarily a source of a high cash flow. Depending on questions of subordination and participation, the investor can obtain other features in such investments, but their most usual characteristic is their high cash flow.

3   Undeveloped land is primarily a speculation for future appreciation and capital gains. It may well have a negative cash flow, requiring the investor to increase the amount invested each year until the property is sold.

Such different types of property will complement one another in an investor's portfolio. We can see how this works in three separate cases. Consider an investor who has bought a new apartment house to achieve tax shelter for his high current income—say, for example, the doctor discussed in Chapter 1. He now finds himself with a large tax-free cash flow. He may now become a candidate to acquire speculative land for future appreciation because he has protected his current income and can risk investing for capital gains. However, over time, as he adds to his landholdings, he may need additional cash to pay their holding costs. Land leases, which generate high cash flow, might be an ideal source for providing this cash. By choosing his types of investments carefully, he succeeds in making each complement his income and future needs.

As another example, consider a woman who seeks immediate cash income and achieves it through a commercial land lease. She will have a high pretax cash flow. If, after a time, she desires to shelter this cash flow, she will find an investment in a first-user apartment property an appropriate complement in her portfolio to achieve that objective. Once she has sheltered her cash flow from taxes, she may become interested in obtaining future appreciation, which she might accomplish through a speculative land investment.

Finally, we can examine the investor who has committed his funds to speculative land for future gain. He will face the need to generate cash to pay the holding cost of his land investment. As suggested above, land leases are an effective vehicle for achieving immediate cash flow. But once this investor has covered his holding costs through cash income from commercial leases, he will soon find that his taxable income has risen and that he needs a tax shelter. First-user apartment projects are now appropriate for his consideration.

As seen from the above discussion, all three investors start out with distinct and separate objectives and utilize different property types to achieve them. But with time, assuming they are successful, their very success creates the need to emphasize another investment objective, thus requiring the addition of a different property type to their portfolio. Eventually each one may use all three property types; yet at the start, one was highly preferable.

Although this illustration is greatly simplified, it does effectively make a point. At different periods one property type may be more suitable than another, but over time, assuming an adequate investment base with which to work, nearly every property merits careful consideration for inclusion in an effective overall investment strategy.

While the investor's characteristics and objectives often provide a useful starting point for portfolio planning, there are also other "building blocks" that should be looked at. At times certain market areas may be more attractive than others. Different property types will offer more investment potential at some times than at others. And while every investment strategy should be based on a carefully formulated program of action, it must also be opportunistic. By this we mean investors must position themselves to be willing and able to respond to an unusually attractive investment opportunity when one comes along. Because not every eventuality can be anticipated, it may be highly rewarding to revise an overall investment program in order to capitalize on an attractive deal.

SUMMARY

Real estate investment is not simple. Making a million dollars or any other large sum is possible, but it requires skill, hard work, and luck. There is always a danger of paying too much for any venture, even when it has all the proper ingredients for success. Many investors are not successful because they habitually overpay for what they get. The old investment maxim that profits are made by buying low and selling high still holds. The trick is to be able to project values so that you know when you have a good buy.

Real property has many investment advantages. Any degree of risk can be chosen. Investors can ''go for broke'' by picking high-leverage situations, or they can opt for safe income on leases from major companies with only a small inflationary hedge in terms of residual values. To many, the main reason for owning a property is to assure their own future living conditions at noninflationary levels. To others, tax incentives are the primary appeal. Still others are attracted by the management job that goes with the ownership of property. Many find that they make their profits by reviewing enough offers to be able to pick the occasional jewel.

Because real estate investment opportunities are so numerous and so diverse, success is far more likely if investors know what they are looking for and why, that is, if they have an investment strategy. With an understanding of what creates profits and values, investors can select the securities or properties that meet their individual needs and give the greatest prospects of high returns.

SELECTED REFERENCES FOR PART SEVEN

Clurman, D.: *The Business Condominium* (New York: Wiley-Interscience, 1973).

Cobleigh, I. U.: *All about Investing in Real Estate Securities* (New York: Weybright & Talley, 1971).

Cohen, J. B., and A. W. Hanson: *Personal Finance: Principles and Case Problems,* 5th ed. (Homewood, Ill.: Irwin, 1975).

Crandell, L. (ed.): *Corporate Real Estate Development and Management* (New York: President's Publishing House, 1971).

Doane's Agricultural Services, Inc., and L. G. Mosburg, Jr.: *New Opportunities in Agricultural Investments* (San Francisco: RESD Publications, 1974).

Friedman, H. C.: ''Real Estate Investment Portfolio Theory,'' *Journal of Financial and Quantitative Analysis,* April 1970.

Friedman, M. R.: *Friedman on Leases* (New York: Practising Law Institute, 1974), 2 vols.

Goldstein, C. A. (ed.): *Commercial and Industrial Condominiums* (New York: Practising Law Institute, 1974).

Goodkin, L. M.: *When Real Estate and Homebuilding Become Big Business* (Boston: Cahners Books, 1974).

Harrison, H. S.: *Houses* (Chicago: National Institute of Real Estate Brokers, 1973).

Kinnard, W. N., and S. Messner: *Industrial Real Estate* (Washington: Society of Industrial Realtors, 1967).

Levine, S. N. (ed.): *Financial Analyst's Handbook* (Homewood, Ill.: Dow Jones–Irwin, 1975).

Lorie, J., and R. Brealey (eds.): *Modern Developments in Investment Management* (New York: Praeger, 1972).

Mackay, C.: *Extraordinary Popular Delusions and the Madness of Crowds* (Wells, Vt.: Fraser Publishing Co., 1841).

Mossin, J.: *Theory of Financial Markets* (Englewood Cliffs, N.J.: Prentice-Hall, 1973).

Nickerson, W.: *How I Turned $1,000 into Three Million in Real Estate—In My Spare Time* (New York: Simon and Schuster, 1969).

Oppenheimer, H. L.: *Land Speculation* (Danville, Ill.: Interstate, 1972).

Price, I.: *Buying Country Property: Pitfalls and Pleasures* (New York: Harper, 1972).

Rachlis, E., and J. E. Marqueace: *The Landlords* (New York: Random House, 1963).

Renwick, F. B.: *Introduction to Investments and Finance* (New York: Macmillan, 1971).

Roulac, S. E.: *Due Diligence in Real Estate Transactions* (New York: Practising Law Institute, 1974).

————: "Real Estate and Common Stock: Return and Risk," *Journal of Portfolio Management*, Winter 1976.

Seldin, M., and R. H. Swesnik: *Real Estate Investment Strategy* (New York: Wiley-Interscience, 1970).

Smith, W. F.: *Housing: The Social and Economic Elements* (Berkeley: University of California Press, 1970).

Wendt, P. F., and S. N. Wong: "Investment Performance: Common Stocks versus Apartment Houses," *Journal of Finance,* December 1965.

Wolf, H. A.: *Personal Finance,* 4th ed. (Boston: Allyn and Bacon, 1975).

Zeckendorf, W., with E. McCreary: *The Autobiography of William Zeckendorf* (New York: Holt, 1970).

Glossary of Real Estate Financing Terms*

Abstract of title A summary or digest of the conveyances, transfers, and any other facts relied on as evidence of title, together with any other elements of record which may impair the title.

Acceleration clause A clause in a trust deed or mortgage giving the lender the right to call all sums owing him or her to be immediately due upon the happening of a certain event.

Acknowledgment A formal declaration before a duly authorized officer by a person who has executed an instrument that such execution is his or her act and deed.

Administrator A person appointed by the probate court to administer the estate of a person deceased.

Ad valorem Latin for "according to value."

Adverse possession The open and notorious possession and occupancy under an evident claim or right, in denial of, or opposition to, the title of another claimant.

Agent One who represents another from whom he or she has derived authority.

Agreement of sale A written agreement or contract between seller and purchaser in which they reach a meeting of minds on the terms and conditions of a sale.

Amenity That which contributes satisfaction rather than money income to its owner.

Amortization The liquidation of a financial obligation on an installment basis.

Appraisal An estimate and opinion of value.

Assessed value A valuation placed upon property by a public officer or board as a basis for taxation.

*Acknowledgment is made to the *Savings and Loan Fact Book* and the State of California Division of Real Estate *Reference Book*.

Assessment   The valuation of property for the purpose of levying a tax or the amount of the tax levied.

Assignee   One to whom property is transferred.

Assignor   One who assigns or transfers property.

Assumption of mortgage   The taking of title to property by a grantee, wherein he or she assumes liability for payment of an existing note secured by a mortgage or deed of trust against the property, becoming a coguarantor for the payment of a mortgage or deed-of-trust note.

Attachment   Seizure of property by court order, usually done to have it available in the event a judgment is obtained in a pending suit.

Balloon payment   The final installment payment on a note when that payment is greater than the preceding installment payments and pays the note in full.

Beneficiary   (1) One entitled to the benefit of a trust; (2) one who receives profit from an estate, the title of which is vested in a trustee; (3) the lender on the security of a note and deed of trust.

Blanket mortgage   A single mortgage which covers more than one piece of real estate.

Borrower   One who receives a loan with the intention of repaying.

Broker   One who for a commission or fee brings parties together and assists in negotiating contracts between them.

Capitalization   In appraising, determining the value of property by considering net income and percentage of reasonable return on the investment.

Capitalization rate   The rate of interest which is considered a reasonable return on the investment and is used in the process of determining value based upon net income.

Collateral   Stocks, bonds, evidence of deposit, and other marketable properties which a borrower pledges as security for a loan. In mortgage lending, the collateral is the specific real property which the borrower pledges as security.

Commission   An agent's compensation for performing the duties of his or her agency; in real estate practice, a percentage of the selling price of property, percentage of rentals, etc.

Commitment   A pledge or a promise or firm agreement to make a loan.

Compound interest   Interest paid on original principal and also on the accrued and unpaid interest which has accumulated.

Conditional sale contract   A contract for the sale of property stating that delivery is to be made to the buyer, title to remain vested in the seller until the conditions of the contract have been fulfilled.

Condominium   A system of direct ownership of a single unit in a multiunit structure. The individual owns the unit in much the same manner as if it were a single-family dwelling; he or she holds direct legal title to the unit and a proportionate interest in the common areas and the underlying ground. (*See* Cooperative.)

Constant rate   A level payment on a mortgage which includes both interest and principal payments.

Construction loan   A loan which is made to finance the actual construction of improvements on land.

Contract   An agreement, either written or oral, to do or not to do certain things.

Contract of sale   An agreement to transfer title after certain payments or conditions have been met.

Conventional loan   A mortgage loan made by a financial institution without insurance or guarantee by the FHA or VA. It is called a conventional loan because it conforms to accepted standards, modified within legal bounds by mutual consent of the borrower and lender.

Conveyance   The transfer of the title of land from one to another. An instrument which carries from one person to another an interest in land.

Cooperative   A system of indirect ownership of a single unit in a multiunit structure. The individual owns shares in a nonprofit corporation which holds title to the building; the corporation in turn gives the owner a long-term proprietary lease on the unit.

Corporation   A group or body of persons established and treated by law as an individual or unit with both rights and liabilities distinct and apart from those of the persons composing it.

Debentures   A form of bond or note.

Debt   A sum of money due by certain and express agreement.

Deed   A written instrument which, when properly executed and delivered, conveys title.

Deed of trust   A conveyance of the title to land to a trustee as collateral security for the payment of a debt with the condition that the trustee shall reconvey the title upon the payment of the debt and with power of the trustee to sell the land and pay the debt in the event of a default on the part of the debtor.

Default   Failure to fulfill a duty or promise or to discharge an obligation.

Deficiency judgment   A judgment given when the security pledge for a loan does not satisfy the debt upon its default.

Demand mortgage   A mortgage which is payable on demand of the holder of the evidence of the debt.

Depreciation   Loss of value in real property brought about by age, physical deterioration or functional or economic obsolescence. Broadly, a loss in value from any cause.

Discount   Interest or a fee deducted from a loan at the time it is made or sold.

Disintermediation   The process that takes place when savers build up their holdings of direct market instruments—such as United States government and agency issues, stocks, and bonds—and slow down their additions to savings or time accounts at financial institutions.

Easement   The right, privilege, or interest which one party has in the land of another.

Economic life   The period over which a building will yield a return on its investment.

Eminent domain   The right of the government to acquire property for necessary public or quasipublic use by condemnation; the owner must be fairly compensated.

Encumbrance   Anything which affects or limits the fee simple title to property, such as a mortgage, an easement, or a restriction of any kind. Liens are special encumbrances which make the property security for the payment of a debt or obligation, such as a mortgage or taxes.

Equity   The interest or value which an owner has in real estate over and above the liens against it.

Equity of redemption   The right to redeem property during the foreclosure period, such as a mortgagor's right to redeem within a year after foreclosure sale.

Escrow   The deposit of instruments and funds with instructions to a third, neutral party to carry out the provisions of an agreement or contract.

Estate   The degree, quantity, nature, and extent of interest which a person has in real property.

Execute   To complete, to make, to perform, to do, to follow out; to execute a deed is to make a deed, including especially signing, sealing, and delivery; to execute a contract is to perform the contract, to follow out to the end, to complete.

Farmers Home Administration (FMHA)   An agency of the federal government which makes, participates in, and insures loans for rural housing and other purposes.

Federal Home Loan Bank (FHLB)   One of the 12 federally chartered regional banks of the Federal Home Loan Bank System. A bank's primary function is to supply credit to member institutions.

Federal Home Loan Mortgage Corporation (FHLMC)   A secondary market facility of the

FHLB System, which is authorized to buy and sell conventional, FHA, and VA loans and participating interests in blocks of such loans.

Federal National Mortgage Association (FNMA, also called "Fannie Mae") A quasigovernmental corporation which supplements private mortgage funds by buying and selling FHA and VA loans.

Federal Savings and Loan Insurance Corporation (FSLIC) An instrumentality of the federal government which insures the savings accounts in member institutions.

Fee The highest type of interest a person can have in land. Fee denotes absolute ownership of land (subject to laws) with the right to dispose of it or pass it on to the owner's heirs as he or she sees fit. The term "fee" is of Old English derivation.

Fee simple In modern estates, the terms "fee" and "fee simple" are substantially synonymous.

Fiduciary A person in a position of trust and confidence.

Financial intermediary A financial institution which acts as an intermediary between savers and borrowers by selling its own obligations for money and, in turn, lending the accumulated funds to borrowers. The classification includes savings associations, mutual savings banks, life insurance companies, credit unions, and investment companies.

Foreclosure A procedure whereby property pledged as security for a debt is sold to pay the debt in the event of default in payments or terms.

Forfeiture Loss of money or anything of value due to failure to perform, for instance, under an agreement to purchase.

Garnishee To attach a specified sum from wages to satisfy a creditor.

Government National Mortgage Association (GNMA, also called "Ginnie Mae") A government corporation that provides special assistance for certain FHA and VA loans and guarantees securities backed by mortgage loans.

Graduated lease A lease which provides for a varying rental rate, often based upon future determination; sometimes rent is based upon the result of periodic appraisals. It is used largely in long-term leases.

Grantee The purchaser of property; a person to whom a grant is made.

Grantor The seller of property; one who signs a deed.

Gross Income The total income from property before any expenses are deducted.

Hundred percent location A city retail-business location which is considered the best available for attracting business.

Hypothecate To give a thing as security without the necessity of giving up possession of it.

Income property A property which produces a money income to the owner.

Installment note A note which provides that payments of a certain sum be made on the dates specified in the instrument.

Interest rate The percentage of a sum of money charged for its use.

Involuntary lien A lien imposed against property without consent of an owner.

Joint tenancy Joint ownership by two or more persons with right of survivorship; all joint tenants own equal interest and have equal rights in the property.

Judgment The final determination of a court of competent jurisdiction of a matter presented to it; money judgments provide for the payment of claims presented to the court or are awarded as damages.

Junior mortgage A lien that is subsequent to the claims of the holder of a prior mortgage.

Land contract A contract ordinarily used in connection with the sale of property in cases where the seller does not wish to convey title until all or a certain part of the purchase price is paid by the buyer; often used when property is sold on small downpayment.

Lease A contract between owner and tenant, setting forth conditions upon which the tenant may occupy and use the property and the term of the occupancy.

Leasehold   The estate held by virtue of a lease.

Lessee   One who contracts to rent property under a lease contract.

Lessor   An owner who enters into a lease with a tenant.

Lien   A form of encumbrance which usually makes property security for the payment of a debt or discharge of an obligation. Examples are judgments, taxes, mortgages, and deeds of trust.

Liquidity   The cash position of an association measured by the cash on hand and securities quickly convertible into cash.

Loan   A sum of money lent at interest to be repaid.

Loan fee   The charge made at the granting of a loan in addition to required interest.

Market value   (1) The price at which a willing seller would sell and a willing buyer would buy, neither being under abnormal pressure; (2) as defined by the courts, the highest price estimated in terms of money which a property will bring if exposed for sale in the open market, allowing a reasonable time to find a purchaser with knowledge of the property's use and capabilities for use.

Mechanic's lien   A claim, created by statutory law in most states, existing in favor of mechanics or other persons who have performed work in, or furnished materials for, the erection or repair of a building.

Moratorium   The temporary suspension, usually by statute, of the enforcement of liability for debt.

Mortgage   An instrument recognized by law by which property is hypothecated to secure the payment of a debt or obligation; procedure for foreclosure in the event of default is established by statute.

Mortgage company   A private corporation whose principal activity is the origination and servicing of mortgage loans which are sold to financial institutions.

Mortgagee   One to whom a mortgagor gives a mortgage; a lender.

Mortgage insurance premium   The amount paid by the borrower for insurance of a loan.

Mortgagor   One who gives a mortgage on his or her property to secure a loan or assure performance of an obligation; a borrower.

Net income   That part of the gross income which remains after the deduction of all charges or costs.

Net yield   That part of the gross yield which remains after the deduction of all charges or costs including necessary reserves.

Nominal interest rate   The interest rate stated in the loan agreement.

Note   A signed written instrument acknowledging a debt and promising payment.

Obsolescence   Loss in value due to reduced desirability and usefulness of a structure when its design and construction become old-fashioned and are no longer in keeping with modern needs. Obsolescence can result from physical deterioration, changing relationships to social or economic conditions, or changing functional needs.

Open-end mortgage   A mortgage which states the intention of the borrower and of the lender that the mortgage shall stand as security not only for the original loan but also for future advances that the lender may be willing to make.

Option   A right given for a consideration to purchase or lease a property upon specified terms within a specified time.

Participation loan   A mortgage loan in which more than one association has an interest. One association makes the loan, and one or more associations purchase an interest in it.

Partnership   As between partners themselves, a contract of two or more persons to unite their property, labor, skill, or some of these, in prosecution of some joint and lawful business, and to share the profits in certain proportions.

Percentage lease   A lease on property the rental for which is determined by the amount of business done by the lessee; usually the rental is a percentage of gross receipts from the business, and there is a provision for a minimum rental.

Personal property   Any property which is not real property.

Points   The amount of a discount stated as a percentage.

Prepayment penalty   A penalty for the payment of a debt before it actually becomes due.

Present value   The current value of an amount to be received in the future.

Principal   The amount of debt.

Proration of taxes   The division of taxes equally or proportionately to time of use.

Purchase-money mortgage or trust deed   A trust deed or mortgage given as part or all of the purchase consideration for property.

Quitclaim deed   A deed to relinquish any interest in property which the grantor may have.

Real estate investment trust (REIT)   A special arrangement under federal and state law whereby investors may pool funds for investments in real estate and mortgages and yet escape corporation taxes.

Reconveyance   The transfer of the title of land from one person to the immediately preceding owner. This particular instrument is commonly used when the performance or debt is satisfied under the terms of a deed of trust and the trustee conveys the title he or she has held on condition back to the owner.

Recourse   The right to claim against a prior owner of a property or note.

Redemption   Buying back one's property after a judicial sale.

Release clause   A stipulation that upon the payment of a specific sum of money to the holder of a trust deed or mortgage, the lien on a specific described lot or area shall be removed from the blanket lien on the whole area involved.

Reserves   Those portions of earnings which have been set aside to take care of possible losses in the conduct of business; listed in the balance sheet as a liability item.

Right of way   A privilege operating as an easement upon land, whereby the owner, by grant or by agreement, gives to another the right to pass over the land, to construct a roadway, or to use as a roadway a specific part of the land; or whereby the owner gives the right to construct through and over the land telephone, telegraph, or electric power lines or gives the right to place underground water mains, gas mains, or sewer mains.

Risk   The probability of future loss.

Risk rating   A process by which various risks are evaluated, usually employing grids to develop precise and relative figures for the purpose of determining the overall soundness of a loan.

Sale-leaseback   A situation where the owner of a piece of property wishes to sell the property and retain occupancy by leasing it from the buyer.

Sales contract   A contract by which buyer and seller agree to the terms of a sale.

Sandwich lease   A leasehold interest which lies between the primary lease and the operating lease.

Savings and loan association (S & L)   A financial intermediary which receives savings and invests these savings mainly in mortgage loans. Always a corporation, it may be either a mutual or a capital stock institution and may be either state-chartered or federally chartered.

Savings bank   A financial intermediary which receives savings in the form of deposits and invests these deposits in mortgages and other securities allowed by law. The banks, with the exception of a few in New Hampshire, are mutual institutions and are governed by self-perpetuating boards of trustees.

Secondary financing   A loan secured by a second mortgage or deed of trust on real property.

Security   Something given, deposited, or pledged to make secure the fulfillment of an obligation or the payment of a debt.

Servicing   The collection of payments on a mortgage. Servicing by the lender also consists of operational procedures covering accounting, bookkeeping, insurance, tax records, loan-payment follow-up, delinquent-loan follow-up, and loan analysis.

Sheriff's deed   A deed given by court order in connection with the sale of property to satisfy a judgment.

Sinking fund   A fund set aside from the income from property which, with accrued interest, will eventually pay for replacement of the improvements.

Statute of frauds   A state law which provides that certain contracts must be in writing in order to be enforceable at law. Examples are real property leases for more than 1 year; and an agent's authorization to sell real estate.

Subject to mortgage   When a grantee takes title to real property subject to mortgage, he or she is not responsible to the holder of the promissory note for the payment of any portion of the amount due. The most that the grantee can lose in the event of a foreclosure is his or her equity in the property.

Subordination clause   (1) A clause in a junior lien permitting retention of priority for other liens; (2) a clause in a first deed of trust permitting it to be subordinated to subsequent liens, for example, the liens of construction loans.

Tenancy in common   Ownership by two or more persons who hold undivided interest, without right of survivorship; interests need not be equal.

Title   Evidence that the owner of land is in lawful possession of it; an instrument evidencing such ownership.

Title insurance   Insurance written by a title company to protect a property owner against loss if title is imperfect.

Trust deed   *See* Deed of trust.

Trustee   One who holds property in trust for another to secure the performance of an obligation.

Trustor   One who deeds property to a trustee to be held as security until he has performed his obligation to a lender under the terms of a deed of trust.

Usury   On a loan, claiming a rate of interest greater than that permitted by law.

Valuation   Estimated worth or price; the act of valuing by appraisal.

Vendee   A purchaser, or buyer.

Vendor   A seller, or one who disposes of a thing in consideration of money.

Waste   Damage to property by neglect or otherwise.

Zoning   Specification by city or county authorities of the type of use to which property may be put in specific areas.

Index